*Adrift on an Inland Sea*

# ADRIFT ON AN INLAND SEA

*Misinformation and the Limits of Empire in the Brazilian Backlands*

Hal Langfur

STANFORD UNIVERSITY PRESS
*Stanford, California*

STANFORD UNIVERSITY PRESS
Stanford, California

© 2023 by Hal Langfur. All rights reserved.

No part of this book may be reproduced or transmitted in any form or by any means, electronic or mechanical, including photocopying and recording, or in any information storage or retrieval system without the prior written permission of Stanford University Press.

Printed in the United States of America on acid-free, archival-quality paper

Library of Congress Cataloging-in-Publication Data

Names: Langfur, Hal, author.
Title: Adrift on an inland sea : misinformation and the limits of empire in the Brazilian backlands / Hal Langfur.
Description: Stanford, California : Stanford University Press, 2023. | Includes bibliographical references and index.
Identifiers: LCCN 2022010220 (print) | LCCN 2022010221 (ebook) | ISBN 9781503632844 (cloth) | ISBN 9781503633964 (paperback) | ISBN 9781503633971 (ebook)
Subjects: LCSH: Misinformation—Brazil—History—18th century. | Misinformation—Brazil—History—19th century. | Brazil—History—1763–1822. | Portugal—Colonies—America—Administration.
Classification: LCC F2534 (print) | LCC F2534 (ebook) | DDC 981/.032—dc23/eng/20220926
LC record available at https://lccn.loc.gov/2022010220
LC ebook record available at https://lccn.loc.gov/2022010221

Cover design: Rob Ehle
Cover image: "Virgin Forest: Banks of the Paraíba River." Source: Jean Baptiste Debret, Voyage pittoresque et historique au Brésil (Paris: Firmin Didot frères, 1834), vol. 1. Courtesy of the John Carter Brown Library. Licensed under CC-BY 4.0.
Typeset by Newgen North America in 10/15 ITC Galliard Pro

*For Kerry, Bridger, and Devon, my anchors*

# CONTENTS

*List of Illustrations* ix
*Acknowledgments* xi
*Note on Conventions* xv
*Map of Southeastern Brazil, ca. 1800* xvi

INTRODUCTION
Navigating the Imperial Unknown . . . . . . . . . . . . . . . . . 1

PART 1. **Making the Wilderness Wild:
The Authority of Misinformation**
27

1. Civilization, Barbarism, and the Tall Tale . . . . . . . . . . . 29
2. Turning Frontier Fictions into Private Property . . . . . . . 53

PART 2. **All That Glitters:
Forest Informants and Regal Dreams**
73

3. Forest Knowledge Networks . . . . . . . . . . . . . . . . . . . 77
4. Natives, Smugglers, Soldiers, Spies . . . . . . . . . . . . . . 102
5. Sovereign Rule and Its Disenchantments . . . . . . . . . . . 129

**PART 3. Science for the Sertão:
New Modes of Inquiry, Old Uncertainties**
153

6. The Enlightened Savant and the Black Prospector King   157
7. Diamonds, Love Songs, and the Alchemy of Exploration   181

**PART 4. The Good Sense of Cannibals:
Further Dispatches from the Atlantic Forest**
215

8. Anthropophagy and the Body Politic   219
9. Ethnological Misadventures   250
   EPILOGUE
   How to Tame an Empire   283

*Abbreviations Used in the Notes* 301
*Notes* 303
*Bibliography* 387
*Index* 421

# ILLUSTRATIONS

**Map**
    Southeastern Brazil, ca. 1800      xvi

**Figures**
| | | |
|---|---|---|
| 1.1. | Enslaved miners near Vila Rica, capital of the captaincy of Minas Gerais | 37 |
| 1.2. | The western savanna | 45 |
| 2.1. | Map of the Campo Grande region of western Minas Gerais | 58 |
| 2.2. | São Gonçalo quilombo | 62 |
| 3.1. | Inhabitants of the coastal forest | 81 |
| 3.2. | Mountains above Rio de Janeiro | 92 |
| 4.1. | Members of colonial militias, a source of troops for backcountry missions | 113 |
| 4.2. | Panning for gold | 121 |
| 5.1. | Forest dwellers at Cantagalo | 136 |
| 5.2. | Clearing the forest | 142 |
| 6.1. | Mineralogical tools and instruments | 163 |
| 6.2. | Prospecting for diamonds | 171 |
| 7.1. | En route to the western backlands | 183 |
| 7.2. | Free and enslaved women labored in a full range of occupations | 192 |
| 7.3. | State-controlled diamond mining | 208 |
| 8.1. | Fording a river | 227 |

| | | |
|---|---|---|
| 8.2. | A Botocudo family | 241 |
| 9.1. | A naturalist's assistants | 256 |
| 9.2. | Near Fort Arcos the German prince observed Botocudo combat | 259 |
| 9.3. | Wied hunting with his Botocudo informant Guack | 265 |

# ACKNOWLEDGMENTS

THIS BOOK CONCERNS HOW colonizers and those they sought to control wielded information in the distant past. Completing it at a time when the manipulation of what is known and unknown has become so problematic, I feel especially grateful for the many professional and personal relationships built on trust that have sustained this project over many years.

Research and writing were made possible by the generosity of various institutions and fellowship programs. A Fulbright research and teaching fellowship based at the Universidade Federal de São João del-Rei (UFSJ) in Minas Gerais, Brazil, gave an essential push to the project at its inception. The University at Buffalo (UB), my home institution, provided two sabbatical leaves and a research fellowship from its thriving Humanities Institute. Further support came from the Newberry Library, which hosted me as a National Endowment for the Humanities Fellow, and the John Carter Brown Library, where I was the R. David Parsons, Donald L. Saunders Research Fellow. At more than twenty archives, most of them underfunded, dedicated staffs made the hunt for sources rewarding on three continents.

Of the numerous debts incurred to those who took an interest in this study, I am able to describe only a few in any detail. In my own department Erik Seeman has been unwaveringly eager to read portions of the manuscript, offer incisive commentary as a fellow Atlanticist, and extend his valued friendship. Laura de Mello e Souza, now at the Sorbonne, first alerted me to the far-reaching possibilities of examining forgotten eighteenth-century expeditions to the *sertões* (backlands) as important social, cultural, and political phenomena. Although our paths have crossed infrequently, her work has been a constant source of inspiration. The late John Monteiro encouraged an entire generation of scholars to take up the challenge of centering Native peoples in Brazil's colonial history. He helped deepen my understanding of the sertões as contested territory, a premise that applied even as this study extended to include peoples of African descent. I was privileged to co-teach a course in Indigenous history at UFSJ with Maria Leônia Chaves de Resende. Her knowledge as a historian and openheartedness as a friend proved decisive at key moments. Leônia, along with Pedro Cardim, Ângela Domingues, Pablo Ibañez Bonillo, and others associated with the Centre for the Humanities (CHAM) at the Universidade Nova de Lisboa, unrivaled as a collaborative environment for scholars of the Lusophone world, invited me on several occasions to present my research in progress. The Luso-American Development Foundation funded one of these visits. Cynthia Radding and Danna Levin Rojo welcomed me into the remarkable international cohort of scholars they assembled for two colloquia that resulted in *The Oxford Handbook of Borderlands of the Iberian World* (2019). Chapters 3 and 5 herein include portions of a text that appeared in their edited volume. Mark Harris and Silvia Espelt-Bombín hosted a similarly productive workshop at the University of St. Andrews, leading to a dedicated issue of *Ethnohistory* (October 2018) on Amerindian spaces in Brazilian history. Parts of my contribution to that collection have been reworked and refocused in chapter 9. Oxford University Press and Duke University Press kindly granted permission to republish this material.

For engaged criticism, invitations to present research, and other forms of academic and personal generosity in the United States, Brazil, and Portugal, I also wish to thank Camilo Trumper, Dalia Antonia Caraballo Muller, Ndubueze Mbah, Victoria Wolcott, Jonathan Dewald, David Castillo, Henry Berlin, Carine Mardorossian, David Alff, Richard Graham, Sandra Lauderdale Graham, Carlos Rodriguez, Brian Bockelmen, León García Garagarza, Amy Turner Bushnell, Neil Safier, Mary Karasch, Judy Bieber, Heather Roller, Sebastián Díaz Angel, Surekha Davies, Fabrício Prado, Chi-ming Yang, Ana Hontanilla, Lisa Voigt, Mariana Dantas, Ray Craib, Alison Bigelow, Lauren Benton, Gabriel de Avilez Rocha, Yuko

Miki, Kris Lane, Tamara Walker, Dain Borges, Kenneth Mills, James Green, Alida Metcalf, Susan Sleeper-Smith, Izabel Missagia de Mattos, Luciano Raposo, Júnia Ferreira Furtado, Márcia Motta, Marina Machado, Valter Sinder, Vania Belli, Andréa Doré, Belmiro Nascimento, Carmen Alveal, Eduardo França Paiva, Maria Regina Celestino de Almeida, Aílton Krenak, Ricardo dos Anjos, Rodrigo Bentes Monteiro, João Pacheco de Oliveira, Cristina Brito, Pablo Sánchez León, Nina Vieira, André Morgado, and Tiago C. P. dos Reis Miranda. Students in my graduate seminar on frontiers and borderlands read a draft, offering helpful suggestions.

With reassuring enthusiasm, expertise, and efficiency, Margo Irvin took on this project at Stanford University Press, ably assisted by Cindy Lim, Tiffany Mok, and others. Barbara Sommer and Kirsten Schultz read the manuscript for the press with meticulous care, each sharing insights that improved the final version. Erin Greb produced the map, Dawn Hall applied her precise pen as copyeditor, and Kate Mertes constructed the index..

Friends, family, and fellow musicians kept things in perspective and sustained me even when the project slowed, especially Bob Campbell, Tom and Peg Sullivan, David and Sigrid Fertig, Joe and Jen Mattimore, Jo and Dick Sanders, the entire Reynolds clan, Maleeka Manurasada, and David Nicholson. My wife Kerry Reynolds read the full manuscript with a perceptive eye. She held me in her heart at every turn, as did my children Bridger Langfur and Devon Reynolds, as do I them, in the end the achievement that matters most. To these beloved three, I dedicate this book.

# NOTE ON CONVENTIONS

FOR TEXTUAL CONSISTENCY, I have adopted contemporary Brazilian orthography but retained diverse original spellings, grammar, and punctuation in citations of historical manuscripts and imprints. The names and spellings of Indigenous groups follow those most widely used by Brazilian scholars, although they, too, vary widely in the notes according to the original sources. The *real* (pl. *réis*) was the basic unit of currency in colonial Brazil. One *mil-réis* equaled one thousand réis, and was written 1$000. One *conto de réis* (or simply one *conto*) equaled one million réis, and was written 1:000$000. Throughout the second half of the eighteenth century, the Portuguese Crown set the value of one *oitava* of gold (an eighth of an ounce) at 1$200 in Minas Gerais. A diamond weighing one oitava equaled 17.7 carats.

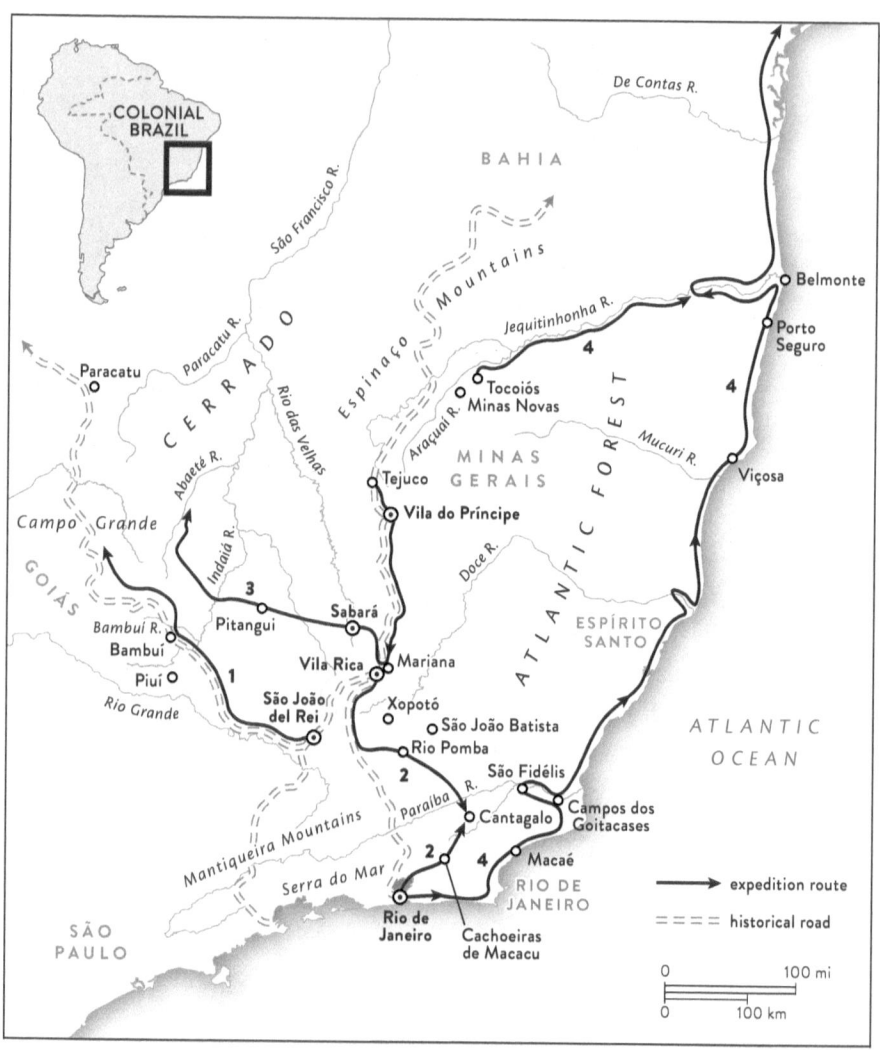

Map of Southeastern Brazil, ca. 1800, with approximate routes of the primary expeditions discussed in the four parts of this study. Numbered routes correspond to these expeditions.

*Adrift on an Inland Sea*

INTRODUCTION

# NAVIGATING THE IMPERIAL UNKNOWN

ON A DAY OF SEEMINGLY LIMITLESS visibility in early 1801, the mineralogist José Vieira Couto ascended a ridge in Brazil's southeastern interior and marveled at the view. "Toward the frontier, looking west, as if it were a vast ocean," he wrote, "one sees the sky and the earth comingle on the smoky and smooth horizons." In the company of his fellow voyagers, the young savant was returning from those horizons, concluding an exploratory mission of nearly ten months in search of diamonds. Now following the Espinhaço Mountains southward toward Vila Rica, the gilded capital of the captaincy of Minas Gerais, Portuguese America's principal mining region, Couto dutifully continued to make his diary entries. Passing through "haunted corridors of tall cliffs" relieved now and then by peaceful meadows and crystalline rivers, he recorded sighting not only dramatic scenery but also potentially profitable copper reserves. In this more traveled country, back from the west, he was still keen to find evidence of mineral wealth to supplement what he knew some critics, perhaps even his monarch, would consider the disappointing results of a long, expensive expedition.[1]

Prince Regent João, ruling the Portuguese Empire for his incapacitated mother, Queen Maria I, had honored Couto with the appointment to investigate unconfirmed reports of the discovery of extensive new diamond fields. After an arduous search the Brazilian-born, Portuguese-trained scientist had located only a few low-quality deposits. In the course of their journey, expedition members had encountered vexing difficulties. They had been forced to rely on a band of impoverished prospectors who served as their backcountry guides, men and women of African descent, former slaves, descendants of slaves, and in some cases possibly fugitives from slavery. White, highly educated, the beneficiary of wealth and privilege, Couto avowed little faith in his unlikely chaperones. At best he dismissed them as rustics; at worst, as conniving frauds. Returning all but empty-handed, the scholar-scientist was left grasping for something positive to report to his royal patron.

The endless vistas he surveyed from the ridgeline offered at least the possibility of future attainments. His association of these tropical wooded grasslands with the immeasurable sea was a fitting image. They comprised the small, visible portion of the immense *sertões*, thinly colonized backlands that at the beginning of the nineteenth century, three hundred years after the Portuguese first set foot on South American shores, still accounted for most of the Brazilian interior. Once stewards of a seaborne empire of global scale, the Portuguese had long ago seen their predominance in intercontinental trade eclipsed. In Couto's time colonial Brazil endured as the remaining stronghold of a gloried imperial past. The colony's sertões beckoned as a potentially revivifying field of conquest.[2]

Well into the future, the promise of their sealike immensity would endure. Pondering the backlands more than a century later, the statesman and abolitionist Rui Barbosa imagined himself "a navigator at the edge of an unknown sea." Invoking the "honor," "destiny," and quest for nature's "opulent treasures" that the sertões and sea called forth, he proclaimed that there was, in both, "the same greatness, the same grandeur, the same inscrutability. Over one and the other extends that same enigma of indecipherable majesties. From one and the other issues the same expression of energy, strength, and power that cannot be resisted. One and the other stares at us, in the same way, like two unfathomable and inexhaustible reservoirs of life."[3] Such poetic yearning and the collective memory it summoned, we will come to see, had their concrete, place-based histories as well as their counternarratives.

During the first half of the eighteenth century, the unearthing of astonishing quantities of gold and diamonds along the Espinhaço cordillera, which stretches more than a thousand kilometers from south to north, had helped sustain an empire. Enslaved laborers shipped from Portuguese Africa kept the region's minerals flowing to Lisbon. During the century's second half, however, as bust followed boom, the Portuguese faced deepening economic challenges that grew more worrisome as revolutionary currents began to circulate in the Atlantic world. One response was a redoubling of efforts to colonize and govern the sprawling, still-unincorporated spaces of the continental interior. The Portuguese thereby hoped, in accordance with the era's mercantilist orthodoxies, to extract the untapped wealth these lands were thought to contain, putting colonial labor and resources at the service of metropolitan prosperity. From the century's midpoint until Brazil gained its independence in 1822, this inland sea, these unsurveyed lands, legally secured but never effectively controlled, became the arena of a diffuse but decisive struggle over the limits of empire.

In this book I demonstrate that the Portuguese drive to assert dominion over swaths of the South American interior was significantly more vigorous than generally appreciated even as the resulting challenges to imperial expansion proved correspondingly more disruptive. Accompanying the progress of quasi-private, military, and scientific forays into ostensibly unknown areas, the chapters that follow assess the objectives, limitations, disorientation, and ultimate dissolution of renewed colonizing ventures as they stretched from Portugal into Brazil's southeastern backlands. Although rarely achieving their aims when authorized to integrate internal frontiers more firmly into the imperial domain, these missions merit close scrutiny because they defined and delimited key capacities of an early modern, transatlantic state. Even as the Portuguese crown honed its practice of long-distance power politics in an era of European absolutism, it was forced constantly to settle for meager gains and make unintended concessions at the effective outer limits of its American possessions.

By following expeditions as they departed the captaincy's urban realm to march through unfamiliar grasslands and forests, we can better grasp this tension between consolidation and attenuation. We can explore apparent contradictions between the foci and the boundaries of colonial administrative potency, between overbearing yet underpowered institutions, between the sertões' putatively subjugated yet practicably unmonitored inhabitants. These overland enterprises demonstrate the workings of a Portuguese monarchy at once forceful in its drive to secure and extract wealth from its boundless American colony yet constrained by distance, limited resources, geographic ignorance, and the machinations of its own vassals. They highlight the activities of those who interacted along what amounted to myriad inland edges of empire. They allow us to glimpse otherwise invisible, wandering subjects and potential subjects, many of them still effectively stateless, in the act of challenging policies and practices aimed at territorializing Portuguese sovereignty.

In Brazil's southeastern interior the specter of mining's collapse lent a special gravity to journeys to the sertões that tested the reach of governing institutions. As the search for new mineral deposits and profitable alternatives intensified, expedition leaders were recruited to extend the effective jurisdiction and fortify the claims of their faraway sovereign. Departing from a discontinuous colonial domain, they carried orders to execute the crown's bidding in matters deemed central to the control of territory. These tasks, endorsed by avid functionaries of Portugal's transatlantic state, included subduing independent Indians, rounding up enslaved Africans who escaped their masters, surveilling small-scale prospectors, crushing contraband rings, reconnoitering reported gold and diamond strikes, and conducting scientific surveys. In the process officials and their backcountry envoys sought to secure new lands for mining, farming, ranching, and commerce, imposing civil, military, and ecclesiastical order. Although they described their aims in terms more common to the era in which they lived, they aspired to territorialize the empire, to ground the claims of the Portuguese monarch on the land.[4] This objective proved elusive, not only as an outcome but also in the act itself.

As these roving mobilizations moved over great stretches of uncontrolled lands still in the process of being colonized, problems surfaced and purposes shifted according to the twisting of the trail and the lengthening separation from royal supervision. Reflecting on the construction and maintenance of Portuguese transatlantic governance in the eighteenth century, Laura de Mello e Souza has urged historians to attend more carefully to Lisbon's dependence on individuals "who obeyed the norms and decisions emanating from the center of power, but who recreated them in daily practice, sometimes rendering the point of arrival so distinct from the point of departure that, not infrequently, the original idea and *sense* were obscured or even lost."[5] Overland expeditions gauge this transformation with unique spatial and temporal precision. They were conceived in palace pronouncements and trailside prose as archetypal conquest missions, consciously framed in the epic tradition of Homer, Camões, and venerated early Brazilian explorers. But they veered off course. The more Portugal's financially strapped state worked to assert dominion over Brazil's internal expanses, the more malleable its authority became.

Neither colonizers nor the colonized served as pliant participants in this resurgent endeavor as it played out over more than half a century. Men charged with exploring and establishing royal authority in zones targeted for internal colonization conducted themselves in ways that proved difficult to regulate. Representing the crown, respected vassals, soldiers, frontier administrators, and scientific experts found themselves ambivalently positioned at the nexus of royal directives, local realities, and personal ambition. In pursuit of mixed objectives, they in turn encountered marginalized frontier actors operating beyond the purview of the state: seminomadic Native peoples, escaped slaves, itinerant poor, and those deemed vagabonds and criminals. These men and women—for women appear frequently enough in the sources to confirm they were a constant presence even if their voices were largely silenced—sometimes cooperated with but more frequently frustrated authorities bent on controlling them. They eluded, defied, redirected, and time and again tamed Lisbon's imperial aims. The ship of Portugal's transatlantic state was cast adrift, attempting to navigate unknown seas, encountering subjects and circumstances its captains could not control or sometimes even comprehend.

For practical and methodological reasons that will become evident—and because it is a history largely untold—I have set out to measure

Lisbon's projection of power against a particular obstacle: imperial information gathering. This data-driven barrier to royal ambitions took shape as a confusion of rumors, distortions, claims, conflicting reports, and disputed facts. Or, better perhaps, it refused to take shape, exerting its force in its amorphousness. The transmission of ambiguous and contradictory reports from the interior derived from an array of cross-purposes and competing projects. As its consequence, a campaign orchestrated by a series of monarchs, viceroys, and governors to secure territory and establish unchallenged rule was subverted during its preliminary acts of reconnaissance. Those bent on colonialism's foundational undertaking, the absorption of unconquered lands, saw projects falter at their inception.

Easy distinctions contrasting elites and nonelites do not adequately capture what occurred. Problematic intelligence and communications confounded royal emissaries dispatched into the backlands. As a result expedition leaders contributed to the swirl of contradictory intelligence, wishful thinking, and fabrication that destabilized the very missions they were ordered to carry out. Their yearning for royal recognition and personal gain made them flawed proxies of an autocratic yet overextended administration. Simultaneously provoking official bewilderment were those already inhabiting lands targeted for colonization. Indians, Africans, Europeans, and their mixed descendants lived at distances that placed them beyond the capacity of imperial bureaucracies to gather and convey trustworthy, actionable intelligence about them. Among their most effective strategies to forestall unwanted royal impositions was to mediate the flow of information issuing from the backlands.

As in frontier settings throughout the Americas, intermediaries played an outsize role in determining the outcome of projects aimed at territorial appropriation and consolidation.[6] Of particular importance for forays into the sertões were those who possessed local knowledge about topography, natural resources, and unsurveilled human activity. The drive to exercise metropolitan sovereignty over the inhabitants of distant forests, savannas, mountains, and river valleys hinged on the reliability of backcountry informants. These individuals stand at the center of this study. As specialists in the possibilities and pitfalls of a vast realm beyond the secured enclaves of colonial settlement, expedition leaders and the peoples they encountered together formed an expertise continuum. Even though they were from strikingly different social origins and often at odds, those who led colonizing intrusions and those they intruded on jointly contributed to the operational intelligence sought by the imperial administration.

To advance its quickening ambitions, the crown required, as a precondition for success, reliable information about places so poorly known they were only beginning to appear on manuscript maps. We "need better information concerning the physical and political state of the ultramarine dominions," an exasperated minister for colonial affairs declared in 1796 from Lisbon.[7] Other tenuously controlled areas in Africa and Asia attracted similar attention, but the Brazilian interior was the largest and most assiduously surveyed of these imperial spaces, where Portuguese administrators, applying Enlightenment principles to overseas statecraft, devised more ambitious and systematic means to collect data deemed essential for wealth extraction and effective governance.[8] To this end, purveyors of backcountry expertise were summoned to report on developments in zones otherwise impervious to official investigation and intelligibility. Sometimes eager, sometimes reluctant, sometimes coerced, occasionally making names for themselves because of the understanding, exaggerations, or obfuscations they imparted, but more often remaining little known and even unnamed in the surviving sources, a panoply of information brokers exercised a vital yet largely unrecognized role in the Portuguese Empire's unfulfilled drive to consolidate and exploit its South American holdings. They shared with each other and with higher authorities what they knew, thought they knew, and pretended to know. When intimidated and interrogated, they confirmed or denied what they were purported to know. Together they contributed to an accelerating early modern cataract of information and misinformation crossing the South Atlantic. Increasingly studied as a European phenomenon transforming metropolitan administration, commerce, and spheres of learning, this flow of communications over great distances begs further attention as a critical component of colonial governance. For here, at the intersection of "political intelligence and indigenous knowledge," as C. A. Bayly discerned about another early modern empire, "colonial rule was at its most vulnerable." As producers of unevenly reliable intelligence, linking the Brazilian interior to the places where Portuguese policy took shape, these individuals advance our understanding of imperial expansion, cohesion, and decay.[9]

With respect to the methodological challenges inherent in recovering relevant voices, any inquiry into colonial informants rightly raises postcolonial anxieties about the possibility of deciphering evidence collected from them. The agents of European empires could not function without local informants. Authorities singled them out, sought to install them where they were absent, coaxed and coerced them, miscast them as envoys of their clans and communities, and misrepresented or suppressed their views when they did not coincide with official imperatives. The resulting falsifications and silences ramify in archives that selectively store accounts of their words and documented actions. But these repositories also contain more evidence than commonly recognized of the reactions, adaptations, negotiations, and countermeasures of backcountry denizens. There are legitimate concerns about what can be gleaned from bullied, nonliterate knowledge brokers. Yet the fundamental problem hampering scholarship about such individuals is not the error of overestimating the value of the documentary record. It is not, in other words, a pervasive misreading of sources the motivations of whose subjects historians naively deem transparent. Incaution in the archives is always concerning. The far greater problem, however, is that scholars have tended to sidestep the task at hand. Diverse groups inhabiting great stretches of the colony's interior have been consigned to the murky margins of history on the mistaken assumption that sources documenting their struggles are unavailable, insufficient, or insuperably untrustworthy. More troubling than the problem of misreading, in short, is the fact that many sources remain unread with an eye for the import of such individuals.[10]

My argument about the capacity exercised by those who supplied backcountry intelligence to challenge, redirect, and delay colonization efforts can be delineated in four parts. First, that the years between 1750 and 1822 witnessed a concerted imperial mobilization, the scope of which remains underappreciated, aimed at transforming multiple internal frontier zones into governed territory. Second, that this attempt to project the crown's sovereign rule brought to prominence a sizeable contingent of backcountry adepts, elites and nonelites alike, who variously appropriated, evaded, and contested the state's objectives, especially through the provision or withholding of critical information about lands, peoples, and resources, the nature of which ranged from fact to pure fantasy. Third, that the persistent inscrutability of the intelligence that reached captaincy, viceregal, and imperial halls of power from the distant sertões altered the course of empire, undermining efforts to incorporate zones deemed to be strategically significant. Finally, and more speculatively, I propose in an epilogue that the consequent inability to project territorial authority over sprawling lands beyond the Atlantic coast merits a prominent place it has not received among the factors explaining Portugal's swift loss of its most important colony on Brazil's independence two hundred years ago.

### Brazil's Internal Frontiers

If a single year can mark a sea change, 1750 best serves as the juncture at which the territorial formation of Brazil turned in on itself. When the Portuguese and Spanish crowns signed the Treaty of Madrid in that year, they established boundaries between the Iberian empires in South America that correspond to a remarkable degree to Brazil's present international borders.[11] Border disputes and further negotiations lay ahead, concerning, for instance, the Río de la Plata basin in the south and French Guiana in the north. Annulled in 1761, the treaty was later superseded, yet also generally reaffirmed, by the Treaty of San Ildefonso in 1777. This high-stakes diplomatic wrangling, however, can divert attention from another, far larger theater of territorializing activity demarcated by the struggle for dominion over lands within the colony, rather than along its interimperial borders. Those borders rimmed a colony within which great expanses remained beyond Lisbon's capacity to govern. Before 1750 the distinction between Brazil's external and internal frontiers was more ambiguous. But as Portugal steadily resolved the problem of its colony's external boundaries, a profusion of ungoverned internal realms, areas having nothing or almost nothing to do with Spanish or other foreign competitors, became the insistent object of royal preoccupation.

The era's centrifugal tendencies were, in an anxious back-and-forth, both animated and held in check by a doggedly centralizing state in the thrall of the reformist autocrat Sebastião José de Carvalho e Melo, the marquis of Pombal, first minister to the insubstantial José I. Pombal set out to remedy what he perceived as Portugal's lack of political and economic control over Brazilian territory. Subsequent administrations followed his lead.[12] Throughout the colony, stretching into the nineteenth century, expeditions moved like so many probing tentacles to extend the crown's dominion. This expansionist impulse drew force from Pombal, his ministerial successors, and colonial administrators who promoted exploration for profitable alternatives to existing inland mining operations and coastal sugar plantations. Yet it also provoked tensions and systemic contradictions when they sought to contain what they had fostered, apprehensive about colonists who slipped outside their surveillance. A scholarly tendency to highlight the general accord struck between colonial elites and their metropolitan benefactors has tended to downplay such points of friction.[13] Compared with their imperial rivals, moreover, the Portuguese confronted an especially wide gap between what was planned and what was possible in the realm of territorial consolidation. Despite its diplomatic triumphs in codifying ample South American borders, Portugal lacked the financial resources, military might, administrative strength, and sustained migratory stream necessary to achieve the kinds of integrative territorial gains made in Spanish and especially British America before independence movements fractured all three Atlantic empires.[14]

Well-consolidated Portuguese enclaves—islands and archipelagos of inland settlement, to use another maritime metaphor historians frequently invoke—places where state authority prevailed and where a functioning commercial economy was subject to at least a semblance of efficient taxation, accounted for a comparatively small portion of Brazil's unevenly colonized domain. Much of its sparsely populated space remained feebly incorporated, socially and culturally discontiguous, the province of independent Indians as well as escaped slaves, straying subsistence farmers, and small-stakes miners. In a concerted policy shift, the intricacies of which remain poorly understood, the crown redoubled its efforts in the second half of the eighteenth century to control these outlying peoples, seeking to count them, tax them, conscript them for military service, bind them to parish churches, and map and profit from the lands they occupied. In every major region of the colony, authorities struggled to extend Portuguese rule over zones lying firmly within the interimperial border yet beyond the crown's ambit. To measure the trajectory and significance of Portuguese America's territorial consolidation, in short, we must abandon the notion of a proto-national perimeter within which royal authority held sway. Instead, we must place greater emphasis on these interior precincts. The spaces separating settler enclaves, the colony's internal frontiers, did far more than is generally recognized to define colonial Brazil.

The precise nature of the inland zones scrutinized in this study will become evident in the following chapters. The term *frontier*, however, cannot be deployed without some initial explanation. Although Couto, the mineralogist returning from the west, did so in his diary entry, only rarely did Lusophone writers of his era use the word *frontier* in anything like the way scholars of imperial and national expansion use it today. In the eighteenth and nineteenth centuries, the Portuguese cognate *fronteira* referred to a boundary between geographic jurisdictions. These jurisdictions might be the separate captaincies that together constituted the whole of Portuguese America. They might be different empires or nation-states. A frontier, that is, was a borderline or border zone. Both in the Americas and Africa, when the Portuguese wished to identify lands unsettled or thinly settled by colonists, they instead favored the term *sertão* or its plural *sertões*. Of uncertain etymology, this term is customarily translated into English as backlands, backcountry, interior, wilderness, or, perhaps confusingly, frontier. It is now generally reserved for describing Brazil's impoverished, semiarid, northeastern interior. Throughout the colonial period, however, it had a much broader application, describing any of the immense lands beyond Brazil's Atlantic coast considered incompletely incorporated. Imbued with intimations of the uncivilized, of a domain of wild animals and savage Indians, a neglected realm consisting of uncultivated, unexcavated, unclaimed land, the term was freighted with colonialist presuppositions. Similar associations have for many years troubled scholars who fret over continuing to use the term *frontier*, even as it persists in the absence of a more suitable alternative. Recognizing the contested nature of these concepts, I cautiously use them both, frontier and sertão, as well as backlands, backcountry, and interior, finding such contemporary academic substitutes as *contact zone, middle ground, Native ground,* and *borderland* no less imperfect for my purposes.[15] Except to emphasize its imaginary qualities devised as a justification for seizure and occupation, I avoid the term *wilderness*, as connoting a place untouched by human habitation. While some early modern Portuguese commentators cast the sertões as unpopulated, they never were.

As an additional refinement, the term *internal frontier* is meant not simply to designate any frontier in the continental interior. Rather, it is intended to distinguish this sort of frontier from those variously described by historians as external frontiers, strategic frontiers, or borderlands, where two or more imperial powers vied for control of disputed territory, sometimes to the detriment, sometimes to the advantage, of those inhabiting these contested spaces. Assessing the centuries-long competition between Portugal and Spain in South America and Iberia, historian Tamar Herzog observes that the distinction between internal and external frontiers can be overdrawn. Frequently, she notes, "the struggle to occupy the land and control its inhabitants (the so-called internal frontier) coincided with and was simultaneous to fixing the border vis-à-vis neighbors (the so-called external frontier)."[16] This caveat holds for many zones but not the ones examined in this book, which by the second half of the eighteenth century lay securely within the borders of the Portuguese Empire, unaffected except in the most indirect way by Spanish designs or by Portuguese measures meant to counter those designs. Despite their imperial internality, however, these frontiers remained stubbornly beyond the reach of Lisbon's military, legal, fiscal, and ecclesiastical institutions. The imperviousness of such areas to metropolitan authority became ever more troubling as European monarchs learned to stress dominion over bounded territories, gradually broadening an older preoccupation with jurisdiction over groups of subjects. In Latin America this expanded notion of a sovereign's power to include exclusive rule over contiguous territory was a product of the eighteenth and nineteenth centuries.[17]

And yet, during the period under study, in counterpoise to this absolutist, territorializing tendency, the internal frontier zones considered in this book moved only haltingly, and often seemingly not at all, toward the establishment of colonial settlements, integrated extractive economies, and consolidated sovereign authority as envisioned by Lisbon. They cannot not be construed as having been overtaken by an imagined leading edge of an expanding empire. Rather, they persisted as unstable spaces of conflict, mediation, negotiation, and appropriation. These were areas where the Portuguese state exhibited scant power to enforce its laws. Officials found it nearly impossible to foster the conditions necessary to establish a pliable labor force sizeable enough to impel the work of colonization. These internal frontiers tended to be located in comparatively unfamiliar ecological zones of difficult access to Portuguese explorers, soldiers, and settlers. The presence of Indigenous peoples often remained pivotal, yet what unfolded in these spaces cannot be limited to the confines of Indigenous history. Understanding their presence requires that we also follow the paths of wandering peoples of African, European, and mixed origins whose conduct sometimes tested royal objectives and challenged imperial absorption more than Native peoples did.[18] Finally, and of particular interest for my purposes, the enduring impenetrability of these expanses elevated the significance of basic imperial intelligence gathering, including the production, exchange, withholding, and manipulation of the knowledge of places and peoples critical for colonization schemes.

Framed in this way, the present study contributes to a creative reappropriation of frontier historiography by scholars of the Latin American past. A new generation of historians is hard at work rethinking how their predecessors studied frontier zones, contributing to a resurgence of research focused on both the colonial and postcolonial periods. Improving on older approaches, working to strip away ethnocentric and nationalistic excesses from their conceptualization of frontiers, historians have turned their attention to areas ranging from the Sonoran Desert to the Amazon rainforest to the Patagonian grasslands. They have done so in dialogue with historians of other hemispheric and global frontiers, and with those who employ the concepts of borderlands and settler colonialism as their preferred analytical tools. They have demonstrated greater sensitivity to the agency of peoples of both Native and African descent in such zones. They have noted the centrality of ethnically hybrid intermediaries in areas where cultures met, clashed, and cooperated. They have pondered new ways to conceptualize and compare frontiers as distinct places and as creations of shared historical processes.[19]

The topic has particular relevance in Brazil, where incursions into Indigenous lands and primeval rainforests by wildcat miners, loggers, cattle ranchers, soy farmers, land speculators, and impoverished squatters continue to this day in the most recent wave of an inland migration lasting half a millennium. Despite this long history of internal colonization, Brazilian scholars often rejected the frontier as an analytical concept. They did so in response to the excesses they perceived in its application to the history of the United States, where during the first half of the twentieth century it became something of an academic obsession. Their reservations proved prescient, as their North American colleagues would come to share many of these same objections. In relegating the idea to the margins, however, Brazilian scholars often ended up neglecting the tension between internal expansion and its hinderances as a central feature of the colonial period.[20] The renewal of scholarly interest in the subject has corresponded with an accelerating effort to study Indigenous history, until the 1990s a pursuit largely relegated to anthropologists, although it should be noted that the Native presence was never limited to colonial Brazil's frontiers, shaping its urban and agricultural districts as well. Interest in these many zones reflects a growing conviction that colonial history cannot be adequately rendered without close attention to internal territorial consolidation, whether or not the term *frontier* is used to describe this process. The history of Portuguese America, in short, cannot be reduced to its established, export-oriented coastal plantation and inland mining complexes.

## Forays

In order to better illuminate the issues at stake in this territorial struggle, I have narrowed my geographic scope to the sertões within and around the southeastern captaincy of Minas Gerais (today a state covering an area larger than France). Four distinct internal frontiers will be considered, areas located roughly in the region's southwest, southeast, west, and northeast. In these four zones, separate sectors of what contemporaries categorized broadly as the captaincy's western and eastern sertões, the royal push to transform long-standing assertions of sovereignty into effective governance occurred with particular intensity. These areas were not confined by the unsurveyed and still-disputed internal borders Minas Gerais shared with neighboring captaincies. Rather, they straddled these borders, extending into Goiás to the west, São Paulo to the south, Rio de Janeiro to the southeast, Espírito Santo to the east, and Bahia to the northeast. This meant that expeditions probing for resources, fugitives from slavery, renegade vassals, and stateless autochthons did not march exclusively outward from the region's central mining zone, where most colonists originally settled as a consequence of the Espinhaço cordillera's prolific gold and diamond deposits. Key operations also proceeded from the outside in, that is, ascending inland in the direction of Minas Gerais and Brazil's Central Plateau from the seaboard (see map, "Southeastern Brazil, ca. 1800").

Of the many undertakings meant to enforce Portuguese claims, four forays into the sertões, corresponding to the book's four parts, will be examined with the aim of illustrating the range and evolving objectives of state-sponsored projects over the course of more than half a century. Their origins, outward progress, accomplishments, and shortcomings will be considered, paying special attention to the problematic acquisition and transmission of intelligence about places, peoples, and resources, and the consequences of these communications for the metropolitan making and frontier unmaking of Portuguese territorial control. The ventures are presented as aggregated microhistories, linking distant places, small incidents, and individual lives to large-scale historical processes. This method avoids the potential deficits, on the one hand, of a study so widely framed as to miss the salience of individual actors' idiosyncratic conduct in particular environments and, on the other, one so narrowly drawn as to ignore systemic contexts, transatlantic implications, and transcontinental comparisons. Together these microhistories accomplish what any one of them alone would not: revealing from the ground up, yet in geographic and temporal breadth, the mechanisms of internal colonization.[21] Their selection was determined by the comparative richness of the surviving documentation and their power to illuminate important aspects of the larger problem. All of these endeavors entailed various expeditions, although for coherence and concision, the emphasis in each part will be on one or two primary voyages.

In the first of the four missions, an ambitious merchant commissioned by the crown looked west to the wooded grasslands known as the *cerrado* along the ill-defined border dividing Minas Gerais and Goiás. Of the half-dozen expeditions he organized, one merits special attention. Setting out in the late 1760s with a retinue of settlers and enslaved laborers, he ordered a scribe to craft an unusual diary documenting his voyage, replete with paeans declaimed by rural poets and trailside cadenzas played by musicians. Polished for royal authorities, the diary trumpeted the merchant's heroic search for Indian adversaries, escaped slaves, and undiscovered gold. Despite making exaggerated promises, he encountered mere flakes of precious metal and only vestiges of the foes he sought. These unimpressive results did not stop him from claiming extravagant rewards for phantom conquests. He managed to assemble vast holdings in the form of multiple royal land grants, circumventing laws designed to limit such excessive accumulations of private property. The measure of his accomplishments lay less in his feats as a frontiersman than in his ability to extract advantages from an imperial administration so eager to register territorial gains it surrendered caution for credulity.

In the second, a series of explorers chased after rumored mineral deposits in the mountainous tropical forest separating Minas Gerais from Rio de Janeiro. Basic reconnaissance of this area, not far inland yet hard to reach because of its rugged terrain, extended over many years. Native informants proved critical to the sharing and withholding of knowledge concerning forest routes and illicit mining activity. They were also suspected of participating in the contraband trade. Lisbon responded with contradictory orders, until reports of persistent criminal activity could no longer be ignored, prompting the mobilization of military expeditions in the mid-1780s. These deployments targeted a notorious smuggler rumored to possess supernatural powers, whose clandestine gold washings infuriated authorities and captured the attention of the Inquisition while attracting impoverished rural laborers from surrounding districts. Converging on the area from the north and the south, soldiers raided the site then attempted to promote supervised settlement. An ensuing military occupation, made possible by the grueling toil of enslaved porters, did not produce the desired transformation, leaving its commander's reputation tarnished. The site's mineral deposits turned out to be overstated, embellished by the same Native informants influential in prompting official action in the first place, and by those who coerced or inflated their testimony. Belatedly, authorities discovered they could convince few settlers to cooperate in their planned colonization scheme.

In the third foray, the one that found José Vieira Couto musing about the sealike sertão, the crown-appointed mineralogist was called on to provide his scientific expertise on a journey to investigate reports of diamond strikes in western Minas Gerais. The advent of scientific inquiry as an instrument of frontier exploration, heralded as an antidote to the disappointments of earlier intelligence failures, did not suddenly provide the clarifying, impartial information Lisbon desperately sought. The mineralogist was guided by a company of Black and racially mixed prospectors, men and women operating outside the law but angling for royal favors. Cognizant of the machinations of a system that dispensed rewards unequally, they exchanged what they knew only guardedly, seeking advantage in their unrivaled knowledge of terrain. The mineralogist found himself drawn into a penurious realm inhabited by informants he distrusted but could not disregard because of their expertise. His frustrated search for the mineralogical evidence that would make his quest worthwhile vied with his desire to impress his superiors and, like his prospector guides, receive royal recompense. Unable to acknowledge the meager results of his explorations, the scientist transmitted improbable findings that again left the crown susceptible to costly illusions about undiscovered mineral wealth. After investing in excavating the area, authorities were forced to abandon it when it failed to yield anything approaching the expected profits. Science in the service of empire offered no easy antidote to the flow of misinformation from the backlands.

In the fourth, frontier authorities explored for gold and pushed a trade route down a remote river valley linking northeastern Minas Gerais with coastal Bahia. The valley was controlled by highly mobile Indigenous foragers whose presumed savagery prompted a royal declaration of war. The conflict provided an early test of royal power and territorial dominion after Napoleon's invasion of Portugal in 1807 forced the ruling Bragança family and its court to flee to Brazil. State actors sought to assert their strength in this frontier zone, but their actions betrayed their unmistakable weakness. They could not dictate policy in interior realms they ostensibly governed. When the valley's Natives demonstrated a willingness to interact, the resulting exchanges destabilized the policy of military conquest, as some officials urged a less belligerent approach. The peaceable conduct of the valley's Indigenous groups also attracted a new set of adventurers: northern European natural historians. These visitors further implicated scientific inquiry in the struggle over the colony's internal frontiers. Foremost among them was a German prince who led an expedition up the same river valley in order to study its Natives. Hailed as uniquely enlightened, his ethnographic account contributed to the popularization of harmful stereotypes about Amerindians among an international readership. His claims of scientific precedence also ignored earlier Portuguese exertions and Indigenous responses to them. His account and its reception exemplify how backcountry histories were subject to erasure and reinscription on the eve of Brazil's independence, during an era that emphasized new modes and measures of progress.

In selecting these four forays, I have skirted a coeval military campaign focused on the Doce River watershed, which drains Minas Gerais to the east, having examined the deadly assault on the Indigenous inhabitants of this sector of the Atlantic Forest in an earlier book.[22] Although repercussions of this struggle will become evident at various points in the present study, the backcountry expeditions considered herein did not engage in warfare with Indians in any conventional sense. As such, these episodes present a different face of the crown's drive to establish inland territorial sovereignty, less starkly bellicose but equally important for understanding the broader characteristics and significance of attempted territorial consolidation. The assault on the Indians inhabiting the Doce River basin was an especially violent case of a more comprehensive project to exert control over all of the colony's inland inhabitants and the lands they occupied. Some Native peoples faced particularly harrowing pressures, but those who avoided armed conflict, as well as marginalized subjects of African and European descent, also felt the Portuguese crown's attempt to tighten its grip across multiple geographic zones.

For Portuguese America as a whole, a satisfactory comprehensive account of the sweeping, post-1750 push toward colony-wide internal territorial consolidation has yet to be written; indeed, historians have struggled simply to delineate and name it.[23] An initial conquest era slowly wrested much of Brazil's long coastline from the Tupinambá and other Indigenous peoples in the sixteenth century. This feat established the foundations on which the *bandeirantes*—explorers and hunters of Indian slaves—pushed deeply but impermanently into the interior over much of the following century, while cattle herders and missionaries initiated a more lasting inland presence in a number of areas. When the gold strikes in Minas Gerais (first announced in the 1690s) led to subsequent discoveries farther west in Mato Grosso (1718) and Goiás (1725), the regions now defined as Brazil's southeast and central-west together became the primary, though not exclusive, loci of territorializing efforts until the middle of the eighteenth century, especially areas where mineral deposits and their provisioning zones lay. By this rough periodization, expeditions roaming the interior in the second half of the century constituted a fourth wave of expansionary activity, one that has received the least scrutiny. A few of the era's most prominent overland and river-borne expeditions have generated focused studies, and an understanding of regional variations has coalesced over time, particularly with respect to the Amazon basin and the colony's southern borderlands.[24] But scores of smaller, local and regional initiatives involving a greater range of actors and objectives have been treated as curiosities rather than as part of a coordinated transatlantic project.[25] The expeditions selected here for close examination are replete with curiosities, but taken together they tell a larger story, connecting the ground-level machinations of territorial formation to the state-building practices of imperial integration.

### Contexts and Sources

Migrants from Portugal, its Atlantic islands, and the Brazilian coast first swarmed to the landlocked region that came to be called Minas Gerais in the early eighteenth century, joining the largest gold rush in the history of the colonial Americas. With them, in even greater numbers, came enslaved Africans. Together they made this region vital to the South Atlantic system. The discovery of massive diamond deposits in the 1720s further strengthened the flow of colonists and captives. Minas Gerais became Portuguese America's most populous captaincy, with an estimated 340,000 inhabitants by the 1770s. It also became home to what was by far Brazil's largest regional population of enslaved men, women, and children. During the final quarter of the century, free people of color became the fastest growing segment of the captaincy population. Whites comprised less than a fifth of all inhabitants in 1786. Consequentially, this demographic composition meant that every colonizing venture depended on people of color, both enslaved and free.[26]

As the mining bonanza waned after 1760, the most accessible alluvial riches exhausted, a transformation occurred that had far-reaching implications for the distribution of the captaincy's population across its territory. Once seen as a decline into decadence, the nature of this economic and geographic reconfiguration has long been debated by historians, some questioning its structural depth, notwithstanding the jeremiads of local elites who fostered a sense of crisis as they sought tax relief from the crown. The mining sector did in fact enter a period of disruptive decline as gold yields collapsed. However, the expansion of other sectors—including ranching, agriculture, small-scale commerce, light manufacturing, and interregional trade—ameliorated this steep slide. The prosperous few sought new sources of wealth to sustain their fortunes; the dispossessed many, by contrast, did well simply to secure their basic subsistence. Relocating if they could marshal the means, internal migrants swelled existing settlements in the captaincy's south, favoring farming and ranching areas that had first emerged to feed the mining camps. These areas continued to provision the growing regional and coastal populations. Coinciding with this migratory impulse, pressure also built to absorb new lands in the thinly settled sertões, both western and eastern, resuscitating colonization efforts in both directions.[27] A considerable scholarly literature documents the changes associated with the end of the mining boom. Historians have explored Lisbon's tortuous response; the local elite's nativist stirrings; the slave system's transition from mineral to agricultural production; the accompanying growth of a free population of color; and the divergence of Old Regime and Enlightenment prescriptions for renewal, to name some of the most well-worn areas of research.[28] But far less attention has been devoted to the interactions of those who vied for land and resources beyond the limits of existing colonized enclaves.[29]

To find in Minas Gerais an enormous gulf between imperial plans and frontier constraints is particularly telling, because the captaincy has traditionally been described as the place where Portugal's overseas governance assumed its most authoritarian form.[30] This heightened absolutism ostensibly derived from the need to stanch what crown officials perceived as the smuggling, corruption, and criminality endemic to turbulent and resource-rich mining camps even as they grew into substantial towns. While the captaincy's urban realm earned a reputation among scholars for imperious administration, its sprawling hinterlands were cast as lawless zones beyond Lisbon's reach.[31] The legacy of this urban-rural binary long precedes modern historiography. A French naturalist who visited the interior in the early nineteenth century put the equation this way: "In unsettled regions, where policing becomes impracticable and the laws almost do not function, certain men, by their audacity, their intelligence, or their fortune, acquire over their neighbors a great ascendance, becoming veritable tyrants."[32] Such a view should give us pause to the degree that it echoes condescending complaints of the urban elites and government officials whose voices fill the colonial archives.

Tightly regulated colonial settlements and uncontrolled peripheries: What explains this interpretive disjuncture? How could the state be deemed so strong in the region's population centers and so weak beyond them in the sertões? A plausible hypothesis is that transatlantic absolutism was neither as unchallenged in the captaincy's intensively administered towns and villages, nor as inconsequential in its weakly colonized outer reaches, as has been generally imagined. In recent decades historians have adopted the first element of this revisionist position, but they have overlooked the second. The state's ineffectualness in the backlands continues to be mistaken for its absence. Correspondingly, the effectiveness of those who hindered Lisbon's drive to secure outlying zones—a countervailing force that was cumulative if not always collective—continues to be underestimated and understudied.

Readers will note a disparity in the language employed by expedition leaders who portrayed themselves as braving unexplored lands even as they registered the presence along their routes, in greater or lesser numbers, of isolated Portuguese colonists, slaves and self-emancipated fugitives, and roving Indigenous bands well practiced in cross-cultural communication and exchange. References to the sertão as a trackless sea depended on such concealments. This incongruity had its origins in the foundational contradiction of European discovery claims. By the second half of the eighteenth century, the long-practiced discursive excision of an aboriginal presence on the land had accumulated specific overlays in and around Minas Gerais. For more than a century before the first alluvial gold strikes were announced, expeditions from the coast had scoured the southeastern interior. As long as the search for mineral wealth proved fruitless, raiding for Indigenous slaves kept backcountry explorers occupied. The region's Indigenous peoples were decimated but not eliminated. Their numbers remained significant, particularly in the forbidding coastal forests covering much of the eastern third of the captaincy, where tens of thousands of foragers and hunters, mostly speakers of associated Gê-based languages, sought uncertain refuge.[33]

As gold and then diamond mining intensified, drawing Portuguese migrants and enslaved Africans into the interior, authorities did what they could to keep the captaincy population concentrated near the most productive mineral washings. To reduce contraband and facilitate tax collection, travel between the primary mineral washings and the coast was restricted by law to just three routes: the Caminho Velho to São Paulo and the port of Parati, the Caminho Novo to Rio de Janeiro, and the Caminho do Rio São Francisco to Bahia. A fourth route, the Picada de Goiás, ran northwest to Goiás. Great swaths of the sertões extending both east and west of the central mining zone were barred to unauthorized settlement. But the impracticality of securing such massive terrain meant that enforcement was always partial. Toward the coast, felling the ancient forest, colonists pressed tentatively into fertile agricultural zones. Toward the continental interior, ranching and agriculture continued to spread across the savanna. In both directions secondary gold and diamond strikes were exploited despite repeated edicts outlawing unsupervised prospecting. As a consequence, state-sponsored forays into the backlands during the second half of the century traversed zones already partly explored and, however feebly, colonized. In other words, places described as untraveled were home not only to surviving Native peoples; they had also been crisscrossed by earlier expeditions, excavated by transient prospectors, farmed by peripatetic squatters, grazed by cattle and sheep, and reconnoitered for hiding places by fleeing slaves and their pursuers. The move definitively to possess these internal frontiers was a significant commitment for the Portuguese crown after 1750, but it was neither the first time nor the only way colonists made their presence felt in these areas.

In Brazilian and Portuguese colonial archives evidence of the struggle over imperial ambitions and backcountry neutralization of those ambitions is preserved in partial and fragmentary form. The very nature of such archives limits what can be known about the day-to-day conduct of mostly nonliterate, frequently nonsubject peoples operating outside the ambit of the early modern bureaucratic state. These documentary repositories preserve what became intelligible to record keepers charged with official duties, individuals often unable to monitor precisely the sort of far-flung activity they sought to govern. What can be more readily culled from surviving sources, however, is evidence of these inland actors' unrivaled knowledge of the areas they explored and inhabited, and the way they used such knowledge to defend their autonomy and ameliorate their vulnerable positions in the colonial social hierarchy. What they claimed to know, what they denied knowing, what they shared of what they knew, and what was verifiable and misleading in what they shared—these critical components of backcountry interactions can be recovered. This is because state officials and the literate few to whom they delegated the task of territorial consolidation were especially keen to gather such intelligence from their informants and transmit it, albeit in altered form, to their superiors and patrons.

The policies that advanced this expansionist project issued respectively from the imperial, colonial, and captaincy capitals of Lisbon, Rio de Janeiro, and Vila Rica, although not always in this order. These policies activated civilian and military expedition leaders who wrote about their voyages and issued their own field orders. In turn, soldiers, settlers, Indigenous guides and translators, enslaved porters, muleteers, hunters, and specimen collectors communicated with these deputized individuals. The diverse documentary sources generated in this exchange of information allow us to gauge the extension and consequent attenuation of imperial power with spatial and temporal precision. Expedition chronicles, military communiqués, requisition orders, camp dispatches, trailside investigations, Inquisition interrogations, ministerial inquiries and directives, land claims, manuscript maps, itineraries, scientific field notes, and early ethnographic studies are among these many sources. Combined, they provide fine-grained, day-by-day, league-by-league portraits of the shifting relationship between Lisbon, its overland emissaries, and those individuals living at the empire's fringes.

In each of the four advances into the backlands to be considered, Portugal's campaign to project power over distant expanses exposed the empire's contradictions and susceptibilities, especially those created by its dependence on negotiating with and assimilating information provided by an array of backcountry actors in pursuit of diverse objectives. The present study explores this historical legacy, deepening our understanding of the transatlantic and hemispheric processes in which power was deployed, appropriated, challenged, and sometimes tamed at distances beyond the consolidated limits of early modern states and empires.

# PART 1

# Making the Wilderness Wild
## *The Authority of Misinformation*

THE RISE TO POWER OF Sebastião José de Carvalho e Melo, the Marquis of Pombal, coincided with declining gold production in Minas Gerais after 1760. A relentless and autocratic reformer as first minister to King José I, Pombal considered Portugal's desultory control over its South American dominions a cause of the monarchy's waning power in Europe. As part of his plan to modernize the administration of Portuguese America, extracting its resources more efficiently, he sought to draw more firmly into the imperial fold not only its strategic frontiers bordering Spanish America but also its many internal frontiers.

To achieve this goal the crown had to depend on unpredictable proxies, local notables charged with conveying to distant places the real and symbolic powers of a centralizing transatlantic state. Beginning in the 1760s the imperial drive to rule contiguous territory rather than a patchwork of settler enclaves provided the impetus for the exploits of a flawed adventurer. Leader of a series of backcountry expeditions, he advanced across the tropical savanna encompassing most of the western two-thirds of Minas Gerais. West of the headwaters of the São Francisco River, the area targeted for colonization included traditional hunting grounds of the seminomadic Kayapó Indians. Low mountains, riparian forests, and isolated grasslands also attracted many self-emancipated fugitives from slavery who sought to distance themselves from the extractive economy that dominated established mining towns and their agricultural hinterlands.

Inácio Correia Pamplona, the wealthy merchant who led these ventures, promised to clear these western sertões of such "enemies" while searching for deposits of precious minerals.

A carefully crafted conquest narrative of his most ambitious expedition in 1769 shaped his reputation as a frontiersman. Communicated in the form of a diary documenting the herculean feats he claimed to have accomplished, the account formed the basis of his decades-long campaign to be compensated with royal favors and honors. He did not receive everything he asked for, but he did manage to become one of the captaincy's largest landholders. The crown rewarded him with multiple land grants, setting aside its own restrictions on the excessive accumulation of landed property. Making the best of Lisbon's quest for imperial renewal, Pamplona turned the narrative of his own voyage into a tale of the kind authorities most wished to hear.

Chapter 1 introduces Pamplona and follows him west. A humble immigrant from the Azores who married the freeborn daughter of a former slave, he ascended to prominence as a merchant, muleteer, and rancher. Drawing on literary and historical traditions of exploration and conquest, touting his search for hostile Indians and gold, performing masculine honor, he accentuated and embellished elements of his venture calculated to garner royal support while exploiting legislative and legal openings. Chapter 2 examines Pamplona's disregard for colonists who preceded him and his search for individuals fleeing from slavery, further components of his self-fashioning. His rewards far exceeded his achievements in the backlands, as he maneuvered to gain enormous expanses of private property. His diary, frontier communiqués, and insistent letter writing to high officials reveal his skill in manipulating their expansionist aspirations and ignorance of far-off places. His exploits demonstrate how privileged adventurers put royal policies to the test even as they invoked imperial mandates.

CHAPTER I

# CIVILIZATION, BARBARISM, AND THE TALL TALE

SUMMARIZING HIS DEEDS toward the end of his life in 1805, the wealthy merchant Inácio Correia Pamplona spoke of having devoted forty years to "opening and populating" the western sertões of Minas Gerais, leading six expeditions to do so, arming and feeding "innumerable men" without any aid from the royal treasury. He had transformed the region from a place "infested" with "wild Indians," "runaway slaves," and "desperados" into one of the captaincy's "most useful expanses of territory." It was he who "routed" Indians, "dismantled" *quilombos* (communities of those who fled slavery), and "stimulated people to establish themselves" in the region. Spending great sums of his own money, he had built churches, chapels, military garrisons, and a jail. For these services, he sought acknowledgment, honors, and sinecures from the Portuguese crown.[1] Close reading of the archival record, however, offers scant evidence of his primary claims. We are left to explain by some other means his success in attracting state patronage, which made him the foremost landowner in the region. In that explanation lie some of the hidden dynamics of Portuguese territorial expansion during this period. The absence of convincing evidence for Pamplona's purported accomplishments as a frontiersman serves paradoxically as evidence of both the empire's growing expansionist assertiveness and the opportunities for self-promotion and accumulation this reorientation offered to local notables with backcountry experience.

Authorized by a series of governors to lead the colonization of lands drained by the headwaters of the São Francisco River, Pamplona produced an unusually detailed archival record. Documentation is particularly strong concerning his most important expedition, which set out in 1769 from a ranch near São João del Rei, one of the oldest mining towns in southeastern Minas Gerais.[2] The mission's planned destination was a portion of the captaincy's western *cerrado*, or savanna, not far from an ill-defined internal border contested by the neighboring captaincies of São Paulo and Goiás. Already known as a man of means and influence, Pamplona was charged with exploring this region and establishing settlers there. His actions testify to the tight bonds forged between the crown, the captaincy administration, and privileged vassals to advance the process of territorial incorporation; they also reveal his determination to exploit this colonial compact for personal gain. The adventures and misadventures that his unidentified scribe recorded in his expedition diary—a restyled, dramatically heightened version of the verbose letters Pamplona wrote along the trail—portray a member of the elite at pains to attract crown favor in conventional ways.[3] Yet they also expose an insistent search for new negotiating tactics on this internal frontier, one of many and multiplying contested edges of Portuguese imperial dominion and knowledge. An increasingly activist transatlantic state provided openings for a man like Pamplona, particularly after crown and captaincy officials handed him all meaningful legal authority as their backcountry regent. He would embrace this opportunity physically, financially, and rhetorically. His vision epitomizes what one historian describes as a conception of the sertão as a "space in the perpetual state of becoming," where the conversion of that space into territory "is achieved to the degree that settlement advances and intensifies." Pamplona pledged not to rest until he fulfilled his "sweet hopes" of recreating in these lands "a small portrait of Europe," replete with wheat and rye harvests, fertile orchards, and thriving livestock.[4]

### Noble Adventurer

Pamplona's wanderings in a wilderness more imagined than real demonstrate how disproportionate wealth and social advantage, in this case measured especially in accumulated land, could be extracted from a state struggling to territorialize its dominion over areas perceived as—or better, constructed as—unsettled, wild, and lawless. The interplay of cooperation and manipulation, of patronage and self-interest, shaped the crown's attempts to control such regions and play a role in the legitimation of private landholdings. Such interdependency was inscribed in the very language, full of exaggerated and self-deprecatory praise, men like Pamplona adopted to express fealty and curry favor. Yet even in the context of the era's epistolary culture of encomium, his was an extreme case. Replying to the first letter received along the trail from the captaincy governor, he effused: "With the most respectful and keen desire and unutterable pleasure, I received the honorable letter with which Your Excellency deigned to elevate my useless insignificance."[5] Less apparent than the obsequiousness of such performances is how much the state, in turn, relied on ambitious vassals to enlarge its domain, how their official accounts hid as much information as they revealed, and how they excluded other claimants from the lands they ostensibly settled. Aware of the opportunities his position afforded, Pamplona did not hold back when writing the governor, referring to himself in the third person as "your Pamplona."[6] Unrestrained obeisance became a literary device tailored to amass property and status.

Born in the Azores in 1729, the same year the discovery of diamonds in Minas Gerais added new incentives to a gold rush by then several decades in the making, Pamplona migrated to Brazil as a child. From a family of modest means, he arrived under the care of an uncle, a Franciscan friar, who on their arrival sent him to live in Minas Gerais with another uncle, a traveling merchant and muleteer. As an adolescent, Pamplona accompanied his guardian on journeys to sell supplies and provisions. Gradually establishing himself as a cattleman and merchant in his own right, he married in his early twenties. His wife, Eugênia Luisa da Silva, was the mixed-descent daughter of an enslaved mother shipped to Brazil from the Mina Coast (present-day Ghana). Accumulating resources in the food marketing business, although on a much smaller scale than Pamplona, the mother had purchased her own freedom, thereby assuring that Eugênia and her sister would themselves be born free. Pamplona's financial wherewithal increased throughout his twenties and thirties. As he was approaching forty, he began acquiring large tracts of land in the western sertões, becoming one of the captaincy's most formidable rural potentates and an exceptionally wealthy man. In later regional historiography, Pamplona would be best known, and reviled, for serving as a government spy, first likely participating in and then joining two other informers who betrayed the 1789 nativist intrigue known as the Inconfidência Mineira (Minas Conspiracy), a failed plot to assassinate the governor and declare an independent republic. But in the mid-eighteenth century, he was focused on expanding his provisioning business. His livestock, foodstuffs, and other goods helped supply not only the captaincy population, including its military forces, but also coastal residents in Rio de Janeiro. Eventually becoming the owner of what he maintained was the largest mule herd in Minas Gerais, he also organized the transport of gold and diamonds for the crown from the inland captaincy to the coast and the awaiting Portuguese fleet.[7]

It was on one of these commercial ventures, while in Rio de Janeiro, probably in 1762, that Pamplona was asked by António Gomes Freire de Andrade, the count of Bobadela (1733–63), then serving as governor of both captaincies, to mount his first expedition to western Minas Gerais. During his long tenure, Bobadela served Lisbon as an unrivaled champion of extending the crown's authority and rationalizing its administrative and fiscal powers over Brazil's interior expanses as well as securing its borders with Spanish America. As a substantial incentive, the governor provided Pamplona with twenty enslaved laborers skilled in masonry, carpentry, and blacksmithing, along with a flock of five hundred sheep seized from Jesuit missionaries, who had recently been expelled from the colony as part of the consolidation of state power over Brazil's most remote lands orchestrated by Sebastião José de Carvalho e Melo, the future marquis of Pombal, first minister to José I (r. 1750–77). Promised continued financial support by Bobadela's successor, Minas Governor Luís Diogo Lobo da Silva (1763–68), Pamplona assigned one of his subordinates to lead the first expedition, and then made the journey himself in 1765. Noting the "excessive" drain on his own financial resources, he set out across the wooded grasslands filled with an "ardent desire" to distinguish himself in service to the crown.[8] His efforts, he frequently claimed, were self-funded. This assertion of independence from the royal treasury would take its place among the many half-truths and outright falsehoods he repeated to burnish his reputation. It was not only state-supplied slaves and sheep that helped him launch his western enterprise but also his manipulation of debts he owed the crown. During the period in which he amassed his extraordinary holdings, he fell so far behind on tax remittances that the crown moved to collect the debts he owed, ordering the seizure of farm buildings, feed, livestock, and numerous enslaved workers.[9]

The diary of Pamplona's subsequent expedition across the savanna, written in 1769, two years after he had already received six land grants (*sesmarias*) for his initial services, offers the most complete narrative of the deeds on which he based his claims. The basic elements of the mission can be quickly summarized. The expedition set out from one of Pamplona's ranches. Thirteen men on horseback led about two hundred settlers westward, although some may have followed later. Most but not all of the participants were male. Apart from Pamplona's daughters, the diary lists another six females. One can assume that many of the colonists brought slaves. Their presence may explain Pamplona's much higher tally of four hundred expedition participants in a later document, although his proclivity for exaggeration may also have been at work. He armed and equipped fifty-eight of his own captive workers for the journey. He also brought eight musicians, all but one of them enslaved, to provide stirring, sacred music when required. He employed a chaplain, a surgeon, and a scribe and mapmaker. More than fifty of his mules were laden with supplies. Some 240 sheep made the trip as well.[10]

Those setters who reached the farthest point of the journey and then returned with Pamplona traveled about one thousand kilometers overland. The round trip took more than three months. Much of the trek crossed the *cerrado* (the shortened term for *campo cerrado* or closed field), the now-vanishing tropical savanna of Brazil's Central Plateau, comprising a variety of ecosystems including grasslands, shrublands, wetlands, dry forests, and riparian forests, crosscut by streams, rivers, and low ridges.

After leaving established trails, the travelers faced daunting terrain. "Lots of slaves went in front with bill-hooks, axes, and hoes to push through the forests, open trails, and make bridges over streams and small rivers, through which the troop could pass," the scribe wrote of an especially grueling day. "Trail-blazing and pushing through the forest with much work, we reached the edge of the São Francisco River. All of us were on foot, without any horses, while over half of our troop and all of our horses and train, pack mules, everything, were scattered across fields and woods, as they could not overcome the obstacles of several streams, woods, and swamps." The merchant and his family were not the only ones to accumulate land as a reward for these efforts. Invested with the powers of agency for the governor and king, he distributed grants to dozens of settlers at the westernmost point of their journey.[11]

Identifying Pamplona's other achievements is less straightforward. When the expedition reached those lands, he sought Indians to conquer, but contrary to his later recollections they evaded his armed lieutenants. He searched for gold but found none of any significance. He attempted to root out runaway slave settlements, but their occupants vanished into the forests. He erected a sizeable bridge across a tributary of the São Francisco River, but an accident during its construction killed more than fifty workers, most of them surely enslaved, when a massive beam crashed through scaffolding. He also built a church, and he cleared a trail for pack animals across a particularly remote stretch of the cerrado.[12] Eager to proclaim his accomplishments, he invited rural poets to sing his praise and recorded their stanzas for royal authorities to read. In short, to enhance his fame as a frontiersman, he enacted a series of conquest rituals, which the crown read as meritorious and worthy of uncommon recompense, despite these modest results. His greatest feat was one he never mentioned: enlisting the state in his campaign to appropriate land just beyond its effective jurisdiction. At such distances, where royal authority became exceedingly tenuous, the crown could do little but delegate its powers. A full range of royal favors, rewards, and privileges encouraged loyalty, yet practices developed over the course of more than two centuries of inland exploration had begun to lose their currency as the mining economy lost its vigor. Designed to project sovereignty where it was not convincingly established, the colonial legal regime, with its peculiar blend of obsolescence, malleability, prohibitions, and incentives, created opportunities that Pamplona seized. Looking more closely at certain elements of his expedition, we can better understand his ability to exploit his powers as a backcountry representative of the crown.

Pamplona situated his expeditionary activity within a long tradition of exploration and raiding for Indigenous slaves. This tradition shaped his actions and informed the support he received for them. Historians of colonial Brazil refer to the most famous of the ventures that struck out for the continental interior as *bandeiras*. The term translates literally as banners or flags. First during the medieval reconquest of the Iberian Peninsula, then during the sixteenth and seventeenth centuries in Brazil, it was used to describe paramilitary expeditions, presumably because troops carried flags to announce their presence and quasi-official status. Historians conventionally tie the end of the bandeira era to the onset of the gold cycle. The mineral strikes at the turn of the eighteenth century redirected the energies of those most active in this enterprise, wilderness adventurers and slavers from the captaincy of São Vicente, later São Paulo. These Paulista *bandeirantes*, as they came to be known, were the first to reconnoiter much of the geographic expanse formalized by Portuguese diplomats as Brazilian territory in the treaties signed in Madrid in 1750 and San Ildefonso in 1777. They were also the first to discover major gold deposits in the lands that became Minas Gerais. But they found themselves quickly pushed aside by a tide of fortune-seekers from Portugal, its Atlantic islands, and coastal cities like Rio de Janeiro and Salvador, who followed the trails they had opened into the interior. Associating the Paulistas with the origins of Brazil as a modern nation, historians celebrated their feats, which in many accounts border on the mythical. At the same time, scholars demoted the study of many subsequent expeditions and their territorializing activity to a matter of little consequence.[13] Setting the example, Diogo de Vasconcelos, patriarch of the scholarly history of Minas Gerais, bemoaned the extinguishing during the first half of the eighteenth century of the "last sparks of the Paulista spirit."[14]

Pamplona and his ilk understood the bandeirante inheritance differently. He explicitly located his activities within this heroic tradition by referring to the exploratory patrols he dispatched to the wilderness as bandeiras. His 1769 expedition occurred at a time when many others, notwithstanding their absence from the historiography, were being deployed to the sertões. As the mining economy began to slow, miners, ranchers, farmers, and merchants enlisted the captaincy government to support the search for new lands to exploit. A succession of governors responded enthusiastically, their own status at court hinging on the revenues the region produced for the crown. Although wary of the legendary if often overstated self-sufficiency of the bandeirantes, they hoped the renewal of the Paulista tradition by courageous settlers would help revitalize the captaincy. Geographic reconnaissance of the sertões, likely requiring clashes with independent Indians and those in flight from slavery, was seen as a starting point for such a revival. Paulista bandeirantes' backcountry pursuits had in the previous century led to the discovery of buried riches. The same would happen again if exploration activity resumed, according to this hopeful version of the past.

Economic motives cannot alone explain this new burst of bandeira activity. The task of forming, funding, provisioning, and deploying armed expeditions, which often depended on the labor of enslaved and free people of African descent and Indians living within colonial society, constituted a considerable and contested mobilization of limited public and personal financial resources and manpower. Furthermore, late colonial expeditions achieved far from decisive results, measured in terms of new mineral discoveries and permanent occupation of new lands. Undeterred, those who advocated the use of expeditions drew on myth, tradition, tropes of masculinity, and historical memory to bolster economic impulses, investing the bandeira with the status of a ritual endowed with deep symbolic meaning.[15]

The renowned Minas poet Cláudio Manuel da Costa extolled the bandeirantes in his epic poem "Vila Rica," completed in 1773:

> Driven by fervor, which the breast contains
> You see the Paulistas, spirited ones,
> Who for the King seek luminous metal
> With their own hands to enrich the treasury.

## CIVILIZATION, BARBARISM, AND THE TALL TALE    37

FIGURE 1.1. Enslaved miners near Vila Rica, capital of the captaincy of Minas Gerais. Source: Johann Moritz Rugendas, *Voyage pittoresque dans le Brésil* (Paris: Engelmann, 1835). Courtesy of the Biblioteca Nacional, Rio de Janeiro.

Referencing the bandeira leader thought to have sparked the gold rush with his discovery in the 1690s of alluvial deposits at the site of an Indian village, the poem continues:

> See how the noble adventurer scorns,
> Bonds and betrayals awaiting him,
> The greedy hunger of the bloody savage.[16]

Costa drew on his own experience in the backlands, having traveled in 1764 to the captaincy's western sertões with Governor Silva, whom he served as secretary. This reconnaissance expedition raised expectations for Pamplona's explorations.[17] The poet's lines summoned the imagined geography into which the merchant and his company marched. The bandeirante mythos evoked adventurers who had once entered the sertão, defeated Native antagonists, and unearthed gold, producing extravagant fortunes on both sides of the Atlantic. A new generation of noble frontiersmen might do the same, reenacting past successes, sustaining the same faith in conquest and the yearning for wealth and glory that had impelled the colonization of Brazil from its earliest days.

Pamplona would prove a master at staging a venture that captured this distinctive moment in the region's history, when a heroic past answered the concerns of an anxious present. Cultivating connections at the highest reaches of captaincy government, he insisted on an account of his trek that bound conquest myths to official purposes. References to backlands enemies, gold-bearing lands, and virile acts would fill the pages of his expedition diary. The narrative skills of his scribe would be put to the test as Pamplona sought favor and fortune, maneuvering within colonial administrative and legal norms to earn the largesse he craved, even as he discovered neither Indians nor gold.

### Indian Adversaries, Real and Imagined

Appointed by the governor as regent (*regente*), militia field commander (*mestre-de-campo*), and mines inspector (*guarda-mor*) of the western sertão, Pamplona was empowered to conduct a remarkable range of administrative, regulatory, and judicial tasks, his authority over the zone exceeded only by the governor, to whom he answered directly. Encompassing military and civil governance, his responsibilities included the command of militia members, tax collection, and Indian relations as well as the regulation of mining and settlement activities, from the distribution of individual mineral claims, to the allocation of water rights, to the provisional concession of land grants. Confirming the appointment, José I resorted to language Pamplona used to describe himself, praising him for his "important service," which he had carried out "with great effort, risk of life, and considerable expense . . . , settling wild Indians into village life in order to foster the cultivation of land and the discovery of the best places for the extraction of gold." As regent and field commander, Pamplona would enjoy "all of the honors, privileges, liberties, exemptions, and exceptions [from taxes and duties] which thereby accrue to him and which are enjoyed by paid infantry colonels in [the king's] armies."[18]

The state administrative structure relevant in this region, as in others, comprised four loci of control: the crown, its ministers, and its overseas governing institutions in Lisbon; the viceroy, recently arrived in Rio de Janeiro after the colonial capital moved south from Salvador, Bahia, in 1763; the captaincy governor in Vila Rica; and the municipal council of São João del Rei, head town of the southern *comarca* or judicial district of Rio das Mortes. As in all four of the captaincy's comarcas, a superior judge (*ouvidor*) administered justice, overseeing circuit judges and other law enforcement officials based in towns and villages, depending on their size. A high appeals court (*Relação*) was created in Rio de Janeiro in 1751, largely in response to complaints from officials in Minas Gerais about the long delays in cases heard by the first of these courts in far-off Salvador. By appointing Pamplona his regent, the governor superseded this elaborate formal structure. The appointment placed all administrative and judicial matters in the rancher's hands, subject to the governor's approval. Although couched in terms that asserted the strengthening of state authority, the arrangement underscored the incipience of legal institutions and even the law itself on this internal frontier. Paradoxically, it also created a jurisdictional vacuum, a fictive wilderness out of lands already populated, by preempting existing institutional structures and threatening to erase preexisting claims. Pamplona and the governor, with the crown's vaguely informed approval, could thereby endeavor to impose a new order. Thus, one of Pamplona's first acts after his expedition reached western Minas Gerais was to order that all landholders in the region present their property titles for validation, even if previously confirmed by the crown. Conveniently ignoring his own expanding holdings, he insinuated to the governor that some of these individuals had deceived officials to accumulate more land than they could use productively.[19]

To clarify how Pamplona used these appointive powers to accumulate his massive family ranches in the west, it is helpful to consider the function of Indian conquests as a legal basis for personal advantage and legitimization of private property. This stratagem dated to the beginnings of Iberian colonization in the Americas. In the second half of the eighteenth century, its permutations continued to animate frontier settlers from Patagonia to California, and beyond, across New France and British America. In Portuguese America's inland mining region, a midcentury rewriting of colonial Indigenous legislation, which professed to bolster Native freedoms, presented men like Pamplona with an opening. Offering their services as agents of the crown, they proposed to extend the reach of the new laws over still-independent Indians and the lands they occupied. Doing so afforded them special authority in lands where royal sovereignty was more an aspiration than a fact. The prospect of exercising such power tempted more than a few to overstate minor gains as lofty feats. It provided cunning colonists the mechanism they needed to stretch and even circumvent the law, the very law they claimed to be imposing on ungoverned zones.[20]

Beyond customary "rights of conquest," the enhanced legal authority Pamplona could anticipate from reporting successful incursions into Indian lands derived from major changes in Portuguese Indigenous legislation and from his own immediate experience. Historians have long noted the contradictory nature of crown Indigenous policy from the earliest days of colonization. A fundamental tension between those policies fostering conquest and others promoting benevolent protection characterized Portuguese rule from the moment the crown dispatched its first royal governor-general to Brazil in 1549. Tomé de Sousa (1549–53) carried with him royal orders to prevent colonists from provoking Indians to war then enslaving those taken captive, in accordance with the medieval concept of "just war." A precursor of future Janus-faced legislation, these orders simultaneously directed Sousa to discipline Indians who resisted subjection, "destroying their villages and settlements, and killing and enslaving whatever part of them you consider sufficient." Over the course of the colonial period, royal edicts repeatedly prohibited Indigenous slavery, and colonists repeatedly ignored them.[21]

In the eighteenth century policies aimed at the nexus of Indigenous relations and territorial dominion proved just as discordant. Crown and captaincy policies were based on the so-called Law of Liberty and its elaboration in the Diretório dos índios, or Indian Directorate. José I promulgated the Directorate in 1758 after Pombal's brother, Francisco Xavier de Mendonça Furtado (1751–59), implemented its provisions unilaterally the year before while he was serving as governor of the Amazonian state of Grão-Pará and Maranhão. The new rules appointed lay directors to oversee Native villages until then governed by missionaries. Intended to check the rising influence of the Jesuits on the eve of their expulsion from the colony, this legislation empowered secular administrators to "civilize these hitherto unhappy and wretched" Indigenous peoples, hastening their incorporation into colonial society, making them "useful to themselves, to the colonists, and to the state." First focused on the village Indians of the Amazon basin, the Directorate was extended to the rest of Brazil the following year, remaining in place until the end of the century.[22]

In Minas Gerais, Governor Silva, the enthusiastic sponsor of Pamplona's first ventures to the west, demonstrated particular aptitude in adapting the law to fit local circumstances. He had gained experience using this same legislation to amplify his administrative powers over territory within and beyond the borders of the northeastern captaincy of Pernambuco, where he previously served as governor.[23] Eyeing the eastern forests of Minas Gerais, he invoked the law to justify the conquest of the independent Botocudo, Puri, and other Native groups. Despite the law's emphasis on village Indians, he reasoned that only by "reducing the heathen"—that is, subduing nonsedentary groups by violent means if necessary—would the state succeed in "making use of their great utility for the benefit of the people and His Royal Treasury."[24] In 1764 Silva ordered a series of armed expeditions deployed to the eastern sertões to effect this conquest. In this same year he traveled with some of his top aides, including the poet Cláudio Manuel da Costa, to the southwest on his own reconnaissance mission. After his return, he called on Pamplona to begin the task of "colonizing" the region lying along the Goiás border, warning him of the "danger of [runaway] slaves and heathens."[25] As a confidant and client of the governor and a keen observer of his expansionist policies, Pamplona understood that a successful campaign against the captaincy's western Indians, especially the feared Kayapó, seminomadic Gê speakers, would be well received. It is little wonder, therefore, that he stressed his courage in the face of Indian resistance as often as possible. It would be Governor Silva who signed off on the land grants Pamplona claimed for himself, his family, and his earliest associates in this effort. As the governor tailored crown Indigenous policy to accommodate his conviction that a push into Native lands would help rescue the captaincy from gold mining's decline, Pamplona took advantage of this expansionist project to advance his own cause.

A year before the rancher launched his major expedition, further impetus was provided by a new governor, José Luís de Meneses Castelo Branco e Abranches, the count of Valadares (1768–73), to whom Pamplona addressed his polished chronicle and his letters from the trail. Pursuing his predecessor's policies in the eastern forests, Valadares called on his military officers to press forward with their "conquest of the barbarous heathen." Soldiers were to do what they could to subdue Indians "in a kind and gentle fashion." If opposed, however, they were to "terrorize them with force and by any means necessary."[26] Such policies encouraged Pamplona to insist he was carrying out a parallel conquest in the west, whether or not he actually encountered any Kayapó.

In orders directed to Pamplona in advance of his 1769 expedition, Valadares conjoined the task of territorial reconnaissance to Indian submission. Pamplona was to keep a daily record and create a map of his westward march, documenting distances and geographic features, making special note of evidence of gold deposits discovered along the route. He was to record the claims of any Portuguese colonists already established in the area. All of this depended, however, on asserting authority over the region's Indians. "Since this country is penetrated by and infested with heathens," the governor wrote, Pamplona should exercise great care in treating them amicably, while "making them perceive the spiritual benefit that they obtain by reducing themselves to the community of Christianity." Should they resist these overtures, the use of arms as a defensive measure was permissible. In such cases members of the expedition were authorized to respond by "subduing them up to the ultimate end," by which the governor evidently meant their extermination. To oversee those who submitted, Pamplona was to appoint administrators to "civilize" them, instruct them "in our mode of work," and "eliminate the infamous idleness in which they live."[27]

From the 1760s to the end of his life, Pamplona trumpeted his accomplishments as an Indian fighter. That he could point to little hard evidence to substantiate his assertions did not prevent him from repeatedly touting what he cast as daring acts. Members of his expedition relied on a number of Native guides. Otherwise, his account contained vague allusions to Indigenous "enemies" but few references to actual encounters with Natives, and these encounters were anything but heroic. The Indians mentioned by the expedition scribe remained figments of the imagination, threatening the party from a distance. For instance, once at nightfall, while hunting alone, Pamplona became lost on the savanna. Expedition members who spent the anxious hours searching for him until he found his way back to camp around midnight "did not know whether he had encountered some danger posed by blacks, heathen Indians, or some beast," his scribe reported. Some days later, in another bit of evidence later used to substantiate exaggerated claims, a priest and admirer praised him for his actions in a region inhabited by "embattled heathens."[28]

If Pamplona hoped that this expedition would produce actual conquests, he was surely disappointed. Self-promotion rather than documented triumphs in armed clashes bolstered his status. Repeatedly claiming to have "routed" the region's Indians during the period preceding his successful request for land, he offered few specifics. He was untroubled by the contradiction of having to mount his 1769 expedition and much later ones in 1781 and 1782 with the same objective of subduing the region's Natives. These subsequent actions responded to officials who accused Kayapó warriors of killing travelers, attacking at least one ranch, alarming settlers, and stalling colonization.[29] It is from this later period that Pamplona offered the clearest description of actual contact with the Kayapó, who at one point followed his entourage from a distance for eleven days. Even in this instance, his account was devoid of specifics. All he could muster was, "This enemy tends to attack in the dead of night," arriving without warning, setting fires to panic their adversaries, shooting arrows at all who flee.[30] More than two decades later, supporting Pamplona's petition for further honors, one ally credited him with pacifying the Kayapó by compelling them to cease wandering and congregate in an *aldeia* (village).[31] Again little documentary support for the claim survives. Other evidence points to ongoing Native resistance west of the São Francisco River. In 1807 an official described the border area between Minas Gerais and Goiás as an unsettled expanse inhabited solely by "wild heathens who cause great damage to travelers who pass through those lands."[32]

Part of the difficulty differentiating fact from fiction, information from misinformation, stems from the lack of scholarly certainty about the Kayapó presence in western Minas Gerais. Most lived across the disputed captaincy border in Goiás, although this jurisdictional boundary certainly did not signify the geographic divide for highly mobile Native peoples that it did for settlers. Paulista bandeirantes enslaved thousands of Kayapó in Goiás in the 1740s. Decades of intense conflict followed, until the governor sued for peace, encouraging many Natives to settle into state-run villages in the 1780s. As settlement pressures increased, warfare returned to the area in the early nineteenth century.[33] Some reports, as noted, stressed ongoing conflict after Pamplona's interventions, and others underlined the collapse of Native society before his arrival. According to one regional historian, "the truth . . . is that Pamplona encountered the Kayapó already practically dispersed and nearly decimated."[34] Based on the evidence Pamplona presented in his communiqués, it is hard to make the case that his actions as an Indian fighter made much difference. The growing presence of settlers, their roads and fields, and especially their cattle herds did far more to disrupt what remained of Kayapó itinerancy.

Regardless of actual encounters with Indigenous foes, Pamplona knew that Indian attacks from an earlier era had thrown into doubt the claims to land grants abandoned by colonists who had preceded him to the region. For instance, written days before his 1769 expedition departed, and apparently received several weeks later, a letter to Pamplona by one interested party described five such vacated properties in vague geographic terms. The letter's author asked for help in investigating the status of this land, one of the claimants to which was the governor of Portuguese Angola, Francisco Inocêncio de Sousa Coutinho.[35] For Pamplona, such uncertainty presented opportunities. In the royal court in Lisbon, pondering the laws

CIVILIZATION, BARBARISM, AND THE TALL TALE   45

FIGURE I.2. The western savanna. Source: Rugendas, *Voyage pittoresque*. Courtesy of the Biblioteca Nacional, Rio de Janeiro.

governing Indian relations, a crown minister could wax poetic about "becoming familiar with and associating with these heretofore unfortunate peoples who, because of the tyranny with which they have always been treated, find themselves in the ignorance in which they were born."[36] But with enterprising men like Pamplona as the colonial administration's favored frontier informants, it was inevitable that laws would be stretched beyond their stated intention and appropriated for personal gain. Thus the canny merchant exaggerated what Indigenous resistance did occur, invented it where it did not exist, and claimed credit for ridding the region of it, whether it was real or imagined.

### Gold and Glory

The expedition's search for gold similarly illustrates the increasingly long, assertive, but clumsy reach of the law and the state in the backlands. This search began in earnest about a month into the journey, when

Pamplona dispatched two smaller exploratory bandeiras, together numbering seventy-six "soldiers," armed to defend themselves during "encounters with the enemy." When these men returned empty-handed nearly a month later—fearful, they admitted, of provoking just such an encounter with hostile Indians or runaway slaves—he could not contain his disappointment. Having all but promised the governor a major new mineral discovery in a prior letter, he issued a strong, public rebuke to one of his lieutenants.[37] He then sent out another group of prospectors. The scribe explained that they were ordered to conduct "a detailed examination of caves and of holes [dug] to the depths of the gravel and shale." Pamplona remained behind, occupied with other duties, including the clearing and planting of land to provision future expeditions. Knowing his leader was never one to be cast in a supporting role, Pamplona's scribe depicted him spending "all day in the hot sun . . . , working and laboring alongside [others], making the others work." So "violent" was this effort that "he sweated three shirts."[38] When the beleaguered prospectors returned again without success, Pamplona resolved to accompany them, and he ordered the expedition chaplain to join him, hoping perhaps that a demonstration of piety might yield results. At night he refused to return to camp, making everyone sleep in the open so that work could resume at daybreak. The outcome, however, "was always the same." Another week passed. Pamplona continued to make "repeated and painstaking inspections" of the places that seemed most promising, but "no gold was found in them, nor anything that looked like it." After still another week, the prospectors had turned up nothing more than a flake or two, amounts too small to justify continuing their labors.[39]

One cannot help but wonder why these details of persistent failure were related. The expedition diary was a carefully constructed document, highlighting incidents that served Pamplona's purposes. The discovery of gold-bearing lands was portrayed as a key objective of the venture. It is possible the whole search was an act, particularly given Pamplona's ample previous experience in the area. Yet his narrated frustrations seem genuine. Certainly he had to report something about his effort to unearth gold. Indeed, in his letters he admitted to these disappointments before the scribe's pen reshaped them in the diary into valiant acts.[40] Having failed to obtain that which the governor and the crown most desired, Pamplona would be forced to rework the storyline. He would convey the impression of unflagging determination. He would insinuate that his recruits were less than capable. His finished version of events would focus on his exertion and, crucially, his honorable conduct whenever his actual accomplishments fell short.[41] From this perspective, we can explain the triumphal heroism attributed by his scribe to Pamplona's modest accomplishments.

This aspect of the expedition chronicle is worth pausing over, because it highlights the importance of traditional appeals to honor and status as a strategy for channeling the power of the state as the crown strove to exert a governing presence in remote areas. Appended to the expedition diary was a summary itinerary drafted for the governor by the scribe and cartographer. The document introduces Pamplona as follows: "Lord Field Commander Regent and Mines Inspector of All the Trails to Goiás, Bambuí, and Piuí." (Bambuí and Piuí, or present-day Piumhi, were nascent settlements in the regions Pamplona was charged with exploring.) The scribe opens the itinerary pleading for the patience of his readers. His training as a chronicler was insufficient for the task before him. He feared his lack of talent as both a writer and a mapmaker left him unprepared to describe the expedition's feats. Yet his choice of words was perfect when, searching for a suitable adjective, he described the party as it set out on its quest not as grand but "grandiose."[42]

At various points along the route, recorded in the diary, poems were read to great applause and shouts of "viva" by those who wished to honor Pamplona and his anticipated acts. It is easy to disparage these poems as rustic doggerel. They derive from the Arcadian tradition, the transatlantic literary movement positioned against the baroque, emphasizing, among other elements, the bucolic countryside and the dignity of nature's Native inhabitants. Pombal himself was an advocate and sponsor of the movement. He identified in its tendencies themes that coincided with his desire to renew the empire, wrest it from its obeisance to overweening religious and especially Jesuit authority, and proclaim as heroes prominent individuals prepared to join him in doing so. Beginning in 1768, a group of prominent Arcadian poets based in the urban centers of Minas Gerais began to publish their works, among them Cláudio Manuel da Costa, following his return from his own journey to the captaincy's west in the governor's company. Like Costa and his fellow literati, the rural poets who dedicated their stanzas to Pamplona embraced the genre idiosyncratically, portraying the region's uncolonized land as a realm bereft of civilization rather than an Arcadian idyll. Its Indigenous inhabitants were not models of noble simplicity but corrupted savages. To the hero who tamed these spaces, royal and even eternal merit would accrue. In Pamplona's virile guise, the Portuguese Empire arrived in the inhospitable sertão, extending its benevolent reign, establishing order, redeeming those who lived outside its purview.[43]

The trailside poems that graced the expedition's progress do not translate readily, but a sense of their purpose can be gleaned from selected phrases, images, and metaphors. The initial poem, a sonnet, sets the tone. An acrostic poem, each of its first thirteen lines begins with a letter of Pamplona's first name, spelled with a *g* as the variant *Ignácio*, and his first surname, spelled without an *i*, Correa.[44] His second surname begins the final line, completing the melodramatic form. The sonnet describes Pamplona as "illustrious," a "famous flower" whose aroma "negated" all others. "The heavens sent you to this land," the poet gushes, to transform everything into "great opulence." The poem's final phrase describes Pamplona as a "fifth essence," that is, as ether, the fifth element after earth, fire, water, and air, which in ancient and classical cosmology filled the universe above the terrestrial sphere. This use of the sonnet, which had fallen from fashion in much of Europe, summoned the peripatetic sixteenth-century chronicler of Portuguese imperial expansion, Luís Vaz de Camões, considered by many Portugal's greatest poet and a preeminent practitioner of the sonnet form.[45]

The second poem, declaimed on the third morning of the voyage as the explorers prepared their mounts, left no doubt about the mythopoeic tradition imbuing their actions with special meaning. The poem was written in decasyllabic ottava rima, with an ABABABCC rhyme scheme. Giovanni Boccaccio's fourteenth-century innovation, this form was used two centuries later by Camões in *The Lusiads*, Portugal's national epic.[46] First published in 1572, *The Lusiads* related in odyssean grandeur Portugal's seaborne voyages of exploration. Camões portrays Bacchus, friend of Portugal's legendary founder Lusus, as jealous of Vasco da Gama and his bold mariners, who set out to conquer new lands, renouncing lives of homebound ease degraded by "souls effeminate," choosing instead the manly hardships and noble deeds that lead to true fame. Convinced they will rival the gods, Bacchus conspires with African Muslims and Neptune to destroy the adventurers. His plot fails when Vasco da Gama reaches India, aided by Venus. The epic profoundly influenced colonial Brazilian poets, including those in Minas Gerais who wrote about inland exploration.[47]

By employing Camões's form and themes, the eighteenth-century rural poet fixed Pamplona's position in a pantheon of Portuguese imperial heroes. He called Pamplona the "Son of the Sun." His "conquest" of the "wild sertão" would allow civilization to flourish. "We have until now suffered the total disregard of human beings," the trailside bard decried, "enduring the roar of beasts in a solitude utterly tyrannical." That these beasts were construed not merely as animals is evident in another line. They were inhabitants of the wilderness who, having "ceased to be people" had now become "chimeras." Pamplona would subdue them because he was "capable of ruling everyone." His livestock would overspread the countryside. He would transform the wilderness into a "garden." Its riches would be revealed because his valor merited the discovery of "hidden treasures" that "were not until now deserved."[48] This last line, as we will see, was particularly telling: until Pamplona arrived, the region's treasures were not deserved.

Hyperbole advanced with the expedition. A later poem exclaims, "How intrepid, how ardent, how astounding" to witness "a new Hero seeking the high summit / where fame had erected his honored temple."[49] Such excess alerts the present-day reader to resist treating this expedition chronicle as even remotely impartial. Yet the temptation to relinquish skepticism and join the adventure is profound. Even in more skeptical times, wilderness adventures retain their appeal, judging from their popularity. Readers are drawn to daring exploits of larger-than-life explorers, extraordinary individuals who brave nature and flout social stasis to strike out beyond the confines of empire, colony, and nation. But the puffery of Pamplona's diary, the would-be myth in the making, is unmistakable. In this chronicle's poetry and prose alike, the reader cannot miss the textual inconsistencies, the details that do not live up to the legend, the treasures never found.

References to an imminent prosperity punctuate the diary. This was Minas Gerais, it must be remembered, where gold and diamonds produced some of the greatest fortunes in the Portuguese Empire. Over the preceding half century, this wealth had adorned the captaincy's baroque churches, rehabilitated the colony, and reinvigorated the empire. Portugal's greatest palaces had been erected with the taxes levied on this treasure. Leveled by an earthquake, tsunami, and fire fourteen years earlier, Lisbon was still being rebuilt on these funds. It is no wonder, therefore, that Pamplona and others like him found it impossible to resist making a show of searching for gold, even when none was to be found. The governor had invested him with his extraordinary appointive powers in hopes that the mounting evidence that gold production was waning could be pushed aside by new discoveries. Pressed by Lisbon to increase production, the governor had every reason to embrace an unctuous, well-off vassal as determined to produce results as Pamplona.

The literary and the legal, the symbolic and the pragmatic, the cultivation of valor and the imposition of sovereign rule over mineral claims, laborers, and land—all of these worked together in a region in which the state still struggled to assert its authority. From the earliest days of alluvial mining in Minas Gerais, being the first to strike gold at a new site was neither a sufficient nor even necessary act to be designated its discoverer. In Portuguese America, as in other early modern Atlantic societies, riches and honors accrued to the rich and honorable. While the act of discovery may have masqueraded as a concrete fact and a private achievement, it was like other valuable prizes in the colony a consequence, more often than not, of intensive negotiation and alliance-building between powerful colonists and agents of the state. The history of the mining boom is replete with accounts of claim jumping in which those who curried favor with higher authorities preempted others who arrived first at gold or diamond deposits. Such favor could be acquired through clientage relationships. It could be purchased by sharing the profits of mining operations with the high-ranking officials charged with their regulation. After being designated discoverers of mineral deposits, these fortunate individuals further enhanced their position by petitioning the crown for royal pensions, sinecures, contracts, land grants, and other honors and privileges, such as administrative posts, militia patents, or membership in one of Portugal's esteemed military orders.

At the same time, from the earliest days of mining in the region, Portuguese laws levied draconian penalties on those caught prospecting without official permission. In 1711 an early crown edict intended to curtail such activity stipulated a fine and prison for prospectors caught entering the "sertões and discovering gold" without reporting their finds to authorities. A 1736 ruling by Gomes Freire de Andrade, the governor who years later encouraged Pamplona to venture west, forbade miners from staking claims in "the unpopulated extremities of the captaincy" without permission. In this fraught social and legal milieu, those who aspired to uncover mineral wealth and then be authorized as designated discoverers to benefit from it wooed, manipulated, competed, and collaborated with each other and with ranking authorities in the process of opening up terrain targeted for exploration and colonization. The exhaustion of mining areas in the second half of the eighteenth century gave new potency to such transactional entrepreneurship, creating openings for a man like Pamplona if he could win and maintain official favor. The inflated language of his expedition diary must be understood in this context, too.[50]

Laws designed to order this exchange of power and prestige included distinctive provisions governing the lands that were the source of wealth. As stipulated in the royal mining code, Pamplona's position as mines inspector empowered him to divide any newly discovered gold deposits into three types of claims. The richest claim at any site was reserved for the crown but then auctioned off to the highest bidder. Only the already well-to-do could afford to purchase such a claim. If Pamplona was not to be that individual himself, his privileged appointive position ensured that it would have to be someone who earned his sympathies. The second claim was allotted to the designated discoverer. All remaining claims were to be divided among free settlers in a lottery. Each claimant received two claims, plus an additional one for each enslaved miner he or she held captive.[51] Those who were named discoverers often managed to direct these mining claims to family members, associates, and clients in a system knit together by webs of patronage. As noted, the naming of a discoverer is better understood as an attained status than an accomplished fact. Pamplona genuinely may have wished to discover gold. He may even have believed he would do so on his 1769 expedition. Either way, as he sweated his many shirts and forced his enslaved laborers to sleep in the open, he was positioning himself publicly to claim the prerogatives of discovery and thereby to preempt those who preceded and followed him to this sector of the western sertões.

All of these provisions excluded those who owned no slaves and had no patrons. If such individuals attempted to mine independently, failing to attach themselves to elite benefactors if free, or steeling away from one's enslaver to excavate an unsupervised site if held in bondage, the mining code condemned them as petty prospectors, transforming them into criminals. Just as wealth came to the wealthy, and honors to the honorable, in this hierarchical, patrimonial society, the margins devolved to the marginalized. This is what the poet meant, or at least channeled, when he proclaimed that the sertão's "hidden treasures . . . not until now deserved" would surely be revealed to Pamplona because his valor merited their discovery. Such valor was not built on deeds alone. It depended on the possession of many slaves, which was as much a prerequisite for conduct deemed meritorious as was the favor of powerful patrons. When his scribe portrayed enslaved porters marching behind Pamplona as he rode out across the western savannah, he was sending an unmistakable message all the way to Lisbon. The expedition chronicle functioned as a virile performance of Pamplona's honor and wealth, aimed at imperial administrators who could aid his continued social ascent.

CHAPTER 2

# TURNING FRONTIER FICTIONS INTO PRIVATE PROPERTY

FOR THE FIRST-TIME reader of the 1769 expedition diary, there is no more disorienting moment than when, one night, after two weeks of arduous travel, the voyagers end up on Pamplona's own ranch. This was a property he had been granted two years earlier. There the party spent much of the next six weeks, using the ranch as a base camp for forays farther into the backlands. The comforts may have been modest, but they suggest at least some improvement of the ranch in previous years and call into question the portrayal of the region as an unsettled wilderness. This conceit in the diary effaced not only an Indigenous presence predating the arrival of colonists but also a plodding, spotty, but nevertheless preexisting Portuguese presence. Pamplona's discourse contrasting barbarity and civilization, the wild sertão and the settled order he heralded, beckons as a narrative temptation. To admit our own tendency to be seduced by such a drama is to understand something more of the image of a wilderness, at once terrifying and alluring, that the shrewd merchant hoped to impress on distant captaincy and crown officials in order to reap benefits associated with his effort to extend the empire's territorial dominion.

### Settlers, White, Black, and Brown

If Pamplona's morality play had its protagonist, it also required its mise-en-scène. For the sertão to become a garden, for valorous Pamplona to harvest its untapped riches, it had to be wild and unexplored. But consider the rural poets again. Who were they anyway? The scribe identified the authors of six of the fourteen sonnets as three local ranchers. Three priests from the region recited another five of the poems. The remaining four were unattributed. Where did these men come from—and all the others who peopled Pamplona's account as he advanced westward? If he was "capable of ruling everyone," as one poet wrote, the implication was that he would find someone to rule. The closer one studies Pamplona's progress, the more jarring the contradiction between this language of taming the wild backlands and the characteristics of the region described, not the least of which was the constant presence, albeit thinly distributed, of settlers already occupying most of the areas traversed.

For a good part of their voyage, until they reached the headwaters of the São Francisco River, the troop traveled along the Picada de Goiás, the trail that, since the 1730s, had been designated by the crown as the authorized route from Minas Gerais to the secondary goldfields farther west in Goiás and Mato Grosso. Almost half a century earlier, in the 1720s, settlers already had begun to receive land grants in the vicinity of the São Francisco headwaters. Others quickly established themselves along the new trail after its completion, particularly cattle ranchers and farmers who used it to transport their livestock and foodstuffs to market. Twenty-five land grants were distributed among these early colonists. In the 1740s and 1750s, they were followed by gold seekers and more ranchers, who acquired land in and around Piuí, one of the regions over which Pamplona would come to exercise jurisdiction as regent.[1] Two years before the expedition set out, another twenty grants were conceded to Pamplona and his associates, including those that went to his family members. In other words, Pamplona and some who accompanied him had been active in the region long enough to receive these prized concessions even as he portrayed his venture as a mission of discovery.

Beyond the major landholders in the region, there was the ubiquitous presence of those who, according to the diary poet encountered in the preceding chapter, had "ceased to be people," becoming "chimeras." The reference suggested something more historically specific than Homer's "grim monster," a beast "all lion in front, all snake behind, all goat between, / terrible, blasting lethal fire at every breath."[2] The Minas poet was alluding to the growing and dispersing population of free people of color, often racially mixed and, not coincidentally, often derogatorily labeled *cabras*—that is, half-breeds or, literally, goats. Such individuals inhabited the margins of Pamplona's account. While lingering at his ranch, for instance, he faced a veritable onslaught of discontented colonists seeking his intervention in local land disputes and other problems. Gathered before him on a single occasion were, his scribe recorded, "87 white persons apart from numerous colored and black folk."[3]

During this period of economic instability whites accounted for just over a fifth; free people of color, almost a third; and enslaved persons, nearly half of the total population of Minas Gerais. The captaincy's white population was actually declining, as those with a certain wherewithal departed for more promising destinations, while the enslaved population and especially the free Black and racially mixed population continued to grow.[4] This demographic shift contributed to a deepening unease among whites, which pervaded the elite discourse of the era. Such foreboding had a strong spatial and geographic content, expressing particular anxiety about those peoples of African descent, frequently described as *feras*, or beasts, who sought to distance themselves from the main centers of slave-based production by migrating as subsistence farmers to outlying lands. Parishes throughout the central mining zone were characterized by the marked presence of these free Black and multiracial migrants, and innumerable edicts and laws were designed to criminalize them, keep them in place, and command their labor. With respect to their presence in the sertão, the lands they occupied could be construed as wild only to the extent that their existence was vilified or ignored. For its part, the crown preferred vilification, issuing a 1766 order to the governor, instructing him to crack down on the "cruel and atrocious offenses that *vadios* and criminals have committed in the sertões of this captaincy, where they live as beasts separated from civil society and human commerce." The deprecatory term *vadio*, or vagabond, referred to a drifting, unmastered, impoverished individual. In colonial parlance such individuals were construed as nonwhite. "With the exception of a small number of whites," explained one official, "they are all mulattos, cabras, mestizos [*mestiços*], and free blacks."[5]

The frontier was a destination for another threatening sector of the population, *quilombolas* (self-emancipated fugitives from slavery). With more men, women, and children enslaved than any other captaincy by the second half of the eighteenth century, Minas Gerais faced a profusion of quilombos, the term used to describe a temporary encampment or more permanent settlement of such fleeing captives. The vast spaces of the inland captaincy made flight a perennial strategy for escaping from servitude, as did the relative autonomy that many slaves exercised in mining operations compared to plantation agriculture. No fewer than 160 quilombos have been documented throughout Minas Gerais in the eighteenth century. Such communities ranged in size from just a few individuals to hundreds, although smaller groups were the rule, given the greater ease with which they could remain hidden and provide for themselves. They derived their sustenance from many sources, including agriculture, animal husbandry, fishing, hunting, clandestine mining, illicit commerce, thievery, and raiding. Among the assets they sometimes seized from neighboring farms and ranches were other captives. Access to the goods afforded by towns and hamlets meant that many quilombos, particularly the smaller ones, formed near such settlements rather than in remote forests and grasslands. This interrelationship has led some historians to view the phenomenon as an integral part, rather than a fracturing, of the slave system.[6] Even so, enslavers never wavered in condemning quilombos as a threat to the system's very existence.

Legislation to repress quilombos proliferated over the course of the century. Crown charters, royal orders, and town council provisions permitted quilombolas to be publicly whipped, branded, and otherwise mutilated when apprehended. The law spared individuals the prescribed punishments when evidence showed they had been brought to a quilombo against their will. Related measures prohibited the enslaved from bearing arms and moving about at night. In the early years of the mining boom, one governor proposed the death penalty for runaways, but masters resisted and annulled the measure, fearing the permanent loss of their investment in captive human capital. Later, the crown instituted the punishment of branding with an *F*, for fugitive, those caught in flight on their first offense. Those caught a second time had an ear cut off. The crown also empowered ranking judicial figures to collect sizable sums from local enslavers to fund expeditions sent out to attack quilombos.

Colonial legislation established an elaborate incentive system to encourage hunting for and destroying fugitive communities, which were known to provide refuge not only to those in flight but also to some freed persons as well as Indians who sought protection. Free men of African descent composed a sizable minority, between 15 and 40 percent, depending on the location, of those empowered by the crown to track down quilombolas. These were the so-called *capitães* and *soldados do mato* (bush captains and soldiers). The captains received royal commissions after they were selected by local town councils, while their soldiers were compelled to serve as a form of militia duty. According to regulations adopted in 1722, runaway slave hunters received payment from masters based on the distance traveled in completing a successful mission. Payment ranged from as little as four *oitavas*, or about 14 grams of gold for a self-emancipated person caught within the vicinity, to as much as 25 oitavas or 88 grams of gold for one caught far from the master's property. A slave hunter earning ten payments of the larger sort could amass a sum equal to the average price of an enslaved adult. Set at 20 oitavas, or about 70 grams of gold, remuneration was also high for fugitives found at any distance dwelling in quilombos and brought back alive, because the risks associated with their recapture were considered extreme. Those killed in attacks on quilombos brought a smaller fee. Bush captains were known to carry on a trade in the salted and preserved ears and severed heads of dead quilombolas. The law encouraged authorities to exhibit these trophies publicly on pikes as a warning to others. That abuses accompanied the position of runaway slave hunter was acknowledged in other regulations, which prohibited such men from seizing enslaved men and women who were not in fact in flight, and from failing to return actual escapees to their masters within fifteen days after their apprehension. While the practices associated with hunting those fleeing bondage might seem "barbarous," admitted a crown advisor, they were necessary given the captaincy's distinctive geographic and economic circumstances.[7]

Well before Pamplona arrived on the scene, the ill-defined western border region that separated Minas Gerais from Goiás became infamous for its large and numerous quilombos. The conventional vocabulary used to describe territorial expansion rarely considers these fugitives as settlers, but that is what they were. Tacitly acknowledging this reality in explaining how quilombos may have ameliorated social tensions, historians have employed the traditional language of frontier social history, describing the pervasive presence of quilombos as an "escape valve."[8] As migrants to the sertão, self-emancipated runaways lend new meaning to the trope that associates the frontier with freedom. Just as colonists used the trails to the west to extend settlement, so too did men and women in flight from

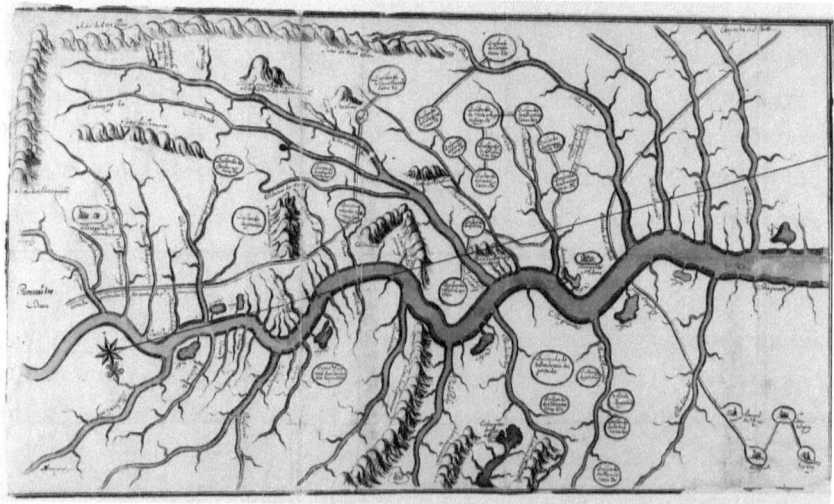

FIGURE 2.1. Map of the Campo Grande region of western Minas Gerais, depicting twenty-five quilombos (fugitive slave communities) as encircled sites along the Rio Grande and its tributaries. Source: "Extrato do Mapa de Todo o Campo Grande," 1765, MS copy, YAP-023-016. Courtesy of Instituto de Estudos Brasileiros, Universidade de São Paulo, Yan de Almeida Prado Fund.

captivity. As more estates were established on land grants in the region traversed by the trail to Goiás, more enslaved laborers absconded from those properties to disappear into outlying lands.

Minas authorities launched two major operations, in 1746 and 1759, against a network of quilombos in the region known as Campo Grande, an area west of the headwaters of the São Francisco River and north of the Rio Grande. The largest of these runaway communities, indeed the largest in the captaincy, was called the Ambrósio Quilombo, the location of which seems to have shifted over time.[9] Justifying the first of these two actions, Governor Gomes Freire de Andrade raised the specter of Palmares, the famed network of quilombos in northeastern Brazil, the largest in the colony's history. Throughout the seventeenth century Palmares provided refuge for thousands of runaways. Its eventual destruction by Paulista bandeirantes contracted by the crown established a tradition of rewarding the heroes of such actions with royal land grants. The governor noted that the Campo Grande fugitives had attacked property and murdered slave owners for more than twenty years, living "barbarously" under the command of their own king and queen. The governor first estimated their numbers at more than six hundred when writing to local officials. This figure increased to more than one thousand when he wrote Lisbon, pressing for crown support for the expedition of more than four hundred well-armed men dispatched to destroy the region's quilombos.[10] The need for the second major expedition just over a decade later testified to the failure of the first to make a lasting difference. The second venture again included as many as four hundred members, among them approximately three hundred free men of color and fifty mission-dwelling Bororo Indians. Its commander, the prominent miner and explorer Bartolomeu Bueno do Prado, whose family had suffered an attack in the area staged by quilombolas and Kayapó Indians reputed to be cannibals, complained that most of the fugitives, well informed of his movements, fled before his troop arrived, leaving them with little more to do than burn the abandoned fields and dwellings. Even so, although palpably disappointed, the governor reported some twenty-five dead and eighty captured runaways in a series of attacks.[11]

60   CHAPTER TWO

Seven years before Pamplona received his first royal land grants in the region, Prado and other leaders of this earlier expedition filed petitions for their own grants, which the governor approved in recognition of their services in effecting the "extinction of the *calhambolas*" (a related term for fugitives).[12] Pamplona encountered even greater difficulties than Prado in pursuing the same mission. Men and women in flight from slavery proved no easier for him to locate than Indians and gold, yet experience had shown that they, too, could reinforce his claim on land that came as a royal reward. If he could not effect their capture, he might still win favor by casting himself as uniquely competent to do so. Once again, a performance convincing enough to captivate distant patrons would serve him well even when his results fell far short of his promises.

On his 1769 expedition Pamplona did make a genuine effort to round up quilombolas. To increase his chances of success, he brought with him a number of Native guides, who, like free Black men, were considered particularly adept at this task. The expedition scribe referred to these individuals as "tapejaras," a Tupi term meaning "skilled on the trail."[13] Such individuals, as one observer stereotypically described them, "go around scarcely dressed and barefoot. In this form they penetrate virgin forests and thorny thickets." They had such sharp eyesight and expert tracking skills that they could identify "the slightest change made by the smallest footprint in a pasture." They could tell where someone had recently passed by observing the disturbance of leaves. Some were so proficient in their vocation that they could "follow the tracks of any slave who flees, ten and twenty leagues," unfazed even by fugitives who crossed rivers to confuse them.[14] On Pamplona's journey, however, the talents of these Native guides did not free them from being derided as "fearful and timorous." At one point, "judging that many blacks were near our entourage," the guides "feared to go and discover them or scout them out, no matter how much [Pamplona] tried to persuade them to do so. They replied every time by pointing to the great danger, saying the quilombos were many in that direction." In the end, their assistance did not yield the hoped-for bounty in recaptured runaways.[15]

In mid-October, eight weeks into their expedition, now reduced to "57 whites, 38 slaves," and 45 mules, Pamplona's troop struck out into less accessible lands.[16] By then the party had lost at least seventeen canoes to quilombolas who stole or sunk them. Accounts of facing down these backcountry adversaries now buttressed the triumphant narrative that the search for hostile Indians and buried treasure increasingly failed to sustain. Vestiges of those fleeing enslavement were everywhere. The scribe registered trails they had trampled, areas deforested, fires burning on distant ridges. At one point, the party reached the abandoned quilombo identified as Ambrósio, previously razed. They were astounded by its size and sophistication. They "wondered at the ruined buildings and the multiple camouflaged trenches studded with spikes."[17] On a crude sketch of the site, the scribe, now acting as mapmaker and illustrator, drew these and other features. The quilombo's outermost structure was a curving wall where lookouts could be stationed. Within lay wooded embankments that further concealed the site. A marsh fortified with pits and spikes protected one side. Planted fields extended from the other three sides, providing an unimpeded view for guards stationed at walled interior posts. Any enemy who managed to cross these fields would encounter an inner fortification with another band of spikes, a moat, still more spikes, and a deep trench, defending more than thirty structures or "houses" at the center of the establishment.[18]

Pamplona's patrols stumbled on numerous other sites. Some were little more than temporary encampments, like the quilombo of Santos Fortes. Others indicated greater permanence. One included structures that housed looms, suggesting a network of trade with other fugitive communities or perhaps even with colonists. Another building was labeled "Council House," indicating some sort of communal governance. Cotton was cultivated at yet another site, and a "Casa do Rei," or king's house, identified the residence of the quilombo leader. More elaborate still was the quilombo of Sambabaia with its surrounding fields and its internal garden plots. Along with a central meeting house, this settlement included a tannery and a forge. The quilombo of São Gonçalo featured particularly

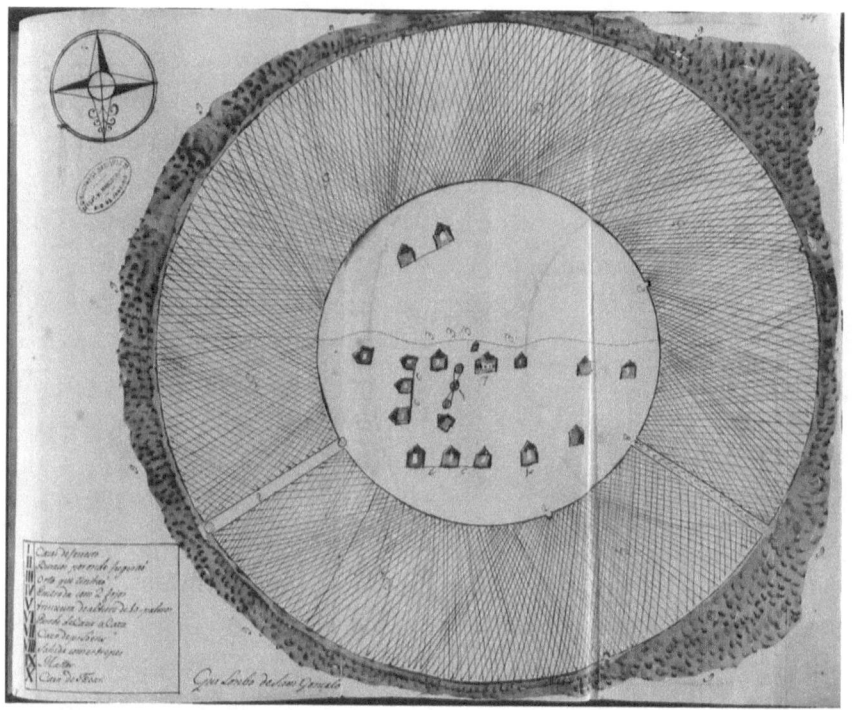

FIGURE 2.2. São Gonçalo quilombo. Source: A Expedição do Campo Grande, Cuyeté, e Abayeté D[istrito] de Paracatú, 1769, BNRJ, SM, CV, cód. 18, 2, 6. Courtesy of the Biblioteca Nacional, Rio de Janeiro.

complex fortifications, consisting of a circular trench with spikes covered with brush, two well-concealed escape tunnels, and two larger passageways that could be readily barricaded.

Besides the mapping of these sites, which deceptively presented some of them as still standing even though they had been previously destroyed, the effect of Pamplona's intrusion into the region's fugitive persons network, like his Indian chasing and gold prospecting, is difficult to measure in concrete terms. He ordered eight quilombos burned or reburned, and he appropriated their fields. But in almost every instance the residents of these communities anticipated his arrival and fled to more isolated hiding places. Rarely did his troops capture even a single individual. For years to come, authorities in Portugal continued to consider the deployment of troops necessary to prevent fleeing slaves from becoming a "clear threat to life" for colonists who crossed through or settled in these lands, where the forest and brush served as a "fortress" for those seeking concealment.[19]

Despite these mitigating circumstances, Pamplona's preoccupation with the quilombos was reported in the same ardent language his scribe used to narrate other feats. For instance, on the day the party reached the Ambrósio quilombo, two men interrupted Pamplona as he was shouting at his workers, presumably for their lack of effort or skill. The men had noticed the tracks of "blacks who were spying" on the troop. "From this rumor," wrote the scribe, "there arose . . . a good deal of fear, each one murmuring according to the valor or cowardice that graced him." Pamplona, characteristically, became "furious at all, even at his trusted friends," appalled by how easily they succumbed to their anxieties. His courage, the scribe marveled, "quickly undid the intrigue that the fearful ones had woven."[20] The anecdote was another story crafted to promote Pamplona's pursuit of official recognition for honorable conduct.

One might imagine that his efforts to counter quilombos would be welcomed by settlers already established in the surrounding region. This was not necessarily the case. Control of the movement, recapture, and disposition of apprehended fugitives was no less a disputed prerogative than control of the regular trade in enslaved individuals. Those who benefited from interacting with fleeing men and women, whether by capturing them and reaping rewards, or by trading with or harboring them for personal gain, did not always welcome the presence of a powerful interloper like Pamplona. One of the slave hunters already active in the area found himself arrested by Pamplona and remitted to the governor in far-off Vila Rica, pointing to just this sort of rivalry.[21] Pamplona accused the man of stealing others' slaves, as well as their land, and generally spreading "terror" throughout the region.[22] In one revealing exchange, Pamplona told an assembled group that, by contrast, he was "engaged in extinguishing" the quilombolas who inhabited these lands "in order to create the *res publica* and establish its well-being." His effort should be seen as "a service of great utility to relieve them of such prejudicial and damaging fears." And yet "the reward he got for such sustained zeal and penitential self-discipline was the ordinary calumny with which people spoke ill of him." He had taken action, he said, "in pure obedience to the only one who could make him undo [what he had done], . . . the Most Illustrious and Excellent Count of Valadares, Governor and Captain General of this Captaincy."[23] Once again, we note the appeal to higher authority to the exclusion of all other claimants, the basis of Pamplona's own legitimacy in the region, the source of his past and potential success, and the reason authorities, or at least most of them, put up with his self-serving actions and his questionable versions of events.

## A Landed Empire

As an emerging magnate operating in a zone beyond the geographical and administrative competencies of captaincy and crown officials, Pamplona took advantage of this indulgence by royal authorities to assemble his landed empire. He managed to stretch the Portuguese land tenure regime beyond its intended limits, appealing to a system of patronage forged between the crown and its favored subjects. His efforts were repaid with a remarkable eight sesmarias. Marking off large tracts of territory, these land grants also delimited the legal and symbolic intersection of private property and royal sovereignty in the backlands. Although only one was registered in his own name, he exercised effective control over the others, most of which were contiguous, distributing the grants among five daughters, a son, and a son-in-law.[24] Particularly blatant as a violation of the spirit of royal restrictions on such excessive property accumulation was his administration of the grants allocated to four of his five daughters, who spent their adult lives secluded in a convent, a substantial expansion of which Pamplona helped fund and construct.[25] Six of the grants each measured at least three square leagues (130.7 sq. km); the remaining two, one-quarter square league (10.9 sq. km). Together, they amounted to at least 806 sq. km (200,000 acres), placing Pamplona in control over more land than perhaps any other colonist in Minas Gerais. The land area of the US state of Rhode Island (2,590 sq. km) is less than three and half times as big as the property Pamplona acquired, and Singapore, Bahrain, and dozens of other nations are smaller. He also owned three cattle ranches in the captaincy's more densely inhabited southeast, including the grand Medanha fazenda as well as a residence on the outskirts of São João del Rei.[26]

Pamplona did encounter some constraints on his ambitions. The crown repeatedly denied him the honors he most coveted in his final years, membership for himself and his son, the priest Inácio Correia Pamplona Corte Real, in the august Military Order of Christ. The vast majority of merchants in Minas Gerais who sought entrance into the Order of Christ were disqualified on the grounds that their occupation, associated with the stigma of manual labor, was ignoble. Other sinecures and pensions he requested for his children also did not materialize. For instance, Pamplona asked that his son be provided a salaried post in Mariana and that three of his daughters receive pensions. The crown's Overseas Council ruled his requests too "onerous," leading him to submit multiple petitions reasserting his meritorious service. If these disappointments registered the limits of his social ascension, his land grab to the west measured its realization.[27] Indeed, even though a surfeit of unclaimed land in the boundless interior of Portuguese America long depressed its monetary value, royal land grants had always occupied a privileged place in reproducing social hierarchies overseas and cementing patrimonial loyalties between colonial elites and the crown.[28]

Yet Portuguese law, however ineffectually, aimed to prevent accumulations of private property as excessive as Pamplona's. Throughout his lifetime jurists attempted to address the problem. In a system that considered land a royal patrimony, service to the monarch combined with social and economic status to determine who received a sesmaria, where, and of what size. The concession of property by the crown cultivated fidelity among its privileged vassals. Land grant recipients, who were overwhelmingly well established to begin with, were expected to fulfill another element of the transaction, generating taxable profits and products from the land through the application of capital and enslaved laborers.[29] As the crown strove to impose restrictions on landholders, they in turn found ways to circumvent them. As early as the 1720s, legislation specified that a standard grant should not exceed one-quarter square league. A legal elaboration in 1738 made an exception for grants in the sertões, where unclaimed land was considered abundant. These grants could extend up to nine square leagues (392 sq. km). A subsequent 1744 revision again limited even these distant concessions to the smaller size.[30] Enforcement proved elusive, even in the colony's better supervised areas. One viceroy admitted to the "constant and notorious . . . confusion" prevailing in the area of land grant regulation, resulting in "continuous doubts and conflicts." In the coastal captaincy of Rio de Janeiro, the chaotic situation spurred the viceroy to order a comprehensive survey and review of all claimed land, titled and untitled.[31]

Restrictions pertained not only to the size of grants but also to their number. Designed to curtail the "fraud" perpetrated by individuals who obtained "many land grants in different names," royal orders empowered local town councils to impede such schemes. Ongoing abuses prompted the creation of regional land grant judgeships (*juízes de sesmaria*) to provide greater oversight.[32] The grants conceded in the names of Pamplona's children exemplified the problem. With their father in his mid-thirties, even the eldest of the five would have been an adolescent. Teodora, for instance, was fifteen years old when she received her land, ostensibly awarded, like those of her sisters, for her role in advancing the "conquest and settlement of the unoccupied sertão."[33] Neither she nor any of her siblings could have met the legal standard that required grantees to own enough slaves to guarantee that a sesmaria was put to productive use. Moreover, when his daughter was nineteen, Pamplona installed Teodora and her three unmarried sisters in the Macaúbas Convent north of Vila Rica, far from the properties the law charged them with improving.[34] The land in his son Timóteo's name was even more problematic. There is no record of this grant having been confirmed by the crown, a required final step in the bureaucratic process that validated lands conceded by the governor. Indeed, apart from a reference in the original grant to the boy being Pamplona's "legitimate son," along with another appearance of his name on a list of settlers who came west with Pamplona, there seems to be no further record of this child. He was not among the six children named in Pamplona's last will and testament, which mentioned only one son, Inácio, the priest. It is possible Timóteo died before Pamplona wrote his will. In any case Pamplona appears to have absorbed this tract into his own holdings.[35]

In a particularly explicit admission that land barons and speculators continued to gain the upper hand throughout the period that Pamplona assembled and legitimated his latifundia, Queen Maria I (r. 1777–1816) issued a royal charter in 1795 in response to the "abuses, irregularities, and conflicts that have raged, are raging, and will continue to rage throughout the State of Brazil over the aggrieved object of its land grants," which had never been regulated by a comprehensive code. Among its many provisions, the new legislation favored the distribution of smaller grants to benefit a greater number of settlers. It required those who had earlier accumulated more than one sesmaria to sell or otherwise dispense with their excess property, if it remained unproductive, at the risk of having it seized. The charter was not well received. Within a year, concerned about alienating some of her most powerful colonial vassals, the queen revoked the charter, citing the "complications and inconveniences that could result from [its] immediate execution." Even so, a less forceful push to rationalize the land tenure regime proceeded. Grantees throughout the colony were compelled to survey and register their holdings in accordance with provisions in the nullified law.[36] In Minas Gerais, as elsewhere, officials struggled to devise ways to end what they deemed the ongoing chaos and criminal conduct surrounding landholding practices, both among squatters and those claiming, often fraudulently, to hold formal title.[37] From the 1760s to his death in 1810, Pamplona took steps to conform to the letter of imperial property law. But his ability to accumulate such vast holdings in the western sertões made a mockery of its spirit.

A pas de deux between state and prominent vassal—the first dependent on but suspicious of a local notable, the second eager for but rarely satisfied with royal recompense—allowed the merchant rancher to overcome legal restrictions that applied to other subjects. His original land grant petition, like those of his children, spoke of the lands he had "discovered" in the sertão at the headwaters of the São Francisco River, incurring "great losses" and "considerable expense." On these lands, which lay beyond the captaincy's most distant western customhouse, Pamplona had received the governor's permission in 1767 to establish, in the language of the royal property concession, his "large number" of slaves, cattle, horses, mules, and sheep. The monarch and governor thereby supported the merchant's claim that the lands he already owned to the east, in the captaincy's original settlement zone, were "not sufficient," given how many captives and how much livestock he possessed. The disproportionate size of the grants was also in recognition of the costs Pamplona had incurred to settle this portion of the interior and the "utility for royal interests and the common good that would follow from such settlement."[38]

At the farthest extent of his journey to the west, it was thus in the process of securing sprawling latifundia that Pamplona reported founding a new hamlet and beginning the construction of a church amid quilombos reduced to ashes. Like a distant echo of the conquistadors who built colonial structures atop the ruins of Aztec and Inca temples, these founding rituals invoked a heroic past familiar to authorities of every European empire that colonized what they deemed their New World, a memory still powerful as settlers pushed back frontiers across the Americas during the second half of the eighteenth century. As acts of legal posturing, these well-worn rites augured the advancement of crown interests and activated an exchange for future patronage. They also cultivated ecclesiastical approbation, for the religious authorization of territorial conquest retained its elemental significance. It did so even though Pombal was pursuing a secularizing agenda and, in the case of Minas Gerais, was doing so in a captaincy from which Roman Catholic missionaries, although not parish priests, long-ago had been banned because of their suspected participation in gold and diamond smuggling.[39]

Atop a ridge Pamplona "ordered us all to dismount," wrote the scribe. Enslaved drummers beat out a cadence. From a massive tree, workers "hewed four crosses" and erected an altar. "After the most holy images of Our Lord and Our Lady were placed on it, the Reverend Chaplain had us all kneel and pray." In a loud voice Pamplona announced that he was taking "possession of that place to which he had come by order of the [governor]." The distribution of land grants to other settlers, the merchant's prerogative as regent, began immediately. Finally, Pamplona declared that "no farther advance into the wilderness would be possible without first populating this place so that those who did go farther would have access to supplies." The order might also prevent subsequent adventurers from preempting the merchant rancher as he was preempting others. A few days later, already retracing his route, he reminded those still in his company that "his intention had been only to carry out, as a faithful vassal, the instructions of the [governor], to honor all of them, and not to offend anyone."[40] With that, he parted company with them and rode toward his frontier ranch and then toward his home far to the east, followed by his captive workers and baggage train.

Rituals of this sort notwithstanding, Pamplona's adventure can hardly be construed as a conquest in any conventional sense, even though this was the term he used. It was an appropriation of previous claims and an earlier occupation. The Portuguese legal claim to this territory dated from the late fifteenth century, secured with the signing of the Treaty of Tordesillas. In the sixteenth and seventeenth centuries, bandeirantes from São Paulo had enslaved or chased off many if not all of its Indigenous inhabitants. Prospecting, ranching, and farming in the region dated, at the latest, to the early eighteenth century. By midcentury, dire reports of runaway activity had become commonplace, and expeditions were dispatched to destroy quilombos. Pamplona and his associates had been active and acquired land grants there before his own primary expedition set out in 1769. Struck from the record in his revised diary, but evident in his correspondence, Pamplona followed directions provided by explorers who had visited even the most distant points of his route before him. Reconnoitering the area around his final destination, for instance, he used a *roteiro* (itinerary) provided by an individual identified as "Senhor Brandão." This informant seems have been Alexandre Pereira Brandão, who a few days earlier had caught up with Pamplona on the trail to challenge his land claims. Pamplona argued dismissively and successfully that the documents in his possession, having been issued by the crown, legally invalidated any claim Brandão might make to having previously possessed the same land.[41] In light of such prior exploration and colonization, Pamplona's assertion of precedent must be questioned.

By casting his mission as a heroic conquest in the tradition of the bandeirantes and, before them, the early Portuguese mariners, Pamplona enhanced his appeal to a chain of officials stretching from Vila Rica to Lisbon, superiors who could decisively amplify his future power and prosperity. Thus he would assert his role as agent of a distant state whose antagonists and vassals alike had strayed into zones beyond its reach, ostensibly extending that reach in his own person. He would portray the area as still uncivilized and all but uninhabitable as a consequence of fierce resistance by Indians and runaways, vindicating his status as "Lord Field Commander Regent and Mines Inspector of All the Trails to Goiás, Bambuí, and Piuí." By the 1780s, after two decades of activity in the western sertões, utterly convinced of his own preeminence, relentlessly seeking additional royal honors and privileges, he would go so far as to describe Portuguese settlers of this region as "his subjects."[42] We may see only sycophancy and self-promotion, but we may also recognize a man working with the legal, administrative, and discursive tools Portugal's early modern state, eager to expand its territorial projection, put at his disposal when he embodied its authority and acted as its privileged surrogate. Pamplona would portray himself as the most daring and deserving of subjects, even as he returned with mere flakes of gold and a few recaptured quilombolas. One can scarcely imagine a narrative that accounted more valiantly for those meager gains.

As he pressed his claims over ensuing decades, seeking ever-more extravagant favors and privileges from the crown, the ministers who ruled on such matters in Lisbon gradually saw through his exaggerations. After José I's death in 1777, a general bureaucratic reassessment of some of the more ambitious projects of the Pombaline era did not help his cause. In a soberer time when constraints on Portuguese monarchical and imperial power had become more evident, Pombal himself would be satirized as an

Inimitable creator of gigantic words,
Amplifier of nothings,
A virtuoso in speech,
An addict of plans,
Abundant in projects lacking in execution.[43]

When in 1805 Pamplona again petitioned for membership in the Order of Christ for himself and his son, adding a request that tax revenues collected not only in the western sertão but also over a wider region be directed to his family, the crown's Overseas Council issued a repudiation reminiscent of the satirist's scorn. Not even the greatest military heroes of the colony's past had shown the temerity to request such pecuniary rewards, the councilors responded. "The supplicant's services were not conducted in the face of enemies, bullets whizzing, confronting death." This phrase must have stung the aging rancher, since he had long claimed precisely such feats, minus whizzing bullets, in confronting Indians and runaways. His accomplishments were, by contrast, "sedentary and peaceful," the councilors concluded. The recompense he sought was "arbitrary," exceeding the value of his services.[44]

Historians of Brazil generally now eschew a traditional view of the past that posited ever-intensifying strains between colonial elites and the transatlantic state that structured their lives. Most now emphasize the compact these privileged subjects forged with Lisbon. Cooperation usually turned out to be a more secure and effective instrument than conflict. One celebrated essay long ago described this phenomenon as the "internalization of the metropolis." A more recent iteration of this interpretive strain emphasizes the empire's "political economy of privileges" or "moral economy of favor" by which local elites and the crown, bound together as clients and patron, exchanged services for rewards.[45] Notwithstanding the limits he confronted toward the end of his life, we readily see the compact at work in Pamplona's case.

His allegiance to Lisbon would ultimately bring him infamy as a consequence of his service as a government spy, traitor to a group of mostly elite individuals who sought in the Minas Conspiracy of 1789 to assassinate the governor and break with the monarchy. A likely member of the original cadre, he seems to have been convinced to betray them in exchange for profits promised for supplying provisions to royal troops deployed from the coast to counter the seditious plot. Making personal or business calculations that escaped the historical record, he was conspicuously absent when ordered to testify against the conspirators, falsely claiming the governor had dispatched him on yet another mission to the western sertões.[46]

Despite his affinity for seeking official favor, we should not forget that the merchant rancher acquired eight land grants for himself and his family, seven of them finally confirmed, from a crown that was supposed to prevent him from amassing so much private property. Pamplona was in this sense a grandiloquent master at maneuvering in a system that not only co-opted men like him but could in turn be co-opted by them. The sertão, cast as unsettled and uncivilized, served him by providing a poorly supervised space perfect for overreaching and mythmaking. Colonial authorities were eager to command remote expanses they could barely comprehend. Men like Pamplona, privileged raconteurs of frontier facts and fictions, of information and misinformation, could provide access and understanding in ways and words calculated to achieve enormous personal gain. In counterpoise to the colony's internalization of its metropolis, these individuals refigured, revalorized, and repossessed the backlands, pressing Lisbon to accept altered terms. Instead of submissive proxies sharpening the distant Leviathan's gaze, we find wily negotiators clouding, diverting, and transmuting that gaze in an imagined wilderness, painting scenes that featured themselves as commanding figures.[47] The prerogatives seized by such backcountry agents and the legal clout delegated to them, legacies of a patrimonial state's search for expanded domain, offered cover for actions the crown found difficult to direct. As the last of the trailside poets to extoll the expedition leader's accomplishments exclaimed, "through you, the Empire expands without dispute."[48] The empire did expand through Pamplona and others like him, although certainly not without dispute. The intertwined struggles to secure private property and territorialize royal sovereignty in the continental interior, conditioned by problematic intelligence from self-interested subjects who informed the crown about its far-flung peoples and possessions, laid bare Lisbon's unstable connection to its colony's vast inland spaces.

PART 2

# All That Glitters
*Forest Informants and Regal Dreams*

AT ABOUT THE SAME time Inácio Correia Pamplona launched his expeditions to the west, the perceived need to secure the southeastern sertões of Minas Gerais sparked even greater concern among imperial administrators. This internal frontier, because of its strategic location between the mining heartland and the colonial capital and port city of Rio de Janeiro, provoked a particularly fretful, sustained response from Portugal's centralizing state. Part of Brazil's Atlantic Forest, a lush and verdant biome starkly different from the drier western cerrado, inhabited by itinerant Indigenous groups with long experience of intermittent interactions with colonists, the region had been largely bypassed by the gold rush of the early eighteenth century. A series of official investigations and countermeasures now ensued, aimed at addressing the threat of colonists conspiring with Indians to move untaxed gold and gemstones through the mountains to seafaring contrabandists. As in western Minas Gerais, interest was fueled by a belief that Natives guarded knowledge of undiscovered mineral deposits in lands they still controlled.

Royal authorities wavered between banning access to the zone and striving to exploit its resources. No matter which policy prevailed, Lisbon had to rely on Indigenous informants to understand events deep in the tropical forest, at locations which, despite their relative proximity to coastal settlements, remained challenging to access and surveil. Although many of the motivations shaping Native accounts and their silences remain difficult to ascertain, officials drew their own conclusions, susceptible to hearsay that fed fantasies of untapped riches, and disdainful of evidence that did not accord with imperial purposes. After decades of frustrated efforts to impede illegal conduct in the zone, the crown acted more decisively in the mid-1780s, deploying military expeditions from both the interior and the coast to arrest an infamous criminal and his band, and to lay hold of the area once and for all. Despite being led by career officers less prone to the same kinds of personal schemes that impelled Pamplona in the western sertões, these missions succeeded in their proximate but not their ultimate goal. After disrupting the illegal mining operation, the state found its effort to exert sovereign rule and promote supervised settlement undermined by the gaps between what was knowable, what was indecipherable, and what was achievable when the empire was forced to rely on forest dwellers who had long resisted submission.

Concentrating on the coastal and inland sides of this internal frontier, respectively, chapter 3 and chapter 4 explore the contested mastery of backcountry geographic and strategic intelligence. Gathering information and evaluating its reliability were the critical first steps in controlling these lands. The crown's struggle to decipher distant developments hinged on interactions between imperial agents, backwoodsmen, enslaved Africans, and especially seminomadic as well as settled, village Indians. Reconnaissance efforts focused on illicit gold mining, especially the outlaws operating under the leadership of the accused smuggler Manuel Henriques, bearer of the sinister nickname Mão de Luva (Gloved Hand) and a target of the Holy Office of the Inquisition. Mounting concerns prompted Lisbon to launch a surprise military raid from Minas Gerais to destroy the operation. Native expertise proved vital both before and after this action, as it did during a much larger troop deployment on the coastal side of the mountains, the subject of chapter 5. This force was charged with establishing the crown's permanent presence in the interior, securing a monitored space in which legal settlement could proceed. Over the course of this episode, Lisbon demonstrated its growing willingness and wherewithal to intervene in the interior, even as its objectives proved elusive.

As backcountry actors steered developments in unanticipated directions, uncertainty and suspicion prevailed. Seeking to spur the development of a slave-based extractive economy in the forest, officials found themselves distrustful of one another and fending off accusations of profiting from the trade in contraband gold.

CHAPTER 3

# FOREST KNOWLEDGE NETWORKS

FROM A GEOPOLITICAL STANDPOINT, arguably the most important of Portuguese America's internal frontiers during the second half of the eighteenth century lay just inland from the colonial capital Rio de Janeiro. Densely forested and mountainous, this zone divided or joined, depending on one's perspective, Brazil's two most dynamic southeastern captaincies. The captaincy of Rio de Janeiro bore the same name as Brazil's fastest-growing major city and foremost commercial entrepôt, which became the residence of the viceregal court after 1763. Immediately to the north Minas Gerais had for more than half a century poured mineral wealth into the Atlantic world while maturing into the colony's most populous region. Between these areas of concentrated settlement, a rugged coastal escarpment long served royal purposes by creating a forest environment perilous for colonists fearful of its itinerant Native occupants and unaccustomed to its teeming flora and fauna. Officials considered the combination of terrain and terror an impediment to unsupervised travel into and out of the colony's mining heartland. In the 1760s, with reports circulating of gold strikes in the forest, the crown moved to chase colonists from this inland area between captaincies, where jurisdictional authority remained ill-defined. Officials thereby hoped to stanch contraband gold and diamonds flowing, they believed, through the coastal mountains to seafaring smugglers.[1]

Whether viewed from the coastal or the inland captaincy, the outcome of multiple incursions into this strategically important zone reveals that its Indigenous occupants wielded what remains an underappreciated influence in shaping Portugal's overseas ambitions and constraints after 1750. Of particular salience was their mastery of backcountry knowledge, including intelligence concerning clandestine mining operations, forest routes, and smuggling activity. Native expertise in these matters, as well as official perceptions and misperceptions of their proficiencies, could advance or hinder vital imperial projects. In this way another of Brazil's internal frontiers became a testing ground for state capacities. Conflict and negotiation with Indians in these zones exposed frailties in imperial rule that in settled enclaves remained veiled. As the crown strove to assert dominion over the colony's unincorporated areas, it assumed a more active presence in the backlands than historians have recognized. But in the process royal authority was also made exceedingly malleable. It depended on the cooperation of Native peoples precariously in possession of the lands into which state emissaries ventured. The enigmatic content of the knowledge Natives shared, under varying conditions of consent and coercion, would confound Portuguese interlocutors. Beset by imperial anxieties resulting from this uncertainty, yet stirred by age-old fantasies of concealed riches in Native lands, Lisbon gradually moved to lay claim to the coastal mountains from both sides of the captaincy border.

**Indians of an Uncertain Nature**

The Indigenous peoples living along the border between the captaincies of Minas Gerais and Rio de Janeiro did not fit easily into standard colonial categories or expectations. They were neither fully mobile nor permanently settled in one place. They were both adepts of the tropical forest and experienced in dealing with colonists. They maintained many of their traditional practices but stocked their encampments with imported manufactured goods. Some spoke Portuguese; some did not. Some had been baptized; most had not. Rather than moving along the path of progressive accommodation with settler society, some seem to have been following a reverse trajectory that led back into the forest after a period of intensive contact with missionaries in the past. During the second half of the eighteenth century, even as some asserted their rights to certain legal protections as Christian Indians, many others lost connection with, concealed, or found themselves stripped of this identity amid intensifying pressures to assimilate. Whether church or civil officials labeled a man or woman of Indigenous ancestry an Indian, a *mestiço* (mestizo), a *pardo* (person of color), or a *branco* (white) could vary from place to place, depending on the circumstances. The designation often hinged on bureaucratic expediency, that is, on whether immediate institutional advantage could be gained by documenting one ethnoracial identity rather than another.[2]

Long-held myths about the inveterate enmity of Native peoples just beyond the edge of enclaves of European settlement in the inland mining region and along the Atlantic seaboard were quickly dispelled as the Portuguese converged from the north and south on the forested mountains separating Minas Gerais and Rio de Janeiro. Just as quickly dashed were any hopes for the Indians' ready subordination and compliant cooperation with imperial plans. The Natives did not respect the captaincy boundaries, jurisdictional lines, and crown sovereignty that the incorporation of the region was supposed to enforce. They uncomfortably fit the description of Indians "living in the darkness of ignorance," far removed from colonial influence, which served as a justification written into royal legislation for ongoing aggression against Native groups elsewhere. They could be both valuable informants and liabilities for anyone who sought to enter into their confidence.[3]

Such circumstances help clarify why scholars have only begun to make sense out of the sorts of encounters documented in the backlands between the two captaincies. Until quite recently, historians and anthropologists devalued the study of Indigenous groups whose experience of colonialism left them neither fully autonomous nor fully integrated into settler or missionary enclaves. A German naturalist visiting the area in the middle of the nineteenth century foreshadowed this scholarly attitude. Acknowledging that "completely savage tribes, still maintaining their primitive customs, no longer exist in these parts," he lamented he would have to "be satisfied with a visit to semicivilized Indians or, as the Brazilians call them, '*indios mansos* [tame Indians],' as opposed to the true savages, '*índios bravos* [wild Indians].'"[4]

In Brazil, as elsewhere, scholars have slowly acknowledged that an earlier search for a pristine Native viewpoint, unadulterated by contact with intruders, had little to do with the indeterminacy of many colonial encounters. The term *colonial Indians*, rather than an oxymoron, is now widely used to describe the condition of some peoples of Indigenous descent who traversed histories of the sort recounted in the following pages.[5] Their presence and resilience is increasingly recognized as a constant over the colonial period. They resided in or interacted with missionary villages established along the coast and deep in the interior beginning in the sixteenth century. Their knowledge of the forests, mountains, savannas, and waterways aided the inland exploration efforts and slaving missions of the Paulista bandeirantes. They joined militias formed to combat French, Dutch, and Indigenous adversaries. They became refugees gathered within, as well as soldiers deployed against, fugitive slave communities. They entered the towns and villages that began as mining camps in Minas Gerais, Goiás, and Mato Grosso, forming minority populations.[6] Only more recently have historians and historical anthropologists begun to appreciate the ongoing importance of their presence during the final century of Portuguese rule.[7]

It has slowly become apparent that many eighteenth-century colonial Indians maintained relations with Indigenous groups outside the purview of settled society. Accumulating evidence threatens to destabilize even further the divide once thought to separate acculturated from autonomous Indians. Colonists imposed this problematic distinction when they contrasted *gentio* (heathens) and índios bravos with índios mansos, those Indians considered domesticated, settled, or civilized. Indigenous legislation presupposed this binary, establishing one set of policies for Natives settled in villages under church or state supervision, and separate, more coercive policies for those resisting such integration.[8] Generations of historians and anthropologists adopted the same dualistic thinking. Even when they turned their attention to colonial Indians, they glossed over the porous boundaries between the village and the forest, between the sedentary and

FIGURE 3.1. Inhabitants of the coastal forest. Source: Rugendas, *Voyage pittoresque*. Courtesy of the Biblioteca Nacional, Rio de Janeiro.

the itinerant, between Indigenous rural agriculturalists and backcountry fishers, hunters, and foragers. The conduct of Natives in the region where Minas Gerais and Rio de Janeiro converged shows the degree to which such conventional distinctions can obfuscate, inherited as they were from colonialist discourse and practice. To understand such conduct we must endeavor to make sense of archival sources, sometimes little more than suggestive fragments, reporting "communication," as one regional official in the 1770s put it, between "tame" and "wild" Indians.[9]

The mountainous zone into which a number of exploratory and punitive expeditions would march provided inconstant refuge for two Native groups that exemplified backlands proficiencies even as they negotiated contacts with colonial society. The Coropó and Coroado demonstrated they could sometimes subvert, sometimes buttress, and sometimes even inspire imperial designs. We should assume they did so not as gullible rustics, shortsighted collaborators, or duplicitous conspirators but primarily as pragmatists, seeking to ensure their individual and communal well-being according to their own logic and contingencies. In many cases, their objectives remain ambiguous because their actions and purported intentions reach us through the filter of official sources. What is certain is that the area they occupied, although at the outer edge of the jurisdictional capacities of the two captaincy administrations, had not escaped the effects of colonial expansion. Given the zone's proximity to the coast, we can surmise that waves of smallpox, measles, and other contagions spread their ravages as early as the sixteenth century, when epidemic disease brought by the first colonists struck the littoral and spread inland as tentative exploration of the interior began. After all, the first expedition from the coast that crossed these low mountains into the expanse that would much later become Minas Gerais is thought to have occurred in 1531.[10]

Apart from the impact of European diseases, the upland forests remained largely beyond the direct grasp of Portuguese settlers and the colonial administration. The major gold and diamond strikes of the mining boom occurred farther inland to the north. The completion of the Caminho Novo in 1725 encouraged the development of numerous farms, some quite sizeable, along this authorized route through the Mantiqueira Mountains. But this commercial corridor lay 100 kilometers farther west along the coastal escarpment from the area where rumored gold strikes and illicit mining became the object of persistent imperial interest during the second half of the century. By then, on the Minas side of the border, crown and captaincy authorities had designated the forests of the eastern sertões "Forbidden Lands [*Áreas Proibidas*], in accordance with the theory," as one governor put it, "that the said sertões serve as a natural barrier that protects this captaincy against smuggling."[11]

Yet colonization exerted a steady influence. Disruptions came from both the coast and the interior, provoking a range of Indigenous responses that combined resistance, strategic engagement, and flight. From the seventeenth century and likely earlier, pressures from settlers gradually ascending river valleys from the coastal plain reverberated inland. According to some accounts, displaced Goitacá Indians had conquered the upland Coropó and Coroado. According to others, these groups themselves were fragments or "mixtures" of Goitacá bands. Farther inland during the late 1750s, as the search for gold-bearing and agricultural lands in southeastern Minas intensified, these Indians fought what one of the era's most respected observers described as a "barbarous and bloody war."[12] It was surely no coincidence that this violence corresponded to the opening, despite royal prohibitions, of what by then were so many new trails through the mountains that, as a leading Brazilian-born crown advisor put it, a "cordon" of guards "many thousands" strong would be insufficient to impeded smuggling of gold and diamonds out of the interior.[13]

The Coropó and Coroado also faced competition from the semi-nomadic Puri and Botocudo Indians, reputed cannibals. Puri hunting grounds stretched northward from the Paraíba River (Paraíba do Sul). By 1800, if not sooner, apparently pressured by the Botocudo, the Puri had also migrated south of the river, where they encroached on Coropó and Coroado domain. All of these peoples were speakers of associated languages of the Macro-Gê linguistic stock. According to a naturalist who spent time among them in the 1810s, the Coropó, Coroado, and Puri communicated readily. They shared cultural traits but contended with the pressures of dwindling territory and resources that exacerbated interethnic conflict. The very names ascribed to these Indigenous groups, or "nations," as many contemporaries referred to them, are products of contact and territorial compression. Imposed by outsiders, whether colonists or Indigenous enemies, such ethnonyms should not be assumed to reflect primeval, fixed ethnic identities. For example, Coroado, which means "crowned" in Portuguese, referred to what colonists perceived as the distinctive way members of this group cut their hair. Both the Coroado and Puri, moreover, were said to call each other Puri, a pejorative term meaning thief or cannibal. Colonists' application of the term to one group and not the other reflected a conviction that Coroado bands were more tractable than groups designated as Puri.[14]

Some Coropó and Coroado responded to the pressures of diminishing territory by seeking protection from authorities in both captaincies. In the late 1750s, they made overtures to a priest and explorers who passed through the region on an expedition from the coast. They also presented themselves to settlers in southeastern Minas Gerais. One headman and his followers traveled as far as Vila Rica, where he and others requested baptism and sought to enlist the governor's aid. Few details survive of this and other voyages made by Indians to settler enclaves, a reminder that even the most assiduous archival prospecting leaves important perspectives inaccessible. To accommodate these travelers while gaining access to their verdant, mineral-bearing foraging grounds, the governor established a large central mission village where they could settle and benefit from provisions and protections offered by the crown. Some already spoke rudimentary Portuguese. Some were identified as refugees dispersed from coastal Jesuit missions after the religious order's expulsion in 1759.[15] Official enthusiasm about incorporating these Natives and their territory remained tempered by concerns that increased activity in the area might open new smuggling routes through the mountains to the sea.

Yet the Indians, presumed to possess special knowledge of the area's mineral wealth, might also lead colonists to new gold-bearing lands. The belief that Amerindians controlled and concealed undiscovered treasures emerged with the discovery of the New World as a defining European conceit. For the Portuguese, this idea was deeply ingrained. The association of prolific resources with territory seized from ethnic others considered heathens dated to the medieval Reconquista, when over the course of centuries fortunes were won and power accumulated by appropriating territory from non-Christian antagonists. When crusaders laid siege to Lisbon in 1147, expelling Muslims from the city, one chronicler described the Tejo River as a river "on the banks of which one encounters gold" and in the depths of which there existed "such an abundance of fish that local inhabitants believe that two-thirds of the current is water, one-third fish." The famous letter of Pêro Vaz de Caminha, which in 1500 first announced the Portuguese arrival in Brazil, recounted the intrepid mariners' unsuccessful attempts to glean from the Tupi coastal peoples "if there is gold or silver or any other kind of metal or iron." The historical memory of Brazil's mining boom nurtured these instincts given that, after more than a century of raiding the interior for slaves, Paulista bandeirantes had struck gold and later diamonds in Native domain. As the mining bonanza languished after 1760 and Lisbon pressed for increased colonial revenues, the desire to locate new mineral deposits rekindled the association between terra incognita and what colonists mysteriously referred to as *haveres incognitos*, buried wealth presumed to be concealed by Indians.[16] For Portuguese officials steeped in this tradition, it thus came as no surprise that an illegal mining and smuggling operation would appear in an Indigenous refuge zone. Any accurate information about the place and its resources would require gathering intelligence from these Natives. Preliminary reconnaissance of the region occurred amid reports not only that its aboriginal inhabitants could be hostile but also that they possessed special knowledge of the area's mineral wealth.

## Reconnaissance and Retreat

Tales passed down by backwoodsmen described as "old Paulistas" and gold specimens presented by an Indian familiar with the region along the captaincy border animated the first intensive, postboom exploration attempts. Explorers gained access to the zone from the coast by following Native trails. The source of the gold was thought to lie somewhat south of the Paraíba River at a spot where "barbarous" Indians of the "Orosó nation" resided. This ethnonym, unattributable to any forest dwellers known to modern scholarship, may indicate that this group disappeared or melded with others. At the time of these exploration attempts, the governor of Minas Gerais had estimated that some 150 separate "nations" inhabited the southeastern reaches of his captaincy.[17] The figure was probably exaggerated but it pointed to the multiple small bands characterizing the social organization of these peoples. It also hints at the limits of official knowledge, as well as our own, about Native communal commonalities and divisions. It seems likely that the ethnonym Orosó was a corruption of Coroado or Coropó, or even Croato or Cropó, alternative eighteenth-century names for the Coroado and Coropó, used especially in Minas Gerais.

Based on an accumulation of rumors and clues, Maurício José Portugal, a prospector from Cachoeiras de Macacu, a hamlet at the foot of the mountains, below the falls on the Macacu River on the Rio side of the border, requested official permission to reconnoiter the area in 1763. He had spoken with various "indomitable Indians" belonging to the "barbarous nations" that inhabited the mountainous zone, individuals who periodically made visits to the coastal plain. Particularly helpful had been an Indian "captain" who used the Christian name Joaquim. Despite the "rusticity of his behavior," this leader exhibited "some signs of humanity." When questioned about the lands where he lived, his responses were "so meaningful and congruent" that the prospector "came to understand that in his savage condition" the Native informant had "developed a greater intelligence" than that possessed by other Indians. The colonist's opinion of Joaquim was further enhanced when the headman told him that he "knew of places where there was much gold" and twice turned over samples.[18]

Before the year was out, his petition granted, the prospector had explored the area accompanied by associates and enslaved laborers. The perennial shortfalls of the royal treasury meant that little could be spared to fund uncertain ventures. The prospector knew this and made a point of promising he would pay for his own expenses, while keeping authorities well informed of the expedition's results, including turning over for inspection any gold collected in the mountains. Permitted just two months for his exploratory voyage, he returned well compensated. After paying the crown's *quinto*, the 20 percent tax levied on the production of gold and diamonds, he walked away with almost 12 ounces of gold. At the time, a sum of this amount would have been understood as enough to purchase one or possibly two enslaved workers, the ultimate measure of colonial wealth. He also gained official recognition as discoverer, promising the potential privileges and rewards—among them a pension, land grant, and military honors—that crown legislation bestowed on such individuals.[19]

Belatedly recognizing the unintended consequences of these events, authorities quickly tried but failed to stop what they had first allowed. The decision to permit the initial reconnaissance and prospecting came from a lesser authority, the captaincy's mining superintendent, during a period of administrative turmoil and interim governance corresponding with the transfer of the colonial capital from Salvador to Rio de Janeiro. The crown soon reversed course, realizing how easily gold could be moved out of the mountains without detection or taxation. José I chastised colonial officials responsible for the misstep, recalled the mining superintendent to Lisbon, and replaced him with a successor considered more prudent. He further ordered vacated all lands already claimed by miners moving into the zone, their rural properties razed. Thereafter not even representatives of the state were to enter the region. Not even the memory of the discovery was to be preserved in official documents. Attempts to control historical memory were a central feature of Portugal's authoritarian state, selective narratives of the past vital to its maintenance of power.

But colonists did not easily forget. Their recollection turned out to be fleeting when it came to royal orders, more lasting when nurtured by the attractions of finding gold. The decision to maintain the area as a no-man's-land backfired. Prospectors, now in far greater numbers, many of them armed and crossing the border from Minas Gerais, took advantage of the absence of state authority to return. After a new viceroy, Antônio Álvares da Cunha, the Count of Cunha (1763–67), assumed office in the new capital, he wrote Lisbon to express dismay that everyone knew the crown had banned access to this sector of the tropical forest, yet "despite this knowledge, everyone pretends to be unaware." Individuals eager to enrich themselves continually petitioned officials to be permitted to prospect in the restricted zone.[20]

The historical record does not preserve these prospectors' impressions of the terrain they penetrated. Their disorientation among the towering trees, experienced again and again by those who followed, can be imagined with the help of others. "We make our way along [the forest] floor, stumbling between the legs of giants, much less dexterously than in open fields. Even in the dry season the morning dew falls in a steady drizzle, soaking the slippery litter and turning the earth to mud," wrote an eminent historian of the Atlantic Forest, a forest now cleared, fragmented, and reduced to a fraction of its original size. "Tangles of roots and vines slow our feet. Lianas, bristling with thorns, scrape our arms. To advance a kilometer is to clamber over fallen trunks a score of times or more. Along the streams, legions of bloodsucking ticks, mosquitoes, sand flies, some of them parasitized by microbes . . . lethal to us hairless mammals—pursue relentlessly. Centipedes, scorpions, and urticating caterpillars dare us to touch them." The visitor to the forest concludes with a mixture of alienation and longing: "Amid this chaos, this wreckage, these dangers, we peer upward at the distant light that filters wanly through the foliage. It is an unsatisfactory view, unlike the clear sweep of the horizon we enjoy in the grasslands. The life that teems in the canopy is beyond our ken."[21]

Those who managed to reach the area from Minas Gerais in defiance of the ban on exploration and settlement, officials later recounted, chose an Indian village as the place most suitable for their mining camp. There they "extracted extremely copious riches."[22] By their choice of location, it seems evident they continued to count on the same Indigenous geographic knowledge that had guided Maurício José Portugal and other early prospectors. They may have also made use of Indigenous labor, although the Indians were rumored to have withdrawn "out of fear" of the numerous migrants, both white and Black, and their increasing number of dwellings and planted fields.[23] One document from the period describes more assertive Natives. Following the crown's 1765 orders to bar access to the area, soldiers had apprehended two Carmelite missionaries known to be mining gold in the area, thereby antagonizing rather than Christianizing Indians, who had "thrown [the friars] out of those districts by force." The viceroy ordered the clerics arrested and sent as prisoners to Lisbon.[24] Given the sparse and contradictory source material, assessing the Indigenous response to intrusions into their lands is a fraught exercise. Later reports would document amicable relations and intensive cooperation between the Natives and prospectors who came to depend on them for help as they sought buried gold. If evidence from similar encounters elsewhere can serve as a guide, all three modes of interaction—flight, resistance, and cooperation—likely occurred, perhaps even simultaneously.[25]

The site of the illicit mining and contraband operation was first portrayed vaguely on manuscript maps drawn around this time. It was thought to lie some 30 leagues (200 kilometers) northeast of the capital city. As the crow flies the actual distance is about 150 kilometers. One map commissioned by the viceroy, completed in 1767, depicted the region covered by forests, a "sertão occupied by wild Indians." Another notation on the map described "fazendas that were demolished," indicating that the king's order to raze properties had been successfully executed.[26] Further details appeared on a second, undated map by an anonymous cartographer. This map featured the "Minas Novas do Castelo" (New Mines of the Castle), far to the north in the interior of what is now the coastal state of Espírito Santo. Despite the distance separating the two mineral strikes, they came to be seen as two poles of a sprawling region subject to illegal prospecting. Both maps exemplified manuscript cartographic production from this period that illustrated colonial ambitions to colonize zones ringing Minas Gerais. The maps reveal how uncertain officials remained about the geography of this inland region, having little sense even of the size of the area they were trying to control. The maps also capture colonists' expectations that, the presence of Indians notwithstanding, the forested uplands separating Minas Gerais from the coast would soon be thrown opened to mining.[27]

Acting on the king's decree to evacuate the mountains northeast of Rio de Janeiro, the Marquis of Pombal charged his brother Francisco Xavier de Mendonça Furtado, now serving as the empire's secretary of state for overseas affairs, with conveying the crown's displeasure to the viceroy about allowing activity in the zone. Yet even as Furtado banned further incursions into Indian domain, he approved nearly identical activity farther north. There, he endorsed actions by Minas governor Luís Diogo Lobo da Silva to attract and subdue forest Indians along the headwaters of the Doce River basin. He did so even though colonization in that zone was likewise ostensibly forbidden. He couched royal support for this colonization effort in the language of protection and religious duty. The king, he wrote, was interested in more than commercial ends: "spiritual" benefits would also accrue to the area's Indians. For this reason the monarch approved of "associating with these heretofore unfortunate peoples who, because of the tyranny with which they have always been treated, find themselves in the ignorance in which they were born."[28] The divergent crown policies, one restricting territorial expansion along the border between Minas Gerais and Rio de Janeiro, the other promoting it just to the north, indicate how local conditions and the persuasiveness of individual officials could sway Lisbon as it attempted to administer remote areas and devise policies concerning their autonomous Native inhabitants.

The official ban on activity in the mountains northeast of the colonial capital continued during the 1770s, under the leadership of a new viceroy, the capable marquis of Lavradio (1769–79), and a new secretary of state for overseas affairs, Martinho de Melo e Castro, who served from 1770 to 1795. Melo e Castro earned his powerful position in imperial governance as a neo-mercantilist reformer. He proved even more rigid than Pombal in his determination to tighten the reigns of metropolitan control over the colony and its internal frontiers, pursuing this goal long after Pombal fell from power on the death of José I in 1777. The viceroy, for his part, adhered to the old assumptions about maintaining a buffer zone, free from colonizing activity, to secure the southern and eastern perimeter of the inland mining zone. He called off a planned conquest of Indians occupying the area stretching northward from the Paraíba River to the Doce River, because "the king had prohibited entering into and founding establishments" in these lands.[29]

Throughout this period Natives in the coastal mountains continued to shape the state's response as rumors of contraband activity circulated unabated. Officials continued to depend on them for intelligence gathering while also coming to suspect them of participating in the illegal extraction, transit, and exchange of gold. Authorities conjectured that "barbarous Indians" were trading gold with settlers in Cachoeiras de Macacu. Adding to these worries were repeated cases of soldiers deserting their posts, presumably to try their luck as prospectors.[30] Despite these persistent concerns, it would not be until Lavradio's successor took office that new information gathered from the backlands provoked Lisbon to act.

### General Inquest

From the beginning of his term in office in 1778, Viceroy Luís de Vasconcelos e Sousa, the Count of Figueiró (1778–90), made a resolute effort to collect such intelligence, ordering his mining superintendent to conduct a wide-ranging investigation, a "general inquest," questioning officials and other informants in outlying districts. The results only deepened concerns about the extent of gold smuggling. It was in the documentation generated by this investigation that the name of Manuel Henriques, frequently referred to by his sobriquet Mão de Luva (Gloved Hand), gained transatlantic notoriety among ranking imperial authorities in Rio de Janeiro and Lisbon as the villainous leader of the clandestine mining operation. One militia field commander estimated that two hundred free prospectors worked under the supervision of this backcountry renegade from Minas Gerais, each of whom possessed three to five slaves. Some were striking out for the clandestine site from the coastal Campos dos Goitacases region. They ascended the Paraíba River in canoes until impassable falls forced them to travel overland through the "wild forest." Some arrived "nearly dead from hunger." The ascent could take thirty days, ending in an area we now know lies about 35 winding kilometers south of the river. The descent by way of Cachoeiras de Macacu was much faster, cutting the transit time to ten or twelve days. Slave owners mined together communally, divided into separate "companies" overseen by their respective leaders. They pooled their gold, dividing it at week's end according to the number of enslaved laborers each contributed to the operation.[31] In this way the work regime entailed a peculiar correspondence to legal conventions, given that the royal mining code apportioned claims at authorized mineral washings on the basis of how many slaves individual claimants possessed, full claims going only to those who demonstrated the seriousness of their interest by dedicating more than a dozen captive workers to a site.[32]

Troubled by these reports, the viceroy questioned the field officer Miguel Antunes Ferreira, who fourteen years earlier had executed the king's order to destroy all backcountry properties. Now the embodiment of the crown's futile effort to stamp out even official memories of the proscribed mines, Ferreira recalled climbing above the falls and meeting two Indian men and two women. The history of Portuguese America is replete with Indigenous women who acted as intermediaries and peacemakers between their kin and colonists.[33] Perhaps because the women Ferreira

FIGURE 3.2. Mountains above Rio de Janeiro. Source: Rugendas, *Voyage pittoresque*. Courtesy of the Biblioteca Nacional, Rio de Janeiro.

encountered were with nursing infants, they stayed behind when he convinced the men to guide him further into the mountains. Two days later, they came on the isolated residence of a cleric working to convert the region's Natives. A white overseer and some enslaved Blacks were present, tending livestock and fields of subsistence crops, which could be used to provision unauthorized miners. The field officer evacuated and demolished the property, as he had already done with fazendas operated by Maurício José Portugal and his associates, the prospectors who first received permission to explore the area. Following a "heathen trail," the only route through an area surrounded by "impenetrable ranges" and "dangerous waterfalls," the officer's party advanced for another dozen days until they reached the Rio Grande, a southern tributary of the Paraíba. Beyond the river, Ferreira recounted, repeating what the Indians told him, lay mountains laden with "the greatest of riches," never explored or exploited because of the presence of "the most numerous and most barbarous and warlike nations that abound in that sertão." His Indigenous informants identified these antagonists as the Puri and the Xopotó, another group of Gê speakers related to the Botocudo.[34]

During the final days of his expedition, Ferreira collected still more tantalizing intelligence. Vulnerable to attack by the Puri, finding no sign of smugglers, contending with sick soldiers in his party, and lacking specific orders to proceed, he never crossed the Rio Grande. But he did explore downriver some distance along a scarcely discernible Native trail. There he encountered a "wild Indian" who informed him, presumably by way of his Indigenous guides, that various Native villages lay to the north, three-days distant. The field officer offered warm garments to the informant, provided gifts for the man's "cacique" and his wife, and dispatched a scouting party composed of his two guides and one soldier to enter into contact with other Indians. The scouts soon returned accompanied by a "copious number of barbarous heathens of the Orosó nation," including five headmen.

Ferreira further reported that the Indians, at least one of whom spoke Portuguese, confirmed that to reach their villages required three days' travel. Another five days' journey brought travelers to the Paraíba River and the captaincy border. The entire region on both sides of the border, they told him, was "extremely abundant in gold, wherever one searches." It was not even necessary to dig for the metal, because streams in the area exposed "infinite flakes" easily retrieved. The field officer repeated his questions about these details many times and always received the same response. In addition, the Indians told him about a large lake where "infinite precious stones are discovered." These gems were "so resplendent that they disturb the view when the sun shines." The potential for farming and ranching was equally promising. The only impediment to exploiting the region, Ferreira remarked, was that it was "inhabited and possessed by innumerable wild heathen of diverse nations, all of them living pitifully in the same disgrace, ignorance, and misery."

Despite their "proud and formidable" appearance, Ferreira judged these forest Indians "flexible and tamable." He convinced the headmen and many of their followers to return with him to Rio de Janeiro to meet with the viceroy. Although no known records survive of this high-level meeting, we can assume the information exchanged corresponded to the stories collected by Ferreira in the mountains. We cannot know the extent to which either the Indians or Ferreira exaggerated what they told the viceroy. There was always incentive to do so, considering the crown's thirst for precious metals and stones and the rewards conferred on those who discovered them. What is clear is that the description of the region attributed to the Indians fed the fantasies of Portuguese authorities and colonists. Although he never managed to confirm or rule out reports that the region's Indigenous inhabitants were participating in the contraband trade, Ferreira would be called on to repeat what he had learned to three successive viceroys, all keen to understand the character of the backlands.[35] Vasconcelos e Sousa was the third of these viceroys to hear Ferreira's account. It was he who pushed Lisbon, increasingly bent on tightening neo-mercantilist control over its colony, to act.

As the viceroy gathered more backcountry intelligence, suspicions redoubled on both sides of the Atlantic that Indians were participating as intermediaries in the smuggling operation thought to be moving gold from the interior to the coast. The fact that the illegal miners had settled at the site of a Native village only deepened these concerns. An attempt to impede smuggling by placing a guard post near a village of "tame" Indians, well above the last authorized settlement on the lower Paraíba River, was put at risk by what another officer described as a war party of "wild heathen." Sounding a horn and armed with bows and arrows, they descended the river in seven canoes. Violence was averted only when leaders of the so-called tame Indians intervened to "frustrate" the surprise attack. The officer despaired of the possibility of combating such foes, given their habit of withdrawing into the forest when pursued. Indians he interviewed said they feared that the growing presence of Portuguese soldiers in the area, part of the viceroy's measures to gain control of the situation, threatened their control of territory.[36]

The officer also extracted a confession from an individual of Indigenous descent caught leading prospectors into the sertão. Identifying himself by the Christian name Domingos, he was described as either an Indian or a mestiço, and a *lingua* (tongue), that is, a translator. His village of "tame Indians," located in the mountains between the coast and the mining camp, was led by a cacique described as a pardo, a term usually reserved for individuals of African as opposed to Indigenous descent. Its use in this case captures the fluidity of racial classification and Indigenous identity, whether imposed or self-ascribed, in a region where Native peoples, colonists, and enslaved and free people of color had interacted for more than two centuries. Domingos described his village as the gateway to a route that connected it, by trail and canoe, to a series of more distant Native aldeias. Other trails reached this village from the captaincy's coastal Indian settlements, former Jesuit missions. He admitted to helping guide four prospectors—three woodcutters from one of these coastal settlements and a sailor—to the illegal mining area. One of the woodcutters was José Gomes, whose testimony would also soon cause a sensation. Another Indian, their lead guide, had brought them to Domingos's village. Serving as a paid translator, Domingos helped them pass unharmed through the Native villages upriver.

Domingos recalled approaching the clandestine mines along the captaincy border as night fell. The party was met by "a tall man . . . with a gloved hand," Manuel Henriques himself, wielding a pistol "under his arm and a machete in his hand." The guide estimated that about twenty men, whites and Blacks, many of them armed, were working at the mining camp, not including the new arrivals. A shortage of provisions at the site meant that the party was obliged to descend to Cachoeira de Macacu in search of manioc flour, evidence of the commercial network the operation required to sustain itself. Three weeks into the journey, angered that he had not received payment for his services, Domingos returned to the coast, where the officer ordered him arrested, recorded his confession, and turned him over to higher authorities for further questioning.[37]

The *sertanista* (backwoodsman) José Gomes provided especially disconcerting information contributing to the decades-long accumulation of backlands knowledge that would soon prompt Lisbon's tactical shift to military mobilization. This secret evidence was coerced from Gomes, one of the woodcutters in league with Domingos and other Indians identified in the viceroy's general inquest.[38] For six months Gomes was held prisoner in Rio de Janeiro's Carmelite convent before being transferred in chains to Lisbon in 1781 to face interrogation by the Holy Office of the Inquisition. Denounced to clergymen employed by the Inquisition in the colony, he was accused of sacrilege and conspiring with the backcountry miners. Seeking protection against the dangers of his inland travels and associations with men operating outside the law, he had absconded with a piece of the Eucharist. He did so by removing the consecrated host from his mouth after receiving communion. He then returned to the forest in possession of this sacred edible, convinced it would safeguard him while he worked with Henriques and his accomplices. When soldiers apprehended Gomes, they seized, along with the stolen Eucharist, some flakes of gold and a large diamond. They then turned him over to church authorities. Under interrogation, he claimed Henriques and a coconspirator had incited him to commit the crime. His confession provided crucial details about the clandestine mining operation. The testimony was considered so sensitive that the viceroy's mining superintendent, rather than employ a scribe, copied it himself when reporting to Lisbon.[39]

During this transatlantic investigation, Inquisition interrogators identified Gomes as white not Indian. Much evidence, however, including his place of residence, his visit to Domingos's village, and what he knew about the sertão, established that he regularly communicated with Natives and moved easily among them. It is possible this was a case of the kind of bureaucratic expediency that commonly labeled Christianized Indians as white. The Inquisition only reluctantly and in rare cases moved against Indians, officially considering them guileless innocents, and thus would have had a stake in classifying Gomes as a non-Indian were he of mixed descent. For their part, local civil administrators in league with colonists took advantage of the assimilationist objectives of royal legislation. They often declared Indians white, mestiço, or pardo in a move to erase legal protections such as Native rights to communal land.[40] Other factors may also have been at work. For instance, Gomes seemed uncertain about his own origins. Categories that modernizing state bureaucracies worked to reify, because they made individuals like Gomes legible and governable from a distance, appear to have had little relevance for the sertanista. He could not confidently respond when asked his age. Inquisitors deemed him to be about thirty years old, "more or less." He also could not name his deceased grandmothers or his godmother. Nor could he specify with certainty the birthplace of his late parents.[41] Such disjunctures make discerning his ethnic identity problematic.

Of further import was the nature of Gomes's alleged misconduct. A crime against the sacraments frequently prosecuted by the Inquisition, theft of the consecrated host, exemplified what Laura de Mello e Souza describes as the "yawning gap" separating "the religious stiffness of the watchful Portuguese Inquisition and the Catholicism lived by the colonists every day." The illicit use in popular Catholicism of small pieces of the unleavened bread of communion to ward off quotidian dangers can be traced back hundreds of years in Europe. The practice became widespread in Brazil by the mid-eighteenth century. Although colonial inhabitants of all stripes believed in the Eucharist's magical properties, those who risked their lives in the backlands had particular reason to secret away pieces of the host, chips of the marble altar stone, and other sacred objects. Transgressive reverence for these items was one way of "seeking protection from the routine, everyday hardships they encountered: ferocious animals, flooded rivers, and the arrows of fierce Indians." Through these magical materials, "they created a parallel universe where the obstacles of daily life dwindled in strength."[42]

Gomes's case corresponded with this tendency. Living on the margins of state legibility and control, a widower of scant means and barely literate, as the ragged signature he appended to his testimony attests, he was described variously as a subsistence farmer, woodcutter, miner, and coarse itinerant without domicile or possessions. His crime occurred at the São João da Barra Chapel, where priests ministered to the rural population at the foot of the mountains northeast of Rio de Janeiro, a gateway to the backlands. Parishioners included residents of the Ipuca aldeia, whose

Native inhabitants were suspected of maintaining ties with the mining operation. The day he pilfered the host, Gomes described his new treasure to an acquaintance as "the best thing in the world."[43] As was often the practice in such cases, he placed the morsel in a pouch that he hung around his neck. Under interrogation, facing charges of superstition, sacrilege, and sorcery, he described adding to the pouch bits of wood, iron, silk, and soil, a piece of an altar stone, and some dust he believed contained dried breast milk from the Virgin Mary, threads of her shawl, and fragments of a prayer by Saint Augustine. Ignoring warnings from his friends, he did all this "on the advice of certain persons for the sole purpose of freeing himself from the dangers he feared might harm him in the sertão."[44]

The company he kept exacerbated his transgression. His mentor in crime, he claimed, was none other than Manuel Henriques, Mão de Luva, who wore a similar pouch and promised such pouches to others. Under increasing pressure, Gomes came to insist that he was "obliged" to work at the illegal mines, implying that the infamous accused contrabandist had threatened to kill him if he did not follow his detailed instructions about how best to steal the host without getting caught. We can only speculate whether Henriques was in fact in the business not only of mining gold but also collecting valuable objects believed magical to distribute or sell to collaborators. Gomes's allegations about the accused smuggler led the investigation from the Inquisition's secret prison in Lisbon back to Brazil. Prominent clergymen pursued the charges, interviewing witnesses who had worked with Henriques and who attested to his flouting of Catholic orthodoxy. A pact with the devil, some said, explained his purported supernatural powers, including the ability to leap over houses on horses he enchanted, help prisoners escape from locked jail cells, avoid perils in the forest, outwit his enemies, and exert a spellbinding influence over those he commanded. The inability of church and civil authorities to apprehend Henriques only added to his mystique, which spread widely in Minas Gerais and Rio de Janeiro.[45] Gomes was less successful in eluding punishment. After more than a year in the Inquisition's prison in Lisbon, he was sentenced to a public whipping "without the spilling of blood." He was then to serve in the royal galleys for five years. The punishment quickly left him sick, hospitalized, and facing his "ultimate ruin." Sympathetic doctors eventually appealed successfully for his release, after which his actions become impossible to trace with any certainty. He requested to serve out his sentence in "any part of America," that is, any part of Portuguese America. The inquisitors commuted his sentence but insisted he remain in Lisbon.[46]

Along with its revelations about events deep in the coastal forest and the lengths to which individuals went to protect themselves from its hazards, this case helps clarify how the state and church worked hand in hand in an attempt to project their power beyond their effective geographic reach. When notified about Gomes's detention, the viceroy ordered clergymen to broaden their questioning beyond church matters. His correspondence reveals how readily he tapped this testimony for his own secular purposes related to security and territorialized sovereignty. Gomes provided by far the most detailed descriptions of trails leading to the illegal mining operation from the coast, and he added to what authorities knew about northern access from Minas Gerais. He had traveled the routes that climbed to the mines from the southwest, starting from the capital city and passing through Cachoeira de Macacu. He also knew the routes from the southeast, starting from Macaé. He displayed an unparalleled knowledge of backcountry topography. He seemed to know every bend in the trail, every rise and descent, every Native encampment, protected sleeping place, false summit, pass, bog, and river crossing, and the distances between them. He knew names for the most obscure geographic features, drawn from both colonial and Indigenous sources, names such as "Burned Hill," "Santa Teresa Creek," "Jequitibá Ranch." He could identify rocks, skulls, tree trunks carved with crosses, and other signs placed by Indians and smugglers to orient themselves as they traveled.[47]

Gomes's familiarity with the region's mineral wealth and unsupervised mining activity was no less impressive. He reported the amounts of gold dust and grains, the size of "small shotgun lead," drawn from an average day's work panning in various streams. He described the quantity, color, and shape of gemstones found in the area, ranging from sky blue to topaz to crystalline. "In one afternoon," he recounted, according to the priest who questioned him, miners "removed a *libra* [pound] of precious stones, among which were some they said were diamonds." A pardo prospector who had "spent twenty years roaming this sertão" once "took out a diamond weighing thirty-three *oitavas*" (117 grams or 585 carats uncut).[48] The accused backwoodsman identified the precise locations of various mineral washings, including Henriques's personal claim. He described a trail leading to the property in Xopotó, Minas Gerais, where the accused contrabandist resided with his family, five days distant from the illegal mining site. Although only eleven prospectors were working at the site the last time Gomes visited, dozens had recently abandoned it because of rumors circulating about an approaching official crackdown. He admitted to having worked directly with Henriques for a full year, coming and going from the mineral washings numerous times. Helping secure his status as a reliable witness, he further told his interrogator that he "had not said everything that he knew about the great riches of this vast expanse of land" because he did not wish to repeat unverified information acquired "only from the statements of others." He knew what he said he knew from "having seen it himself."[49]

Gomes had seen and communicated enough to make a new course of action seem urgent. After nearly two decades of information gathering on the coastal side of the backlands separating Rio de Janeiro and Minas Gerais, state officials had assembled a case the implication of which could no longer be minimized. The case was built on the backcountry expertise of Indigenous informants and their interlocutors. These individuals lived both in the mountains and on the coastal plain. During the second half of the eighteenth century, they traversed a period in the colony's history when changes in Indigenous legislation combined with long-term pressure from coastal settlers required difficult choices about autonomy and cooperation. The information they shared with authorities was revelatory but could not always be trusted. The reports colonial authorities in turn transmitted to Lisbon introduced further lacunae, biases, and distortions. Within this communications matrix, linking forest dwellers to palace dignitaries, it became increasingly impossible for coastal authorities, the viceroy foremost among them, to maintain that the crown's evolving restrictions were working to impede illicit activity in the mountains looming over the settled littoral. For some, the very integrity of the empire seemed at stake. If Lisbon could not exert its authority over areas immediately inland from the coast, if it could not stop the flow of smuggled gold and diamonds through the mountains, the fundamental calculus of mercantilist rule and colonial submission to a sovereign throne seemed at risk.

CHAPTER 4

## NATIVES, SMUGGLERS, SOLDIERS, SPIES

AS ON THE COASTAL PLAIN, when authorities on the far side of the mountains in landlocked Minas Gerais sought information about the secretive gloved smuggler Manuel Henriques, they found themselves engaging Indigenous intelligence networks. From the 1760s efforts to convert Native peoples and gather them in state-sponsored mission villages helped open large stretches of the captaincy's southeastern backlands to colonization. Both conflict and collaboration with the Coroado and Coropó Indians resulted. Under the Forbidden Lands policy the crown prohibited settlement in these expanses covered by the Atlantic Forest. But the reality on the ground differed. Colonists flouted the restrictions in their search for economic alternatives. Attracted by unsettled land, they migrated away from waning mining towns, clearing the forest for subsistence and then commercial farming. They also opened new smuggling routes, exploiting Native trails. This unmonitored migration drew the state in its wake. Although at first hesitant, imperial administrators concluded they had to establish an official presence in the area. In the mid-1780s, with rumors rife about Henriques and his criminal associates, officials moved more decisively to extend the crown's authority to the sector of the sertões east of the Caminho Novo along the captaincy border.

An accelerating exchange of information about contraband flowing through these lands was both a precursor to and by-product of the move to exercise greater territorial control. Contacts with the Coroado and

Coropó confirmed the existence of a network of trails linking southeastern Minas Gerais to the lands across the captaincy border—a jurisdictional division that mattered little to mobile Indigenous groups. These trails provided access to the zone where Henriques's illegal gold washings were located. From there transport routes extended to the coast. Smugglers and their enslaved workers, officials learned, were likely using the same routes and opening their own. With concerns about illegality intensifying, the crown came to view its own lack of dominion over the cross-border region as no longer tolerable. It was at this juncture that Henriques's notoriety attained outsize, transatlantic proportions. Lisbon authorized the Minas governor to launch a surprise military raid to capture Henriques and his criminal associates. As soldiers prepared for the operation, the governor himself fell under suspicion of profiting from the illicit activity. After the raid concluded, as authorities sought to establish government rule over the area, Indians continued to provide vital intelligence, navigating the fraught terrain between concealment and cooperation.

### Indigenous Confidants

Even before state emissaries began probing what Indians knew about illegal mining and contraband activity in the area, prospectors, too, depended on Native geographic expertise. Recall the 1767 map describing as a "sertão occupied by wild Indians" the region between the coastal range and the Paraíba River, the same region from which rumors of gold smuggling began to circulate. Recall, too, that gold specimens and information gathered from Indians spurred the initial state-authorized exploration of the region from the coast, before it was called off, and that testimony acquired in the process documented exchanges between prospectors and Natives. On the coastal side of the border, official contacts with Natives and settlers suspected of smuggling continued into the 1780s.

It is difficult to imagine that Henriques did not by necessity, from his first arrival in the area, interact extensively with Indians. The nature of such contacts, however, remains elusive. The clandestine character of the mining operation works against the clarity we seek. Many rumors but little reliable information circulated during the earliest days of suspected mining in the zone. Attempts to bar access to the area, deliberately shortening the reach of precisely the institutions whose bureaucracies would have generated crucial sources, shaped what can and cannot be known.

Despite the fact that Indians were said to have fled when Henriques and his band first entered Rio de Janeiro from Minas Gerais, setting up camp in the Native village, there is also evidence they later returned and that amicable relations ensued, even leading some of the Indians to learn to pray under the smuggler's tutelage.[1] It seems likely that the invasion of prospectors and enslaved laborers disrupted Native hunting, foraging, and other activities, resulting in the same sort of tensions such encounters produced elsewhere. If evidence collected in neighboring zones provides a model for what might have occurred, we can hypothesize that interactions included some combination of gift-giving, information gathering, guide services, misunderstanding, misdirection, and coerced displacement. Undoubtedly this was no forest utopia. Yet it seems reasonable to conclude that Henriques and his fellow miners could not have established themselves without ample reliance on the forest's aboriginal inhabitants.

In the mid-1760s, soon after the earliest reports of the contraband mining operation began to provoke official anxieties, Minas governor Luís Diogo Lobo da Silva intensified efforts to incorporate Native bands in the eastern sertões, just as he did to the west. He placed a militia captain and the intrepid priest Manoel de Jesus Maria in charge of the area most susceptible to smuggling. They managed to establish several state-controlled mission villages where Indians settled, supplied with goods purchased by the royal treasury. In the face of the mounting settler migration, significant numbers of Coroado and Coropó took up residence at the aldeias of São Manuel do Rio Pomba and São João Batista do Presídio. Padre Maria remained active in Christianizing the Coroado and Coropó for more than forty years. He appealed to authorities repeatedly over the decades to impede settler encroachment on lands he considered part of the Native villages. Yet his own activities, not the least of them his preoccupation with extending roads to improve transport and communications, helped open the region to such settlement.[2]

The son of an enslaved woman from Angola and her owner, freed under unknown circumstances before he sought ordination, Padre Maria was an enslaver himself by the time he received permission from the governor to set out for the forests, aided by Native translators. The cleric became a key agent of the mutually reinforcing consolidation of church and state in this frontier zone, defined by the course of the Pomba River as it tumbled toward the Paraíba at the captaincy border.[3] When he first entered the area, as he later recalled, he had "walked the entire way on foot, suffering hunger and hardships, and sleeping in the open," twice nearly drowning on stretches of the route barely navigable by canoe. He and the settlers who followed him took "great risks" by exposing themselves to the "inconstancy of the Indians." He quickly accumulated regional fame for his successes in "Christianizing, civilizing, and reducing the Indians to the faith of Christ."[4] More than one thousand Indians were baptized in the priest's newly created parish between the late 1760s and early 1790s.[5]

Padre Maria missionized and enlarged existing Coroado and Coropó villages with the help of Natives who sought his protection from intruding settlers. This activity gave him an acute understanding of developments in the more distant forests along the captaincy border. He administered the sacraments to those who established themselves under his care, sought state funds to clothe and feed them, provided for their basic education, and denounced settlers to higher authorities for seizing lands set aside for Native dwellings and food production. In return, the Indians joined him and other colonists on expeditions deeper into the forest to attack the Puri, their common enemy, hunt fugitives from slavery, search for mineral deposits, and establish relations with other Coroado and Coropó, coaxing and sometimes coercing them to relocate to the state-administered villages.[6]

Through the 1770s captaincy officials continued to support missionizing these groups in keeping with crown Indigenous policy. At the same time they were at pains to demonstrate compliance with Lisbon's ban on settlement in peripheral areas vulnerable to smuggling. Key figures during this period were the family of Captain Francisco Pires Farinho, who provided military support to Padre Maria and served as lay director of the Rio Pomba aldeia, becoming the godparent of the Indigenous youth Jacinto at his baptism. The officer, members of his family, and dependents, including Jacinto and other village Indians, staged incursions into Coroado and Coropó hunting grounds and attacked quilombos. At least two family members received royal land grants in the region.[7] In 1778 Governor Antônio de Noronha (1775–80) chastised the captain for permitting his brother, Manoel Pires Farinho, to lead an expedition into prohibited areas, risking opening up a contraband route. The reprimand had no lasting effect. In 1781 he led another unauthorized expedition, attacking a group of Puri, killing ten. Governor Rodrigo José de Meneses, the Count of Cavaleiros (1780–83) rebuked Captain Farinho for permitting this raid on Indians who had given no "immediate motive for being treated as enemies." While stopping short of prohibiting all subsequent expeditions into the same region, the governor warned against waging similar attacks "in any case other than natural defense."[8]

By the early 1780s the logic of the Forbidden Lands policy looked increasingly antiquated as gold production continued to decline and the captaincy population shifted increasingly to agropastoral production. Both to the north and west of the zone in which Henriques established his rogue mining operation, Governor Meneses activated plans to advance colonization of the sertões that Minas Gerais shared with the coastal captaincies of Espírito Santo, Rio de Janeiro, and São Paulo. He attempted to do so without rankling ministers in Lisbon. Meneses investigated claims of new gold and diamond strikes, conceded land grants in regions previously off-limits, and sought both to incentivize and compel impoverished single males and families to occupy these remote areas. In areas accessible to the Caminho Novo, little state incentive proved necessary because proximity to the major transportation route provided commercial opportunities that drew farmers and miners voluntarily. Indeed, before the Minas government recognized the scope of what was occurring, settlement to the east and west of the royal road extended over significant stretches of the Mantiqueira Mountains, notwithstanding the crown's ongoing prohibitions. Arguing to Lisbon's secretary of state for overseas affairs, Martinho de

Melo e Castro, that the original settlement ban had been "based on totally impracticable principles, whose observance would result in the ruin of this captaincy," the governor insisted that the crown should acknowledge this reality, formalize land tenure by issuing land grants, and dispatch soldiers to guard against contraband activity.[9]

The governor considered the issue urgent enough that he decided to visit the area to the west of the Caminho Novo himself with a party of officers, soldiers, and aids. Over the course of a month, traveling an arduous route on horseback and then in canoes, exposed to "great danger" while descending rapids and falls, the party explored for gold deposits, which they found, and identified numerous paths the smugglers used. The party observed many squatters already established in the area, miners and farmers of both ample and meager means, with and without captive workers. Flocking to the governor's trailside command post, more than seven hundred individuals and families submitted petitions for land grants and mining claims, most of which the governor approved, convinced that it was better to formalize what had already occurred rather than attempt to turn back the tide of advancing frontier settlers. He appointed officials to govern the zone and ordered military patrols to surveil it as an obstacle to illegal activity.[10]

While pursuing his active interest in gaining control of the sertões, Governor Meneses revealed his knowledge of and support for at least some of Henriques's activities before the latter became a criminal pariah in the captaincy. Although Henriques was already being investigated and condemned by Viceroy Luís de Vasconcelos e Sousa, the governor mentioned him in a 1782 communiqué to a cavalry commander, evincing no knowledge of Henriques's involvement in illicit activity. The governor discussed assigning him an unspecified mission, an order he was now rescinding, apparently to prioritize the commander's plans to secure outlying districts. The following year, now resorting to Henriques's shadowy nickname Mão de Luva, the governor wrote another commander to seek assistance in apprehending an escaped criminal. If Mão de Luva could be located, the commander was to place him in charge of this operation.[11] While cryptic, these communiqués make it clear that Governor Meneses had official dealings with the accused smuggler during a period just before the crown ordered his arrest. The governor treated him as a reliable aid in distant areas he sought to bring under state control. If he knew of Henriques's clandestine mining camp, he did not say so.

After taking office in late 1783, Governor Luís da Cunha Meneses (1783–88), later the Count of Lumiares, less politically astute than his predecessor, promoted what the viceroy quickly denounced as an imprudent push to establish an official presence in the lands to the east of the Caminho Novo, that is, just north of the site of the illicit mining operation. Struggling to keep pace with migrants abandoning exhausted mining towns, and pressured to do something about Henriques in the wake of the viceroy's general inquest, Cunha Meneses ordered the deployment of a reconnaissance mission to the area in 1784. He did so even as rumors circulated about possible collaboration in the smuggling operation by captaincy soldiers, including the officer he charged with commanding the mission, Sergeant Major Pedro Afonso Galvão de São Martinho. Also participating was the dragoon officer Joaquim José da Silva Xavier. Better known to history as Tiradentes (Tooth-Puller), Silva Xavier was later implicated in the Minas Conspiracy of 1789, executed, and eventually transformed into a hero of Brazilian independence. The officers were to examine areas previously set off limits by the crown. In an intersection of military reconnaissance, policing, and natural history fieldwork increasingly typical of state-sponsored advances into the backlands during this era, Silva Xavier assumed responsibility for mapping the lands, rivers, and other features of the southeastern border region, while registering the number of settlers who had ignored crown restrictions to migrate there. He was also ordered to catalog all the trails and roads penetrating the area, especially any crossing the captaincy border. Finally, he was to recommend the most strategic places to dispatch military patrols and establish checkpoints.[12]

As part of this reconnaissance, Sergeant Major São Martinho questioned Padre Maria. The priest's presence in the region since the 1760s made him an ideal informant. His expertise was especially prized because of his knowledge of Indigenous groups inhabiting the captaincy periphery. Asked about any illicit activity along the border, the priest reported the existence of a "wide trail" connecting the region in question with the Caminho Novo, facilitating transport, provisioning, and presumably smuggling. The priest also recalled seeing a party of some thirty miners, including enslaved laborers, heading into the region. The group's leader claimed to have official permission from the current governor's predecessor to search for gold with Henriques along the Paraíba River.[13]

This claim may have been nothing more than a ploy by these men to avoid punishment, but it raises the possibility that the group in league with Henriques believed their operation to have the captaincy administration's imprimatur. Nevertheless, this authorization would almost certainly not have permitted prospecting on the Rio de Janeiro side of the border. It is conceivable, given what was then the still indeterminate location of the border, that the miners believed their mineral washings were in Minas Gerais. Some evidence for this interpretation can be found in the previous governor's communications with Henriques. Furthermore, in ongoing negotiations with Lisbon, Governor Meneses had advocated pushing the border as far south as possible. For the captaincy such a move would mean enhanced tax revenues drawn from expanded territory. For Henriques and his associates this possibility added another reason to hope their secret claims might one day be deemed legal.[14]

Padre Maria's testimony concerning Native movement across the captaincy border validated Lisbon's worst fears about the ease with which malefactors might smuggle gold and diamonds to the Atlantic seaboard. He spoke of Indigenous exchange networks stretching from the outer edge of settlement in Minas Gerais, crossing the mountains, and reaching the coast. Material proof came in the form of ornamental beads. Coroado and Coropó living along the captaincy border, he said, communicated with relative ease with members of "the same nation" who lived in the Campos dos Goitacases region on the coastal plain northeast of Rio de Janeiro. While these groups sometimes clashed with the Puri, they managed to conduct trade that moved beads from the littoral, "passing from one group to another," across the border, and into the priest's parish. Movement through the mountains in both directions was thereby confirmed. Sergeant Major São Martinho relayed this intelligence to the governor in

Vila Rica, who passed it on to the viceroy, who in turn, when the news arrived in Rio de Janeiro more than three months later, forwarded it to Lisbon. If the bead trade was any indication, intelligence from Native villages in Minas Gerais to those in Rio de Janeiro, even those as far away as the former Jesuit missions along the coast, moved much faster.[15]

Acquired from and intensifying suspicions about the area's Indians, interwoven with and inseparable from stories about untapped gold and diamonds, these accounts from Minas Gerais combined with those from Rio de Janeiro to form a corpus of documents that crossed the Atlantic, compelling the crown to adopt a new approach. Bolstered with details gathered by smaller patrols and other backcountry sources, the intelligence convinced the empire's ranking authorities that their attempt to establish a lowland "blockade" around the vast mountainous region accessed by trails from various directions had failed.[16] In Rio de Janeiro the viceroy acknowledged "the great difficulty of impeding any smuggling" through the mountains, "despite all measures I have taken in this respect." The time had come to use more forceful means to punish the "scandalous company" of armed men operating with ever greater temerity.[17]

In Lisbon, Secretary of State Melo e Castro concurred. He doubted whether the policy of barring access to the zone, a policy initiated long before he assumed his office, had ever made sense. The resulting absence of state power over the area simply encouraged what the ban on settlement and government surveillance was intended to prevent: the unauthorized activity of prospectors, contrabandists, and others who felt at liberty to defy the crown. As a result, an ostensibly "deserted and uninhabited" sertão now served as a "secure refuge so that the smugglers can freely do their prospecting there, without risk of being seen." Even if the viceroy succeeded in barring access from the coast, mounting evidence made it clear that various points of access allowed prospectors, merchants, settlers, and the enslaved to enter the unsurveilled region from Minas Gerais. The time had come to territorialize royal sovereignty, deploying military expeditions from both the north and the south.[18]

In his orders to the viceroy and the governor of Minas Gerais to mobilize militarily, Melo e Castro made repeated reference to the information previously acquired from Indians. He also quoted extensively from the Inquisition prisoner José Gomes's testimony analyzed in the preceding chapter, acknowledging that the region had been thoroughly "penetrated and invaded from various directions." Gomes's assertion that the contrabandists maintained their home base in Minas Gerais bore "every appearance of truth," the secretary of state concluded. It was this information that convinced him, following the viceroy's reluctant recommendation, to allow soldiers from Minas Gerais to take the lead in mounting a surprise attack even though the mining camp lay outside the governor's jurisdiction.[19]

How reliance on Native backcountry knowledge, evasion, and cooperation both catalyzed and vexed attempts to consolidate territorial control becomes especially evident when we take the secretary of state at his word, recognizing that the ensuing mobilization to occupy the zone was premised not merely on capturing Henriques and his fellow miners but on establishing effective state hegemony throughout the region comprising this internal frontier. For decades reports from and about Indians had pointed to the area's untapped wealth. The potential for a royal windfall had been inflated by those who consulted with Indians or coerced their testimony, and by officials who took this intelligence to heart. Had the ranking authorities in both the colony and the metropolis been less credulous, less subject to the colonial conviction that Indians and undiscovered riches went hand in hand, the troop deployment that followed would likely have been much more limited and practicable. The mission's origins and outcome rested on dreams founded on rumors. Both could be traced to Indians whose purposes officials took for granted but could rarely comprehend.

## In Pursuit of the Gloved Hand

No longer able to tolerate mounting evidence of illegal mining and smuggling, the crown deemed it time to assert its territorial dominion over the backlands linking the two captaincies, Minas Gerais and Rio de Janeiro. The Portuguese staged two sizeable military expeditions into the area, the first, a rapid strike from the north; the second, a plodding, prolonged occupation from the south. The secretary of state planned and propelled the major elements of this joint operation from Lisbon in conjunction with royal authorities at the highest levels of the imperial and colonial administrations. In the first operation officials envisioned a surprise attack designed to capture Henriques and his associates. Scholars have rendered the move to apprehend him primarily as a colorful episode in the regional history of Minas Gerais or Rio de Janeiro, culminating in the smuggler's arrest. To the degree that some historians have acknowledged broader implications, they have concentrated on the state's absenteeism.[20] But the state acted vigorously, albeit belatedly, especially if we consider the Minas raid in tandem with a second operation staged from Rio de Janeiro. This larger, longer, and costlier mission, designed to established a permanent official presence in the mountains, is the subject of the following chapter.

The secretary of state ordered the initial raid on the illicit mining camp be launched from Minas Gerais because the area was more readily accessible from the north. From one perspective it would have been common practice and crown policy for the government to move in quickly whenever and wherever news circulated of an unsupervised mineral strike. The royal mining code provided the legal mechanisms and incentives to do so. In keeping with the code's stipulations, the crown quickly appropriated and auctioned off its royal claim, designated discoverers received theirs, and petitioners moved in to control all remaining claims distributed according to the number of captive laborers they pledged to put to work. The initial secrecy of new discoveries thus tended to fade quickly as well-capitalized competitors displaced small-stakes miners. It was precisely this process that, during the final decades of the century, after the best deposits had already been exploited, pushed much low-level prospecting to the remotest areas of Minas Gerais. Many of these areas lay along the captaincy's vaguely mapped border or, as in the case of the gloved villain Henriques, just beyond that border.[21]

From another perspective Governor Cunha Meneses's assumption of responsibility for capturing Henriques was deeply problematic. Almost from his arrival in Minas Gerais in 1783, suspicions and denunciations dogged the governor. Self-promoting, despotic, and despised by prominent vassals, he was accused of reaping profits for himself, his cronies,

FIGURE 4.1. Members of colonial militias, a source of troops for backcountry missions. Source: Carlos Julião, [Oficiais do Terço], late 18th century, BNRJ, SI, C.I,2,8. Courtesy of the Biblioteca Nacional, Rio de Janeiro.

and his dragoon officers by permitting contraband operations in exchange for a share of their illegal profits. While charged by Lisbon with cracking down on Henriques, the governor was tarnishing his reputation elsewhere by turning a blind eye as his friends and military accomplices benefited from a smuggling ring in the diamond-mining center of Tejuco. His misdeeds were denounced to the secretary of state by detractors even as Lisbon authorized him to spearhead the cross-border raid.[22]

In May 1784, while in Rio Pomba, the mission village where he questioned Padre Maria, Sergeant Major São Martinho had first proposed such a raid and took preliminary steps to block supplies flowing to the Henriques's criminal band. The commander interrogated three men arriving from the direction of the captaincy border, where they admitted to helping provision the mining camp. He set out the next day to seize fields where crops were ripening to feed the miners. But reinforcements would be required, he wrote, to cross the Paraíba River and capture Henriques and his co-conspirators. São Martinho estimated a modest force of an additional dozen soldiers would be sufficient, half of them to guard the approach route and half to proceed to the mining camp. He would need more rifles and two canoes or a larger craft to cross the river safely. Awaiting further orders from the governor, he also recommended that the viceroy take measures to prevent the provisioning of the mining camp from the south side of the border, predicting that no further supplies would reach the miners from Minas Gerais once his own forces secured the river crossing.[23]

Another eight months passed before Lisbon issued the orders that would give him permission to proceed, authorizing a far more elaborate mission than he originally envisioned. Overruling the viceroy, who expressed concerns about entrusting the operation to Cunha Meneses, the secretary of state ordered the Minas governor to put an end to the rogue mining operation, apprehending its leaders and sending them to Rio de Janeiro to face punishment. Stressing that these orders came directly from the queen, he authorized the governor to assemble as many paid cavalry, infantry, and auxiliary troops as he thought necessary to attack the site. He was to dispatch this force with the utmost haste and secrecy. Based on the intelligence gathered by São Martinho and informants on the south side of the border, the secretary of state deemed the evidence incontrovertible that Henriques had established himself as the leader of a "great number of contrabandists and smugglers," who had crossed over the Paraíba River through the Forbidden Lands. These criminals were either so brazen, so convinced captaincy officials condoned their actions, or so dismissive of the captaincy government's power to enforce its authority that they scarcely bothered to conceal their activities. Rather than limit their comings and goings to a single clandestine route, they traveled openly along multiple trails to reach the border. They carried on extensive business relationships in Minas Gerais to sustain the operation. Property owners sold them captive workers. Muleteers rented them pack animals to transport food and materiel to the Minas border. Enslaved porters moved the goods the remaining distance, crossing into the captaincy of Rio de Janeiro. Families collaborated in this criminal conduct, deplored the secretary, "without any concealment or dissimulation." Parents knew of their children's involvement yet willingly sent them off from their homes with supplies and slaves in search of untaxed profits. Such ties with familial and supply networks in Minas Gerais further justified assigning the interdiction mission to the Minas governor, even though the site in question lay across the border in Rio de Janeiro, the viceroy's jurisdiction. Were troops to approach first from the coast, the criminals would surely withdraw into Minas Gerais along the very network of trails used to support their operation. Their social and commercial connections would render their capture all but impossible. Moreover, soldiers from Minas Gerais could avail themselves of the same routes the miners used to travel through the backlands.[24]

Even as he ordered the initial raid staged from Minas Gerais, the secretary of state felt compelled to admonish Governor Cunha Meneses, reminding him that royal legislation dating to the early decades of the gold and diamond boom prohibited colonists from mining at locations unsupervised by captaincy authorities. The queen had therefore further ordered the governor to rescind any authorization he or his predecessors had given to miners seeking to exploit such areas. If he knew of any other such sites being excavated, especially any with overland access to coastal ports, he was to report them immediately. The secretary pointedly reminded the governor that "the riches of Brazil, regulated and managed according to the inviolable observance of [royal] orders and laws, and with the vigilant care, zeal, and disinterest of [captaincy] governors, constitute the property of this kingdom and this state." When contrabandists and smugglers absconded with this wealth, these very same riches ensured "the ruination of Portugal and Brazil."[25]

The secretary's reasoning merits scrutiny. He pointed to long-standing legislation designed to limit access to remote precincts where the state did not fully preside. He cited a 1730 crown resolution banning mining at "sites totally separated by great distances" from existing mining operations. He further cited a 1750 law, which reconfirmed a 1733 charter, prohibiting the opening of new roads leading into or out of Minas Gerais from or toward any neighboring captaincy. The law prescribed severe punishment for anyone who traveled along such unauthorized routes, treating them as common smugglers. Authorities were to seize their possessions as contraband and divide it equally between the royal treasury and any informants whose collaboration led to such arrests.[26] By the 1780s, however, colonization of the backlands without state oversight had cleared the way for precisely what the earlier legislation was meant to prevent: unsupervised prospectors operating without fear of consequences, extracting precious metals and stones, secreting this wealth through the mountains to seafaring smugglers. In other words, even as the crown ordered the governor to enforce existing prohibitions, it effectively acknowledged their failure. Invoking the past, the state set a new course, intervening in areas from which it previously kept its distance, asserting a newfound determination to territorialize its rule. But another year would elapse between the time that the crown authorized the attack on the clandestine mining camp and its execution.

As for Manuel Henriques—Mão de Luva, as the official sources from the period commonly referred to him—his depiction in scholarly works, local lore, and popular fiction has oscillated between that of tyrannical outlaw and anticolonial rebel, lowly brute and Portuguese Robin Hood. Products of or responses to colonialist discourses, these interpretive tendencies owe their origins and motifs to denunciations by crown authorities.

The secretary of state condemned Henriques and his followers as "violent criminals" who should be cleared from the sertão.[27] The viceroy, seeking to increase pressure on the governor of Minas Gerais to act, demanded Cunha Meneses "repress the contumacy of these aggressors, who gathered with many armed people and were ready to defend themselves in those forbidden places," their power becoming "absolute and increasingly reckless" under the leadership of Henriques."[28] Both officials stressed the group's illegality and amorality. These were not merely violent criminals but treasonous rebels.

A favorite topic of European travelers who visited Minas Gerais and the mountains of Rio de Janeiro in the nineteenth century, Henriques continues even to this day to captivate local storytellers, poets, and filmmakers. A historically minded town councilman in Cantagalo, the town now standing on the site of the former mineral washings, ascribed to these stories the status of an origin myth, which simplifies to intelligibility the many ambiguities of an era that first brought the region to the crown's attention as Lisbon struggled to respond to the exhaustion of the alluvial wealth that had defined Minas Gerais and its place in the empire.[29] Henriques is remembered in the names of local geographic features and descriptions of tourist attractions such as the Caves of Bom Jardim, which no light of any kind can penetrate, as local legend has it, thus frustrating the search for the treasure he supposedly buried there. He has been romanticized as the protagonist of multiple novels. One fictional conceit casts him as a charismatic nobleman caught in an ill-starred romance with Princess Maria, before she succeeded her father José I to the throne. Banished to Brazil after being accused of plotting to assassinate the monarch, Henriques vowed never to remove the glove he donned to cover the hand that received the princess's parting kiss. His exile is rendered as an injustice, proof of the crown's oppressive rule. In some retellings he is portrayed as a freedom fighter, transformed into a precursor of Brazilian independence and even a harbinger of postcolonial campaigns for social justice. Following his arrest after the government's surprise raid, he supposedly endured the viceroy's dungeons on the Ilha das Cobras (Snake Island) in Rio de Janeiro's Guanabara Bay, which weakened him beyond recovery. Again exiled, this time to Africa, he never returned or, alternatively, he died before the ship transporting him could leave the bay, his body thrown overboard, his hand still donning the black glove, a testament to his enduring love for Maria, now his queen. Another version of the story has him losing his hand while clashing with an army platoon dispatched to arrest his band of three hundred men. Some were killed, others taken prisoner, but Henriques escaped into the forest, only to be captured several years later and banished to the colony's southern borderlands. Still another version describes his glove as concealing a deformation. Archival evidence supports this less dreamy explanation, but not yet another embellishment, which identifies leprosy, contracted during his transatlantic flight from Portugal, as the cause of his misshapen hand.[30]

The punitive raid launched from Minas Gerais and especially the intriguing villain who provoked it have attracted their share of attention from regional historians. Researchers have sought, with varying success, to distinguish the archival record from the myths surrounding it. While much of the substance of Henriques's life before and after his arrest remains a mystery, the recent discovery of documents concerning his marriage in the 1770s erases any lingering doubts that fueled speculation about his origins, proving he was not of noble birth. Nor, it seems, was he born in Portugal but rather in Minas Gerais, where he married Maria da Silva, a widow described with the honorific "Dona," indicating her standing among the respected and comparatively well-off residents of the parish of Guarapiranga in the southeastern reaches of the captaincy. In securing such a marriage, we can assume Henriques, too, enjoyed a respectable status. While not an aristocratic voyager, he was a notable local.[31]

Even as historians have dispelled myths surrounding the outlaw's career, they have perpetuated his larger-than-life image by framing his arrest as a key moment in the long history of uncontrolled smuggling and banditry that plagued colonial Minas Gerais. Recent studies tend to reject as too uncritical depictions casting him as a Hobsbawmian social bandit, compelled by a repressive regime to commit illegal acts in search of basic survival and freedom. Scholars generally hew, nevertheless, to interpretations influenced by the official exaggerations of the era, inflating his influence as a backcountry strongman who by dint of his personal power and lack of scruples challenged the authority of colonial governors and crown ministers. According to such interpretations, a corrupt, weak state gave rise not to a freedom fighter but to a tyrannical rural chieftain dedicated not to social justice but to building a personal fiefdom, enriching himself and his family, intimidating challengers, and cultivating local clients for protection received and returned.[32]

Understood in a broader context, the gloved Henriques looks less imposing. By the time São Martinho's military action led to his arrest, he was less the serious threat to imperial authority that the secretary of state and viceroy portrayed him to be than a modest aggravation. He was more a symptom than a source of imperial incapacities in the backlands. As Lisbon grew increasingly determined to do something about his violations, he became more of a symbol than a cause of the drive to assert control over the empire's internal frontiers. Fictional and scholarly accounts alike neglect the assessment of historian Diogo de Vasconcelos, who more than a century ago described the accused contraband chief in less than elevated terms. On the eve of his arrest, Henriques was no longer the "potentate" described by the viceroy and secretary of state. Rather, wrote Vasconcelos, "he was old and suffered from numbness in his feet and a scabrous nose," a possible reference to syphilis. Rumors of impending arrest frightened him, spurring him to travel to Vila Rica to beg the governor for mercy. The governor proceeded to humiliate the "fallen regulus," pledging lenience while falsely describing the covert military action bearing down on his distant camp as a friendly mission that would legalize his mining claims. Casting the ringleader as responsible for his own demise, the historian portrayed a gullible outlaw who opened "the gates of his kingdom to the Trojan Horse."[33] Although respected for his archival research, Vasconcelos did not adequately cite the documents supporting this ignoble portrait. Yet in his attention to timing and recognition of official hyperbole, he presented needed but neglected nuance to official denunciations that overstated the influence of an individual smuggler in order to reinforce the empire's drive to consolidate state power over unsurveilled forests. From this perspective, while it is true that the crown pursued Henriques because of his criminal activities, it did so in this place and at this time because it was ever more determined to impose its sovereign will over an expanse that had until the late eighteenth century remained beyond its reach.

Information about the smuggler's activities continued to filter out of the forests during the years immediately preceding the raid on his mining camp. Spurred by intensifying evidence of illegality and the erosion of the Forbidden Lands policy, the state's military, bureaucratic, and legal reach slowly did touch and transform the region, however haltingly. Although differing in their priorities and methods, the secretary of state, the viceroy, and the governor together acted to impose control, determined to assert royal sovereignty. The state could not be everywhere at once but it could make its presence felt almost anywhere, no matter how remote, when determined to do so. In this sense Henriques and the other backcountry inhabitants whose lives we can reconstruct in the colonial archives remain creations of the surviving sources, almost all of them saturated with official bias. The gloved leader of the accused contraband ring—his criminality, defiance, treachery, violent behavior, and even his alleged supernatural powers—crystallized in these sources in direct proportion to the determination of authorities in Lisbon, Rio de Janeiro, and Vila Rica to extend colonial governance over the rugged mountains and river valleys lying between the mining heartland and the coast.

## Deployment and Seizure

Mounting delays in effecting Lisbon's orders left Viceroy Vasconcelos e Sousa suspicious that the Minas governor might be abetting Henriques and his criminal operation. In support of this theory, the viceroy pointed to reports that the governor had ordered Sergeant Major São Martinho to enlist the smugglers' help in clearing a road leading to the border area, improving access. The viceroy considered this road nothing less than an encouragement to the flow of contraband, which the governor strongly denied. He maintained he was simply attempting to fool the criminals by having soldiers appear to cooperate with them. By this scheme captaincy soldiers supposedly had infiltrated the operation over several months.[34] Some historians find the viceroy's view credible; others find the evidence

FIGURE 4.2. Panning for gold. Note the presence of female vendors (see chap. 7). Source: Rugendas, *Voyage pittoresque*. Courtesy of "Slavery Images: A Visual Record of the African Slave Trade and Slave Life in the Early African Diaspora," accessed January 16, 2022, www.slaveryimages.org/s/slaveryimages/item/924. Licensed under CC-BY-NC 4.0.

insufficient, attributing the viceroy's criticism to jurisdictional disputes, ambition, and personal animosity.[35] Raising further questions about who was in league with whom were intercepted letters between one of Manuel Henriques's brothers, Antônio Henriques, and one of the governor's supposed military spies, Sebastião Craveiro de Faria. Faria described himself as a "servant" and "beloved dear friend" of the Henriques brothers. He mentioned gold dust, tools, salt, tobacco, shot, gunpowder, and other provisions, as well as slaves, exchanged between soldiers and miners working at the site.[36]

Depositions gathered from enslaved Africans interrogated along the main trail leading from the mineral washings into Minas Gerais deepened suspicions about dealings between soldiers and the outlaws. Caught carrying small quantities of gold, the individuals were identified as illiterate captives from west central Africa. One was just thirteen years old. Some testified that, with the full knowledge of soldiers manning the river crossing, they had passed over the captaincy border to work the mines and tend the fields that provisioned the encampment. Others traveled the network of trails ascending from the coast, often under the cover of night, sleeping in the forest or in the homes of "poor people," following orders from their enslavers. One of these enslavers was the soldier Sebastião Faria, whom the interrogated slaves said had spent months at the site and was a close associate of the accused contrabandists, although the governor insisted he was a spy. The enslaved informants further testified that the "whites" working there feared that "war was coming from Rio de Janeiro." Hailing from both captaincies, the alluvial miners planned to abandon their work before the troops arrived, hiding in the forest until it was safe to travel. These captives were communicating rumors about the larger deployment underway in the colonial capital, rumors that had already reached the governor's desk. He had heard that a force of six thousand infantrymen had assembled in the colonial capital, a figure that dramatically exaggerated the truth, which was that 332 soldiers, auxiliaries, and enslaved porters were approaching from the coast.[37] This testimony is a reminder of the extent to which the enslaved played a vital role, replicated throughout the captaincy, in the development of the mining camp, carrying out its most burdensome labor. Like the region's Indigenous inhabitants, they also served as leery sources of backcountry expertise, coerced to offer intelligence or doing so voluntarily for their own purposes.

After delaying as long as he dared in order to conceal his involvement, as the viceroy saw things, or acting with prudence as he gathered more information from his spies and waited for the rainy season to relent, as the governor maintained, Cunha Meneses finally ordered Sergeant Major São Martinho to execute the raid. The cross-border mission was carried out during April and May of 1786, departing from Vila Rica. The governor detailed 126 troops to this force. Hailing from Vila Rica and seventeen towns and villages across the southeastern portion of the captaincy, 105 of these soldiers participated in the actual raid on the illegal mining camp. The remainder manned key posts at river crossings and trails leading to the site, maintained supply routes, and guarded against the escape of fugitives. The force leading the attack included sixty-two criminals (*apenados*) impressed for military service in punishment for their misdeeds as well as a dozen porters, presumably all enslaved men.[38]

As the final step in his scheme, the governor dispatched a squadron corporal, a soldier, and eight enslaved porters, all of them feigning collaboration, on a visit to the mines, ostensibly to deliver supplies. Once in the mining camp, the infiltrators were secretly to seize the primers of and thereby render useless as many firearms as possible in advance of a surprise midnight attack by forces led by São Martinho. After some confused shouting, scuffling, and crossfire, Henriques and his men surrendered, surprised that soldiers they considered their partners in crime had betrayed them. "We are defeated!" Henriques reportedly shouted. "We surrender. No one resist." São Martinho immediately reported the success of his mission in a field communiqué, expressing hope that the governor would see fit to honor him with a promotion.[39]

Scholars who have studied this episode have all but ignored what happened next. Almost as soon as the raid was over, Joaquim, apparently the same Christian Indian "captain" who more than two decades earlier had informed coastal officials of the region's wealth, presented himself to São Martinho to plead with the officer "not to hurt him [Joaquim] or Sir

Manuel," that is, Manuel Henriques. The gloved leader of the mining camp, Joaquim insisted, was a good man and had "taught his people to pray," a fact the officer thought confirmed when the Native headman was observed reciting prayers. Two days later another Indian, unnamed in São Martinho's report, revealed to a soldier the hiding place of a "free mulatto" who had fled the mining camp during the confusion of the nighttime raid. The pair led a group of Indians into the forest, capturing the escapee. The same unnamed individual promised the soldiers that the Indians would track down five enslaved Blacks who had similarly fled. The Indians requested permission from the governor to cross into Minas Gerais with the runaways, once they were apprehended. They pledged to deliver them to a newly established guard post strategically placed at a crossing along the Paraíba River.[40] Presenting themselves as friends of Henriques and, at the same time, allies of the troops who arrested him and his fellow miners, the Indigenous inhabitants of this zone, once again, proved to be central if mercurial actors in the affairs of imperial consolidation.

Excluding the enslaved, those apprehended during the raid, all of them male and the majority from Minas Gerais, totaled twelve whites and three free pardos. Another white conspirator who supplied captive laborers to the mining camp was captured in Minas Gerais. Among the arrested were Henriques and three of his brothers. All were dispatched to Vila Rica, then to Rio de Janeiro to stand trial. Five more miners known to be active at the site were absent on the night of the raid. Of the twenty-nine enslaved workers arrested, fourteen were owned by just two miners, both of whom were absent. The Henriques brothers together held seven slaves, two of them on loan from a priest. The remaining seven people of modest means who owned few or no slaves accounted for the majority of site's free, non-Native inhabitants. Almost a third of the apprehended slaves were described as ill from one malady or another. Seven managed to flee during the raid, two of whom were quickly recaptured and counted among those arrested. The remaining five were those the Indians promised to pursue. One of the conspirators, Manuel Teixeira, was distinguished from the others as not living in one of the three ranchos at the site, but rather as someone who "wanders with the Indians." He, too, could not be located after the raid.[41] Ordered to arrest anyone caught fleeing the site, troops closer to the coast later apprehended a "half-breed" considered an associate of the accused smugglers.[42]

The soldiers seized just over 85 ounces of gold dust, a substantial sum. Henriques and his brothers held almost half of this treasure. Shotguns, pistols, swords, machetes, and knives were confiscated. A full assortment of tools, additional mining supplies, corn and beans from nearby fields, and roosters and hens were likewise inventoried and taken as state property. From this plunder the Indians received a knife, a cauldron, hoes and axes, barrels, roosters, bacon, and other foodstuffs, presumably a reward for their cooperation, including that aid that they had already given and that which officials wished to encourage in the aftermath of the ambush. Before leaving the mineral washings, São Martinho ordered razed the miners' residences, their slave quarters, and other structures.[43] He also recommended severe punishment for the soldiers manning the nearest crossing point along the Paraíba River. He did so citing the intensive commerce they had carried on with the miners, an exchange that became obvious during the collection of evidence following the operation.[44] Apparently, even the commander, like the viceroy, was uncomfortable with what the governor claimed was part of his lengthy plot employing these soldiers to fool Henriques and his accomplices.

In the months that followed, Viceroy Vasconcelos e Sousa did not relent in his criticism of Cunha Meneses, accusing him of violating the law in his pursuit of his supposed secret plan. He questioned the governor's delays, his motives, his "arrogance," the "fantasy" of his interpretation of royal orders, and the conduct of the troops under his command. The viceroy pressed unsuccessfully to try as accomplices seven soldiers and one corporal who ostensibly had acted as the governor's spies. Even if they claimed they were only following orders as operatives in a scheme to learn more about the illicit operation, in doing so they had committed blatant crimes, including helping provision the mining camp, allowing contraband gold to pass their checkpoints, and other violations. It was one thing to spy on the smugglers, quite another to aid and abet them. The viceroy also sought to discipline the enslaved persons who had labored at the mineral washings, a number of them owned by the Minas soldiers. These captives were jailed in Vila Rica. Unconvinced they would be properly punished, Vasconcelos e Sousa wanted them transferred to the colonial capital. He also demanded the governor remit to him the gold seized in the raid. Caught in this jurisdictional dispute, the secretary of state sought to balance competing claims. He agreed with the viceroy that the governor's military spies should be included among the accused, given their active participation in the contraband operation, but he advocated pardoning them. After all, whatever the governor's motives had been, and notwithstanding the soldiers' problematic behavior, together they had executed a plan that crushed the smuggling ring, and they apprehended its primary perpetrators without loss of life. Swayed by this logic, after a long delay, the queen issued the pardon in 1788. No action was taken to reprimand Cunha Meneses, whose term as governor ended earlier that year.[45]

Conspicuously absent in these communications was any mention of Indians among the accused. The viceroy wished to punish not only Henriques and his free associates at the mining camp but also collaborating soldiers and slaves, and anyone else on either side of the border who transported supplies and bondsmen to the mineral washings, secreted away its gold, or contributed to maintaining the secrecy of the operation. Yet he did not target Indians. Neither he nor the governor acted to bring the force of colonial legal institutions to bear on the area's forest dwellers, despite accumulating evidence of their interaction with Henriques and his co-conspirators. The fact that such interaction may have been compelled did not dissuade the governor from jailing, and the viceroy from seeking to interrogate, bring to trial, and punish the enslaved African laborers captured at the site. Why did authorities not insist on the same consequences for the Indians?

A likely explanation is that, as imperial officials, they functioned in a milieu that treated Indians recently brought under the authority of the state as children and rustics. They were considered a subordinate laboring class, otherwise ill-prepared for full participation in colonial society as vassals. Despite being declared free in a sequence of edicts over the course of the colonial period, their legal status was defined in practice as something closer to indentured servitude than full vassalage. Considered intellectually inferior and morally immature, they were relegated to the juridical status of orphans—that is, wards of the state—when classified as no longer living in their traditional or state-supervised villages or not engaged in remunerative labor.[46] From Portuguese America's founding, they were considered irrational, "inconstant" (a descriptor Padre Maria had used), and ill-equipped for understanding the complex codes and customs governing daily life in the colony. They were thus deemed unreliable witnesses in ecclesiastical and civil court trials. Although not entirely exempt from prosecution by the Inquisition, only in rare cases did they suffer its punitive repercussions, precisely on the grounds of their lesser status.[47] Under these circumstances, they were unlikely to face legal action of the kind the viceroy demanded for whites and Blacks caught up in the raid. As the empire's institutions extended into new territorial jurisdictions, Native peoples suffered grave consequences, but the perils of formal legal proceedings were not foremost among them.

To the degree that their perspectives can be gleaned from these events and the skewed sources that document them, the Indians must have considered the state most deserving of the inconstancy label. For decades prospectors had been straying into their mountainous domain from both the coast and Minas Gerais in search of precious stones and metals. Joaquim and the Indians whose community cohered under his authority must have found it difficult to distinguish these early, unsanctioned colonists from those who operated with the full authority of the state in areas along the coast and in closer proximity to the established towns and villages of the legal inland mining areas. By the second half of the eighteenth century, most Native occupants along the captaincy border seem to have concluded that both direct confrontation with and complete isolation from Portuguese intruders and the Africans they brought with them was untenable or even undesirable. Instead, they sought to engage prospectors by serving as guides, accepting gifts in return for peaceful cooperation, and perhaps even laboring in fields or mineral washings to achieve some level of mutual benefit.

As religious, military, and, eventually, civil authorities made their presence known in this zone, imperial policies would have remained difficult for the Indians to decipher. Even as the crown sought to restrain colonists from entering the area, early missionizing efforts helped open it to those prepared to ignore such restrictions. Prospectors and their enslaved workers became more numerous, trails and cultivated fields proliferated, and merchants transported an increasing variety of goods back and forth. Although soldiers were ordered to enforce the Forbidden Lands policy, some found that the resulting lack of rigorous surveillance offered remunerative opportunities. Whether authorized or not by the governor, they delivered captive labor and supplies to the illegal mining camp in a trade the magnitude of which could not have gone unnoticed by the Indians. Even soldiers profited from the contraband moving past the checkpoints they manned.

If the secretary of state, viceroy, and governor had difficulty agreeing on what was unfolding in the region just beyond the state's effective reach, if they debated what its response should be, the Indians surely found their own way forward fraught, requiring the utmost caution, flexibility, and pragmatism. From their vantage point, it was not themselves but a strange assemblage of miners, farmers, merchants, priests, soldiers, and distant officials who acted unreliably and incomprehensibly in pursuit of conflicting and changing objectives. Given such a milieu, Joaquim and his Native community could praise Henriques for his kindness while promising fidelity to those who came to arrest him. The transactional nature of colonial rule, especially as it arrived in the forests with greater force, meant that the smartest option was often to play to multiple sides. Observers decried this behavior as Indigenous inconstancy, but the sources suggest it was the inconsistent nature of official policies that encouraged Indians sometimes to placate, sometimes to evade, sometimes to confide in, and sometimes to withhold information from both illegal prospectors and the state authorities who came to punish them. Such relations would further complicate Lisbon's attempts to assert its sovereignty in the backlands.

CHAPTER 5

# SOVEREIGN RULE AND ITS DISENCHANTMENTS

FOLLOWING MANUEL HENRIQUES'S arrest, the location of his rogue mining operation south of the captaincy border meant that the larger task of securing the region would fall to troops from Rio de Janeiro. The resulting military deployment from the colonial capital, under the command of Lieutenant Colonel Manoel Soares Coimbra, has all but escaped scholarly notice.[1] Although less dramatic than the surprise attack from Minas Gerais, Coimbra's efforts constituted a much more extensive projection of power, involving a far greater commitment of resources and manpower. The undertaking also more fully reflected the larger goals of the mission. The order to dismantle the contraband ring was but a first step, focused on those who could be caught in flagrante delicto. More challenging was Secretary of State Martinho de Melo e Castro's directive to take possession of the area by establishing a permanent military presence and then to open the region to colonization under the full supervision of the state. To emphasize the raid from Minas Gerais outside the context of this larger mission is to miss a key policy shift. Rather than continuing to bar access to this expanse of the Atlantic Forest, the crown now acted to territorialize its sovereignty.

In the crown minister's words, experience had shown that it was "absolutely useless and impractical"—given the size of the area, the degree to which it already had been explored and exploited, and the impossibility of patrolling its periphery—"to compel [colonists] to leave it." The crown exercised virtually no control over the zone, despite its proximity to the capital and the strategic access it provided to and from the interior. According to the secretary of state, such unincorporated terrain, hemorrhaging mineral riches diverted from the royal treasury, placed the very strength of the empire at risk.[2] The point of Lieutenant Colonel Coimbra's larger operation, in short, was not simply to put an end to illicit mining in the region along the captaincy border, but to encourage legal, regulated mining and agriculture. The crown's goal was not merely to capture a criminal but to incorporate an internal frontier, populate it with vassals, extract and tax its wealth, impose the rule of law, and establish the empire's dominion.

## Ascent into the Mountains

Not always in agreement with the secretary of state as to methods and tactics, Viceroy Vasconcelos e Sousa had reluctantly relinquished responsibility for the initial raid to Governor Cunha Meneses in Minas Gerais. As the force from Rio de Janeiro made its preparations, and throughout its journey, the viceroy demonstrated his commitment to decisive action, maintaining a watchful, hands-on approach. Helping transform this internal frontier into territory and property, cartographers were to prepare a detailed map of all significant natural and man-made features in the area. On their way from the coast into the mountains, troops were to prevent anticipated escape attempts by criminals fleeing the raid from the north. To achieve this goal, soldiers were to secure all routes leading from the backlands to the coast. Once the region was firmly under crown control, legal mining claims and land grants were to be surveyed and distributed among "useful and industrious vassals abiding by rules and regulations."[3] The change in strategy from forbidden access to controlled colonization embodied Lisbon's determination to imbue with real substance its authority over the sertão linking the two vital captaincies.

The viceroy placed more than four hundred troops at Coimbra's disposal, from which the commander selected a force that numbered fifty-one salaried soldiers, sixty-two impressed auxiliaries, and sixty-nine supporting soldiers stationed at strategic points along the route. Even more numerous were the 150 enslaved porters impressed into service, rented or on loan from the region's planters.[4] An army officer with long experience, Coimbra led his troops up into the imposing coastal range, which rises more than two thousand meters to the northwest of the capital city.[5] At first attempting to synchronize its movements with the soldiers dispatched from Minas Gerais, Coimbra's force ended up much delayed and in distrustful competition with those troops. The hardships of moving troops, supplies, and heavy equipment up a slippery, sloping forest floor proved greater than anyone anticipated.

Like his co-commander in Minas Gerais, Coimbra relied on Indigenous informants for military intelligence critical to his mission. All but silenced in official correspondence is how Indigenous groups were moved by their own purposes—their long histories of contact with colonists, their search for subsistence and security, their hopes and fears. But the sources make clear they became empowered as informants. What they communicated, as we have seen, helped trigger the mobilization of substantial resources from the imperial, viceregal, and captaincy administrations. Without their knowledge, the costly expedition launched from Rio de Janeiro might never have been deployed. As the military made its way into the mountains, they continued to shape projections of imperial power.

Even before his troops began their ascent, Coimbra enlisted the counsel of a priest who, when still a young man, had wandered through the captaincy border region "reducing Indians." For the past seven years, he had ministered to residents of the coastal aldeias. Arguing that this cleric would make a more useful chaplain than the one already assigned to the expedition, Coimbra convinced the viceroy to approve the substitution. He also called on the services of a soldier born in the area, who, before joining the military, had participated in more than one expedition to Indian aldeias in the mountains. Such experience, he insisted, made men like these indispensable.[6]

In his direct interactions with Natives, the commander found them cooperative, especially when he offered them gifts. Nevertheless, despite what Indians had said over the decades, or were said to have said, he remained skeptical about their stories. And despite what the viceroy and secretary of state seemed to believe, he doubted that the Orosó, if such a group still existed, or the Coroado or Coropó would lead his men to rich new mineral deposits. This wariness put him in a difficult position. He perceived that it might not be as easy as his superiors imagined to act on intelligence gathered from Indigenous peoples who continued to assert their autonomy. At the same time he became the target of critics who emphasized the unreliable and even subversive nature of the colony's Indigenous inhabitants. By the time his operation concluded, he would be accused of conspiring with the same Indians in his own contraband scheme.

The surprise attack from Minas Gerais occurred in mid-May of 1786. Coimbra had received his marching orders two months earlier, but time spent in preparations meant his troops did not set out from the city of Rio de Janeiro until May 8, less than a week before the raid. Delays in communications, however, obscured this sequence of events. News had to travel from the site of the raid to the governor in Vila Rica, and then from the governor to the viceroy. The report did not reach Rio de Janeiro until early July. From there, in great haste, the viceroy dispatched a messenger who caught up with Coimbra in the mountains. The viceroy's communiqué ordered Coimbra to advance immediately to the site.[7]

After learning of the raid, Coimbra continued to gather intelligence from and about Indians. This information would help the crown build its case against the accused malefactors. At his trailside headquarters, he conducted a detailed inquiry, questioning a number of individuals known to have collaborated with Indians. He interrogated a colonist from Cachoeira de Macacu, Joaquim da Silva, who claimed that, more than a year earlier, an Indian guide named José Gomes "had induced him" and six of his companions to travel together to the clandestine mineral washings. Despite his matching name and shared vocation as a backwoodsman, this José Gomes cannot be identified definitively as the same backcountry informant condemned by the Inquisition. After the commutation of his sentence in 1782, might the homologous Gomes have somehow managed to regain his health, return from Portugal, and resume his perilous exploits in the sertão? Such a return would have violated the terms of his release, which required him to remain in Lisbon. Yet, given the right circumstances, we can readily imagine an individual of such humble origins slipping aboard a vessel bound for Brazil, unnoticed by authorities. The Inquisition's prisoner had been identified as white not Indian, although such designations, as we have seen, could be imprecise, expedient, and mutable. It is certainly possible, therefore, that the Gomes identified in Coimbra's trailside inquiry as recently leading prospectors to the mines had by then been to Lisbon and back.[8] What can be known from the documentation is that the Native guide named José Gomes, when questioned by Coimbra, recalled promising to lead Joaquim da Silva and his associates to a stream filled with precious stones. They set out, covering difficult terrain on foot, then traveling long stretches by canoe. They crossed the Rio Grande on a makeshift bridge. There they encountered more Indians and followed a trail Gomes told them would lead them to the mining zone. In the opposite direction, it connected to the coast, skirting military checkpoints. Proceeding for several more days, the party never located the promised riches. Instead, they became convinced of the Indian guide's "deceit."[9]

Silva decided to continue after his companions turned back. His guide had left him very near to Henriques's mining camp. The prospector came on no fewer than six separate mineral washings, five of them operational. Under interrogation by Coimbra, he offered names and other critical details. Two of the washings were run by Joaquim, Dionísio, and José Lopes, three brothers found missing on the night of the raid by the Minas troops. Although from Minas Gerais, these miners maintained ties with associates in Cachoeiras de Macacu and family members in Magé, near the capital city. A third washing was operated by Miguel Moniz, also from Minas Gerais. Henriques and his kin ran the two largest placer mines and were developing another. In total some thirty laborers were active at the site, most of them armed, including whites, free men of color, and about a dozen captives. Cleared fields were planted with corn, beans, and rice to sustain the miners.[10]

Silva had worked in the illegal operation for a month while recovering from a gunshot wound suffered in a dispute with the Lopes brothers. At the time Henriques was away in Minas Gerais, said to have been summoned to Vila Rica by the governor. Silva claimed he witnessed substantial gold extracted during his brief stay, and he was told that additional deposits of precious stones and silver could be found nearby. Aside from one "half-breed" toiling at the site, the prospector reported no sign of Indigenous workers. He did attest, however, to communications between members of the Henriques clan and the Native villages along a trail descending to the coast. One family member had recently visited these aldeias in search of a fugitive slave. Silva said soldiers from Minas Gerais periodically visited the illegal operation to transport gold to military officers in Vila Rica. The outlaws also negotiated for provisions and mules with soldiers posted along the Caminho Novo. Others questioned by Coimbra produced similar stories, adding other details. The commander learned, for instance, that prospectors throughout the area hoped the gold washings would liberate them from poverty. Mão de Luva had managed the venture with a forceful hand for years. Yet several witnesses remarked they were unimpressed by the quantity of gold recently being excavated at the site.[11]

These details help explain the viceroy's suspicions concerning misdeeds by the Minas governor and the royal troops under his command. In hindsight they also have the strange quality of dreams that refused to die even after the mining operation had been destroyed. At the end of his trailside inquest, Coimbra summarized the proceedings for the viceroy and counseled restraint. Apart from the rumors spread by Indians, or by those who claimed to have communicated with them, there was little evidence to sustain the conviction that great mineral wealth remained to be, or perhaps ever had been, extracted from the region. None of the visitors to the area reported anything approaching the two hundred prospectors, each with three or more captive laborers, originally believed to be working there. Most risked travel to the site because they were poor and easily lured into any scheme that might alleviate their misery. Some were coerced. When they left for the sertão, they were largely "ignorant of the offenses" in which they became involved. They returned exhausted, abused, sometimes wounded and without their promised pay. If the viceroy wished to proceed against everyone who had visited the illegal operation, Coimbra concluded, it would be necessary to "punish almost the entire district."[12]

## Cantagalo

It was not until the commander finally arrived at the illegal site in early August 1786 that he had the chance to weigh all of the talk by and about Indians against their actual behavior. His superiors, like many colonists, harbored the conviction that Native peoples of the backlands possessed an almost preternatural knowledge of hidden gold and diamond deposits. The viceroy and secretary of state had embraced this view by quoting testimony gathered from Native informants about easily obtainable wealth, while ignoring evidence to the contrary. Coimbra's sober communiqués, by contrast, suggest he did not expect a great deal when he reached the site at the upper reaches of a narrow valley, nestled among low mountains. An anticlimactic conclusion to the mission, months behind schedule, must have seemed inevitable. The troops from Minas Gerais had long since come and gone, burning many structures to cinders. Henriques and key members of his criminal band had been arrested; others had fled. Although surprised by the midnight raid from Minas Gerais, they seem to have known, even before soldiers set out from Rio de Janeiro, that a mobilization was underway. It was in this context that Coimbra first made direct contact with Indians, initiating interactions that set the tone for his final, dismal assessment of the costly effort to assert an official presence at the site, now renamed Cantagalo. The new name was yet another sign of problematic intelligence, in this case intelligence that morphed into lore, or vice versa. It referenced a crowing rooster that supposedly revealed the location of Henriques and his co-conspirators during the ambush staged by the soldiers from Minas Gerais. But military communiqués demonstrate knowledge of the location well before the raid occurred.[13]

Coimbra did not go looking for Indians; they found him, making their presence evident almost immediately. They repeatedly appeared before the commander and his troops without warning and disappeared without explanation. Coimbra received them in friendship. At least one Indian in the first group that visited spoke Portuguese, allowing the lieutenant colonel to request a meeting with their "captain," who soon appeared with a larger group. Coimbra counted thirty men, women, and children. He gave them

FIGURE 5.1. Forest dwellers at Cantagalo. Source: Debret, *Voyage pittoresque*. Courtesy of the John Carter Brown Library. Licensed under CC-BY-SA 4.0.

clothing, food, and beads and engaged in "other similar gallantries with which they were very pleased." Additional members of this larger band spoke Portuguese and had been baptized, including their leader Joaquim, who had previously interacted with the troops from Minas Gerais and, before the raid, with Henriques and his fellow miners. The Indians spent the night at the encampment Coimbra's troops had begun to construct, departed the following morning, and promised to return, initiating a period of regular visits. The commander's thoughts turned to the potential for more permanent contact and exchange. If the viceroy desired that the region's forest dwellers "be reduced to the faith," he wrote, a modest material investment would be required, consisting of knives, other gifts, and more clothing, "because all of them go around nude."[14]

Before two weeks had elapsed, Coimbra registered increasing competition for material goods as well as other grounds for concern. The Indians visited almost every day and eagerly sought more gifts, including machetes, knives, hoes, and *aguardente* (spirits distilled from sugarcane juice). The resulting tool shortage hampered efforts by the troops to plant and cultivate foodstuffs. Meanwhile, having learned of Coimbra's actions, including his liberal distribution of warm clothes during the cool winter weather, members of another Indigenous community began to visit the military encampment, appearing in groups of as many as a dozen or more at a time and sometimes spending the night. This group followed a Christian Indian named Martinho. In a telling convergence, his godfather was one of the soldiers participating in the expedition, an indication of the social webs that tied those of Native, mixed, and non-Native descent in the area. Martinho explained that his people had once lived below the falls in the vicinity of Cachoeiras de Macacu. They later resettled in the more remote captaincy border area but had been forced to abandon this new aldeia along the Paraíba River, a day's journey from Cantagalo, because of the "poor treatment and abuses" suffered when prospectors from Minas Gerais arrived. The Indians had resorted to "wandering in this sertão without having a fixed home," surviving by hunting and gathering. The departure of the criminal gang now presented the possibility of returning to their former dwelling place. Short on supplies for his own troops, Coimbra could not grant their request for clothing and farm implements, "despite seeing all of them nude." He believed these wanderers deserved the state's "compassion" and its recognition of the "great necessity that they have for some way to cultivate the land." He appealed to the viceroy for aid.[15]

The commander qualified this request with a final observation. In their clothing preferences, he noted, the Indians were "very inclined to the colors blood-red and light blue."[16] It was an offhand remark, but it captured the delicacy of the situation. From the moment Coimbra left the realm of rumors and coerced intelligence and began to deal with the specific needs of Indians who sought his aid, a new dynamic took hold, one that had precedents in countless previous encounters, not only in Brazil but throughout the Americas. As Natives assessed the prospects of adopting—or in this case readopting—sedentary ways, some were attracted by the trappings of settler society, some became dependent on manufactured goods and provisions, and some used them as a basis for new negotiating tactics. If officials were serious about appealing to these forest peoples, they would have to make commitments that were bound to strain state resources, norms, and patience. In its effort to transform Natives into Christian agriculturalists, the state would create its own expectations and obligations, and in the process some authorities would come to resent Native demands.

An example of this dynamic was a plan Viceroy Vasconcelos e Sousa proposed to relocate these mobile communities to the São Fidélis aldeia, a recently established, state-supported village administered by Capuchin missionaries, approximately 100 kilometers to the northeast along the Paraíba River. Opposing the Indians' desire to reoccupy their former home, the viceroy favored congregating them at this well-supervised settlement. The strategy offered the prospect of clearing territory for the colonists the viceroy hoped would now move into the backlands under state supervision. Coimbra predicted the Indians would not bow readily to this scheme. They retained negative memories of past attempts to enter colonial society, episodes in which "the greater part of them had perished." As if to underline the developing tensions between official plans and Native expectations, when the viceroy agreed to the latest of Coimbra's requests for supplies and sent a shipment of colorful cloth to the encampment, the commander considered the response insufficient. Barely suppressing his exasperation, he pressed for additional items he thought the state should logically provide: thread, buttons, and needles, as well as a tailor to fashion the cloth into garments.[17]

Nearly three months after the expedition arrived in Cantagalo, long enough to dash any hopes harbored by its commanding officer for a prompt reassignment, interactions with the Indians inexplicably ceased. The itinerant communities that had regularly visited no longer appeared, putting Coimbra on the defensive. He was already fending off sharp questions from the viceroy about his treatment of soldiers, auxiliaries, and captives, queries prompted by the desertion of some of his troops and the flight and deaths of a number of enslaved porters. Coimbra knew that the viceroy would assume the Indians had withdrawn because they were dissatisfied with their treatment. With little to show for all the state funds and effort expended on his mission, he could ill afford an incident that might be interpreted as evidence of his incompetence or his abusive command.[18]

Even before he reported the disappearance to the viceroy, Coimbra sought his own explanation. In a reversal of the once routine visits by the Indians to his backcountry military headquarters, he twice dispatched troops to search for them in the forest. They could not be found. His soldiers spotted signs along a trail indicating that the Indians had departed in the direction of the coast. The only other remnants of their presence were a field planted in corn, beans, potatoes, and bananas, and an array of possessions left behind in one of their encampments. Coimbra inventoried these items—machetes, hoes, knives, plates, barrels, hammocks, woolen shawls, sieves made of vegetable fibers, wooden bowls, jars, a rooster, and some chickens—and safeguarded them for their return.[19]

Increasingly frustrated, the lieutenant colonel struggled to explain what had happened. Reporting to the viceroy, he insisted that the Indians "had no motive that might compel them to flee from our friendship." They could only have appreciated "the fine hospitality with which I treated them." He had shared his table with some and distributed gifts and provisions to others. According to those with long experience of Native "character and customs," particularly the priest whom Coimbra had enlisted to join the expedition precisely for such insights, there was no reason to be alarmed. Among the items they had left behind were tools they valued so highly that they were sure to return. The Indians were known to "regulate themselves" according to the phases of the moon. They had a tendency to plant foodstuffs in several areas at once, wandering from place to place as crops matured. This was the time of year when they left their cabanas to hunt for insects they prized. The more explanations Coimbra offered, the less convincing he seemed. He tried to convey a sense of unruffled confidence but ended sounding fretful. "I certify to Your Excellency that I always treated them with the greatest kindness possible." He had even prevented his soldiers from visiting the Natives in their encampments "in order to avoid any turmoil that might occur among them because of their wives and daughters." The commander concluded with a plea: "I want

Your Excellency to believe me that if the Indians had any motive to withdraw, I am totally unaware of it." If the viceroy wished him to pursue them, Coimbra would gladly do so, tracking them through the forest.[20]

In addition to the commander's concern about his personal and professional honor, his chagrin at the Indians' disappearance made sense in the context of crown Indigenous policy, which would have made him sensitive to any suggestion he had harmed them. These assimilationist policies, originally devised for the village Indians of the Amazon basin, had a distinct meaning in the sertão between southeastern Minas Gerais and Rio de Janeiro. The policies did not prevent ongoing violence against autonomous seminomads, such as the Kayapó to the west or the Puri and Botocudo to the north.[21] Coimbra and the viceroy, however, could not hope to justify the same aggressive posture with respect to the more accommodating Indians encountered at the seized mining camp, and there is no indication he wished to do so. The benevolent face, however changeable, of crown Indigenous policy impelled the commander to be cautious. His direct interactions with these Indians revealed them to be open to exchange and largely sedentary, cultivators of subsistence crops, enthusiasts of manufactured goods, and in more than a few cases already baptized Christians and Portuguese speakers. The law called for such Indians to be gathered in aldeias, where local authorities would guarantee them "the liberty of their persons, possessions, and commerce," rights that were not to be "interrupted or usurped under any policy or pretext." Individuals caught mistreating such Indians were to receive prompt punishment.[22] To the west and the north, officials dodged such checks on violent conquest; Coimbra and the viceroy did not. The viceroy hoped to relocate the Indians, a move that would cause them serious disruptions, but he did not wish to attack them militarily.

The commander's concern about their whereabouts also reflected their proven and potential value as informants and laborers. The jailed outlaws were unlikely to volunteer many details about their illegal operation. Backwoodsmen had similar reasons to be reticent, even though Coimbra had managed to pry information from some of them. By comparison the

Indians had an unmatched hold on backcountry knowledge. Even if they were sometimes less than forthright, they had long demonstrated their familiarity with clandestine activity in the area, subject as they were to prospectors' intrusions going back many years. To the extent that more was to be learned about smuggling operations, it was reasonable to expect that Indians would continue to serve as primary informants. Assuming relations remained amicable, the possibility they might labor as boatmen, porters, woodcutters, and agricultural workers to advance the cause of frontier colonization further enhanced their collaborative value. Coimbra singled out the Indians as a solution to what authorities quickly perceived as a labor shortage. The viceroy was less optimistic. "This cast of people," he averred, was "barely subjugated." They tended to "desert and abandon the work in which they are employed" unless subjected to rigorous discipline. Even so, faced with the increasing need for workers to effect Lisbon's plans, he approved Coimbra's proposal to employ some Indian as day laborers. They would have to be brought up to the site from the coastal aldeais, where they had long experience working for daily wages, at least until the Indians at Cantagalo showed an inclination to return.[23]

The challenge of assembling workers at this remote location pointed to a related problem, inherent in any attempt to incorporate the internal frontiers of a colony thoroughly tied to slavery. Almost as soon he reached his destination, the commander requested additional slaves, beyond those 150 already serving his expedition, in order to speed the work of transforming the site into a permanent, legal settlement. Coimbra had depended on enslaved laborers from the outset. Captive porters determined the very feasibility of his mission. Their backbreaking conveyance of supplies and military materiel made possible the troop's movement up steep, mud-slicked, overgrown trails. When planters in the greater region failed to deliver sufficient hands in a timely fashion, the forward progress of the expedition stalled. Facing one such delay, Coimbra pleaded with the viceroy for more assistance. Without more enslaved workers, he wrote, "nothing can be done." They were "the sole carriers worthwhile to us."[24] The food they carried likewise came from enslaved labor. The viceroy

142  CHAPTER FIVE

FIGURE 5.2. Clearing the forest. Source: Rugendas, *Voyage pittoresque*. Courtesy of the Biblioteca Nacional, Rio de Janeiro.

requisitioned manioc flour from dozens of farm owners, both male and female. They in turn directed captive men, women, and children at work in their fields to meet these quotas.[25]

In the early days of the military occupation of Cantagalo, enslaved porters continued to ferry manioc flour, corn, beans, knives, machetes, and other supplies requisitioned from settlements on the coastal plain. Although enslavers received some remuneration, they grumbled about orders that "obliged them to contribute" to this long-distance provisioning effort. A lack of mules and canoes meant that the reliance on captive porters would continue.[26] The government also sought enslaved men with special knowledge of excavation and panning techniques. Eager to produce revenues to justify the spiraling expense of the military mobilization, the viceroy ordered an emissary to acquire bondsmen with such skills in

Minas Gerais. Governor Cunha Meneses blocked the purchase, arguing that no such individuals could be spared because their expertise was required in his captaincy.[27] In Rio de Janeiro the royal treasury completed another transaction for forty slaves, dispatching them to the mountains under the supervision of a soldier slave driver.[28] The costly purchase illustrates just how committed Lisbon remained to the achievement of its aims, and how thoroughly these aims depended on captive labor. At the most basic level, it was enslaved Africans who carried out the work of frontier colonization.

Replicating a slave-based economy in this outpost of empire brought with it the social harm that inevitably accompanied the system's bodily exactions. Predictably, for example, officials suspected enslaved porters of stealing foodstuffs and other supplies. In one incident Coimbra dismissed from service, rather than physically punish, a group of captives accused of thieving. Among the items that went missing were soldiers' provisions as well as gifts intended to cement relations with the Native population, including beads, knives, and scissors. Coimbra expressed frustration that he could "neither tolerate nor impede the great thefts [the enslaved] continually commit while moving cargo from one region to another." Traveling the trail through the mountains, the porters accused in this instance had fled into the surrounding forest. When they were recaptured, they were "nearly dead" from starvation. For the remainder of the journey, they had to be carried on the backs of others. All who completed the voyage were severely malnourished. In their desperation some ingested substances "improper for humans." Four died along the way.[29]

As in the case of the disappearing Indians, these events forced Coimbra to defend himself. Charged with negligence and cruelty, he insisted on his "compassion." He assured the viceroy that the troop's captive laborers "never had reason to complain." They were given daily manioc and bean rations equal to those they received while working on their masters' farms, he explained, and some were so lazy they did not even cook the beans they received. It apparently did not occur to him that disorienting exhaustion and starvation may have explained this behavior. In addition to withholding a lashing for repeated thefts, Coimbra rewarded those who finished the journey with a ration of alcohol and two rolls of tobacco, which he paid for himself. He personally made sure the weakened, recaptured runaways received a portion of dried meat to help restore their strength. Three of those who perished had succumbed to disease not hunger, he claimed, just as they were prone to sicken and die under their masters' care. The fourth had drowned while attempting to cross a river in an inadvisable place. The real problem, the commander insisted, was not that he and his officers mistreated bondsmen but that their masters, seeking to minimize disruptions to their own enterprises, assigned their least capable workers to the military mission, those who were sick, weak, and elderly. Thus deaths were to be expected. He pointed to an earlier communiqué he sent to a sergeant tasked with distributing rations to the porters. Reprimanding this subordinate for inadequately caring for those who had fallen ill, Coimbra had erupted, either you are the "most inhumane man there is or you are crazy!" Yet no matter how much the lieutenant colonel fashioned himself a caring custodian of government slaves, he had failed to prevent the loss of life along the trail.[30] In the backcountry, no less than on plantations, compassion and slavery never made easy bedfellows.

## Backcountry Disillusionment

Coimbra and the viceroy theorized about substituting African with Native labor in their colonizing project, but the Indians had moved on. As the problems of assembling enslaved labor at such an inaccessible site became increasingly evident, the lieutenant colonel's attempts to understand why these potential workers had vanished after such promising initial exchanges proved futile. The decisive role they had played from the inception of his mission had ended. Although he would remain deployed at Cantagalo until April 1787, almost a year after he first ordered his troops to begin their march, he would report no further contacts of any consequence.

It must have struck him as the cruelest of ironies, therefore, to be accused of conspiring with the Indians to smuggle gold out of the area. Suspicions about Indian misconduct ran as deep as fantasies about their access to hidden treasure. For many years, officials had "conjectured," in the words of one officer, that the Natives were participants in the contraband gold trade. Information that surfaced in inquiries before and during Coimbra's expedition reinforced this distrust. The distance between the colonial capital and the commander's military base in the mountains, his long absence from the city, the rumors of extensive gold deposits, and envy exacerbated by official secrecy: these factors combined to spawn rumors and misrepresentation, especially among those resentful of Coimbra's position or eager to gain access to the region. Further allegations came from the governor of Minas Gerais, part of his endless quarrels with the viceroy. The governor alleged that smuggling continued under Coimbra's watch, under the guise of developing the site for settlement. In a letter to the viceroy, Coimbra defended himself.[31] There is no indication that this gossip damaged his record in any permanent way. He would continue his successful career, within five years becoming governor of the southern captaincy of Santa Catarina and eventually earning a promotion to brigadier. However, by the end of 1786, having spent three months leading the expedition into the mountains and another five months at Cantagalo, he admitted in a rare personal letter to a trusted friend to a "profound state of melancholy."[32] Once again, the Indians had a role.

Coimbra believed he had conducted himself as a model officer. He had proved himself loyal, circumspect, and proficient, if sometimes severe with his troops and not as prompt in achieving his objectives as the viceroy desired. Undoubtedly, he anticipated the usual rewards for a military commission successfully executed: official commendation, perhaps a promotion. Military officers were immersed in the same exchanges for state patronage that helped keep other elites steadfast. Low military salaries and high returns for smuggling meant that officers charged with protecting the mining district's porous borders were particularly susceptible to exactly the sort of criminal activity they were supposed to suppress. The surest way to encourage their fealty, suggested one advisor to the monarch, was to exploit the traditional compact that guaranteed royal favors for services rendered. Officers deployed in anticontraband missions should be confident in the crown's "infallible promise that, fulfilling their duty, they will surely be promoted immediately to [higher] posts." Whatever the personal satisfactions of a job well done, "nothing stimulates the honor of men in taking charge of their obligations more than the expectation of a reward."[33] Coimbra surely was not immune to such expectations, but the ample correspondence he drafted during his command betrays nothing of the entitled pleading for royal recompense that suffused the frontier dispatches of less duty-bound vassals. If there was theater here, the leading actor was trained to underplay his role to enhance his personal and professional honor.

Yet, in proportion to each league his soldiers cut through the primeval forest, he had become increasingly dispirited, convinced that his superiors were finding his performance lackluster, despite its rigors. In the candid letter to his friend, he rejected, one by one, a compendium of allegations of his incompetence, which had spread through the city and wider region. His detractors accused him of physically abusing and underfeeding his soldiers, which he denied. Any corporal punishment meted out to the troops had been limited and deserved. Any hunger they experienced was a result of the demands of the mission rather than his withholding of rations.

As for the accusations that he was conspiring with Indians, he scarcely knew how to respond. The expedition chaplain returned from a visit to Rio de Janeiro to recount that more than once he had been asked if Coimbra "was still maintaining a tavern in this place," insinuating he was involved in illicit commerce, "and if it was true that Captain Joaquim [the Indian headman] had given [Coimbra] a container filled with gold and various precious stones." Losing his accustomed composure, Coimbra despaired, "They want to annihilate me." Acknowledging feelings of isolation and gloom, he wrote, "I have never been in a more desperate post than this, and I would gladly trade this place for one with the greatest risk of facing the enemy."[34] Nearly four months later, when the viceroy unceremoniously granted Coimbra "permission to withdraw," he left his garrison without pausing to write a final communiqué.[35]

Coimbra summed up his mission with a personal lament, but his experience reflected much larger issues. From the vantage point of captaincy, colonial, and imperial policy, the problem of contraband gold and diamonds flowing out of Minas Gerais continued undiminished through the

1780s.³⁶ Stopping the illegal operation at Cantagalo was not expected to solve this problem, but it also did not result in a partial remedy anywhere equal to the commitment of state resources brought to bear on the area. And despite ongoing expenditures, it would take decades to bring the kind of commercial development and administrative consolidation to the zone that the secretary of state and viceroy aimed to achieve with their ambitious mobilization.

By early 1787 the viceroy was already expressing his disappointment at the pace of progress, blaming insufficient funding available from the royal treasury as well as a lack of initiative on the part of the first colonists arriving under state supervision. These supposedly "useful and industrious vassals" imagined gold could be found at the site with little labor, even though by then the area had been excavated and panned illegally for more than twenty years. In accordance with the royal land tenures and mining codes, land grants and mining claims were rapidly distributed among applicants according to the number of slaves they owned. But the most obvious and accessible claims had been mined out by the clandestine miners who preceded these legal migrants. This reality, according to the viceroy, accounted for the quick disillusionment of those whose expectations had been inflated by "vague rumor" that circulated concerning "great riches" easily accumulated. For these impatient settlers, the result was a steady abandonment of their claims and of the region. The viceroy hoped that a more persistent brand of colonist would eventually settle and thrive, those who understood the need to cultivate crops and raise cattle to sustain sufficient numbers of captive laborers to effect a more thoroughgoing exploitation of the area's mineral wealth.³⁷

Eager to foster such a future, the viceroy persevered. Patrols and guard posts were established and fortified to prevent smuggling. Storage facilities were constructed to guarantee food supplies for the troops. The difficult task of cutting roads through the forest from the coast continued. Officials were appointed to occupy key supervisory positions, none perceived as more important than that of the new mining superintendent. But the meager gold unearthed did not come close to offsetting the required expenditures.³⁸ Until the end of his tenure in 1789, when he urged his successor to "advance and promote" the project begun in earnest by Coimbra's expedition, Viceroy Vasconcelos e Sousa continued to maintain that the mineral washings at Cantagalo "will not fail to be of great benefit, not only for the abundance but the quality of their gold."[39] The viceroy, it must be noted, seemed oblivious of the irony of his own conduct. He ridiculed rumors of easy riches yet continued to fuel them by insisting more buried wealth would soon be unearthed. Such rumors, his own included, had spurred official action from the earliest days. State support for occupying the once-forbidden zone, he seemed to forget, had begun in overoptimistic exchanges between hopeful explorers and prospectors, officials determined to pursue buried treasure, and the Native peoples attempting to navigate the resulting territorial incursions, coercive questioning, and material offerings.

The renewal of mining anticipated by the viceroy was not to be. As a historian of the town that later took root there observed, "The fabulous riches of the sertão . . . never existed." Of the modest wealth that Manuel Henriques and his criminal band extracted, "only vestiges remained." Yet hope, buttressed by fantasy, sprung eternal. As late as 1806, two decades after Coimbra's expedition reached its destination, despite years of royal outlays that exceeded revenues at Cantagalo, Prince Regent João received an anonymous report in Lisbon, a copy of which he forwarded to Rio de Janeiro that singled out Cantagalo's development as the most promising project in the entire colony in need of the monarch's support.[40]

Three years later, when the British naturalist John Mawe visited the parish, he described a feeble settlement, where "so little gold is at present found" that the tax revenue collected on its production "scarcely pays the officers and soldiers appointed to receive it." The place was "very poorly stocked with cattle"; it sent low-value foodstuffs to the capital city; and its environs, "destitute of inhabitants," remained the province of "half-civilized aborigines . . .but one remove from the anthropophagi." Their refusal to labor for colonists accounted, as Mawe saw it, for "the low state of agriculture in the district."[41]

It would be slave-based export agriculture, not mining, that eventually transformed the area. Private initiative and outside investment capital catalyzed the change, not projects managed by a transatlantic state vigorously trying but ultimately unable to direct activity within this and other internal frontiers. There is some evidence that gold mining did contribute to the earnings of a few early legal migrants who persisted at Cantagalo, most of them continuing to cross into the captaincy from Minas Gerais. This migration seems to have pressured still-autonomous Puri Indians to encroach on Coroado hunting grounds, increasing hostilities between the two groups. The imperial administration, however belatedly, abandoned its emphasis on the settlement's chimerical buried gold, declining to appoint a new mining inspector when the official occupying the post died in 1805. The new source of wealth arrived during the following decades, unforeseen by Indigenous peoples, small-stakes prospectors, foodstuffs farmers, and the many state actors who had dedicated their energies to inhabiting, exploiting, concealing, or securing the site. Cantagalo's transformation hinged on the growth of the coffee export trade, which took hold of the Paraíba River valley, enriching large landholders and investors based in Rio de Janeiro. The first coffee bushes appeared in the area about the time Mawe lamented its destitution. Investment tied to fortunes deriving from the transatlantic slave trade followed.[42]

At midcentury, aptly drawing on a metaphor tied to gold, a visiting German naturalist, Hermann Burmeister, called Cantagalo the "Eldorado" of coffee. Such enthusiasm suggested he imagined that the export boom that produced prosperity for plantation owners would continue indefinitely. He was unaware that soil erosion, blight, and the availability of better land elsewhere meant its decline had already begun, another dream undone. The visitor stopped for several days in a mission village founded by Franciscans along the Paraíba River. He encountered many Coroado families still living in the region. The older they were, he found, the more likely they were to be "given over to the vice of alcohol, becoming, in this way, repugnant and even animalesque." This was especially true of those old enough to have lived through the changes that unfolded once the state legalized colonization in the aftermath of Coimbra's expedition. Satisfied by the modernization he admired, but lamenting a lost opportunity to observe the Indians in their former condition, the naturalist commented, "To find them in a completely savage state is [now] nearly impossible."[43]

Burmeister's assessment foreshadowed later scholarly trends. Until quite recently historians have paid little heed to these Indigenous groups and those who lived along the coast in the former Jesuits missions. Such groups did not fit scholars' assumptions about Native peoples meriting study. But late in the eighteenth century, more than two hundred years after European settlement first took hold along the not-so-distant coast, the Indigenous inhabitants of the internal frontier separating the colony's burgeoning capital from its mining heartland retained considerable sway over the crown's ability to impose its sovereign dominion. They largely determined what could be known, what remained a mystery, what could be accomplished, and what was beyond reach in this strategic mountainous expanse. Living on the margins of imperial authority, cautious purveyors of backlands knowledge, they could influence the success or failure of state exploration, law enforcement, taxation, and colonization efforts. Imperial interactions with autonomous and semiautonomous Indians in such zones exposed both the aspirations and limitations of Portuguese territorializing projects, revealing the state's constrained ability to project power over this zone relatively close to the administrative center of Portuguese America, as well as many other zones much more distant. Orchestrated at the highest levels of the imperial administration, the operation's inglorious outcome in the mountains above the colonial capital became a measure not only of imperial overreach but of Native proclivities to engage, redirect, and sometimes tame Portuguese territorial ambitions. The enduring resilience of the Coroado, the Coropó, and dozens of other groups in zones undergoing parallel processes of incorporation, turned Brazil's internal frontiers into largely unacknowledged testing grounds and, in some cases, dissolution zones for the projects of a centralizing, territorializing transatlantic state.

Even so, Lisbon would not relent. Secretary of State Melo e Castro lost interest in Cantagalo when it failed to produce a bonanza. The fiasco in the backlands only deepened his suspicions about colonial administrators, especially those who governed inland mining areas. In 1788 he issued instructions to the new governor of Minas Gerais, Luís Antônio Furtado de Mendonça, the Viscount of Barbacena (1788–97), the viceroy's nephew. The secretary cautioned him to guard against the "carelessness" and "negligence" with which the captaincy had been governed. This disregard led to pervasive "indifference and abuses" by the region's vassals. The consequence was the crown's inability to reap advantages from the "great benefits with which nature endowed the captaincy." Barbacena was to impose order on the captaincy's territory, including taking "all possible measures to prevent contraband and smuggling," a task made especially difficult because of the sertões ringing the mining zone, the many overland routes penetrating those sertões, and the limited number of troops to patrol these vast areas at the limits of imperial control. A redoubling of imperial authority should be the governor's highest priority, achieved through more forceful governance. "Among all the people who comprise the different captaincies of Brazil," the crown minister continued, "perhaps none has cost more to subjugate and reduce to the obedience and submission vassals owe to their sovereign than those of Minas Gerais."[44]

These words would come to seem prescient the following year, when Barbacena stymied the 1789 Minas Conspiracy, the nativist plot hatched by a cadre of urban white elites, with the exception of the dragoon officer Joaquim José da Silva Xavier, who was white but less well off. That plot, as noted, has received much attention. Far less examined is how the minister's concerns would continue to play out in the sertões, where a more diverse set of actors contended for much longer with intensifying crown impositions.

# PART 3

## Science for the Sertão
### *New Modes of Inquiry, Old Uncertainties*

BY THE TURN OF THE NINETEENTH century, scientific reconnaissance had come to play a central role in Portugal's efforts to exploit untapped resources in the Brazilian interior. Striving sons of the colony's leading families, a generation of naturalists dedicated themselves to the task. After taking their degrees in Europe, especially at the venerable University of Coimbra, they fanned out across Portuguese America's inland expanses to survey flora, fauna, and mineral deposits for commercial potential. Enlightenment aspirations assumed a distinctive character in their thought and actions. Science, they believed, should serve the empire. Knowledge drawn from the direct observation of nature should guide policy reforms to address the major problems of colonial governance, financial management, investment, and trade. Portugal might thereby avoid the disjunctures that were severing transatlantic empires in the northern hemisphere and stirring discontent in South America. This reformist agenda could also advance personal ambitions. If the state-sponsored naturalists succeeded in their backcountry missions, the crown would surely reward them well.

A disproportionate number of these savants hailed from Minas Gerais. The mutually beneficial exchange of scientific knowledge between elite vassals and the imperial administration underlay multiple proposals for restoring the captaincy to its former prosperity. Some began to see expanded agropastoral production as the only viable response to mining's decline.

Others held fast to the belief that gold and diamond mining could be revived. Scion of a family that made its wealth in the mining sector, the mineralogist José Vieira Couto was among those who advocated redoubling the search for precious stones and metals. His reputation earned him a royal commission to serve as the scientific expert on an expedition to the captaincy's western sertões.

Couto found himself forced, however, to depend on another source of expertise. Impoverished Black and multiracial prospectors had first announced new diamond discoveries to the west. Their unrivaled knowledge of the region made them indispensable informants. Ordinarily denigrated and criminalized by authorities who wished to ensure their subservience, they seized the opportunity circumstances afforded them to reap rewards for their services as guides and laborers. A deeply problematic overland investigation resulted. State-sponsored scientific exploration was supposed to ensure transparency and the sober evaluation of mineral resources. Instead, skewed power dynamics distanced the state from its scientific expert, and the expert from his mistrusted informants.

Chapter 6 considers the personal, social, and political contexts in which the mineralogist and his prospector-guides, known as *garimpeiros*, became entangled in each other's lives. Returning to Minas Gerais from his university training in Coimbra, Couto established himself as a leading authority on minerals and mining. The governor and prince regent sought his technical knowledge for the proposed mission to the west, sparked by a massive diamond turned over by Couto's backcountry counterpart, Isidoro de Amorim Pereira. Achieving fame as a "black prospector king," Isidoro led a remarkable life in the backlands, but not the one attributed to him by later legends. For men of his ilk, diamonds could bring salvation but were more often the source of misery. Chapter 7 turns to the reconnaissance mission itself. Notwithstanding its scientific agenda, the expedition was conditioned by historical precedents that portended problematic findings. The heroic tradition of backcountry conquest narratives made objectivity elusive. In the field, moreover, Couto's distrust of his hardscrabble guides deepened. They contributed their route-finding labor but produced little in the way of new discoveries. Nevertheless, indefatigably confident and eager to impress, Couto issued a promising report. Swayed by knowledge brokers of strikingly different sorts—a cosmopolitan university graduate and a toughened backcountry specialist—the crown invested in preliminary excavations only to be quickly disappointed

CHAPTER 6

# THE ENLIGHTENED SAVANT AND THE BLACK PROSPECTOR KING

DURING THE FINAL DECADES of the eighteenth century, Portuguese imperial administrators turned to what we now call scientific exploration to overcome misconceptions about the interior and more efficiently extract resources from the backlands. The organization of expeditions in pursuit of knowledge about the natural world coincided with the reformist tendencies of the age, as Enlightenment thought influenced colonial governance. Inland reconnaissance by learned investigators—natural philosophers and natural historians—appealed to policy makers in Lisbon, as in other European capitals, who sought to institute an empirically grounded, less personalistic, more cost-effective regime for appropriating the wealth of Portuguese America's seemingly limitless inland expanses. Even more thoroughly than its European counterparts, the Portuguese crown succeeded in co-opting cadres of enlightened naturalists. Especially critical to this effort were those born in Brazil but, by necessity, educated in the emerging earth and life sciences in Europe, since the colony had no university. Far from elevating the observation of nature for the sake of pure knowledge, the scientific reconnaissance of the colony by these savants on their return to Brazil was tightly integrated into neo-mercantilist modernization schemes.[1] Promising to remedy the shortcomings of ventures led by self-interested adventurers, and less costly than large-scale military operations, such exploration developed as an attractive alternative to earlier intelligence-gathering methods. Serving as skilled backcountry investigators and specimen collectors, trained naturalists might avoid the pitfalls of their predecessors, ushering in a new era of imperial prosperity.

Since the production of scientific knowledge cannot be separated from its social and political context, many of the challenges that hampered earlier territorializing efforts continued to limit the effectiveness of this new type of state-sponsored mission. Like their forerunners, erudite voyagers to Brazil's internal frontiers were susceptible to competing incentives and objectives. Actors with agendas of their own, they were members of social networks and patronage hierarchies that shaped their perspectives and influenced their conduct. Their cosmopolitanism, while a bulwark against provincialism, could leave them ill-equipped to find their way, literally and figuratively, in the sertões, especially when they needed to rely, as was frequently the case, on unlettered backcountry guides whose aims rarely prioritized dispassionate empirical inquiry.

No scientific mission better illustrates the challenges encountered by the crown in this altered context than the expedition dispatched to the western reaches of Minas Gerais in 1800. Its objective was to investigate reports of new mineral discoveries, especially diamonds. It relied on the expertise of José Vieira Couto, a mineralogist born in the captaincy and trained in Portugal, dependent on royal patronage, and led into the backlands by a company of free Black and racially mixed prospectors engaged as guides, individuals who otherwise operated outside the law. Their charismatic leader, Isidoro de Amorim Pereira, although derogated by the mineralogist, acquired mythical stature and lived on in local lore. To understand the uneasy partnership forged between these two men, we must begin by examining the trajectories, both personal and social, that landed them side by side on a circuitous hunt for gemstones.

### An Education for the Backlands

Born in 1752 to Portuguese parents in Tejuco (present-day Diamantina), the administrative center of the captaincy's renowned Diamond District, José Vieira Couto traveled as a young man to Portugal, like many other sons of the colony's wealthiest families, to study at the University of Coimbra.[2] He pursued his education during a transformational period in the institution's history, just after Pombal enacted sweeping educational reforms. José I's tireless first minister aimed to expand instruction to include certain practical realms of Enlightenment thought while tightening the ties between the university and the Portuguese state. As part of these reforms, Pombal bolstered the university's curriculum in the physical and life sciences, the disciplinary boundaries of which were far less distinct than they are today. The changes connected integrally to the autocratic minister's plans for imperial renewal. He sought to cultivate a corps of Brazilian scholar-authorities to serve the metropole on their return to the colony. He viewed the accumulation of more extensive and precise knowledge concerning Portuguese America's natural resources as a linchpin of his efforts to centralize control over and extract greater revenues from the colony.

To oversee the expansion of natural science instruction, Pombal brought the Italian scholar Domingos Vandelli to Coimbra. Vandelli's writings provide a primer to the education received by students who attended the university during these years. Preparation included practical training in mounting scientific expeditions, known as "philosophical voyages." Of particular relevance for the young scholar from the Diamond District was Vandelli's guidance on locating, identifying, and extracting gold and diamonds in Minas Gerais. Although the Italian educator sought to remain aloof from political debates about the proper role of mining in the captaincy's changing economy, he argued that the administration of mineral resources could no longer be relegated to "people ignorant of mineralogy." At the time mineralogy was roughly equivalent to the branch of knowledge now known as earth sciences. Only as the nineteenth century advanced would the term *geology* be used widely to describe this realm of scientific study. The new mode of inquiry was in its earliest stages of development in Portugal and its American colony. In Minas Gerais, maintained Vandelli, the lack of trained experts to manage the captaincy's prodigious mineral resources redounded "to the grave prejudice of the state." Drawn to this vision of a revivified mining sector, Couto found a focus for his life's work. He opted for a degree in philosophy, the field added to the university curriculum as the umbrella discipline for the study of nature and the physical universe. Concentrating on mathematics and natural history, he graduated in 1778, the year after José I died and his daughter Maria I assumed the throne.³

Although Pombal was pushed from power, ministerial-level interest in scientific reconnaissance, colonial resource development, and rational management of the mining economy only intensified. Lisbon's Royal Academy of Sciences (Academia Real de Ciências), founded in 1779, ensured the continuous promotion of the Enlightenment's scientific turn throughout the empire. Enjoying crown sponsorship, it cultivated reformist rather than radical solutions. Under its aegis intellectuals authored a profusion of memorials (*memórias*), reports evaluating the state of the kingdom and its overseas dominions. Their emphasis was on commerce, trade, and economic modernization. Many openly acknowledged that Portugal was lagging behind its northern European rivals, especially the industrializing British. Authors explored a variety of responses, analyzing the colonial economy in its broadest sense. Detailed studies examined not only the agricultural and mining sectors but, in keeping with the less rigid epistemological divisions of the era, also matters of climate, geography, and local customs, often simultaneously. With respect to Minas Gerais, the collapse of gold production was the foremost concern of memorial writers. Some advocated developing alternative commodities, especially agricultural products. Others proposed new policies and technologies to modernize and reinvigorate mining.

More than a gathering place for sedentary thinkers and theorists, the Royal Academy encouraged correspondents to reconnoiter Brazilian territory and communicate their findings. In this way they would speed the transfer of practical knowledge from the colony to the metropole that would help rationalize resource administration and maximize royal revenues. As a rule, despite growing revolutionary discontent in the Atlantic world, memorial writers proposed incremental reforms intended to foster cooperation between powerful metropolitan and colonial interests. Owing their scientific missions to the Portuguese state, they were not inclined to dissent. Many viewed the scientific enterprise as a means to an end, a way to foster an illustrious administrative career and secure the privileges associated with high position.[4]

It was in this transatlantic milieu that Couto, on his return from Portugal to Minas Gerais, assumed his place among a generation of Brazilian naturalists, political economists, and legal scholars promoted to influential bureaucratic and advisory roles as part of a conscious effort to stifle rumblings of nativism and republicanism in the colony. That these currents had reached Brazilian shores became manifest in the foiled Minas Conspiracy of 1789. A second failed plot, later known as the Tailor's Conspiracy, proved even more worrisome. Inspired by the French Revolution and the slave rebellion in Saint-Domingue, conspirators posted anonymous handbills around the urban center of Salvador, calling for the founding of a Bahian republic. In contrast to the white elites involved in the Minas Conspiracy, most of these plotters were free people of color, including soldiers, and artisans of middling means, among them many tailors. Some foresaw an end to slavery. The plot was discovered in 1798, its participants brutally punished.

With these troubling events as his frame of reference, Secretary of State for Overseas Affairs Rodrigo de Sousa Coutinho, later the Count of Linhares, moved to redirect the restless energies of colonial intellectuals toward imperial projects in which they had a stake. Coutinho assumed his position as crown minister in 1796, commissioning some of the most influential scientific and economic memorials of his era. A committed neo-mercantilist at this point in his political career, he took up the task of reasserting, while updating, projects Pombal had devised to engage Brazilian elites in imperial modernization. This agenda made him particularly receptive to hopeful memorials from Brazilian literati, including those predicting that backcountry exploration would uncover unexploited mineral reserves, restoring Minas Gerais to its position as a cornerstone of imperial prosperity. He personally monitored and issued directives regarding the status of mining and the collection of mineral samples from the captaincy. His elevation of Couto to serve among his favored experts was part of this larger effort. Such state-sponsored knowledge production encouraged memorialists like the mineralogist from Tejuco, aspiring men who sought the crown's favor, to craft proposals that promised rapid returns for the royal treasury.[5]

The high point of Couto's service to the crown was the expedition to the western sertões and the São Francisco River watershed organized by the captaincy governor, Bernardo José de Lorena (1797–1803), the Count of Sarzedas. Expedition members were to accompany the mineralogist on a trek that would last nearly ten months. Couto's assignment was to investigate news of precious mineral and especially diamond strikes reported by local garimpeiros, small stakes prospectors operating in violation of laws that made diamond mining a state monopoly. His training made him a natural for this mission, but his family's involvement in local business and politics meant factors other than scientific expertise were never far from his mind. A decade before the expedition, notes historian Kenneth Maxwell, the Diamond District's ranking royal administrator had accused the Couto family of engaging in "extensive pilfering of and contraband in diamonds." Couto himself had placed captive laborers in the district's military guard, "doubtless with the protection of [the family's] illegal interest in mind."[6] Thus Couto had to balance his inclinations as a scientist and his family's commercial concerns against a backdrop of increasing anxiety about mining's decline. His approach to his backcountry investigations and his resulting reform proposals were uneasy amalgams of these influences.

Couto's study, travel, collecting, and metallurgical experiments resulted in a handful of significant manuscripts drafted for the crown. In 1799, the year before the expedition set out, he submitted his *Memória sobre a Capitania das Minas Gerais; seu território, clima e produções metálicas* (*Memorial on the Captaincy of Minas Gerais: Its Territory, Climate, and Metallurgical Production*). In late 1801, after he returned, he completed his report on the exploration mission to the west. Its title was similar, *Memoria sobre as minas da capitania de Minas Geraes; suas descripções, ensaios e domicílios próprios, à maneira de itinerário . . .* (*Memorial on the Mines of the Captaincy of Minas Gerais: Their Description, Mineral Assays, and Specific Locations, in the manner of an Itinerary . . .*), but its content differed markedly. Forwarded almost immediately to Lisbon but not published until 1842, this text chronicled Couto's journey from Tejuco to Vila Rica,

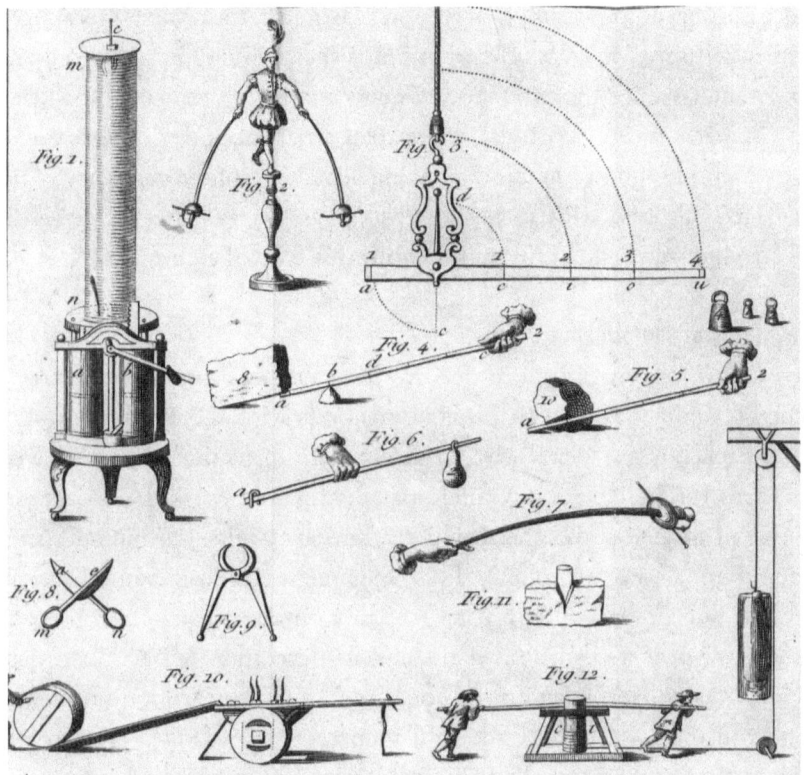

FIGURE 6.1. Mineralogical tools and instruments. Source: Torbern Bergman, *Manual do mineralogico, ou esboço do reino mineral, disposto segundo a analyse chimica* (Lisbon: João Procopio Correa da Silva, 1799). Courtesy of the John Carter Brown Library. Licensed under CC-BY-SA 4.0.

then to the São Francisco River and points westward, some 300 kilometers distant. The report included a lengthy appendix on his geographic, mineralogical, and metallurgical studies of Nova Lorena Diamantina, a sprawling expanse he renamed for the governor. In these and other works, despite what by then amounted to decades of accumulated evidence to the contrary, Couto insisted that the future wealth of the region, and its contribution to the prosperity of the empire, would continue to hinge on the extraction of precious minerals. He believed the systematic examination of nature, the application of the latest mining methods, and the advent of a more rational administration of resources would return Minas Gerais to its former fortunes.[7] Even as others conceded that mining's heyday would not return, he believed the extraction of gems and metals remained the key to a prosperous future. Portugal, more than any rival power, had reason to redouble its emphasis on mining, taking advantage of the captaincy's "rich lands that abound with metals" and its "vast sertões that never will be effectively settled and cultivated without this type of commerce."[8]

### The Informant's Informant

No association proved more decisive for Couto's prospects as a proponent of mining's revival than his interactions with the Black and multiracial backcountry adepts who would guide him to the captaincy's western sertões. These were the much-maligned garimpeiros, the prospectors whose position on the social and territorial margins of mining society made them a constant source of disparagement and suspicion. Historians have all but ignored their pivotal role in Couto's journey.[9] But it would never have occurred without them, and its outcome—what it uncovered, what it missed, and what conclusions could be drawn from months wandering in the sertão—depended on their local knowledge. Their role as information brokers impelled Couto's efforts and impeded his success. As historians have come to recognize was frequently the case in such scientific endeavors, the learned and the vernacular operated hand in hand.[10] The erudite informant to the crown required, even as he scorned, his own informants in the sertão.

On the very first day of his voyage, Couto would encounter the enforcement apparatus set up to surveil and punish the sort of individuals on whom he would rely. Just six leagues (40 km) out of Tejuco, his party passed a military garrison. The soldiers, Couto wrote, were charged with searching travelers for smuggled diamonds and patrolling the area for illegal "*grimpeiros.*" Couto was using an alternate spelling here, which made more plausible the etymological explanation he proposed. The word derived from *grimpa*, he asserted. Now commonly signifying a weather vane, at the time it also was a synonym for a summit or a mountain slope, presumably linked to the French *grimper*, to climb. Those who prospected for diamonds clandestinely, Couto explained, were called grimpeiros because of their habit of "living and wandering hidden among the mountain summits." The term may also have alluded to these miners' itineracy, their tendency, as a period dictionary had it, "to be very inconstant, like a weathervane that turns with the wind, that changes and varies."[11] Most of Couto's contemporaries spelled the word as it is spelled today, garimpeiros. Still widely used, it refers to impoverished precious metals and gem prospectors who continue to dig for buried wealth in Minas Gerais and elsewhere.

In the past, as it does today, the term presupposed the illicit. The naturalist and mineralogist John Mawe, who became the first Englishman permitted to visit the Diamond District in 1809, made this association explicit. Prince Regent João provided him letters of introduction and a military escort during his voyage; in exchange, he put his expertise at the empire's service. Garimpeiros, he wrote, did not "give notice" of their mineral strikes or solicit legitimate claims from the government to excavate them. They were therefore "treated as smugglers." Enslavers evinced outrage, he noted, when the term came up in polite conversation during his visit to Tejuco. He thought their reaction a charade. Eager to avoid suspicion of profiting from using their own bondsmen for such illegal prospecting, the elite "shudder with horror and distort their features, calling on the Virgin to witness their abhorrence of a crime to which the Government has attached the greatest disgraces and punishments."[12] Consistent with this response, Francisco Beltrão, the mining intendent of Sabará and the ranking royal official accompanying Couto's expedition, did not conceal his contempt for such individuals. To be a garimpeiro, he maintained, was to be a "thief and killer."[13]

Thus it was no small or single irony that Couto, a member of a notable family accused of profiting from contraband diamonds and suspected of placing men he held as slaves in the Diamond District's military guard to aid in such trafficking, had been appointed to investigate unmonitored diamond strikes in the west, and that this assignment required him to rely on a particularly notorious group of garimpeiros. At the head of this hardscrabble company was Isidoro de Amorim Pereira. Archival sources from the period usually referred to him by his first name only, a convention adopted in the discussion that follows. Deeply threatening to the established order during his lifetime, useful to government critics decades later as a symbol of antiauthoritarian resistance, Isidoro acquired a fame the archives could not contain. The legend he inspired, originating in his supposed backcountry proficiencies and defiance of Portuguese tyranny, is to this day a feature of popular memory in Diamantina, the former Tejuco, where Couto began his journey. It merits retelling, stripping away its generational accretions, because it foregrounds the blurring of fact and fiction that frequently compromised information originating in the sertão. The mystique surrounding Isidoro made it difficult for the university-trained mineralogist, the governor, and the crown to discern the truth. It also has made things difficult for historians.

Isidoro came to be known as the "black prospector king." According to one popular version of the myth, he cut a commanding figure. His enslaved and freed "companions nurtured a mystical respect for him, as if [he] were a black prince who had arrived with a shipment of slaves captured by a caravan in the unknown deserts of Africa." Purportedly a friar's captive who grew up in the Diamond District, Isidoro was seized from his master after being accused of illegal prospecting. He was then forced to work in chains in the diamond washings. Despite close supervision, he escaped, disappearing into the surrounding mountains, initiating his long career as a fugitive. He hewed to a strict moral code, as the legend had it, gathering other runaways under his leadership. Together they congregated at a fortified quilombo. Working at night by torchlight, they unearthed gold and diamonds, using the proceeds to strengthen their community and purchase the freedom of fellow slaves. Disguising himself in order to fool authorities, Isidoro traded precious stones and gold dust with eager buyers in Tejuco. He "dreamed of forming a strong black redoubt," the story held, "and he also dreamed of the liberation of all of those of his race," while refusing to resort to violence or mere thievery to achieve these aspirations. With the profits he earned, he secured the freedom of the woman he loved, Maria, and the son born of their secret liaisons, paying three times the owner's asking price for the boy. The surplus, he demanded, was to be distributed among the town's poorest residents.[14]

Isidoro's fame grew in the early nineteenth century, and his quilombo attracted more fugitives from slavery. Troops dispatched to locate and destroy the community were repeatedly repelled until, eventually, Isidoro was betrayed. Soldiers captured him in a bloody battle, mortally wounding him, but not before he managed to hide his accumulated treasure in gold and diamonds in a cave. Bleeding profusely, he was marched through the streets of Tejuco. Residents who admired his struggle for freedom and justice came out of their homes, exclaiming, "There comes the martyr, the persecuted innocent!" After suffering many days of torture, bound to a wooden frame, whipped, exposed to the elements, "his body transformed into an open wound," Isidoro refused to reveal the names of the townsfolk who collaborated with him. At the hour of his death, it was not Isidoro but the official overseeing his punishment who repented. The despotic Diamond District intendant, Manuel Ferreira da Câmara, came to his side to ask forgiveness for treating him so cruelly. Isidoro's cave, according to this legend, "continues to test the courage of many adventurers who have struggled futilely to penetrate its depths."[15]

Although it accrued embellishments over time, this tale can be traced to an account of the 1860s of Isidoro's life, purportedly based on first-hand testimony, published by the jurist, statesman, journalist, and regional historian Joaquim Felício dos Santos. In the pages of the newspaper he founded in Tejuco decades after the end of colonial rule, Santos described the "act of barbarity" that resulted in the death of this "leader of a troop of [runaway] slave garimpeiros." Having labored in mining from his childhood, Isidoro was thoroughly familiar with the richest diamond deposits in the area. Santos emphasized his band's righteousness. Although they traded in illicit diamonds, they did so for their very survival. They never treated their buyers unfairly, even though these residents of Tejuco were their former enslavers, who stole their liberty, "the greatest of possessions." As a result, the garimpeiros lived in harmony with the Diamond District's leading residents, whom Santos contrasted with the venal Portuguese authorities who governed them.[16]

Even before Intendant Câmara's arrival in Tejuco, Santos explained, crown officials launched a campaign to apprehend Isidoro. Câmara intensified the hunt, declaring a "bloody war" against the garimpeiros, whose capture became an obsession and a point of honor. He deployed military patrols to search the backlands, threatened locals suspected of protecting Isidoro, and encouraged others to betray him. When one of Isidoro's compatriots finally succumbed to this pressure and revealed his whereabouts, the intendant pounced, ordering a detachment of soldiers to attack his hiding place. To the end, Isidoro fought back, resisting the raid "alone and valorously." After a long battle, he finally fell, struck by three bullets, taken prisoner, and then beaten by soldiers who treated him "as one treats a wild animal." Santos dated the arrival of the prisoner in Tejuco to June 1809. During his interrogation, asked why he had first fled enslavement, Isidoro answered simply that it was unjust. Asked who purchased the diamonds he and his followers unearthed, he refused to say.

Thus began his torture. Santos penned a lurid description: "Soon the flesh tears, the blood dapples, and the still-fresh wounds reopen." But Isidoro neither protested nor revealed the identity of a single collaborator. A lesser man would have died more quickly, but the prisoner, "robust and athletic," endured several more days of agony. When the end came, his fame as a martyr spread. Concluding with the tale of Isidoro's lost mine and hidden treasure, Santos assured his readers that his account was based on testimony he received from "trustworthy, impartial," eyewitnesses.[17] Accuracy, however, was not always Santos's guiding principle.

Portuguese America's sparsely colonized inland frontiers often hid from view what historians would most like to know. As we have seen in previous chapters, the sertões provided fertile ground for the elaboration of myths and legends. Other than a few points of agreement, the existing documentary evidence recording Isidoro's actions departs sharply from the lore. This is to be expected. More surprising is how little scholars have done to correct the record. Santos's nineteenth-century fable about Isidoro is presented as fact in more than one scholarly history.[18] The sources Santos interviewed, individuals who had supposedly witnessed the prospector's demise, would have been at least in their sixties, recounting events that happened when they were small children. Upon his purported capture and torture, Isidoro himself would have been aging and weakened, near or even past seventy, hardly the powerful figure Santos described. From other accounts he published in his newspaper, we know that Santos never let facts stand in the way of a good story. The most famous of his refashioned colonial characters was Chica da Silva, an enslaved woman and Tejuco resident who won her freedom from one of the wealthiest men in the Portuguese Empire. Historians have labored to correct the falsehoods Santos spread about her in stories designed to attract readers and popularize the journalist's criticism of Brazil's nineteenth-century ruling class.[19] Isidoro has not been the subject of similar reconsideration. To understand his role as Couto's backcountry informant, we must differentiate his historical and fictional personas.

To begin with, there is no indication in the documentary record that Isidoro was either enslaved or a fugitive from slavery.[20] As we will see, in possession of a huge diamond he discovered, Isidoro appealed to the governor, and the governor to the crown, requesting a pardon for past crimes in exchange for the gemstone. Had he been a fugitive, he would have asked first for his freedom, which a captive could expect as the primary reward for turning over such a valuable diamond. The governor made no suggestion that Isidoro was ever anything other than a freeman. Nor did others, including Couto, who spent many days with the prospector. Intendant Francisco Beltrão, who disdained Isidoro, considering him to be little more than a conniving criminal, similarly never suggested he was a runaway. The governor, Couto, and others called him "captain," a title they applied neither ironically nor merely honorifically. Isidoro was an actual captain, the commander of a free Black militia unit. In that official position he could not have been a runaway.[21] Whether some of the garimpeiros among his followers had escaped their owners is less certain. It seems unlikely, however, that such individuals would have risked joining a venture accompanied by government soldiers who would be rewarded handsomely for apprehending escapees.

Furthermore, no verifiable archival evidence of Isidoro's purported martyrdom has been found, and the incident did not appear in the detailed travel account published by Mawe, who visited Tejuco just a few months after it supposedly occurred. Mawe stayed in the home of and freely exchanged information with the Diamond District's intendant, who, according to Santos, had ordered Isidoro tortured. To the contrary, in 1802, seven years earlier, during the period that, according to the legend, the garimpeiro would have been at the height of his powers, Governor Lorena described him as a man sapped by disease and "very poor." Whatever his past misdeeds may have been, his vulnerable physical state guaranteed his future obedience, the governor believed.[22] Isidoro simply was no longer capable of the strenuous mining activities that had once placed him outside the law.

Less than a year before Couto's expedition departed, however, the governor did acknowledge Isidoro's renown, describing him as a "celebrated pardo." The ambiguities of his conduct and character nourished the stories that later evolved into legends. Then in his sixties, he was called "Captain" or simply "The Pardo" by subordinates and detractors. The governor evinced a grudging respect. He wrote, for instance, that Isidoro had "always been obedient" when soldiers ordered him to leave areas where mining was restricted. Of course, this implied Isidoro repeatedly violated such restrictions, even if he withdrew when caught. His obedience, that is, apparently vanished the moment soldiers looked the other way. Still, the governor described him as a man of "many moral virtues" who "never offended anyone" and who "gave alms generously to the poor." He had never been caught in possession of illegal gems or gold. As for the marginal individuals who benefited from Isidoro's largesse, Governor Lorena was convinced they protected him from punishment, helping him conceal his dealings in contraband, and even hiding him when necessary. "I have made the greatest effort to apprehend him," the governor wrote, but to no avail.

It therefore came as quite a surprise when Isidoro presented himself voluntarily to Governor Lorena. Emerging without warning from the "desolate sertões" in the company of an associate, the son of a prominent family from São Paulo, the historical Isidoro said that he and his fellow garimpeiros had discovered lands rich in diamonds, gold, and silver. As

FIGURE 6.2. Prospecting for diamonds. Source: Carlos Julião, [Escravos britadores de pedra para a extração de diamantes], late 18th century, BNRJ, SI, C.I,2,8. Courtesy of the Biblioteca Nacional, Rio de Janeiro.

proof he turned over a diamond weighing more than two oitavas, a quarter of an ounce or approximately 35 carats. He said he wished to make a gift of the diamond to the royal treasury. Whether the garimpeiro leader turned himself in as a response to the constant pressure from soldiers tracking his whereabouts or out of a sincere desire to cooperate, the governor could not be certain. The large, high-quality diamond he turned over, however, was enough to preclude his arrest. Isidoro explained that he had "come to subject himself" to the governor and to offer his services as a loyal vassal "obedient to the sovereign laws of Our Lady the Queen." He promised to lead an official party to lands in the vicinity of the Abaeté River, a tributary of the São Francisco, where many more diamonds could be found, along with major deposits of gold and silver. Governor Lorena quickly conveyed the news to Secretary of State Coutinho in Lisbon. With it he sent Isidoro's diamond.[23]

As much as he may have wanted to believe in the existence of undiscovered treasure that would spell a better future for the captaincy and empire, Governor Lorena did not fully trust Isidoro. After all, he should not have been in the area where he made his discoveries in the first place. The high esteem in which locals held the prospector, the governor confided to the secretary of state, "obliges me to believe him" and to order the region explored. Nevertheless, there were further concerns. The garimpeiro chief stood accused of participating in a confrontation with soldiers on patrol in the western sertões eight years earlier. The troops had surprised a group of prospectors in the midst of illegal activities, shots were fired, and several men on both sides fell dead, including the patrol's commander. An official investigation pointed to Isidoro's involvement. Along with others alleged to be his associates, he was accused of murder. Governor Lorena urged the crown to drop the charges and take the garimpeiro leader up on his offer of assistance. As justification, he noted, first, that Isidoro's "humane conduct" was inconsistent with the behavior of a murderer. Second, he said it "was widely known" that Isidoro was never seen at the site of the violent encounter and that the man he allegedly killed had in fact been shot by "an old black man, crippled in one leg." Having as yet received no reward for the diamond he turned over, or for his promise to guide officials to the source of this treasure, Isidoro deserved the crown's pardon as long as he desisted from unsupervised prospecting in the future.[24]

Considering how rarely the machinations of justice in the colony favored men and women of color, the governor's stance was unusual. Perhaps Isidoro was convincing in his claim of innocence. Perhaps the governor felt uncommonly magnanimous. The possibility of a mutually advantageous agreement between the two men must also be considered. Isidoro retained significant leverage as a backcountry specialist who could reveal or withhold his geographic expertise. The knowledge he possessed prepared him both to lead and mislead. Governor Lorena, avid to prove his worth to the crown by helping stem the relentless decline in mineral production, had ample reason to enlist Isidoro's aid as an expedition guide. Direct personal gain might also be forthcoming. In the end we cannot know whether the two men struck a covert bargain, although such corruption was endemic.[25]

A complicating factor was that officials in charge of the royal diamond diggings, who might seem the most qualified to oversee the reconnaissance operation, were not to be trusted either. According to the governor, they feared the discovery of precious stones to the west might require them to leave their comfortable lives in the "civilized" town of Tejuco and relocate to the "uncultured and deserted sertão." The governor recounted rumors suggesting that these Diamond District officials, whose orders to answer directly to Lisbon created ill will with multiple captaincy governors, had covered up the results of their own exploratory expeditions. Marching enslaved laborers to the west to carry out excavations, they had examined the region's potential for profitable mining, but on their return they announced they had discovered nothing worth pursuing. For this reason, the governor argued he needed to stage another expedition, under his own authority. As its lead fiscal officer, he planned to appoint, not one of the Diamond District officials suspected of malfeasance, but Intendant Francisco Beltrão of Sabará, whose jurisdiction encompassed the region in question. A complete and accurate account of this expedition's findings would be provided to Lisbon. The governor concluded his communiqué with a pledge. He assured the secretary of state that, because of his unstinting efforts, the captaincy's diamond-bearing lands were now "entirely free of troops of garimpeiros."[26] Subsequent events would prove otherwise.

Receiving authorization to proceed, Governor Lorena began to organize the expedition that Couto would join as mineralogical expert, appointed by Prince Regent João himself. Its departure was scheduled for the beginning of the dry season in April of 1800. Couto and the intendant would be escorted by some thirty soldiers under the command of a sergeant major. They in turn would be guided by Isidoro and his company of garimpeiros, who were to be encountered en route. The governor's correspondence left no doubt as to the impetus for this initiative. Isidoro's testimony, he wrote, was the primary "cause of the reconnaissance and source of the knowledge revealed."[27]

Stated differently, against all odds, Isidoro convinced the governor of the value of his hard-earned backcountry expertise, aided by a multicarat prop. So persuasive was his performance that he captivated not merely the governor but also a transatlantic audience that included the secretary of state and the prince regent. As a consequence Couto would be called on to stage his own performance, assuming the role of the skillful investigator for which his university training had prepared him. For both Isidoro and Couto, uneasy partners in an exchange of information that linked the sertão to the metropole, transmission of their specialized knowledge promised prestige and social enhancement. Yet the burdens inherent in seeking patronage from a transatlantic state bent on consolidating its control over the interior would leave each of them susceptible to misjudgments and exaggerations when clear-sighted expertise was supposed to be their stock in trade.

**Treacherous Diamonds**

The portion of the backlands to be explored as a result of Isidoro's overture to the captaincy government had long been known to conceal diamonds. Sometimes called the Abaeté Sertões, for the river that meandered through the area in a northeasterly direction until it joined the São Francisco, its vulnerability to unsupervised and untaxed prospecting had prompted authorities to post crown soldiers there some forty years earlier.[28] In 1784 Governor Luís da Cunha Meneses issued orders to verify reports of such activity to officials in both Tejuco and Paracatu, a substantial gold-mining town to the northwest of the zone in question, along the Goiás border. They were to investigate rumors of diamond strikes, control illegal migration to the area, and increase the military and militia presence in this "exceedingly vast sertão." They were also to apprehend and expel any garimpeiros and determine whether circumstances merited establishing a state-supervised mining operation. The lawless prospectors themselves would act as unwitting guides, the governor schemed, because evidence of their diggings along certain stretches of the river would indicate where officials should focus their own efforts. Intelligence gathering was slow, but in early 1788 Governor Cunha Meneses informed Lisbon of the likelihood of a state-run mining operation yielding "extraordinary riches in diamonds as well as gold and other valuable gemstones."[29]

For that wealth to benefit the crown, a "tumult of garimpeiros" who were "invading" the area had to be controlled. As news spread of new discoveries in the area, anticipated to be the largest in recent memory, these illusive prospectors were setting out from Tejuco, Paracatu, and other towns. A government edict posted in these towns warned against such adventurism. Anyone wishing to travel to the restricted area or to leave the captaincy would require an official passport. Colonists in the sertão could expect to be stopped and searched if they traveled without military authorization. The region was to be mapped and its garrisons reinforced.[30]

An infantry officer familiar with the area who possessed nearly three decades' experience in diamond mining outlined plans to establish a royal mining installation along the Abaeté River. The river would have to be diverted so that its bed and banks could be profitably excavated. He estimated that 130 slaves would be sufficient to carry out this engineering project within four months, after which mining could begin. Approximately 15 percent of the laborers could be expected to lose their lives in completing this dangerous river diversion. Deducting this expense and others, including the cost of paying for an administrator, a chaplain, slave drivers, blacksmiths, carpenters, mules, and other necessities, the operation could still be expected to yield an attractive profit over the first nine months. Doubling the number of captive workers would double the returns.[31]

In 1789, as Lisbon pondered this proposal, hundreds of prospectors rushed to the area as word spread of additional diamond and gold strikes. Faced with a shortage of troops, Governor Luís Antônio Furtado de Mendonça, the Viscount of Barbacena (1788–97), Governor Lorena's immediate predecessor, admitted his inability to monitor the migrants. Still less feasible was the possibility of forcing them to withdraw. The governor called on the viceroy to help remedy the problem by sending soldiers from Rio de Janeiro to reinforce those already mobilized from Vila Rica.[32] Reports of both collusion and conflicts between soldiers and garimpeiros also dated to this period. By the early 1790s, Isidoro figured in some of these reports, including the one that led to the charges for which Governor Lorena requested his pardon.[33] In an incident indicative of the precariousness of the situation and deemed concerning enough to report to the queen, a pair of deserters made off with the daily wages sent to sustain the isolated military detachment.[34] It was also at about this time, according to Couto, that the two major expeditions led by Diamond District officials entered the area. But after more than two years of expensive reconnaissance and test excavations, they had returned all but empty-handed, declaring the region "poor and of no utility." The initiative was scrapped, the guards posted there reduced in number, and the territory "almost totally abandoned to the garimpeiros who knew better how to make the best of it." As noted, Governor Lorena suspected Diamond District officials of downplaying the true scale of the region's precious mineral deposits.[35] Instead, he placed his trust in Isidoro and the garimpeiros. Since standard procedures had not delivered the expected windfall to the state, perhaps unconventional methods would.

The risks involved in this gem-burdened collaboration were not borne merely by the governor, the mineralogist, and the crown. A great deal was at stake for Isidoro and his company of backcountry prospectors. If they were lucky, one way garimpeiros made the best of their perilous circumstances was to turn over to authorities particularly large diamonds, as Isidoro did. Similar cases illustrate the possibilities. Just a few years before he presented his gemstone to the governor—and contributing to the sensation it sparked—several prospectors, one of them a man of color, had come forward with a stone far larger than Isidoro's, so large that experts speculated it might be "the largest diamond in the world."[36]

News of this remarkable find circulated for many years. When Mawe, the British mineralogist, visited the Diamond District in 1809, local officials were still talking about it. By then, like so many accounts of gold and diamond strikes originating in the sertão, the story had taken on a life of its own, accumulating many adornments. Even so, no exaggeration was involved when Mawe learned the stone weighed nearly an ounce uncut. Government officials registered it as just short of that weight at 7 3/4 oitavas (135.6 ct). The stone was valued at 8:000$000, worth an immodest fortune at the time.[37]

Like Isidoro, the three men who made this discovery had been condemned as criminals. Banished from their homes and left to wander the backlands for more than six years, they nourished dreams of finding buried riches and their redemption. They exposed themselves to "a double risk, being continually liable to become the prey of the Anthropophagi, and in no less danger of being seized by the soldiers of [the] Government," Mawe wrote. During a drought that exposed portions of the Abaeté riverbed, their search bore fruit. While panning for gold, they found the remarkable diamond. After seeking guidance from a priest, they brought their treasure to Vila Rica, approached the governor, and "threw themselves at his feet." At first he could not believe the evidence placed before him. When experts confirmed that the stone was in fact an enormous diamond, he acted swiftly. "Being thus, by the most strange and unforeseen accident, put in possession of the largest diamond ever found in America, he thought it proper to suspend the sentence of the men as a reward for their having delivered it to him." After receiving the gem in Lisbon, the largest of any in the crown's possession, Prince Regent João confirmed the pardon in the name of his incapacitated mother, Queen Maria.[38]

The discoverers received substantial rewards in addition to their exoneration. The prospector credited with leading the operation received 1:200$000; his second in command, 1:000$000; the priest, 600 mil-reis, respectively. More than two dozen others who assisted in the excavations each received 200 mil-reis. No fewer than fourteen enslaved porters and miners who carried out the bulk of the manual labor required to unearth the diamond received their freedom from the crown, as well as 100 mil-reis each. Of the initial party of three, the two white discovers received remunerative government posts in addition to their monetary prizes, as did another seventeen white officers and soldiers credited with aiding the find. In contrast, the third of the three original associates, along with ten free colored soldiers involved in the operation, found himself excluded from such a sinecure on the basis of his color.[39] Petitioning the crown, he complained that the "accident of his color" unfairly barred him from his just reward. Although the outcome of his petition is not known, transatlantic negotiations continued for several years, during which the Abaeté region was once again reinforced with soldiers, and authorities again mounted an exploratory expedition to the area, including some two hundred enslaved individuals. As had occurred in the past, however, the operation yielded disappointing results, only to be abandoned by the government.[40] Nevertheless, from the perspective of individual garimpeiros, such happenings, however rare, kept alive dreams of a life-altering discovery.

Mawe provided other glimpses of the stakes involved for individual miners marginalized by colonial hierarchies. If an enslaved laborer at the royal mineral washings found a diamond weighing an oitava (17.5 ct), "much ceremony takes place," the Englishman explained. "He is crowned with a wreath of flowers and carried in procession to the administrator, who gives him his freedom," compensating his owner for the cost of manumission. For lesser finds, captives received new clothes. Two shirts, a new suit, a hat, and a knife were awarded for stones weighing more than eight carats. During his visit to the washings, Mawe observed how excited everyone grew one day when an enslaved man found a particularly large gem. "It was pleasing to see the anxious desire manifested by the officers that it might prove heavy enough to entitle the poor negro to his freedom." When it turned out to weigh "a carat short of the requisite weight, all seemed to sympathize with his disappointment."[41]

For such individuals, it must be remembered, disappointment was the rule; life transformation, the exception. Another telling incident occurred just before Mawe left Rio de Janeiro for Minas Gerais. The Portuguese royal family had recently taken up residence in the city after fleeing Napoleon's armies in 1807 and crossing the Atlantic under the escort of British warships. The British mineralogist found himself summoned to determine the authenticity of a stone said to be a gigantic diamond, which a man of color had presented to the prince regent after journeying to the coastal capital from Vila do Príncipe in Minas Gerais, a voyage of some 750 kilometers. The freeman had written the monarch to request that he be allowed to deliver the gem in person, having received it from a deceased friend. The reported size of the stone "was such as to raise imagination to its highest pitch." Along the royal road leading from the mining district to the colonial capital, now the effective center of the empire, "all who had heard the report hailed [the freeman] as already honored." He was rushed to the royal palace as soon as he arrived in Rio de Janeiro. "In a few moments," Mawe wrote, "the hopes which he had for so many years indulged would be realized, and he should be exalted from a low and obscure condition to a state of affluence and distinction." Such, "no doubt, were the thoughts which agitated him during the moments of suspense" after he "threw himself at the Prince's feet."

The monarch's ministers marveled at the size of the stone, some speculating it would greatly enrich the royal treasury. Others raised doubts. The following day Mawe appeared at the royal treasury to conduct an appraisal. He was led into a grand chamber, where the treasurer and his secretaries awaited. Together, they passed through a series of "apartments hung with scarlet and gold" to reach the innermost room, where "there were several strong chests with three locks each, the keys of which were kept by three different officers, who were all required to be present at the opening." Out of one of these chests, the object in question, more than an inch in diameter, was removed and "in great form" placed in front of the Englishman. He knew immediately that it was nothing more than a "rounded piece of crystal." This he proved by scratching it with one of the genuine diamonds held in the vault. Signing a document to certify his finding, he worried how the setback would affect the prince regent, upon whose permission to visit Minas Gerais the natural historian's voyage depended. The prince, however, proved "too noble-minded to manifest any chagrin at the disappointment." Not so for the "poor negro." He was "deeply afflicted by this unwelcome news; instead of being accompanied home by an escort, he had to find his way thither as he could." Mawe assumed he would face "the ridicule and contempt of those who had of late congratulated him on his good fortune."[42]

These incidents provide glimpses of the charged atmosphere that surrounded any discovery of the sort Isidoro made. A single gemstone of substantial size might secure emancipation for an enslaved person, redemption for a vagabond, exoneration for an accused criminal. Free poor prospectors, even if they were Black, might win a monetary reward large enough to purchase one or more enslaved laborers, thereby fundamentally improving their social status and life chances. (A small but significant minority of enslavers in virtually every region of the colony were themselves free persons of color, especially among small farmers and artisans.)[43] A white soldier or official credited with having a hand in the delivery of the gem could expect promotion. A governor could expect royal attention, the most desirable of benefits for an already high-ranking servant of the crown.

For garimpeiros near the bottom of the social hierarchy, like those who escorted the mineralogist José Vieira Couto to the western sertões, the sight of diamonds, the mere rumors of their proximity, occasioned dreams of freedom from the travails of daily life in the colony, an escape from poverty, an enhanced position in colonial society. Yet the pursuit of every dream came laced with the prospect of bitter failure, the potential consequences of illegality, and the vulnerability of revealing secrets to, or hiding them from, associates and authorities whose trustworthiness could not be guaranteed. The carbon allotropes that crystallized into diamonds might be all but unbreakable, but the projects they sparked were easily shattered, both for the individuals and the empire that pursued them. This treacherous reality is distilled in an adage still heard around the region once demarcated as the Diamond District: "A diamond cuts gold, a diamond cuts iron, a diamond cuts the heart."[44]

CHAPTER 7

# DIAMONDS, LOVE SONGS, AND THE ALCHEMY OF EXPLORATION

EVEN WHEN ACQUIRED BY HIGHLY trained experts and subjected to rigorous verification, the geographic, economic, and political knowledge that flowed from the Brazilian backlands to Lisbon continued to mislead as much as clarify. As Lisbon pressed to consolidate its control in the western reaches of Minas Gerais, scientific reconnaissance epitomized the empire's modernizing campaign to assert territorial sovereignty over the colony's internal frontiers. Yet a more rationalist approach to the backlands did not signal a radical break with the past. It absorbed rather than dispensed with older understandings and ways of being in the backlands. The new mode of inquiry exemplified the state's evolving capacities, but it also reinscribed tenacious limitations.

The exploratory expedition that united the Coimbra-trained savant and the charismatic garimpeiro leader in temporary common cause exposed the vulnerabilities of a transatlantic state drawn into negotiations with marginalized frontier intermediaries, in this case Isidoro and his followers, primarily impoverished men of African descent. Normally persecuted by the very authorities who now sought their assistance, these small-stakes miners made the best of an unusual opportunity. When the mineralogist communicated improbable findings about the magnitude of the region's diamond deposits, he left royal councilors on uncertain footing, subject to wishful thinking, implementing impracticable plans. Although deeply skeptical of his prospector guides, the mineralogist and most of his superiors, including the prince regent, ended up swayed by their claims.

### Heroic Mineralogy

Couto's orders from the governor instructed him to explore the "wild sertões" of the captaincy's far west.[1] Some preliminary observations about the mineralogist's assumptions as a thinker and his techniques as a writer will help clarify how his journey unfolded in practice and prose. Like other natural historians of this era, mineralogists often relied on the conventions of travel writing. In the course of chronicling their journeys, they melded their scientific investigations to reflections on the social, political, and economic circumstances they deemed relevant to their purposes. Such intellectual expansiveness prevailed because Enlightenment sciences remained enmeshed in other spheres of action and thought.[2] Couto's recourse to this approach was further stamped by regional idiosyncrasies. Like those intent on exploring the sertões who preceded him, he made much of Brazil's bandeirante past. In doing so at the turn of the nineteenth century, he epitomized the gradual transformation of this legacy into myth. He construed his study of rocks, minerals, the earth, and its landforms as an extension of the colony's long history of exploration, conquest, mining, and territorial incorporation, a history rendered in heroic terms. He spoke of the western sertões as though they lay outside the captaincy, beyond the empire's reach, empty of colonists, unexploited by miners loyal to the sovereign crown.[3] He believed scientific progress and imperial prosperity would be simultaneously advanced in the pursuit of backcountry conquests, secured by opening "bandeira routes" with which "the Lusitanian throne elevates and sturdies itself."[4]

Like the bandeirantes of old, or at least like their incarnations in his imagination, he emphasized the arduous crossing of a forbidding wilderness and the promise of mineral strikes that inspired his quest. As the captaincy's leading authority on the formation, classification, utilization, and regional distribution of minerals, he considered himself uniquely qualified to help restore mining to the central place it merited. "It is left to me above all to discover and examine more lands than we have yet seen and

FIGURE 7.1. En route to the western backlands, travelers rounded the southern end of the Espinhaço Mountains. Source: Rugendas, *Voyage pittoresque*. Courtesy of the Biblioteca Nacional, Rio de Janeiro.

examined," he wrote. "Immense places still exist on which human feet have not trodden."[5] These realms must be cleared of subhuman and nonhuman foes impeding progress. "Already the ugly monsters, already the indomitable people, who inhabit these places withdraw and, what is more, leave us these new and extremely fertile lands, which will be the source of new farming and mining operations and of new riches for the state."[6] Such language inescapably tied Couto's ambitions to a valiant past. The work of the natural historian became the latest chapter in the great epic of Portuguese imperial expansion. Mineralogy became the science of new conquests.

Couto was not alone in linking inland exploration in Minas Gerais to future prosperity. Distrustful government ministers in Lisbon might blame the mining sector's decline on smugglers, labor shortages, the indolence of the poor, or a feckless local elite. By contrast, Brazilian-born literati like Couto pressed for greater state initiative and royal incentives to spur a renewal of the conquering spirit. Attempting to stir collective historical memory, they called on the crown to reinvigorate the backcountry energies of a bygone era, a spirit of exploration that had resulted in the discovery of the region's great gold and diamond reserves.[7] Born in the captaincy of São Paulo, José Bonifácio de Andrada e Silva became professor of mineralogy and metallurgy at the University of Coimbra and intendant of mines and metals in Portugal. Writing from Lisbon, the future ideologue of Brazilian independence likewise stressed the historical import of the bandeirantes. "In a word, almost the whole of the interior of Brazil, with its immense riches, would have been still unknown but for them. The metropolis at present enjoys the fruit of their eccentric activity and hazardous discoveries. Constantly with their arms in their hands to defend themselves against the savages, in the midst of impenetrable forests and solitary wastes, exposed for . . . years to famine and the inclemency of the seasons, they overcame every obstacle: nothing could check their unconquerable spirit."[8] Extolling the economic potential of exploring the sertão in 1798, the Minas-born educator, poet, and diplomat José Eloi Ottoni prophesied the discovery of riches surpassing all of the gold and diamonds previously extracted from Minas Gerais. "The greatest treasures are yet to be discovered," he wrote. Like Couto, linking the fervor of former explorers to desired reform, he called on the crown to encourage a new generation of "*bandeiristas*" [sic] to enter the sertões in search of gold. He advocated "stimulating the project of making new discoveries by means of favors, privileges, and grants," which would inspire those "inflamed by patriotic zeal." Their efforts, he believed, would usher in of a new era of unprecedented prosperity.[9]

In Minas Gerais no memorialist outdid Couto in making explicit the desire to meld the bandeirante ethos, the Enlightenment spirit of commercial reform, and the scientific impulse to study nature. No other intellectual combined these discursive strands in a form that had greater implications for the troubled emergence of science as a realm of knowledge and praxis in the colony. The consequences for Couto's account of his voyage to the west are evident from its first pages. The epigraph he chose, drawn from Virgil's *Georgics*, left little doubt about the message he wished to convey to Lisbon. Translated from the Latin, it read, "In this rich land / Deep veins of silver show, and ores for brass, / With lavish gold." With these lines Virgil extolled what one classicist has called the "patriotic regeneration" that impelled the territorial expansion of imperial Rome.[10] Couto believed the greatness of the Portuguese Empire could similarly be restored.

For Couto the policy of limiting access to the sertão, for fear of unsupervised mining and contraband, no longer made sense. Concerns about smuggling had originally prompted this confining wariness. But smuggling, he believed, was "inevitable," considering the ease with which contraband moved through the captaincy's backlands, "so vast and impracticable to guard."[11] Like other reformers he wished the crown to shed its draconian controls, which were impeding commercial development. The state, "as the foremost father of families," should assume its paternal duty, valorizing the most far-flung corners of Portuguese America. It should "force nature, compelling her to give that which she wants to refuse to men, all the better to lay hold of advantageous portions of lands so fertile and so extensive."[12] As in much colonialist discourse, masculinist metaphors proliferated.

In keeping with the bandeirante tradition, Couto presented the narrative of his 1800–1801 expedition "in the manner of an itinerary" (*à maneira de itinerário*), as its subtitle asserted. Doing so was another way in which he tapped into the bandeirante peripatetic tradition, adopting a form whose resonances would have been unmistakable for the royal officials who read his report. Although the literary technique suited his purposes as a voyager, it also reflected sheer artifice. The account unfolded as a diary in which daily movement along the trail led the reader not only deeper into the sertão but nearer to the fulfillment of Couto's promised contribution as a trained naturalist: objective validation of the alleged diamond deposits. Close analysis of the manuscript, however, reveals that the daily textual divisions establishing the travelogue conceit were imposed after the fact. Evidently, Couto kept some sort of daily field notes on his journey, but in the finished manuscript his observations along the trail were interspersed with and subordinated to material that could only have been written on his return. Back in Tejuco he could consult reference works in his extensive private library, which he frequently cited; assay soils, rocks, metals, and gems collected en route in his personal laboratory; reflect on the import of the mission's findings; reconcile his observations with those advanced two years earlier in his 1799 memorial; and devise final recommendations for the prince regent, to whom he dedicated the text. Indeed, there are stages of the narrative, spanning weeks at a time, during which Couto drops the format of the journal entry entirely. Conversely, there are passages crafted as daily entries in which he interrupts his narration of the journey with long passages concerning philosophical, political, economic, and social matters, obviously written either before or after the fact.

The entry for the seventh day of travel out of Tejuco offers a telling example. It began, "I continued my march, which extended over eight leagues, until Vila Rica. As soon as I left . . . I began observing along the road many specimens of copper, which continued to become more abundant until a place called Agua Quente, a distance of half a league from [the town of] Catas Altas. Here the extent of copper is immense." Couto proceeded to describe the route, the settlements observed along the way, the topography, the flora and fauna, and something of the history of the area traversed. He then interrupted his own account of the day's journey with a digression that dwarfed the rest of the entry. He subtitled the long aside "Considerations Concerning the Two Most Important Classes of Settlers in This Captaincy, Which Are Those of Miners and Farmers, and the Manner by Which to Animate Them."[13] Such juxtapositions typified Couto's eclectic approach, and they reflected his times. He had learned his craft during an era when "neither natural history nor the power dynamics shaping New World colonialism operated in a vacuum," writes one historian. "The classifications that underpinned early modern systems of knowledge in the Atlantic world embraced both plants and people and reflected a yearning for order that transcended any division between science and statecraft."[14]

Couto's narrative leaped from mundane trailside observations to sweeping calls for state intervention, insisting that a renewed push into the backlands would "fill the coffers of the state."[15] At one point his "considerations" on animating miners elicited a prayerlike earnestness as he urged more favorable policies for the region's miners, including the abolition of the royal fifth, the steep tax on gold production. Eliminating this levy would promote greater investment in mining by law-abiding vassals, reversing the sector's decline. "My Lord," he wrote, pleading with the monarch to attend to local needs, "lower your eyes upon the most precious, the most faithful, and the most innocent lot of people who inhabit these, your sertões. Cast your eyes over these, your rich and vast dominions, over these proud hills riven with caverns. . . . Your name, like that of an angel savior, will sound above the blare of these waterwheels, these carts, these handspikes; will thunder from cavern to cavern; will rend the air and ascend to the Heavens."[16] In light of such ecstatic yearning, it is perhaps no wonder that his descriptions of the mining district's natural resources displayed as much activist passion as they did rationalist prudence.[17]

Although the search for diamonds was Couto's primary objective on his journey west, his interest in copper along the way was also insistent and revealing. Should the promise of precious gems prove illusive, Couto could fall back on this less rarified source of mineral wealth as a new means to engage imperial dynamism. On just the second day of his journey, he mused that gold, silver, and diamonds, which had formerly constituted the Americas' greatest wealth, were soon to be joined by copper, which he hailed as the "new perfect metal." In his earlier memorial of 1799, he had mistaken copper deposits for iron. The abundance of the metal had contributed to his error, he explained in the later expedition report, given that deposits of this magnitude had never before been encountered. The European naturalists he relied on as authorities had dismissed the possibility of such deposits, both in their extent and their location. He acknowledged that his own rushed experiments had contributed to initial miscalculation. In passages revised in the wake of laboratory experiments conducted after his journey to the west, he described observing "entire mountains" of exposed copper, gray in color and unadulterated by any other soil or mineral. By the fourth day of the journey, presumably as the purity of the ore increased, red copper replaced the gray, glowing as the sun rose. By the seventh day, he wrote, "All of the land is reddish, either lighter or darker," marveling at the colors with which "the ochre of copper tinges all of the land's surface." If he had once thought he was seeing iron, he could scarcely be blamed. Even the great Swedish chemist and mineralogist Johan Gottschalk Wallerius, whom Couto cited, had noted the difficulties of distinguishing the two substances.[18]

The only problem with Couto's observations in these passages is that they were dead wrong. He was not discovering copper. He was mistaking it for iron. His findings had been accurate in the 1799 text, mistaken in his 1801 memorial, despite his more thorough experiments. A similar error occurred a few years later, when he became convinced that Minas Gerais contained massive cobalt deposits. That discovery launched the mineralogist into excited predictions that Minas Gerais would compete with other regions of the world for dominance in supplying cobalt's famed blue pigments.[19] Again Couto had misidentified his specimens, which further tests in Portugal proved, once more, to be iron. The episode led José Bonifácio, the royal mining advisor, to ridicule Couto, albeit affectionately. Then in his mid-fifties, Couto was a mere "boy," the professor wrote. He was hardworking and zealous, but not to be taken seriously as a naturalist, even if some of his findings might still prove useful to the state. Over the years, José Bonifácio had examined four separate specimen shipments sent from the Diamond District to Lisbon by Couto. In each case the mineralogist from Tejuco had misidentified some if not all of the samples.[20] Historians of science have been more charitable, noting that, as one of the colony's first mineralogists, Couto lacked reagents and laboratory equipment necessary to conduct accurate experiments.[21]

It is hard to escape the conclusion, however, that the flaws in Couto's science also derived from his willingness to skew his analysis to accord with his visions of personal and imperial grandeur. This would come as no surprise. Many Brazilian naturalists of his generation, subject to the same conflicts between sober fieldwork and state patronage, including appointments to prestigious offices, cut short or otherwise compromised their investigations to appeal to royal sponsors and advance their careers. Maintaining the pact between colonial and metropolitan elites that preserved transatlantic loyalties, they sacrificed sustained, clear-eyed scientific investigation.[22] In addition to the truths his descriptions and analysis revealed, Couto's account served as a vehicle for his personal advancement and favor-seeking for himself and family members. For example, in a letter accompanying a shipment of Couto's specimens to Lisbon, Governor Lorena recommended that the mineralogist be rewarded for his investigations with promotion to the post of militia cavalry coronel. The governor later backed Couto in his quest to be honored with induction into the prestigious Order of Christ.[23] The mineralogist made this mutually reinforcing exchange of information for royal favor all but explicit when dedicating his memorial on cobalt to the prince regent: "Behold, Lord, in a short while not a few discoveries made in mineralogy, made only by your command, and owed to you, discoveries of interest to the sciences and arts, will one day be so many sources of wealth for the state."[24] On such ground, elevated yet transactional, where the crown's beneficence could make or break a career, copper and cobalt were sure to capture the prince's attention in ways that mere iron never would—diamonds even more so.

### Fieldwork and Its Discontents

The project sparked by Isidoro's massive diamond offering entailed more than the urgent organization of yet another expedition to the western sertão. It again embroiled the captaincy government in the decades-long policy struggle over whether to focus on barring access to the zone or opening it up for state-supervised mining if not settlement. Governor Lorena's decision to deploy the expedition demonstrated the evolving official view: the first step toward resolving the status of this expanse of unsupervised territory must be to assert the crown's sovereignty over it. The participation of the Coimbra-trained savant, he hoped, would make this the venture that determined, once and for all, "the utility that the state can still expect from this same country."[25]

After Couto traveled from Tejuco to Vila Rica, the party set out from the captaincy capital in late April 1800, planning to rendezvous with Isidoro and his associates along the west bank of the São Francisco River. Advancing toward this meeting point, passing through ever more thinly settled lands, Couto reflected on the misery besetting colonists in this portion of the captaincy, now that mining's glory days had passed. Passing from hamlet to hamlet, shocked at the "extreme decadence" of the region, he witnessed "everything in ruins, every place depopulated." Left in the wake of this economic catastrophe were a "people of degenerate customs, themselves or their parents once slaves, who do not work because they judge this fitting only for slavery." These "people of color," he continued, "serve only as a weight on the state, living by theft and alms."[26]

Hardened by the prejudice pervasive among the region's leading families, the mineralogist was not disposed to a favorable view of the garimpeiros he would soon encounter. From Vila Rica it took fifteen days, traversing the wooded grasslands of the cerrado on horseback, to reach the appointed rendezvous location. Nine days more elapsed waiting for Isidoro and his party to appear. When the garimpeiros finally arrived, Couto did not hide his contempt. The company consisted of "a multitude of 60 to 70 individuals," he wrote, "a very motley blend of different colors, including whites, mulattos, cabras, and blacks, all of the lowermost sort, and with such customs as required by their wretched and unhappy way of life."[27]

Isidoro's adult son Bento was at his father's side, and the pair was not the only family unit. Intendant Beltrão, the crown's fiscal representative, recoiled at what he described as an assemblage of "all colors and both sexes." Without providing details, he repeatedly noted the families and children of the male garimpeiros joining the expedition.[28] This observation was unusual. As the mission's natural historian charged with recording its every detail, Couto neglected even to mention the women and children among the garimpeiros. Prospector cadres were—and still are—almost always portrayed as associations of men. A paucity of scholarship on these small-stakes miners means that we know less than we might about their social composition. Their habit of operating beyond the colonial state's ability to describe and document them, except in pejorative and punitive terms, contributes to our ignorance.

After the initial decades of the gold and diamond rush, when young males, both free and enslaved, disproportionately flooded the region's mining camps, a highly skewed sexual imbalance gradually gave way to a more demographically stable society centered on nuclear and extended families. Critical to the maintenance of the mining economy, women of African descent toiled as fieldworkers, food producers, vendors, peddlers, cooks, seamstresses, laundresses, sex workers, domestic laborers, wet nurses, and childcare providers. In the primary mining camps, the triumvirate of enslaver, church, and patrimonial state oversaw sexually divided labor and legal regimes. To date, little evidence has surfaced to suggest widespread participation of women in the work of excavation, panning, sluicing, and sifting.[29]

Next to nothing is known about the presence in the sertões of female prospectors, *garimpeiras*. Their numbers were certainly reduced, not least because remote mining sites, even late in the colonial period, tended cyclically to replicate the gender imbalances of the early decades of the mining boom.[30] Yet far away from established population centers, it is conceivable that females, though fewer in absolute numbers, more commonly assisted in the physically demanding work of placer mining. Small-scale garimpeiro labor tended to be organized around kin and informal associations of the kind Intendant Beltrão observed at the rendezvous point. While inferences across centuries are always risky, researchers have noted the presence of women and children in more recent prospecting operations in the interior. One scholar found impoverished men predominant in the exploration for new mineral strikes in the Brazilian Amazon. They also tend to be the earliest to migrate great distances to exploit them. But women quickly follow, gathering at secondary deposits, in some cases taking over the manual tasks of *batear* (panning for gold) and *requiar* (collecting mineral-bearing gravel). Children often work at their sides.[31]

In and around Diamantina, the renamed Tejuco, where low-level prospecting continues to this day and hardware stores sell the pans, picks, and other basic equipment necessary to outfit individual garimpeiros,

FIGURE 7.2. Free and enslaved women labored in a full range of occupations essential to the mining economy. Source: Carlos Julião, [Negras vendedoras de rua], late 18th century, BNRJ, SI, C.I,2,8. Courtesy of the Biblioteca Nacional, Rio de Janeiro.

preconceptions prevail regarding the presence of female miners in the past. Claiming descent from generations of garimpeiros, the prospector and guide Belmiro Nascimento explained when interviewed that it was always considered "bad luck" for male prospectors to have women near their diggings.[32] But his account contradicts the popular wisdom of male miners in the eighteenth century, when it was in fact considered good luck to search for gold in the company of enslaved women, specifically those from the Mina Coast, the embarkation point for captives seized in or transshipped from what is now Ghana. These women's technical know-how, acquired from gold mining in the west African interior, is now thought to be the source of what was once considered a colonial superstition. Enslaved men from the Mina Coast seem to have been prized for the same reason.[33]

Notwithstanding Couto's lack of interest in the female garimpeiras—and, for that matter, in the males who did not serve as his primary interlocutors—the mineralogist closely observed Isidoro. Described as a charismatic pardo, over fifty years of age, he cut a commanding figure. His voice and gestures were enough to sway those who followed him. He uttered "very few words," but when he did speak his manner was "respectful, soft, and courteous." Yet he was "artful and shrewd," his "endowments lending him the prerogative to always dominate great swarms of such people." Simultaneously impressed and suspicious, Couto would become increasingly wary as the journey progressed. An intimation of what was to come, this initial character sketch reminds us how careful we must be as we strive to understand the Black leader and his followers, considering that all descriptions of their conduct reach us from the pens of white elites.[34]

Beyond the São Francisco River crossing, Isidoro took over as the expedition guide. Behind him trudged the combined party: the six or seven dozen garimpeiros, the thirty-odd soldiers and their officers, an unspecified number of enslaved porters and miners, the intendant, and the mineralogist. A single mention of an expedition chaplain marks the sources, a sign perhaps of the religious impulse losing ground to scientific practice. The party set out in mid-May for the site of the purported diamond strikes, the leaders on horseback, the others on foot, and their baggage train stretched out along the trail. In an unmistakable reference to the racial composition of the garimpeiros and foot soldiers, Couto described the assemblage as a "long cordon blackening the verdure of the meadows." To the west, under a blue sky, the low mountains lying in the direction of the captaincy of Goiás came into view. It was toward this internal frontier and captaincy borderland that the expedition now headed.[35]

As with other portions of his text that chronicled the troop's overland progress, Couto presented this segment as a diary, accounting daily for distances traveled, natural features observed, rivers crossed, ascents and descents safely managed, and other challenges overcome. The rising and setting sun imposed his narrative structure, but because the whole account was subject to revision and elaboration once the voyage ended in order to impose a more scientific aesthetic on the text, it is unclear exactly when the mineralogist came to suspect that Isidoro and his prospectors were intentionally leading the official party astray. After the entry recounting the first day spent in the garimpeiros' company on the trail, Couto inserted a footnote signaling his impatience to the high-ranking readers he expected to consult his manuscript. He deplored what he already had begun to consider a charade. "The actual route" through this territory, he explained, headed north to a regional military barracks, and from there to more distant frontier garrisons. The most remote of these sites, a guard post known as Ascenção, where they would finally end up after much meandering, could have been reached on established roads. "But our discoverers," Couto scoffed, "wanting to astonish us with the roughness of the trails, and at the same time to lend an air of novelty to their so-called *discoveries*, took us on an unnecessary detour where, moreover, no roads existed, which greatly increased our fatigue and worries." He underlined the word *discoveries* in his manuscript to emphasize his contempt.[36]

This was no minor deviation through a particularly inhospitable stretch of the cerrado. For two weeks, crossing rolling hills and brush-choked plateaus, deciduous forests and grasslands, the party entered an "unknown wilderness, whose harshness, unhealthy airs, and other equally dreadful aspects our guides greatly amplified." By the fourth day, the fading trail had disappeared entirely, forcing workers in the lead to take up machetes and sickles to penetrate the brush. On more than one day, the task of moving the pack animals up and down the steep slopes of high ridges brought the expedition nearly to a standstill. A hazardous crossing of a large stream at the bottom of a ravine shortened the distance covered on one of these days to a mere three kilometers. When the inclines eased and the vegetation opened, mud-covered paths impeded the troop, as did obstacles created by countless creeks that snaked through the watershed in every direction. It was not uncommon to cover more distance circumventing such barriers than advancing in the desired direction. To aid their progress the troop resolved to follow ridgelines whenever possible. But the need to camp near water entailed the additional labor of clearing thickets that flourished along the streams. The work created a cacophony of falling trees and snapping branches as the men swung their machetes to prepare the night's camp. The mineralogist kept his eye on the composition, topography, and the fertility of the land. In one river, the Indaiá, a test excavation produced results that seemed promising enough for Couto to conclude that the river was likely "rich in diamonds."[37]

As experimental digging and panning began, Couto did not specify whether the garimpeiros, unaccustomed to working under the supervision of soldiers and state authorities, had to conform to rules imposed on the gangs of enslaved Africans that labored at the primary placer deposits of the Diamond District. There, captives worked "entirely naked excepting a cloth round their middle, in order that they may not embezzle any of the diamonds."[38] Along the Indaiá River, outnumbered and, it seems, outsmarted—a condition Couto's narrative unintentionally presses on the reader—the official observers more likely adapted to garimpeiro customs. The prospectors on this occasion extracted more than forty gemstones from a small hole opened for the purpose. One weighed three-quarters of an oitava (13.1 ct), another five-eighths of an oitava (10.9 ct). The concurrent search for gold was less encouraging. Even in the stream where they panned the most, the total yield amounted to "very little." Over much of this route, deposits of copper again struck Couto as "immense," although he apparently continued to confuse copper with iron.[39]

After Couto had traveled for more than a week with Isidoro, his men, and their families, the trail again became more apparent. A few days later they passed the Ascenção guard post, which seemed to promise an easier journey ahead on more traveled roads. As if on cue, Isidoro now informed the official party that a new route would have to be opened through dense scrub in order to reach the perfect point for prospecting along the Abaeté River. The expedition halted, waiting for an advance party to cut through the vegetation. Couto again expressed dismay. "A little higher up or a little lower down, we could very easily have approached the said river where it passed through meadows, but our discoverers, who always wanted to show us the most foul and admirable things, purposefully led us into the middle of these forests." It took five days for the trail to be readied, the distance traversed a mere three kilometers.[40]

The place Isidoro and his men chose to pitch camp along the east bank of the broad Abaeté River seemed to the mineralogist as inappropriate as the route they had selected to get there. Couto described it as a "hideous" site, a low depression, noisy because of the rushing waters, overgrown, stifling, lightless. The party spent the next three weeks cutting back the forest and burning brush to make room for a series of makeshift huts. It was not until late June that Isidoro and his men deemed it time to begin their excavations. And then, to Couto's surprise and further consternation, they did not do so at the site that had been cleared with so much tribulation. Instead, they chose a point nearly seven kilometers downriver, requiring the preparation of a second encampment.[41]

A mere two sentences in Couto's account summarized the strenuous but futile efforts of the next three weeks, anticipating greater disappointments that lay ahead. The Abaeté and surrounding rivers, he pronounced, held nothing like the "widespread and continuous" diamond deposits that gave the Tejuco region its fame. The precious stones unearthed by the garimpeiros, despite many days of prospecting, amounted to a "very insignificant" discovery.[42] A scientist's equanimity is evident at this critical juncture in the narrative. At what would seem, up to this point, to have been the moment of his greatest frustration, Couto presented himself as a detached observer of nature. He acknowledged the objective reality of a painstaking but so far fruitless investigation. He resisted, for the moment at least, the exaggerated claims of so many exploration accounts. Doubtless his years as a resident of Tejuco, the Diamond District's epicenter, had accustomed him to a milieu in which fantasies about undiscovered mineral wealth competed with the relentless evidence of declining returns. Gold production in Minas Gerais had peaked no later than 1760; diamond production, somewhat later, by the early 1770s.[43] Metropolitan demands to increase mining revenues had for several decades clashed with the common sense of colonists with firsthand experience of exhausted alluvial deposits, realists who believed that mining's boom years would not return and that alternatives must be sought in other places or other activities. Like many members of the Minas elite, Couto reconciled this tension in his own thinking by seeking a middle ground. He was eager to please if not parrot the crown and thereby cultivate its support for his scientific investigations. Yet he was more aware than most, because of his training and direct experience, of the failure of mining activity in its current state to undergird the regional and imperial economies as it once had.[44] Rather than express dismay that the venture into the backlands had thus far failed to fulfill royal expectations, Couto concentrated on crafting as dispassionate an account as he could muster, but one that continuously proposed alternatives to Lisbon's relentless fixation on gold and diamonds.

Before the full expression of this compromise coalesced in the final draft of his memorial, however, Couto would have to proceed still farther under the now wholly unwelcome tutelage of the garimpeiros, an imperial investigator at the mercy of his guides. After weeks of unsuccessful prospecting, Isidoro announced the time had come to head deeper into the sertão, where the search would turn from diamonds to gold and silver, which he again promised would be found in abundance. This vow professed he was as confident as ever, but his actions suggested otherwise. Having apparently reached the limits of his own patience, he delegated leadership of the next stage of the voyage to his son Bento. Couto described Bento as "the opposite of his father, abundant in words, always talking tough, and with none of the fineness of spirit and shrewdness" evident in Isidoro. But like his father, Bento insisted that a valuable discovery lay ahead. The journey that followed, he promised, would reveal "immense wealth," resulting in the ultimate satisfaction of the entire party. The garrulous young garimpeiro warned that they would have to proceed with utmost caution, that the sertões they would now cross were the most rugged yet encountered. The party would enter lands "infested" by "wild Indians and quilombos of runaway slaves." They would cross high peaks and expanses devoid of game, and their "hunger would be cruel."

Couto was unmoved. His growing experience of his informants had by now trained him to pay little heed to such admonitions. "We did not give much credit to these bad omens," the mineralogist wrote, as he described the mid-July departure of a much-reduced party, including Bento, himself, and fourteen soldiers and slaves.[45] Given the many disappointments of the past weeks, the naturalist gave just as little credit to Bento's pledge that a fabulous discovery would in the end justify the undertaking. Yet, as if unable to admit total defeat, the party set off down the Abaeté River, heading north in three canoes. The many rapids along the river threatened to shatter the vessels.

The disciplined Couto continued to focus on his investigations—or at least he later crafted a manuscript that accentuated such a focus. He shifted from impatient stories of slow progress along a route he doubted to austere notes befitting his university training. For instance, he interrupted his daily narrative to insert a specimen inventory. It was structured according to a now-abandoned taxonomic system taught at the University of Coimbra. The system combined two contrasting approaches. The first, based on the botanical classifications of Carl Linnaeus, emphasized the external properties of minerals and metals; the second, favored by Linnaeus's Swedish contemporaries, Wallerius and his student Torbern Olaf Bergman, extended beyond such properties as color, form, taste, and smell to focus on chemical composition.[46]

Couto classified the rocks and minerals he collected along the river by their "genera" and "species," as in the following excerpt:

| | |
|---|---|
| *Spatum* | *compactum.* |
| | *calcarium.* |
| *Talcum* | *lamellare*: the greater part of the river's gravel is formed of fragments of this rock, which is dominant in this region. It is gray in color, more or less dark: the pebbles, even when rolled by the waters, remain always flat, polished, and rounded along their edges. |
| *Quartzum* | *hyalinum*: imperfect crystals. |
| | *lacteum, opacum*: pebbles. |
| | *nobile*: water drops. |
| *Silex* | *pyromachus*: shotgun stones. |
| | *calcedonius* [*sic*]: milk stones, some quite transparent and clear: agates.[47] |

This list continued for another nine "genera" and accompanying "species." Translated from the Latin to correspond to what at the time were the English equivalents, the genus *Spar* (spatum) appeared in two species, subdiaphanous compact (compactum) and calcareous spar (calcarium); soap-rock (talcum) in a single species, gray plated soap-rock (lamellare); quartz (quartzum) in four species, pellucid rock (hyalinum), milky (lacteum), opaque (opacum), and pebble quartz (nobile); and flint (silex) in two species, gun flint (pyromachus) and chalcedony (chalcedonius).[48] In this fashion Couto identified the minerals he later assembled for shipment to Lisbon, occasionally adding further descriptive commentary.

Wherever possible Couto continued to search for diamonds and other valuable minerals. At one site, he uncovered three small diamonds. After descending the Abaeté River for eleven days, expedition members spied the mouth of a small tributary Bento had been seeking, a stream too shallow and broken with falls to ascend in canoes. Trekking up its banks several kilometers, the men selected a spot at Bento's urging to begin their excavations in earnest. After a half-day's labor, with eight men digging, panning, and sifting, they located nothing noteworthy. "Not a flake did we see of gold, and only four or five very tiny [flakes] of platinum," wrote

Couto. As for gemstones, they found fragments of red and yellow crystals but not a single diamond.[49]

What was most striking at this pivotal point in the voyage, however, was the young guide's behavior. At precisely the moment Bento might have been expected to sink a shovel into the ground and reveal glimmering gems or gold-laced gravel, he threw himself down and "remained," wrote Couto, "for the entire time that we were working, stretched out on the ground beneath a leafy thicket without paying the least attention to whether the riches he had promised were verified or not." While the crew labored, he lay about bellowing love songs, "completely out of tune, gullet opened wide." His melodies, Couto marveled, "concerned him more than tending to the fulfillment of his promises." Eventually Bento tired of his diversions. At this point he was the first to conclude that the effort was in vain, that food was running low, and that they should return to their base camp as quickly as possible. Trudging back to their canoes, the men traveled a little farther downriver and then spent several days "breaking through the bush and opening a trail at times with the force of our own bodies."[50]

Apart from the exasperation evident in these passages, Couto did not comment further on Bento's behavior. Like his father, albeit with a bluster Isidoro did not share, Bento had maintained until the moment of ultimate resignation that he possessed exclusive and specific knowledge concerning the whereabouts of abundant mineral wealth. Also like his father, he led the crown's representatives on what can only be judged a fool's errand. We are left to speculate about his motivation as we imagine him sprawled out and singing in his leafy thicket. What passed through the young prospector's mind as he crooned his melodies of unrequited love and as, hour after hour, he watched the others laboring in the sun, turning up nothing? His behavior suggested he was not at all surprised by the final failure to unearth buried treasure. Yet all along he had assured the official party that he was leading them toward a great discovery. He had lied, we might reasonably conclude, or at least counted on luck to make him honest. In the end he realized the game was up. The temptation of providing the backcountry intelligence that officials most wished to hear proved irresistible, even if doing so meant deceiving those he guided as long as possible in hopes of discovering something, anything. After all, the right story embraced by the right person, bearing fruit at the right time, promised to alter his life, rescuing him from the margins of respectability. Bento's social position may have differentiated him from the patronage-seeking savant who scorned him, but similar motives and strategies shaped their itinerant tales.

Another possibility is that, rather than lie, Isidoro, Bento, and their fellow garimpeiros told the truth to the extent that it did not undermine their proprietary interests. The long history of official attempts to crack down on illicit mining by small-stakes prospectors in Minas Gerais convinced authorities that there was every reason to take these men seriously. For decades reports of diamond strikes in the western sertões had attracted official interest. Having originally presented his impressive diamond to the governor, Isidoro provided the hard evidence necessary to justify organizing what was but the latest in a series of expeditions to set out in search of the supposed deposits from which it came. As the explorers advanced, they had noticed the upturned earth that further substantiated rumors of profitable, if unsupervised, mining throughout the region. As the expedition entered lands the garimpeiros knew better than anyone, perhaps they sought to mete out the truth in such a way that would garner rewards without revealing the primary sources of their earnings from illicit mining. As long and as convincingly as possible, perhaps they prolonged the theatrics of doing the state's bidding, even leading officials to sites they knew to contain only meager gold and diamond deposits. But they had no intention of revealing the locations of their most productive diggings. If this was their strategy, they calculated that they could make more from their clandestine prospecting than from any recompense they might reap from the crown.

Without underestimating the hardships of their lives, it is conceivable that some also preferred the modest freedoms of an existence on the fringes of a colonial society in which most poor men and women of color found their geographic and social mobility sharply curtailed. In one form or another, to preserve what they most valued, perhaps they were willing to suffer the consequences of being ostracized as liars and charlatans. To lead officials to the source of their wealth, to relinquish their existence as prospectors operating beyond the empire's enforcement capabilities, would be to throw their futures into even greater doubt. Some might earn prizes for their aid as discoverers, informants, guides, and laborers. But many others might end up losing the material source of their sustenance and their hard-earned if always constrained autonomy. For their part Isidoro and Bento might surrender more than they thought reasonable of the knowledge and consequent power that made them leaders of the rough-hewn backcountry itinerants who followed them. Evocative of such a calculus is a work song still chanted, according to a local folklorist, by Black miners in northeastern Minas Gerais in the early twentieth century. A boy in the song shouts to his father that he has discovered a diamond; the father admonishes him to hide the stone and keep quiet.[51]

Although many weeks of travel lay ahead, including additional detours over demanding terrain to investigate further tales of rich deposits of diamonds, gold, and platinum, Bento's anticlimactic acquiescence marks a turning point in the exploration chronicle. For the rest of the journey, the garimpeiros fade from view. Couto continued to reflect on their generalized presence in the region, but they all but ceased to merit his commentary as active participants in his quest. Indeed, from this point forward, their absence suggests that the official party became so disenchanted with their prospector guides that they left most or all of them behind. Isidoro and his son disappear from the narrative, and they largely vanish from the historical record, the father to be rehabilitated decades later as a rebellious hero. In the end Couto would classify the garimpeiros as individuals willing to deceive, cheat, rob, and even kill each other in their desperate pursuit of buried riches.[52]

The naturalist did not elaborate further on his evident conviction that the garimpeiros had conned the government. His reticence on this point is understandable. To denounce the father, son, and their fellow prospectors as frauds was to expose the captaincy governor as their dupe. To admit that the entire venture had been a waste of time, manpower, and royal funds was to relinquish any hope of having contributed to the knowledge of nature's bounties, which might benefit the empire while distinguishing him in the eyes of higher authorities. In this inclination he had much in common with his garimpeiro guides, notwithstanding his training in enlightened modes of verification. Thus, nearing the end of his journey, atop a ridgeline in the Espinhaço Mountains, he would look west to the "smoky and smooth" horizon, imagine the sertão as a "vast ocean," and hone his message. "A thousand reflections fed the tumult of my spirit!" he thought two days later, setting eyes on his natal Tejuco for the first time in nearly ten months. Cloistered in his library in the months that followed, transforming his field notes into a polished manuscript for his monarch, he would resolve to emphasize possibilities over practical realities, ratifying imperial yearnings for readily exploitable diamonds, despite all evidence to the contrary.[53]

### Taking Stock, Shifting Stories

Governor Lorena was equally committed to casting the expedition as a success. Immediately upon its return from the backlands to the captaincy capital, before Couto proceeded to Tejuco, Lorena ordered a declaration to this effect drawn up, under his direct supervision, before members of the Board of Royal Finance (Junta da Real Fazenda), the captaincy's highest fiscal organ. He brought Beltrão, Couto, and the expedition's military officers before the board. Isidoro, proudly bearing his militia title, Captain of the Free Colored Regiment of Vila Rica, was also present. Explaining how leadership of the expedition had been organized in the field, the governor pronounced that Isidoro had served not only as guide but also as "director" of all exploratory excavations.

The gathered men were required to respond to three questions, worded to achieve the desired effect. They were asked, first, whether the region explored was sufficiently rich in diamonds to warrant further mining that would prove of "great utility to the royal patrimony"; second, whether adequate measures had been taken to prevent falsifying the records of the expedition, misappropriating its funds, and absconding with any diamonds; third, whether the government troops assigned to the mission had acquitted themselves honorably in a way befitting the monarch. Everyone present registered their assent to each query, with their sole qualification being that the excavations conducted had been of necessity cursory, given limited time and resources. The officials also tallied the diamonds collected during the months spent wandering the sertão. They totaled seventy-five stones of various sizes, together weighing just over 5 1/2 oitavas (96.3 ct).[54] To place this sum in context, these diamonds would probably have been included in the shipment from Rio de Janeiro to Lisbon on the royal fleet scheduled for late 1801. This shipment, which arrived late, stirring great concern in the imperial capital, contained diamonds weighing 4,813 oitavas (84,227.5 ct). In other words the expedition diamonds would have accounted for a mere tenth of 1 percent of that single delivery.[55]

More than a year later, Governor Lorena was still trying to make the case to Lisbon that the results were more significant than they seemed. He acknowledged to the secretary of state that the total haul in precious stones was in itself unimpressive. To offset this disappointing reality, he stressed the high quality of the individual stones and the poor quality of the labor force assembled to unearth them. An inadequate number of garimpeiros under Isidoro's authority and their "lack of aptitude" had to be taken into consideration. Making this argument, the governor openly contradicted his original contention that the garimpeiros, considering their unequalled knowledge of the backlands, were precisely the men best suited to find diamonds in the region. Now he insisted that greater wealth would have been uncovered had the party been able to establish more permanent diggings supported by a greater number of laborers, greater know-how, and greater funding.[56]

By contrast, in an unusually candid letter to a confidant and key member of the secretary of state's staff, the nominal leader of the expedition, Intendant Beltrão, described the entire journey as a fiasco and Isidoro as an "impostor."[57] The intendant's attack on the credibility of the operation represented not just an opposing view but a mobilization of power from an arm of the state functioning as a bureaucratic counterweight to the enormous personal authority of the governor. By law, intendants answered not to the captaincy governor but to one of two general intendants based in Rio de Janeiro and Salvador. As the official selected by the crown to direct the intendancy based in the mining town and judicial district (*comarca*) of

Sabará, Beltrão administered one of the captaincy's most important fiscal jurisdictions. Its enormous territory ranged from the heart of the primary mining zone to the captaincy's western border, a boundary whose location would not be fully resolved until long after the colonial period ended. The relative administrative independence of the post, and the fact that he was newly arrived in Minas Gerais, help explain the intendant's willingness to express his unencumbered criticism to his confidant in Lisbon. That the governor remained unaware Beltrão had called his competence into question seems clear from the fact that he continued to praise the intendant's leadership.[58]

Beltrão wrote that he had been selected to lead the expedition before taking up his new post and without being consulted. Several other candidates already residing in the captaincy had refused the commission. They were either wary of the intelligence on which it was based because of the suspect character of the prospector who delivered it, or they were fearful of the dangers of the backlands, which Isidoro exaggerated. Beltrão believed he had been given the assignment because, still aboard ship crossing the Atlantic, he could not say no and was not yet aware of Isidoro's misdeeds. Government soldiers, he had since learned, had chased the garimpeiros out of the Diamond District, where they engaged in "continuous thefts." In flight, they invaded the western region he was charged with administering. The captaincy's border with Goiás proved no barrier to their crimes, as they "continued to make their furtive forays" in both jurisdictions, taking advantage of the uncertain geographic limits of each. In the most distant reaches of the captaincy where they circulated, they were to blame for "immense thefts" and "many deaths," as they pursued their illicit extraction of gemstones. All attempts to control them had proven unsuccessful.[59]

Isidoro, Beltrão was convinced, did in fact have a hand in the killing of the patrol commander for which he stood accused and sought to be pardoned. The intendant also hinted Isidoro had managed to bribe soldiers as he was about to be captured, presumably offering them illegal diamonds. Whether or not this was the case, soldiers connected with the discovery of any major diamond deposit, or even a single large stone, could expect to be rewarded by the crown, and thus their interactions with garimpeiros were always suspect.⁶⁰ When the accused approached Governor Lorena, he knew he could count on powerful protectors to avoid arrest. His promise to reveal the source of more diamonds like the one he delivered to the governor was nothing but a ruse to "escape the gallows." Without any attempt to determine the veracity of Isidoro's claim, the governor had precipitously decided to mount what would prove to be a costly and pointless expedition. Further compromising the mission, the commander of the soldiers assigned to it was the same officer Beltrão suspected of colluding with Isidoro instead of capturing him, an officer who made his contempt for the intendant evident from the outset.⁶¹

Beltrão underlined what struck him as the absurdity of setting out for an unknown destination guided by an untrustworthy military commander and criminal prospectors. When queried, none of the garimpeiros would inform Beltrão where precisely they were leading the party. Like Couto, he complained of the hardships of the trail and noted the presence of existing military outposts. It struck Beltrão as ludicrous that the garimpeiros had led them to an area known for years to contain diamond deposits, which is why guards had been posted there in the first place. For Couto and the governor, the modest results of the expedition's excavations suggested the need for a more thoroughgoing approach. For Beltrão, the failures spoke for themselves. For months, pursuing Isidoro's leads, the garimpeiros engaged in the "most sluggish and poorly directed work one can imagine," the intendant wrote his correspondent in Lisbon. The result: a few unimpressive diamonds, and no gold or silver whatsoever. When these initial efforts proved "fruitless," instead of conceding failure, the party extended its excavations to other sites. These tests, too, were "absolutely frustrated."

Beltrão evinced more respect for Couto than for any other member of the expedition. But the naturalist's escapade with Bento to yet another site where riches were promised inspired in the intendant nothing of the expectations for future success the mineralogist still sustained. Couto's tests there had turned up just three small diamonds. Hoping to salvage something from the expedition and to recoup some of its expenses, Beltrão ordered a more extensive excavation at this site, which lasted another two months. The weight of diamonds extracted totaled 3 1/4 oitavas (56.9 ct). One of these uncut diamonds weighed a full oitava (17.5 ct), about half the size of the stone Isidoro had initially presented. The enslaved miner who found it gained his freedom in accordance with customary practice, the cost of reimbursing his master included as an official expense. The rest of the stones were very small. Insignificant quantities of gold and platinum found at the site did not promise to offset the cost of the labor required to extract these metals. In a final stab at making the voyage worthwhile, Beltrão ordered excavations at a location previously mined under the official auspices of the Diamond District administration. Over the course of three weeks, two oitavas (35 ct) of very small stones were pulled from the banks of the Indaiá River before the onset of the rainy season inundated the diggings, making further work impossible.[62]

Despite Beltrão's efforts to economize, the expedition had been expensive. Those participants who were not enslaved, both civilians and soldiers, were paid a daily wage over the course of seven months, including the two months spent marching to and from the western sertões. Apparently, in other words, the large number of prospectors accompanying Isidoro were among those who earned wages, which helps explain their interest in participating. All had to be fed, requiring a large number of rented mules to ferry provisions from distant markets. Beltrão calculated the total allocation for the venture from the royal treasury at nearly 9:000$000, a figure that far surpassed the value of the diamonds extracted.[63] The intendant's calculation of costs was significantly greater than the governor's, who tallied total expenses of 6:525$000, including a stipend for the chaplain, medical care for the expedition members, and the manumission of the enslaved worker rewarded for finding the single large diamond located during the months of labor.[64] Even this lower figure left the venture looking like a questionable exploit.

Notwithstanding the small-stakes prospecting that still attracted garimpeiros to the area, any significant deposits had long since been extracted by the Diamond District administration, Beltrão continued. Widespread evidence of abandoned diggings left no doubt that every other place expedition members explored had been previously worked over by garimpeiros.

FIGURE 7.3. Unlike small-scale prospecting, state-controlled diamond mining depended on significant capital investment and an enslaved workforce. John Mawe, *Travels in the Interior of Brazil* (London: Longman, 1812). Courtesy of the John Carter Brown Library. Licensed under CC-BY-SA 4.0.

Any effort to exploit even less accessible sites in the beds of deep rivers or in their rapids or falls would require a great commitment of skilled labor including carpenters and blacksmiths, and large numbers of slaves. The region's climate was hot and unhealthy, characterized by "pestiferous airs," its "burnt" terrain hostile, and its distance from the nearest cattle herds great enough that provisioning workers would present a constant problem.[65]

Perhaps the only valuable result of this misguided enterprise was a map the intendant ordered made, detailing the area's geographic features. The map depicted rivers, the route taken by the expedition, and the sites excavated. It identified the outer limits of colonial settlement, noting isolated fazendas and guard posts. Based on Couto's observations and replete with a cartouche portraying cherubs admiring treasure chests laden with gems, it also specified the location of presumed deposits of platinum, copper, and lead.

Beltrão viewed the whole "unpleasant and useless journey" as proof not only of Isidoro's and Bento's individual treachery but of a pervasive conspiracy to deceive Lisbon, a conspiracy in which he hinted prominent locals participated. He argued that military detachments in the area served no positive purpose. Soldiers and commanders used theses postings to enrich themselves, exacting bribes from the garimpeiros in exchange for allowing them to continue prospecting, a corrupt practice "scandalously well known." Such was the "theater" in which Isidoro had operated for many years, perpetrating his "thefts, killings, challenges to justice, and other criminal offenses against the law for which he intends to be not only pardoned but even rewarded." The unscrupulous prospector's scheme should be seen as a blatant and outrageous attempt to hoodwink the governor, the royal treasury, and the public. Henceforth, the governor and others should be less gullible, less ready to "believe in only the words and promises of a few black and mulatto garimpeiros." With this unsparing conclusion, theatrical in its own right, the intendant staged his counter-performance, soliloquizing the troubled history of a white elite's skewed understanding of free Black prospectors in a mining economy organized around captive labor.[66]

Beltrão intended his utterly antiheroic assessment of the expedition to be relayed to the prince regent. It presented a stark contrast to the old bandeirante stories and other standard chronicles of backcountry ventures, a gloomy challenge to incautious imperial expansion to the colony's internal frontiers. It serves us as another useful corrective to such tales, highlighting their inflated rhetoric. Couto's narrative mélange of science, social commentary, and reformist prescription may have been marginally more subdued than the usual discovery and conquest narratives. He too heaped criticism on his garimpeiro guides. The Tejuco savant, however, left no doubt about the benefits he believed would accrue to the royal treasury, whether in the form of diamonds, gold, platinum, copper, or cobalt, from further state-supported incursions into the backlands. In an attempt to restrain this buoyant view, Beltrão warned that others might offer the crown an account of the expedition written "with greater eloquence," but no one would report on it "with greater truth."[67] The warning called into question the scientific objectivity of Couto's account and the intelligence it was designed to deliver—ostensibly unbiased findings that were supposed to distinguish this foray into the sertão from those that preceded it.

Couto renamed the region, formerly the Sertões of Abaeté, Nova Lorena Diamantina. This renaming attributed to the governor the exploration and commitment to the future development of a new resource-rich territory. The new map of the area revealed the region's enormous extent. From east to west, it spread from the São Francisco River to the captaincy's border with Goiás; from north to south, from the Paracatu River to the Bambuí River and Campo Grande, the area that had been the focus of government-sponsored exploration beginning in the 1760s.[68] The map and accompanying memorial made this zone legible to a distant monarch, but to what extent did the region end up producing significant wealth in precious stones and metals? Scholars have disagreed. One study asserts, without citing substantiating sources, that Couto's predictions proved accurate and that diamonds "were subsequently exploited by the crown for huge profits." Another concludes that in the nineteenth century "gold and diamonds were no longer encountered in abundance."[69]

The documentary evidence from the years following the expedition favors the second position. From the moment the voyagers returned, the governor admitted that they had come back from the sertão with only a modest collection of stones, more notable for their quality than quantity.[70] Intendant Beltrão disputed even the quality of the gems, and in this assessment Couto conditionally agreed.[71] Perhaps as a result of these inconclusive findings, but surely also because of the deepening crisis in Napoleonic Europe that in 1807 would prompt the royal family's flight from Lisbon to Rio de Janeiro, the crown did not rush to exploit the area's mineral deposits. Once official operations finally began, the difficulties of mining the distant location immediately became evident. Diamond District officials transferred several hundred captive workers, as well as overseers and administrators, to the area to initiate placer mining along the Abaeté and

Indaiá Rivers. When the diamonds extracted failed to offset expenditures, these efforts were quickly abandoned.[72]

In late 1808, responding to the order to shutter the operation, a new captaincy governor, Pedro Maria Xavier Ataíde e Melo, later the Viscount of Condeixa (1803–1810), expressed his "great sorrow" that the crown's ample investment in the region was to be lost. He attributed this unfortunate outcome in part to the memorial authored by Couto and the influence this report had exerted among government officials. Couto remained the site's "leading apologist," the governor continued, but his scientific work was not to be trusted.[73] This pessimistic assessment was reaffirmed by the British naturalist John Mawe. Although he intended to visit the region explored by Couto, illness prevented him from doing so, leaving him to rely on information gathered from officials in Tejuco. From Intendant Câmara, Mawe learned that the area drained by the Abaeté River had "produced many large diamonds, though generally of inferior quality."[74]

Calculations based on government sources must be considered partial, however, because the zone remained particularly prone to contraband. Its vastness, remoteness, inhospitable environment, and the resulting attenuated character of military, judicial, and fiscal oversight meant a great deal occurred that escaped official surveillance. The lackluster results of the expedition and the subsequent abortive crown effort to exploit the region leave open the possibility that its wealth continued to be secreted away by small-stakes prospectors, smugglers of greater means, and even soldiers and other state officials taking advantage of their positions to cheat the royal treasury and enrich themselves and their protectors and patrons. Since the colonial period, local historians have continued to promote versions of this narrative.[75] The trope of criminal elements absconding with the region's resources flourishes to this day.

As with so many other aspects of life in the sertão, the garimpeiros probably knew better than anyone how many diamonds had been found along certain stretches of the area's many streams and rivers. More than eighty years later, in 1885, when a mining engineer retraced Couto's route, seeking to gauge the region's development and prospects, he singled out the gap between the expertise of individual backcountry prospectors and large-scale, state-backed mining projects. Reflecting on the ruins of guard posts abandoned earlier in the century, witnessing small groups of miners still active in the area, he opined, "Only the persistent garimpeiro, stubborn, accustomed to privation, and knowledgeable of every nook and cranny—on the ridges, along the rivers, in the caverns—satisfied always with the meager results of hard work, could eke profits from this kind of mining."[76] Into the twentieth century garimpeiros continued on occasion to unearth huge diamonds along the Abaeté River, some many times larger than the one Isidoro presented to Governor Lorena.[77] These gemstones appeared as products of grueling work, luck, desperation, and backcountry know-how. The garimpeiros' mode of existence ensured that the expertise necessary to locate such diamonds remained among kin and confidants, local day laborers and their stealthy bosses. By definition, the state bureaucracy, the archive, and the historian register only fragments of this knowledge.

Despite the expedition's modest results—or, rather, despite its losses—Couto evaluated its significance with the enthusiasm of a discoverer of new worlds, a conquistador, a bandeirante. The area explored "will one day be a very populous and happy region," yielding the crown "incalculable profits," he insisted, ultimately unrestrained by the sober aesthetic of the scientific training he deployed in service of his monarch. "Diamonds will always be a principal object supporting these inhabitants and the interests of the state." Especially because of its profusion of oversized gemstones, the region would prove more important than the Diamond District itself, which for decades had produced great riches for Portugal. Couto thought it likely that the crown would, as a result, come to "possess the largest and rarest diamonds in the universe." All that was required was for the state to establish an enlightened, rational administration over this distant zone.

Couto had a specific individual in mind who possessed the expertise necessary to direct such an enterprise: himself. The task could never be managed by "men bound by routine"; it demanded "those who have exhausted themselves in the study of nature."[78] The proper management of mineral wealth, along with the preliminary task of gathering reliable information to locate that wealth in the distant backlands, required a new kind of informant, a practitioner of the modern science of mineralogy, Coimbra-trained.

To arrive at this inevitability in Couto's thought need not entail mocking colonial science or its practitioners. It need not return us to the discredited, condescending view according to which all early modern rationalism worth its name emanated from Europe. Historians who have highlighted Couto's contribution are not mistaken. Furtado makes a fair point when she writes that the realities of the colonial compact forced him to employ "skillful rhetoric" to conceal "iconoclastic thoughts," the most daring of which was his call for the abolishment of the royal fifth.[79] Science historian Clarete Paranhos da Silva is also right to maintain that we learn less about a colonial natural historian like Couto by holding him up to an abstract standard of scientific objectivity than we do by contextualizing his science as a quotidian practice, fundamentally shaped by his "here and now," and by recognizing the Portuguese crown's resolve to "seek in science a solution for the problems that presented themselves in that moment."[80] Within and beyond the Portuguese Empire, both in the Americas and Europe, naturalists during this period were motivated less by science's theoretically objectivist foundations than by the drive to achieve mastery over the natural world.[81] The pressures Couto faced as a Brazilian-born savant, as well as the opportunities to be seized, shaped his investigative practice and his findings.

Heir to a heroic view of colonialism's past, proponent of a future reformed by Enlightenment rationality, Couto was bent on producing knowledge that would allow the crown to absorb and exploit territory it possessed but did not control. Like the mineral composites in the metamorphic rocks he collected, these inclinations marbled his persona as a forward-thinking natural philosopher charged with helping reinvigorate the mining economy and with it an unsteady Portuguese Empire. His endeavor hinged, however, on intelligence provided by individuals whose experience departed sharply from the educated elites who grudgingly turned to them for practical guidance. What the crown hoped to learn from its erudite expert depended in turn on what he could glean from backcountry intermediaries. Most of these informants were men of African descent, denigrated, criminalized, and dispossessed by royal officials and privileged vassals. These itinerants sought a means of survival in the sertão. In doing so they stepped outside the law. A few, like Isidoro, were mythologized as rebels, but most are better understood as refugees from a repressive mining economy and administrative edifice founded on the exploitation of enslaved labor. They agreed to join an official operation only in exchange for a daily wage and guaranteed sustenance. They conceded the know-how requested of them only guardedly. The gulf between them and those who sought their secrets hindered the transfer of reliable data from the interior to the metropole. The result was an informational alchemy in which hints and whispers about buried minerals combined in a potent elixir. When imprudently consumed, this tonic destabilized Portugal's drive to expand its imperial domain.

PART 4

# The Good Sense of Cannibals
*Further Dispatches from the Atlantic Forest*

IN THE FINAL DAYS OF NOVEMBER 1807, fleeing Napoleon's Iberian invasion, the Portuguese royal family and its court and retinue, numbering some 10,000 migrants, evacuated Lisbon, sailed across the Atlantic, paused in Salvador, Bahia, and finally disembarked in Rio de Janeiro in March 1808. For the next thirteen years, the colonial capital functioned as the crown's tropical home in exile, the new metropole from which the drive to assert a more potent sovereignty over Portuguese America's immense interior radiated. The sertões ringing Minas Gerais remained a focus of this effort, especially the tropical forest separating the mining heartland from the coast. Earlier efforts to colonize the mountainous backlands between Minas Gerais and Rio de Janeiro intensified and extended to the north, targeting the great forests separating Minas Gerais from the coastal captaincies of Espírito Santo and Bahia. A reprise of earlier reconnaissance methods demonstrated the cyclical, processual nature of internal colonization as it spread to new zones. Although exploration for gold and diamonds continued on a diminished scale, imperial and captaincy authorities now concentrated on opening trade and transportation routes along river valleys to the sea. If adequately surveilled and protected by the state, these routes would promote the flow of taxable commodities into and out of the interior and secure new lands for agricultural development. The area in question, however, was controlled by highly mobile hunters and foragers considered hostile to Portuguese rule. Thus one of the crown's first acts upon arriving in Brazil was to declare war against these forest dwellers, accusing them of cannibalism and other abominations.

Even before the resulting military conflict subsided, a new class of informants arrived to harvest knowledge from these rugged lands and their threatened Indigenous communities. Northern European naturalists, invited by the crown to explore regions from which they previously had been excluded, descended on the coastal forests to pursue botanical, zoological, and ethnological investigations. Their audience, no longer limited to Portuguese authorities, included a wider, non-Lusophone public eager for information about distant places and unfamiliar peoples. Among the most able of these visitors was the German Prince Maximilian Alexander Phillip von Wied-Neuwied who, beginning in 1815, mounted a two-year expedition that culminated in his voyage up the Jequitinhonha River, ultimately reaching the point where it exited northeastern Minas Gerais. Along the river he conducted research at military installations frequented by the Botocudo, the most feared and reviled of the zone's Native occupants. Framing his sojourn as an encounter with Indians still living in their natural state, he minimized to the point of erasure preceding decades of Portuguese and Indigenous interactions. This narrative sleight of hand helped him establish himself as an authority possessing unrivaled knowledge of the Botocudo, while recasting them as exotic primitives and dismissing their demonstrated capability to shape their historical circumstances, even when faced with military conquest.

Chapter 8 examines the transatlantic conjuncture, both political and intellectual, that afforded the German prince the opportunity to conduct his investigations in the Brazilian interior. It then shifts to developments that prompted the declaration of war against the Botocudo, a decisive test of the crown's postrelocation territorializing agenda. Along the upper reaches of the Jequitinhonha River, prolonged exchanges between Luso-Brazilian explorers, soldiers, and the Botocudo resulted in a tense peace, in contrast to the pervasive violence that characterized the conflict elsewhere. When the Botocudo demonstrated themselves amenable to cooperation, frontier officials contested the war footing, calling into question the legitimacy of royal policies that treated the Natives as irredeemable savages. Chapter 9 turns to the German prince's voyage, exploring the consequences of his dismissal of this history. His scientific renown depended on portraying his ethnological fieldwork as unprecedented, even though he conducted it at forts established before his arrival, where interaction with the Botocudo was already a fait accompli and inconceivable without their initiative. Violating grave sites and returning to Europe with a young Botocudo informant he sought to reeducate, the naturalist made a name for himself contributing to a nascent, global anthropological enterprise that, for an international reading public, would reinscribe Brazil's backlands as an abode of problematic, now racially impaired, exotic primitives in desperate need of the promise of European progress. Although modernized, this perspective testified to the crown's ongoing limitations in territorializing its rule, as the colonial era came to an end.

CHAPTER 8

# ANTHROPOPHAGY AND THE BODY POLITIC

DURING THE FIRST QUARTER of the nineteenth century, no region became more critical for testing state-directed efforts to subdue autonomous Indigenous groups and incorporate their lands than the sparsely settled tropical forest standing, now like an unwanted guest, between the colonial capital of Rio de Janeiro, the northeastern sugar plantations of coastal Bahia, and the inland mining, farming, and ranching expanses of Minas Gerais. Colonization efforts concentrated on the river valleys that cut through this area, including the valley carved by the Jequitinhonha River.[1] This valley constituted the major watershed draining northeastern Minas Gerais, descending more than 1,000 km from its source near Tejuco in the Espinhaço Mountains to the coast.

As the state redoubled its campaign for dominion over internal frontiers that remained beyond its reach, an array of new informants became influential.[2] Indigenous guides, translators, and participants in gift exchanges figured among the valley's forest peoples whose perspectives the archives preserve, at least in muted form. Recaptured fugitives returned to slavery and free people of color added their voices, likewise faintly because they reach us almost always by way of government sources. Frontier officials and soldiers secured a more prominent archival presence as privileged representatives of settler society who communicated with imperial administrators. Finally, the last to arrive in the valley, yet claiming pride of place, a new breed of scientific explorer also played a decisive role, hailing from northern Europe and no longer concerned primarily with serving the Portuguese Empire. Combining erudition with Eurocentric prejudice directed at both their Indigenous and Portuguese interlocutors, these visiting naturalists were prone to interpretive lapses as they built their transatlantic scientific reputations. Such was the case of the German Prince Maximilian Alexander Phillip von Wied-Neuwied (1782–1867), despite being among the most astute of these travelers.[3]

Before the prince arrived in the river valley, and largely unperceived by him, the Portuguese and the Indians had reached an accommodation that made his presence possible and colored all he observed. Significant discord divided state actors charged with implementing plans to transform the region's seminomadic foragers into submissive subjects. In particular, disagreements arose over the appropriate response to accusations of cannibalism. For the Portuguese crown and most of its ranking functionaries, the only response considered adequate to this outrage was a full-scale armed assault, enshrined in the declaration of war issued in 1808. For a few state actors, however, military conquest was ill-advised. Although always a minority, these officials advocated a level of restraint that may seem surprising. Despite our contemporary inclination to think that the charge of cannibalism served as little more than a pretext for subjugation, the perspectives of those acquainted with the backlands were more nuanced. Even as they conceded the reality of Botocudo cannibalism, some frontier officials advocated a peaceful advance on the forest. These officials managed to curb the state's bellicose inclinations, at least in this river valley. Importantly, the divide between a crown mobilized for war and its official critics can be traced to the conduct of the Botocudo. Their resourcefulness in the face of mounting aggression shifted the terms of the debate and mitigated the worst of the violence. Like the crown, the visiting naturalist stressed Native incommensurability with civilized society. Botocudo backcountry diplomacy suggested otherwise.

## Informant to the World

The flight to Brazil of Queen Maria I, her son Prince Regent João, and the administrative organs of the Portuguese Empire cleared the way for a new legion of informants reporting on the interior. They arrived as a flurry of visiting northern European natural historians—German, French, and English, among others. Mineralogists, zoologists, botanists, and ethnologists, some better trained than others, some hewing to their specialties, others more scattershot in their observations, these men of science and commerce drew support from the Portuguese crown as the colony increasingly opened to the non-Lusophone world. They wrote primarily for an audience of fellow naturalists and non-Portuguese European readers eager for reports from the tropics concerning the esoteric and exotic. These peripatetic naturalists, all of them male, as was overwhelmingly the case among those afforded formal education in natural history in Europe, revealed much that was unknown and fascinating to readers unfamiliar with Portuguese America. They also disseminated stereotypes originating in their own biases and conceits. They influenced nineteenth-century Brazilian elites and policy makers, individuals enamored of scientific progress, who read their works before they were ever translated into Portuguese. Historians, too, relied extensively on their Eurocentric assessments to diagnose what distinguished Brazil and Brazilians from what would come to be called the developed world, and why the country did not join the ranks of leading Atlantic powers in the nineteenth and twentieth centuries.[4]

Non-Lusophone natural history flourished in Portuguese America as circumstances dictated a loosening of the restrictions that had barred prominent foreign naturalists in earlier years. Rebuffed by suspicious authorities in Rio de Janeiro, Joseph Banks, future president of Great Britain's Royal Society, managed to sneak ashore for a single day when James Cook, sailing to the Pacific, paused in Guanabara Bay to resupply the HMS *Endeavour* in 1768. He had only hours to collect plants and hunt birds. The viceregal government obliquely accused Cook of trafficking in contraband and sent him on his way. Later, Alexander von Humboldt, traveling under Spanish and French auspices, was ordered arrested if caught crossing into Portuguese America during his Spanish American expedition (1799–1804). Portuguese authorities, protective of the colony's resources, treated non-Lusophone naturalists as little more than enemy spies, prying into state secrets.[5]

This wariness all but evaporated with the throne transferred to Rio de Janeiro and Brazil's ports opened to friendly nations in 1808. While still in Salvador, where he first set foot in the colony, pressured to secure new trading partners while Portugal remained under the occupation of Napoleon's forces, Prince Regent João effectively abolished the prevailing mercantilist system by permitting friendly nations access to the ports. As the colonial compact with Portugal collapsed, attempts to monopolize access to and knowledge of the continental interior also no longer made sense. The shift accelerated with the formal elevation of the colony to a kingdom enjoying co-equal status with Portugal in 1815. It was further hastened the following year when Maria I died and the prince regent was crowned João VI, King of the United Kingdom of Portugal, Brazil, and the Algarves.[6] The application of the newest scientific methods to territorial reconnaissance now was seen as befitting a colony that had become the tropical seat of the empire. Just as the ports had opened to foreign shipping, so would the interior be opened to men of science. Valorizing European expertise above all, the monarch turned to outsiders to advance the task of cataloging Brazil's boundless natural resources in order to better exploit this wealth. European savants were pleased to comply. Stimulated not only by the Portuguese crown but also by the final defeat of Napoleon, by improvements in shipping, mass printing, and lithography, and by the accompanying impulse, both scientific and imperialist, to collect and catalog, they hurried to Brazil to explore newly accessible areas of South America.

Of particular interest to João VI and his advisors were the presumed mineralogical, botanical, and zoological assets of Brazil's Atlantic Forest, particularly the portion encompassing eastern Minas Gerais and the coastal captaincies from Rio de Janeiro north to Bahia. No longer valued primarily as an impenetrable buffer zone barring access to and egress from the interior's now largely exhausted alluvial mining fields, these forests became a prized object of scientific study. For both the practical purposes of commercial development and the symbolic task of rebuilding the post-Napoleonic image of the Portuguese Empire, the king moved to welcome some of Europe's leading natural historians to mount missions to explore these forests, providing them with financial and logistical support.

From the perspective of the visiting savants, this domain—lying just inland from the coast yet long shielded from aggressive settlement and inhabited by Natives cast as archetypal primitives—presented an irresistible opportunity. Brazil's Atlantic Forest "was at last to be the subject of *curiosity*," wrote Warren Dean, the preeminent historian of the destruction of this rainforest over the span of half a millennium. "Thus was rent the curtain that had been drawn over this immense natural realm."[7] However, considering all the activity and intelligence gathering that preceded the flurry of foreign naturalists, Dean's assessment seems excessive, captive to the very impression the northern European visitors wished to foster. To the degree that their fieldwork did represent an altered knowledge regime, it would simultaneously absorb, replicate, and ultimately obscure many of the accomplishments and failings of earlier Portuguese efforts to understand the lands, vassals, and nonstate actors positioned at the limits of official reconnaissance capabilities while overlaying these past legacies with new representations, some more accurate than others.[8]

Concerning the botanical and zoological abundance of the eastern forests, as well as the Native peoples who inhabited them, the German prince established himself as the most able and widely read of these erudite travelers upon publishing the findings of his 1815–17 voyage from Rio de Janeiro to Salvador, with several excursions into the interior. Scion of the ruling family of the Principality of Wied-Neuwied, a decorated major in the Prussian Army who fought more than a dozen battles against Napoleon's forces, Wied trained as a naturalist before entering the military and hastened to pursue this vocation on the cessation of continental hostilities. He would seek guidance in interpreting his Brazilian scientific findings from his former professors at the University of Göttingen, the renowned botanist Heinrich Adolf Schrader and the comparative anatomist and craniometrist Johann Friedrich Blumenbach, a founding theorist of physical anthropology and its discredited subfield racial anthropology. Inspired to explore the Portuguese colony by his friend and mentor Humboldt, also a Blumenbach protégé, Wied sailed from London to Rio de Janeiro, arriving in mid-1815.[9] He disembarked in the tropical capital as a "true representative," in one historical geographer's phrasing, of an epochal "European scientific reconnaissance," a scientific traveler who "dissects, categorizes, measures, and classifies the natural history he observes, whether flora, fauna, meteorology, geology, or even comparative anthropology." At a time when modern disciplinary specialization was still unknown, such travelers "set off to distant shores to map a dazzling 'New World' and to make order out of perceived chaos."[10]

Although financing much of his mission himself and far less dependent on official patronage than the Luso-Brazilian naturalists who preceded him, Wied received essential protection and authorizations from the relocated Portuguese crown. The very possibility of his presence in the tropical colony and now co-equal kingdom underpinned his sense of indebtedness to João VI. "What a contrast is there between the liberal policy of the present government, and the ancient system, when the traveler, upon his landing in Brazil, was surrounded with soldiers, and cautiously watched!" he exclaimed. "In the name of my countrymen, and of all other European travelers, I cannot do less than thus publicly express my gratitude towards a Monarch who has adopted measures equally wise and popular." This shift in attitude, Wied predicted, would "be attended with incalculable advantage to the sciences, in which the whole civilized world will participate."[11] Wied fashioned himself an informant to that civilized world.

Government aid came in other forms as well. First minister and secretary of state for foreign and overseas affairs, António de Araújo e Azevedo, the Count of Barca, himself respected for conducting scientific investigations, provided Wied with passports and generous letters of introduction to governors, military officers, and other officials. These endorsements ensured almost universal assistance from local authorities en route, helping the expedition secure provisions, shelter, porters, military escorts, guides, hunting and collecting assistance, shipping, and transport. The ornithologist Georg Wilhelm Freyreiss and the botanist and illustrator Friedrich Sellow, two German naturalists already in Rio de Janeiro, agreed to join forces with Wied for portions of his journey. Both were employed by the state as naturalists, receiving annual stipends from the royal treasury.[12] Accompanying Freyreiss on the expedition was his "attendant" Francisco, a Coropó Indian and the party's most skilled hunter. With later royal support, including granted land, livestock, and tools, Freyreiss would return to a stretch of the southern Bahian coast traveled with Wied, where he helped found a settlement with other German and Swiss immigrants. Sellow would later drown collecting specimens on the Doce River.[13]

In Rio de Janeiro the thirty-three-year-old prince assembled his entourage with little delay. The party included the three naturalists, two family servants who accompanied Wied from Europe, and another ten men engaged to serve as hunters and tend the expedition's pack animals, among other tasks. All were armed. Each of sixteen mules were outfitted with wooden chests wrapped in leather designed to protect foodstuffs, gunpowder, general supplies, and the collections of plants, birds, reptiles, insects, and mammals to be acquired along the way. Wied traveled under a pseudonym, Max von Braunsberg, in order to disguise his noble lineage and attract less attention. His expedition would proceed northeastward through the captaincies of Rio de Janeiro, Espírito Santo, and Bahia, covering a distance of well over 2,000 kilometers, including his inland detours, before he sailed back to Europe from Salvador.[14]

The prince's writings about the Native peoples inland from Brazil's southeastern and central coast—among them the Coroado, Puri, Kamacã, and especially the Botocudo—would come to be considered his most important intellectual contribution. On several of his inland excursions, the prince conducted the ethnological investigations that secured his international renown. To do so, he relied on military escorts and local Native guides and hunters to enter territory that soldiers, land-hungry settlers, and clergy were in the process of wresting from these aboriginal peoples. Soon after setting out, for instance, still in the captaincy of Rio de Janeiro, he passed two days observing the Coroado, Coropó, and Puri in the environs of the state-run São Fidélis mission on the Paraíba River. Wied traded for bows, arrows, and baskets. Freyreiss took advantage of this occasion to purchase a Puri youth—to serve as another attendant and object of study—for a shirt, two knives, a handkerchief, glass beads, and some small mirrors. Untroubled by his countryman's willingness enter into this transaction, Wied instead remarked on the indifference displayed by the boy, which he cited as evidence that Amerindians were moved only by their stomachs, not by affective bonds. Toward the end of his excursion's journey, Wied also briefly paused to study Kamacã villagers, south of the Contas River in Bahia.

Between these two episodes, Wied received authorization for a month-long sojourn on Cachoeirinha Island, up the Jequitinhonha River. Here he achieved what he had hoped for from the beginning: extended contact with the Botocudo. Clashes between settlers, soldiers, and the Botocudo along the Doce and Mucuri Rivers twice prevented such direct observation earlier in the trip. At last afforded this opportunity along the Jequitinhonha, he relished the chance finally to study groups he described as "pure Indians," those "still in the rude state of nature," individuals whose "hoards" continued to wander, hunt, fish, and forage in the surrounding woods.[15] Before he ventured upriver, replicating Freyreiss's methods, he acquired his own Botocudo youth, who served as his translator and cultural insider.

Narrating the progress of his expedition northward along the coast, Wied early on prepared his readers for the extended encounter that would follow. The Botocudo "were the real tyrants of these wildernesses," he averred, repeating the premise that had made these Natives the focus of a declaration of war by the crown in 1808. As the party questioned colonists met along the way, local authorities and settlers related tales of Botocudo attacks directed at the Portuguese and at other Natives. Wounded Puri, for instance, had recently emerged from the forests in one river valley, and dozens of settlers were said to have lost their lives in raids in another. Upon reaching the Doce River valley, the conflict's deadliest theater, the party questioned a subaltern officer who had served at an outpost upriver before being seriously wounded in a skirmish with the Botocudo. Noting their "custom of eating human flesh," and "their warlike spirit," Wied left no ambiguity about his view of Botocudo depredations, but neither did he spare the colonizers his condemnation. Since their war declaration, the Portuguese had shown "no mercy." The Botocudo "have been extirpated, wherever they have been found, without respect to age or sex."[16]

Scholars of travel writing have noted the tendency of nineteenth-century German voyagers to combine these critiques—of indigenes

FIGURE 8.1. Fording a river. Source: Debret, *Voyage pittoresque*. Courtesy of the Biblioteca Brasiliana Guita e José Mindlin, São Paulo.

and their colonizers—especially when it came to Spanish and Portuguese America, although they were certainly not the only northern Europeans to do so. Rejecting the Enlightenment trope of the noble savage, the visiting naturalists found in their writings much to dislike about Native cultures, while simultaneously castigating Iberians as oppressors. Mary Louise Pratt describes this phenomenon as narrating an "anti-conquest," a representational strategy by which such writers sought to "secure their innocence in the same moment as they assert[ed northern] European hegemony," crafting narratives that distanced themselves from "older imperial rhetorics of conquest associated with the absolutist era." These writers sought knowledge of the natural world in remote zones where conquistadors—or bandeirantes—once sought gold or Indians to enslave, and settlers still sought land. For the anticonquistador, the discovery of such knowledge became the currency of reputation and readership at a time when travel literature was an increasingly desired source of information by readers unable themselves to undertake great voyages and encounter distant peoples. The genre rested on and gave new life to a version of the Black Legend that northern Europeans had long before crafted to smear Spanish imperial history as uniquely inhumane, a version now directed at the Portuguese, portrayed as "fallen, degenerate, and imbecile people," in the words of the sociologist and legal scholar Boaventura de Sousa Santos.[17]

Along the Jequitinhonha River, however, things were different, Wied learned. There, the enlightened policies of officials responsible for this more northern sector of the coastal forest had established the groundwork necessary to avoid the worst of the conflict. Above all, the governor of Bahia, Marcos Noronha e Brito, the count of Arcos (1810–18), had demonstrated that the "incorrigibility" of the Botocudo proceeded "as much from the manner in which they have been treated, as from their native rudeness." If on the Doce River a cycle of raiding and retaliation still churned nearly a decade after the declaration of war, on the Jequitinhonha River peace prevailed. Wied credited Governor Brito with initiating that peace, acting in accordance with his "moderate and humane" character. It seems likely that the German traveler was persuaded in this view by the governor himself, whom Wied praised after receiving a warm welcome to Salvador from this fellow aristocrat at the end of his overland journey.[18]

Wied's understanding of the origins of peaceful relations along the Jequitinhonha River valley allowed for no agency by the Botocudo themselves. His suppositions erased a history of incursions into Native territory by backcountry explorers and soldiers on the upper reaches of the river that established the circumstances into which his expedition ventured. Not only were the Botocudo he encountered and deemed "pure" and "still in the rude state of nature" well acquainted with the Portuguese, they had also played a significant role in cultivating the amicable relations that allowed Wied to conduct his investigations. To understand their actions, we must shift the focus away from the German prince and his entourage for the remainder of this chapter, returning to events surrounding the crown's 1808 declaration of war, which elsewhere in the forest made it impossible for him to interact with the inland Native peoples he so desired to study.

## A Declaration of War

To the detriment of any satisfactory understanding of the import of Indigenous agency and territorial autonomy during the final years of colonial rule, two of the crown's earliest actions after the royal family's arrival in Brazil have received unequal scholarly attention. The first was the opening of Brazilian ports to friendly nations. This move favored England, Portugal's exigent ally, whose warships had escorted the royal family across the Atlantic. As a harbinger of political and economic changes that unfolded over the nineteenth century, including England's intensifying push to dominate South Atlantic markets and end the transatlantic slave trade to Brazil, this policy has figured prominently in independence-era historiography.[19] In contrast, the second action, the declaration of war against Indigenous adversaries, seemed to hark back to the earliest days of Portuguese settlement in the sixteenth century. It has attracted comparatively little attention from scholars riveted by the period's dramatic transformations. Yet the two apparently unrelated decrees stemmed from the same impulse to adjust to the crown's dislocation to the tropics. Imperial geopolitics impelled both policies. The first pointed outward to commercial changes in the Atlantic system; the second aimed to integrate inland areas into that larger world. The first acknowledged the breakdown of exclusive trade between the colony and its incapacitated metropole; the second belatedly recognized the end of Brazil's mining boom by deeming the coastal forests no longer critical as a buffer zone that prevented the smuggling of gold and diamonds from the interior. Earlier state-backed incursions, as at Cantagalo, had penetrated areas deemed strategically critical. Now, in their entirety, the forests offered a new field of conquest and colonization promising new sources of wealth for an empire in disarray.

Blocking this territorial integration project was the presence of more than a dozen Native groups that shared many cultural traits, including their associated Macro-Gê languages. Among the most successful at opposing colonial expansion were the Puri, Pataxó, and Botocudo. To the south, Puri domain extended from the Paraíba River and its tributaries, where they encountered the Coropó and Coroado, with whom they competed for hunting and gathering grounds. To the north, they inhabited the southern banks of the Doce River and the valleys carved by its headwaters. Farther north, the Pataxó inhabited lands dividing Minas Gerais from settlements along a narrow coastal strip in Espírito Santo and Bahia.

Vying for much of this same territory were the roving bands considered most formidable, known by the mid-eighteenth century as the Botocudo. The imposed ethnonym derived from *botoque*, the Portuguese word for the wooden disks these Indians inserted in their ear lobes and lower lips. In practice, the name took on a generic quality as colonists collapsed diverse groups into one. Any group resisting conquest could be decried as Botocudo, particularly as attempts at colonization from both the interior and the coast destabilized the region and pressed separate bands in on one another. Highly mobile, hunting and foraging over large areas, these bands tended to fissure and fight back when cooperation required capitulation. Adept at hit-and-run tactics, male warriors struck isolated farmsteads and, more rarely, soldiers on patrol. While settlers, officers, and state authorities exaggerated their aggressiveness, there is no question that they proved remarkably successful at holding territory. By the nineteenth century, colonists considered them "the paradigm of the wild Indian."[20]

On his arrival from Portugal, determined to incorporate the coastal forests of the strategic triangle defined by northern Rio de Janeiro, eastern Minas Gerais, and southern Bahia, Prince Regent João set out to subdue the Botocudo once and for all. Condemning mounting "invasions" by these "cannibal" Indians, he invoked the timeworn principle of just war, pledging a military offensive until they submitted to the rule of law, accepting life as settled Christian vassals.[21] The state would not formally revoke this policy until 1831. According to frontier authorities who had urged the crown to act decisively for decades, Native violence did not merely exact a heavy toll on colonists in terms of casualties and material possessions. It also repeatedly forced the abandonment of Portuguese settlements over significant stretches of the coastal forests. Most officials saw military action as a natural and required response.

As the crown viewed the conflict from its newly established throne in Rio de Janeiro, cannibalism served as the principal basis for deeming lawful the 1808 decision to pursue what would be the final instance of a so-called just war declared in Portuguese America. If fears about roving cannibals had once served royal interests by discouraging access to this forested no-man's-land, the presence of hostile autonomous Indians during the final decades of the colonial era no longer seemed tolerable. Enacted just two months after the royal court disembarked in Rio de Janeiro, the 1808 military mobilization signaled the crown's adoption of policies of territorial conquest that had first emerged at the local and regional levels. The determination to quell Native resistance and assert the sovereign's reach by doing so—rather than relegate this activity to captaincy elites—corresponded with centralizing imperatives characteristic of the era's modernizing states. To the extent that state consolidation required symbolic power to undergird overt coercive might, strident official condemnation of and mobilization against cannibalism assumed an importance unequaled since Brazil's anthropophagi first became the stuff of Portuguese and greater European ambitions, fears, and fantasies in the sixteenth century.[22]

As the prince regent expressed the problem, Indian aggression forced his hand. Issuing his declaration to the governor of Minas Gerais, Pedro Maria Xavier Ataíde e Melo, he condemned the "invasions that the cannibal Botocudos [were] practicing daily," driving colonists to flee the captaincy's eastern reaches "at great loss to themselves and to my royal crown." The Indians had perpetrated "the most horrible and atrocious scenes of the most barbarous cannibalism." They had dismembered their victims, drunk their blood, and consumed their "sad remains." They had demonstrated "the uselessness of all human efforts" to civilize them, to settle them in villages, and to persuade them "to take pleasure in the permanent advantages of a peaceful and gentle society." As a consequence, the crown would adopt a policy of "just" and "offensive war," a war that would "have no end," until settlers returned to their habitations and the Indians submitted to the rule of law, "promising to live in society" and becoming "useful vassals." To secure the region, the prince regent ordered the governor to deploy detachments of foot soldiers charged with effecting the "total reduction" of this "cruel cannibal race." Armed Indians who were captured in these actions would be considered prisoners of war and enslaved for ten years. In practice this restoration of legalized Indigenous slavery fell particularly hard on surviving women and children after adult male warriors lost their lives in combat. Although the decree singled out the Botocudo, the crown made it clear that these provisions applied to the "reduction and civilization . . . of other Indian races" in the eastern forests.[23]

According to the crown, cannibalism made the war legal. As was perennially the case with such accusations, the monarch demonstrated little interest in gathering evidence to evaluate this charge. Only after the declaration was issued did Rodrigo de Sousa Coutinho, now serving as minister of war, order the governor of Minas Gerais to send to the royal court, under strict security, one Botocudo male and one female to satisfy the monarch's "curiosity to see this cannibal race."[24] Cannibalism once again played its customary role in colonial conquest as a representation of radical alterity that threatened the social order. It also served the purposes of a monarchy eager to reconfigure and reassert its power, militarily and symbolically, from its fugitive throne in Rio de Janeiro. Yet to limit analysis to machinations in the royal palace is to misconstrue the complex foundations of imperial policy during this period. Aspects of that policy ascended the chain of command to Rio de Janeiro from the backlands, where the besieged Indigenous inhabitants of the eastern forests attempted to manage a crisis that threatened their territorial autonomy and, in turn, their existence.

Most ranking regional authorities lauded the new terms of military engagement. They had impelled the shift in royal policy in the first place. Governors of Minas Gerais had pressured the crown for decades to scrap its ban on colonizing the easternmost reaches of the captaincy. Charged with revitalizing the mining district as its gold and diamond production declined, they had focused on the incorporation of Indian territory as a solution to the region's economic ills. From the 1760s on, virtually all of them authorized attacks against Indigenous forest dwellers, usually cloaked in the language of retaliation. To affirm the state's power over this zone, the prince regent had merely put his imperial imprimatur on practices already in place at the regional and local levels.[25]

The ability of captaincy authorities to draw the imperial state into the conflict becomes evident in the actions of governors preceding the declaration of war. From Lisbon in mid-1801, as a prelude to full-scale military mobilization, the crown responded to complaints about Indian hostilities communicated by Minas governor Bernardo José de Lorena. The reply authorized him to conduct offensive warfare against the Botocudo. The governor was to divide the area "infested" by these Indians into military districts that would form the basis for the full-scale troop deployments that would follow in 1808. In this way the 1808 declaration constituted an expansion of this preceding ruling in Minas Gerais, as well as similar orders issued in 1801 and 1806 to Bahian authorities contending with clashes between settlers and Indians along the coast.[26] Governor Lorena had already anticipated the change, moving vigorously to secure the opening of the Doce River and its fertile valley to navigation and settlement, predicting the development of a profitable commercial corridor to the Atlantic seaboard. Taking advantage of royal approbation, he established a customhouse far down the Doce River and deployed a detachment of troops there to monitor and collect duties on the anticipated trade with the captaincy of Espírito Santo. After basing another detachment upstream, he declared the river route "free of savages."[27] The claim was premature. The Doce River valley would become the most violent theater of the coming war.

The governor was on firmer ground in asserting a growing consensus that identified the opening of underexplored reaches of the captaincy to all manner of commerce, rather than gold and diamond extraction only, as nothing less than a necessity for future prosperity. By the 1790s the long-held notion that the barrier created by the rugged eastern forest—or the eastern sertões, as they were known in Minas Gerais—served the interests of the state had given way. In its place the belief arose that little had been attempted in pursuit of territorial expansion to the east, that Native resistance rather than royal proscription was to blame for this state of affairs, and that trade with coastal settlers and the Atlantic world would restore the opulence local elites had once enjoyed when gold and diamonds poured forth from the earth. Among the impatient memorialists who sought to remedy the captaincy's land-locked economic isolation and dispense with Native antagonists, the mineralogist José Vieira Couto described the eastern sertões as "an extensive cordon of dense forests inhabited solely by barbarous and wild peoples," running along "the entire eastern side" of the captaincy, a combined natural and human barrier that "prevents communication" with the coast.[28]

The new view focused especially on river valleys, seen as natural transit routes to the coast. "Everything will take on a new vigor," enthused Couto, no less an advocate of this eastward expansion than he was of its westward counterpart. Importuning the crown to promote the opening of the Doce and Jequitinhonha River valleys to colonization and trade, he could scarcely maintain the sobriety of his academic training. "What abundance, what new sources of wealth!" he exclaimed. "Today these rivers serve only as drinking places for the ugly monsters and dispersed bands of barbarous people who inhabit their shadowy banks."[29] Writing to Governor Lorena's successor the year before war was declared against the zone's Native inhabitants, another memorialist, Diogo Pereira Ribeiro de Vasconcelos, emphasized the importance of these routes for the profitable exchange of a full range of commodities. Recognizing that barriers, both "moral and physical," stood in the way, he nevertheless urged officials to move aggressively. "Incalculable are the advantages in terms of exports and imports that can come to the captaincy by way of navigation" of the rivers flowing out of Minas Gerais to the coast, argued the Portuguese-born Vasconcelos, who occupied numerous high government posts. "Apart from commerce, we would equally obtain the vast riches that cover those lands," which he described as a nothing less than "a new India," so abundant were their precious stones and metals.[30] This conviction, recalling the long tradition of projecting dreams of the future onto lands unconquered in the past, increasingly extended beyond Minas Gerais to crown ministers in Lisbon and to officials in the coastal captaincies of Espírito Santo and Bahia.[31]

Governor Melo, Lorena's successor, justified warlike actions with increasingly shrill accusations of cannibalism. He described "wild and insatiable carnage," which resulted when settlers were "attacked, killed, and devoured by the barbarous, anthropophagous, heathen Botocudo." In 1806 the captaincy's treasury board, under Melo's direction, submitted a report to Lisbon fulminating against undeterred Indian raids. The forest Natives were forcing settlers to "abandon their farming and mining fazendas after having cultivated these lands at the expense of their labor." The board had received numerous appeals from these settlers, which testified to the "excessive costs" to the crown in the loss of tax revenues and in the attempt "to expand the captaincy" to the east. Received approvingly by a leading crown minister who decried the "barbarous cruelty of the anthropophagous Indians," this argument found its way into the text of the declaration of war after the Portuguese court arrived in Brazil and prompted the creation of new frontier squadrons to oppose Botocudo "invasions."[32]

The exaggeration and then attempted eradication of the internal Indian threat offered a decisive test for Portugal's transplanted monarchy as it experimented with the altered political geography of state consolidation from its new residence in Rio de Janeiro. The seemingly unassailable logic of the crown's opposition to cannibalism provided the justification required to address for its own political purposes the anxieties of regional authorities. These authorities pressed the central state to act; by acting, the state then strengthened its hand over regional authorities. They, in turn, responded to the determination of Native peoples to hold onto forests and river valleys essential for hunting and foraging. The more authorities felt compelled to mount an invasion of the eastern forests, the more they acknowledged the success of Indian opposition. Enduring Native proficiencies, especially the ability to attack weak points along the edge of settled territory, striking at the illusion of colonial dominion in the sertão, convinced regional officials and eventually the crown itself to resort to open warfare. However, we should not confuse official ambitions with frontier realities. A great divide separated imperial and regional justifications for the policy of war from the complexities of interethnic conflict and cooperation in the eastern forests.

### Consumption, Communication, and Conciliation

From the earliest era of colonial settlement, charges of cannibalism proliferated when Europeans sought to seize territory. This correlation reminds us to exercise extreme caution in accepting such accusations at face value. Scholars who continue to debate the veracity of the accusations leveled against Brazil's eastern Indians are far from the first to do so.[33] In the aftermath of the declaration of war, the cadre of eager northern European naturalists that descended on the eastern forests took particular interest in verifying the practice of cannibalism, but they arrived at no consensus concerning its pervasiveness or characteristics. It will likely never be known exactly to what extent, in which circumstances, or even definitively whether, the Botocudo, the Puri, and other groups in the region engaged in this practice. Some of the foreign visitors accused Brazilian settlers and officials of inventing denunciations to justify the appropriation of land and the enslavement of seminomadic forest dwellers. Others gathered evidence to support these claims. Among the most thorough in his investigations and circumspect in his conclusions, Wied, the German prince and naturalist, posited what for the era was something of a compromise position. He rejected the idea that the Botocudo ate human flesh as part of their subsistence diet. He even questioned whether the practice was part of their ancestral tradition. He did not doubt, however, that it existed as an Indigenous resistance strategy, sowing terror among colonists.[34]

The enduring question of verification and its implications for royal policy can draw attention away from a related issue even more pertinent for understanding relations between these Native peoples and the state. For the crown and its highest authorities, charges of cannibalism justified extermination and enslavement where assimilation proved impossible. But as numerous sources emerging from frontier encounters attest, there was nothing inevitable about this connection between cannibalism and violent conquest. A number of dissenting local officials put into practice approaches counter to the violent ones espoused by the crown. Like the ranking captaincy and imperial administrators who devised the justification for war, most lower-level authorities active in the eastern forests shared the belief that the Botocudo and other Native peoples consumed their adversaries. Nevertheless, some interpreted this conclusion in ways that asserted the potential for peaceable exchange leading to the Botocudos' voluntary incorporation into settler society.

One such official, by no means alone in his methods, administered the small Indian aldeia and nascent settler village of Tocoiós in northeastern Minas Gerais. Originally inhabited by a group of Malali Indians, the settlement was about 50 kilometers by a winding trail from Minas Novas, the nearest sizeable town. From the village the trail extended northeast to the confluence of the Araçuaí and Jequitinhonha Rivers. At the beginning of the nineteenth century, still covered by the Atlantic Forest, this area constituted the outer reaches of settlement, the upper reaches of the river valley that Wied would later ascend from the coast. To the east the Jequitinhonha River plunged into the Atlantic Forest, descending through rugged, mountainous terrain, eventually spilling into the ocean north of the town of Porto Seguro. Gold had been discovered in the area no later than the 1720s by bandeirantes from São Paulo. Colonization of the surrounding forests stalled, however, in part because of resistance from the region's Indigenous peoples and in part because of the crown's concerns about smuggling. Settlers again moved into the area in the early nineteenth century, abandoning declining mining camps, attracted by the possibility of cotton cultivation and the prospects of opening a thriving trade corridor down the watershed to the coast.[35]

A respected frontier administrator appointed by the governor in 1799 to serve unremunerated as the Tocoiós village regent, a man of means, well-educated and well-connected, José Pereira Freire de Moura became preoccupied by a series of encounters with the Botocudo, which he documented in a report issued in 1809, as soldiers worked to secure the Jequitinhonha River valley for further colonization and for the transport of goods.[36] Moura's conviction that the Indians seen in the area were Botocudo stemmed from allegations of cannibalism, which he maintained went hand in hand with their proclivity for irrational hostility. He recalled one confrontation years earlier between fifty Botocudo warriors and more than two hundred armed colonists. The Indians had "fought until they had used up all of their arrows." All of them died in battle, except one, "who grabbed hold of the trunk of a tree to avoid being killed. He refused all food for three days and in the end beat his head against the tree trunk so many times that he died."

Evidence of cannibalism was recent and verifiable, wrote Moura. In an incident occurring around the turn of the century, a band of Botocudo had devised a plot to devour three escaped slaves. The Indians convinced the fugitives to follow them to a spot along the banks of the Jequitinhonha River, promising that gold could be found there in abundance. They killed two of the three Blacks at the site. The third escaped to Tocoiós and described the murders. A group of colonists who pursued the Indians investigated his account. Reaching the scene of the attack, they discovered the vestiges of a cannibal feast. The remains of the victims consisted of "heaps of bones . . . scorched by a fire and thoroughly gnawed." The crime remained fresh in the memory of local settlers for years. The pursuers had brought back the skull of one of the victims and placed it in the settlement's cemetery, where it stood as a reminder of Native atrocities.

Although the unfortunate escapees did not speak for themselves, their presence in Moura's report is evidence of how legal status differentiated persons of color as frontier informants. Fugitives from slavery were not obvious or common sources of backlands intelligence, at least not to white authorities. Those who hunted them needed to know the backcountry well. Those in flight guarded their knowledge of forest routes, hideouts, and natural and human hazards from their potential pursuers with a rigor expected of individuals whose freedom hung in the balance. Free persons of color, by contrast, were perceived as providing crucial communications concerning outlying lands frequented by Native hunters, fishers, and foragers. The value of their reporting, for example, led regional officials to balk in 1810 when pressed by the crown to fulfill military recruitment quotas, which perennially fell on the unprotected free poor, often men of African descent. Members of the town council of Vila do Príncipe, the distant seat of government for the jurisdiction encompassing Minas Novas and Tocoiós, complained that removing such men from the region for military service would endanger its nascent development. The promising eastern edge of the region, they explained in a letter addressed to the prince regent, was "surrounded by Botocudo and other wild heathen." Mulattos, mixed-bloods, and creoles, as the councilmen described the bulk of this area's free settler population, might be provoked by a recruitment drive to join the Indians in rebelling against outnumbered whites. Furthermore, those potential recruits who could be trusted, "despite being among the excluded class because of the quality of their color, are in one form or another necessary in this land." Forming a strategic buffer between white colonists and hostile Indians, these impoverished subsistence farmers could be relied on as "the first to send news of insurrections and skirmishes" involving Indians. Accustomed to "wandering the forests and enduring the rigors of the seasons and of hunger," free persons of color survived such backcountry violence more readily than whites, the councilmen averred. According to this argument, the ability to withstand the ravages of life in the eastern sertões made free Afro-descendants critically important as vanguards of colonization and as sources of information about threats deep in the forests.[37] In this context it is possible that townsfolk in Tocoiós concocted the story about cannibals, either to discourage the enslaved from running away, to undermine a feared alliance between Blacks and Indians, or simply to attract official attention and state resources. The documentary evidence leaves no doubt that Moura took the matter seriously, yet his reaction was not the usual call for retaliation. Instead, he became convinced that the proper response demanded something other than the customary armed retaliation.

In 1800, the year after he assumed his administrative position, he ordered troops based at Tocoiós to form a bandeira and descend the Jequitinhonha River in search of the Botocudo. Contact occurred in the forest without violent incident. Then, beginning in 1804, as his superiors were gearing up for war, he provided instructions to a series of expeditions aimed at coaxing the Botocudo peacefully into colonial society. The first of these missions descended the Jequitinhonha River some 20 leagues (about 130 km) under the leadership of a corporal, Manoel Rodrigues Prates.[38] On an island deemed suitable for the planned encounter, he established an encampment with a portable forge. Using steel and iron carried to the site, his troops fabricated machetes and fishhooks. When expedition members sighted wandering Botocudo along the far bank of the river, they approached them with the help of a Native translator and gained their friendship by giving them tools.

At first the Indians proved wary. One of them, described as a male covered in black dye, made it clear he suspected a trap. They would all be captured and killed, he warned, just as his wife and all his children had once been murdered by whites. After some delay, ultimately convinced by the soldiers' assurances, the others crossed to the island on canoes. Corporal Prates urged them to travel upriver where they would be provided with more tools. Sometime later they appeared in Tocoiós, where Moura welcomed them and distributed gifts. Over the course of the next two years, the Indians returned for further visits. Then, mysteriously, they disappeared. The corporal led forest patrols every year for three consecutive years in an attempt to contact them, but they were not to be found. Moura suspected that they were purposefully avoiding contact, because fresh signs of their presence in the forest were always evident. They likely remained hidden as a response to the dangers presented by the intensifying mobilization for war.

Moura had personal reasons for his accommodating approach, for seeking backcountry intelligence from the Botocudo rather than advocating revenge. A plan he was orchestrating stood little chance of success without their cooperation. It originated in his discovery of an undated document among the papers of his deceased father. The document described a route down the Jequitinhonha River and then overland through the dense forests to a place described as Lagoa Dourada, the Golden Lagoon. Like a map to Eldorado, the document was a signed, first-person description of an expedition manned long ago by bandeirantes from São Paulo. They had wandered through the region, perhaps a century earlier, and uncovered evidence of ample gold deposits, which purportedly they had not had the time or wherewithal to unearth. Moura wished to retrace their steps, but increasing age and infirmity prevented him. Instead, he sought to mount an expedition led by one of his sons in search of the site.[39]

FIGURE 8.2. A Botocudo family. Source: Rugendas, *Voyage pittoresque*. Courtesy of the Biblioteca Nacional, Rio de Janeiro.

While Moura may in fact have possessed the document he described, he also summoned with its invocation a classic trope of the era and region that portrayed an explorer, often a Paulista bandeirante, at the moment of his death whispering to a trusted friend the route to his clandestine gold or diamond strike. But as historian Franciso Eduardo de Andrade has demonstrated, the political and social power of such knowledge to the living usually mattered more than any geographic secrets: "itineraries to supposed riches were . . . well utilized during the active life of the explorer or backwoodsman, who, allied with his relatives and friends, wanted to reap benefits from the Portuguese crown and establish or reinforce prestige with other groups."[40] Discovery accounts, often accompanied by maps, became a currency used to enhance the status of individuals, families, their clientele, and their official patrons. With the aid of well-placed patrons, such accounts were also used to preempt potential competitors lacking powerful sponsors, who might claim precedence in finding the same treasure or some other treasure in the same region. The function of a document like Moura's was in this sense not only to conquer the backlands but also, with privileged information, to conquer the state as it strove to exercise greater control over the colony's unincorporated inland spaces.

The quest Moura proposed entailed descending the Jequitinhonha River in canoes to a point where falls made it impassable. The troops would then march overland, making contact with various fractured Indigenous groups known to be living in the area. Moura described these groups as the "remains of nations . . . fleeing their total destruction" in raids launched by Botocudo bands from the Doce River basin to the south. The region he was attempting to explore "always was the one most exposed to invasions by the Botocudo." Although he had managed to win the friendship of some, they could easily launch a "treasonous" attack if they sensed weakness or became dissatisfied. "In this case," he explained, "I and my family will be the first ones sacrificed." Nevertheless, he remained convinced of the merits of conciliating rather than waging war against these denizens of the forest.[41]

To ensure the success of his plan, Moura sought to out-maneuver the regional officials to whom he was supposed to answer. Bypassing these superiors, who balked at his efforts to venture into unsupervised forests, he appealed directly to the highest authorities in Brazil, sending to Rio de Janeiro another son with a letter addressed to War Minister Coutinho. The letter testified to the "great wealth" that could be found if the expedition were allowed to proceed. He pressed the minister to request authorization from the crown. In addition to financial support, he sought a series of orders from the prince regent, requiring the captaincy governor and other officials to cooperate. His letter made it clear that he had been stymied by the frontier chain of command, facing resistance from local military officers and the governor, authorities he suspected of plotting to foil his attempt to locate the site of the hidden treasure. Among other advantages, royal backing would allow him to round up recruits, by force if necessary, and press them into service. With such support, he predicted his mission would be of "great utility" to the crown's vassals and its treasury.[42]

These machinations paid off. A substantial expedition soon set out from the frontier outpost where Moura dreamed of untapped gold deposits, undeterred by an accelerating turn in much of the exhausted mining heartland to other sources of wealth. A note listed more than three dozen men as participants, some of them identified as "prisoners." An unsigned document, evidently written by Moura, contained orders issued to his son. The orders stipulated that expedition members must "never attack the Indians without previous provocation from them." Their "good treatment" was to be guaranteed by the distribution of machetes, fishhooks, knives, and trinkets. If possible, the Botocudo were to be invited to join the mission. The document referred to a separate order issued by the prince regent to purchase supplies.[43]

The available evidence, in short, suggests Moura succeeded in his efforts to sway the crown not only to back the foray into the forest but also to attempt to placate rather than wage war against presumed cannibals. Such methods contradicted the basic premise of official Indigenous policy, namely, that the man-eating Botocudo eschewed all interactions with civilized society. As the prince regent pursued his war elsewhere in the eastern forests, the dislocations caused by the military assault likely explained why some Natives sought out the kinds of tentative, diplomatic interactions documented along the Jequitinhonha River.

Accusations of cannibalism, it seems, could be deployed by state actors for a range of purposes. With what he claimed to be immediate and gruesome experience of such atrocities, Moura might have judged the Indians irredeemable, candidates for enslavement or annihilation in accordance with prevailing policies. This was not his conclusion. Instead, he attempted to woo the Botocudo into the village he administered, believing that with patience and persistence they could be assimilated. While labeling Indians cannibals may have always served the empire's overarching aim to control territory, Moura's approach indicated how individual state actors rejected the crown's reflexive recourse to violent conquest. His personal ambitions, and perhaps his moral inclinations, suggested another approach, as did his direct knowledge of amicable interactions within the large but shrinking space the Botocudo still dominated. The conduct of the Botocudo in this northern theater of the conflict revealed options that the crown knew it had at its disposal but at first largely ignored. What is striking about Moura's account is not just his own willingness but also that of the Botocudo bands to negotiate. As more evidence accumulated of this gap between official denunciation of Native savagery and the actual behavior of Indians in the forests, it would challenge the credibility the state's war policy. Further details from the encounters at Tocoiós are instructive in this regard, as are other instances of interethnic cooperation in the eastern sertões.

Several times during 1809, the year following the declaration of war, small groups of a dozen or so Natives again made contact with troops in the surrounding forest and with Moura in his village. The Natives were always treated hospitably, he reported, but he could not keep up with their desire for metal tools. The Indians told him that they planned to return in greater numbers, that they would bring their children in order to receive more fishhooks and other gifts, and that they found the village an agreeable dwelling place, particularly since food was more readily accessible there than in the forest. This exchange concluded with a startling revelation. The Botocudo told Moura that "without doubt" they would settle permanently at the village if it were possible to convince their wives. But their wives "were very wild," Moura reported the men saying, "and feared they would be killed and eaten."[44]

The statement is worth pondering. Botocudo women, particularly the elderly, influenced decisions of great import in their various bands. The power they held included their sway over any deliberations that concerned entering colonial settlements, which they associated with disease, death, and dark magic.[45] In the case of Moura's village, was there a basis for their fears? Would the Botocudo be consumed if they took up residence at Tocoiós? Since their ancestors, the Aimoré, first came into contact with the Portuguese along Brazil's Atlantic coastline in the sixteenth century, they had been the victims of innumerable depredations perpetrated under the rationale of "just wars." They had been massacred and taken captive. They had watched from the woods as Portuguese soldiers cut off the ears of their fallen kin as proof of victory in battle. Men like those who conferred with Moura had seen women and children of their kin groups marched off in an expanding slave trade along the Jequitinhonha River. When family members vanished in this way, it made sense to suspect the worst. After all, Botocudo origin myths and religious beliefs expressed the terror of being eaten not only by wild animals but also non-Botocudo cannibals.[46]

Whatever the basis for their fears of Portuguese cruelty may have been, the Botocudo demonstrated in their conduct a full range of responses. Some fought back. Some entered colonial society. If the statements Moura recorded are to be believed, some struggled with a dilemma not unlike that of their colonial antagonists, striving to convince wary kin that the white enemies they encountered in the forest, while violent and untrustworthy, could best be dealt with as if they were rational human beings.

As the militarization of the conflict accelerated, a new detachment of soldiers garrisoned along the Jequitinhonha River in 1810 continued to maintain amicable relations with the river valley's Botocudo bands.

These soldiers participated in a burst of road-building activity, designed to link the northern reaches of the mining district with the coast, slashing through the heart of Botocudo hunting and gathering grounds. Numerous accounts of contacts between soldiers, settlers, and the Botocudo were recorded.[47]

The commander of the new detachment, Lieutenant Julião Leão, who also spent time searching for the golden lagoon depicted on Moura's old bandeirante map, sent detailed reports to the prince regent describing these interactions. Having extended a road more than a hundred kilometers down the river valley into Indian territory, Leão adopted the practice of gift exchange that Moura had found effective. He described the enthusiasm of the forest dwellers for such items as knives, fishhooks, and manioc flour. Communicating by way of Native interpreters, he promised that colonists would teach them "an easy way of life," helping them to build dwellings and cultivate crops. The number of Indians emerging from the forest steadily increased. They presented their own gifts, including coconuts, hearts of palm, and boar meat. Some worked for a few hours clearing fields. They ate, slept, and played games with the soldiers. Some even slept in the commander's tent. Leão sent his translators deeper into the forest to communicate good tidings and promises of further gifts to those still wary about approaching the road-building expedition. He visited one distant encampment himself at the Natives' invitation.

After almost two months of such exchanges, he calculated that he had befriended more than a hundred Indians, male and female, the young and the old, headmen and their followers. These Natives demonstrated a willingness to follow orders. They instructed the soldiers on hunting methods and how to move safely through the forest. They warned that "wild Botocudos" threatened the security of the soldiers to the south, and they pledged their aid in the event of an attack. Some of the adult males offered their daughters in marriage. Leão expressed frustration that the state could not better fund his efforts as the demand for gifts outstripped the supply. The experience left him convinced of the Natives' amity and the ill-conceived premises of the crown's war policy. The Botocudo "absolutely do not want war," he wrote the prince regent, "and I should not wage it against them." Leão's alternative approach, it should be noted, did not otherwise guarantee interethnic harmony. Later in his career, he would be accused of abusing Indian laborers and transferred to another command.[48]

Incursions by soldiers and colonists into the forests led increasing numbers of Indians to opt to settle in state-supported villages, like the one Moura supervised, or even to join military forces based at a line of unimpressive forts established by the crown to secure control over both the Doce and Jequitinhonha River valleys. Such recently settled Indians were "the most appropriate" soldiers to prevent the hostilities of those who remained outside the control of authorities, according to one group of local officials who reported to the crown.[49] Field officers had made use of such Indigenous soldiers from the earliest stages of their move into the eastern sertões, a tactic common to tribal zones targeted for colonial invasion.[50] For example, an unspecified number of "tame Indians" participated as enlisted soldiers in a bloody punitive ambush led by the commander of the garrison established along the Doce River by Governor Lorena.[51] The success of the operation led the commander to urge the governor to enlist more "tame Indians" than those already being employed, since they were particularly skilled in tracking and surrounding the unconquered Botocudo.[52] More than a decade later, when he traveled through the area, the importance of such individuals in the zone of conflict was still evident to Wied, the German naturalist. Accompanying a military expedition dispatched to work on one of the roads linking the coast to northeastern Minas Gerais, he was struck by "the various races of men" laboring together as foot soldiers. "There were in our company negroes, creoles, mulattos, mamelukes [i.e., mamelucos or mestizos], Natives of the coast, a Botocudo, a Malali, some Maconis, and Capuchos, all [Native] soldiers from Minas Gerais."[53]

It did not take long for the crown to concede the possibility that the Indians it condemned as cannibals could be approached and welcomed to settle in villages, then acculturated, if only very gradually. Within months of declaring war, it issued provisions allowing for the settlement,

Christianization, and supervised agricultural labor of those Natives who submitted to the pressures of military occupation. This second edict authorized the allocation of royal land grants to settlers along the length of the Doce River, reserving plots for Indians who voluntarily sought "royal protection." On this land the Puri, Botocudo, and others could cultivate crops for their own subsistence and for the emerging market. Profits from their labor would allow them to purchase clothing, tools, and other supplies, minimizing their dependence on the state or settlers. Taxes on Indian production would pay for priests to oversee the task of conversion and education. Ideally, local landholders would also assume these responsibilities in exchange for the privilege of putting Indians to work on their farms and ranches. Adult Natives allocated to such individuals were to be required to work in this capacity for a dozen years, children under twelve for twenty years. Even after this prolonged period of unremunerated labor expired, landholders who took on Indians as dependents could receive payments for contracting their labor out to other settlers.[54] Slavery by another name, such working conditions meant that most of these individuals likely never again attained their freedom, although little is known about their fate.

Much like the link between the offensive war policy and the conquest previously set in motion by captaincy political elites in collaboration with the crown, these settlement provisions wedded the aspirations of the state to the ambitions of local landholders. As soldiers patrolled the forests, flushing out Indians from their traditional dwelling places, authorized to attack even without provocation, the possibility of retaining control over hunting, fishing, and foraging zones became ever more imperiled. The war, Wied wrote, "was maintained with the greatest perseverance and cruelty, since it was firmly believed that [the Botocudo] killed and devoured any enemy who fell into their hands."[55] But the disingenuousness of this official stance was increasingly apparent to those frontier authorities disposed to think more flexibly. Indian conduct simply did not conform to the image of unbending savagery that continued to underpin royal policy.

Over time the crown would learn to relinquish its displays of violence and adopt alternative frontier policies throughout the eastern forests. Well before 1831, when the war on the Botocudo and other groups officially ended, the military approach to territorial incorporation gave way to less centralized and, importantly, less expensive methods that met the needs of a state increasingly aware of its inability to marshal the necessary funds and soldiers for a prolonged conquest. In the Jequitinhonha River valley, the divergence from the 1808 declaration of war prevented the bellicose proclivities of the state from subsuming fragile interethnic relationships. The appeal of arguments by men like the civilian Moura and the army officer Leão against the use of military force and the evidence of the practical results of their conciliatory approach gradually found their way out of the valley to be taken up by influential advisors who urged the crown to reevaluate its position. As events along the Jequitinhonha River showed, the Botocudo had demonstrated a willingness to respond to amicable overtures all along. The degree to which they succeeded in communicating this capacity along information channels running from the forests to the halls of power proved vital to their security and survival, at least temporarily. Their actions made possible the truce with soldiers along the river, which in turn allowed visiting naturalists like Wied to conduct investigations precluded elsewhere by interethnic violence. The German prince, however, brought his own misperceptions with him to the forest, skewing what the wider world would come to know about the Botocudo.

CHAPTER 9

# ETHNOLOGICAL MISADVENTURES

THE FINAL CHAPTER OF THIS study explores departures and continuities as the German prince took up his role as information broker, shaping understandings of the Brazilian interior and its inhabitants. Aimed at an audience located beyond Brazil's shores, his writings heralded a new iteration of the informant's role, that of the scientifically inclined, non-Portuguese interloper. Considered the most capable ethnologist among northern European travelers to write about the besieged Botocudo in the early nineteenth century, Prince Maximilian von Wied-Neuwied promoted a perspective on the backcountry information he accumulated that, predictably, was captive to ethnocentric biases. Elevating the Botocudo as objects of excited transnational scientific interest, he contributed what he learned about them, bolstering emerging theories of scientific racism. He did so while projecting an aura of erudite authority that persists to the degree that scholars still treat the data he collected, if not his less palatable conclusions, with due respect. Drawing on multidisciplinary scholarship that reconsiders the worldwide natural history and collecting expeditions characteristic of this period, we can uncover much that this reputation obscures.[1]

While Wied's investigations were wide-ranging, two components of his work are particularly revealing, one related to the dead, the other to the living; one artifactual, the other incarnate. The first concerned his efforts to procure a Botocudo skull to present to his academic mentor on returning to Europe. The second involved his acquisition of a young Botocudo informant named Guack. Taking advantage of the crown's relegalization of Indigenous slavery following its 1808 declaration of war against the Botocudo, Wied purchased Guack and included him in his traveling entourage. When Wied returned to Europe to write up his findings, Guack accompanied him. Ensconced in the secure setting of his family palace along the Rhine River, the naturalist continued to rely on his young Botocudo informant. Guack served as a living, physical specimen, available for uninterrupted questioning and observation, as Wied refined his theories and polished his account of his Brazilian travels to wide acclaim.

Wied's reports were also significant because of their characterization of Portuguese settler colonialism as it advanced tentatively inland from the coast, and coastward from Minas Gerais. His sustained ethnological investigations at two military installations along the Jequitinhonha River resulted in the most probing study of the valley's foragers during the years prior to Brazil's independence from Portugal in 1822. But his writings evinced little interest in events that preceded his arrival in the valley, and he ignored the legacy of Native efforts to influence the course of these events. Heavy reliance on Indigenous informants served Wied and fellow traveling naturalists in establishing credibility with readers, but at the cost of promoting a view of the Indians as remnants of a barbarous past outside history. As uncivilized relics of an early stage of human development, they could be spared annihilation only if they bowed to the promise of European progress. As Brazil relinquished mercantilist restrictions and opened to the world, not only as a source of international commerce but also of shared knowledge, the idea that the Botocudo themselves might have shaped the comparatively peaceful circumstances that allowed Wied to conduct his research entirely escaped the naturalist's perception.

### Forest Sojourn

Wied's party had their first sustained contact with the Botocudo along the coast, soon after proceeding northward from Espírito Santo into Bahia. Shocked by this meeting, the German prince dropped all pretense of scientific detachment. "The sight of the Botocudos astonished us beyond all expression; we had never before seen such strange and singularly ugly beings. Their original countenances were farther disfigured by large pieces of wood which they wore in their lower lips and in their ears." These were the ornamental plugs—the botoques—that more than any linguistic, cultural, or physical feature, accounted for colonists' classification of diverse forest-dwelling bands under the generic ethnonym Botocudo. "The lip is thus made to project very much, and the ears of some of them hang like large wings down to their shoulders. Their brown bodies were covered with dirt." No longer autochthons of the forest, these Natives were youths gathered in the town of Viçosa at the offices of the *ouvidor* (royal judge). From what can be gleaned from Wied's description, most if not all were male. They may have been enslaved under the terms of the war declaration, although this fate more commonly awaited women and children. Wied reported merely that the judge always kept these youths with him "in order to gain their confidence." Emaciated, many bore scars, evidence of recent bouts with smallpox. They were terrified of the disease, Wied learned. He recounted a story he heard of a planter who had scattered clothes contaminated by the virus in the woods, hoping to spread the contagion. Before this encounter ended, the judge pressed his wards to sing for the visitors. The music, Wied wrote, resembled "an inarticulate howling." Even as his familiarity with the Botocudo increased over time, he never shed his conviction that their language was "wild and barbaric."[2]

In August 1816 Wied hired five boatmen and two canoes to paddle his party and baggage from the town of Belmonte up the Jequitinhonha River to Fort Arcos, a five-day journey. It was at Fort Arcos and, briefly, at Fort Salto that the German prince would conduct his month-long study of the Botocudo. Before setting out Wied and his fellow travelers made sure they were well stocked with brandy as a remedy against forest "fevers." Illness would weaken them nonetheless, one by one. They were immediately sapped by the heat and humidity and tormented by mosquitos. Regaled by the cries of monkeys and parrots, they marveled at the profusion of forest flora and fauna. By day they landed paid hunters on the riverbanks to track unusual species for their collections; by night they lit cooking fires and built makeshift huts covered with cocoa leaves to protect them against mosquitos, predators, and the drenching rain. Limited knowledge of the surrounding area left them subject to basic geographic errors. Passing a tributary, for instance, they misidentified it as the Salsa River and mistakenly believed it connected the Jequitinhonha with the Pardo River to the north.[3]

After five days of paddling, they finally arrived at Fort Arcos, ready to study "pure Indians" living in "the rude state of nature." By the time the travelers made their appearance in the valley, however, more than a decade had elapsed since the aging explorer and frontier administrator José Moura at Tocoiós first dispatched his expeditions down this same river from Minas Gerais. The military effort to open a secure transportation and trade route down the valley under the command of Julião Leão was also well underway. Extensive interaction between Leão's soldiers and multiple Botocudo kin groups entailed constant contacts, both cooperative and conflictual, between and among these groups over the length of the river. The captaincy border presenting no barrier to Botocudo itineracy, upriver threats to their territorial control reverberated among downriver groups. Wied would consistently downplay the degree to which these preceding and concurrent intrusions had transformed the world of the groups he encountered. He was singularly uninterested in reflecting on the strategies they adopted to manage increasing pressure on their hunting grounds and competition for food and manufactured goods distributed by the Portuguese. Such considerations would have exposed the limits of his claim that the Botocudo with whom he interacted were all but unaffected by colonial society.[4]

He also scarcely registered a complex inter-Indigenous contest for territorial control, pitting the Botocudo against other Native groups, which set the context for encounters in which he participated at Fort Arcos and Fort Salto. Seeking to reap any advantage this struggle might afford while working to secure safe passage along the valley to Minas Gerais, the Bahian governor and his subordinates had calculated that the Botocudo could be enlisted as allies to fight the Pataxó, whose long-standing skirmishes with settlers in southern Bahia were deemed more immediately concerning than tension with the inland Botocudo. With this objective in mind, following the lead of Minas authorities, the Bahian governor offered the Botocudo gifts—knives, axes, cloth, caps, handkerchiefs, and other articles and tools—as well as refuge at the two forts. Additional forts upriver under Leão's command, constructed along Native trails descending the valley, functioned in tandem with these military outposts. Together the installations protected river transport, a portage around falls near the border dividing the two captaincies, and a rudimentary mule trail newly linking Minas Novas to Belmonte at the river's mouth. When Wied passed through Belmonte, before embarking upriver, the town had just begun receiving shipments of millet, salt pork, gunpower, cotton, and other provisions from Minas Gerais.[5] Neither the governor's attempted manipulations of intertribal rivalries in the valley, nor Wied's rose-tinted attributions of humanitarian zeal to this policy, recognized that the Botocudo, facing pressure from all sides, might have had their own reasons for seeking peaceful relations with the growing number of Portuguese intruders, while attempting to do so, as much as possible, on their own terms.

Occupying the downstream end of Cachoeirinha Island, Fort Arcos had been carved out of the tropical forest more than two years earlier on the Bahian governor's orders. Wied's letter of recommendation from the foreign ministry ensured a generous reception from its commanding officer. The modest installation consisted of a few wattle-and-daub huts with thatched roofs, surrounded by fields cultivated to feed a squadron of troops, fields dwarfed in turn by the towering hardwoods of the enveloping forest. Banana and papaya groves had been added for the purpose of attracting wandering Botocudo bands. The fruit was free for the taking, but no one at the post complained about the terms of this transaction. What settlers elsewhere considered raiding of their properties, here was accepted and encouraged "in order not to disturb the peaceable footing" on which the soldiers lived with the Indians. Recent tensions, however, had led "four hordes" of Botocudo to withdraw from the environs into the woods. One band was known to have migrated upriver to Minas Gerais, along the new trail that ascended from a point across from the island on the river's southern bank. There a priest migrating in the opposite direction from the inland captaincy had established a modest compound, planting corn, manioc, rice, cotton, and other crops. This forest fortification, thus sturdied on the pillars of church and state, made it possible for Wied's party to conduct its hunting, collecting, and ethnological probing over the following weeks.[6]

The soldiers manning the fort were "chiefly people of color, natives, or mulattos," the naturalist observed, registering their harsh daily lives. They were poorly paid and inadequately armed. Half the squadron had deserted, leaving only about ten men. The Native soldiers were especially adept at tracking and other military operations in the tropical forest. As a consequence, they suffered the dangers and indignities of men considered collaborators. "The civilized natives behave well as soldiers against their savage brethren," Wied noted. "The latter therefore bear a violent hatred against them, and are said to aim at them first, because they consider them as traitors to their country."[7] The European sojourners would find them indispensable as translators and guides.

The prince's daily excursions into the forest surrounding Fort Arcos began immediately. He focused on gathering plants and animals for his collections and learning everything he could about the Botocudo. His initial interactions with a Botocudo band occurred first in the forest within walking distance of the fort, and then at the fort itself. Believing the Botocudo absent from the area, he set off on foot one morning to examine some huts they had abandoned "at a considerable distance from the river, in the inmost recesses of the wilderness." At this encampment a young Botocudo, apparently a guide assigned to the party by the fort's commander, pointed out a grave in a clearing under some tall trees, covered by thick pieces of wood. Without hesitating Wied and his companions removed the wood and began pulling bones from the earth. The young guide "loudly expressed his dissatisfaction," forcing them to suspend their work.[8] Thus began the enactment of one of Wied's central preoccupations. Seeking Botocudo bones, above all a skull, he aspired to contribute to the nascent field of comparative anthropology, an outgrowth of the study of natural history to the extent that its practitioners, still mostly amateurs rather than academics, added the observation and classification of human

FIGURE 9.1. A naturalist's assistants. Source: Debret, *Voyage pittoresque*. Courtesy of the Biblioteca Brasiliana Guita e José Mindlin, São Paulo.

variation to that of minerals, flora, and fauna, extending the ambit of their data collection into increasingly accessible colonized lands.[9]

Some days later, the explorers again set out for the site, wielding pickaxes and shotguns, hoping to finish disinterring the remains before the absent "savages" returned. Without warning, several Botocudo, armed with bows and arrows, "naked and brown like the beasts of the forest," appeared on the path immediately behind the prince, interrupting the hypnotic greens of the tropical flora. "My surprise, I confess, was not small," he wrote. "Had they been inimically disposed, I should have been pierced by their arrows before I could have suspected they were near." Struggling to maintain his composure, he "advanced boldly towards them, and repeated what words I knew of their language." His overture produced the desired effect. They embraced him, clapping him on the shoulder, eyeing the party's guns. Women now appeared, equally nude, laden with heavy loads, carrying infants on their shoulders, leading older children by the hand. A member of Wied's party, someone who understood something of their language, helped ease the tension. This translator was likely a different Indigenous guide, since the one who had accompanied them the day before had expressed his strong displeasure with the party's actions. This translator explained that several of the forest dwellers' kinsmen had just returned to Fort Arcos after a long voyage in the company of a royal judge to Rio de Janeiro, having been invited to meet with members of the royal court. Excited by the news, the Botocudo hurried away in the direction of the fort. Wied expressed relief, "for if the savages, who had to pass close by the grave, had surprised us when engaged in our intended examination, their resentment might have involved us in great danger." Concerned about offending the subjects of his investigation, yet unwilling to be thwarted, Wied resolved to defer his grave site collecting until a more favorable opportunity presented itself.

A final meeting occurred on this day along the trail before Wied returned to the fort. The band's leader, known as Captain June to the Portuguese, called by his own people Querengnatnuck in Wied's rendering, appeared as suddenly as had the others. An "old man of rough appearance, but of a good disposition," panting under the weight of a massive burden of arrows and unworked reeds needed to make additional arrows, he wore lip and ear plugs noticeably larger than the others. These disks extended "four inches and four lines English in diameter," Wied wrote. He confirmed this observation when the headman later allowed him to measure the disks. Querengnatnuck inquired after his kinsmen who had traveled to Rio de Janeiro. Learning of their return, he, too, reacted joyfully and hurried away to the fort.

When Wied and his companions caught up with the Natives, "a great number" had installed themselves at the fort, inside and outside its simple structures. They struck Wied as ravenous, as they busied themselves stripping the papaya trees of their fruit, consuming the ripe fruits on the spot, and roasting or boiling the unripe ones over an open fire. They also ate manioc distributed by the soldiers. The Botocudo were visibly curious about the European newcomers. "A great part of them were contemplating with astonishment my people, whose appearance was very singular to them. They were not a little surprised at their white skin, light hair, and blue eyes." Wied lost no time building his ethnological collection. Offering "them knives, red handkerchiefs, glass beads, and other trifles, he traded with the Indians for their "arms, sacks, and other utensils." He noted they "manifested a decided preference for everything that was made of iron." These exchanges marked the beginning of the month of intensive interaction between the naturalist and the forest dwellers amid an uneasy but generally friendly relationship proceeding from initial Portuguese efforts to secure the valley.

The naturalist was struck by the marked contrast between relations with these peoples who were "so little feared" and those to the south in the Doce River basin who "manifest[ed] such irreconcilable hostility." In the company of these northern Botocudo, he explained, "people have even ventured to go several days' journey with them into the great woods to hunt, and to sleep with them there in their huts: such experiments however are not yet very frequent, as the distrust entertained of them cannot easily be quite overcome." For their part, the Botocudo liked "to be near the Europeans on account of the advantages they derive from them." They even demonstrated a willingness to adopt agricultural practices to supplement their hunting and gathering and their access to handouts at Fort Arcos, which were often scarce. Not far from the fort, for example, they had planted their own bananas. Such experience showed that "the Botocudos already begin to make advances towards civilization." Equally evident, however, was the certainty that it would prove "very difficult for them to renounce their natural roving hunter's life, since they so easily return to it even from plantations which they have themselves made." In a telling conclusion to these reflections, Wied added, "Nothing but the increasing population of the Europeans, and the contraction of [the Natives'] hunting grounds, can induce them to a gradual change in their mode of life."[10]

During his brief excursion to Fort Salto, a three-day paddle upriver, he resumed his quest for Botocudo bones. This fort, guarding the portage that skirted an unnavigable cataract at the border between Bahia and Minas Gerais, had been the original site chosen by the Bahian governor when he moved to establish a presence along the river to interdict

FIGURE 9.2. Near Fort Arcos the German prince observed rival Botocudo clans engage in ritualized combat. Source: Wied, Travels. Courtesy of the John Carter Brown Library. Licensed under CC-BY-SA 4.0.

contraband, protect itinerant merchants, tax intercaptaincy trade, and signal to the Botocudo the extension of Portuguese dominion over the lower reaches of the valley. The governor had based about sixty soldiers there, many of them of Indigenous origins, but their mounting discontent from unspecified causes prompted their relocation downriver to Fort Arcos. Julião Leão, the officer from Minas Gerais who had by this point engaged in extensive contact with the Botocudo upriver, moved to assume responsibility for Fort Salto. This transfer of authority made administrative sense since the fort stood on land claimed since 1811 by Minas Gerais, and the government of the inland captaincy had been the first to establish a military presence there after the 1808 declaration of war. One of Leão's subalterns commanded about a dozen men at the garrison, but when Wied and his party arrived, all but two, not counting the officer, a man of color, had left for duties upriver. In the soldiers' absence the fort was filled with

Botocudo men and women who were pausing there to receive provisions meant to keep them on good terms.[11]

Taking advantage of this opportunity to obtain the skull he so desired, Wied learned of a burial site a short distance from the fort. With pickaxes in hand he and his companions made short work of the task, unearthing the cranium of a young warrior. "We observed at the first sight an osteological curiosity," he wrote with practiced equanimity. "The large piece of wood, worn on the underlip, had not only pushed the lower fore-teeth out of their places, but even pressed together and effaced the alveoli or sockets of the teeth." This was unexpected in such a youthful skull. Normally such deformation happened "only to very old people."

Wied tried to keep the grave site operation secret, but word of it quickly spread among Fort Salto's occupants. It "excited a strong sensation among the unenlightened people," he reported. "Impelled by curiosity, and yet with a secret terror, several of them came to the door of my lodging and desired to see the head." But he had hidden the prized find in his trunk, and he hastily departed the next morning, returning to Fort Arcos. From there, he dispatched the skull to the coast, where waiting assistants added it to his growing collections. Reflecting further on the episode, Wied noted that "the Botocudos had taken less offense at this proceeding than the soldiers," who "refused to assist in the operation."[12] By comparison the Botocudo harbored neither superstitions about nor attachments to the bones of their dead, he averred. Ironically, their purported indifference would reinforce his dismal view of their place in the hierarchy of human civilizations. A short, final stay at Fort Arcos, during which the naturalist witnessed a violent but nonlethal ritual combat between two rival bands, concluded his time spent among the Botocudo.[13]

From the Jequitinhonha River, the expedition would proceed for another six months, including a final prolonged journey into the interior during which he explored scrublands farther north along the border between Bahia and Minas Gerais. The German prince then descended from the sertão to the coast for the last time. Before reaching Salvador, his party, now reduced to just six members, the others having gone their separate ways, was briefly detained by suspicious local authorities and escorted under guard to Nazaré, located across the Bay of All Saints from the Bahian capital. After gaining his release, nearly two years after first arriving in Brazil, he left Salvador in May 1817. He sailed for Portugal, England, and Belgium before making his way overland to his family palace on the Rhine in the foothills of the Westerwald.

## Birth Pangs of Anthropology

The skull Wied carried with him would figure as part of the evidence he deployed in a key chapter of his travel account titled "Some Words Concerning the Botocudos," considered by scholars to be, as one put it, the "first serious anthropological monograph on any Brazilian tribe."[14] This was the sole portion of his work in which he abandoned the travelogue conceit, replacing it with the determinedly analytical aesthetic of an ethnographic treatise. The chapter exhibited his expertise as an ethnologist, a new kind of informant reporting on the colonization of the eastern forests, an anticonquistador, to apply Pratt's term. He was not, that is, a colonist himself in any conventional sense, and he frequently criticized the Luso-Brazilian state's colonizing practices when it came to the treatment of the Botocudo. Yet he could not have carried out his work in the absence of the state's support and military protection, which he received from the displaced imperial administration as it advanced the work of territorial consolidation. Unlike the traditional conquistador, he sought knowledge, not land or riches. Instead, he wished to gather data to advance the fledgling enterprise of comparative anthropology, bolstering its scientific ambitions. To do so he would document Botocudo traditions before they vanished, as in his view they inevitably would. To the state and his readers at large, he also proffered advice for orchestrating Botocudo cultural dissolution in the least violent way possible, clearing the backlands for settler society. Like Moura, Leão, and others active upriver before him, he came to believe the Botocudo might be acculturated rather than exterminated.

Presenting his Indigenous subjects as "pure" Indians living in their natural state, Wied's ethnological treatise was in reality a sketch of a people facing existential threats, testing out ways they might approach intruders without losing their lives and lands.[15] As anthropologized informants, they would have their individual voices all but silenced, subsumed by Wied's detached synthetic analysis. In their collective actions, however, they persisted in making strategic overtures, building on the exchanges they had experimented with over the preceding decades. These actions influenced the conclusions Wied drew about their potential assimilability. As the Indigenous scholar Margaret Bruchac has described this dynamic in the North American context, anthropologists' Indigenous informants "observed the actions and motivations of the 'other-than-Indian' persons who came into their worlds, and attempted to mediate contacts with these strangers in ways that might prove the most beneficial and least harmful."[16]

When it came to cranial analysis, Wied did not possess the highly specialized expertise of Johann Blumenbach, his mentor at Göttingen, to whom he presented the most treasured artifact in his collection, the Botocudo skull unearthed, like a precious diamond, from the grave near Fort Salto. In preparations for publication, the illustrators of his travelogue would transform it into a startling lithograph. Adding it to a profusion of skulls sent to him by his students and other collectors from around the world, Blumenbach classified Wied's contribution as lying somewhere between the cranium of a man and that of an orangutan. He ordered a "race-bust" fashioned, a plaster-cast used to aid in studying "the outward forms of races."[17] With its dental deformations, the skull, now classified by Blumenbach, served Wied as the basis for a broader consideration of Botocudo appearance, physiognomy, racial type, and culture. The prince's wide-ranging analysis assessed the Natives' distinguishing use of lip plugs; the way they cut their hair; how they painted their bodies; the arms, tools, and utensils they used; their methods of constructing huts and encampments; their hunting, foraging, and dietary habits; their martial practices, including the differences between their deadly attacks on colonists and the ritual combat he had witnessed between rival bands; their territorial disputes with neighboring Indigenous groups; their familial, kinship, and polygynous marital customs; the singing and games they favored during hours of leisure; their ways of managing illness and death; their medical and religious beliefs; and the nature of their language.[18]

The treatise also included an assessment of the characteristic considered by virtually every early nineteenth-century commentator on Botocudo behavior as their most condemnable, cannibalism. Accusations of cannibalism had been decisive in the crown's 1808 declaration of war, a move Wied repeatedly criticized as misguided. In support of his recommendations of an alternative policy, he did not deny the existence of anthropophagy. Evidence of the practice, extensive at the time as hearsay but meager as documented eyewitness testimony, has been called into question by contemporary anthropologists and ethnohistorians.[19] Wied's investigations led in another direction, one consonant with the consensus of his time. While acknowledging that some of the evidence was suspect, he asserted that his own research had convinced him that the Botocudo did, in fact, consume human flesh. Referring to both the Botocudo and Puri, he wrote, "They cut the meat of their enemies into slices, cook it in a pot or roast it." Celebrating their victories in battle, he continued, they then removed cooked heads from this preparation, placing them on stakes and dancing around them while singing and shrieking. After sucking on the remaining bones, they hung them from the roofs of their cabanas. "It is difficult to believe, as some affirm, that they eat human flesh as a matter of preference," but "there is no doubt," he concluded, "that out of revenge they devour the flesh of their enemies killed in battle."[20]

The naturalist never witnessed these acts himself, but he consulted with Indigenous informants who led him to what he considered his undeniable finding: Botocudo, Puri, and possibly even Coroado anthropophagy was a reality. How he arrived at this conclusion exposes the frequently tortuous passage of information from informant to ethnologist. Many of his Native interlocutors denied the existence of the practice. But not Guack, the young Botocudo who became Wied's confidant. Following the model of his companion Freyreiss, Wied had acquired Guack, who was then twelve years old, in a transaction made along the coast, not long before the expedition's foray up the Jequitinhonha River.[21] The young Botocudo, despite his tender age, offered evidence about cannibalism the German prince considered incontrovertible. Under pressure to explain the practice in detail, Guack extinguished "any doubt in this respect," wrote Wied.[22]

To arrive at this conclusion, notwithstanding his search for confirmation from Guack, Wied favored European over Indigenous testimony and coaxed an answer consistent with that testimony from his primary Botocudo informants. While interviewing Puri Indians early in his voyage along the Paraíba River, his Native informants "would never confess to us that they eat human flesh." Some pointed to their Indigenous rivals as the only ones who persisted in doing so. But as Wied gathered what he considered somehow more "authentic testimonies" from his compatriot Freyreiss and a Portuguese priest, he concluded that Puri denials "cannot have much weight." With respect to Guack's testimony, Wied explained that the young Botocudo had for a long time refused to speak the truth, fearful of the consequences. He relented only after the naturalist assured him that he was not accusing his confidant of engaging in cannibalism. It had become clear in the course of Wied's research, he told Guack, that the youth's own band had long since abandoned the practice. It was at this point that Guack related the story of a Botocudo "chief" of another band who had captured a Pataxó rival. In celebration the chief's kinsmen prepared and consumed the body in the manner Wied reported as a customary "cannibal feast." Guack also described a second such incident.[23]

These direct exchanges with individual Natives concerning cannibalism were exceptional in that Wied usually acknowledged only obliquely how much he relied on Indigenous informants to enlighten him. This was typical for the European naturalists of his era. In the chronological, diary-like narration of his Fort Arcos stay, he briefly mentioned multiple interactions with an assistant he called Ahó, whom he characterized as "my Botocudo." Ahó served as a boatman and hunter, yet he did not reappear as an informant in Wied's subsequent ethnological ruminations.[24] Conversely, Wied did not once mention Guack in his account of the Fort Arcos visit. That the young Botocudo was with him throughout this period becomes clear to the reader only in the subsequent chapter—that is, in the analytical treatise on Botocudo culture. Here, Wied introduced Guack similarly, as "one of my Botocudos." He also credited Guack with explaining a few mysteries other than cannibalism. The informant responded, for instance, to Wied's

FIGURE 9.3. Wied hunting with his Botocudo informant Guack. Source: Johann Heinrich Richter, Prinz Maximilian zu Wied-Neuwied mit Joachim Quäck auf der Jagd im brasilianischen Urwald, oil on canvas, 1828, Brasilien-Bibliothek der Robert Bosch GmbH, Stuttgart, public domain, https://upload.wikimedia.org/wikipedia/commons/a/af/Prinz_Maximilian_zu_Wied-Neuwied_mit_Joachim_Qu%C3%A4ck_auf_der_Jagd_im_brasilianischen_Urwald.jpg.

queries about Botocudo dancing. The youth also explained that, counter to what some maintained, his people knew no cure for snakebites. At least until the pair began to learn something of each other's languages, these exchanges would have required third-party translation. Wied further acknowledged conferring with Botocudo "captains" or chiefs on a number of occasions, communication that similarly would have occurred through a translator.[25]

But these instances of acknowledged person-to-person communication were few and fleeting when weighed against the voluminous data collected by the erudite traveler in innumerable interactions with what must have been a procession of Indigenous subjects during his month-long stay at Fort Arcos. One can hardly help but wonder how he came to understand what he witnessed. How did he come to know things that could not be gleaned through visual observation alone? Who explained the intricacies of Botocudo customs and conduct? He must have benefited from, not merely an acknowledged few, but an almost ceaseless stream of information originating from Indigenous men and women mediated by an unspecified number of translators of varying ability, including Indigenous soldiers and other intermediaries.

An obfuscating breach between what Wied learned and how he learned it looms over the ethnological treatise. A few examples will suffice to elucidate this hidden transfer of knowledge from the anthropologized to the anthropologist. Wied explained that the respect afforded the "chiefs" in charge of the various Botocudo "hoards" that wandered up and down the Jequitinhonha River valley hinged on their "warrior qualities." How did he know? In years past, he added, these headmen adorned themselves with headdresses of a dozen or more feathers, which made for a "beautiful contrast to the denigrated color of their hair," but which they no longer used. How could he know? "The masculine sexual organs appear to be always of moderate size among the native peoples of South America." Had he inspected enough of these unclothed men to support such generalization? "The love of a life of freedom, rude and independent," he wrote of Botocudo children, "is inscribed profoundly from early on in the spirit of the young, and remains as such throughout their lives." Did the children really express this sentiment to Wied, even through translators? When a member of their band died, the Botocudo grieved with "dreadful moans," women in particular behaving as if they were "crazy." Their pain evidently did not penetrate deeply, however, because the next day they appeared unaffected, "resuming their habitual lives." Even with visual cues, how did Wied divine his male and female subjects' innermost feelings?[26] Such assessments presented as facts proliferated in the prince's treatise. They rely on information he could have obtained only from Indigenous informants whom he almost always neglected to identify. The added explanation—that he also relied on the published accounts of other travelers, the conventional wisdom of Portuguese colonists, pernicious stereotypes, and his own unsubstantiated assumptions—is obvious in some if not all of these instances. Either way, the silenced presence of Indigenous interlocutors and translator-intermediaries loomed throughout an ethnography hailed as one of the most perceptive ever written about the Botocudo, a text that secured Wied's fame.

Although the naturalist mentioned him only rarely after he left the river valley, Guack traveled with Wied for the remaining six months of his overland journey. After crossing the Atlantic and taking up residence in the Wied family palace, now speaking rudimentary German, the adolescent presumably spent day after day answering the prince's queries about words to be included in the Botocudo vocabulary appended to the text.[27] He also helped clarify the meaning of myriad puzzling actions and behaviors Wied had recorded in his field notes. As had been the case during the pair's interactions in Brazil, whatever the mechanisms of this palace exchange may have been, it ended up all but effaced in the final publication.

Such erasure comes as no surprise. It has been a vexing problem for the ethnographic enterprise since its foundation, thoroughly debated for decades by anthropologists, incisively criticized by Indigenous scholars, and deconstructed by literary critics. The Indigenous literary critic and German studies scholar Renae Dearborn, who has written about Wied's North American travels, views such silencing as contributing to the project of "fictionalizing the indigenous in German travel literature," although the problem was by no means restricted to German writers.[28] This

268 CHAPTER NINE

feature of backlands information gathering must be registered as a critical determinant of what the German prince managed to know and communicate about the Native peoples he studied, including their response to the growing presence of Portuguese soldiers, long-distance traders, and the first colonists attempting to establish themselves in the heart of their territory. Such knowledge transfers, Pratt reminds us, rested on "radically asymmetrical relations of power," which frequently subverted communication.[29]

In the concluding paragraphs of the chapter dedicated to Botocudo ethnology, Guack was ultimately transformed into a different kind of informant. Installed in Wied's palace, he became a living exemplar of the forest peoples the prince strove to render faithfully in prose, an animate specimen available for physical inspection. The ongoing possibility of such direct contact, Wied maintained, set his work apart from other accounts authored by those who had never "personally observed" the Botocudo. With this walking, talking evidence at his disposal, he turned to his culminating reflections on Botocudo racial typology, beginning with the question of skin color. Dismissing what some surmised about the possibility that the Botocudo were born white, their skin subsequently darkening through exposure to the tropical sun and other climatological factors, Wied insisted there was no basis for this view. They were never born "white like us." He based this conclusion "on information from my Botocudo Guack," who rejected the possibility.

From his own observations Wied acknowledged that their hue did vary widely, just as the shape of their foreheads, height, and weight varied. Striving to explain this physical differentiation, Wied consulted those with greater expertise. He turned to his scientific mentors Blumenbach and Humboldt, among others, concerning this and other enigmas of comparative anthropology, including the problem of human origins that so fascinated scientists of his era. These authorities, whom he mentioned in his text and cited in footnotes, assured him that the physiognomy and color of the Botocudo, as well as other "tribes," matched "perfectly with those of indigenous nations of North America." Even so, substantial change was possible if they were removed from their Native environment. Guack again stood in as evidence incarnate, demonstrating "in an eloquent manner the influence of climate over skin color." During the sunny Rhineland summer, his face appeared brown, but in winter it lightened to a tone so "clear," his cheeks slightly reddening, that some even mistook him as European. "I must recall, however," Wied added, he "does not belong to the darkest race of Botocudos." In the end, the naturalist admitted, it was "extremely difficult to decipher the mystery of the origin of many racial groups in the Americas."[30]

Ultimately, his accumulated reading, travel, and fieldwork, along with this opportunity to observe Guack in a different setting for an extended period, confirmed Wied's embrace of the monogenism advocated by many thinkers of his day, those, like Blumenbach and Humboldt, who posited the common descent of all humankind from a single originary pair, regardless of racial differences. The acceptance of monogenism did not in itself translate into racial tolerance. While for Humboldt it underlay a radical vision of human equality, for Blumenbach monogenism supported conclusions that established him as a precursor of scientific racism. Even Humboldt's position should not be mistaken for the cultural relativism embraced by anthropologists only a century later. Although he attributed to the depredation of European oppression and colonialism what many of his scientific contemporaries theorized as Indigenous peoples' innate racial and cultural inferiority, he did not hesitate to condemn cannibalism, infanticide, and other practices he thought revolting.[31]

Like Humboldt, Wied decried colonial persecution, but he was much more willing to denigrate the subjects of his fieldwork on the Jequitinhonha River as culturally inferior. In this realm his ethnological interpretations hinged on a number of assumptions. Well before he reached the forts on the Jequitinhonha River and spent weeks in the company of the Botocudo—or at least before he did so in the course of the carefully constructed narrative he later authored—he had become convinced that the royal campaign to exterminate or forcibly pacify the Botocudo was misguided. Furthermore, he believed a more compassionate approach, epitomized in his view by the Bahian governor, could achieve the government's desired control over the eastern forests without bloodshed.

Such humane action, however, would have to proceed in the face of what he acknowledged to be the implacable savagery of the Botocudo. "The most brutish sensuality dominates their intellectual faculties, which does not impede them at times from being capable of sensible judgement and even a certain acuity of spirit," he wrote, summing up his view of the moral character of his anthropological subjects. It was true that those made to live among "whites" exhibited positive alterations in behavior, engaging in a comic mimicry of the actions they observed, being particularly keen students of dance and music. However, "as they are neither guided by any moral principle, nor subject to any social restraint whatsoever," the Botocudo were inevitably prone to "yield entirely to their five senses and their instincts, just like jaguars in the forest. The irrepressible urges of their passions, vengeance and envy in particular, are all the more fearful in them, as they erupt quickly and suddenly."

Additional character traits of the adult males who, from what he had observed, dominated the women and children in their bands, included an obsession with seeking retribution for the most minor offense. This short-fused vengeance produced an uncontrollable, murderous anger and a lack of concern for the value of human life. Yet the Botocudo also conceded a ready fealty, even obeisance, to those who treated them kindly. Finally, "one of the traits most characteristics of these savages is their laziness." Spurred from their natural indolence only when hungry, even then the males insisted on the "rights" they claimed based on their physical dominance, leaving for women and children most tasks other than hunting and warfare. The women constructed encampments, foraged in the forest, carried heavy loads, cared for children. Forced to obey their husbands, wives displayed scarred bodies that testified to the beatings they received when they failed to do so. Maximilian, of course, was ill-prepared to diagnose Botocudo gender relations. His "patriarchal *Weltanschauung*" and "ethnocentricity," in the words of one scholar who has studied his later glosses of Indigenous women in North America, combined to corrupt his objectivity as a natural historian, interfering with his "Linnaean discourse. Instead of starting with a blank page in his narrative, the Prince's ideological framework predetermine[d] his observations."[32]

Ultimately, Wied's dim, ostensibly scientific view of Botocudo culture diverged only slightly from the dominant Portuguese colonialist discourse. The crown and the naturalist agreed on the savagery of the forest Indians and the irreconcilability of Botocudo lifeways in their present state with the imperatives of progress. Even the naturalist's recommendation for responding to their intransigence not with violence but with patient benevolence had precursors in Portuguese Indigenous policies dating to the sixteenth century and, more immediately, to Pombal's Indian Directorate. For Wied, the justification for such a response did not spring from any sympathy for their character and conduct but rather from a solution-seeking conviction, nearly as impatient with Iberians as it was with Amerindians, a conviction characteristic of the northern European anticonquistador, that the best way to correct the defective behavior of the Botocudo was to encourage their peaceable transformation into vassals and citizens. All of Wied's reporting on official efforts to draw the Jequitinhonha River valley into the crown's sovereign domain was colored by these opposing notions: that the Botocudo, "whose stage of civilization is the lowest of all," might nevertheless "gradually progress to a more advanced degree of culture." With an expanding colonial population pushing them westward from the coast and eastward from landlocked Minas Gerais into ever-shrinking forest hunting grounds, there could be little doubt, Wied concluded, that the Botocudo would, one way or another, finally "march along the road to civilization."[33]

Some have argued that Wied separated himself from other scientific travelers of the early nineteenth century era by acknowledging the possibility of Botocudo humanity. But in this fundamental respect concerning Botocudo perfectibility, Wied's perspective matched the discursive conventions of his fellow natural historians, adventurers who sought out peoples they considered Brazil's most primitive indigenes. He contrasted Indigenous and northern European societies, representing the latter as paragons of civilization while proposing strategies for integrating the former into colonial society as productive vassals and citizens.[34] As Wied articulated the basis for this position, "One cannot really expect to find in the raw nature of these men the feelings of delicacy and tenderness that culture and education have developed in us; but, for that reason, we should not think that the attributes have been completely dulled that distinguish man from irrational beings."[35] Some also argue that most of these northern European visitors demonstrated greater interest in and optimism regarding Native peoples as potential industrious citizens than did the Portuguese. But we have seen how some Portuguese frontier authorities—men like Moura and Leão—who arrived in the Jequitinhonha River valley well before the German prince were already practicing what he preached, favoring assimilation over extermination.

## Backlands Transnationalized

Wied's reputation, connections, and personal wealth helped guarantee the promotion of and intense interest in the published narrative resulting from his expedition. Multiple translations of the original two-volume German edition (1820–21) into English, French, Dutch, and Italian appeared almost simultaneously. The first Portuguese translation did not appear until 1940, limiting readership in Brazil to bilingual, book-buying elites for more than a century.[36] Hemispheric awareness of Wied's work strengthened in the 1830s, after he mounted another scientific voyage, in the company of Swiss artist Karl Bodmer, traveling from St. Louis, up the Missouri River, to the American Fur Company's westernmost outpost at Fort McKenzie, near present-day Loma, Montana.[37]

Even before the narrative of his Brazilian journey appeared in print, news of the prince's travels captivated the press in Europe and the United States. Upon Wied's return to Europe, a Boston newspaper heralded "the superb collection of plants and minerals" he brought with him. Rumor, distortion, and sensationalism accompanied the news, echoing the fictions that had always surrounded information transferred from the Brazilian backlands, notwithstanding the scientific aspirations of the era. Citing a French report, the same Boston newspaper falsely claimed Wied was accompanied back to his homeland by "a young female savage of the tribe of Boutoucondus [*sic*], who would feed on human flesh, in preference to any other, if she could procure it." Another report maintained he had returned with an entire "royal Indian family, consisting of the king, queen, and an infant prince" of the Puris. The Puris, "being at war with the tribe of Botiludos [*sic*], killed their kings." In this fashion the Puri leader supposedly in Wied's company had acquired his queen, who, "by right of war, became the prize." A more circumspect notice in a New York City newspaper, representative nonetheless of the excitement generated among literati on both sides of the Atlantic on the 1820 publication of the first volume of Wied's account, described it as "one of the most important [works] that has yet appeared respecting this interesting, but hitherto imperfectly known country." Ensuring the value of his contribution, he had examined "totally unknown regions along the east coast of Brazil," places that "had not yet been penetrated into by any traveler, with a scientific view."[38]

Wied cultivated the sensation surrounding his travel account by emphasizing this trope of journeying into the unknown. He made it the central justification for his voyage and a primary claim for the importance of his contribution. Before the royal court's precipitous migration to the Americas, he wrote in his introduction, Brazil as a whole had remained a place apart from the circuits of European intellectual exchange. In the sixteenth century Portuguese mariners and a few northern European visitors like Jean de Léry, the French Huguenot, and Hans Staden, the Hessian sailor, had conveyed some limited information concerning the natural history of the tropical colony. Jesuit missionaries added to these early reports, as did the natural historians Willem Piso and Georg Marcgrave in the first half of the seventeenth century during the Dutch occupation of northeastern Brazil. Only recently had the first northern European naturalists been permitted to visit inland Minas Gerais. "On my arrival in Brazil, therefore, I thought it best to select the East coast, which was still quite unknown, or at least not described," wrote Wied. Of particular interest, he noted, were "the aboriginal inhabitants [who] yet live there in their primitive state, undisturbed by the Europeans."[39]

He framed his venture, in other words, as a mission to study a realm of nature hitherto not subjected to the sort of intelligence gathering that would make it intelligible to European readers. Such a conceit ignored Portugal's aggressive efforts, especially since the mid-eighteenth century, to accumulate experience in and knowledge of the continental interior.

Against all historical precedent it construed the coastal zone as one of the colony's least-known realms, even though it was the longest and most thoroughly colonized of Brazil's regions. Furthermore, Wied recast the Indigenous occupants of the coastal forests not merely as primitives, which the Portuguese also believed, but as the objects, along with rocks, plants, animals, and insects, of scientific investigation rather than as the historical subjects they were.

In the political realm Wied's critique of official Indigenous policy was similar to that of authorities like Moura, Leão, and a few others who effected the work of frontier incorporation for the crown but were willing to speak out against its methods. His position also differed as a backcountry informant in that he was comparatively independent of government patronage. His primary audience was no longer the imperial administration, and the advice he proffered regarding inland colonization was not his central purpose. The advent of accounts like his and those published subsequently by German, French, British, Austrian, Russian, and other erudite voyagers pointed to a new era in the flow of information out of the Brazilian interior to the global north's armchair adventurers, scientists, and merchants eager for news about potentially profitable commodities available for exploitation in a transformed colony, soon to be an independent nation, in which the old mercantilist restrictions no longer obtained.

A generation ago historians still heralded this new knowledge regime as evidence of the young nation's embrace of modernity. As one scholar proclaimed, the spate of scientific expeditions opened "new horizons for the life the country," as some of the world's leading savants "put their learning at the service of understanding the flora, fauna, geography, geology, paleontology, and ethnology, of this portion of the New Continent."[40] More recently and skeptically, scholars have underlined the preconceptions such scientific voyagers brought to their investigations. Aristocratic, romanticist, European, white, wealthy, and patriarchal, Wied could not escape his social and ideological biases as he described the natural world he explored. His purpose was not simply to render his Indigenous subjects faithfully, but to establish his own status as an authority able to reveal truths about Natives whom he maintained others had previously failed to understand, sometimes diminishing as untrustworthy even what the Botocudo themselves told him. He distanced his putative European objectivity from what he construed as Amerindian primeval illogic. Assuming the persona of an intrepid, clear-eyed discoverer, he cast life in the tropical forest as antithetical to modernity, fortifying the developmentalist imperatives subsequently used to justify the eastern forest's environmental degradation as it was cut down and transformed into unevenly arable land.

Allowing that the Botocudo could be shorn of their cultural defects and peaceably integrated into civilized society, his simultaneous insistence on their radical alterity reinforced the prevailing derogation of their nomadism and tribalism, among other practices essential to their survival, while lending legitimacy to efforts to colonize their territory. Upon his return to Europe, his dressing, coiffing, and displaying of Guack enacted this vision of European dominion over tropical nature and its uncivilized inhabitants. So did the oil portrait of a Europeanized Guack that the noble naturalist commissioned and hung in his palace, the young, dark-eyed informant staring solemnly at the viewer from the canvas, head angled to exhibit a distended earlobe, its large perforation the only evidence of the wooden disk he had once donned. Taught to speak German, the more he learned, the more he was able to help Wied understand the intricacies of his own language, prolonging his service as cultural insider, interpreter, and research collaborator. Guack died in 1833, still living with Wied. His remains became the object of further scientific study.[41]

In concluding his travelogue Wied encouraged others to follow in his footsteps. He appended recommendations for naturalists planning future expeditions in Brazil, along with a corrected map of the region he had traveled.[42] His collections of vegetable, animal, and mineral specimens kept him busy with the work of classification for decades, during which he published numerous scientific papers, identifying many new species. These specimens, along with his collection of Indigenous weapons and other ethnological materials, found their way into museum cases in Europe and the United States. They were the harbinger of new knowledge networks linking the Brazilian interior to a wider world. They served to satisfy the curiosity, as historian Ângela Domingues has written, of a "cultured and cosmopolitan" European elite for an "an immense territory that, even at the beginning of the nineteenth century, was poorly understood." The advent of works by traveling naturalists like Wied would help close this gap, drawing two continents together, a Europe "considered intellectually and technologically superior" and a South America that one day might likewise be civilized.[43]

In the Brazilian interior, meanwhile, the incorporation of the internal frontier of the Atlantic Forest remained far from complete. Violence perpetrated locally by soldiers and especially settlers against Indians persisted through the 1820s and well beyond. On the upper Jequitinhonha River in Minas Gerais, notwithstanding Wied's sanguine narrative of amicable relations, another scientist-voyager, the French botanist Auguste de Saint-Hilaire, witnessed continuing "horrible abuses" a decade after the war declaration, exacerbated by its clause relegalizing Indigenous slavery. "Mulattos and even whites buy [Indian] children from their parents for trinkets, or carry them off by force, and then sell them in the villages of the interior," he lamented, although he, too, doggedly sought a Botocudo child for his own, acquiring first a girl, later exchanged for a boy, whom he, like Freyreiss and Wied before him, referred to as "my Botocudo" before the youth finally fled. Along the stretch of the river he traveled, "there were already no children left in those tribes that communicate most with the Portuguese; and in order to be able to sell more children, those tribes make war on others farther distant."[44]

Like Wied, Saint-Hilaire denounced offenses perpetrated by the Portuguese against the Botocudo, and his recipe for resolving the conflict similarly revealed his racial determinism. Brazilian authorities, he advocated, should "seek to encourage legitimate unions of Botocudo damsels with free negro and mulatto men" in order to "obtain, thereby, a mixed race, more capable than the Indians of resisting the superiority of the whites, a race that will be more in harmony with our degree of civilization." He also recorded an Indigenous twist on Portuguese logic. The Portuguese fashioned the Botocudo along the Jequitinhonha River as friendly and those along the Doce River as inveterate enemies. The Botocudo thought the problem originated in Portuguese hostility, not their own. From his

Indigenous informants the Frenchman learned that the northern and southern bands perceived themselves as getting along well. The latter informed the former of the Portuguese attacks they suffered, leading the Botocudo of the Jequitinhonha River valley to conclude there were "two species of Portuguese, the good ones they know, and the bad ones" responsible for the ongoing aggression to the south.[45]

Against these odds, the Botocudo persisted. Wied recognized their enduring potential power. "Europeans are still very weak in the immense forests of eastern Brazil," he wrote. If the diverse Native peoples who still resided there were to "unite among themselves," coordinating attacks against the Portuguese, their "common enemy," it would not take long for the entire region of the central coast and its interior to fall back into their hands.[46] But this reversal was not to be.

Brazil ended its colonial subordination to Portugal in 1822, uniquely retaining the rule of its royal dynasty under a hastily assembled constitutional monarchy led by Emperor Pedro I, son of João VI. With the advent of this independent Brazilian Empire, the most powerful critic of royal Indigenous policy was José Bonifácio de Andrada e Silva, naturalist, statesman, and leading ideologue of a new national sovereignty as well as the mineralogist José Vieira Couto's old detractor. In his capacity as first minister to the emperor, he found himself allocating provisions destined for Indians, which frontier agents were requesting as they searched for nonviolent solutions to ongoing conflicts in the eastern forests. He released state funds to purchase, among many other items, mirrors, knives, hoes, nails, scissors, tobacco, beads, utensils of various sorts, paper products, bolts of cloth, images of saints, medicines, and even rifles for a company of Native soldiers.[47] He stuck to this tactic even though ranking regional officials informed him that settlers in the forest had "suffered greatly from those anthropophagi." The officials continued, "When at war they are terrifying, when at peace they are pernicious." When offered provisions the Botocudo merely "devoured" these handouts at great sacrifice to colonists.[48]

José Bonifácio famously proposed in 1823 a less bellicose approach to Brazil's Indigenous peoples, focusing on the revitalization of a mission village system meant to improve on colonial precedents. In doing so, despite being exiled the following year during the political turmoil that followed independence, he helped nudge the young nation to adopt Indigenous policies emphasizing exactly the kind of stance that Moura, Leão, and Wied advocated, a position then disseminated by the German naturalist to observers far beyond Brazil. "Even the Botocudos and Puris, against whom we have recently declared a cruel war, are becoming domesticated," José Bonifácio wrote. In some sectors of the eastern forests, military men had managed to gain their trust. In others, open warfare had produced limited gains. Reason and experience dictated that, "although the wild Indians are a mean, lazy, and to a great extent an ungrateful and inhumane race of men," they were "capable of civilization, as long as one adopts proper methods and employs constancy and true zeal."

Like the warfare strategy, this alternative approach had first gained adherents on a regional level, percolating up from the backlands to the central government in Rio de Janeiro. By 1823, when José Bonifácio articulated his vision, the state was already adopting milder legislation governing the treatment of the Indians of Minas Gerais and Espírito Santo, even though the declared war would not end officially until 1831. He was well aware of experiments, highlighted in his policy recommendations, like those along the Jequitinhonha River, in which nonviolent, or at least less violent, methods proved successful. It seems all but certain, considering his polyglot literacy, voracious scientific interests, concern for territorial consolidation, and commitment to absorbing Brazil's Native peoples as citizens, that he had read Wied's account, which by then had been published in five languages. Like Wied, he believed in the present savagery yet potential perfectibility of Brazil's Native peoples, a transformation that could occur only following their submission to Brazil's colonizing neo-European state and settler society.[49]

Only after years of state-sponsored aggression did the crown adopt this alternative policy amid mounting financial strains on the royal treasury. The push to foster material exchange with the region's Natives came to correspond with the search for solutions other than military conquest. Fiscal considerations alone cannot explain this reevaluation. The crown considered the war a useful tool for extending its power over unincorporated lands and linking the interior with burgeoning Atlantic markets, but the complex character of interethnic exchanges limited its success. No small part of the policy reversal stemmed from the capacity of the eastern Indians to forestall state-organized conquest, at least in the Jequitinhonha River valley, through strategic engagement with territorial intruders in ways that diffused conflict. However inequitable or coerced, such exchange required more than one willing party. Every instance of harmonious relations cited as promising by those who sought to colonize the valley required Botocudo participation. By demonstrating a willingness, even if under conditions of extreme duress, to entertain interactions that some officials recognized as rational, the Indigenous peoples of Brazil's eastern forests undermined a war policy and imperial geopolitics that denied them their humanity.

During the final years of colonial rule and the early years following independence, in the towns and villages of Minas Gerais, a small but significant population of Indians and individuals of partial Native descent lived side by side with colonists, daily proving themselves adept at navigating the passage into settled society, despite official discourse that continued to brand them as irrationals. They made up as much as 3 percent of the population of many urban enclaves in Minas Gerais. In parishes on the edge of the eastern forests, this percentage could be substantially higher. Such was the case in São João Batista and its subdistrict of São Januário, where in 1825 settled Indians identified in a parish census made up 14 and 21 percent of the population, respectively. By then, independence having arrived on the frontier with little fanfare, this was the route that increasing numbers of Botocudo, Puri, Coroado, and others were traveling, as the possibility of sustaining lives devoted to hunting and gathering diminished. Taking up residence in state-financed villages, at first intermittently and gradually with greater permanence, they tapped into supplies of food, tools, and other provisions in exchange for peaceful coexistence.[50]

A comprehensive resolution to the region's interethnic tensions, however, remained far in the future. Some would argue it never arrived. Maps drafted as late as the 1860s still characterized extensive swaths of this inland frontier as "unsettled lands" and "little-known forests inhabited by indigenes." By the 1880s the great bulk of the estimated remaining twelve to fourteen thousand Botocudo were described by a British anthropologist as "still in the savage state, forming the most numerous and one of the fiercest wild tribes in East Brazil," and still practicing cannibalism. Put differently, the Botocudo remained in control of substantial if diminishing hunting, fishing, and gathering grounds, especially to the north of the Doce River, a testament to their ability to withstand concerted efforts to reduce them to submission, whether by military means or material dependence.[51] Often at great risk to their security, the Indigenous occupants of this zone continued to devise strategies to ensure their survival. Measured in terms of the more than three centuries that they prolonged their hold on forests just inland from the Atlantic coast and extending across much of eastern Minas Gerais, they succeeded.

Accusations of cannibalism had provoked the declaration of just war in 1808, yet the Native peoples condemned for this practice had asserted, in turn, a territorial autonomy that ultimately outlasted the crown's willingness to prosecute that war. Moura, Leão, Wied, José Bonifácio, and a few other non-Indigenous critics assailed the legitimacy of the war, striking out at the official consensus. Their vision of luring Native foragers into Brazilian society without recourse to state violence can be said to have prevailed to a limited degree. The purpose here, however, is not to lionize a handful of comparatively flexible officials who advocated peaceful methods. These same individuals never wavered in their conviction that the colonial state had every right to insist on the political, economic, and cultural subordination of independent Indigenous peoples. All were prone to deprecatory, ethnocentric notions about Indigenous cultures. All believed that the Native peoples of the eastern forests practiced cannibalism, which they saw as an unconscionable defect as well as a justification for the incorporation, as rapidly as possible, of the backlands into colonial and, later, national domain. Together, moreover, their narratives universally obscured the role of Native peacemaking, which restrained the state's most violent inclinations in its drive to consolidate territorial sovereignty. Despite being accused of a practice viewed by others as placing them beyond the purview of frontier diplomacy, the Native inhabitants of the Jequitinhonha River valley embraced conciliatory methods. They convinced a handful of key officials and visiting naturalists that less coercive methods could succeed.

Throughout these decisive years the aboriginal inhabitants of the Jequitinhonha River valley and surrounding coastal forests mattered not merely as tenacious antagonists to colonial domination. They mattered because their presence preoccupied the highest ranks of the Portuguese state; because their conduct exposed the spuriousness of state policies; because their absorption into the body politic challenged notions of who counted as royal vassals and citizens; because their knowledge of the lands they controlled was unparalleled; and not least because they asserted their humanity, even when decried for engaging in innumerable acts of savagery. Cast as both irrationally violent and fatally powerless, naive, and doomed, they exercised remarkable influence over the course of events, transforming their verdant lands into a space in which royal imperatives were contested, altered, and sometimes even nullified.

The state's inability to impose its will in the backlands through military means should not be mistaken for an outcome that permanently favored the Native peoples of the eastern forests. By midcentury the failure of an independent Brazil's central government to secure the frontier resulted in increasing private violence, as settlers continued their drive to control land, labor, and resources.[52] By the turn of the twentieth century, few forest dwellers remained who had not entered Brazilian society.

Notably, of all the regions studied in these chapters, none remains to this day more impoverished than the Jequitinhonha River valley, none more impervious to the kind of transformative modernization that imperial administrators, colonists, and naturalists envisioned in the early nineteenth century. In 2011 Guack's remains, long exhibited at the University of Bonn, were repatriated to the Krenak, struggling descendants of the Botocudo, who reside on federally protected lands along the Doce River. The area was devasted in 2015 by a mining disaster that polluted the river with tailings and toxic chemicals.[53] Meanwhile, craniometric studies of Botocudo skulls collected in the nineteenth century continue, now including DNA analysis, leading one group of present-day scientists to conclude that the Botocudo descended from paleolithic cave dwellers who inhabited the famed Lagoa Santa archeological site in central Minas Gerais some ten thousand years ago. Without consent, in the form of their remains, the Botocudo thereby still serve the scientific community as informants.[54]

EPILOGUE

# HOW TO TAME AN EMPIRE

AFTER DESCENDING THE Jequitinhonha River valley in late 1816 and proceeding northward along the Bahian coast, Prince Maximilian von Wied-Neuwied had the opportunity to consider the "many legends" he had heard over the course of his voyage concerning the ranges rising to the west. Even at this late date, decades after the mining boom, these mountains were thought to be "rich in gold and precious stones." Some still believed a "fabulous Eldorado" lay inland, where with little effort "great riches" could be found, rivaling the imagined abundance of the mythical South American site sought by Spanish conquistadors in the sixteenth century. Such tales led the German naturalist to ponder the distance between rumor and reality, the same gap in information exchanges that had long vexed Portuguese imperial administrators in their struggle to extend royal sovereignty over the continental interior. "European adventurers, avid for gold, excited by these fabulous narratives, risked wandering all parts of the New World in search of this paradise so ardently desired," he mused. "To find it, they penetrated the most distant forests of this vast continent, and many never returned." The result of this obsession, paradoxically, was that the Portuguese, like the Spaniards, had acquired only "a few incomplete notions" concerning South America's "conditions and geography."[1] Had this herald of European anthropology, botany, and zoology known about the frontier administrator José Moura and his search for the Golden

Lagoon, or had he known that Lieutenant Julião Leão had taken up this same search for riches while establishing the state's military presence along the upper Jequitinhonha River valley, Wied might have closed his eyes, shaken his head, and lamented the folly of yet two more men driven by their thirst for material gain.

Traveling in Minas Gerais, the French botanist Auguste de Saint-Hilaire did know about these two officials, having visited the region where they were active. He recognized that the Americas were not the only place where "ambition made men chase after chimeras." Still, he thought it "very strange that, in such a vast extension of the New World," treasure hunters had so consistently linked the idea of an inland body of water "to imaginary riches that gave rise to so many adventurous expeditions." He cited Humboldt's theory that the myth of Eldorado could be tied to the sparkling mica-laden sediments found in some South American lakes. Thus explained, these fables epitomized the "illusions that so often seduce and agitate men," the botanist concluded.[2]

The British mineralogist John Mawe made similar observations, stressing the need for a more systematic approach to the interior's untapped potential. When in 1812 he published the account of his visit to Minas Gerais, he emphasized the generalized ignorance of the region's populace. He criticized the "want of science" that prevented them from benefiting from abundant resources. The government should establish learned societies in the captaincy's principal towns, modeled on European counterparts, to encourage inquiry into "the useful arts," develop technical knowhow, design mining and agricultural machinery, distribute relevant publications, promote commerce, and ameliorate the harsh working conditions of the enslaved. Patronized by the crown, such societies should, in short, "promote the cultivation of science among the inhabitants." The state would thereby awaken a "spirit of enquiry" in its people, who would "learn to appreciate the blessings with which nature has enriched their country." They would soon make "modern improvements" commensurate with European standards, as science effected "a total change in the moral character and general habits of the Brazilians." The prospects for the future were manifold, "for no territory perhaps in the world is so rich in natural products, and at the same time so neglected for want of an enlightened and industrious population."³

For these northern European naturalists who rushed to Brazil when it opened to non-Lusophone explorers following the transfer of the court to Rio de Janeiro, the interior was a realm first dreamed by the Portuguese, then squandered. The contradictory image of Luso-Brazilian lassitude and greed-driven magical thinking that German, French, and British observers promoted in the early nineteenth century said more about their own condescension and self-fashioning as authoritative explorers than it did about Portugal's exertions or purported lack thereof in the southeastern interior. Drafting the introduction to his account, while hewing to the narrative conventions of scientific reconnaissance, Wied made a preposterous assertion about the reason he had chosen to travel northward along the coast, gaining access to the interior by way of several river valleys. This coastal realm, he claimed, was "still quite unknown, or at least not described. Several tribes of the aboriginal inhabitants yet live there in their primitive state, undisturbed by the Europeans."⁴ With this assertion he formulated a basic obfuscation. He minimized the difference between places and peoples that were genuinely unknown to Europeans and those merely unfamiliar to his non-Lusophone readers, between realms undisturbed by colonial intrusions and those merely unvisited by non-Lusophone explorers. The coast was in fact the longest-occupied, best known, and most thoroughly described region of Brazil. Its aboriginal inhabitants had adjusted to incursions since the onset of colonization. Portuguese explorers had first ascended the Jequitinhonha and other river valleys leading to the interior in the sixteenth century. Soldiers, colonists, and a priest or two had asserted their permanent presence in the valley in a particularly determined fashion for at least a decade and a half before Wied arrived.⁵ Wied's narrative obscured this history, downplaying the prelude of conflict and collaboration that determined what he found when he arrived. The dogged efforts of Moura, Leão, unnamed boatmen and muleteers, enslaved laborers, Portuguese and Indigenous soldiers, and untold others up and down the valley faded into the background as the German naturalist worked to sustain his conceit of pursuing the Indigenous "lords of these solitary wildernesses" about whom "until now no traveler has furnished precise information."[6]

After independence the sense of mission articulated by northern European scientific travelers would appeal to Brazil's newly empowered elites. Scanning their country's immense expanses, they honed their coastal gaze. Many were captivated by British and French models of progress and disdainful of inland inhabitants, whom they perceived as less European, less white, less modern, less moral, less civilized. It is little wonder, then, that the redoubled efforts of the preceding half century by the Portuguese crown to tighten its hold on the backlands were minimized, deemed insufficient, and largely forgotten. It is even less surprising that the conduct of peoples of Indigenous and African descent who contested, diverted, and sometimes embraced and advanced this project for their own purposes would be forgotten. Not until the late nineteenth century did the study of the backlands seem a fitting subject for a few of Brazil's leading historians. This lapse of historical memory helped sustain a postindependence conviction that the sertões with their backward inhabitants would impede national development as long as they remained outside the reach of the new national government.[7]

The northern European visitors were not wrong to notice a yearning for undiscovered riches that motivated many forays into the sertões; however, any suggestion that this was an Iberian idiosyncrasy ignored colonialism's worldwide fixation on wealth accumulation. The credibility of reports of gold and diamond strikes had a particular staying power in the southeastern interior not because of a gullibility or greed peculiar to the Portuguese but because such reports had proven accurate for so long. For much of the eighteenth century, Minas Gerais had secured its place as the world's foremost supplier of both of these precious substances.[8] There was every reason to imagine that ever-more-thorough exploration of the sertões both west and east of the depleted Espinhaço cordillera would produce additional strikes. The relentless pursuit of new deposits appeared misguided only when the alluvial wealth that had sustained the bonanza for so long definitively waned. Increasingly remote backlands beckoned.

Adventurers responded. Their perseverance seemed like folly only to the degree it went unrewarded.

More surprising than the ongoing search by individual explorers for undiscovered gold and diamonds was the Portuguese imperial administration's determination to investigate such activity in the most inaccessible reaches of the sertões. After 1750, time and again, royal officials on both sides of the Atlantic sought to underwrite reconnaissance missions sent out to substantiate reports of distant discoveries. Stirred to action by Pombal's interventionist agenda, crown ministers, colonial governors, military officers, and frontier administrators did not retreat from this commitment after his fall. The progressive exhaustion of the old mining centers accentuated how dependent Lisbon had become on the wealth they produced. For decades, the state's avidity for discovering additional deposits increased in inverse proportion to mining's decline. A redoubtable but also mythologized bandeirante past, wherein backcountry boldness had once produced prosperity, deepened the sense of destiny that impelled this drive. Officials persisted despite mounting evidence that the pursuit of rumored buried fortunes was amounting to little or nothing.

More often than not, reconnaissance activity ultimately discredited initial reports that spurred the crown to order, organize, and finance backcountry expeditions. In none of the expeditions documented in this study did mineral deposits of any significance compensate for the funds and labor allocated to verify purportedly unexploited treasure. Except for the most skeptical among them, officials did not anticipate these failures, and only rarely did they acknowledge unsuccessful ventures when they occurred. Instead, they turned their attention to the next alluring foray, hopeful that further efforts would produce results. Some persisted out of genuine loyalty to the empire. Others did so because they knew that success promised to enhance their own status in the eyes of the crown. New discoveries could also contribute to their own wealth, given the tangled patronage and corruption networks that made it possible for a patrimonial regime to rule at such great distances. Absent the separation of public and private finances characteristic only of a later period, the prospect of enticing Lisbon to back the search for a lucrative mineral strike almost always outweighed the risk of failure.[9]

But the state's resurgent dedication to backcountry exploration cannot be reduced simply to a reimagined bandeirante inheritance or a very real pecuniary allure. Like Spanish, British, and French imperial competitors during this post-1750 era, Portugal's transatlantic, centralizing imperial administration sought to assert control over multiple internal frontiers even where they did not yield compensating treasure.[10] Any notion that the Portuguese crown was somehow uniquely inactive or even uninterested in consolidating territorial claims in the continental interior—that it neglected the interior's potential "for want of an enlightened and industrious population," to repeat Mawe's view—simply does not hold up. The crown devoted substantial energies to inland exploration and governance during this period, one the historiography generally has cast as an era of abandonment, portraying the sertões as a legal and jurisdictional vacuum filled by the arbitrary, violent, private power of local potentates and rural bandits.[11] The difficulties successive royal administrations encountered consolidating territorial gains should not be confused with inaction. Portugal cannot be accused of ignoring the backlands.

In each part of this study, we have tracked the crown's concerted effort to wrest territory from Indians and runaway slaves, to extend its bureaucratic ambit, to monitor straying vassals, to crack down on backcountry criminality, to map and scientifically survey remote expanses, and to open regions for commercial development, thereby increasing tax revenues. All this occurred in tandem with its investigations of newly reported mineral deposits. Yet if the empire did not ignore the backlands, neither did it manage to maintain its course. In every frontier foray we have followed, state authorities found themselves co-opted, deceived, disappointed. No mirage caused by mica glinting in a lake suffices to explain this outcome. Instead, we must recognize the countervailing influence of the individuals, both privileged and persecuted, on whom overseas administrators relied. The determination with which the Portuguese sought to seize hold of the interior is also the measure of the capacity of diverse inland actors to divert the ship of state. Over the decades, misadventures multiplied, widening the gap between what the crown sought to accomplish and what remained beyond its capabilities. The impediments to its colonizing projects came less frequently from outright antagonists than from those who bent orders to serve their own purposes, those who offered officials what they most wished to hear even when such information had little grounding in backcountry realities, and those who evaded strict compliance in distant zones where the state's ability to enforce its rule was limited.

Commissioned to help colonize the western savanna of Minas Gerais, the entrepreneurial Inácio Correia Pamplona trumpeted clearing the sertão of hostile Kayapó warriors and runaway slaves, while making a show of his search for gold. The enemies he claimed to hunt never appeared, and the gold never surfaced. Undeterred, he concentrated his energies on amassing ranchlands, becoming one of the captaincy's great land barons in spite of legislation meant to prevent such excess. Relentless exaggeration and self-promotion enabled him to reshape a mission conceived as an assertion of the monarch's territorial authority into a scheme for personal enrichment.

In the southeastern coastal mountains, acting on intelligence gathered from Coroado and Coropó Indians, Lisbon moved to secure an area penetrated by illegal miners and smugglers. The ensuing military operations yielded discouraging results. Troops dispatched by the governor of Minas Gerais were implicated in the smuggling network. Those mobilized from the coast by the viceroy established a base in the highlands with little else to show for their labors. If gold had ever been mined there in significant quantity, it was exhausted by the time the soldiers arrived. Commanding officer Lieutenant Colonel Manoel Soares Coimbra ended up thoroughly disillusioned, and the crown soon lost interest. Throughout, Native peoples retained their ability, within limits, to shape events.

By the end of the eighteenth century, embraced as a remedy for earlier missteps and disappointments, scientific reconnaissance came to play a greater role in backcountry ventures. At every step, however, continuities were evident. Those who now pursued scientific goals still advanced imperial aspirations to dominate lands and peoples. The university-trained mineralogist José Vieira Couto answered his sovereign's call to authenticate the claims of free Black prospectors. Distrusted itinerants, they led Couto on an all but fruitless expedition to the west. Disinclined to issue a negative report, he employed the discourse of scientific rigor to recast the mission as a journey to an exceptionally promising region, where further exploration was certain to yield elusive treasure. The state committed resources for excavations, but the region never produced its promised windfall.

To the northeast, frontier authorities again enlisted the cooperation of Native peoples while searching for gold and a secure route to the coast. The Botocudo of the Jequitinhonha River valley chose the course of diplomacy, avoiding the interethnic warfare engulfing the forests to the south. Although undermining belligerent crown policies, they could not have predicted that the relative calm prevailing in the valley would attract a new breed of scientific explorers, first among them a German prince. Fashioning himself the harbinger of northern European expertise, Wied ascended the valley to harvest specialist knowledge. He cast the Botocudo not as deft survivors but as anthropologized primitives, setting the course for an era in which backcountry inhabitants would be further marginalized by the misleading and destructive discourse of scientific racism.

As the end of the colonial period arrived, strenuous imperial endeavors in the backlands were relegated to obscurity. Accounts published by a spate of foreign travelers entranced Brazil's coastal elites in no small part because they passed judgment on peoples increasingly considered racially suspect and historically backward. Claiming precedence and primacy, northern European scientific explorers dismissed the importance of the preceding era during which Luso-Brazilian adventurers, soldiers, and naturalists engaged, confronted, coaxed, and coerced autonomous Native peoples, fugitive and free Blacks, and others who resisted, evaded, deceived, and sometimes cooperated.

While the remedies proposed by foreign visitors were often self-serving, their diagnosis contained a degree of truth. During successive chapters of its post-1750 drive to exercise expanded territorial control, the imperial administration's circumscribed ability to gather reliable information about lands and peoples targeted for absorption proved a decisive obstacle to its colonizing projects. The church, although essential for its endorsement of territorial conquest, exhibited its own limitations. Rarely absent from major overland reconnaissance missions, clergymen generally acted as pliant servants of the state. Pombal's secularizing policies checked their power in the backlands, as did the ban on missionary orders operating in Minas Gerais. With the rise of scientific exploration, they were further sidelined. As a result, whereas in an earlier era or another region missionaries might have served as vital sources of intelligence, other sorts of backcountry informants found themselves much sought after for their real or perceived knowledge.

For some of these knowledge brokers, this valorization was empowering; for others, a source of abuse. They might be elite or plebian, voluntary or coerced, candid or calculating. They might be closely tied to the state bureaucracy or effectively stateless. Their individual and collective understanding of backcountry geography, opportunities, and perils merged into an information stream that ran from the sertão to Vila Rica, Rio de Janeiro, and Lisbon, where government authorities found it difficult to distinguish fact from fiction. Credible reporting became entangled with fabrication and concealment. A confusing amalgam of intelligence, contradictory and incomplete, occasioned the mobilization of state resources that might be either insufficient or excessive. Miscalculations stemmed from officials' own misperceptions and from frontier informants' pursuit of personal and communal objectives distinct from those of the state. The interplay and disjunctures between the two constrained the territorialization of royal sovereignty.

Rather than the consequence of an inactive state, the power of diverse proprietors of valued backcountry expertise increased precisely to the degree that Portugal asserted its presence in zones previously peripheral to its interests. These adepts of the sertão became the eyes and ears of empire. They shared what they saw and heard, but they did so according to their individual and collective circumstances and within the context of particular backcountry histories. At their least compliant, they slowed imperial expansion to a crawl. At their most cooperative, when acting as eager proxies and partners, their collaboration was frequently a performance masking other motives. Empowered to mediate the flow of information from the backlands, they limited the crown's campaign to transform internal frontiers into governed territory. Although integral to the mechanisms of governance at a distance, these enigmatic colonial informants left metropolitan rule on a shaky footing.[12]

The inability to project its sovereign authority over Brazil's sprawling interior would seem an obvious contributing factor to Portugal's singular powerlessness to retain its most important colony when independence arrived in 1822. Histories of the nation's birth, however, almost never register this possibility. Brazil's independence was achieved with little fighting. Battles to hold inland expanses—not just coastal ports or capital cities—characterized all the hemisphere's independence movements except Brazil's. As an island nation, Haiti's small size contributed to much of its domain being consumed by revolutionary warfare when it split from France. More telling, given the enormity of their respective mainland colonies, are contrasts with British and Spanish America. For years, England and Spain fought revolutionaries over extensive inland battlefronts. Portugal did not. It could not. A thoroughgoing analysis of this geopolitical difference would be a subject for another book; however, the present study offers at least a partial explanation for Portugal's failure to mount a defense of its territorial dominion beyond the Atlantic seaboard.

The relative importance of factors contributing to Portugal's loss of Brazil continues to spark debate two hundred years after the event. Yet in virtually all historical accounts, independence brews and boils over as a coastal phenomenon. Among neither the underlying nor proximate causes of independence do historians contemplate the empire's fragile hold on the colony's enormous interior, where consolidated settler enclaves remained dwarfed by immeasurable sertões.[13] Scholars of the period teach us that the preservation of territorial integrity was not a foregone conclusion, given the great economic, political, and historical diversity of Brazil's regions, and that a binding sense of nationhood did not emerge for several decades. Even so, their narratives remain fixed on urban, coastal dynamics. Rarely do they remind us that the Brazil that became independent, although delimited by an international border endowing the new nation with near-continental proportions, was a Brazil then still consisting primarily of scarcely integrated sertões. They highlight the spread of Enlightenment liberalism in coastal cities, growing friction between Brazilian- and Portuguese-born elites, the lure of freer trade with England. They note the special status Brazil enjoyed during the crown's long sojourn in Rio de Janeiro, including its elevation to a co-equal kingdom in 1815. Its threatened demotion to colonial subordination again when João VI returned to Lisbon in 1821 fanned anticolonial sentiments, as did the gathering tide of independence movements throughout Spanish America. A comparatively smooth break with Portugal seemed possible when João's eldest son Pedro stayed behind to govern as prince regent. The prospective maintenance of dynastic authority bolstered the willingness of powerful planters and merchants to back a move to sever ties. Pedro's presence would invest the new government with a legitimacy otherwise unimaginable, and the agricultural export economy and its structural bulwark, slavery, could continue to function without severe disruption. In the view of most historians of the period, when Pedro finally declared independence on September 7, 1822, the momentum building for more than a decade made his decision all but inevitable. In the port of Salvador, Bahia, Portuguese forces waged a brief fight against local insurgents, who were reinforced by Brazil's newly formed army and navy. Besieged and outnumbered, the garrison sailed for Europe in mid-1823, quickly followed by troops based in the northern ports of São Luís and Belém.[14]

As to the significance of internal territorial dominion among these factors, the contrasts with British and Spanish America are striking. In the hemisphere's first independence war, the British had attempted to roil internal frontiers where they cultivated Native allies and colonists. These lands became so important that, in the view of historians Erik Hinderaker and Peter Mancall, "Britain's American empire eventually collapsed under the weight of a backcountry grown too large and complicated to administer or control." In 1778, however, this outcome remained in doubt, as British soldiers mounted raids, for example, with Delaware, Shawnee, Iroquois, and other Indigenous allies against isolated settlements and patriot militia outposts in the upper Ohio Valley and frontier Pennsylvania. Native warriors who joined these maneuvers sought to avenge relatives or regain lands lost to the relentless encroachment of surveyors and squatters from the East. Village-level reprisals and imperial mobilizations intertwined. At Wyoming on the Susquehanna River, loyalist commander John Butler, Seneca war chief Sayenqueraghta, and their combined British-Iroquois fighting force of five hundred took two rebel forts without firing a shot. They then lured some two hundred Pennsylvania militiamen and Continental Army regulars into an ambush, slaughtering and scalping them. The victory cleared the way for further depredations, which the British surmised would force the Continental Army to defend western settlers, thereby diverting resources from the war's eastern theater. In response the Continental Army rampaged through the backcountry. Marching up the Susquehanna to New York's Finger Lakes and Genesee Valley in 1779, General John Sullivan commanded a patriot army of three thousand men that left a path of fire, rape, and murder, destroying Seneca and Cayuga villages, cornfields, and orchards.[15]

Struggles over frontier lands likewise accompanied the fracturing of imperial authority in Spanish America. Great distances, rugged terrain, and unfamiliar climates and ecosystems impeded communications, transportation, and the uncontested imposition of decisions crafted by urban elites, whether they resided along the coast or in highland capitals. A prominent example was the Venezuelan *llanos*, the sparsely populated subtropical plains watered by the Orinoco River. The pastoralists of this region, primarily men and women of mixed African, Indigenous, and European ancestry, became the objects of repressive restrictions after Spain suffered Napoleon's incapacitating invasion. Bereft of their dethroned monarch, coastal creoles convened a congress, drafted a constitution, and declared independence in Caracas in 1811, becoming the first to do so in Spanish America. The congress, dominated by plantation and hacienda owners, considered the forceful control of these cattle-raising lands and toughened herdsmen, subsistence farmers, indebted peons, and fugitives from slavery essential to preserving the country's social order. Distrust was mutual. The *llaneros*, writes historian Jaime E. Rodríguez, "bitterly resented the white republicans who had earlier attempted to reduce them to serfdom."[16] Free Blacks and armed slaves would fight on both sides of the conflict, the latter petitioning for their emancipation in compensation for their military service. The region witnessed a devasting royalist uprising by a cavalry force ten thousand strong composed mainly of multiracial horsemen armed with lances and machetes. As the conflict evolved they shifted to the insurgent cause when Simón Bolívar established his base of operations in the interior along the lower Orinoco. Disavowing slavery and discrimination based on race, promising bonuses and lands seized from royalists, he forged an alliance with the llaneros that positioned the plains beyond the reach of imperial rule. Far from the coast this internal frontier provided a protected staging ground for expanding republican armies. It was from here that Bolívar launched his epic surprise attack on Bogotá in 1819, traversing flooded lowlands and crossing the Andes to inflict a shattering defeat on Spain.[17]

The examples cited for British and Spanish America could be multiplied. As the Thirteen Colonies fought for independence, the conflict played out along the frontiers of New York, Pennsylvania, Virginia, North and South Carolina, and Georgia, as well as in Kentucky, Tennessee, the Ohio Valley, and the Illinois country. To a lesser but still significant degree it was also contested along strategic frontiers where British and Spanish America met, and where settlers, fugitives from slavery, free Blacks, and Indigenous peoples vied for advantage. Affected zones extended into British Florida and Spanish Louisiana.[18] Decades later, during the Spanish American independence wars, struggles over the control of territory, populations, and resources considered vital to either the rebel or royalist causes disturbed numerous frontiers. Comanche, Wichita, and Lipan Apache raiding parties eroded Spanish authority over much of northern New Spain in the years preceding Mexican independence in 1821, seizing the advantage as Mexican insurgents and royalist forces clashed. When Comanche and Spanish objectives coincided, however, some warriors joined royalist soldiers, at least until funds designated for gifts and diplomacy dwindled. Farther west, the Ópata saw an opportunity to challenge the viceregal regime, capturing a presidio, occupying several settlements, and threatening much of eastern Sonora, until a combined royalist force defeated them at the Battle of Arivechi in 1820. In Florida during the First Seminole War (1816–19), the last of a series of violent conflicts pitting an expansionist United States against Spain, the Iberian empire was unable to defend Black and Indigenous settlements in the interior. Having reclaimed the Spanish throne, Ferdinand VII (r. 1808, 1813–33) ceded Florida to the expanding United States in 1821 as the crown moved to abandon the Americas with the exception of Cuba and Puerto Rico. Further examples in South America include the pampas of Río de la Plata (later Argentina), the interior reaches of the Banda Oriental (Uruguay), and lands in central Chile, all of which involved Indigenous peoples allying with one side or the other and, as was often the case, militating for their own objectives. Another distinctive case was the Pacific lowland region of western New Granada (Colombia), explored and exploited by wealthy landowners based in the Andes to the east. In this gold-mining frontier enslaved Afro-descendants seized the mines and staged a decade-long rebellion in defense of the crown against forces seeking independence, including their own masters.[19]

Nothing remotely approaching these contests occurred in the interior of Portuguese America during its independence struggle in the early 1820s.[20] Competition over Brazil's tenuously colonized internal frontiers galvanized neither those determined to keep the empire whole nor those seeking to break away. Naval and coastal engagements were the only meaningful military contests that affected the conflict's outcome. In Minas Gerais, where densely settled enclaves made it the most populous captaincy of the period, neither side mounted efforts to control the sertões that had any significant bearing on independence. More precisely, neither side displayed the capacity to draw outlying regions into the fray. One can imagine strategic reasons for doing so, particularly along the captaincy's southeastern flank where still-unincorporated backlands extended over the border shared with the captaincy of Rio de Janeiro. In a prolonged independence war these lands, which included the zone where smuggling and illicit mining had so troubled imperial officials in the 1780s, might have been deemed critical for provisioning the coastal capital and, more generally, for maintaining or severing the link between the two vitally important southeastern captaincies. Undergoing a shift from a thinly settled frontier to agricultural hinterlands feeding growing populations on both sides of the coastal mountains, the region was essential not only for these reasons but also because of incipient coffee cultivation. As planters felled and burned its primeval forests, the new crop already accounted for more than a sixth of Brazil's export earnings on the eve of independence. Within a decade coffee would come to dominate the export economy. Prince Regent Pedro, soon to be Pedro I of the independent Empire of Brazil, understood these matters even though he exercised little power over the zone. It was no accident that, only months before declaring independence, he traveled with a retinue on horseback across this rugged region on his way to visit Vila Rica. At this critical juncture his presence ensured the support of elites in Minas Gerais, where a governing junta had briefly flirted with backing Portugal.[21]

Had the struggle to sever ties with Portugal been more protracted, had João VI and his court not resided in Brazil until the year before separation occurred, had his heir not remained to ensure that independence arrived more as a transition than a trauma, perhaps key portions of the backlands would have been pulled into a broad contest over territorial control between patriots and royalists. It is also worth considering the opposite possibility. Had Portugal been able to muster frontier troops or militias, had it been able to marshal the support of Indian, Black, and multiracial allies dispersed in the sertões, perhaps it could have mounted a more robust defense of transatlantic unity. As we have seen, this was beyond Portugal's capabilities.

Despite having secured imperial borders that cut deeply into the continent, Portugal could not consolidate its power over the internal frontiers within its American domain. Despite its prodigious efforts over the previous half century, Portugal could not navigate much less dominate the sertões of Portuguese America. In case after case, throughout the unincorporated zones ringing the most economically and demographically important of its inland regions, it could not even effectively communicate orders or gather reliable intelligence. Unable to accomplish with any certainty the basic task of backcountry reconnaissance, it could not hope to devise effective policies to achieve its aims. Nor could it do much more than try either to intimidate or coax and accommodate frontier elites and nonelites, proxies and nonstate actors, who pursued their own interests and retained what Edward Said called "the power to narrate."[22]

The advent of scientific exploration to stanch the flow of information considered inaccurate did not solve the problem. Scientific narratives could be manipulated, too, especially in a social context in which its practitioners depended on royal patronage. Notwithstanding all of these impediments to exercising effective territorial sovereignty, it bears repeating that one should resist the tendency among scholars to posit the state's backcountry absence. Undeniably, officials struggled to establish control over many isolated zones and failed to achieve Lisbon's objectives, but a preponderance of evidence reveals an increasingly assertive rather than an absent state. Coordinated efforts by officials on both sides of the Atlantic to project the empire's authority over the sertões demonstrates a determination to govern areas beyond the reach of imperial institutions. Indeed, denunciations of unchecked private power, criminality, and Indigenous savagery surged in direct proportion to the state's expansionist project. The distinction is subtle but important. It accounts for the enormous official energies expended, and the occasional advances achieved, in establishing dominion and imposing the rule of law. In this sense, too, the Brazilian backlands assume characteristics comparable to the internal and strategic frontiers of other transatlantic empires, which increasingly, though with uneven results, pushed to territorialize royal sovereignty during the second half of the eighteenth century.[23]

The four forays examined in this study as aggregated microhistories highlight the activities of those who interacted along trails and riverine routes—along what amounted to innumerable edges of empire. Reversals at the territorial limits of the empire's administrative capabilities became the measure of an idiosyncratic transatlantic statecraft, absolutist overreach, and unforeseen compromises required of the crown and its backcountry agents. Results differed strikingly from original plans. The combined ability of backcountry denizens in these many zones to thwart or redirect Lisbon's expansionist exertions elevates to historical significance their incapacitation of imperial territorial dominion. They evaded, misinformed, manipulated, and sidetracked expedition leaders who entered their realms. The required negotiations and modifications, undermined by problematic geographic intelligence, exposed the instability of metropolitan power, loosening the state from its moorings. What in thoroughly colonized areas may have seemed like the genius of a transatlantic enterprise responsive enough to bend without breaking, in the backlands looked unmistakably ineffectual. After 1750, beyond Brazil's coastal strip and established inland enclaves, the Portuguese Empire cast about, veered off course, and faltered, adrift on an inland sea.

Much would change in the Brazilian interior over the succeeding centuries, although the country's international borders remained remarkably similar to the boundaries established in 1750. Internal frontiers would be colonized and contested within those boundaries to the south, west, and north. Acting as an agent of order, progress, and pillage, the national government would continue its territorializing efforts. Now, two hundred years since independence, with the Amazon burning, Native land reserves invaded by loggers and miners, and federal authorities confident they are in control, the postcolonial state's projection of power over great expanses, first from Rio de Janeiro, later from Brasília, remains a flawed and unfinished project.

# ABBREVIATIONS USED IN THE NOTES

The following archives are abbreviated in the Notes.

| | |
|---|---|
| *ABNRJ* | *Anais da Biblioteca Nacional do Rio de Janeiro* |
| ACSM | Arquivo da Casa Setecentista, Mariana, Brazil |
| AHEx | Arquivo Histórico do Exército, Rio de Janeiro |
| AHM | Arquivo Histórico Militar, Lisbon |
| AHMB | Arquivo Histórico do Museu Bocage, Lisbon |
| AHMCUL | Arquivo Histórico do Museu de Ciência da Universidade de Lisboa |
| AHU | Arquivo Histórico Ultramarino, Lisbon |
| AIHGB | Arquivo do Instituto Histórico e Geográfico Brasileiro, Rio de Janeiro |
| AMRSJDR | Arquivo do Museu Regional, São João del Rei, Brazil |
| ANRJ | Arquivo Nacional, Rio de Janeiro |
| ANTT | Arquivo Nacional do Torre do Tombo, Lisbon |
| APEB | Arquivo Público do Estado da Bahia, Salvador, Brazil |
| APM | Arquivo Público Mineiro, Belo Horizonte, Brazil |
| Arq. | Arquivo |
| ATC | Arquivo do Tribunal de Contas, Lisbon |
| AUC | Arquivo da Universidade de Coimbra, Portugal |
| BA | Biblioteca da Ajuda, Lisbon |
| BACL | Biblioteca da Academia das Ciências, Lisbon |
| BNL | Biblioteca Nacional, Lisbon |
| BNRJ | Biblioteca Nacional, Rio de Janeiro |
| BPE | Biblioteca Pública, Évora, Portugal |
| CC | Arquivo Casa dos Contos |

| | |
|---|---|
| CM | Cartografia Manuscrita |
| Cód. | Códice |
| CP | Coleção Pombalina |
| CV | Arquivo Conde de Valadares |
| Cx. | Caixa |
| DB | Documentos Biográficos |
| Doc. | Documento |
| DSFND | Decretamentos de Serviço Fiscalizados e Não Decretados |
| ER | Erário Régio |
| Fot. | Fotograma |
| GMD | Geography and Map Division |
| IL | Inquisição de Lisboa |
| JCBL | John Carter Brown Library, Providence, RI |
| LC | Library of Congress, Washington, DC |
| Liv. | Livro |
| MR | Ministério do Reino |
| NL | Newberry Library, Chicago, IL |
| NM | Negócios Militares |
| OLL | Oliveira Lima Library, Catholic University of America, Washington, DC |
| PP | Processos dos professores |
| PT | Portugal |
| *RAPM* | *Revista do Arquivo Público Mineiro* |
| RGM | Registo Geral de Mercês |
| *RIHGB* | *Revista do Instituto Histórico e Geográfico Brasileiro* |
| Rio | Rio de Janeiro city |
| SC | Seção Colonial |
| SCP | Seção Colonial e Provincial |
| SI | Seção de Iconografia |
| SM | Seção de Manuscritos |
| TSO | Tribunal do Santo Ofício |
| TT | Torre do Tombo |

# NOTES

### Introduction

1. José Vieira Couto, *Memoria sobre as minas da capitania de Minas Geraes: Suas descrições, ensaios e domicílios próprios, à maneira de itinerário* . . . (Rio de Janeiro: Laemmert, 1842), 100. Couto completed this long-unpublished account in 1801.

2. For an insightful discussion of the term *sertão*, including its uncertain origins, unstable meaning, and usage in colonial Minas Gerais, see Cláudia Damasceno Fonseca, *Arraiais e vilas d'el rei: Espaco e poder nas Minas setecentistas* (Belo Horizonte: Universidade Federal de Minas Gerais, 2011), chap. 1.

3. Rui Barbosa, "A Conferência de Alagoinhas (1919)," in *Obras completas de Rui Barbosa*, ed. Américo Jacobina Lacombe (Rio de Janeiro: Fundação Casa de Rui Barbosa, 1988), vol. 46, tomo 3, 35–37. Souza notes that the twentieth-century historians of colonial Brazil, Alcântara Machado and Sérgio Buarque de Holanda, also were fascinated by the natural, psychic, and cultural connection between the sea and the sertões. Laura de Mello e Souza, *O sol e a sombra: Política e administração na América portuguesa do século XVIII* (São Paulo: Companhia das Letras, 2006), 325. For more recent invocations of this metaphor, see Tamar Herzog, *Frontiers of Possession: Spain and Portugal in Europe and the Americas* (Cambridge, MA: Harvard University Press, 2015), 1, 42; Mary C. Karasch, *Before Brasília* (Albuquerque: University of New Mexico Press, 2016), 141, 303.

4. Works that have contributed to my understanding of Portugal's late eighteenth- and early nineteenth-century state and the challenges its representatives encountered while attempting to govern over great distances, particularly in Minas Gerais, include Souza, *O sol e a sombra*, esp. chap. 1; Júnia Ferreira Furtado, *O Livro da Capa Verde: O regimento diamantino de 1771 e a vida no Distrito Diamantino*

*no período da real extração* (São Paulo: Annablume, 1996); Júnia Ferreira Furtado, *Homens de negócio: A interiorização da metrópole e do comércio nas Minas setecentistas* (São Paulo: Hucitec, 1999), esp. 15–27; Fonseca, *Arraiais e vilas*, esp. chap. 4; Francisco Eduardo de Andrade, *A invenção das Minas Gerais: Empresas, descobrimentos e entradas nos sertões do ouro da América portuguesa* (Belo Horizonte: Autêntica, 2008), esp. chap. 8; Kenneth R. Maxwell, *Conflicts and Conspiracies: Brazil and Portugal, 1750–1808* (Cambridge: Cambridge University Press, 1973); Roderick J. Barman, *Brazil: The Forging of a Nation, 1798–1852* (Stanford, CA: Stanford University Press, 1988); Jeremy Adelman, *Sovereignty and Revolution in the Iberian Atlantic* (Princeton, NJ: Princeton University Press, 2006). Also see Timothy Mitchell, "Society, Economy, and the State Effect," in *State/Culture: State-Formation after the Cultural Turn*, ed. George Steinmetz (Ithaca, NY: Cornell University Press, 1999), 77, 85–89; Pierre Bourdieu, "Rethinking the State: Genesis and Structure of the Bureaucratic Field," in *State/Culture: State-Formation after the Cultural Turn*, ed. George Steinmetz (Ithaca, NY: Cornell University Press, 1999).

5. Souza, *O sol e a sombra*, 14, emphasis in original.

6. For an insightful interpretation of Brazil's first century as a Portuguese colony focusing on such intermediaries, see Alida C. Metcalf, *Go-Betweens and the Colonization of Brazil, 1500–1600* (Austin: University of Texas Press, 2006). Also see Judy Bieber, "Mediation through Militarization: Indigenous Soldiers and Transcultural Middlemen of the Rio Doce Divisions, Minas Gerais, Brazil, 1808–1850," *The Americas* 71, no. 2 (2014); Adriano Toledo Paiva, *Os indígenas e os processos de conquista dos sertões de Minas Gerais (1767–1813)* (Belo Horizonte: Argumentum, 2010); Heather F. Roller, "River Guides, Geographical Informants, and Colonial Field Agents in the Portuguese Amazon," *Colonial Latin American Review* 21, no. 1 (2012).

7. Rodrigo de Sousa Coutinho, quoted in Gabriel Paquette, *Imperial Portugal in the Age of Atlantic Revolutions: The Luso-Brazilian World, c. 1770–1850* (Cambridge: Cambridge University Press, 2013), 52.

8. For parallel efforts, see Catarina Madeira Santos, "Administrative Knowledge in a Colonial Context: Angola in the Eighteenth Century," *British Journal for the History of Science* 43, no. 4 (2010); William J. Simon, *Scientific Expeditions in the Portuguese Overseas Territories (1783–1808) and the Role of Lisbon in the Intellectual-Scientific Community of the Late Eighteenth Century* (Lisbon: Instituto de Investigação Científica Tropical, 1983); Márcia Moisés Ribeiro, "Ciência e império: O intercâmbio da técnica e o saber científico entre a Índia e a América portuguesa," in *A "Época Pombalina" no mundo luso-brasileiro*, ed. Francisco Falcon and Claudia Rodrigues (Rio de Janeiro: Editora FGV, 2015), 499–522; Ângela

Domingues, "Para um melhor conhecimento dos domínios coloniais: A constituição de redes de informação no Império português em finais do Setecentos," supplement, *História, Ciências, Saúde—Manguinhos* 8 (2001).

9. On the emerging field of early modern information history, see Ann Blair and Devin Fitzgerald, "A Revolution in Information?," in *The Oxford Handbook of Early Modern European History, 1350–1750*, ed. Hamish M. Scott (Oxford: Oxford University Press, 2015), vol. 1, esp. 249–53. Also see the seminal C. A. Bayly, *Empire and Information: Intelligence Gathering and Social Communication in India, 1780–1870* (Cambridge: Cambridge University Press, 1999), quoting 2; C. A. Bayly, "The First Age of Global Imperialism, c. 1760–1830," *Journal of Imperial and Commonwealth History* 26, no. 2 (1998); Paul Slack, "Government and Information in Seventeenth-Century England," *Past and Present*, no. 184 (August 2004): 33–68; Robert Darnton, "An Early Information Society: News and the Media in Eighteenth-Century Paris," *American Historical Review* 105, no. 1 (2000): 1–35; Jacob Soll, *The Information Master: Jean-Baptiste Colbert's Secret State Intelligence System* (Ann Arbor: University of Michigan Press, 2009); Brendan Dooley, ed., *The Dissemination of News and the Emergence of Contemporaneity in Early Modern Europe* (Farnham, UK: Routledge, 2010); Katherine Grandjean, *American Passage: The Communications Frontier in Early New England* (Cambridge, MA: Harvard University Press, 2015); Alejandra Dubcovsky, *Informed Power: Communications in the Early American South* (Cambridge, MA: Harvard University Press, 2016); María M. Portuondo, *Secret Science: Spanish Cosmography and the New World* (Chicago: University of Chicago Press, 2009); Sylvia Sellers-García, *Distance and Documents at the Spanish Empire's Periphery* (Stanford, CA: Stanford University Press, 2013); Daniela Bleichmar, *Visible Empire: Botanical Expeditions and Visual Culture in the Hispanic Enlightenment* (Chicago: University of Chicago Press, 2012); Neil Safier, *Measuring the New World: Enlightenment Science and South America* (Chicago: University of Chicago Press, 2008); Ângela Domingues, *Monarcas, ministros e cientistas: Mecanismos de poder, governação e informação no Brasil colonial* (Lisbon: CHAM/FCSH/UNL and Universidade dos Açores, 2012). On the decisive participation of information brokers, colonial go-betweens, local experts, informants, and translators in forging "the contents and paths of knowledge" that accompanied worldwide empire-building during the period covered by the present study, see Simon Schaffer et al., eds., *The Brokered World: Go-Betweens and Global Intelligence, 1770–1820* (Sagamore Beach, MA: Science History Publications, 2009), quoting x.

10. Gayatri Chakravorty Spivak, *A Critique of Postcolonial Reason: Toward a History of the Vanishing Present* (Cambridge, MA: Harvard University Press, 1999), esp. chaps. 1 and 3; Florencia E. Mallon, "The Promise and Dilemma of Subaltern

Studies: Perspectives from Latin American History," *American Historical Review* 99, no. 5 (1994); Hal Langfur, "Índios, territorialização e justiça improvisada nas florestas do sudeste do Brasil," in *Os indígenas e as Justiças nas Américas*, ed. Maria Leônia Chaves de Resende, Ângela Domingues, and Pedro Cardim (Lisbon: Centro de História da Universidade de Lisboa, 2019), 184–85.

11. For a fascinating study of the cartographic history informing the treaty negotiations, see Júnia Ferreira Furtado, *Oráculos da geografia iluminista: Dom Luís da Cunha e Jean-Baptiste Bourguignon D'Anville na construção da cartografia do Brasil* (Belo Horizonte: Universidade Federal de Minas Gerais, 2012).

12. For an introduction to Pombal, his policies, and the historiographical debates that surround his rise to power, see Kenneth R. Maxwell, *Pombal: Paradox of the Enlightenment* (Cambridge,: Cambridge University Press, 1995); A. R. Disney, *A History of Portugal and the Portuguese Empire: From Beginnings to 1807*, 2 vols. (Cambridge: Cambridge University Press, 2009), vol. 1, chap. 13. On his and his successors' determination to better control Brazilian territory to enhance metropolitan power, see Paquette, *Imperial Portugal*, 50–57; Kirsten Schultz, *Tropical Versailles: Empire, Monarchy, and the Portuguese Royal Court in Rio de Janeiro, 1808–1821* (New York: Routledge, 2001), 22–27; Nívia Pombo, "D. Rodrigo de Sousa Coutinho e a formulação do princípio de unidade política," in *Em terras lusas: Conflitos e fronteiras no Império Português*, ed. Márcia Motta, José Vicente Serrão, and Marina M. Machado (Vinhedo: Horizonte, 2013); Antonio Cesar de Almeida Santos, "Poder e territorialização na América portuguesa (segunda metade do século XVIII)," *Revista de Historia Moderna: Anales de la Universidad de Alicante*, no. 36 (2018).

13. On the pact between the crown and colonial elites, see Júnia Ferreira Furtado, *Diálogos oceânicos: Minas Gerais e as novas abordagens para uma história do Império Ultramarino Português* (Belo Horizonte: Universidade Federal de Minas Gerais, 2001); Maria Odila Leite da Silva Dias, "A interiorização da metrópole," in *A interiorização da metrópole e outros estudos* (São Paulo: Alameda, 2005); João Fragoso, Maria Fernanda Bicalho, Maria de Fátima Gouvêa, eds., *O Antigo Regime nos trópicos: A dinâmica imperial portuguesa, séculos XVI–XVIII* (Rio de Janeiro: Civilização Brasileira, 2001); Maria Fernanda Bicalho and Vera Lúcia Amaral Ferlini, eds., *Modos de governar: Idéias e práticas políticas no Império português, séculos XVI–XIX* (São Paulo: Alameda, 2005). For incisive criticism of this consensus model, see Souza, *O sol e a sombra*, 58–70; Adelman, *Sovereignty and Revolution*, 33–35.

14. See, for example, Barman, *Brazil*, chap. 1; Adelman, *Sovereignty and Revolution*, 125–31. For Spanish and British American comparisons, see David J. Weber, *Bárbaros: Spaniards and Their Savages in the Age of Enlightenment* (New Haven,

CT: Yale University Press, 2005); Daniel K. Richter, *Facing East from Indian Country: A Native History of Early America* (Cambridge, MA: Harvard University Press, 2001), chap. 6; D. W. Meinig, *The Shaping of America: A Geographical Perspective on 500 Years of History*, vol. 1 (New Haven, CT: Yale University Press, 1986), 288–95.

15. For the revival of the concept of the frontier in North American historiography, see Stephen Aron, "Convergence, California, and the Newest Western History," *California History* 86, no. 4 (2009): 6. Also see Mary Louise Pratt, *Imperial Eyes: Travel Writing and Transculturation* (London: Routledge, 1992); Richard White, *The Middle Ground: Indians, Empires, and Republics in the Great Lakes Region, 1650–1815* (Cambridge: Cambridge University Press, 1991); Kathleen DuVal, *The Native Ground: Indians and Colonists in the Heart of the Continent* (Philadelphia: University of Pennsylvania Press, 2006); Pekka Hämäläinen and Samuel Truett, "On Borderlands," *Journal of American History* 98, no. 2 (2011).

16. Herzog, *Frontiers of Possession*, 261. Herzog does not entirely discard the distinction between such frontiers, arguing that "what transpired in the American interior was an ideologically motivated divide between an internal and an external frontier, allowing actors to apply different criteria when dealing with rival Europeans and when facing natives" (13). Also see Weber, *Bárbaros*, esp. 22, 85–90; Amy Turner Bushnell, "Gates, Patterns, and Peripheries: The Field of Frontier Latin America," in *Negotiated Empires: Centers and Peripheries in the Americas, 1500–1820*, ed. Christine Daniels and Michael V. Kennedy (New York: Routledge, 2002).

17. Peter Sahlins, *Boundaries: The Making of France and Spain in the Pyrenees* (Berkeley: University of California Press, 1989), 6–7; Lucien Febvre, "*Frontière*: The Word and the Concept," in *A New Kind of History: From the Writings of Lucien Febvre*, ed. Peter Burke (New York: Harper and Row, 1973), 208–17; Jeffrey A. Erbig Jr., *Where Caciques and Mapmakers Met: Border Making in Eighteenth-Century South America* (Chapel Hill: University of North Carolina Press, 2020), 3, 175n3.

18. My understanding of these zones continues to evolve, building on earlier efforts to discern their characteristics in Hal Langfur, *The Forbidden Lands: Colonial Identity, Frontier Violence, and the Persistence of Brazil's Eastern Indians, 1750–1830* (Stanford, CA: Stanford University Press, 2006), 4–7; Hal Langfur, "Frontier/*Fronteira*: A Transnational Reframing of Brazil's Inland Colonization," *History Compass* 12, no. 11 (2014). Although they prefer the umbrella term *borderlands*, my thinking has most recently benefited from the incisive essay by Cynthia Radding and Danna Levin Rojo, "Borderlands: A Working Definition," in *The Oxford Handbook of Borderlands of the Iberian World*, ed. Cynthia Radding and Danna Levin Rojo (New York: Oxford University Press, 2019), esp. 1–7.

19. For overviews of the Latin American frontier and borderlands historiography, as well as the theoretical and comparative underpinnings of the wider scholarly field, see Cynthia Radding and Danna Levin Rojo, eds., *The Oxford Handbook of Borderlands of the Iberian World* (Oxford: Oxford University Press, 2019); Fabrício Prado, "The Fringes of Empires: Recent Scholarship on Colonial Frontiers and Borderlands in Latin America," *History Compass* 10, no. 4 (2012); Langfur, "Frontier/*Fronteira*"; Hal Langfur, "Introduction: Recovering Brazil's Indigenous Pasts," in *Native Brazil: Beyond the Cannibal and the Convert, 1500–1889*, ed. Hal Langfur (Albuquerque: University of New Mexico Press, 2014); Márcio R. A.ced os Santos, *Rios e fronteiras: Conquista e ocupação do sertão baiano* (São Paulo: Universidade de São Paulo 2017), chap. 11; José de Souza Martins, *Fronteira: A degradação do Outro nos confins do humano* (São Paulo: Contexto, 2009); Jeremy Adelman and Stephen Aron, "From Borderlands to Borders: Empires, Nation-States, and the Peoples in between in North American History," *American Historical Review* 104, no. 3 (1999); James H. Merrell, "Indian History during the English Colonial Era," in *A Companion to Colonial America*, ed. Daniel Vickers (Malden, MA: Blackwell, 2003); Hämäläinen and Truett, "On Borderlands."; Nathaniel Millett, "Borderlands in the Atlantic World," *Atlantic Studies* 10, no. 2 (2013); Lorenzo Veracini, *Settler Colonialism: A Theoretical Overview* (New York: Palgrave Macmillan, 2010); Walter L. Hixson, *American Settler Colonialism: A History* (New York: Palgrave Macmillan, 2013).

20. Prominent exceptions proved the rule. See, for example, Sérgio Buarque de Holanda, *Caminhos e fronteiras* (Rio de Janeiro: J. Olympio, 1957). Holanda used the term *fronteira* in this work to indicate a place in between—in between landscapes, populations, customs, institutions, techniques, and languages that came face to face with one another. However, he warned against any wholesale application of the concept to colonial Brazil, eschewing the triumphalism with which it had been invested by historians of the United States. On Holanda's interest in the idea of the frontier, see Robert Wegner, *A conquista do oeste: A fronteira na obra de Sérgio Buarque de Holanda* (Belo Horizonte: Universidade Federal de Minas Gerais, 2000). Other classic works that examined frontier processes in colonial Brazil without necessarily adopting this terminology include João Capistrano de Abreu, *Caminhos antigos e povoamento do Brasil* (Belo Horizonte: Itatiaia, 1989); Basílio de Magalhães, *Expansão geographica do Brasil colonial*, 2nd ed. (São Paulo: Companhia Editora Nacional, 1935); Cassiano Ricardo, *Marcha para Oeste: A influência da bandeira na formação social e política do Brasil* (Rio de Janeiro: José Olympio, 1940); Clodomir Vianna Moog, *Bandeirantes and pioneers*, trans. L. L. Barrett (New York: G. Braziller, 1964). For a more detailed discussion of these historiographical issues, see Langfur, "Frontier/*Fronteira*."

21. On aggregation as a remedy for analytical problems that compromise some microhistorical approaches, see Rebecca Jean Emigh, "What Influences Official Information? Exploring Aggregate Microhistories of the Catasto of 1427," in *Small Worlds: Method, Meaning, and Narrative in Microhistory*, ed. James F. Brooks, Christopher R. N. DeCorse, and John Walton (Santa Fe: School for Advanced Research Press, 2008). Also see Lara Putnam, "To Study the Fragments/Whole: Microhistory and the Atlantic World," *Journal of Social History* 39, no. 3 (2006); Rebecca J. Scott, "Small-Scale Dynamics of Large-Scale Processes," *American Historical Review* 105, no. 2 (2000); Hans Medick, "Turning Global? Microhistory in Extension," *Historische Anthropologie* 24, no. 2 (2016).

22. Langfur, *Forbidden Lands*.

23. Contributions pointing in the direction of such an account have come from John Hemming, who catalogs internal colonization in his survey of the era's Indigenous history; from Ângela Domingues, who emphasizes the development of new "information networks" developed by naturalists and colonial officials, connecting Lisbon with many of the most remote areas of the Portuguese Empire; from Ronald Raminelli, who similarly examines what he terms "government at a distance" in his study of itinerant naturalists who functioned as a kind of intelligence-gathering corps as the crown strove to understand and administer its American possessions; and from Tamar Herzog, whose sweeping study of South American and Iberian territorial formation concentrates on borderland areas disputed by Spaniards and Portuguese. John Hemming, *Amazon Frontier: The Defeat of the Brazilian Indians* (Cambridge, MA: Harvard University Press, 1987); Ronald Raminelli, *Viagens ultramarinas: Monarcas, vassalos e governo à distância* (São Paulo: Alameda, 2008); Herzog, *Frontiers of Possession*; Domingues, "Para um melhor conhecimento." Domingues's essay was later reprinted in her collection of essays on governance and information in Portuguese America, Domingues, *Monarcas, ministros e cientistas*. On colonial mapmaking as a critical component of understanding Minas Gerais and Brazil as a geographic whole, see João Carlos Garcia, ed., *A mais dilatada vista do mundo: Inventário da colecção cartográfica da Casa da Ínsua* ([Lisbon]: Comissão Nacional para as Comemorações dos Descobrimentos Portugueses, 2002); Antônio Gilberto Costa et al., eds., *Cartografia das Minas Gerais: Da Capitania à Província* (Belo Horizonte: Universidade Federal de Minas Gerais, 2002); Júnia Ferreira Furtado, "Um cartógrafo rebelde? José Joaquim da Rocha e a cartografia de Minas Gerais," *Anais do Museu Paulista* 17, no. 2 (2009). Beyond the Brazilian case, John Lynch adopted the phrase "second conquest of America" to describe the coeval centralizing policies of the Spanish crown associated with the Bourbon Reforms. David Weber showed how the reforms emphasized greater administrative and economic control of Spanish America's peripheral regions and

their Native inhabitants. Although mentioning neither Portugal nor Brazil, C. A. Bayly proposed the moniker "the first age of global imperialism," from about 1760 to 1830, an era of empire-building he considers neglected yet singularly important. John Lynch, *The Spanish American Revolutions, 1808–1826*, 2nd ed. (New York: Norton, 1986), 7–24; Weber, *Bárbaros*; Bayly, "First Age," 28.

24. Perceptive studies, for example, treat the expeditions charged with fixing Brazil's international borders after the treaties of Madrid and São Ildefonso; conquest of the southern Guarapuava plains in the 1760s; military missions dispatched to fortify the colony's southwestern border in the 1760s and 1770s; and the scientific expeditions of Charles Marie de La Condamine, Alexandre Rodrigues Ferreira, and other geostrategic and scientific ventures in the Amazon River basin in the 1780s and 1790s. See Erbig, *Where Caciques and Mapmakers Met*; Mário Olímpio Clemente Ferreira, *O Tratado de Madrid e o Brasil meridional: Os trabalhos demarcadores das partidas do sul e a sua produção cartográfica (1749–1761)* (Lisbon: Comissão Nacional para as Comemorações dos Descobrimentos Portugueses, 2001); Ana Maria de Moraes Belluzzo et al., *Do contato ao confronto: A conquista de Guarapuava no século XVIII* (São Paulo: BNB Paribas, 2003); Glória Porto Kok, *O sertão itinerante: Expedições da Capitania de São Paulo no século XVIII* (São Paulo: Hucitec, 2004); Ângela Domingues, *Viagens de exploração geográfica na Amazónia em finais do século XVIII: Política, ciência e aventura* (Lisboa: Instituto de Historia de Além-Mar, FCSH-UNL, 1991); Ronald Raminelli, "Do conhecimento físico e moral dos povos: Iconografia e taxionomia na Viagem Filosófica de Alexandre Rodrigues Ferreira," supplement, *História, Ciências, Saúde-Manguinhos* 8 (2001); Roller, "River Guides."; Barbara A. Sommer, "Colony of the Sertão: Amazonian Expeditions and the Indian Slave Trade," *The Americas* 61, no. 3 (2005); Mary Karasch, "Rethinking the Conquest of Goiás, 1775–1819," *The Americas* 61, no. 3 (2005).

25. Model exceptions include Heather F. Roller, *Amazonian Routes: Indigenous Mobility and Colonial Communities in Northern Brazil* (Stanford, CA: Stanford University Press, 2014); Domingues, *Viagens de exploração*.

26. Laird W. Bergad, *Slavery and the Demographic and Economic History of Minas Gerais, Brazil, 1720–1888* (Cambridge: Cambridge University Press, 1999), 91, 97; Langfur, *Forbidden Lands*, 109; Dauril Alden, "The Population of Brazil in the Late Eighteenth Century: a Preliminary Survey," *Hispanic American Historical Review* 43, no. 2 (1963): 196–200; Altiva Pilatti Balhana, "A População," in *O Império Luso-Brasileiro, 1750–1822*, ed. Maria Beatriz Nizza da Silva (Lisbon: Editorial Estampa, 1986), 28–38; Amilcar Martins Filho and Roberto B. Martins, "Slavery in a Nonexport Economy: Nineteenth-Century Minas Gerais Revisited," *Hispanic American Historical Review* 63, no. 3 (1983): 537–44.

27. For a balanced assessment of the economic shift, highlighting the importance of frontier zones where economic growth occurred, see Ângelo Alves Carrara, *Minas e currais: Produção rural e mercado interno em Minas Gerais, 1674–1807* (Juiz de Fora: Universidade Federal de Juiz de Fora, 2007), 21–30, 240–46. On economic diversification, also see Douglas C. Libby, *Transformação e trabalho em uma economia escravista: Minas Gerais no século XIX* (São Paulo: Brasiliense, 1988), esp. 13–15; Douglass C. Libby, "Reconsidering Textile Production in Late Colonial Brazil: New Evidence from Minas Gerais," *Latin American Research Review* 32, no. 1 (1997): 88–108; João Luís Ribeiro Fragoso, *Homens de grossa aventura: Acumulação e hierarquia na praça mercantil do Rio de Janeiro (1790–1830)* (Rio de Janeiro: Arquivo Nacional, 1992), 104–12; Alcir Lenharo, *As tropas da moderação: O abastecimento da Corte na formação política do Brasil, 1808–1842* (São Paulo: Símbolo, 1979), chap. 2; Martins Filho and Martins, "Slavery in a Nonexport Economy: Nineteenth-Century Minas Gerais Revisited," 539–40; Robert W. Slenes, "Os multiplos de porcos e diamantes: A economia escravista de Minas Gerais no seculo XIX," *Cadernos IFCH UNICAMP* 17 (June 1985): 39–80; Bergad, *Slavery*, 16–25. On the broader late colonial economic disjuncture throughout Portuguese America, of which the decline in mining was but one part, see Fernando A. Novais, *Portugal e Brasil na crise do antigo sistema colonial (1777–1808)*, 2nd ed. (São Paulo: Ed. HUCITEC, 1981); José Jobson de A. Arruda, *O Brasil no comércio colonial* (São Paulo: Ed. Ática, 1980), esp. 115–20, 317–18, 655–62; Maxwell, *Conflicts and Conspiracies*, esp. chap. 2.

28. Outside Brazil, scholarly interest in colonial Minas Gerais has been deceptively limited. Within the Brazilian academy, by contrast, the region perennially generates an abundant, sophisticated literature dedicated to a great variety of themes. For a survey of this historiography from the 1980s forward, see Júnia Ferreira Furtado, "Novas tendências da historiografia sobre Minas Gerais no período colonial," *História da Historiografia* 2 (March 2009): 116–62. For English-language readers, among book-length works focused entirely or substantially on the region, the classic entry points are C. R. Boxer, *The Golden Age of Brazil, 1695–1750: Growing Pains of a Colonial Society* (Berkeley: University of California Press, 1969); Maxwell, *Conflicts and Conspiracies*; A. J. R. Russell-Wood, *The Black Man in Slavery and Freedom in Colonial Brazil* (London: Macmillan Press, 1982). For more recent contributions, including translated works, see Bergad, *Slavery*; Kathleen J. Higgins, *"Licentious Liberty" in a Brazilian Gold-Mining Region: Slavery, Gender, and Social Control in Eighteenth-Century Sabará, Minas Gerais* (University Park: Pennsylvania State University Press, 1999); Langfur, *Forbidden Lands*; Mariana Dantas, *Black Townsmen: Slavery and Freedom in Eighteenth-Century Baltimore, Maryland, and Sabará, Minas Gerais* (New York: Palgrave Macmillan,

2008); Laura de Mello e Souza, *The Devil and the Land of the Holy Cross: Witchcraft, Slavery, and Popular Religion in Colonial Brazil* (Austin: University of Texas Press, 2003); Júnia Ferreira Furtado, *Chica da Silva: A Brazilian Slave of the Eighteenth Century* (Cambridge: Cambridge University Press, 2009).

29. As Furtado articulates the issue, "it remains a challenge for historians to comprehend the relations that the central mining area established with the outer reaches of the captaincy." Furtado, "Novas tendências," 133. There are, of course, exceptions, which suggest a growing interest in the problem. For early contributions, see Oiliam José, *Indígenas de Minas Gerais: Aspectos sociais, políticos e etnológicos* (Belo Horizonte: Imp. Oficial, 1965); Waldemar de Almeida Barbosa, *A decadência das minas e a fuga da mineração* (Belo Horizonte: Universidade Federal de Minas Gerais, 1971). More recently, see Celso Falabella de Figueiredo Castro, *Os sertões de leste: Achegas para a história da Zona da Mata* (Belo Horizonte: Imprensa Oficial, 1987); Haruf Salmen Espindola, *Sertão do Rio Doce* (Governador Valadares: Univale, 2005); Langfur, *Forbidden Lands*; Paiva, *Os indígenas*; Célia Nonata da Silva, *Territórios de mando: Banditismo em Minas Gerais, século XVIII* (Belo Horizonte: Crisálida, 2007); Carla M. J. Anastasia, *A geografia do crime: Violência nas Minas setecentistas* (Belo Horizonte: Universidade Federal de Minas Gerais, 2005); Marcia Amantino, *O mundo das feras: Os moradores do Sertão Oeste de Minas Gerais—século XVIII* (São Paulo: Annablume, 2008).

30. For a critique of this historiographical tendency, see Furtado, *O Livro da Capa Verde*.

31. Examples include Anastasia, *A geografia do crime*; Silva, *Territórios de mando*; Amantino, *O mundo das feras*.

32. Auguste de Saint-Hilaire, *Viagem à Província de Goiás* (Belo Horizonte: Itatiaia, 1975), 142.

33. In the 1820s, following a devastating war waged against them, the surviving population of the Botocudo Indians, the most numerous ethnic group inhabiting the eastern forests of Minas Gerais and neighboring Espírito Santo and Bahia, was estimated at more than 20,000 individuals by the era's leading authority. Guido Tomás Marlière to Provincial President, 28 March 1827, Ouro Preto, *RAPM* 12 (1907): 530.

## Chapter 1

1. Requerimento do coronel Inácio Correia Pamplona, pedindo remuneração com mercês pelos seus distintos serviços, before 17 Sep 1805, AHU, Minas Gerais, cx. 177, doc. 47. For similar language in a letter dating from the early years of his endeavor, see Pamplona to Governor, Estância de Santa Maria de São Francisco de

Salles, 16 Sep. 1769, A Expedição do Campo Grande, Cuyeté, e Abayeté D[istrito] de Paracatú, 1769, BNRJ, SM, CV, cód. 18, 2, 6, p. 45.

2. In combination, I use several iterations of the expedition's records. The most comprehensive is a corpus of manuscripts, most of them letters in Pamplona's hand, together amounting to more than six hundred pages of a codex in the Biblioteca Nacional in Rio de Janeiro. This material is essential for understanding how Pamplona and his scribe selected certain experiences, omitted others, and reshaped the whole in their finished diary. The codex, paginated at a later date, is cataloged as A Expedição . . . , cited in full in the preceding note. The diary itself (pp. 171–264), the source of virtually all of the limited scholarship on the expedition, accounts for less than one-sixth of this material. The diary was transcribed and published as "Notícia diária e individual das marchas[,] e acontecimentos ma(i)s condigno(s) da jornada que fez o Senhor Mestre de Campo, Regente[,] e Guarda(-)mor Inácio Corre(i)a Pamplona, desde que saiu de sua casa[,] e fazenda do Capote às conquistas do Sertão, até se tornar a recolher à mesma sua dita fazenda do Capote, etc. etc. etc., [1769]," *ABNRJ* 108 (1988: 53–113). Portions of the diary were later translated into English by Sandra Lauderdale Graham and published for the benefit of students as "Daily Notice of the Marches and Most Noteworthy Happenings in the Expedition Made by Field Officer Regent Inácio Correia Pamplona," in *Colonial Latin America: A Documentary History*, ed. Kenneth Mills, William B. Taylor, and Sandra Lauderdale Graham (Wilmington, DE: Scholarly Resources, 2002), 337–52. Some members of the expedition departed from São João del Rei to encounter the main group, which began the trek from Fazenda do Capote in present-day Lagoa Dourada. For present locations of places named in the diary, see the painstaking reconstruction of the expedition route by Tarcisio José Martins, *Quilombo do Campo Grande: A história de Minas que se devolve ao povo*, rev. ed. (Contagem: Santaclara, 2008), 982.

3. Direct comparison to Pamplona's letters is but one way to detect the extent to which the expedition diary dramatizes the expedition narrative. Another useful comparison is to the dispassionate journal kept by Luís de Albuquerque de Melo Pereira e Cáceres, as he led an expedition through the region less than three years later in 1772 on his way to occupy the governorship of Mato Grosso. Luís de Albuquerque, Collection, 1772–1789, vol. 1, NL, Vault, Case MS 5043. Historian Francisco Eduardo Pinto speculates that the expedition scribe was Manuel Ribeiro Guimarães, who signed a map of the region explored by Pamplona, completed some fifteen years later. Francisco Eduardo Pinto, "Potentado e conflitos nas sesmarias da Comarca do Rio das Mortes" (PhD diss., Universidade Federal Fluminense, 2010), 67. However, this map by a skilled cartographer may be based

on but in style bears no resemblance to the rudimentary maps that accompanied the 1769 text, preceded by a disclaimer from the scribe about his lack of training as a mapmaker. Further, no individual by this name is listed among the expedition participants. Cf. Manuel Ribeiro Guimarães, "Mappa da Conquista do Mestre de Campo Regente [Chefe de Legião] Ignacio Correya Pamplona," ca. 1784, AHU, CM, Minas Gerais, no. 258/1165; [Mapa de todo o país que fosse avançado na viage . . .], A Expedição . . . , following 255. For the scribe's disclaimer and the diary map, see "Notícia diária," 96, 104–5. For a reproduction of the map, see Guimarães, "Mappa da Conquista," facsimile, Antônio Gilberto Costa et al., eds., *Cartografia das Minas Gerais: Da Capitania à Província* (Belo Horizonte: Universidade Federal de Minas Gerais, 2002), Mapas regionais, pl. 6. A more likely scribe candidate is Jolião da Costa Resende, whose name does appear in the expedition account, followed by the Portuguese abbreviation "Es$^{te}$," used in the eighteenth century to shorten "*escrevente*" (clerk, copyist, or scribe). "Notícia diária," 93; Maria Helena Ochi Flechor, *Abreviaturas: Manuscritos dos séculos XVI ao XIX*, 2nd ed. (São Paulo: Ed. UNESP; Edições Arquivo do Estado, 1991), 166. For the paleography of the original manuscript notation, see "Lista das pessoas que pediram sesmarias pertencentes ao araial de Nossa Senhora da Conceição Conquista do Campo Grande até o dia 19 de Novembro de 1769," A Expedição . . . , 225.

4. Pamplona to Governor, Tejuco, 30 Mar. 1770, A Expedição . . . , 309; Cláudia Damasceno Fonseca, *Arraiais e vilas d'el rei: Espaco e poder nas Minas setecentistas* (Belo Horizonte: Universidade Federal de Minas Gerais, 2011), 54 (Fonseca's italics). Also see Patrício A. S. Carneiro, "Do sertão ao território das minas e das gerais: Entradas e bandeiras, política territorial e formação espacial no período colonial" (PhD diss., Universidade Federal de Minas Gerais, 2013), 316–28.

5. Pamplona to Governor, [Estância de] São Simão, 7 Sep. 1769, A Expedição . . . , 11. Pamplona, too, received letters full of praise from his own subordinates. For an example, see Domingos [illeg.] to Pamplona, Vila Rica, 13 Aug. 1769, A Expedição . . . , 33. On the encomium culture, see Laura de Mello e Souza, *O sol e a sombra: Política e administração na América portuguesa do século XVIII* (São Paulo: Companhia das Letras, 2006), 416–34.

6. For example, Pamplona to Governor, Estância de Santa Maria de São Francisco de Salles, 16 Sep. 1769, A Expedição . . . , 43.

7. On Pamplona's activities in the sertão, as well as his actions as a a spy and probable participant in the 1789 plot, see Laura de Mello e Souza, "Violência e práticas culturais no cotidiano de uma expedição contra quilombolas, Minas Gerais, 1769," in *Liberdade por um fio: História dos quilombos no Brasil*, ed. João José Reis and Flávio dos Santos Gomes (São Paulo: Companhia das Letras, 1996), 193–212; Márcia Motta, *Direito à terra no Brasil: A gestação do conflito, 1795–1824*

(São Paulo: Alameda, 2009), 182–88; Marcia Amantino, *O mundo das feras: Os moradores do Sertão Oeste de Minas Gerais—século XVIII* (São Paulo: Annablume, 2008), 179–200; Waldemar de Almeida Barbosa, *A decadência das minas e a fuga da mineração* (Belo Horizonte: Universidade Federal de Minas Gerais, 1971), 36–38, 117–37; Pinto, "Potentado e conflitos," esp. 54–83; Kenneth R. Maxwell, *Conflicts and Conspiracies: Brazil and Portugal, 1750–1808* (Cambridge: Cambridge University Press, 1973), 152–53, 158, 162–63, 167–68, 193. Assis corrects and adds to Pamplona's biography by referencing his baptism and marriage records, among other archival materials. See Maria Emília Aparecida de Assis, "Inácio Correia Pamplona: O 'Hércules' do sertão mineiro setecentista" (master's thesis, Universidade Federal de São de del Rei, 2014), which includes a revealing account of Pamplona's involvement in and betrayal of the Minas Conspiracy; Maria Emília Aparecida de Assis, "Uma trajetória de conquista e civilização: Inácio Correia Pamplona e o sertão oeste das Minas Gerais setecentista," *Revista Outras Fronteiras* 2, no. 1 (2015): 133–56. Martins has expressed scathing skepticism about Pamplona's claims as a frontiersman, condemning as "tawdry" the expedition he led in 1769 and calling him "one of the greatest liars of our history" and a "scamp." While Martins's attacks are themselves problematic, Pamplona's account cannot be taken at face value, as the present chapter will demonstrate. See Martins, *Quilombo*, 313, 658, 890.

8. Requerimento do coronel Inácio Correia Pamplona, pedindo remuneração com mercês pelos seus distintos serviços, before 17 Sep 1805, AHU, Minas Gerais, cx. 177, doc. 47. In one of the many documents composing this larger, unpaginated petition, Pamplona assembled a thirty-one-paragraph, itemized catalog of these achievements. See, Justificação do coronel Inácio Correia Pamplona, Vila Rica, 3 Jul 1804, AHU, Minas Gerais, cx. 177, doc. 47. In this document Pamplona remembered first being asked in 1763 to lead the mission by Andrade, who during most of his thirty-year tenure as governor of Rio de Janeiro simultaneously administered Minas Gerais. After a month-long illness, Andrade died on January 1, 1763, suggesting that his request to Pamplona came somewhat sooner in late 1762. Also see Barbosa, *A decadência*, 36. For expenses incurred, see, for example, Pamplona to Governor, [Estância de] São Simão, 7 Sep. 1769, A Expedição . . . , 12; Pamplona, "Instrução e despedição qeu faço desta estancia de São Simão do Rio das Ajudas . . . ," 4 Sep. 1769, A Expedição . . . , 13; Pamplona to Governor, Estância de Santa Maria de São Francisco de Salles, 16 Sep. 1769, A Expedição . . . , 43. On António Gomes Freire de Andrade, see Mônica da Silva Ribeiro, "'Razão de Estado' e Pombalismo: Os modos de governar na administração de Gomes Freire de Andrada," in *A "Época Pombalina" no mundo luso-brasileiro*, ed. Francisco Falcon and Claudia Rodrigues (Rio de Janeiro: Editora

FGV, 2015). On the Jesuit expulsion, see Márcia Amantino and Marieta Pinheiro de Carvalho, "Pombal, a riqueza dos Jesuítas e a expulsão," in *A "Época Pombalina", no mundo luso-brasileiro*.

9. Dossiê do sequestro de bens feito ao mestre-de-campo Inácio Correia Pamplona por estar em dívida com a Real Fazenda, 9 Oct. 1775 to 4 Oct. 1777, BNRJ, SM, CC, gaveta I-26-24, doc. 9.

10. The exact number of participants in the expedition is not entirely clear in the diary, which lists the names of 225 colonists. Of these, 140 were identified as "*novo entrantes*," or individuals who had newly entered the region. Of this group nine did not accompany the expedition but arrived from other places. The scribe noted that others belonged to this category but that he did not know their names or how many they numbered. Finally, another eighty-five were identified as having requested land grants in the area by November 15, 1769. The scribe did not specify whether they arrived with the expedition or shortly thereafter, or whether some were elsewhere awaiting a decision from Pamplona or the governor about their requests. "Notícia diária," 91–96. The list of 225 colonists corresponds approximately with a communiqué from Pamplona a month into the journey, in which he tallied 132 "whites, mulattos, and blacks," not including seventy-six men whom he had deployed to explore the region. Pamplona to Governor, Estância de Santa Maria de São Francisco de Salles, 16 Sep. 1769, A Expedição . . . , 39; Pamplona, "Instrução e despedição qeu faço desta estancia de São Simão do Rio das Ajudas . . . ," 4 Sep. 1769, A Expedição . . . , 14. The sheep, not mentioned in the diary, are noted in Pamplona's first letter from the trail, nine days into the journey. Pamplona to Governor, [Paragem do Quilombo, near headwaters of the São Francisco River], 27 Aug. 1769, A Expedição . . . , 1.

11. "Daily Notice," 338–39. The diary suggests that well over one hundred sesmarias were distributed to other members of the expedition. However, historian Francisco Eduardo Pinto, who tracked these names, was able to confirm the concession of land grants in the area to just fifty-three of the settlers. Pinto, "Potentado e conflitos", 90. Also see Justificação do coronel Inácio Correia Pamplona, Vila Rica, 3 Jul 1804, AHU, Minas Gerais, cx. 177, doc. 47. On the cerrado biome, see Ricardo Ferreira Ribeiro, *Florestas anãs do sertão: O cerrado na história de Minas Gerais* (Belo Horizonte: Autêntica, 2005).

12. For an account of the construction accident, see "Daily Notice," 339. The bridge was large enough to convey oxen and carts, making more accessible a trail that shortened an existing route to Bambuí. Expedition members also improved another trail that crossed the savanna for perhaps 175 kilometers toward what would be their final destination near present-day Salitre de Minas. Combining these two stretches, the scribe credited the expedition with having "made a road 49 leagues

[323 km] long," which would seem to be a significant exaggeration based on Pamplona's own estimate. "Notícia diária," 96. For Pamplona's estimate, see Pamplona to Governor, Estância de Santo Estevão, 17 Nov. 1769, A Expedição . . . , 118.

13. An enduring historiography explores bandeirismo in the sixteenth and seventeenth centuries. Representative contributions of an earlier era include, José de Alcântara Machado, *Vida e morte do bandeirante* (1930; reprint, Belo Horizonte: Itatiaia, 1980); Afonso de E. Taunay, *História geral das bandeiras paulistas*, 11 vols. (São Paulo: Ideal, 1924–50); Jaime Cortesão, *Rapôso Tavares e a formacão territorial do Brasil* (Rio de Janeiro: Ministério da Educação e Cultura, 1958); Richard M. Morse, ed., *The Bandeirantes: The Historical Role of the Brazilian Pathfinders* (New York: Knopf, 1965). For works exemplifying revisionist tendencies, see John M. Monteiro, *Negros da terra: Índios e bandeirantes nas origens de São Paulo* (São Paulo: Companhia das Letras, 1994); José Carlos Vilardaga, "São Paulo na órbita do império dos felipes: Conexões castelhanas de uma vila da América portuguesa durante a União Ibérica (1580–1640)" (PhD diss., Universidade de São Paulo, 2010). For trenchant analyses of territorial conquest during the early decades of the mining boom, see Francisco Eduardo de Andrade, *A invenção das Minas Gerais: Empresas, descobrimentos e entradas nos sertões do ouro da América portuguesa* (Belo Horizonte: Autêntica, 2008); Adriana Romeiro, *Paulistas e emboabas no coração das Minas: Idéias, práticas e imaginário político no século XVIII* (Belo Horizonte: Universidade Federal de Minas Gerais, 2008); Márcio Santos, *Bandeirantes paulistas no sertão do São Francisco: Povoamento e expansão pecuária de 1688 a 1734* (São Paulo: Universidade de São Paulo, 2009). On bandeiras in Minas Gerais during the second half of the eighteenth century, see Hal Langfur, "The Return of the Bandeira: Economic Calamity, Historical Memory, and Armed Expeditions to the Sertão in Minas Gerais, Brazil, 1750–1808," *The Americas* 61, no. 3 (2005); Maria Leônia Chaves de Resende, "'Devassas gentílicas': Inquisição dos índios na Minas Gerais colonial," in *Caminhos gerais: Estudos históricos sobre Minas (séc. XVIII–XIX)*, ed. Maria Leônia Chaves de Resende and Silvia Maria Jardim Brügger (São João del Rei: Universidade Federal de São João del Rei, 2005), 9–48; Souza, "Violência e práticas culturais."

14. Diogo [Luís de Almeida Pereira] de Vasconcelos, *História média de Minas Gerais*, 4th ed. (Belo Horizonte: Itatiaia, 1974), 236. The phrase was later quoted approvingly in an influential early history of Brazilian territorial expansion. Basílio de Magalhães, *Expansão geographica do Brasil colonial*, 2nd ed. (São Paulo: Companhia Editora Nacional, 1935), 242.

15. Langfur, "Return of the Bandeira." On Paulista self-sufficiency, see Souza, *O sol*, chap. 3; Júnia Ferreira Furtado, *Homens de negócio: A interiorização da metrópole e do comércio nas Minas setecentistas* (São Paulo: Hucitec, 1999), 151.

Also see Diogo Ramada Curto, "Naturalismo, indigenismo, reformas e relatos de viagem," in *Cultura imperial e projetos coloniais: Séculos XV a XVIII* (São Paulo: Unicamp, 2009), 463–68.

16. Cláudio Manoel Costa, "Vila Rica," in *Obras poeticas de Claudio Manoel da Costa (Glauceste Saturnio)*, ed. João Ribeiro (Rio de Janeiro: H. Garnier, 1903), vol. 2, quoting canto 6, p. 216. On Costa, see Laura de Mello e Souza, *Cláudio Manuel da Costa: O letrado dividido* (São Paulo: Companhia das Letras, 2011); Sérgio Buarque de Holanda, *Capítulos de literatura colonial* (São Paulo: Brasiliense, 1991), 227–405. On the debate concerning whether Antônio Rodrigues de Arzão, whom the poem references, was in fact the first to discover gold in Minas Gerais, see José Joaquim da Rocha, *Geografia histórica da Capitania de Minas Gerais* (Belo Horizonte: Fundação João Pinheiro, 1995), 78–81; Francisco de Assis Carvalho Franco, *Dicionário de bandeirantes e sertanistas do Brasil: Século XVI, XVII, XVIII* (Belo Horizonte: Itatiaia, 1989), 42–44.

17. For the official report on this 1764 expedition, copied by the poet in his role as secretary, see "Termo de junta feito no regresso da diligência a que foi Sua Excelência o Ilmo. e Exmo. Sr. Luís Diogo Lobo da Silva, com o Desembargador Provedor da Real Fazenda José Gomes de Araújo, à Comarca do Rio das Mortes e Jacuí, e os acompanhou o Dr. Intendente do ouro da mesma Comarca Manuel Caetano Monteiro Guedes," Vila Rica, copied 30 Dec. 1767, ANTT, MR, NM, DSFND, maço 210, doc. 26, no. 75, no pagination. Souza identified the first of these sources in her penetrating study of the colony's administrative history. Souza, *O sol*, 335n13. This citation in turn led me to the original account of the expedition written in Costa's hand, Providencias gerais que se deram por todo o circuito da jornada que fazemos na Comarca do Rio das Mortes, 26 Nov. 1764, AHU, Minas Gerais, cx. 84, doc. 47, with appended documents.

18. Pamplona's appointment as regent came in stages, first in a provisional royal order in March 1766 that required further confirmation by José I in January 1771. See ANTT, RGM, José I, liv. 24, 30 Jan. 1771, f. 63. On the duties of a regent during this era, see Paulo Mendes Ferreira Campelo, "Representação," n.d., BNRJ, SM, CV, cód. 18, 2, 26, doc. 198; Governor, "Instrução que hade observar o Comandante . . . ," Vila Rica, 4 June 1765, BNRJ, SM, CV, cód. 18, 2, 6, doc. 203; and Governor to Campelo, Vila Rica, 21 June 1767, BNRJ, SM, CV, cód. 18, 2, 6, doc. 204. The duties of a *guarda-mor* were spelled out in the royal mining code of 1702. See "Regimento Mineral," Lisbon, 19 Apr. 1702, *RAPM* 1, no. 4 (1896): 675. For militia structure, ranks, and responsibilities, see Ana Paula Pereira Costa, "Organização militar, poder de mando e mobilização de escravos armados nas conquistas: A atuação dos Corpos de Ordenanças em Minas colonial," *Revista de História Regional* 11, no. 2 (2006): esp. 111–13. Also see Adriana Romeiro and

Angela Vianna Botelho, *Dicionário histórico das Minas Gerais: Período colonial* (Belo Horizonte: Autêntica, 2003), 252–53.

19. Pamplona to Governor, Estância de Santa Maria de São Francisco de Salles, 16 Sep. 1769, A Expedição . . . , 47; Pamplona to Governor, Estância de Santa Maria de São Francisco de Salles, 7 Oct. 1769, A Expedição . . . , 69–70.

20. For parallel instances in eastern Minas Gerais of conquest motivated by these legal changes, see Hal Langfur, *The Forbidden Lands: Colonial Identity, Frontier Violence, and the Persistence of Brazil's Eastern Indians, 1750–1830* (Stanford, CA: Stanford University Press, 2006), esp. 60–67. Herzog helpfully emphasizes that vassals in both Portuguese and Spanish America routinely leveled accusations about territorial adversaries "meant to capture royal attention rather than necessarily to represent the truth." Tamar Herzog, *Frontiers of Possession: Spain and Portugal in Europe and the Americas* (Cambridge, MA: Harvard University Press, 2015), 21.

21. King João III, "Regimento de Tomé de Sousa," 17 Dec. 1548, in Paulo Bonavides and Roberto Amaral, eds., *Textos políticos da história do Brasil*, 3rd ed., vol. 1 (Brasília: Senado Federal, 2002), 159; Beatriz Perrone-Moisés, "Inventário da legislação indigenista, 1500–1800," in *História dos índios no Brasil*, ed. Manuela Carneiro da Cunha (São Paulo: Companhia das Letras, FAPESP/SMC, 1992), 529–66. Many apparent contradictions in Indigenous legislation stemmed from the difference between relatively more tolerant policies intended for Indians settled in church- or state-run villages and more aggressive ones meant for independent Indians who resisted incorporation. Perrone-Moisés, "Índios livres e índios escravos: Os princípios da legislação indigenista do período colonial (séculos XVI a XVIII)."

22. For the relevant legislation, see "Ley porque V. Magestade ha por bem restituir aos Indios do Grão Pará, e Maranhão a liberdade das suas pessoas, bens, e commercio na forma que nella se declara" (Lisbon, 1755) and "Directorio que se deve observar nas Povoaçoens dos Indios do Pará, e Maranhão em quanto Sua Magestade não mandar o contrario," (Pará, 1757), facsimile reprint in Carlos de Araújo Moreira Neto, *Índios da Amazônia: De maioria a minoria (1750–1850)* (Petrópolis: Editora Vozes, 1988), 161–62, 165–203, quotations 166–68. For the full text of the law extending the Directorate to the rest of Brazil, see "Direção com que interinamente se devem regular os indios das novas villas e lugares erectos nas aldeias da Capitania de Pernambuco e suas annexas," in *RIHGB* 46, no. 1 (1883): 121–69. For Furtado's governorship, Marcos Carneiro de Mendonça, *A Amazônia na era pombalina: Correspondência inédita do governador e capitão-general do estado do Grão Pará e Maranhão, Francisco Xavier de Mendonça Furtado, 1751–1759*, 3 vols. (Rio de Janeiro: Instituto Histórico e Geográfico Brasileiro, 1963). On the

import of these laws in Amazonia, see Rita Heloísa de Almeida, *O Diretório dos índios: Um projeto de "civilização" no Brasil do século XVIII* (Brasília: Universidade de Brasília, 1997); Barbara A. Sommer, "Negotiated Settlements: Native Amazonians and Portuguese Policy in Pará, Brazil, 1758–1798" (PhD diss., University of New Mexico, 2000); Ângela Domingues, *Quando os índios eram vassalos: Colonização e relações de poder no Norte do Brasil na segunda metade do século XVIII* (Lisbon: Comissão Nacional para as Comemorações dos Descobrimentos Portugueses, 2000); Heather F. Roller, *Amazonian Routes: Indigenous Mobility and Colonial Communities in Northern Brazil* (Stanford, CA: Stanford University Press, 2014). On their legal implication in Minas Gerais, see Langfur, *Forbidden Lands*, 60–67. For comparable circumstances in other regions, see Heather F. Roller, "Autonomous Indian Nations and Peacemaking in Late Eighteenth-Century Brazil," in *The Oxford Handbook of Borderlands of the Iberian World*, ed. Cynthia Radding and Danna Levin Rojo (Oxford: Oxford University Press, 2019). For Indigenous legislation more broadly, see Perrone-Moisés, "Índios livres e índios escravos: Os princípios da legislação indigenista do período colonial (séculos XVI a XVIII)," 115–32; Perrone-Moisés, "Inventário da legislação indigenista, 1500–1800," 529–66.

23. José Inaldo Chaves Júnior, "Reforma dos territórios e das jurisdições nas capitanias do Norte do Estado do Brasil: As atuações do capitão-general Luís Diogo Lobo da Silva e do "juiz de fora" Miguel Carlos de Pina Castelo Branco na aplicação do Diretório dos índios (1757–1764)," *Locus: Revista de História* 24, no. 1 (2018).

24. Governor to Francisco Xavier de Mendonça Furtado, Vila Rica, 1 Mar. 1764, AHU, Minas Gerais, cx. 83, doc. 16. Throughout, I translate the Portuguese *gentio* as heathen. On the term's origin, relationship to the English word "gentile," and usage in colonial Brazil, see B. J. Barickman, "'Tame Indians,' 'Wild Heathens,' and Settlers in Southern Bahia in the Late Eighteenth and Early Nineteenth Centuries," *The Americas* 51, no. 3 (1995): 327n6.

25. For the mobilization in the eastern sertão, see "Lista das pessoas que devem e tem obrigação de concorrerem para embaraçar o corso com que o gentio Sylvestre está todos os annos entrando pelas fazendas e sesmarias da Beira do Rio Doce . . . ," Vila Rica, 9 May 1765, APM, CC, cód. 1156, fol. 4; "Petição que fizerão e assignarão os moradores das freguesias ostilizadas," ca. May 1765, APM, CC, cód. 1156, fol. 9–10; Governor to Furtado, Vila Rica, 6 July 1765, AHU, Minas Gerais, cx. 83, doc. 16. On Governor Silva's western journey, see José João Teixeira Coelho, *Instrução para o governo da Capitania de Minas Gerais*, ed. Caio César Boschi (Belo Horizonte: Secretaria de Estado de Cultura, 1994), 248; Souza, "Violência e práticas culturais," 196; Vasconcelos, *História média*, 191–97. For his

orders to Pamplona, see Justificação do coronel Inácio Correia Pamplona, Vila Rica, 3 Jul 1804, AHU, Minas Gerais, cx. 177, doc. 47.

26. Governor, "Memoria do que deve observar na derrota que tem de seguir o Capitam Antonio Cardozo de Souza para a Conquista do Gentio a que vai destinado, e do que hade praticar," Vila Rica, 9 Apr. 1769, BNRJ, SM, CV, cód. 18, 2, 6, doc. 306.

27. Requerimento do coronel Inácio Correia Pamplona, pedindo remuneração com mercês pelos seus distintos serviços, before 17 Sep 1805, AHU, Minas Gerais, cx. 177, doc. 47.

28. "Daily Notice," 344; "Notícia diária," 84.

29. Rocha, *Geografia histórica*, 77. Also see Barbosa, *A decadência*, 127.

30. Quoted in Assis, "Inácio Correia Pamplona", 118.

31. Requerimento do coronel Inácio Correia Pamplona, pedindo remuneração com mercês pelos seus distintos serviços, before 17 Sep 1805, AHU, Minas Gerais, cx. 177, doc. 47.

32. Diogo Pereira Ribeiro de Vasconcelos, *Breve descrição geográfica, física e política da Capitania de Minas Gerais* (Belo Horizonte: Fundação João Pinheiro, 1994), 51. Also see Mary C. Karasch, *Before Brasília* (Albuquerque: University of New Mexico Press, 2016), 62, 121.

33. Mary Karasch, "Interethnic Conflict and Resistance on the Brazilian Frontier of Goiás, 1750–1890," in *Contested Ground: Comparative Frontiers on the Northern and Southern Edges of the Spanish Empire*, ed. Donna J. Guy and Thomas E. Sheridan (Tucson: University of Arizona Press, 1998), 115–34. Also see Robert H. Lowie, "The Southern Cayapó," in *Handbook of South American Indians*, ed. Julian H. Steward (New York: Cooper Square, 1963), vol. 1, 519–20; Odair Giraldin, *Cayapó e Panará: Luta e sobrevivência de um povo Jê no Brasil Central* (Campinas: Unicamp, 1997); Karasch, *Before Brasília*, 59–62, 121–25; Mário Lara, *Nos confins do Sertão da Farinha Podre: Povoamento, conquistas e confrontos no Oeste de Minas* (n.p., 2009), 179–207.

34. Barbosa, *A decadência*, 128–37.

35. Domingos [illeg.] to Pamplona, Vila Rica, 13 Aug. 1769, A Expedição . . . , 33–34.

36. Francisco Xavier de Mendonça Furtado to Governor, [Lisbon], 12 Feb. 1765, AHU, cód. 610, f. 31–31v.

37. "Notícia diária," 59–61. The quotations are from Pamplona to Governor, [Estância de] São Simão, 7 Sep. 1769, A Expedição . . . , 21; Pamplona, "Instrução e despedição qeu faço desta estancia de São Simão do Rio das Ajudas . . . ," 4 Sep. 1769, A Expedição . . . , 14. For Pamplona's optimistic

predictions, see Pamplona to Governor, Estância de Santa Maria de São Francisco de Salles, 16 Sep. 1769, A Expedição . . . , 42. On hostile enemies, see Pamplona to Governor, Estância de São Simão, 10 Oct. 1769, A Expedição . . . , 75.

38. "Daily Notice," 343.

39. "Notícia diária," 69, 72, 76.

40. See, for example, Pamplona to Governor, Estância de Santa Maria de São Francisco de Salles, 5 Oct. 1769, A Expedição . . . , 81; Pamplona to Governor, Estância de São Simão, 10 Oct. 1769, A Expedição . . . , 75–76; Pamplona to Governor, Estância de Santo Estevão, 15 Nov. 1769, A Expedição . . . , 106.

41. Insights concerning the public face of honor in early modern Iberia and Spanish America help elucidate Pamplona's conduct. Ann Twinam, *Public Lives, Private Secrets: Gender, Honor, Sexuality, and Illegitimacy in Colonial Spanish America* (Stanford, CA: Stanford University Press, 1999), 31–34.

42. "Notícia diária," 96–97.

43. See Amantino, *O mundo*, 186–95; Maria Emília Aparecida de Assis, "Inácio Correia Pamplona: Um 'herói' para o sertão mineiro setecentista," *Temporalidades: Revista de História* 6, no. 1 (2014): 67–83; Melânia Silva de Aguiar, "A literatura do Setecentos em Minas Gerais: O Arcadismo," in *História de Minas Gerais: As Minas setecentistas*, ed. Mari Efigênia Lage de Resende and Luiz Carlos Villalta (Belo Horizonte: Autêntica, 2007), vol. 2, 313–33; Holanda, *Capítulos*, 116–74 and part 2. For Holanda, Arcadian elements in Costa's poetry were merely the "outward disguise" (281) of a style still wedded to baroque and classical precursors.

44. Elsewhere in the original diary, Pamplona's name generally appears in a more modern orthography as Inácio Correia Pamplona.

45. "Notícia diária," 53–54.

46. I thank Chi-ming Yang and Ana Hontanilla for alerting me to the formal elements of these poems.

47. Luís Vaz de Camões, *The Lusiads*, trans. Landeg White (New York: Oxford University Press, 2001), canto 1, st. 73–77; canto 6, st. 26–34, 80–99, quoting 96. For Camões's influence, see Moema Cavalcante, *Por mares muito antes navegados: A tradição de Camões na poesia colonial brasileira* (Canoas: Univerdiade Luterana do Brasil, 2001), esp. chap. 4; Patricia A. O. de Baubeta, "Revisiting Camões' Sonnets: Anthologies, Translations, and Canonicity," *Bulletin of Spanish Studies: Hispanic Studies and Researches on Spain, Portugal, and Latin America* 95, no. 2–3 (2018).

48. "Notícia diária," 54–55.

49. "Notícia diária," 56.

50. On the symbolic, social, and political aspects of gold and diamond discoveries, see Andrade, *A invenção*, esp. 333–39. On patronage and prospecting laws,

see Romeiro and Botelho, *Dicionário histórico*, 160–62, 252–53; Marco Antonio Silveira, *O universo do indistinto: Estado e sociedade nas Minas setecentistas (1735–1808)* (São Paulo: HUCITEC, 1997), 169–83.

51. The division of land into mining claims generally conformed to the royal mining code of 1702. Later innovations in the law favored the crown while extending to all enslavers certain advantages previously reserved for those with more than a dozen slaves. The original code stipulated that the initial discoverer enjoyed the right to select the first claim. The second was then allotted to the crown, the third, again, to the discoverer. Subsequent claims were divided according to a lottery system. The original code, moreover, allocated an entire mining claim (*data*) only to those with more than a dozen slaves, but just a fraction of such a claim to those with fewer slaves. See "Regimento Mineral," Lisbon, 19 Apr. 1702, *RAPM* 1, no. 4 (1896): 675. Boxer presents a slightly different apportionment scheme in C. R. Boxer, *The Golden Age of Brazil, 1695–1750: Growing Pains of a Colonial Society* (Berkeley: University of California Press, 1969),

52. Variations apparently stem from the fact that different versions of the code have been published, including Francisco Ignacio Ferreira, *Repertorio jurídico do mineiro: Consolidação alphabetica e chronologica de todas as disposições sobre minas, comprehendendo a legislação antiga e moderna de Portugal e do Brasil* (Rio de Janeiro: Typ. Nacional, 1884), 200–208; Damião Peres, *Estudos de História Luso-Brasileira* (Lisbon: n.p., 1956), 53–63. Also see Afonso de Escragnolle Taunay, *História geral das bandeiras paulistas* (São Paulo: Typ. Ideal and Imp. Oficial, 1924–50), vol. 9–10, 244–48; Francisco Vidal Luna and Iraci del Nero da Costa, *Minas colonial: Economia e sociedade* (São Paulo: Livraria Pioneira, 1982), 3–4; Francisco Vidal Luna, *Minas Gerais: Escravos e senhores: Análise da estrutura populacional e econômica de alguns centros mineratórios (1718–1804)* (São Paulo: Instituto de Pesquisas Econômicas, 1981), 38–40; Romeiro and Botelho, *Dicionário histórico*, 252–53.

## Chapter 2

1. Waldemar de Almeida Barbosa, *A decadência das minas e a fuga da mineração* (Belo Horizonte: Universidade Federal de Minas Gerais, 1971), 29–36, 80–85. Correcting geographic misconceptions repeated by many historians, Barbosa clarifies that the Picada de Goiás ran from São João del Rei, crossed the São Francisco River near its confluence with one of its tributaries, the Bambuí River, continued through the Marcela Mountains (Serra da Marcela), then passed the important mining town of Paracatu along the captaincy's northwestern border. Finally, it continued to Vila Boa in Goiás.

2. Homer, *The Iliad*, trans. Robert Fagles (New York: Viking, 1990), 6.213–15.

3. "Notícia diária e individual das marchas[,] e acontecimentos ma(i)s condigno(s) da jornada que fez o Senhor Mestre de Campo, Regente[,] e Guarda(-)mor Inácio Corre(i)a Pamplona, desde que saiu de sua casa[,] e fazenda do Capote às conquistas do Sertão, até se tornar a recolher à mesma sua dita fazenda do Capote, etc. etc. etc., [1769]," *ABNRJ* 108 (1988): 58. On terms used to describe racial categories in Portuguese America, many of them derogatory, see Muriel Nazzari, "Vanishing Indians: The Social Construction of Race in Colonial São Paulo," *The Americas* 57, no. 4 (2001): 497–524; Stuart B. Schwartz, "Brazilian Ethnogenesis: Mestiços, Mamelucos, and Pardos," in *Le Nouveau Monde, Mondes Nouveaux: L'experience americaine*, ed. Serge Gruzinski and Nathan Wachtel (Paris: EHESS/CNRS, 1996), 7–27; Sheila de Castro Faria, *A colônia em movimento: Fortuna e família no cotidiano colonial* (Rio de Janeiro: Ed. Nova Fronteira, 1998), 135–39; Hebe Maria Mattos, *Das cores do silêncio: Os significados da liberdade no Sudeste escravista—Brasil século XIX*, 2nd ed. (Rio de Janeiro: Nova Fronteira, 1998), chap. 5.

4. Laird W. Bergad, *Slavery and the Demographic and Economic History of Minas Gerais, Brazil, 1720–1888* (Cambridge: Cambridge University Press, 1999), 91, 97; Hal Langfur, *The Forbidden Lands: Colonial Identity, Frontier Violence, and the Persistence of Brazil's Eastern Indians, 1750–1830* (Stanford, CA: Stanford University Press, 2006), 109.

5. Ordem Régia (royal order), Palácio de Nossa Senhora da Ajuda, 22 July 1766, BNRJ, SM, cód. 36, 9, 28, doc. 1; José João Teixeira Coelho, *Instrução para o governo da Capitania de Minas Gerais*, ed. Caio César Boschi (Belo Horizonte: Secretaria de Estado de Cultura, 1994), 149. On vadios, see Laura de Mello e Souza, *Desclassificados do ouro: A pobreza mineira no século XVIII*, 3rd ed. (Rio de Janeiro: Graal, 1990), esp. 51–71, 124–25, 215–22; Langfur, *Forbidden Lands*, 76–85.

6. Carlos Magno Guimarães, "Escravidão e quilombos nas Minas Gerais do século XVIII," in *História de Minas Gerais: As Minas setecentistas*, ed. Mari Efigênia Lage de Resende and Luiz Carlos Villalta (Belo Horizonte: Autêntica, 2007), vol. 1, 439–48; Carlos Magno Guimarães, "Mineração, quilombos, e Palmares: Minas Gerais no século XVIII," in *Liberdade por um fio: História dos quilombos no Brasil*, ed. João José Reis and Flávio dos Santos Gomes (São Paulo: Companhia das Letras, 1996), 139–63; Adriana Romeiro and Angela Vianna Botelho, *Dicionário histórico das Minas Gerais: Período colonial* (Belo Horizonte: Autêntica, 2003), 245–47; Mariana L. R. Dantas, "'For the Benefit of the Common Good': Regiments of Caçadores do Mato in Minas Gerais, Brazil," *Journal of Colonialism and Colonial History* 5, no. 2 (2004); Donald Ramos, "O quilombo e o sistema escravista em Minas Gerais do século XVIII," in *Liberdade por um fio: História dos quilombos no Brasil*, ed. João José Reis and Flávio dos Santos Gomes (São

Paulo: Companhia das Letras, 1996), 164–92. Guimarães's chapters summarize his earlier works. See Carlos Magno Guimarães, "Quilombos: classes, estado e cotidiano (Minas Gerais—século XVIII)" (PhD diss., Universidade de São Paulo, 1999); Carlos Magno Guimarães, *Uma negação da ordem escravista: Quilombos em Minas Gerais no século XVIII* (São Paulo: Icone, 1988). Also see Flávio dos Santos Gomes, "Seguindo o mapa das minas: Plantas e quilombos mineiros setecentistas," *Estudos Afro-Asiáticos* 29 (March 1996): 113–42; Waldemar de Almeida Barbosa, *Negros e quilombos em Minas Gerais* (Belo Horizonte: n.p., 1972); Ricardo Ferreira Ribeiro, *Florestas anãs do sertão: O cerrado na história de Minas Gerais* (Belo Horizonte: Autêntica, 2005), vol. 1, 301–27. For regional variants and overviews of the quilombo phenomenon, see João José Reis and Flávio dos Santos Gomes, eds., *Liberdade por um fio: História dos quilombos no Brasil* (São Paulo: Companhia das Letras,1996); Stuart B. Schwartz, *Slaves, Peasants, and Rebels: Reconsidering Brazilian Slavery* (Urbana: University of Illinois Press, 1992), esp. chap. 4; Flávio dos Santos Gomes, *A hidra e os pântanos: Mocambos, quilombos e comunidades de fugitivos no Brasil (séculos XVII–XIX)* (São Paulo: Polis, UNESP, 2005); Flávio dos Santos Gomes, *Palmares: Escravidão e liberdade no Atlântico Sul* (São Paulo: Contexto, 2005); Flávio dos Santos Gomes, *Histórias de quilombolas: Mocambos e comunidades de senzalas no Rio de Janeiro, século XIX*, rev ed. (São Paulo: Companhia das Letras, 2006); Maria do Carmo Brazil, *Fronteira negra: Dominação, violência e resistência escrava em Mato Grosso, 1718–1888* (Passo Fundo: Universidade de Passo Fundo, 2002), 111–19.

7. Guimarães, "Escravidão e quilombos," 448–53; Romeiro and Botelho, *Dicionário histórico*, 70–71; Dantas, "For the Benefit." The quotation comes from "Reflexões sobre a Ley de 11 de Agosto do presente anno em que se patenteam os prejuisos, que a mesma causa á Real Fazenda, e se dá instrução da gente, de que a mesma Ley trata, e dos seus costumes, e notícia das Tropas, que ha nos Governos de todas as Minas, e da despeza, que cada uma causa, tanto na sua criação, como em o gasto annual de soldos e mantimentos," after 1760, BPE, cód. CV/1–3, fol. 115v.

8. See, for example, Ramos, "O quilombo," 167, 174.

9. Martins identifies two quilombos with the same name, often confused in the sources and by historians, which he distinguishes by their locations as Ambrósio I near Cristais and, to the north, Ambrósio II near Ibiá. See Tarcisio José Martins, *Quilombo do Campo Grande: A história de Minas que se devolve ao povo*, rev. ed. (Contagem: Santaclara, 2008), 620–26.

10. Governor to Town Councils, Vila Rica, 14 June 1746, APM, SC, cód. 84, f. 108v–109; Governor to King, Rio, 8 Aug. 1746, APM, SC, cód. 45, f. 64v–65. Also see Guimarães, "Mineração, quilombos, e Palmares." On Palmares, see,

among many works, Gomes, *Palmares*; Schwartz, *Slaves, Peasants, and Rebels*, chap. 4; Luiz Felipe de Alencastro, *The Trade in the Living: The Formation of Brazil in the South Atlantic, Sixteenth to Seventeenth Centuries*, trans. Gavin Adams and Luiz Felipe de Alencasto (Albany: State University of New York Press, 2018), 242–49; Edison Carneiro, *O quilombo dos Palmares*, 3rd ed. (Rio de Janeiro: Civilização Brasileira, 1966); José da Costa Porto, *Estudo sobre o sistema sesmarial* (Recife: Universidade Federal de Pernambuco, 1965), 144–49.

11. Governor to Town Councils, Vila Rica, 12 Feb. 1757, APM, SC, cód. 116, f. 98–99; Governor to Bartolomeu Bueno do Prado, Vila Rica, 10 Sep. 1759, APM, SC, cód. 123, f. 103–103v. Also see the detailed reconstruction of Prado's activities, including this expedition in Martins, *Quilombo do Campo Grande*, 233, 360–61, 528, 635–55; Diogo [Luís de Almeida Pereira] de Vasconcelos, *História média de Minas Gerais*, 4th ed. (Belo Horizonte: Itatiaia, 1974), 180–81; Ribeiro, *Florestas anãs do sertão*, vol. 1, 302–17. From the late eighteenth century on, accounts by credulous historians ignored this frustrated assessment, crediting Prado with, or decrying him for, killing as many as 3,900 runaways. Martins is among the latest to accept the unsubstantiated casualty figures (793–98). Contrast Francisco de Assis Carvalho Franco, *Dicionário de bandeirantes e sertanistas do Brasil: Século XVI, XVII, XVIII* (Belo Horizonte: Itatiaia, 1989), 312–13. Pamplona, who would have been well informed about the earlier expeditions, if also intent on minimizing their accomplishments, wrote that they had captured and killed very few runaways. Pamplona to Governor, Estância de São Simão, 10 Oct. 1769, A Expedição . . . , 76.

12. See Sesmaria of Bartolomeu Bueno do Prado, 18 Dec 1760, APM, SC, cód. 129, f. 99–99v. There is no evidence that Prado later received the required royal confirmation of his land grant, suggesting that he may have sold the land to someone else. For land grants distributed among Prado's associates, see, among others, Sesmaria of Antonio Francisco França, 18 Dec 1760, APM, SC, cód. 129, f. 98–98v; Sesmaria of Felipe Antonio de Burem, 18 Dec 1760, APM, SC, cód. 129, f. 100–100v (quoted); and Sesmaria of Domingos França, 18 Dec 1760, APM, SC, cód. 129, f. 101–101v.

13. "Daily Notice of the Marches and Most Noteworthy Happenings in the Expedition Made by Field Officer Regent Inácio Correia Pamplona," in *Colonial Latin America : A Documentary History*, ed. Kenneth Mills, William B. Taylor, and Sandra Lauderdale Graham (Wilmington, DE: Scholarly Resources, 2002), 343–44. Also see A[ntônio] Gonçalves Dias, *Diccionario da lingua tupy: Chamada lingua geral dos indigenas do Brazil* (Leipzig: F. A. Brockhaus, 1858), 165.

14. "Reflexões sobre a Ley," BPE, cód. CV/1-3, fols. 114v–115. The author of this document referred to Indian slave hunters as *carijós* (persons of mixed Indian

and European descent or detribalized Indians). Also see Renato Venâncio Pinto, "Os últimos carijós: Escravidão indígena em Minas Gerais: 1711–1725," *Revista Brasileira de História* 17, no. 34 (1997); Dias, *Diccionario da lingua tupy*, 165.

15. "Daily Notice," 343–44.

16. Pamplona to Governor, Estância de São Simão, 10 Oct. 1769, A Expedição . . . , 80.

17. "Daily Notice," 343. On the canoes, see Pamplona to Governor, [Estância de] São Simão, 7 Sep. 1769, A Expedição . . . , 21.

18. For a reproduction of this map, see "Quilombo do Ambrósio," in "Notícia diária," 111.

19. Secretary of State, "Instrucção para D. Antonio de Noronha, Governador e Capitão General de Minas Gerais," Salvaterra de Magos, 24 Jan. 1775, BNL, CP, cod. 643, f. 130, par. 34–37.

20. "Daily Notice," 343. For Pamplona's original account of this episode, see Pamplona to Governor, Estância de Santo Estevão, 15 Nov. 1769, A Expedição . . . , 105. The comparison illustrates the dramatic elaborations characteristic of the later diary.

21. "Notícia diária," 59.

22. Pamplona to Governor, [Estância de São Simão], 7 Sep. 1769, second letter of this date, A Expedição . . . , 23.

23. "Daily Notice," 351–52.

24. In tracing the long and complex land grant concession process, which the governor was empowered to initiate but which eventually required crown confirmation in Lisbon, historians display some confusion as to the number and size of the grants Pamplona received, when he received them, and in whose name. Sources divided among several archives clarify that he and his family received eight grants, six awarded in 1767, two almost thirty years later, although their informal possession dated from the earlier period. For the governor's approval of Pamplona's land grant petition, see Sesmaria of Inácio Correia Pamplona, Vila Rica, 1 Dec. 1767, APM, SC, cód. 156, f. 61v–62. For five grants in the names of his daughters and son, see sesmarias of Simplícia Correia Pamplona, Rosa Correia Pamplona, Teodósia [Teodora] Correia Pamplona, Inácia Correia Pamplona, and Timóteo Correia Pamplona, Vila Rica, 1 Dec 1767, APM, SC, cód. 156, f. 62–63, 63–64, 64–65, 65–65v, 66–66v. For the two smaller grants legalized later, in the names of daughter Bernardina and her husband, a relation, see Sesmaria of Bernardina Correia Pamplona, Vila Rica, 22 Sep. 1796, APM, SC, cód. 265, f. 139–140; Sesmaria of João José Correia Pamplona, Vila Rica, 23 Sep. 1796, APM, SC, cód. 265, f. 140v–141. Conceded by Governor Luís Antônio Furtado de Mendonça in 1796, these grants of 1/2 square league (10.9 sq. km) each were located at places

known as Lagoa dos Servos and Arco, on the east side of the São Francisco River. They were contiguous with two of the larger grants, each at least three square leagues (130.7 sq. km). The other four contiguous grants, each at least three square leagues, lay to the west of the river. Pamplona listed all of these sesmarias in his last will and testament. Inácio Correa Pamplona, Post-Mortem Inventory, 1810–1821, AMRSJDR, Inventários e Testamentos, cx. 100, f. 2–3. When officials ordered a colony-wide validation of land grants at the turn of the century, all but one of the properties was confirmed. Apparently, the grant in the son's name became part of Pamplona's property. Ownership of Pamplona's grant was confirmed and registered by the crown and recorded in Minas Gerais between 1800 and 1802. See Sesmaria of Inácio Correia Pamplona, before 14 May 1800, AHU, Minas Gerais, cx. 153, doc. 4; Sesmaria of Inácio Correia Pamplona, Lisbon, 16 Dec 1801, ANTT, RGM, Maria I, liv. 31, f. 77v–78 [registered 21 Jan. 1802]; Sesmaria of Inácio Correia Pamplona, Vila Rica, 16 Dec 1801, APM, SC, cód. 299, f. 1–2. For confirmation and registration of the grants in the names of his daughters and son-in-law in Lisbon see sesmarias of Simplícia Correia Pamplona, Rosa Correia Pamplona, Teodósia [Teodora] Correia Pamplona [mislabled Teodósio], and Inácia Correia Pamplona, Lisbon, 16 Dec 1801, ANTT, RGM, Maria I, liv. 31, f. 78–78v [registered 21 Jan. 1802]; sesmarias of Bernardina Correia Pamplona and João José Correia Pamplona, Lisbon, 5 June 1800, ANTT, RGM, Maria I, liv. 31, f. 76–77 [registered 21 Jan. 1802]. For the recording of these grants in Minas Gerais, see sesmarias of Simplícia Correia Pamplona, Rosa Correia Pamplona, Teodora Correia Pamplona, Inácia Correia Pamplona, Vila Rica, recorded 23 Nov. 1802, APM, SC, cód. 299, respectively, 4v–6, 6–7v, 2–3, 3–4v; Sesmaria of Bernardina Correia Pamplona, Vila Rica, recorded 23 Nov. 1802, APM, SC, cód. 299, f. 9–10; Sesmaria of João José Correia Pamplona, Vila Rica, recorded 23 Nov. 1802, APM, SC, cód. 299, f. 10–11v. Márcia Motta located evidence in Lisbon that two of these grants—those of Teodora and Simplícia—were nullified when deemed to lie within the land claimed by their father. However, the later records cited above, dated 23 Nov. 1802, show that the two sesmarias, along with the others, were confirmed by the monarch, registered in Lisbon, and recorded in Minas Gerais. The disparity is of import primarily as a matter of inheritance, since during his lifetime Pamplona, not his children, administered the various properties. See Márcia Motta, *Direito à terra no Brasil: A gestação do conflito, 1795–1824* (São Paulo: Alameda, 2009), 187.

25. Maria Emília Aparecida de Assis, "Inácio Correia Pamplona: O 'Hércules' do sertão mineiro setecentista" (master's thesis, Universidade Federal de São de del Rei, 2014), 36.

26. Inácio Correa Pamplona, Post-Mortem Inventory, 1810–1821, AMRSJDR, Inventários e Testamentos, cx. 100, f. 2–3. Also see Laura de Mello e Souza,

"Violência e práticas culturais no cotidiano de uma expedição contra quilombolas, Minas Gerais, 1769," in *Liberdade por um fio: História dos quilombos no Brasil*, ed. João José Reis and Flávio dos Santos Gomes (São Paulo: Companhia das Letras, 1996).

27. Requerimento de Inácio Correia Pamplona, after 1 Oct. 1801, AHU, Minas Gerais, cx. 160, doc. 3; Requerimento do coronel Inácio Correia Pamplona, pedindo remuneração com mercês pelos seus distintos serviços, before 17 Sep 1805, AHU, Minas Gerais, cx. 177, doc. 47. For the crown's denial of Pamplona's requests, see Inácio Correia Pamplona, certidão negativa, 29 Aug. 1805, repeated 3 Mar. 1819, ANTT, RGM, Registo de certidões negativas, Maria I, liv. 1, f. 367v. While the recorded denial is ambiguous, not citing the honor requested, by its date it applied in all likelihood to the above petitions. The negative finding also referenced Pamplona's appointment as regent, more than thirty years earlier. Royal order, 30 Jan. 1771, ANTT, RGM, José I, liv. 24, f. 63. On merchants and the Order of Christ, see Aldair Carlos Rodrigues, "Homens de negócio: Vocabulário social, distinção e atividades mercantis nas Minas setecentistas," *História* 28, no. 1 (2009): esp. 209.

28. Rodrigo Ricupero, *A formação da elite colonial: Brasil c. 1530–c. 1630* (São Paulo: Alameda, 2008), 18–19.

29. Iraci del Nero da Costa, *Minas Gerais: Estruturas populacionais típicas* (São Paulo: EDEC, 1982), 78–82; Stanley J. Stein, *Vassouras: A Brazilian Coffee County; The Roles of Planter and Slave in a Plantation Society* (Cambridge, MA: Harvard University Press, 1958; reprint, 1985), 10–12.

30. See royal order to Governor, Lisbon, 20 Nov. 1725, *RAPM* 30 (1979): 228; Governor, Bando, 8 Aug. 1738, summarized in "Indices dos livros do Archivo Publico Mineiro," *RAPM* 20 (1924): 420. For the 1744 order, see Francisco Gregorio Pires Monteiro Bandeira, Indice cronológico das Leys, Alvarás, Cartas Regias, Decretos, Avizos, e Provizoens, que se expedirão para a Provedoria, e Junta da Real Fazenda da Capitania de Minas Geraes, Título 18, No. 2, 1770, OLL, cód 4.

31. Viceroy, "Edital para a medição e divizão das terras na forma que abaixo se declara," Rio, 30 Dec. 1771, Portarias do expediente do governo do . . . Marquez do Lavradio, Rio, 1771–1774, f. 27v–28v, vault Ayer MS 1814, NL.

32. Romeiro and Botelho, *Dicionário histórico*, 252–53, 275–76, quoting 276. For an overview of land grant legislation in Minas Gerais, also see Ângelo Alves Carrara, *Minas e currais: Produção rural e mercado interno em Minas Gerais, 1674–1807* (Juiz de Fora: Universidade Federal de Juiz de Fora, 2007), 151–54.

33. Sesmaria of Teodósia [Teodora] Correia Pamplona, Vila Rica, 1 Dec 1767, APM, SC, cód. 156, f. 64.

34. For Teodora's age, see "Brazil, Baptisms, 1688–1935," https://familysearch.org/pal:/MM9.1.1/XNYF-QTT, Teodozia [Teodora] Pamplona, 3 Sep. 1752;

citing reference LIV 3 PAG 16V, FHL microfilm 1284523. For the convent, see Waldemar de Almeida Barbosa, *Dicionário histórico-geográfico de Minas Gerais* (Belo Horizonte: Itatiaia, 1995), 191. Also see Francisco Eduardo Pinto, "Potentado e conflitos nas sesmarias da Comarca do Rio das Mortes" (PhD diss., Universidade Federal Fluminense, 2010), 57–58; Motta, *Direito à terra*, 184–87.

35. See Sesmaria of Timóteo Correia Pamplona, Vila Rica, 1 Dec 1767, APM, SC, cód. 156, f. 66–66v; Testament of Inácio Correa Pamplona, 1821, AMRSJDR, Fundo Cartorial, Livro de testamentos, no. 14; "Notícia diária," 93.

36. Alvará (royal charter), 5 Oct. 1795, and Decreto (royal decree), 10 Dec. 1796, in Antonio Delgado da Silva, ed., *Collecção da legislação portugueza desde a ultima compilação das ordenações*, 6 vols., vol. 4 (Lisbon: Maigrense,1825), vol. 4, quoting 242, 341. Prince Regent João reasserted and strengthened these provisions in 1809. Alvará, 25 Jan. 1809, in Cândido Mendes de Almeida, ed., *Codigo Philippino ou Ordenações e Leis do Reino de Portugal*, 14th ed. (Rio de Janeiro: Instituto Filomático,1870), Book 4, 1028–29. Motta, *Direito à terra*, 81–96.

37. See, for example, Joaquim Veloso Miranda to Governor, Vila Rica, 11 Oct. 1800, and Governor to Vila Rica Câmara (Town Council), Vila Rica, 20 Oct. 1800, AHU, Minas Gerais, cx. 161, doc. 24.

38. Sesmaria of Inácio Correia Pamplona, Vila Rica, 1 Dec 1767, APM, SC, cód. 156, f. 61v–62. Much of the language cited, describing the slaves and livestock dedicated to productive enterprise, can be considered pro forma in land grant petitions. The crown required successful petitioners to demonstrate that the lands in question were cultivated and occupied within the span of two years from the date of the original concession. Although frequently unenforced, this deadline may have contributed to Pamplona's desire to lead the 1769 expedition to demonstrate that he was improving his land.

39. An older house of worship may have already stood where Pamplona declared himself the founder. Runaways attempted to burn to the ground the preexisting church in 1760. It suffered another arson attempt, also blamed on runaways, in 1770, the year after Pamplona's rededication ritual. See Martins, *Quilombo do Campo Grande*, 675; Ribeiro, *Florestas anãs do sertão*, vol. 1, 320. Also see Lauren A. Benton, *A Search for Sovereignty: Law and Geography in European Empires, 1400–1900* (New York: Cambridge University Press, 2010), 24–26. On the banning of missionaries and other constraints on the power of the church during this period, see C. R. Boxer, *The Golden Age of Brazil, 1695–1750: Growing Pains of a Colonial Society* (Berkeley: University of California Press, 1969), 180–81; Dauril Alden, *The Making of an Enterprise: The Society of Jesus in Portugal, Its Empire, and Beyond, 1540–1750* (Stanford, CA: Stanford University Press, 1996), 597; Evergton Sales Souza, "Igreja e Estado no período pombalino," in *A "Época Pombalina"*

*no mundo luso-brasileiro*, ed. Francisco Falcon and Claudia Rodrigues (Rio de Janeiro: Editora FGV, 2015), 277–306. On the church's role in territorializing royal and religious authority, see Cláudia Damasceno Fonseca, *Arraiais e vilas d'el rei: Espaco e poder nas Minas setecentistas* (Belo Horizonte: Universidade Federal de Minas Gerais, 2011), chap. 2.

40. "Daily Notice," 348–49. Cf. Pamplona to Governor, Estância de Santo Estevão, 15 Nov. 1769, A Expedição . . . , 106–7.

41. Pamplona to Governor, Estância de Santo Estevão, 15 Nov. 1769, A Expedição . . . , 108; "Notícia diária," 73–74; Carrara, *Minas e currais*, 163–64.

42. Quoted in Assis, "Inácio Correia Pamplona," 62.

43. José Basílio da Gama, [Testamento irónico do Marquês] in [Textos, predominantemente satíricos e jocosos, contra o Marquês de Pombal e a sua política], n.d., BNP, Manuscritos Reservados, cód. 13026, 83–99.

44. Quoted in Assis, "Inácio Correia Pamplona," 65.

45. The classic statement of this perspective, first published in 1972, is Maria Odila Leite da Silva Dias, "A interiorização da metrópole," in *A interiorização da metrópole e outros estudos* (São Paulo: Alameda, 2005). While Dias focuses on the post-1808 period, many other historians have more recently applied her argument to the eighteenth century. For Minas Gerais, concerning individuals, like Pamplona, who achieved social distinction as merchants, see Júnia Ferreira Furtado, *Homens de negócio: A interiorização da metrópole e do comércio nas Minas setecentistas* (São Paulo: Hucitec, 1999); Rodrigues, "Homens de negócio," esp. 208–9. On the "political economy of privileges," see, for example, Maria Fernanda Bicalho, "As câmaras ultramarinas e o governo do Império," in *O Antigo Regime nos trópicos: A dinâmica imperial portuguesa, séculos XVI–XVIII*, ed. João Luís Ribeiro Fragoso, Maria Fernanda Bicalho, and Maria de Fátima Gouvêa (Rio de Janeiro: Civilização Brasileira, 2001), 189–221; Rodrigo Bentes Monteiro et al., eds., *Raízes do privilégio: Mobilidade social no mundo ibérico do Antigo Regime* (Rio de Janeiro: Civilização Brasileira, 2011). For the Spanish American counterpart, see Alejandro Cañeque, *The King's Living Image: The Culture and Politics of Viceregal Power in Colonial Mexico* (New York: Routledge, 2004), 174.

46. Kenneth R. Maxwell, *Conflicts and Conspiracies: Brazil and Portugal, 1750–1808* (Cambridge: Cambridge University Press, 1973), 152–53, 158, 162–63, 167–68, 193.

47. For the British Empire, Kathleen Wilson finds the vantage point of imperial frontiers useful in re-conceptualizing an early modern European state "from the outside in." For continental Europe, too, as Peter Sahlins argues, states and nations emerged from a dialectical process in which impositions from the center were matched and offset by social and political relations along their territorial

perimeters. Kathleen Wilson, "Rethinking the Colonial State: Family, Gender, and Governmentality in Eighteenth-Century British Frontiers," *American Historical Review* 116, no. 5 (2011): 1320; Peter Sahlins, *Boundaries: The Making of France and Spain in the Pyrenees* (Berkeley: University of California Press, 1989), 8–9. For negotiation at the Spanish, British, French, and other Portuguese imperial peripheries in the Americas, see the essays in Christine Daniels and Michael V. Kennedy, eds., *Negotiated Empires: Centers and Peripheries in the Americas, 1500–1820* (New York: Routledge, 2002). Also see the negotiated process of transculturation occurring in such zones as theorized in Mary Louise Pratt, *Imperial Eyes: Travel Writing and Transculturation* (London: Routledge, 1992).

48. "Notícia diária," 87.

## Chapter 3

1. For a preliminary examination of events discussed in part 2, see Hal Langfur, "Native Informants and the Limits of Portuguese Dominion in Late-Colonial Brazil," in *The Oxford Handbook of Borderlands of the Iberian World*, ed. Cynthia Radding and Danna Levin Rojo (Oxford: Oxford University Press, 2019). From the early eighteenth century, authorities fretted about contraband gold and diamonds flowing from the interior through Rio de Janeiro. Ernst Pijning, "The Meaning of Illegality: Contraband Trade in Eighteenth-Century Rio de Janeiro," *RIHGB* 164, no. 419 (2003).

2. Muriel Nazzari, "Vanishing Indians: The Social Construction of Race in Colonial São Paulo," *The Americas* 57, no. 4 (2001); Maria Leônia Chaves de Resende, "Gentios brasílicos: Índios coloniais em Minas Gerais setecentista" (PhD diss., Universidade de Campinas, 2003); Maria Leônia Chaves de Resende, "'Devassas gentílicas': Inquisição dos índios na Minas Gerais colonial," in *Caminhos gerais: Estudos históricos sobre Minas (séc. XVIII–XIX)*, ed. Maria Leônia Chaves de Resende and Silvia Maria Jardim Brügger (São João del Rei: Universidade Federal de São João del Rei, 2005), 9–48; Almir Diniz de Carvalho Júnior, "Índios cristãos: A conversão dos gentios na Amazônia Portuguesa (1653–1769)" (PhD diss., Universidade de Campinas, 2005); Maria Regina Celestino de Almeida, "Land and Economic Resources of Indigenous *Aldeias* in Rio de Janeiro: Conflicts and Negotiations, Seventeenth to Nineteenth Centuries," in *Native Brazil: Beyond the Convert and the Cannibal, 1500–1889*, ed. Hal Langfur (Albuquerque: University of New Mexico Press, 2014), 62–85. Similar inconsistencies, especially a tendency in church records to whiten individuals, can be found in colonial documents labeling free persons of African descent. See Sheila de Castro Faria, *A colônia em movimento: Fortuna e família no cotidiano colonial* (Rio de Janeiro: Ed. Nova Fronteira, 1998), 135–39.

3. See "Ley porque V. Magestade ha por bem restituir aos Indios do Grão Pará, e Maranhão a liberdade das suas pessoas, bens, e commercio na forma que nella se declara" (Lisbon, 1755) in Carlos de Araújo Moreira Neto, *Índios da Amazônia: De maioria a minoria (1750–1850)* (Petrópolis: Editora Vozes, 1988), 161–62. On the centuries-long contacts between these Indians and coastal colonists, see Márcia Malheiros, "'Homens de Fronteira': Índios e Capuchinhos na ocupação dos Sertões do Leste do Paraíba ou Goytacazes (séculos XVIII e XIX)" (PhD diss., Universidade Federal Fluminense, 2008), 112–20.

4. Hermann Burmeister, *Viagem ao Brasil através das províncias do Rio de Janeiro e Minas Gerais*, trans. Manoel Salvaterra and Hubert Schoenfeldt (São Paulo: Livraria Martins, 1952), 121.

5. For a more detailed discussion, see John M. Monteiro, "Tupis, tapuias e historiadores: Estudos de história indígena e do indigenismo" (Livre Docência thesis, IFCH-Unicamp, 2001), chap. 3; Hal Langfur, "Introduction: Recovering Brazil's Indigenous Pasts," in *Native Brazil: Beyond the Cannibal and the Convert, 1500–1889*, ed. Hal Langfur (Albuquerque: University of New Mexico Press, 2014), chap. 1.

6. Within a growing body of scholarship concerned with these early colonial Indians, see Sérgio Buarque de Holanda, *Caminhos e fronteiras* (Rio de Janeiro: J. Olympio, 1957); John M. Monteiro, *Negros da terra: Índios e bandeirantes nas origens de São Paulo* (São Paulo: Companhia das Letras, 1994); Stuart B. Schwartz and Frank Salomon, "New Peoples and New Kinds of People: Adaptation, Readjustment, and Ethnogenesis in South American Indigenous Societies (Colonial Era)," in *The Cambridge History of the Native Peoples of the Americas*, ed. Frank Salomon and Stuart B. Schwartz (Cambridge: Cambridge University Press, 1999); Alida C. Metcalf, *Go-Betweens and the Colonization of Brazil, 1500–1600* (Austin: University of Texas Press, 2006); Cristina Pompa, *Religião como tradução: Missionários, Tupi e Tapuia no Brasil colonial* (Bauru: EDUSC, 2003); Ronaldo Vainfas, *Traição: Um jesuíta a serviço do Brasil holandês processado pela Inquisição* (São Paulo: Companhia das Letras, 2008); Pedro Puntoni, *A Guerra dos Bárbaros: Povos indígenas e a colonização do sertão nordeste do Brasil, 1650–1720* (São Paulo: Hucitec/Edusp, 2002); Stuart B. Schwartz and Hal Langfur, "Tapanhuns, Negros da Terra, and Curibocas: Common Cause and Confrontation between Blacks and Indians in Colonial Brazil," in *Black and Red: African-Indigenous Relations in Colonial Latin America*, ed. Matthew Restall (Albuquerque: University of New Mexico Press, 2005).

7. Ângela Domingues, *Quando os índios eram vassalos: Colonização e relações de poder no Norte do Brasil na segunda metade do século XVIII* (Lisbon: Comissão Nacional para as Comemorações dos Descobrimentos Portugueses, 2000);

Barbara A. Sommer, "Negotiated Settlements: Native Amazonians and Portuguese Policy in Pará, Brazil, 1758–1798" (PhD diss., University of New Mexico, 2000); Mark Harris, *Rebellion on the Amazon: The Cabanagem, Race, and Popular Culture in the North of Brazil, 1798–1840* (Cambridge: Cambridge University Press, 2010); Heather F. Roller, *Amazonian Routes: Indigenous Mobility and Colonial Communities in Northern Brazil* (Stanford, CA: Stanford University Press, 2014); Nazzari, "Vanishing Indians." For works focused on Minas Gerais and Rio de Janeiro, see Maria Regina Celestino de Almeida, *Metamorfoses indígenas: Cultura e identidade nos aldeamentos indígenas do Rio de Janeiro* (Rio de Janeiro: Arquivo Nacional, 2002); Resende, "Gentios brasílicos"; Maria Leônia Chaves de Resende and Hal Langfur, "Minas expansionista, Minas mestiça: A resistência dos índios em Minas Gerais do século do ouro," *Anais de História de Além-Mar* 9 (2008); Adriano Toledo Paiva, *Os indígenas e os processos de conquista dos sertões de Minas Gerais (1767–1813)* (Belo Horizonte: Argumentum, 2010).

8. See, for example, B. J. Barickman, "'Tame Indians,' 'Wild Heathens,' and Settlers in Southern Bahia in the Late Eighteenth and Early Nineteenth Centuries," *The Americas* 51, no. 3 (1995).

9. Manoel Pereira da Silva to Viceroy, São Salvador [dos Campos dos Goitacases], 28 Nov. 1779, Correspondências e documentos relativos às Novas Minas de Macacu, do Rio de Janeiro, de que era superintendente geral Manuel Pinto da Cunha e Sousa, 1786–[17]90, BNRJ, SM, cód. 9, 3, 17, doc. 137.

10. Deadly epidemics were recorded around Guanabara Bay in the 1550s, although it is likely they began to depopulate the area of its Indigenous inhabitants earlier, during the first half of the century. Metcalf, *Go-Betweens*, 131–36. For contacts between backcountry and coastal Indians and settlers, see Malheiros, "Homens de Fronteira," esp. chap. 3; Paulo Mercadante, *Os sertões do leste: Estudo de uma região; A mata mineira* (Rio de Janeiro: Zahar, 1973), 15–20.

11. Quoted in Diogo [Luís de Almeida Pereira] de Vasconcelos, *História média de Minas Gerais*, 4th ed. (Belo Horizonte: Itatiaia, 1974), 275. On the origins of this policy see Hal Langfur, *The Forbidden Lands: Colonial Identity, Frontier Violence, and the Persistence of Brazil's Eastern Indians, 1750–1830* (Stanford, CA: Stanford University Press, 2006), 35–37.

12. José Joaquim da Cunha de Azeredo Coutinho, *Ensaio economico sobre o comerico de Portugal e suas colonias* (Lisbon: Academia Real das Ciências, 1794), 65. Also see "Requerimento de D. José Joaquim da Cunha de Azeredo Coutinho a rainha D. Maria I," ca. 1794, in Alberto Lamego, *A Terra Goitacá á luz de documentos inéditos*, 6 vols. (Rio de Janeiro: Garnier, 1913–41), vol. 2, 505–6; Fernando G. Lamas, "Conflitos agrários em Minas Gerais: O processo de conquista da terra na área central da Zona da Mata (1767–1820)" (PhD diss., Universidade Federal Fluminense, 2013); Mercadante, *Os sertões* chap. 2.

13. Alexandre de Gusmão, "Reparos sobre a despozição da Lei de 3 de Dezembro de 1750, a respeito do Novo Methodo da Cobrança do Qunto do Brazil, abolindo o da Capitação," Lisbon, 18 Dec. 1750, fol. 117, Cartas de Alexandre de Gusmão, Menistro de Estado particular de Sua Mag.e Fedelissima o Senhor Rey Dom Joam 5o, Codex Port. 5, MS, JCBL. For a second copy of this report, see Alexandre de Gusmão, "Parecer de Alexandre de Gusmão sobre a capitação das Minas," Lisbon, 18 Dec. 1750, BPE, cód. CXII/2–7, fols. 95–113v.

14. Alfred Métraux, "The Purí-Coroado Linguistic Family," in *Handbook of South American Indians*, ed. Julian H. Steward (New York: Cooper Square, 1963), vol. 1, 523–30; José Ribamar Bessa Freire and Márcia Fernanda Malheiros, *Aldeamentos indígenas do Rio de Janeiro* (Rio de Janeiro: Programa de Estudos dos Povos Indígenas, Universidade do Estado do Rio de Janeiro, 1997), 21–25; José de Souza Azevedo Pizarro e Araújo, *Memórias históricas do Rio de Janeiro e das provincias annexas a jurisdicção do vice-rei do Estado do Brasil*, 9 vols. (Rio de Janeiro: Imp. Regia, 1820–22), vol. 5, 288–95; Maximilian A. P. Wied-Neuwied, *Travels in Brazil in the Years 1815, 1816, 1817* (London: Henry Colburn, 1820). On scholarly disagreement over linguistic commonalities among groups classified as Gê speakers, see Norman A. McQuown, "The Indigenous Languages of Latin America," *American Anthropologist*, n.s., 57, no. 3, part 1 (1955): 560. Also see Langfur, *Forbidden Lands*, 23–24; Paiva, *Os indígenas*; Malheiros, "Homens de Fronteira," 102, 108.

15. These events are documented in [António Gomes Freire de Andrade] to [José António Freire de Andrade], Vila Rica, late Nov. 1758, AIHGB, Conselho Ultramarino, Arq. 1, 3, 8, fols. 164v–67v; Sylverio Teixeira to [José António Freire de Andrade?], Vila Rica, 25 Nov. 1758, AIHGB, Conselho Ultramarino, Arq. 1, 3, 8, fols. 163v–64v; José António Freire de Andrade to Thomé Joaquim da Costa, Rio, 4 Jan. 1759, AIHGB, Conselho Ultramarino, Arq. 1, 3, 8, fols. 162v–63v. Contextual clues suggest the author of the first letter to be the Minas governor, the Count of Bobadela. In addition, see Coutinho, *Ensaio economico*, 64; Manoel Martinz do Couto Reys, *Manuscritos de Manoel Martinz do Couto Reys, 1785* (Rio de Janeiro: Arquivo Público do Estado do Rio de Janeiro, 1997), 29n93.

16. José Augusto de Oliveira, ed., *Conquista de Lisboa aos Mouros (1147): Narrada pelo Cruzado Osberno*, 2nd ed. (Lisbon: S. Industriais da C. m. L., 1936), 68; Pêro Vaz de Caminha, "Letter to King Manuel I of Portugal [1500]," in *The Brazil Reader*, 2nd ed., ed. James N. Green, Victoria Langland, and Lilia Moritz Schwarcz (Durham, NC: Duke University Press), 16. For references to the Indians' *haveres* or *haveres incognitos* see, for example, "Ordens sôbre arrecadação e despesas, 1768[–1771]," 6 Aug. 1768, BNRJ, SM, CC, gaveta I-10-7, doc. 1; Miguel Antunes Ferreira to Viceroy, Rio, 10 Aug. 1779, Correspondências e documentos . . . , BNRJ, SM, cód. 9, 3, 17, doc. 135. Also see Hal Langfur, "Uncertain

Refuge: Frontier Formation and the Origins of the Botocudo War in Late-Colonial Brazil," *Hispanic American Historical Review* 82, no. 2 (2002): esp. 239–40. For Spanish American parallels, dating to Columbus's encounter with the Taíno, see the fascinating study by Allison M. Bigelow, *Mining Language: Racial Thinking, Indigenous Knowledge, and Colonial Metallurgy in the Early Modern Iberian World* (Chapel Hill: University of North Carolina Press, 2020), esp. chap. 1.

17. Secretary of State to Viceroy, Palácio de Nossa Senhora da Ajuda, 8 Jan. 1785, Correspondências e documentos . . . , BNRJ, SM, cód. 9, 3, 17, doc. 127; Miguel Antunes Ferreira to Viceroy, Rio, 10 Aug. 1779, Correspondências e documentos . . . , BNRJ, SM, cód. 9, 3, 17, doc. 135; Governor to Francisco Xavier de Mendonça Furtado, Vila Rica, 1 Mar. 1764, AHU, Minas Gerais, cx. 83, doc. 16. On the native trails, see Miguel Antunes Ferreira to Viceroy, Rio, 22 June 1773, Correspondências e documentos . . . , BNRJ, SM, cód. 9, 3, 17, doc. 135.

18. Petition of Mauricio José Portugal to interim governors, with appended documents, Rio, 21 May 1763, Correspondências e documentos . . . , BNRJ, SM, cód. 9, 3, 17, doc. 129. The petition was remitted to and approved by the Desembargador Intendente Geral de Ouro (Superintendent of Mines). Settler and Jesuit missionary activity in the area later designated Cachoeiras de Macacu dated to the mid-sixteenth century. Rui Dias de Menezes, "Comfirmações aos cartas e alvarás abaixo declarados," Lisbon, 10 Mar. 1624, ANTT, Cartório dos Jesuítas, maço 90, no. 103.

19. Petition of Mauricio José Portugal to interim governors, with appended documents, Rio, 21 May 1763, Correspondências e documentos . . . , BNRJ, SM, cód. 9, 3, 17, doc. 129. The prospector's accumulated gain after paying the *quinto* tax but before deducting expenses was one *marco* (mark), three *onças* (ounces), six *oitavas* (eighths of an ounce), 28 and 4/5 *grãos* (grains), or just under 12 ounces. One mark equaled eight ounces; one ounce equaled eight *oitavas*; and one *oitava* equaled 72 grains. The sum of five separate amounts of gold turned over to authorities reveals an accounting error in the source. The document states that the Indians and Portugal originally turned over four ounces, but the scribe must have meant four *oitavas*, which would bring to total to the correct amount. For weights of gold, see Rafael Bluteau, *Vocabulario portuguez e latino* (Lisbon: Pascoal da Sylva, 1720), 75. Between 1751 and 1803 the crown set the value of one ounce of gold at 9$600 in Minas Gerais. Thus twelve ounces equaled 114$400. See "Mappa do Rendimento que produzio o Real Quinto do Oiro na Cappitania de Minas Geraes desde o anno de 1700 a 1781 a saber," *RAPM* 8 (1903): 578; Kenneth R. Maxwell, *Conflicts and Conspiracies: Brazil and Portugal, 1750–1808* (Cambridge: Cambridge University Press, 1973), 245. Amid falling prices prompted by a contracting

mining economy, the value of an enslaved male or female between fifteen and forty years old in Minas Gerais averaged approximately 100$000, with males about 15 percent more costly than females. In coastal Bahia, for which reliable figures also exist, a healthy enslaved male purchased for fieldwork in the 1780s also cost about 100$000. Prices in rural Rio de Janeiro appear to have been lower. There an adult male slave born in Africa cost, on average, 73$000 in 1790, 87$000 in 1800, and 95$000 in 1810, while those born in Brazil cost less in 1790 (60$000), but more in 1800 and 1810 (101$000 and 105$000). Laird W. Bergad, *Slavery and the Demographic and Economic History of Minas Gerais, Brazil, 1720–1888* (Cambridge: Cambridge University Press, 1999), 163–76; Laird W. Bergad, "After the Mining Boom: Demographic and Economic Aspects of Slavery in Mariana, Minas Gerais, 1750–1808," *Latin American Research Review* 31, no. 1 (1996): 67–97; B. J. Barickman, *A Bahian Counterpoint: Sugar, Tobacco, Cassava, and Slavery in the Recôncavo, 1780–1860* (Stanford, CA: Stanford University Press, 1998), 139, fig. 10; Manolo Garcia Florentino, *Em Costas Negras: Uma história do tráfico de escravos entre a África e o Rio de Janeiro (séculos XVIII e XIX)* (São Paulo: Companhia das Letras, 1997), 300.

20. Secretary of State to Viceroy, Salvaterra de Magos, 31 Jan. 1765, Negócios de Portugal, Correspondência do vice-reinado para a Corte, ANRJ, cód. 68, vol. 4, fols. 225–25v; Miguel Antunes Ferreira to Viceroy, Rio, 10 Aug. 1779, Correspondências e documentos . . . , BNRJ, SM, cód. 9, 3, 17, doc. 135; Viceroy to Secretary of State, Rio, 25 Aug. 1781, Correspondência do vice-reinado para a Corte, ANRJ, cód. 68, vol. 4, fols. 182–82v; Secretary of State to Viceroy, Palácio de Nossa Senhora da Ajuda, 8 Jan. 1785, Correspondências e documentos . . . , BNRJ, SM, cód. 9, 3, 17, doc. 127; Viceroy to Secretary of State, Rio, 9 Nov. 1765, in *RIHGB* 254 (1962): 342–44, quoted. On memory, see Rui Tavares, "Lembrar, esquecer, censurar: A Real Mesa Censória sob Pombal (Portugal, 1768–1777)," *Estudos Avançados* 13, no. 37 (1999): esp. 146.

21. Warren Dean, *With Broadax and Firebrand: The Destruction of the Brazilian Atlantic Forest* (Berkeley: University of California Press, 1995), 10.

22. Secretary of State to Viceroy, Palácio de Nossa Senhora da Ajuda, 8 Jan. 1785, Correspondências e documentos . . . , BNRJ, SM, cód. 9, 3, 17, doc. 127.

23. Miguel Antunes Ferreira to Viceroy, Rio, 10 Aug. 1779, Correspondências e documentos . . . , BNRJ, SM, cód. 9, 3, 17, doc. 135.

24. Viceroy to Secretary of State, Rio, 9 Nov. 1765, in *RIHGB* 254 (1962): 342–44.

25. On varieties of Indigenous responses, see John M. Monteiro, "Rethinking Amerindian Resistance and Persistence in Colonial Portuguese America," in *New*

*Approaches to Resistance in Brazil and Mexico*, ed. John Gledhill and Patience A. Schell (Durham, NC: Duke University Press, 2012).

26. Manoel Vieira Leão, "Carta topografica da capitania do Rio de Janeiro," 1767, BNRJ, SI, arc. 30, 1, 18 and arc. 30, 1, 21. Leão was a sergeant-major and commander of a fortress in the capital city.

27. "Mapa das Minas Novas do Castelo dos Campos dos Goutacazes," [second half of 18th c.], BPE, gaveta 4, pasta A, no. 16; Miguel Antunes Ferreira to Viceroy, Rio, 10 Aug. 1779, Correspondências e documentos . . . , BNRJ, SM, cód. 9, 3, 17, doc. 135; Superintendent of Mines to Secretary of State, Rio, 16 July 1781, Correspondências e documentos . . . , BNRJ, SM, cód. 9, 3, 17, doc. 128. On the Castelo mines, see Judy Bieber, "Uatú Júpú: A History of the Indigenous Rio Doce," *Brasiliana: Journal for Brazilian Studies* 5, no. 2 (2017): 130–31.

28. Secretary of State to Governor, [Lisbon], 12 Feb. 1765, "Providencias tomadas para a catechese dos Indios no Rio Doce e Piracicaba, Vila Rica, 1764–1767," APM, CC, cód. 1156, fols. 2–3v. Also see Langfur, *Forbidden Lands*, 60–67.

29. Viceroy to [Tomás de Almeida], Rio, 26 Mar. 1773, in Luís de Almeida Portugal, Cartas do Rio de Janeiro, 1769–1776 (Rio de Janeiro: Instituto Estadual do Livro, 1978), 117. Lavradio's full name was nothing less than Luís de Almeida Portugal Soares Alarcão Eça Melo Pereira Aguilar Fiel de Lugo Mascarenhas Silva Mendonça e Lencastre. Scholars, however, generally employ the abbreviated Luís de Almeida Portugal or, more simply, the marquis of Lavradio, which he used when signing letters and other documents. On his administration, Dauril Alden, *Royal Government in Colonial Brazil with Special Reference to the Administration of the Marquis of Lavradio, Viceroy, 1769–1779* (Berkeley: University of California Press, 1968). On Melo e Castro's neo-mercantilism, see Maxwell, *Conflicts and Conspiracies*, 78–79. For his role in the administration of Minas Gerais, see Virgínia Maria Trindade Valadares, *A sombra do poder: Martinho de Melo e Castro e a administração da Capitania de Minas Gerais (1770–1795)* (São Paulo: HUCITEC, 2006).

30. Miguel Antunes Ferreira to Viceroy, Rio, 10 Aug. 1779, Correspondências e documentos . . . , BNRJ, SM, cód. 9, 3, 17, doc. 135.

31. Bartolomeu José Vahia to Viceroy, Rio, 6 Aug. 1779, Correspondências e documentos . . . , BNRJ, SM, cód. 9, 3, 17, doc. 135. This source and related documentation avoid the term *garimpeiros*, commonly used elsewhere to refer to small-stakes prospectors operating outside the law, often men of color, who were a constant provocation to authorities during the second half of the eighteenth century. Instead, the terms favored to describe prospectors in this zone between the two captaincies included *bandidos* (bandits), *criminosos* (criminals), *ladrões* (thieves), *salteadores* (robbers), *contrabandistas* (contrabandists), and *extraviadores*

(smugglers), among others. It seems likely that the distinction rested on the fact that those accused of leading this illegal operation owned slaves and operated at least partially within colonial society rather than entirely outside its purview. It may also have resulted from gold rather than diamonds being the primary object of the mining operation. Cf. Júnia Ferreira Furtado, introduction to José Vieira Couto, *Memória sobre a Capitania das Minas Gerais; seu território, clima e produções metálicas* (Belo Horizonte: Fundação João Pinheiro, 1994), 16n2; Adriana Romeiro and Angela Vianna Botelho, *Dicionário histórico das Minas Gerais: Período colonial* (Belo Horizonte: Autêntica, 2003), 151–52.

32. See "Regimento Mineral," Lisbon, 19 Apr. 1702, *RAPM* 1, no. 4 (1896): 675.

33. For indigenous women go-betweens during the early colonial period, see Metcalf, *Go-Betweens*, esp. 1–2, 85, 97, 270–71. For later examples, see Heather F. Roller, *Contact Strategies: Histories of Native Autonomy in Brazil* (Stanford, CA: Stanford University Press, 2021), 58, 64, 69–70, 79–80, 91; Mary Karasch, "Damiana da Cunha: Catechist and Sertanista," in *Struggle and Survival in Colonial America*, ed. David G. Sweet and Gary B. Nash (Berkeley: University of California Press, 1981), 102–20.

34. Miguel Antunes Ferreira to Viceroy, Rio, 10 Aug. 1779, Correspondências e documentos . . . , BNRJ, SM, cód. 9, 3, 17, doc. 135. On the Xopotó, see Oiliam José, *Indígenas de Minas Gerais: Aspectos sociais, políticos e etnológicos* (Belo Horizonte: Imp. Oficial, 1965), 37.

35. Miguel Antunes Ferreira to Viceroy, Rio, 10 Aug. 1779, Correspondências e documentos . . . , BNRJ, SM, cód. 9, 3, 17, doc. 135. As can be gleaned from this report, Ferreira related his findings not only to Viceroy Cunha, who ordered the mission, but also to the marquis of Lavradio, sometime between 1769 and 1778, and then to Viceroy Vasconcelos, in 1779. It is not clear whether he also shared the information with Viceroy Antônio Rolim de Moura Tavares, the Count of Azambuja (1767–69).

36. Town Council to Viceroy, Santo Antônio de Sá, 26 Apr. 1779, Correspondências e documentos . . . , BNRJ, SM, cód. 9, 3, 17, doc. 132; Manoel Pereira da Silva to Viceroy, São Salvador [dos Campos dos Goitacases] with appended confession, 28 Nov. 1779, Correspondências e documentos . . . , BNRJ, SM, cód. 9, 3, 17, doc. 137, quoted. Rio's superintendent of mines, Manoel Pinto da Cunha e Souza, summarized this and other information gathered from outlying districts in a report to the viceroy. See Superintendent of Mines to Viceroy, Rio, 24 Dec. 1779, Correspondências e documentos . . . , BNRJ, SM, cód. 9, 3, 17, doc. 137. Also see Rodrigo Leonardo de Sousa Oliveira, "'Mão de Luva' e 'Montanha': Bandoleiros e salteadores nos caminhos de Minas Gerais no século XVIII (Matas

Gerais da Mantiqueira: 1755–1786)" (master's thesis, Universidade Federal de Juiz de Fora, 2008), 109–23; José Antônio Soares Souza, "As Minas do Sertão de Macacu," *RIHGB* 326 (1980): 27.

37. Superintendent of Mines to Viceroy, Rio, 24 Dec. 1779, Correspondências e documentos . . . , BNRJ, SM, cód. 9, 3, 17, doc. 137; Manoel Pereira da Silva to Viceroy, São Salvador [dos Campos dos Goitacases] with appended confession, 28 Nov. 1779, Correspondências e documentos . . . , BNRJ, SM, cód. 9, 3, 17, doc. 137.

38. Viceroy to Secretary of State, Rio, 25 Aug. 1781, Correspondências e documentos . . . , BNRJ, SM, cód. 9, 3, 17, vol. 4, fol. 183v.

39. In Rio de Janeiro, the prisoner José Gomes was questioned by two representatives of the Holy Office: Vicente Ferreira de Noronha, vicar of the coastal parish of Maricá, the site of a former Jesuit mission where many Indians continued to live; and the Carmelite friar Bernardo de Vasconcelos. As *comissários* (commissioners) of the Holy Office, both were among a small number of clergymen serving as the highest resident authorities of the Inquisition in Brazil. See Vicente Ferreira de Noronha to Viceroy, before July 1781, Correspondências e documentos . . . , BNRJ, SM, cód. 9, 3, 17, doc. 141; Bernardo de Vasconcelos to Viceroy, n.p., before July 1781, Correspondências e documentos . . . , BNRJ, SM, cód. 9, 3, 17, doc. 142. Also see Superintendent of Mines to Secretary of State, Rio, 16 July 1781, Correspondências e documentos . . . , BNRJ, SM, cód. 9, 3, 17, doc. 128; Secretary of State to Viceroy, Palácio de Nossa Senhora da Ajuda, 8 Jan. 1785, Correspondências e documentos . . . , BNRJ, SM, cód. 9, 3, 17, doc. 127, para. 14. Three sets of documents composed the Inquisition's case against José Gomes after he arrived in Lisbon. See Processo de José Gomes, 1781, ANTT, PT-TT-TSO-IL-028–11509; Correspondência de José Gomes, 1781, ANTT, PT-TT-TSO-IL-028-CX1597–13781; Traslado incompleto de uns autos da justiça contra José Gomes, 23 Jan. 1781, ANTT, PT-TT-TSO-IL-028–18005.

40. Between the late sixteenth and the early nineteenth century, of 1,076 prisoners dispatched from Brazil to Lisbon to stand trial by the Inquisition, thirty-three men and seven women (3.7 percent) were identified as Indigenous or of mixed Indigenous and European descent. The number increases to forty-seven men and thirteen women when the total includes those who were tried in Brazil along with those sent to Lisbon. Of these, only one lived in the captaincy of Rio de Janeiro. The rest lived far to the northeast and north, during periods and in places in which peoples of Indigenous descent composed larger segments of the colonial population. Only six of those tried were prosecuted after 1770. Luís Rafael Araújo Corrêa, "Feitiço caboclo: Um índio mandingueiro condenado pela Inquisição" (PhD diss., Universidade Federal Fluminense, 2003), 205–8; Eduardo Viveiros de Castro, *The Inconstancy of the Indian Soul: The Encounter of Catholics*

*and Cannibals in 16th-Century Brazil*, trans. Gregory Duff Morton (Chicago: Prickly Paradigm Press, 2011). On Indigenous ethnic and racial identity, see Almeida, "Land and Economic Resources," 80; Maria Regina Celestino de Almeida, *Os índios na história do Brasil* (Rio de Janeiro: FGV, 2010), 98–106, 118–19, 126–33; Nazzari, "Vanishing Indians." For Spanish American parallels, see Marisol de la Cadena, "Are 'Mestizos' Hybrids? The Conceptual Politics of Andean Identities," *Journal of Latin American Studies* 37, no. 2 (2005).

41. Processo de José Gomes, 1781, ANTT, PT-TT-TSO-IL-028–11509, fols. 27v–28. Also see James C. Scott, *Seeing Like a State: How Certain Schemes to Improve the Human Condition Have Failed* (New Haven, CT: Yale University Press, 1999).

42. Laura de Mello e Souza, *The Devil and the Land of the Holy Cross: Witchcraft, Slavery, and Popular Religion in Colonial Brazil* (Austin: University of Texas Press, 2003), 87, 138, 140–41. Also see Carvalho Júnior, "Índios cristãos," 316–16; Resende, "Devassas gentílicas," 22.

43. Traslado incompleto de uns autos da justiça contra José Gomes, 23 Jan. 1781, ANTT, PT-TT-TSO-IL-028–18005, fol. 1; Freire and Malheiros, *Aldeamentos indígenas*, 61. On the Ipuca aldeia, see Miguel Antunes Ferreira to Viceroy, Rio, 22 June 1773, Correspondências e documentos . . . , BNRJ, SM, cód. 9, 3, 17, doc. 135.

44. Processo de José Gomes, 1781, ANTT, PT-TT-TSO-IL-028–11509, fols. 47–48.

45. Processo de José Gomes, 1781, ANTT, PT-TT-TSO-IL-028–11509, fols. 20v, 31v (quoted), 63v–64; Processo de Agostinho [de Abreu Castelo Branco] e Manuel Henriques, 1781, ANTT, PT-TT-TSO-IL-028–12969, fols. 11–19. I thank Leônia Chaves de Resende for sharing her transcription of this second case.

46. Processo de José Gomes, 1781, ANTT, PT-TT-TSO-IL-028–11509, fols. 66v, 73–75.

47. Vicente Ferreira de Noronha to Viceroy, n.p., before July 1781, Correspondências e documentos . . . , BNRJ, SM, cód. 9, 3, 17, doc. 141; Viceroy to Secretary of State, Rio, 25 Aug. 1781, Correspondência do vice-reinado para a Corte, ANRJ, cód. 68, vol. 4, fol. 183v.

48. Vicente Ferreira de Noronha to Viceroy, n.p., before July 1781, Correspondências e documentos . . . , BNRJ, SM, cód. 9, 3, 17, doc. 141. The size of an uncut diamond is never a guarantee of the size or quality of the resulting cut gem. For purposes of comparison, the famed De Beers Centenary Diamond, discovered in South Africa, weighed 599 carats (120 g) uncut, 274 carats (55 g) when cut, making it the world's largest colorless, flawless diamond.

49. Vicente Ferreira de Noronha to Viceroy, n.p., before July 1781, Correspondências e documentos . . . , BNRJ, SM, cód. 9, 3, 17, doc. 141; Bernardo

de Vasconcelos to Viceroy, n.p., before July 1781, Correspondências e documentos . . . , BNRJ, SM, cód. 9, 3, 17, doc. 142, quoted.

## Chapter 4

1. Miguel Antunes Ferreira to Viceroy, Rio, 10 Aug. 1779, Correspondências e documentos . . . , BNRJ, SM, cód. 9, 3, 17, doc. 135. São Martinho to Governor, Roça Grande, 17 May 1786, fols. 232–33.

2. Petition of Padre Manoel de Jesus Maria to King, [Mariana?, ca. Nov. 1768], ANTT, Ordem de Cristo, Padroado do Brasil, Bispado de Mariana, maço 5; Ordens sôbre arrecadação e despesas, 1768[–1771]," 23 July and 8 Aug. 1770, 18 Feb. 1771, BNRJ, SM, CC, gaveta I-10-7, docs. 56, 71; Auguste de Saint-Hilaire, *Viagem pelas províncias do Rio de Janeiro e Minas Gerais*, trans. Vivaldi Moreira (Belo Horizonte: Itatiaia, 1975), 276–77; Waldemar de Almeida Barbosa, *Dicionário histórico--geográfico de Minas Gerais* (Belo Horizonte: Itatiaia, 1995), 286–87; Celso Falabella de Figueiredo Castro, *Os sertões de leste: Achegas para a história da Zona da Mata* (Belo Horizonte: Imprensa Oficial, 1987), 11–15, esp. transcription, p. 14n4, of royal order dated 20 Oct. 1779, describing the priest's activities. For the original MS of this order, see APM, SC, cód. 220, fols. 44v–45. Also see Diogo [Luís de Almeida Pereira] de Vasconcelos, *História média de Minas Gerais*, 4th ed. (Belo Horizonte: Itatiaia, 1974), 205–10; Paulo Mercadante, *Os sertões do leste: Estudo de uma região: A mata mineira* (Rio de Janeiro: Zahar, 1973), 40–42; Adriano Toledo Paiva, *Os indígenas e os processos de conquista dos sertões de Minas Gerais (1767–1813)* (Belo Horizonte: Argumentum, 2010), chap. 1.

3. Paiva, *Os indígenas*, 46–62; Vasconcelos, *História média de Minas Gerais*, 203–10.

4. Petition of Manuel de Jesus Maria to Governor Mendonça, [São Manuel do Rio Pomba], no date, with governor's reply, Vila Rica, 8 Mar. 1790, appended to sesmaria of D. Anna Joaquina de Almeida, 1798, ACSM, 1º ofício, cód. 2, auto 87, fols. 11v–12v, 14–15.

5. Paiva, *Os indígenas*, 71–72.

6. Petition of Padre Manoel de Jesus Maria to King, [Mariana?, ca. Nov. 1768], ANTT, Ordem de Cristo, Padroado do Brasil, Bispado de Mariana, maço 5; Petition of Manuel de Jesus Maria to Governor Mendonça, [São Manuel do Rio Pomba], no date, with governor's reply, Vila Rica, 8 Mar. 1790, appended to sesmaria of D. Anna Joaquina de Almeida, 1798, ACSM, 1º ofício, cód. 2, auto 87, fols. 14–15; Ordens sôbre arrecadação e despesas, 1768[–1771]," 23 July and 8 Aug. 1770, 18 Feb. 1771, BNRJ, SM, CC, gaveta I-10-7, docs. 56, 71; Saint-Hilaire, *Viagem pelas províncias*, 276–77; Paiva, *Os indígenas*, 62–78; Castro, *Os sertões de leste*, 11–15. In sources produced in Minas Gerais during this period,

the Coroado and Coropó were more commonly referred to as the Croato and Cropó.

7. For the two land grants, see sesmaria of Clara Pires Farinho, 1773, APM, SC, cód. 172, fol. 200v; sesmaria of Martinho Pires Farinho, 1786, APM, SC, cód. 234. For munitions and other supplies funded by the royal treasury for these initiatives, see Royal Treasury Board, Captaincy of Minas Gerais, [Recibos e faturas referentes a liberação de munições e outros gêneros para guarnecer tropas em bandeiras contra gentios no combate a quilombos], Vila Rica, 1 Apr. 1771, BNRJ, SM, CC, gaveta I-10-3-1, doc. 65. Also see Paiva, *Os indígenas*, 63, 111–12.

8. Governor to Francisco Pires Farinho, Cachoeira, 13 Nov. 1781, APM, SC, cód. 227, fols. 13–13v.

9. Governor to Secretary of State, [Vila Rica], 3 June 1781, APM, SC, cód. 224, fol. 29v; Governor to Felix Vital Noge, [Vila Rica], 14 July 1780, cód. 224, fol. 37. Also see Hal Langfur, *The Forbidden Lands: Colonial Identity, Frontier Violence, and the Persistence of Brazil's Eastern Indians, 1750–1830* (Stanford, CA: Stanford University Press, 2006), 148–54, 223–24.

10. Governor to Secretary of State, Vila Rica, 31 Dec. 1781, APM, SC, cód. 224, fols. 61–64v. Also see José Joaquim da Rocha, *Geografia histórica da Capitania de Minas Gerais* (Belo Horizonte: Fundação João Pinheiro, 1995), 189–91.

11. Governor to Antônio Veloso de Miranda, Vila Rica, 31 Apr. 1782, cód. 227, fols. 26–26v; Governor to Luís Antonio da Silva Velho, Vila Rica, 18 Jan. 1783, cód. 227, fl. 53–53v.

12. Carla M. J. Anastasia, "Salteadores, bandoleiros e desbravadores nas Matas Gerais da Mantiqueira (1783–1786)," in *Revisão do paraíso: Os brasileiros e o estado em 500 anos de história*, ed. Mary Del Priore (Rio de Janeiro: Editora Campus, 2000), 132–33; José Antônio Soares Souza, "As Minas do Sertão de Macacu," *RIHGB* 326 (1980): 45. For an entry point to scholarship on the 1789 Minas conspiracy, see Kenneth R. Maxwell, *Conflicts and Conspiracies: Brazil and Portugal, 1750–1808* (Cambridge: Cambridge University Press, 1973).

13. Pedro Afonso Galvão de São Martinho, "Informação que tirei do Padre Manoel de Jesus," São Manuel do Rio Pomba, 12 May 1784, Correspondência do vice-reinado para a Corte, Negócios de Portugal, ANRJ, cód. 68, vol. 6, fols. 239–41.

14. Governor to Secretary of State, [Vila Rica], 3 June 1781, APM, SC, cód. 224, fols. 31v–32.

15. Pedro Afonso Galvão de São Martinho, "Informação que tirei do Padre Manoel de Jesus," São Manuel do Rio Pomba, 12 May 1784, Negócios de Portugal, Correspondência do vice-reinado para a Corte, Original, ANRJ, cód. 68, vol. 6, fols. 240v–41; Pedro Afonso Galvão de São Martinho to Governor, ANRJ,

cód. 68, vol. 6, fol. 239; Governor to Viceroy, Vila Rica, 19 May 1784, ANRJ, cód. 68, vol. 6, fols. 238–38v; Viceroy to Secretary of State, Rio, 28 Aug. 1784, ANRJ, cód. 68, vol. 6, fols. 236–37. Also see Souza, "As Minas," 39.

16. Superintendent of Mines to Viceroy, Rio, 24 Dec. 1779, Correspondências e documentos . . . , BNRJ, SM, cód. 9, 3, 17, doc. 137. For military patrols, see Alexandre Alves Duarte e Azevedo to Viceroy, Santo Antônio de Sá, 7 June 1780, Correspondências e documentos . . . , BNRJ, SM, cód. 9, 3, 17, doc. 140; Viceroy to Secretary of State, Rio, 28 Aug. 1784, Negócios de Portugal, Correspondência do vice-reinado para a Corte, Original, ANRJ, cód. 68, vol. 6, fol. 236.

17. Viceroy to Secretary of State, Rio, 28 Aug. 1784, Negócios de Portugal, Correspondência do vice-reinado para a Corte, Original, ANRJ, cód. 68, vol. 6, fol. 236.

18. Secretary of State to Viceroy, Palácio de Nossa Senhora da Ajuda, 8 Jan. 1785, Correspondências e documentos . . . , BNRJ, SM, cód. 9, 3, 17, doc. 127, par. 14–25.

19. Secretary of State to Viceroy, Palácio de Nossa Senhora da Ajuda, 8 Jan. 1785, Correspondências e documentos . . . , BNRJ, SM, cód. 9, 3, 17, doc. 127, quoting para. 6 and 17. For material quoted by the secretary of state from Gomes's testimony, see para. 10–13. On the viceroy's wary support for the use of troops from Minas Gerais, see Souza, "As Minas," 41, 44. Anastasia incorrectly claims the viceroy wanted troops from Rio de Janeiro to lead the attack. Carla M. J. Anastasia, *A geografia do crime: Violência nas Minas setecentistas* (Belo Horizonte: Universidade Federal de Minas Gerais, 2005), 102.

20. On Mão de Luva and the raid staged from Minas Gerais, see Sebastião A. B. de Carvalho, *O tesouro de Cantagalo* (Niterói: Gráfica do Colégio Salesiano, 1951); Acácio Ferreira Dias, *O Mão de Luva (fundador de Cantagalo)* (Niterói: Imprensa Oficial, 1953); Vasconcelos, *História média de Minas Gerais*, 277–81; Castro, *Os sertões de leste*, 18–38; Souza, "As Minas," 21–86; Romyr C. Garcia, "O Mão de Luva e os sertões de Serra acima: Garimpos clandestinos e conflitos sociais no Brasil Colônia," *Revista Unifesco—Humanas e Sociais* 4, no. 4 (2018): 246–68; Anastasia, "Salteadores," 117–38; Anastasia, *A geografia do crime*, 96–104; Rodrigo Leonardo de Sousa Oliveira, "'Mão de Luva' e 'Montanha': Bandoleiros e salteadores nos caminhos de Minas Gerais no século XVIII (Matas Gerais da Mantiqueira: 1755–1786)" (master's thesis, Universidade Federal de Juiz de Fora, 2008), esp. chaps. 3–4; Mauro Leão Gomes, "Ouro, posseiros e fazendas de café: A ocupação e a degradação ambiental da região das Minas do Canta Gallo na província do Rio de Janeiro" (PhD diss., Universidade Federal Rural do Rio de Janeiro, 2004), chap. 1; Fernando G. Lamas, "Conflitos agrários em Minas Gerais:

O processo de conquista da terra na área central da Zona da Mata (1767–1820)" (PhD diss., Universidade Federal Fluminense, 2013), 66–85.

21. Garcia, "O Mão de Luva," 247. Also see "Regimento Mineral," Lisbon, 19 Apr. 1702, *RAPM* 1, no. 4 (1896): 675.

22. Maxwell, *Conflicts and Conspiracies*, 100–106.

23. Pedro Afonso Galvão de São Martinho to Governor, São Manuel do Rio Pomba, 12 May 1784, Negócios de Portugal, Correspondência do vice-reinado para a Corte, Original, ANRJ, cód. 68, vol. 6, fol. 239.

24. Secretary of State to Governor, Palácio de Nossa Senhora da Ajuda, 10 Jan. 1785, Correspondências e documentos . . . , BNRJ, SM, cód. 9, 3, 17, doc. 144. For information about the comings and goings of Mão de Luva in Minas Gerais, including his efforts to organize enslaved laborers, provisions, and mule transport for his operation, see Secretary of State to Viceroy, Palácio de Nossa Senhora da Ajuda, 8 Jan. 1785, Correspondências e documentos . . . , BNRJ, SM, cód. 9, 3, 17, doc. 127; Pedro Afonso Galvão de São Martinho to Governor, São Manuel do Rio Pomba, 12 May 1784, Negócios de Portugal, Correspondência do vice-reinado para a Corte, Original, ANRJ, cód. 68, vol. 6, fol. 239, with appended documents.

25. Secretary of State to Governor, Palácio de Nossa Senhora da Ajuda, 10 Jan. 1785, Correspondências e documentos . . . , BNRJ, SM, cód. 9, 3, 17, doc. 144 with appended laws, docs. 145 and 146.

26. Carta Régia (royal edict) to Governor of Rio de Janeiro, Lisbon, 8 Feb. 1730, AHU, cód. 610, fols. 103–3v; Alvará (royal charter), 27 Oct. 1733, AHM, divisão 2, seção 1, cx. 1, no. 15; and Alvará, 3 Dec. 1750, AHU, cód. 610, fols. 103v–4v. In his letter to Cunha Meneses, Melo e Castro cited the 1730 edict in its entirety and the relevant clauses of the 1750 law. See Secretary of State to Governor, Palácio de Nossa Senhora da Ajuda, 10 Jan. 1785, Correspondências e documentos . . . , BNRJ, SM, cód. 9, 3, 17, doc. 144 with appended laws, docs. 145 and 146.

27. Secretary of State to Viceroy, Palácio de Nossa Senhora da Ajuda, 8 Jan. 1785, Correspondências e documentos . . . , BNRJ, SM, cód. 9, 3, 17, doc. 127, par. 15.

28. Viceroy to Secretary of State, Rio, 28 Aug. 1784, Negócios de Portugal, Correspondência do vice-reinado para a Corte, Original, ANRJ, cód. 68, vol. 6, fol. 236.

29. Ana Borges, "Mitos e verdades: Mão de Luva e Tiradentes," Jornal A Voz da Serra, https://www.youtube.com/watch?v=Rn5ye8X-B7A (accessed August 21, 2019).

30. For iterations of these stories, see "Cantagalo (Rio de Janeiro)," Wikipedia, the Free Encyclopedia, http://pt.wikipedia.org/wiki/Cantagalo_%28Rio

_de_Janeiro%29 (accessed March 3, 2012); Instituto Histórico e Geográfico de Bom Jardim, "Lenda: Furnas do Mão de Luva," http://ihgbj.blogspot.com/2009/07/lenda-furnas-do-mao-de-luva.html (accesssed February 13, 2016); Paulo Novaes, *Mão de Luva: Romance* (Rio de Janeiro: Nau Editora, 1996); Vera de Vives, *Descobertos e extravios: História de Maria I e Mão de Luva* (Rio de Janeiro: Editora Record, 1997); Luiz Paiva de Castro, *O galo é um homem que canta: Mão de Luva, Euclides da Cunha, e Antonio Conselheiro* (Rio de Janeiro: Salamandra, 1980); Dias, *O Mão de Luva*; Johann Jakob von Tschudi, *Viagem às Províncias do Rio de Janeiro e São Paulo*, trans. Eduardo de Lima Castro (São Paulo: Livraria Martins, 1953), 83; Hermann Burmeister, *Viagem ao Brasil através das províncias do Rio de Janeiro e Minas Gerais*, trans. Manoel Salvaterra and Hubert Schoenfeldt (São Paulo: Livraria Martins, 1952), 130–31. Also see the review of the 2007 documentary *Mão de Luva*, directed by Sílvio Coutinho, "Documentário 'O Mão de Luva' é exibido em praça pública, em Cantagalo," 100 anos sem Euclides: Projeto cultural, http://www.projetoeuclides.iltc.br/index.php?page=conteudo&conteudo=impre_noticias&id=212 (accessed March 3, 2012). Regarding Mão de Luva's deformed hand, described by the governor of Minas Gerais, see Governor to Viceroy, Vila Rica, 12 Apr. 1786, Negócios de Portugal, Correspondência do vice-reinado para a Corte, Original, ANRJ, cód. 68, vol. 7, fol. 221.

31. Oliveira, "Mão de Luva," 146–49; Sheila de Castro Faria, "Ouro, porcos, escravos e café: As origens das fortunas oitocentistas em São Pedro de Cantagalo, Rio de Janeiro (últimas décadas do século XVIII e primeiras do XIX)," *Anais do Museu Paulista: História e Cultura Material* 26 (2018): 6–7.

32. See especially Anastasia, *A geografia do crime*; Célia Nonata da Silva, *Territórios de mando: Banditismo em Minas Gerais, século XVIII* (Belo Horizonte: Crisálida, 2007). More convinced by Hobsbawm's model is Garcia, "O Mão de Luva," 261. Also see Eric J. Hobsbawm, *Bandits* (New York: New Press, 2000).

33. Vasconcelos, *História média de Minas Gerais*, 279–81. On the link between syphilis and nose sores (*chagas no nariz*) described by Vasconcelos, see J. A. David de Morais, "A sífilis nas 'Centúrias de curas medicinais,' de Amato Lusitano," *Cadernos de Cultura: Medicina na Beira Interior, da Pré-história ao Século XXI* 32 (2018): 29–56. See esp. case 25, detailed on p. 53.

34. Viceroy to Secretary of State, Rio, 21 Jan. 1786, Negócios de Portugal, Correspondência do vice-reinado para a Corte, Original, ANRJ, cód. 68, vol. 7, fols. 11–12.

35. Historian Carla Anastasia affirms the viceroy's critique as part of her larger argument about the Minas backlands as a place of violence, criminality, personal ambition, and official corruption. The backlands, she maintains, were stateless and

lawless, a circumstance contributing to the perpetuation of these negative traits in contemporary Brazilian political culture. Anastasia, "Salteadores," 133–34, 137; Anastasia, *A geografia do crime*, 22–25, 128. For a perspective stressing the merits of the governor's actions, see Souza, "As Minas," 45–47, 61–67.

36. Antonio Henriques to Sebastião Craveiro de Faria, n.d., n.p., ANRJ, Negócios de Portugal, Correspondência do vice-reinado para a Corte, Original, cód. 68, vol. 7, fols. 235v–36; Faria to Antonio Henriques,? May, Quartel do Louriçal, ANRJ, cód. 68, vol. 7, fols. 236–36v; Faria to Antonio Henriques, n.d., n.p., ANRJ, cód. 68, vol. 7, fols. 236v–37. Anastasia, "Salteadores," 133–34.

37. Pedro Afonso Galvão de São Martinho, "Interrogatorios feitos as pessoas que chegarão a este Porto do Cunha, vindo do Descoberto de Macacû," 5, 6, 8, 20 May 1786," Negócios de Portugal, Correspondência do vice-reinado para a Corte, Original, ANRJ, cód. 68, vol. 7, fols. 233v–35. On the actual number of troops, Relasão da tropa que se deve aprontar a ordem do Ilustrisimo e Excelentisimo Senhor Vice Rei," ca. Mar. 1786, Correspondências e documentos . . . , BNRJ, SM, cód. 9, 3, 17, doc. 151; "Mapa das prasas de tropa paga e auxiliary e mais pesoas q. se achão debaixo do comando do Tenente Coronel Manoel Soares Coimbra," 22 July 1786, Correspondências e documentos . . . , BNRJ, SM, cód. 9, 3, 17, doc. 52. On the governor's version of the rumor, Souza, "As Minas," 49.

38. Pedro Afonso Galvão de São Martinho, "Mapa das praças que marcharão para o Descoberto de Macacu, e que ocuparão os mais lugares abayxo declarados," Roça Grande, 27 May 1786, APM, SC, cód. 239, f. 70. On the initial deployment from Vila Rica, Souza, "As Minas," 51.

39. São Martinho to Governor, Roça Grande, 17 May 1786, Negócios de Portugal, Correspondência do vice-reinado para a Corte, Original, ANRJ, cód. 68, vol. 7, fols. 232–33. This letter was transcribed in its entirety and published in Souza, "As Minas," 52–54.

40. São Martinho to Governor, Roça Grande, 17 May 1786, fols. 232–33. Anastasia and Souza mention Mão de Luva's apparently amicable relations with the Indians but do not discuss the matter further. Anastasia, *A geografia do crime*, 98; Souza, "As Minas," 37.

41. São Martinho, "Relação dos homens brancos e pardos forros que foram presos . . . por andarem abrindo picadas novas e extraindo ouro," 19 June 1786, Vila Rica, Negócios de Portugal, Correspondência do vice-reinado para a Corte, Original, ANRJ, cód. 68, vol. 7, fol. 228; José de Deus Lopes, "Nomes das pessoas libertas que se acham no Descoberto," n.d., n.p., ANRJ, cód. 68, vol. 7, fol. 229; São Martinho, "Relação das pessoas que foram presas na noite de 13 de Maio de 1786 no Descoberto," 17 May 1786, Corgo do Cantagalo do Descoberto do Macacu, ANRJ, cód. 68, vol. 7, fols. 230–31. Records from the court proceedings

against Mão de Luva and these twelve co-conspirators have never been found. In a 1789 letter to his successor, the viceroy stated the men had been sentenced for their crimes. Viceroy to José Luís de Castro, *RIHGB*, no. 4 (1842): 24.

42. Manoel Soares Coimbra to Viceroy, Registo da Fazenda do Cônego , 11 July 1786, Correspondências e documentos . . . , BNRJ, SM, cód. 9, 3, 17, doc. 44.

43. São Martinho, "Relação das pessoas que foram presas na noite de 13 de Maio de 1786 no Descoberto," 17 May 1786, Corgo do Cantagalo do Descoberto do Macacu, Negócios de Portugal, Correspondência do vice-reinado para a Corte, Original, ANRJ, cód. 68, vol. 7, fols. 230–31.

44. Garcia, "O Mão de Luva," 256.

45. Viceroy to Governor, "Relação dos réus do extravio do ouro," Rio, 3 Aug. 1786, Negócios de Portugal, Correspondência do vice-reinado para a Corte, Original, ANRJ, cód. 68, vol. 7, fols. 238–38v; Viceroy to Governor, Rio, 14 Aug. 1786, Negócios de Portugal, Correspondência do vice-reinado para a Corte, Original, ANRJ, cód. 68, vol. 7, fols. 239–39v; Viceroy to Secretary of State, Rio, 16? Jan. 1787, Negócios de Portugal, Correspondência do vice-reinado para a Corte, Original, ANRJ, cód. 68, vol. 7, fols. 260–68v, quoting fol. 266. Also see Souza, "As Minas," 61–68.

46. Alcida Rita Ramos, *Indigenism: Ethnic Politics in Brazil* (Madison: Univeristy of Wisconsin Press, 1998), 15–18.

47. Luís Rafael Araújo Corrêa, "Feitiço caboclo: Um índio mandingueiro condenado pela Inquisição" (PhD diss., Universidade Federal Fluminense, 2003), 205–8; Eduardo Viveiros de Castro, *The Inconstancy of the Indian Soul: The Encounter of Catholics and Cannibals in 16th-Century Brazil*, trans. Gregory Duff Morton (Chicago: Prickly Paradigm Press, 2011).

## Chapter 5

1. For scholarly references to Coimbra's expedition, see Rodrigo Leonardo de Sousa Oliveira, "'Mão de Luva' e 'Montanha': Bandoleiros e salteadores nos caminhos de Minas Gerais no século XVIII (Matas Gerais da Mantiqueira: 1755–1786)" (master's thesis, Universidade Federal de Juiz de Fora, 2008), 128–30; Mauro Leão Gomes, "Ouro, posseiros e fazendas de café: A ocupação e a degradação ambiental da região das Minas do Canta Gallo na província do Rio de Janeiro" (PhD diss., Universidade Federal Rural do Rio de Janeiro, 2004), chap. 1; José Antônio Soares Souza, "As Minas do Sertão de Macacu," *RIHGB* 326 (1980): 49.

2. Secretary of State to Viceroy, Palácio de Nossa Senhora da Ajuda, 8 Jan. 1785, Correspondências e documentos . . . , BNRJ, SM, cód. 9, 3, 17, doc. 127, para. 14–16.

3. Secretary of State to Viceroy, Palácio de Nossa Senhora da Ajuda, 8 Jan. 1785, Correspondências e documentos . . . , BNRJ, SM, cód. 9, 3, 17, doc. 127, para. 14–25, quoting para. 16.

4. "Relasão da tropa que se deve aprontar a ordem do Ilustrisimo e Excelentisimo Senhor Vice Rei," ca. Mar. 1786, Secretary of State to Viceroy, Palácio de Nossa Senhora da Ajuda, 8 Jan. 1785, Correspondências e documentos . . . , BNRJ, SM, cód. 9, 3, 17, doc. 151; "Mapa das prasas de tropa paga e auxiliary e mais pesoas q. se achão debaixo do comando do Tenente Coronel Manoel Soares Coimbra," 22 July 1786, Correspondências e documentos . . . , BNRJ, SM, cód. 9, 3, 17, doc. 52.

5. Most of the sources documenting Coimbra's expedition are found in Correspondências e documentos . . . , BNRJ, SM, cód. 9, 3, 17. This codex is the first of five, cataloged as códs. 9, 3, 17–21. Each volume covers a single year's activity, including subsequent efforts to control the zone. The first also contains much preliminary correspondence and relevant royal legislation from earlier years, beginning in 1730 but concentrating on the period after 1760 when the first reports of the contraband ring drew the attention of royal authorities. Selected copies of this correspondence and additional materials concerning the expedition and its aftermath are also found in Correspondência do vice-reinado para a corte, ANRJ, Fundo Negócios de Portugal, cód. 68, vol. 4 (1781), fols. 187–225v; vol. 6 (1783–85), fols. 236–42v; and vol. 7 (1787), fols. 11–13v, 79–80, 217–39v, 263–96v; vol. 8 (1788–90), fols. 54–78; and Secretaria do Estado do Brasil, Correspondência da Corte com o vice-reinado, ANRJ, cód. 67, vol. 15 (1787), fols. 63–112. For the secretary of state's concerns, see Secretary of State to Viceroy, Palácio de Nossa Senhora da Ajuda, 8 Jan. 1785, Correspondências e documentos . . . , BNRJ, SM, cód. 9, 3, 17, doc. 127, par. 15–16.

6. Coimbra to Viceroy, Registo da Entrada da Serra, 17 May 1786, Correspondências e documentos . . . , BNRJ, SM, cód. 9, 3, 17, doc. 9; Correspondências e documentos . . . , BNRJ, SM, cód. 9, 3, 17, Cantagalo, 4 Nov. 1786, doc. 83.

7. Viceroy to Coimbra, Rio, 12 Mar 1786, Correspondências e documentos . . . , BNRJ, SM, cód. 9, 3, 17, doc. 148; Coimbra to viceroy, Vila de Santo Antonio de Sá [present day Cachoeiras de Macacu], 10 May 1786, Correspondências e documentos . . . , BNRJ, SM, cód. 9, 3, 17, doc. 5; Viceroy to Coimbra, Rio, 8 July 1786, Correspondências e documentos . . . , BNRJ, SM, cód. 9, 3, 17, doc. 163; Viceroy to Coimbra, Rio, 10 July 1786, Correspondências e documentos . . . , BNRJ, SM, cód. 9, 3, 17, doc. 164.

8. See chapter 3 herein.

9. Coimbra to [Viceroy], Registo da Fazenda do Cônego, 14 July 1786, Correspondências e documentos . . . , BNRJ, SM, cód. 9, 3, 17, doc. 47. Coimbra questioned eight individuals in total.

10. Coimbra to [Viceroy], Registo da Fazenda do Cônego, 14 July 1786, Correspondências e documentos . . . , BNRJ, SM, cód. 9, 3, 17, doc. 47. Although this testimony mentioned only Joaquim and Dionísio Lopes, their brother José was later implicated by the Indian guide José Gomes, as described in Vicente Ferreira de Noronha to Viceroy, n.p., ca. 1780, Correspondências e documentos . . . , BNRJ, SM, cód. 9, 3, 17, doc. 141. Also see Romyr C. Garcia, "O Mão de Luva e os sertões de Serra acima: Garimpos clandestinos e conflitos sociais no Brasil Colônia," *Revista Unifesco—Humanas e Sociais* 4, no. 4 (2018).

11. Coimbra to [Viceroy], Registo da Fazenda do Cônego, 14 July 1786, Correspondências e documentos . . . , BNRJ, SM, cód. 9, 3, 17, doc. 47.

12. Coimbra to [Viceroy], Registo da Fazenda do Cônego, 19 July [1786, misdated as 1768], Correspondências e documentos . . . , BNRJ, SM, cód. 9, 3, 17, doc. 46. For the number of prospectors estimated in Lisbon to be working at the site, see Secretary of State to Viceroy, Palácio de Nossa Senhora da Ajuda, 8 Jan. 1785, Correspondências e documentos . . . , BNRJ, SM, cód. 9, 3, 17, doc. 127. The estimate relied on a report from a local field officer. See Bartolomeu José Vahia to Viceroy, Rio, 6 Aug. 1779, Correspondências e documentos . . . , BNRJ, SM, cód. 9, 3, 17, doc. 135.

13. John Mawe, *Travels in the Interior of Brazil, Particularly in the Gold and Diamond Districts of That Country* (London: Longman, 1812), 120–21; Souza, "As Minas," 54.

14. Coimbra to Viceroy, Cantagalo, 10 Aug. 1786, Correspondências e documentos . . . , BNRJ, SM, cód. 9, 3, 17, doc. 60.

15. Coimbra to Viceroy, Cantagalo, 19 Aug. 1786, Correspondências e documentos . . . , BNRJ, SM, cód. 9, 3, 17, doc. 61; Coimbra to Viceroy, Cantagalo, 25 Aug. 1786, Correspondências e documentos . . . , BNRJ, SM, cód. 9, 3, 17, doc. 62.

16. Coimbra to Viceroy, Cantagalo, 25 Aug. 1786, Correspondências e documentos . . . , BNRJ, SM, cód. 9, 3, 17, doc. 62.

17. Coimbra to Viceroy, Cantagalo, 22 Sept. 1786, Correspondências e documentos . . . , BNRJ, SM, cód. 9, 3, 17, doc. 67; Viceroy to Coimbra, Rio, 16 Sept. 1786, Correspondências e documentos . . . , BNRJ, SM, cód. 9, 3, 17, doc. 175. The Indians continued their regular visits to Cantagalo through the first days of November. For Coimbra's subsequent comments on providing for their needs, see Coimbra to Viceroy, Cantagalo, 7 Oct. 1786, Correspondências e documentos . . . , BNRJ, SM, cód. 9, 3, 17, doc. 73; Correspondências e documentos . . . , BNRJ, SM, cód. 9, 3, 17,, 4 Nov. 1786, doc. 83. On responses by Brazil's eastern Indians

to trade goods during this period, see Hal Langfur, *The Forbidden Lands: Colonial Identity, Frontier Violence, and the Persistence of Brazil's Eastern Indians, 1750–1830* (Stanford, CA: Stanford University Press, 2006), 230–39. Also see Richard White, *The Roots of Dependency: Subsistence, Environment, and Social Change among the Choctaws, Pawnees, and Navajos* (Lincoln: University of Nebraska Press, 1983).

18. Coimbra to Viceroy, Cantagalo, 4 Nov. 1786, Correspondências e documentos . . . , BNRJ, SM, cód. 9, 3, 17, doc. 83; Viceroy to Coimbra, Rio, 11 Nov. 1786, Correspondências e documentos . . . , BNRJ, SM, cód. 9, 3, 17, doc. 190; Coimbra to Camilo Maria Tonnelot, Cantagalo, 28 Dec. 1786, Correspondências e documentos . . . , BNRJ, SM, cód. 9, 3, 17, doc. 122. For more on desertions, see Coimbra to Viceroy, Cantagalo, 7 Sept. 1786, Correspondências e documentos . . . , BNRJ, SM, cód. 9, 3, 17, doc. 64; Viceroy to Coimbra, Rio, 16 Sept. 1786, Correspondências e documentos . . . , BNRJ, SM, cód. 9, 3, 17, doc. 178; Coimbra to Viceroy, Cantagalo, 22 Sept. 1786, Correspondências e documentos . . . , BNRJ, SM, cód. 9, 3, 17, doc. 67; Viceroy to Coimbra, Rio, 9 Oct. 1786, Correspondências e documentos . . . , BNRJ, SM, cód. 9, 3, 17, doc. 182; Alexandre Alves Duarte e Azevedo to Coimbra, Itaboraí, 4 Nov. 1786, Correspondências e documentos . . . , BNRJ, SM, cód. 9, 3, 17, doc. 87. For more on captive flights and deaths, see Coimbra to Antonio Luiz Pereira, Cantagalo, 8 Sept. 1786, Correspondências e documentos . . . , BNRJ, SM, cód. 9, 3, 17, doc. 87; Coimbra to Viceroy, Cantagalo, 18 Nov. 1786, Correspondências e documentos . . . , BNRJ, SM, cód. 9, 3, 17, doc. 86; Coimbra to Viceroy, Cantagalo, 16 Dec. 1786, Correspondências e documentos . . . , BNRJ, SM, cód. 9, 3, 17, doc. 121. On requisitions of enslaved workers, see Viceroy to José Joaquim da Fonseca [*sic*], Rio, 4 Sept. 1786, Correspondências e documentos . . . , BNRJ, SM, cód. 9, 3, 17, doc. 174; Coimbra to Viceroy, Cantagalo, 29 Sept. 1786, Correspondências e documentos . . . , BNRJ, SM, cód. 9, 3, 17, doc. 70.

19. Coimbra to Viceroy, Cantagalo, 4 Nov. 1786, Correspondências e documentos . . . , BNRJ, SM, cód. 9, 3, 17, doc. 83; Coimbra, "Relasão dos trastes pertencentes aos Indios," Cantagalo, 4 Nov. 1786, Correspondências e documentos . . . , BNRJ, SM, cód. 9, 3, 17, doc. 84.

20. Coimbra to Viceroy, Cantagalo, 4 Nov. 1786, Correspondências e documentos . . . , BNRJ, SM, cód. 9, 3, 17, doc. 83. According to the priest who informed Coimbra about this matter, the Indians found the insects they desired in taquara groves. The plant, bearing a Tupi name, is a genus of bamboo (*Gramineae: Bambusoideae*), which Native peoples throughout South America continue to use in the fabrication of dwellings, baskets, and decorative objects. John Luccock, *Notes on Rio de Janeiro and the Southern Parts of Brazil; Taken during a Residence of Ten Years in That Country, from 1808 to 1818* (London: Samuel Leigh, 1820),

688; Oikos Laboratório, "Taquara e Bambu," Universidade Federal de Paraná, http://www.oikos.ufpr.br/produtos/taquaras%20e%20bambus.pdf (accessed October 24, 2015).

21. For this ongoing violence, see chap. 1 of this study and Langfur, *Forbidden Lands*, esp. 61–67.

22. "Ley porque V. Magestade ha por bem restituir aos Indios do Grão Pará, e Maranhão a liberdade das suas pessoas, bens, e commercio na forma que nella se declara," Lisbon, June 6, 1755, in Carlos de Araújo Moreira Neto, *Índios da Amazônia: De maioria a minoria (1750–1850)* (Petrópolis: Editora Vozes, 1988), 161–62.

23. Coimbra to Viceroy, Cantagalo, 11 Dec. 1786, Correspondências e documentos . . . , BNRJ, SM, cód. 9, 3, 17, doc. 106; Viceroy to Coimbra, Rio, 31 Dec. 1786, Correspondências e documentos . . . , BNRJ, SM, cód. 9, 3, 17,, doc. 211 (quoted). Native boatmen came to work in the mountains from the São Barnabé aldeia, founded by Jesuits in the sixteenth century. The village's proximity to the city of Rio de Janeiro meant that these Indians had long experience serving as laborers. See Maria Regina Celestino de Almeida, *Metamorfoses indígenas: Cultura e identidade nos aldeamentos indígenas do Rio de Janeiro* (Rio de Janeiro: Arquivo Nacional, 2002).

24. Coimbra to [Viceroy], Registo da Fazenda do Cônego, 2 June 1786, Correspondências e documentos . . . , BNRJ, SM, cód. 9, 3, 17, doc. 14; Coimbra to [Viceroy], Registo da Fazenda do Cônego, 12 July 1786, Correspondências e documentos . . . , BNRJ, SM, cód. 9, 3, 17, doc. 45, quoted.

25. Joaquim José da Fonseca to [Viceroy], Vila de Santo Antonio de Sá, 14 Jan., 13 Feb., and 18 May 1786, with appended requisition lists, Correspondências e documentos . . . , BNRJ, SM, cód. 9, 3, 17, docs. 1–4, 12.

26. Coimbra to [Viceroy], Cantagalo, 19 Aug. and 29 Sept. 1786, Correspondências e documentos . . . , BNRJ, SM, cód. 9, 3, 17, docs. 61 and 70; Joaquim José da Fonseca to [Viceroy], Vila de Santo Antonio de Sá, 29 Sept. 1786, Correspondências e documentos . . . , BNRJ, SM, cód. 9, 3, 17, doc. 71; Viceroy to Joaquim José da Fonseca, Rio, 4 Sept. 1786, Correspondências e documentos . . . , BNRJ, SM, cód. 9, 3, 17, doc. 174, quoted. For the regional scope and mounting cost of this provisioning effort, see the lists of supplies, locations, and expenses enumerated in docs. 108 and 110–12. For the treasury's involvement, see Joaquim José da Fonseca to Queen, Vila de Santo Antonio de Sá, 28 Dec. 1786, Correspondências e documentos . . . , BNRJ, SM, cód. 9, 3, 17, doc. 118.

27. Records exist of payments for fourteen enslaved males purchased by the government in two separate instances to work at the site. Their names indicate

they were African-born. The records establish that their average price was 119$500, commensurate with prices in Minas Gerais but more than 60 percent higher than in coastal Rio de Janeiro. Souza, "As Minas," 69–70; Garcia, "O Mão de Luva," 257; Laird W. Bergad, *Slavery and the Demographic and Economic History of Minas Gerais, Brazil, 1720–1888* (Cambridge: Cambridge University Press, 1999), 44; Manolo Garcia Florentino, *Em Costas Negras: Uma história do tráfico de escravos entre a África e o Rio de Janeiro (séculos XVIII e XIX)* (São Paulo: Companhia das Letras, 1997), 300.

28. Viceroy to Coimbra, Rio, 31 Dec. 1786, Correspondências e documentos . . . , BNRJ, SM, cód. 9, 3, 17, doc. 212.

29. Coimbra to [Viceroy], Cantagalo, 4 Nov. 1786, Correspondências e documentos . . . , BNRJ, SM, cód. 9, 3, 17, doc. 83; Coimbra to [Viceroy], Cantagalo, 18 Nov. 1786, Correspondências e documentos . . . , BNRJ, SM, cód. 9, 3, 17, doc. 86.

30. Coimbra to [Viceroy], Cantagalo, 18 Nov. 1786, Correspondências e documentos . . . , BNRJ, SM, cód. 9, 3, 17, doc. 86; Coimbra to Antonio Luiz Pereira, Cantagalo, 8 Sept. 1786, Correspondências e documentos . . . , BNRJ, SM, cód. 9, 3, 17, doc. 99.

31. Miguel Antunes Ferreira to Viceroy, Rio, 10 Aug. 1779, Correspondências e documentos . . . , BNRJ, SM, cód. 9, 3, 17, doc. 135; Coimbra to Viceroy, Cantagalo, 10 Jan. 1787, ANRJ, Negócios de Portugal, Correspondência do vice-reinado para a Corte, Original, cód. 68, vol. 7, fol. 294; Viceroy to Secretary of State, Rio, 16? Jan. 1787, ANRJ, Negócios de Portugal, Correspondência do vice-reinado para a Corte, Original, cód. 68, vol. 7, fols. 260–68v.

32. Coimbra to Camilo Maria Tonnelot, Cantagalo, 28 Dec. 1786, Correspondências e documentos . . . , BNRJ, SM, cód. 9, 3, 17, doc. 122. For documents pertaining to Coimbra's future military career, see Manoel Soares de Coimbra, AHM, processo 394, 1802. Also see Carlos H. Corrêa, *Os governantes de Santa Catarina, 1739–1982: Notas biográficas* (Florianópolis: Universidade Federal de Santa Catarina, 1983), 114.

33. "Reflexões sobre a Ley de 11 de Agosto do presente anno em que se patenteam os prejuisos, que a mesma causa á Real Fazenda, e se dá instrução da gente, de que a mesma Ley trata, e dos seus costumes, e notícia das Tropas, que ha nos Governos de todas as Minas, e da despeza, que cada uma causa, tanto na sua criação, como em o gasto annual de soldos e mantimentos," after 1760, BPE, cód. CV/1–3, fol. 114.

34. Coimbra to Camilo Maria Tonnelot, Cantagalo, 28 Dec. 1786, Correspondências e documentos . . . , BNRJ, SM, cód. 9, 3, 17, doc. 122.

35. Viceroy to Coimbra, Rio, 20 Apr. 1787, Correspondências e documentos . . . , BNRJ, SM, cód. 9, 3, 17, doc. 198.

36. Kenneth R. Maxwell, *Conflicts and Conspiracies: Brazil and Portugal, 1750–1808* (Cambridge: Cambridge University Press, 1973), chaps. 3–4.

37. Viceroy to Secretary of State, Rio, 21 July 1788, ANRJ, Negócios de Portugal, Correspondência do vice-reinado para a Corte, Original, cód. 68, vol. 8, fols. 54–58, published in *RIHGB* 256 (1963): 333–41, quoting 337.

38. Viceroy to Secretary of State, Rio, 21 July 1788, ANRJ, Negócios de Portugal, Correspondência do vice-reinado para a Corte, Original, cód. 68, vol. 8, fols. 54–58, published in *RIHGB* 256 (1963): 333–41.

39. Viceroy to José Luís de Castro, Rio, 20 Aug. 1789, in *RIHGB*, vol. 4 (1842): 24, 27.

40. Souza, "As Minas," 75–80.

41. Mawe, *Travels in the Interior of Brazil*, 122–25.

42. Sheila de Castro Faria, "Ouro, porcos, escravos e café: As origens das fortunas oitocentistas em São Pedro de Cantagalo, Rio de Janeiro (últimas décadas do século XVIII e primeiras do XIX)," *Anais do Museu Paulista: História e Cultura Material* 26 (2018); José de Souza Azevedo Pizarro e Araújo, *Memórias históricas do Rio de Janeiro e das provincias annexas a jurisdicção do vice-rei do Estado do Brasil*, 9 vols. (Rio de Janeiro: Imp. Regia, 1820–22), vol. 5, 288–95; Manoel Martinz do Couto Reys, *Manuscritos de Manoel Martinz do Couto Reys, 1785* (Rio de Janeiro: Arquivo Público do Estado do Rio de Janeiro, 1997), 72; Langfur, *Forbidden Lands*, 23–24, 205–12.

43. Hermann Burmeister, *Viagem ao Brasil através das províncias do Rio de Janeiro e Minas Gerais*, trans. Manoel Salvaterra and Hubert Schoenfeldt (Sa?o Paulo: Livraria Martins, 1952), 131, 144–45. For coffee and slavery in the Paraíba Valley, see Mariana Muaze and Ricardo Salles, *O Vale do Paraíba e o Império do Brasil nos quadros da segunda escravidão* (Rio de Janeiro: 7Letras, 2015). Also see Stanley J. Stein, *Vassouras: A Brazilian Coffee County; The Roles of Planter and Slave in a Plantation Society* (Cambridge, MA: Harvard University Press, 1958; reprint, 1985).

44. Martinho de Melo e Castro, "Instrucção para o Visconde de Barbacena, Luiz Antonio Furtado de Mendonça . . . ," Salvaterra de Mago, 29 Jan. 1788, in *RIHGB*, vol. 6 (1844): 3–59, quoting 4, 14. For the colonial secretary's comments on the sertões, see 20.

## Chapter 6

1. On scientific expeditions in the Portuguese Empire, see Ronald Raminelli, *Viagens ultramarinas: Monarcas, vassalos e governo à distância* (São Paulo: Alameda, 2008); William J. Simon, *Scientific Expeditions in the Portuguese Overseas Territories (1783–1808) and the Role of Lisbon in the Intellectual-Scientific Community of*

*the Late Eighteenth Century* (Lisbon: Instituto de Investigação Científica Tropical, 1983); Ângela Domingues, "Museus, coleccionismo e viagens científicas em Portugal de finais de Setecentos," *Asclepio* 71, no. 2 (2019): 1–19; Ângela Domingues, "Para um melhor conhecimento dos domínios coloniais: A constituição de redes de informação no Império português em finais do Setecentos," *História, Ciências, Saúde—Manguinhos* supplement, 8 (2001): 823–38; Silvia F. de M. Figueirôa, Clarete Paranhos da Silva, and Ermelinda Moutinho Pataca, "Aspectos mineralógicos das 'Viagens Filosóficas' pelo território brasileiro na transição do século XVIII para o século XIX," *História, Ciências, Saúde-Manguinhos* 11, no. 3 (2004): 713–29. On the co-opting of Enlightenment savants in Portugal, see Júnia Ferreira Furtado, introduction to José Vieira Couto, *Memória sobre a Capitania das Minas Gerais; seu território, clima e produções metálicas* (Belo Horizonte: Fundação João Pinheiro, 1994), 14; Raminelli, *Viagens ultramarinas*; Clarete Paranhos da Silva, *O desvendar do grande livro da natureza: Um estudo da obra do mineralogista José Vieira Couto, 1798–1805* (São Paulo: Annablume, 2002), 41–45, 149–50.

2. Studies of Couto and his scientific contributions include Júnia Ferreira Furtado, introduction to Couto, *Memória sobre a Capitania*; Júnia Ferreira Furtado, "Enlightenment Science and Iconoclasm: The Brazilian Naturalist José Vieira Couto," *Osiris* 25, no. 1 (2010); Silva, *O desvendar do grande livro*. For the history of the Diamond District, see Júnia Ferreira Furtado, *O Livro da Capa Verde: O regimento diamantino de 1771 e a vida no Distrito Diamantino no período da real extração* (São Paulo: Annablume, 1996), chap. 8; Júnia Ferreira Furtado, *Chica da Silva: A Brazilian Slave of the Eighteenth Century* (Cambridge: Cambridge University Press, 2009); C. R. Boxer, *The Golden Age of Brazil, 1695–1750: Growing Pains of a Colonial Society* (Berkeley: University of California Press, 1969).

3. Domingos Vandelli, *Memórias de história natural* (Porto: Porto Editora, 2003), esp. introduction and chaps. 1, 2, and 6, quoting 29. Vandelli wrote the first two of the three texts, which are published in this volume as separate chapters, ca. 1790; the third, ca. 1800. Couto's matriculation and four-year training at the University of Coimbra is registered in Livros de Matriculas, AUC, 1774–1775, Filosofia, Primeio ano, fol. 9; 1775–1776, Matemática, Primeiro ano, fol. 13v; 1775–1776, Filosofia, Segundo ano, fol. 50; 1776–1777, Filosofia, Terceiro ano, fol. 43v; 1777–1778, Filosofia, Quarto ano, fol. 61, with a margin note in this final volume stating that he completed his degree in philosophy. For a guide to specimen collecting techniques contemporaneous to Couto's completion of his university training, see [Anon.], Methodo de recolher, preparar, remeter e conservar os produtos naturais, segundo o plano, que tem concebido e publicado alguns naturalistas, para o uso dos curiosos que visitam os certoins, e costas do mar, Lisbon, 1781, MS, AHMB, Res-18. For a list of the animal, plant, and mineral specimens assembled by Vandelli

to train students shortly before Couto's arrival at the University of Coimbra, see Domingos Vandelli, "Breve relação do museu d'historia natural, que o D.r Domingos Vandelli tinha na Ajuda no Real Jardim Botanico, e de que no anno 1772 fiz prezente a esta universidade, e do qual se tem servido athe agora para as lições de historia natural," Coimbra, 15 Mar. 1777, AUC, PP, no. 372. Also see Virgínia M. T. Valadares, *Elites mineiras setecentistas: Conjugação de dois mundos* (Lisbon: Edições Colibri, 2004); Fernando Taveira da Fonseca, "Uma primeira educação do olhar: Universidade e estudantes de Coimbra na transição reformista," in *A universidade pombalina: Ciência, território e coleções científicas*, ed. Ana Cristina Araújo and Fernando Taveira da Fonseca (Coimbra: Universidade de Coimbra, 2017), 35–45; Regina Horta Duarte, "Facing the Forest: European Travellers Crossing the Mucuri River Valley, Brazil, in the Nineteenth Century," *Environment and History* 10, no. 1 (2004): 34. On natural philosophy and natural history, see N. Jardine, J. A. Secord, and E. C. Spary, *Cultures of Natural History* (Cambridge: Cambridge University Press, 1996). In the same volume, on mineralogy, see Martin Rudwick, "Minerals, Strata, and Fossils," in *Cultures of Natural History*, ed. N. Jardine, J. A. Secord, and E. C. Spary (Cambridge: Cambridge University Press, 1996).

4. Júnia Ferreira Furtado, introduction to Couto, *Memória sobre a Capitania*, 15. Also see Cardoso, introduction to Vandelli, *Memórias de história natural*; Silva, *O desvendar do grande livro*, 37, 49–53; Fernando A. Novais, *Portugal e Brasil na crise do antigo sistema colonial (1777–1808)*, 2nd ed. (São Paulo: Ed. HUCITEC, 1981); Raminelli, *Viagens ultramarinas*.

5. Kenneth R. Maxwell, *Conflicts and Conspiracies: Brazil and Portugal, 1750–1808* (Cambridge: Cambridge University Press, 1973), 207–13; Maria Odila da Silva Dias, "Aspectos da Ilustração no Brasil," *RIHGB* 278 (January–March 1968): 105–70; E. Bradford Burns, "The Intellectuals as Agents of Change and the Independence of Brazil, 1724–1822," in *From Colony to Nation: Essays on the Independence of Brazil*, ed. A. J. R. Russell-Wood (Baltimore: Johns Hopkins University Press, 1975), esp. 235–46; Silva, *O desvendar do grande livro*, 51–53. On the Tailor's Conspiracy, see Donald Ramos, "Social Revolution Frustrated: The Conspiracy of the Tailors in Bahia, 1798," *Luso-Brazilian Review* 13, no. 1 (1976); Roderick J. Barman, *Brazil: The Forging of a Nation, 1798–1852* (Stanford, CA: Stanford University Press, 1988), 33–38. For anticolonial agitation during this period in comparative perspective, see Hal Langfur and Charles F. Walker, "Protest and Resistance against Colonial Rule in Iberian America," in *The Iberian World, 1450–1820*, ed. Fernando Bouza, Pedro Cardim, and Antonio Feros (London: Routledge, 2020), 617–34. For the secretary of state's active interest in mining, see Secretary of State to Alexandre Rodrigues Ferreira, Lisbon, 26 Sept. 1799, 2 Oct. 1799, 9 June 1800, 18 June 1800, Livro de registo dos decretos, portarias, avisos, e outras regias

determinaçoens, que baixão ao Real Jardim Botanico . . . AHMCUL, Fundo Real Museu e Jardim Botânico da Ajuda, livro 1863, doc. 78, 80, 108, 110.

6. Maxwell, *Conflicts and Conspiracies*, 66. Also see Couto, *Memoria sobre as minas*, 36–37. Coutinho increasingly abandoned his neo-mercantilist political and economic philosophy after the turn of the century. Richard Graham, *Feeding the City: From Street Market to Liberal Reform in Salvador, Brazil, 1780–1860* (Austin: University of Texas Pres, 2010), 181.

7. See Couto, *Memória sobre a Capitania*, which includes an excellent critical introduction by Júnia Furtado; José Vieira Couto, *Memoria sobre as minas da capitania de Minas Geraes; suas descrições, ensaios e domicílios próprios, à maneira de itinerário* . . . (Rio de Janeiro: Laemmert, 1842). For an MS of the 1799 memorial, see AHU, Minas Gerais, cx. 147, doc. 1. This MS is one among several, the others located in the BNRJ, SM, and the AIHGB, which contain inconsequential differences introduced by copyists. For the original MS of the 1801 memorial, including a map depicting the journey, sent by the governor to Lisbon in 1802, see AHU, Códices, cód. 1819. After this memorial was published in 1842, it was reprinted in *RAPM* 10, no. 1 (January–June 1905): 55–166.

8. Couto, *Memória sobre a Capitania*, 68.

9. Silva and Furtado briefly mention Couto's reliance on these prospector guides. Silva, *O desvendar do grande livro*, 114–15; Furtado, "Enlightenment Science," 208–9.

10. For another example of the conduit between local and metropolitan expertise, see Júnia Ferreira Furtado, "Tropical Empiricism: Making Medical Knowledge in Colonial Brazil," in *Science and Empire in the Atlantic World*, ed. James Delbourgo and Nicholas Dew (New York City: Routledge, 2008), 127–51. Also see Cameron B. Strang, *Frontiers of Science: Imperialism and Natural Knowledge in the Gulf South Borderlands, 1500–1850* (Chapel Hill: University of North Carolina Press, 2018).

11. Couto, *Memoria sobre as minas*, 2n4. The same spelling was used by the renowned José Bonifácio. See José Bonifácio de Andrada e Silva, "An Account of the Diamonds of Brazil," in *Obras científicas, políticas e sociais*, ed. Edgard de Cerqueira Falcão ([São Paulo]: [Empresa Gráfica da Revista dos Tribunais], 1963), 58. For the quoted dictionary definition, see "grimpa" in Antonio de Moraes Silva, *Diccionario da lingua portugueza*, 2 vols. (Lisbon: Typ. Lacerdina, 1813), vol. 2, 101. Also see Antônio de Morais Silva and Rafael Bluteau, *Diccionario da lingua portugueza composto pelo padre D. Rafael Bluteau, reformado, e accrescentado por Antonio de Moraes Silva natural do Rio de Janeiro*, 2 vols. (Lisbon: Simão Thaddeo Ferreira, 1789), vol. 1, 670. Neither grimpeiro nor garimpeiro appear in these editions of this respected Portuguese dictionary, suggesting the terms' colloquial origins. They are similarly absent in another dictionary

published within six years of Couto's expedition. See *Novo diccionario da lingua portugueza: Composto sobre os que até o presente se tem dado ao prelo, e accrescentado de varios vocabulos extrahidos dos classicos antigos, e dos modernos de melhor nota, que se achaõ universalmente recebidos* (Lisbon: Rollandiana, 1806). Further etymological clues are provided in Wilhelm Ludwig von Eschwege, *Pluto brasiliensis*, trans. Domício de Figueiredo Murta, 2 vols. (Belo Horizonte: Itatiaia, 1979), vol. 2, 286n347. For more on garimpeiros in colonial Minas Gerais, who sometimes worked in groups numbering in the hundreds, see Furtado, *O Livro da Capa Verde*, 91–92; Laura de Mello e Souza, *Norma e conflito: Aspectos da história de Minas no século XVIII* (Belo Horizonte: Universidade Federal de Minas Gerais, 1999), 142–47; Ivana D. Parrela, *O teatro das desordens: Garimpo, contrabando e violência no sertão diamantino, 1768–1800* (São Paulo: Annablume, 2009); Aires da Mata Machado Filho, *O negro e o garimpo em Minas Gerais* (Belo Horizonte: Itatiaia, 1985).

12. John Mawe, *Travels in the Interior of Brazil, Particularly in the Gold and Diamond Districts of That Country* (London: Longman, 1812), 2, 120, 252.

13. Francisco de Paula Beltrão to João Filipe da Fonseca, Sabará, 28 Sept. 1801, AHU, Minas Gerais, cx. 158, doc. 22.

14. Mary Apocalypse, "O tesouro de Isidoro, o garimpeiro," in *Estórias e lendas de Minas Gerais, Espírito Santo e Rio de Janeiro*, ed. Mary Apocalypse (São Paulo: Iracema, 1997), 79–83. For another version of the Isidoro legend, see Rubens Fiúza, *O diamante do Abaeté e outros contos* (Belo Horizonte: Imprensa Oficial, 1988), 158–63.

15. Apocalypse, "Estórias e lendas," 79–83.

16. Joaquim Felício dos Santos, *Memórias do Distrito Diamantino da Comarca do Serro Frio (Província de Minas Gerais)*, 4th ed. (1868; reprint, Belo Horizonte: Itatiaia, 1976), 239–42. In his study of colonial Tejuco, the linguist and folklorist Aires da Mata Machado Filho quoted from what he said was a denunciation by an anonymous eyewitness of Isidoro's flogging. This complaint was published in 1821, wrote Machado Filho, but he did not provide a citation detailed enough to locate it. Aires da Mata Machado Filho, *Arraial do Tijuco, cidade Diamantina* (Belo Horizonte: Itatiaia, 1980), 87–89.

17. Santos, *Memórias do Distrito Diamantino da Comarca do Serro Frio (Província de Minas Gerais)*, 239–42.

18. See, for example, Clóvis Moura, *Dicionário da escravidão negra no Brasil* (São Paulo: Universidade de São Paulo, 2004), 218–20.

19. See esp. Furtado, *Chica da Silva*. On Santos's regional pride and antimonarchist, republican political views, which he advanced in the pages of his regional newspaper *O Jequitinhonha* in the 1860s and early 1870s, see Eder Liz

Novaes, "Joaquim Felício dos Santos: Republicanismo e Cultura Historiográfica (1860–1871)" (master's thesis, Universidade Federal de Ouro Preto, 2014).

20. In an otherwise insightful essay on Couto, Furtado describes Isidoro as a runaway slave but cites no documentary support. Furtado, "Enlightenment Science," 208. Environmental historian Ricardo Ferreira Ribeiro also conflates the story of the runaway slave named Isidoro narrated by Santos with the historical figure who guided Couto and his party into the sertão. Ricardo Ferreira Ribeiro, *Florestas anãs do sertão: O cerrado na história de Minas Gerais* (Belo Horizonte: Autêntica, 2005), 331–33.

21. Francisco de Paula Beltrão to João Filipe da Fonseca, Sabará, 28 Sept. 1801, AHU, Minas Gerais, cx. 158, doc. 22. Also see Mawe, *Travels in the Interior of Brazil*. In July 1799, when the prospector first offered to guide the expedition to the site of his discovery, the governor referred to Isidoro as "Captain Isidoro." In November 1800, after the expedition returned, the governor used the full title "Captain of the Free Black [Homens Pardos] Regiment" of Vila Rica. Governor to Secretary of State, Vila Rica, 15 July 1799, AHU, Minas Gerais, cx. 149, doc. 5; Termo (official pronouncement) of Board of Royal Finance, Vila Rica, 19 Nov. 1800, AHU, Minas Gerais, cx. 161, doc. 23. The second of these documents was published in *RAPM* 4 (1899): 296–97.

22. Governor to Secretary of State, Vila Rica, 6 Feb. 1802, AHU, Minas Gerais, cx. 161, doc. 23.

23. Governor to Secretary of State, Vila Rica, 15 July 1799, AHU, Minas Gerais, cx. 149, doc. 5 with appended Board of Royal Finance (Junta da Real Fazenda) declaration drafted in Vila Rica, 21 June 1799. The declaration identified Isidoro by his full name, Isidoro de Amorim Pereira. It specified that he found the diamond along the "Rio Andayá," that is, the Indaiá River, another tributary of the São Francisco.

24. Governor to Secretary of State, Vila Rica, 15 July 1799, AHU, Minas Gerais, cx. 149, doc. 5. For another account of the confrontation with soldiers, see Eschwege, *Pluto brasiliensis*, vol. 2, 107.

25. On the participation of leading Minas officials in contraband schemes, see Maxwell, *Conflicts and Conspiracies*, 66–67, 100–103.

26. Governor to Secretary of State, Vila Rica, 15 July 1799, AHU, Minas Gerais, cx. 149, doc. 5.

27. Governor to Secretary of State, Vila Rica, 6 Feb. 1802, AHU, Minas Gerais, cx. 161, doc. 23. Also see Couto, *Memoria sobre as minas*, 38.

28. Couto, *Memoria sobre as minas*, 36–37.

29. Governor to Secretary of State, Vila Rica, 6 Feb. 1788, AHU, Minas Gerais, cx. 128, doc. 20.

30. José Antonio de Mello to Governor, Paracatu, 27 Jan. 1788, AHU, Minas Gerais, cx. 128, doc. 20; José Antonio de Mello, Edital (edict), Paracatu, 27 Jan. 1788, AHU, Minas Gerais, cx. 128, doc. 20. A decade later, in 1798, spurred by criminality in the sertão among other concerns, the crown strengthened its institutional presence in western Minas Gerais, elevating Paracatu's status from *arraial* (village) to *vila* (town), thereby making it the administrative center of its own *termo* (municipal district). The move responded to the "large population" inhabiting the remote settlement and its surrounding region. The expenses and delays involved in administering justice resulted in "grave disadvantages and irreparable damages," particularly the lack of a resident judge necessary to ensure "tranquility and public security." The change meant that the crown would pay a circuit judge (*juiz de fora*) to be based in the town. Alvará, 20 Oct. 1798, in Antonio Delgado da Silva, ed., *Collecção da legislação portugueza desde a ultima compilação das ordenações*, 6 vols. (Lisbon: Maigrense,1825), vol. 4, 510–11.

31. Valentim José de Carvalho to [Governor], Paracatu, 27 Jan. 1788, AHU, Minas Gerais, cx. 128, doc. 20.

32. Governor to Viceroy, Cachoeira do Campo, 6 May 1789, AHU, Minas Gerais, cx. 131, doc. 54.

33. Governor to Secretary of State, Vila Rica, 15 July 1799, AHU, Minas Gerais, cx. 149, doc. 5; Eschwege, *Pluto brasiliensis*, vol. 2, 107.

34. Representação solicitando a quantia que falta para o pagamento dos soldos do destacamento de Abaeté, devido a um furto na condução dos ditos soldos, Vila Rica, 28 July 1792, BNRJ, SM, CC, gaveta I-25–14, doc. 8, with appended documents.

35. Couto, *Memoria sobre as minas*, 36–37.

36. Mawe, *Travels in the Interior of Brazil*, 140. Governor Lorena mentioned the earlier discovery in his letter to Lisbon announcing the receipt of Isidoro's diamond. Governor to Secretary of State, Vila Rica, 15 July 1799, AHU, Minas Gerais, cx. 149, doc. 5.

37. Mawe, *Travels in the Interior of Brazil*.

38. Mawe, *Travels in the Interior of Brazil*, 242–44. The weight of the stone was registered in the ledgers of Lisbon's ministry of foreign affairs (Secretaria de Estado dos Negocios da Marinha e Domínios Ultramarinos). A certified summary of the entry accompanied a petition filed by of one of the diamond's discoverers, José Rodrigues Neofito, who described himself as a man of color. Petition of José Rodrigues Neofito to Prince Regent, after 8 Jan. 1802, AHU, Minas Gerais, cx. 161, doc. 3.

39. For the 1797 orders distributing rewards for the discovery, see "Premios aos descobridores do Grande Diamante do Abaeté," in *RAPM* 2, no. 1 (1897): 41–44.

For the negotiations that ensued, see Ruling of the Overseas Council, Lisbon, 12 Dec. 1800, AHU, Minas Gerais, cx. 155, doc. 12; Petition of Francisco Xavier de Almeida to Prince Regent, before 28 May 1801, AHU, Minas Gerais, cx. 157, doc. 47; Petition of Antonio Marques dos Reis to Prince Regent, before 16 June 1801, AHU, Minas Gerais, cx. 157, doc. 68; Petition of José Rodrigues Neofito to Prince Regent, after 8 Jan. 1802, AHU, Minas Gerais, cx. 161, doc. 3. The priest involved in the episode also came forward to request a reward. See Overseas Secretary to President of Overseas Council, Lisbon, 12 Dec. 1796, with appended undated petition to crown by Anastasio Gonçalves Pimentel, AHU, Minas Gerais, cx. 142, doc. 56.

40. Petition of José Rodrigues Neofito to Prince Regent, after 8 Jan. 1802, AHU, Minas Gerais, cx. 161, doc. 3. Also see Mawe, *Travels in the Interior of Brazil*, 242–44.

41. Mawe, *Travels in the Interior of Brazil*, 224.

42. Mawe, *Travels in the Interior of Brazil*, 137–41.

43. Herbert S. Klein and Francisco Vidal Luna, *Slavery in Brazil* (Cambridge: Cambridge University Press, 2010), 49–53, 250–60; James H. Sweet, *Domingos Álvares, African Healing, and the Intellectual History of the Atlantic World* (Chapel Hill: University of North Carolina Press, 2011), 93–96.

44. Belmiro Luiz Nascimento, interview by author, along the Ribeirão do Guinda (Guinda Creek), Diamantina, Minas Gerais, 24 July 2014.

## Chapter 7

1. José Vieira Couto, *Memoria sobre as minas da capitania de Minas Geraes; suas descrições, ensaios e domicílios próprios, à maneira de itinerário* . . . (Rio de Janeiro: Laemmert, 1842), 10.

2. E. P. Hamm, "Knowledge from Underground: Leibniz Mines the Enlightenment," *Earth Sciences History* 16, no. 2 (1997): 87; Gillian Beer, "Travel Narratives and Truth Claims," in *Cultures of Natural History*, ed. N. Jardine, J. A. Secord, and E. C. Spary (Cambridge: Cambridge University Press, 1996); Mary Louise Pratt, *Imperial Eyes: Travel Writing and Transculturation* (London: Routledge, 1992), esp. 27–37; Paul Smethurst, *Travel Writing and the Natural World, 1768–1840* (London: Palgrave Macmillan, 2012); Dorinda Outram, *The Enlightenment*, 4th ed. (Cambridge: Cambridge University Press, 2019), 110.

3. Couto, *Memoria sobre as minas*, 76–77.

4. José Vieira Couto, *Memória sobre a Capitania das Minas Gerais; seu território, clima e produções metálicas* (Belo Horizonte: Fundação João Pinheiro, 1994), 91.

5. Couto, *Memória sobre a Capitania das Minas Gerais*, 61.

6. Couto, *Memoria sobre as minas*, 10, 34.

7. Hal Langfur, "The Return of the Bandeira: Economic Calamity, Historical Memory, and Armed Expeditions to the Sertão in Minas Gerais, Brazil, 1750–1808," *The Americas* 61, no. 3 (2005).

8. José Bonifácio de Andrada e Silva, "An Account of the Diamonds of Brazil," in *Obras científicas, políticas e sociais*, ed. Edgard de Cerqueira Falcão ([São Paulo]: [Empresa Gráfica da Revista dos Tribunais], 1963), 58. On Silva's activities as a naturalist, see Alex Gonçalves Varela, Maria Margaret Lopes, and Maria Rachel Fróes da Fonseca, "Naturalista e homem público: A trajetória do ilustrado José Bonifácio de Andrada e Silva em sua fase portuguesa (1780–1819)," *Anais do Museu Paulista* 13, no. 1 (2005): 207–34. Also see Emilia Viotti da Costa, "José Bonifácio de Andrada e Silva: A Brazilian Founding Father," in *The Brazilian Empire: Myths and Histories* (Chicago: University of Chicago Press, 1985), 24–52.

9. Jozé Eloi Ottoni, "Memória sobre o estado actual da Capitania de Minas Gerais," Lisboa, 1798, in *ABNRJ* 30 (1908): 313; Hal Langfur, *The Forbidden Lands: Colonial Identity, Frontier Violence, and the Persistence of Brazil's Eastern Indians, 1750–1830* (Stanford, CA: Stanford University Press, 2006), 51–54.

10. Moses Hadas, *A History of Latin Literature* (New York: Columbia University Press, 1952), 148–49.

11. Couto, *Memoria sobre as minas*, 26n16.

12. Couto, *Memoria sobre as minas*, 81.

13. Couto, *Memoria sobre as minas*, 19, 22.

14. Rebecca Earle, "The Pleasures of Taxonomy: Casta Paintings, Classification, and Colonialism," *William and Mary Quarterly* 73, no. 3 (2016): 431.

15. Couto, *Memória sobre a Capitania*, 80.

16. Couto, *Memoria sobre as minas*, 26.

17. Júnia Ferreira Furtado, "Enlightenment Science and Iconoclasm: The Brazilian Naturalist José Vieira Couto," *Osiris* 25, no. 1 (2010): 195–96.

18. Couto, *Memoria sobre as minas*, 5–20. Also see Couto's discussion of copper in his dedication to Portugal's Prince Regent João, dated 20 Nov. 1801, which immediately precedes the main text, unpaginated. Johan Gottschalk Wallerius, *Mineralogie ou description générale des substances du regne mineral* (Paris: Durand, 1753), vol. 1, 510.

19. José Vieira Couto, Memoria sobre as Minas de Cobalto da Capitania de Minas Geraes, com 35 Exemplares da mesma Mina, Tejuco, 25 June 1805, BA, Lisbon, 54-V-12(3). Another copy of this report, held by the BNL, is slightly compromised, not containing Couto's dedication to the prince regent in its entirety. José Vieira Couto, Memoria sobre as Minas de Cobalto da Capitania de Minas Geraes, com 35 exemplares da mesma mina, Tejuco, 25 June 1805, Papéis

vários, alguns relativos ao Brasil, BNL, CP, MS 720, film 3522, fot. 197–231, esp. f. 31, 39v.

20. José Bonifácio de Andrada e Silva to Secretary of State, Coimbra, 2 Dec. 1806, AHU, Minas Gerais, cx. 182, doc. 53. This letter preceded an appended copy of Couto's "Memoria sobre as Minas de Cobalto."

21. Luciano E. Faria and Carlos A. L. Filgueiras, "A busca por chumbo e prata em Minas Gerais como alternativa às esgotadas minas de ouro e diamantes no século XIX," *Química Nova* 42 (2019): 107.

22. For the seminal study of this phenomenon, see Ronald Raminelli, *Viagens ultramarinas: Monarcas, vassalos e governo à distância* (São Paulo: Alameda, 2008).

23. Governor to Secretary of State, Vila Rica, 20 Aug. 1799, AHU, Minas Gerais, cx. 149, doc. 50; Governor to Secretary of State, Vila Rica, 6 Feb. 1802, AHU, Minas Gerais, cx. 161, doc. 23. Also see Furtado, introduction to Couto, *Memória sobre a Capitania*, 22–23; Clarete Paranhos da Silva, *O desvendar do grande livro da natureza: Um estudo da obra do mineralogista José Vieira Couto, 1798–1805* (São Paulo: Annablume, 2002), 65.

24. Couto, "Memoria sobre as Minas de Cobalto," f. 25v.

25. Couto, *Memoria sobre as minas*, 36–37.

26. Couto, *Memoria sobre as minas*, 23.

27. Couto, *Memoria sobre as minas*, 50.

28. Francisco de Paula Beltrão to João Filipe da Fonseca, Sabará, 28 Sept. 1801, AHU, Minas Gerais, cx. 158, doc. 22.

29. See, for example, Mariana L. R. Dantas, "Black Women and Mothers: Social Mobility and Inheritance Strategies in Minas Gerais during the Second Half of the Eighteenth Century," *Almanack* 12 (January–April 2016): 88–104; Donald Ramos, "Single and Married Women in Vila Rica, Brazil, 1754–1838," *Journal of Family History* 16, no. 3 (1991): 261–82; Luciano R. de A. Figueiredo, *O avesso da memória: Cotidiano e trabalho da mulher em Minas Gerais no século XVIII* (Rio de Janeiro: José Olympio, 1993); Luciano R. de A. Figueiredo, *Barrocas famílias: Vida familiar em Minas Gerais no século XVIII* (São Paulo: HUCITEC, 1997), 138–46; Júnia Ferreira Furtado, *Chica da Silva: A Brazilian Slave of the Eighteenth Century* (Cambridge: Cambridge University Press, 2009); Kathleen J. Higgins, *"Licentious Liberty" in a Brazilian Gold-Mining Region: Slavery, Gender, and Social Control in Eighteenth-Century Sabará, Minas Gerais* (University Park: Pennsylvania State University Press, 1999), esp. chap. 2; Júnia Ferreira Furtado, "Pérolas Negras: Mulhers Livres de Cor no Distrito Diamantino," in *Diálogos oceânicos: Minas Gerais e as novas abordagens para uma história do Império Ultramarino Português*, ed. Júnia Ferreira Furtado (Belo Horizonte: Universidade Federal de

Minas Gerais, 2001); Laird W. Bergad, *Slavery and the Demographic and Economic History of Minas Gerais, Brazil, 1720–1888* (Cambridge: Cambridge University Press, 1999); Eduardo França Paiva, "Bateias, carumbés, tabuleiros: Mineração africana e mestiçagem no Novo Mundo," in *O trabalho mestiço: Maneiras de pensar e formas de viver, séculos XVI a XIX*, ed. Eduardo França Paiva and Carla Maria Junho Anastasia (São Paulo: Annablume, 2002), 81–121. In Spanish America, by contrast, we have ample evidence of both Indigenous and enslaved African women active in colonial mining operations beginning in the early sixteenth century, despite a tendency in the sources to erase their presence. See, for example, Allison M. Bigelow, *Mining Language: Racial Thinking, Indigenous Knowledge, and Colonial Metallurgy in the Early Modern Iberian World* (Chapel Hill: University of North Carolina Press, 2020), esp. 45–49.

30. Langfur, *Forbidden Lands*, 93, 106–18, 158–59.

31. Jeannette Graulau, "Peasant Mining Production as a Development Strategy: The Case of Women in Gold Mining in the Brazilian Amazon," *Revista Europea de Estudios Latinoamericanos y Del Caribe* 71 (2001): 71–106; Francisco Freire da Silva and Marlene Rauber, "Memórias, práticas e degradações garimpeiras em Alta Floresta, MT [Mato Grosso]," *Revista Eletrônica das Faculdades de Alta Floresta* 7, no. 2 (2018), http://refaf.com.br/index.php/refaf/article/view/279 (accessed February 9, 2020); Ana Aranha, "Escravos do ouro," *Repórter Brasil* (2018), https://reporterbrasil.org.br/2018/08/resgate-trabalho-escravo-garimpo-ouro-para/ (accessed February 9, 2020).

32. Belmiro Luiz Nascimento, interview by author, along the Ribeirão do Guinda (Guinda Creek), Diamantina, Minas Gerais, July 24, 2014.

33. Paiva, "Bateias."

34. Couto, *Memoria sobre as minas*, 50–51.

35. Couto, *Memoria sobre as minas*, 51. For a rare instance when Couto mentioned the expedition's enslaved participants, see p. 62. For the chaplain, see Carlos José da Silva, Relação da Despeza paga pertencente a expedição feita nos Certões dos Rios Abaeté e Andayá na exploração de Diamantes e mais haveres, [Vila Rica], ca. 6 Feb. 1802, AHU, Minas Gerais, cx. 161, doc. 23.

36. Couto, *Memoria sobre as minas*, 51n26, emphasis in original.

37. Couto, *Memoria sobre as minas*, 53–54. Indaiá was spelled Andaiá in the memorial.

38. Silva, "An Account," 60.

39. Couto, *Memoria sobre as minas*, 57–58.

40. Couto, *Memoria sobre as minas*, 60.

41. Couto, *Memoria sobre as minas*, 60.

42. Couto, *Memoria sobre as minas*, 61.

43. Bergad, *Slavery*, 4–5; Melânia Silva de Aguiar, "A literatura do Setecentos em Minas Gerais: O Arcadismo," in *História de Minas Gerais: As Minas setecentistas*, ed. Mari Efigênia Lage de Resende and Luiz Carlos Villalta (Belo Horizonte: Autêntica, 2007), vol. 1, 294–97.

44. Roberta Giannubilo Stumpf, *Filhos das Minas, americanos e portugueses: Identidades coletivas na capitania das Minas Gerais (1763–1792)* (São Paulo: Hucitec, 2010), 144, 150–51. Also see Furtado, introduction to Couto, *Memória sobre a Capitania*.

45. Couto, *Memoria sobre as minas*, 61–62.

46. See Couto, *Memoria sobre as minas*, 139; Varela, Lopes, and Fonseca, "Naturalista e homem público," 219–20; Silva, *O desvendar do grande livro*, 87–89.

47. Couto, Memoria sobre as minas . . . , AHU, Códices (1548–1821) e (1671–1833), cód. 1819, 119–29. This copy of the original MS, in contrast to published versions, clarifies Couto's organization of this material on the handwritten page, which I have replicated here.

48. For the English terms used to describe these rocks and minerals near the turn of the nineteenth century, see John Hill, *Fossils Arranged According to Their Obvious Characters; with Their History and Description; Under the Articles of Form, Hardness, Weight, Surface, Colour, and Qualities; the Place of Their Production, Their Uses, and Distinctive English, and Classical Latin Names* (London: R. Baldwin, 1771); Richard Pulteney, *A General View of the Writings of Linnaeus* (London: T. Payne and B. White, 1781); Carl Linnaeus, *A General System of Nature: Through the Three Grand Kingdoms of Animals, Vegetables, and Minerals*, trans. William Turton, vol. 7 (London: Lackington, Allen, 1806). For the erroneous assumptions underlying Linnaeus's mineral classification scheme, see Stephen Jay Gould, "Linnaeus's Luck?," *Natural History* 109, no. 7 (2000).

49. Couto, *Memoria sobre as minas*, 63–65.

50. Couto, *Memoria sobre as minas*, 65–66.

51. Aires da Mata Machado Filho, *O negro e o garimpo em Minas Gerais* (Belo Horizonte: Itatiaia, 1985), 79.

52. Couto, *Memoria sobre as minas*, 131.

53. Couto, *Memoria sobre as minas*, 100, 103.

54. Termo (official pronouncement) of Board of Royal Finance, Vila Rica, 19 Nov. 1800, AHU, Minas Gerais, cx. 161, doc. 23. Established by Pombal in an attempt to rationalize the imperial administration, colonial boards of finance were emblematic of the drive to centralize the Portuguese transatlantic state, curbing the patrimonial power of captaincy governors by bureaucratizing the management of financial affairs. Lorena's influence at this meeting demonstrates the limits of this effort. On the creation and function of these boards, see Kenneth R. Maxwell,

*Conflicts and Conspiracies: Brazil and Portugal, 1750–1808* (Cambridge: Cambridge University Press, 1973), 44–45, 108–10.

55. Royal notice (*aviso*) to Viceroy, Queluz Palace, Lisbon, 19 June 1802, AHU, Minas Gerais, cx. 165, doc. 58.

56. Governor to Secretary of State, Vila Rica, 6 Feb. 1802, AHU, Minas Gerais, cx. 161, doc. 23.

57. Beltrão to Fonseca, Sabará, 28 Sept. 1801, AHU, Minas Gerais, cx. 158, doc. 22.

58. Governor to Secretary of State, Vila Rica, 6 Feb. 1802, AHU, Minas Gerais, cx. 161, doc. 23. On the indeterminacy of the captaincy border, see Francisco Antônio de Salles, "Questões de limites entre os estados de Minas e Goyaz," *RAPM* 9, no. 2 (1904): 795–826.

59. Beltrão to Fonseca, Sabará, 28 Sept. 1801, AHU, Minas Gerais, cx. 158, doc. 22.

60. For an example of such a reward received by a soldier, see Petition of José Rodrigues Neofito to Prince Regent, after 8 Jan. 1802, AHU, Minas Gerais, cx. 161, doc. 3. Also see John Mawe, *Travels in the Interior of Brazil, Particularly in the Gold and Diamond Districts of That Country* (London: Longman, 1812), 138.

61. Beltrão to Fonseca, Sabará, 28 Sept. 1801, AHU, Minas Gerais, cx. 158, doc. 22. Beltrão tallied the number of soldiers at twenty-two, unlike Couto who wrote that about thirty accompanied the mission.

62. Beltrão to Fonseca, Sabará, 28 Sept. 1801, AHU, Minas Gerais, cx. 158, doc. 22. For the purchase of the enslaved man's freedom, which cost the state 150 mil-reis, see Carlos José da Silva, Relação da Despeza paga pertencente a expedição feita nos Certões dos Rios Abaeté e Andayá na exploração de Diamantes e mais haveres, [Vila Rica], ca. 6 Feb. 1802, AHU, Minas Gerais, cx. 161, doc. 23.

63. Beltrão to Fonseca, Sabará, 28 Sept. 1801, AHU, Minas Gerais, cx. 158, doc. 22. Beltrão concurred with the official accounting of the total weight of the diamonds extracted at just over 5.5 oitavas (96.3 ct).

64. Carlos José da Silva, Relação da Despeza paga pertencente a expedição feita nos Certões dos Rios Abaeté e Andayá na exploração de Diamantes e mais haveres, [Vila Rica], ca. 6 Feb. 1802, AHU, Minas Gerais, cx. 161, doc. 23.

65. Beltrão to Fonseca, Sabará, 28 Sept. 1801, AHU, Minas Gerais, cx. 158, doc. 22.

66. Beltrão to Fonseca, Sabará, 28 Sept. 1801, AHU, Minas Gerais, cx. 158, doc. 22. For a published facsimile of the map, see José Vieira Couto, "Carta da Nova Lorena Diamantina (1801)," in *Cartografia da conquista do território das Minas*, ed. Antônio Gilberto Costa (Belo Horizonte: Universidade Federal de Minas

Gerais, 2004), 216. The map's artist is identified as C. R. X. D. Villas Boas. A more skillful artist, C. L. Miranda, drew and painted another version, also in 1801, accessible as digitized from the AHU by way of the BNRJ's Rede Memória project. See http://bdlb.bn.gov.br/redeMemoria/handle/20.500.12156.2/301476.

67. Beltrão to Fonseca, Sabará, 28 Sept. 1801, AHU, Minas Gerais, cx. 158, doc. 22.

68. Couto, "Carta da Nova Lorena Diamantina (1801)," 216; Couto, *Memoria sobre as minas*, 113–14.

69. Furtado, "Enlightenment Science," 209; Faria and Filgueiras, "A busca por chumbo," 114.

70. Governor to Secretary of State, Vila Rica, 6 Feb. 1802, AHU, Minas Gerais, cx. 161, doc. 23.

71. Beltrão to Fonseca, Sabará, 28 Sept. 1801, AHU, Minas Gerais, cx. 158, doc. 22; Couto, *Memoria sobre as minas*, 127.

72. Wilhelm Ludwig von Eschwege, *Brasil, Novo Mundo*, trans. Domício de Figueiredo Murta (Belo Horizonte: Fundação João Pinheiro, 1996), 153.

73. Governor to Secretary of State, Vila Rica, 15 Oct. 1808, in *RAPM* 11, no. 1 (1906): 318–19. For a report on receipts and expenditures, see Governor to João de Almeida Melo e Castro, Vila Rica, 26 May 1809, AHU, Minas Gerais, cx. 187, doc. 38. For the governor's opinion of Couto, see Governor to Secretary of War, Vila Rica, 21 June 1808, in *RAPM* 11, no. 1 (1906): 316–17.

74. Mawe, *Travels in the Interior of Brazil*, 238. Shortly before Mawe's visit, a stone weighing just over three oitavas (52.5 carats) was extracted from the region, in this case not by garimpeiros but by the state-run mining operation. The governor was so impressed, he made a crude drawing of the gem and speculated more such stones were to be found at the same site. Governor to Count of Galveias, Vila Rica, 18 Jan. 1809, AHU, Minas Gerais, cx. 187, doc. 30, with appended drawing. The German naturalist Wilhelm Ludwig von Eschwege did visit the remote region more than once, issuing an unpublished report on its tree species. Eschwege, Discripção florestal de 158 differentes Arvores que crescem no Certão do Abaeté juntamente com huma colecção de madeiras das mesmas offerecidas ao Real Muzeo do Rio de Janeiro no anno de 1819, [Rio de Janeiro, 1819], BACL, Série Azul, 1534.

75. See, for example, Antonio Olyntho dos Santos Pires, "Viagem aos terrenos diamantiferos do Abaeté," *Annaes da Escola de Minas de Ouro Preto* 4 (1885): 107–8; Wolney Garcia, "Nas águas do Indaiá uma história de ambição e ódio," Centroeste Urgente, www.centroesteurgente.com.br/centro-oeste-mineiro/nas-aguas-do-indaia-uma-historia-de-amibicoes-e-muito-odio/ (accessed February 5, 2020).

76. Pires, "Viagem aos terrenos diamantiferos," 107.

77. See entries under "Abaeté Brilliant Diamond" (144 ct), "Abaeté Diamond" (238 ct), "Abaeté Rose Diamond" (118 ct), "Cedro do Abaeté" (194 ct), "Nova Estrela do Sul Diamond" (140 ct), "Tiros I Diamond," (354 ct), "Tiros II Diamond," (198 ct), "Tiros III Diamond," (182 ct), "Tiros IV Diamond," (173 ct), and "Tiros Lilac Diamond" (12 ct) in Mohsen Manutchehr-Danai, *Dictionary of Gems and Gemology* (Berlin: Springer, 2000), 1, 78, 335, 473.

78. Couto, *Memoria sobre as minas*, 130–32.

79. Furtado, "Enlightenment Science," 205.

80. Silva, *O desvendar do grande livro*, 30, 34.

81. Daniel Roche, "Natural History in the Academies," in *Cultures of Natural History*, ed. N. Jardine, J. A. Secord, and E. C. Spary (Cambridge: Cambridge University Press, 1996), 133.

## Chapter 8

1. In the early nineteenth century, east of the border separating Minas Gerais from Bahia, where the Jequitinhonha River becomes navigable along the coastal plain, the river was—and often still is—called the Rio Grande do Belmonte or simply the Rio Grande.

2. For preliminary considerations of some of the issues covered in this chapter, see Hal Langfur, "Cannibalism and the Body Politic: Independent Indians in the Era of Brazilian Independence," *Ethnohistory* 65, no. 4 (2018): 549–73; Hal Langfur, "Elite Ethnography and Indian Eradication: Confronting the Cannibal in Early Nineteenth-Century Brazil," in *Contesting Knowledge: Museums and Indigenous Perspectives*, ed. Susan Sleeper-Smith (Lincoln: University of Nebraska Press, 2009), 15–44.

3. Referring to Wied and others from the territory now comprising modern Germany as German, I follow the convention of scholars who do so because these individuals wrote in German.

4. For a sampling of the extensive scholarship on these northern European travelers, see Alicia V. Tjarks, "Brazil: Travel and Description, 1800–1899; A Selected Bibliography," *Revista de Historia de América* 83 (January–June 1977); Paulo Berger, *Bibliografia do Rio de Janeiro de viajantes e autores estrangeiros, 1531–1900*, 2nd ed. (Rio de Janeiro: SEEC-RJ, 1980); Regina Horta Duarte, "Facing the Forest: European Travellers Crossing the Mucuri River Valley, Brazil, in the Nineteenth Century," *Environment and History* 10, no. 1 (2004); Karen Macknow Lisboa, *A nova Atlântica de Spix e Martius: Natureza e civilização no viagem pelo Brasil (1817–1820)* (São Paulo: Hucitec, 1997); Ângela Domingues, "O Brasil nos relatos de viajantes ingleses do século XVIII: Produção de discursos sobre o

Novo Mundo," *Revista Brasileira de História* 28, no. 55 (2008); David M. Knight, "Travels and Science in Brazil," *História, Ciências, Saúde-Manguinhos* supplement, 8 (2001); Lorelai Kury, "Viajantes-naturalistas no Brasil oitocentista: Experiência, relato e imagem," *História, Ciências, Saúde-Manguinhos* supplement, 8 (2001); Ana Luisa Fayet Sallas, "Narrativas e imagens dos viajantes alemães no Brasil do século XIX: A construção do imaginário sobre os povos indígenas, a história e a nação," *História, Ciências, Saúde-Manguinhos* 17, no. 2 (2010). For brief biographies and a helpful chronology of European explorers, naturalists, and adventurers in Brazil, see John Hemming, *Amazon Frontier: The Defeat of the Brazilian Indians* (Cambridge, MA: Harvard University Press, 1987), 483–511. On the exclusion of women from their ranks, see Londa Schiebinger, "Gender and Natural History," in *Cultures of Natural History*, ed. N. Jardine, J. A. Secord, and E. C. Spary (Cambridge: Cambridge University Press, 1996), 163–64.

5. Knight, "Travels and Science," 814; Dauril Alden, *Royal Government in Colonial Brazil with Special Reference to the Administration of the Marquis of Lavradio, Viceroy, 1769–1779* (Berkeley: University of California Press, 1968), 409–10.

6. An extensive historiography explores these changes. Excellent starting points include Kirsten Schultz, *Tropical Versailles: Empire, Monarchy, and the Portuguese Royal Court in Rio de Janeiro, 1808–1821* (New York: Routledge, 2001); Luís Valente de Oliveira and Rubens Ricupero, eds., *A abertura dos portos* (São Paulo: Senac, 2007); Gabriel Paquette, *Imperial Portugal in the Age of Atlantic Revolutions: The Luso-Brazilian World, c. 1770–1850* (Cambridge: Cambridge University Press, 2013), chap. 2.

7. Duarte, "Facing the Forest," 35–37; Jean M. C. França, "A construção de um público," *Hipólito José da Costa e o Correio Braziliense* 30, vol. 1 (2002): 568–69; Warren Dean, *With Broadax and Firebrand: The Destruction of the Brazilian Atlantic Forest* (Berkeley: University of California Press, 1995), 117, 124, original italics.

8. For a similar critique, see Ângela Domingues, "Notícias do Brasil colonial: A imprensa científica e política ao servíco das elites (Portugal, Brasil e Inglaterra)," in *Monarcas, ministros e cientistas: Mecanismos de poder, governação e informação no Brasil colonial*, ed. Ângela Domingues (Lisbon: CHAM/FCSH/UNL and Universidade dos Açores, 2012), 150–78.

9. The principality of Wied-Neuwied was mediatized to an expanding Prussia in 1806. Scholarship on Wied that proved particularly useful includes Christina R. da Costa, "O Príncipe Maximiliano de Wied-Neuwied e sua Viagem ao Brasil (1815–1817)" (master's thesis, Universidade de São Paulo, 2008); Duarte, "Facing the Forest."; Regina Horta Duarte, "Olhares estrangeiros: Viajantes no vale do rio Mucuri," *Revista Brasileira de História* 22, no. 44 (2002); P. L. R. Moraes,

"The Brazilian Herbarium of Maximilian, Prince of Wied," *Neodiversity* 4 (2009); Sallas, "Narrativas e imagens," which focuses on the iconography that illustrated his work; Paul Schach, "Maximilian, Prince of Wied (1782–1867): Reconsidered," *Great Plains Quarterly* 14, no. 1 (1994); Ângela Domingues, "O Brasil de Maximiliano de Wied-Neuwied," *Oceanos* 24, no. (1995). For Wied's requests to his former professors for help in revising his manuscript, see Wied to H. L. Brönner, Neuwied, 10 July 1818, vault box Ayer MS 979, Newberry Library, including anonymous English translation. On Blumenbach, including his influence on Wied's notions of racial difference, see Nicolaas Rupke and Gerhard Lauer, eds., *Johann Friedrich Blumenbach: Race and Natural History, 1750–1850* (New York: Taylor and Francis, 2019); Ernst Pijning, "O ambiente científico da época e a viagem ao Brasil do príncipe alemão Maximiliano de Wied-Neuwied," *Oceanos* 24, no. (1995): 28; Sara Eigen and Mark Larrimore, eds., *The German Invention of Race* (Albany: State University of New York Press, 2006), chaps. 3 and 5.

10. Michael G. Noll, "Prince Maximilian's *Other* Worlds," *Pennsylvania Geographer* 43, no. 1 (2005): 67. Important contributions concerning the eastern forests and their Indigenous inhabitants made by other traveling northern European naturalists during the final years of colonial rule include Auguste de Saint-Hilaire, *Viagem ao Espírito Santo e Rio Doce*, trans. Milton Amado (Belo Horizonte: Itatiaia, 1974); Auguste de Saint-Hilaire, *Viagem pelas províncias do Rio de Janeiro e Minas Gerais*, trans. Vivaldi Moreira (Belo Horizonte: Itatiaia, 1975); G. W. Freireyss, "Viagens a varias tribus de selvagens na capitania de Minas Geraes . . ." *Revista do Instituto Histórico e Geográfico de São Paulo* 6 (1900–1901); G. W. Freireyss, "Viagem ao interior do Brazil nos annos de 1814–1815," *Revista do Instituto Histórico e Geográfico de São Paulo* 11 (1907); John Mawe, *Travels in the Interior of Brazil, Particularly in the Gold and Diamond Districts of That Country* (London: Longman, 1812); Johann B. von Spix and Karl F. P. von Martius, *Reise in Brasilien auf befehl Sr. Majestät Maximilian Joseph I., königs von Baiern, in den jahren 1817 bis 1820 gemacht und beschrieben*, 3 vols. (Munich: M. Lindauer, 1823). Like Wied, Spix and Martius saw their work quickly appear in English in a truncated edition. Johann Baptist von Spix and Karl F. P. von Martius, *Travels in Brazil, in the Years 1817–1820: Undertaken by Command of His Majesty the King of Bavaria*, trans. H. E. Lloyd (London: Longman, Hurst, Rees, Orme, Brown, and Green, 1824).

11. Maximilian A. P. Wied-Neuwied, *Travels in Brazil in the Years 1815, 1816, 1817* (London: Henry Colburn, 1820), 3. This English translation included only the first volume of the German original, thus it does not contain, for instance, Wied's pathbreaking ethnographic treatise on the Botocudo. The most recent Portuguese translation, also cited in this and the following chapter, provides access to the second volume for those who do not read German.

12. Wied-Neuwied, *Travels in Brazil*, 35–36. Also see Cerue K. Diggs, "Brazil after Humboldt: Triangular Perceptions and the Colonial Gaze in Nineteenth-Century German Travel Narratives" (PhD diss., University of Maryland, 2008); Moraes, "Brazilian Herbarium," 21; Schach, "Maximilian, Prince of Wied," 10–11; Domingues, "O Brasil de Maximiliano," 45.

13. Carlos Oberacker Jr., "Viajantes, naturalistas e artistas estrangeiros," in *História geral da civilização brasileira*, ed. Sérgio Buarque de Holanda (São Paulo: Difel, 1985), tomo 2, vol. 3: 121–22; Yuko Miki, *Frontiers of Citizenship: A Black and Indigenous History of Postcolonial Brazil* (Cambridge: Cambridge University Press, 2018), 37–38. On Francisco, see Wied-Neuwied, *Travels in Brazil*, 41, 92, 110.

14. Wied-Neuwied, *Travels in Brazil*, 35–36; Moraes, "Brazilian Herbarium," 21.

15. Wied-Neuwied, *Travels in Brazil*, 108–26 (Coroado, Coropó, and Puri), 288–326 (Botocudo), quoting 26; Maximilian A. P. Wied-Neuwied, *Viagem ao Brasil*, trans. Edgar Süssekind de Mendonça and Flávio Poppe de Figueiredo (Belo Horizonte: Itatiaia, 1989), 429–38 (Kamacã). Also see Costa, "O Príncipe Maximiliano," 54.

16. Wied-Neuwied, *Travels in Brazil*, 146, 169–70.

17. Diggs, "Brazil after Humboldt," 259, 263–64, 268; Paul Smethurst, *Travel Writing and the Natural World, 1768–1840* (London: Palgrave Macmillan, 2012), 55–56, 98; Mary Louise Pratt, *Imperial Eyes: Travel Writing and Transculturation* (London: Routledge, 1992), 7. For the application of the anticonquest concept to Wied's later travels in North America, see Renae W. Dearhouse, "Fictionalizing the Indigenous in German Travel Literature (1772–1834): The Expeditions of Chamisso, Forster, Humboldt, and Maximilian" (PhD diss., Stanford University, 2007), 2. On the Black Legend, see Boaventura de Sousa Santos, "Between Prospero and Caliban: Colonialism, Postcolonialism, and Inter-Identity," *Luso-Brazilian Review* 39, no. 2 (2002): 21–24.

18. Wied-Neuwied, *Travels in Brazil*, 171; Wied-Neuwied, *Viagem ao Brasil*, 467–71.

19. See, for example, Barman, *Brazil*, 46; Maria de Fátima Silva Gouvêa, "Poder político e administração na formação do complexo atlântico português," in *O Antigo Regime nos trópicos: A dinâmica imperial portuguesa, séculos XVI–XVIII*, ed. João Fragoso, Maria Fernanda Bicalho, and Maria de Fátima Gouvêa (Rio de Janeiro: Civilização Brasileira, 2001), 314.

20. Hal Langfur, *The Forbidden Lands: Colonial Identity, Frontier Violence, and the Persistence of Brazil's Eastern Indians, 1750–1830* (Stanford, CA: Stanford University Press, 2006), esp. chap 7; Manuela Carneiro da Cunha, "Pensar os índios: Apontamentos sobre José Bonifácio," in *Antropologia do Brasil: Mito, história, etnicidade* (São Paulo: Brasiliense/EDUSP, 1986), 169, quoted. Other

contributions to the history of Brazil's eastern Indians during this period include Judy Bieber, "Mediation through Militarization: Indigenous Soldiers and Transcultural Middlemen of the Rio Doce Divisions, Minas Gerais, Brazil, 1808–1850," *The Americas* 71, no. 2 (2014); Maria Hilda Baqueiro Paraíso, *O tempo da dor e do trabalho: A conquista dos territórios indígenas nos sertões do leste* (Salvador: EDUFBA, 2014); Maria Leônia Chaves de Resende, "Gentios brasílicos: Índios coloniais em Minas Gerais setecentista" (PhD diss., Universidade de Campinas, 2003); Haruf Salmen Espindola, *Sertão do Rio Doce* (Governador Valadares: Univale, 2005); Adriano Toledo Paiva, *Os indígenas e os processos de conquista dos sertões de Minas Gerais (1767–1813)* (Belo Horizonte: Argumentum, 2010).

21. "Carta Régia (royal edict) ao Governador e Capitão General da capitania de Minas Gerais sobre a guerra aos Indios Botecudos," 13 May 1808, in Manuela Carneiro da Cunha, ed., *Legislação indigenista no século XIX: Uma compilação (1808–1889)* (São Paulo: Universidade de São Paulo,1992), 57–60.

22. Langfur, *Forbidden Lands*, esp. chap. 1, 262–72; Duarte, "Facing the Forest," 34–36. On the frequent invocation in the sixteenth and seventeenth centuries of "just wars" against the Indians of Portuguese America and their early link to cannibalism, see Beatriz Perrone-Moisés, "Índios livres e índios escravos: Os princípios da legislação indigenista do período colonial (séculos XVI a XVIII)," in *História dos índios no Brasil*, ed. Manuela Carneiro da Cunha (São Paulo: Companhia das Letras, FAPESP/SMC, 1992); Alida C. Metcalf, *Go-Betweens and the Colonization of Brazil, 1500–1600* (Austin: University of Texas Press, 2006), 179–80. See also Mara Loveman, "The Modern State and the Primitive Accumulation of Symbolic Power," *American Journal of Sociology* 110, no. 6 (2005); Mara Loveman, "Blinded Like a State: The Revolt against Civil Registration in Nineteenth-Century Brazil," *Comparative Studies in Society and History* 49, no. 1 (2007).

23. "Carta Régia," 13 May 1808, in Cunha, *Legislação indigenista*, 57–60. On the Botocudo war, see Langfur, *Forbidden Lands*, chap. 8; Hemming, *Amazon Frontier*, 92–93, 99–100; Maria Hilda B. Paraíso, "Os Botocudos e sua trajetória histórica," in *História dos índios no Brasil*, ed. Manuela Carneiro da Cunha (São Paulo: Companhia das Letras, FAPESP/SMC, 1992), 417–23; B. J. Barickman, "'Tame Indians,' 'Wild Heathens,' and Settlers in Southern Bahia in the Late Eighteenth and Early Nineteenth Centuries," *The Americas* 51, no. 3 (1995): 359–65. On the enslavement of Botocudo captives, see Miki, *Frontiers of Citizenship*, 52–60.

24. War Minister to Governor, Rio, 4 Aug. 1808, AHEx, Livros da Capitania, Minas Gerais, 1808–1811, cód. I-1, 1, 34, fol. 23v.

25. Langfur, *Forbidden Lands*, esp. chap. 5.

26. Diogo Pereira Ribeiro de Vasconcelos, *Breve descrição geográfica, física e política da Capitania de Minas Gerais* (Belo Horizonte: Fundação João Pinheiro,

1994), 155n24. Also see Barickman, "Tame Indians," 360n98; Paraíso, "Os Botocudos e sua trajetória histórica," 416.

27. Governor to Antônio da Silva Brandão, Vila Rica, 10 Feb. 1802, APM, SC, cód. 277, fol. 103v; Governor to Luís Pinto de Sousa Coutinho, Vila Rica, 17 Apr. 1801, APM, SC, cód. 276, fols. 82v–83.

28. José Vieira Couto, *Memória sobre a Capitania das Minas Gerais; seu território, clima e produções metálicas* (Belo Horizonte: Fundação João Pinheiro, 1994), 53. For other memorialists who shared Couto's views, see Jozé Eloi Ottoni, "Memória sobre o estado actual da Capitania de Minas Gerais," *ABNRJ* 30 (1908): 313; Vasconcelos, *Breve descrição*, 144–49, 157.

29. Couto, *Memória sobre a Capitania*, 80.

30. Vasconcelos, *Breve descrição*, 144–49.

31. For views expressed in Lisbon, Espírito Santo, and Bahia, see Luís de Vasconcelos e Sousa to Junta da Fazenda of Minas Gerais, [Lisbon], 16 Jan. 1807, ATC, ER, cód. 4074; Anon. to Crown, Discursos sobre a decadencia em que se acha a nosa America relativos aos seos estabalecimentos e comerçio, [n.p., second half of 18th c.], ANTT, Papéis do Brasil, maço 78, nos. 14, 18; Anon. to Queen, Considerações sobre o estado dos sertões brasileiros, [n.p., end of 18th c.], ANTT, Papéis do Brasil, maço 78, no. 22; [Governor of Espírito Santo to Governor of Minas Gerais, Quartel da Vitória, 23 April 1800, AHU, Espírito Santo, cx. 6, doc. 438; Memoria sobre a abertura do Rio Doce, e sua navegação . . . e Extração das Madras ao Longo delle . . . , [1804?], APEB, SCP, maço 585.

32. Treasury Board (*junta da fazenda*), Report (*termo*) to Prince Regent on Botocudo hostilities, Vila Rica, 1 Feb. 1806, AHU, Minas Gerais, cx. 179, doc. 36. For the response to this report, see Luís de Vasconcelos e Sousa to Junta da Fazenda of Minas Gerais, [Lisbon], 16 Jan. 1807, ATC, ER, cód. 4074. See also the declaration of war, "Carta Régia," 13 May 1808, in Cunha, *Legislação indigenista*, 57–60.

33. The extent to which cannibalism in Brazil, the early modern Americas, and the non-Western world in general constituted a reality or a myth, propagated to justify conquest and enslavement, has long intrigued scholars in various disciplines. Notable contributions to this debate include W. Arens, *The Man-Eating Myth: Anthropology and Anthropophagy* (New York: Oxford University Press, 1979); Frank Lestringant, *Cannibals: The Discovery and Representation of the Cannibal from Columbus to Jules Verne*, trans. Rosemary Morris (Berkeley: University of California Press, 1997); Francis Barker, Peter Hulme, and Margaret Iversen, eds., *Cannibalism and the Colonial World* (New York: Cambridge University Press,1998). For research specific to Portuguese America, see Beth A. Conklin, *Consuming Grief: Compassionate Cannibalism in an Amazonian Society* (Austin: University of Texas

Press, 2001); Metcalf, *Go-Betweens*, esp. 47–48, 71, 177–80; Donald W. Forsyth, "Three Cheers for Hans Staden: The Case for Brazilian Cannibalism," *Ethnohistory* 32, no. 1 (1985).

34. Wied-Neuwied, *Viagem ao Brasil*, 313–15, 322.

35. Raimundo José da Cunha Matos, *Corografia histórica da província de Minas Gerais (1837)*, 2 vols. (São Paulo: Itatiaia, 1981), vol. 1, 194 and vol. 2, 168; Saint-Hilaire, *Viagem pelas províncias*, 271–72, 279, 284n428; Johann Baptiste von Spix and Carl Friedrich Phillipp von Martius, *Viagem pelo Brasil, 1817–1820*, trans. Lúcia Furquim Lahmeyer, 3 vols. (Belo Horizonte: Itatiaia, 1981), vol. 2, 56–60.

36. Except where otherwise indicated, the following account is recorded in José Pereira Freire de Moura, "Notícia e observaçoens sobre os Índios Botocudos que frequentão as margens do Rio Jequitinhonha, e se chamao Ambarés, ou Aymorés," Tocoiós, Dec. 1809, *RAPM* 2, no. 12 (1897): 28–31. See also Espindola, *Sertão do Rio Doce*, 133–35. On Moura's appointment and local prestige, see Bieber, "Mediation through Militarization," 236.

37. Town Council [Joaquim Joze Farneze, Antonio Felicianno da Costa, Manoel da Silva Pereira, Simeão Vas Mourão, and Antonio de Brito Teixeira] to Prince Regent, Vila do Príncipe, 9 Feb. 1810, BNRJ, SM, cód. 8, 1, 8, doc. 1. On military recruitment during the late colonial period and nineteenth century, see Maria Beatriz Nizza da Silva, *Sistema de casamento no Brasil colonial* (São Paulo: T. A. Queiroz, Universidade de São Paulo, 1984), 56–58, 189; Joan E. Meznar, "The Ranks of the Poor: Military Service and Social Differentiation in Northeast Brazil, 1830–1875," *Hispanic American Historical Review* 72, no. 3 (1992); Hendrik Kraay, "Reconsidering Recruitment in Imperial Brazil," *The Americas* 55, no. 1 (1998); Hendrik Kraay, *Race, State, and Armed Forces in Independence-Era Brazil, Bahia, 1790s–1840s* (Stanford, CA: Stanford University Press, 2001).

38. Moura identified this corporal by name in Moura to War Minister, Tocoiós, 5 Jan. 1810, *RAPM* 2, no. 1 (January–March 1897): 32.

39. Moura to War Minister, Tocoiós, 5 Jan. 1810, and José de Sousa Caldas, "Copia do roteiro para se procurar a Lagoa Dourada," n.d., *RAPM* 2, no. 1 (January–March, 1897): 31–34. For another account of Moura's search for the Golden Lagoon and of others attempting to follow such routes to legendary buried riches in northeastern Minas Gerais during the early nineteenth century, see Saint-Hilaire, *Viagem pelas províncias*, 264–65.

40. Francisco Eduardo de Andrade, *A invenção das Minas Gerais: Empresas, descobrimentos e entradas nos sertões do ouro da América portuguesa* (Belo Horizonte: Autêntica, 2008), 235.

41. Moura to War Minister, Tocoiós, and José de Sousa Caldas, "Copia do roteiro," *RAPM* 2, no. 1 (January–March, 1897): 31–34. See also Bieber, "Mediation through Militarization," 236.

42. Moura to War Minister, Tocoiós, and José de Sousa Caldas, "Copia do roteiro," *RAPM* 2, no. 1 (January–March, 1897): 31–34.

43. Moura to War Minister, Tocoiós; Moura, "Lista dos homens q. pedi de auxilio ao Com.ᵗᵉ do Districto de S. Domingos"; "Instruçoens q. se darão ao chefe da bandeira q. for procurar a Lagôa-Dourada," *RAPM* 2, no. 1 (January–March, 1897): 35–36.

44. Moura, "Notícia e observaçoens."

45. Izabel Missagia de Mattos, *Civilização e revolta: Os Botocudos e a catequese na Província de Minas* (Bauru: EDUSC, 2004), 156–67; Izabel Missagia de Mattos, "Considerações sobre política e parentesco entre os Botocudos (Borún) do século XIX: Uma interpretação da articulação de uma rede social e simbólica," *Revista de Antropologia da Universidade Federal de São Carlos* 5, no. 1 (2013): 82–96.

46. Langfur, *Forbidden Lands*, esp. chap. 7; Langfur, "Elite Ethnography"; Saint-Hilaire, *Viagem pelas províncias*, 250; Curt Nimuendajú, "Social Organization and Beliefs of the Botocudo of Eastern Brazil," *Southwestern Journal of Anthropology* 2 (1946).

47. See, for example, *Idade de Ouro do Brasil*, 17 December 1811, 2–3; 20 December 1811, 3. See also Barickman, "Tame Indians," 355; Espindola, *Sertão do Rio Doce*, 135–36.

48. Julião Fernandes Leão to Prince Regent, Quartel Geral de Palma, 1 Oct. 1811, BNRJ, SM, cód. 8, 1, 8, doc. 75; Saint-Hilaire, *Viagem pelas províncias*, 248–50, 264–65; Bieber, "Mediation through Militarization," 234–37.

49. Câmara to Prince Regent, Mariana, 30 Dec. 1801, AHU, Minas Gerais, cx. 160, doc. 82.

50. Manoel de Jesus Maria to Governor, Rio Pomba, 27 Aug. 1799, BNL, CP, cód. 634, fol. 573v; [Manoel Vieyra Nunes] to Campelo, Cuieté, [ca. May 1769], BNRJ, SM, CV, cód. 18, 2, 6, doc. 187. On ethnic soldiering, see R. Brian Ferguson and Neil L. Whitehead, "The Violent Edge of Empire," in *War in the Tribal Zone: Expanding States and Indigenous Warfare*, ed. R. Brian Ferguson and Neil L. Whitehead (Santa Fe: School of American Research Press, 1992), 21–23; Stuart B. Schwartz and Hal Langfur, "Tapanhuns, Negros da Terra, and Curibocas: Common Cause and Confrontation between Blacks and Indians in Colonial Brazil," in *Black and Red: African-Indigenous Relations in Colonial Latin America*, ed. Matthew Restall (Albuquerque: University of New Mexico Press, 2005).

51. Quartermaster Elesbão Lopes Duro described this ambush in Duro to Governor, Antônio Dias Abaixo, 15 July 1802, APM, SC, cód. 277, fols. 111v–12v. Governor Lorena offered his congratulations to Duro in Governor to Duro, Vila Rica, 13 Aug. 1802, APM, SC, cód. 277, fols. 112v–13; and to Duro's commanding

officer in Governor to Antônio da Silva Brandão, Vila Rica, 13 Aug. 1802, APM, SC, cód. 277, fol. 113.

52. Duro to Governor, Antônio Dias Abaixo, 15 July 1802, APM, SC, cód. 277, fols. 111v–12v.

53. Wied-Neuwied, *Travels in Brazil*, 226.

54. Carta Régia, 2 Dec. 1808, in Cunha, *Legislação indigenista*, 68–69; Espindola, *Sertão do Rio Doce*, 125–32.

55. Wied-Neuwied, *Travels in Brazil*, 170.

## Chapter 9

1. From this extensive body of scholarship in the disciplines of history, anthropology, geography, and literary, visual, science, and Indigenous studies, particularly applicable works include Edward W. Said, *Orientalism* (New York: Vintage Books, 1979); Mary Louise Pratt, *Imperial Eyes: Travel Writing and Transculturation* (London: Routledge, 1992); James Clifford, *Routes: Travel and Translation in the Late Twentieth Century* (Cambridge, MA: Harvard University Press, 1997); Paul Smethurst, *Travel Writing and the Natural World, 1768–1840* (London: Palgrave Macmillan, 2012); Harry Liebersohn, *Aristocratic Encounters: European Travelers and North American Indians* (Cambridge: Cambridge University Press, 2001), esp. part 3; Karen Macknow Lisboa, *A nova Atlântica de Spix e Martius: Natureza e civilização no viagem pelo Brasil (1817–1820)* (São Paulo: Hucitec, 1997); James Delbourgo and Nicholas Dew, eds., *Science and Empire in the Atlantic World* (New York: Routledge, 2008); N. Jardine, J. A. Secord, and E. C. Spary, *Cultures of Natural History* (Cambridge: Cambridge University Press, 1996); Daniela Bleichmar, *Visible Empire: Botanical Expeditions and Visual Culture in the Hispanic Enlightenment* (Chicago: University of Chicago Press, 2012); Margaret M. Bruchac, *Savage Kin: Indigenous Informants and American Anthropologists* (Tucson: University of Arizona Press, 2018); Renae W. Dearhouse, "Fictionalizing the Indigenous in German Travel Literature (1772–1834): The Expeditions of Chamisso, Forster, Humboldt, and Maximilian" (PhD diss., Stanford University, 2007).

2. Maximilian A. P. Wied-Neuwied, *Travels in Brazil in the Years 1815, 1816, 1817* (London: Henry Colburn, 1820), 204–5; Maximilian A. P. von Wied-Neuwied, *The North American Journals of Prince Maximilian of Wied*, trans. William J. Orr, Paul Schach, and Deiter Karch, 3 vols. (Norman: University of Oklahoma Press, 2008–12), vol. 1, 228.

3. Wied-Neuwied, *Travels in Brazil*, 279–88.

4. The French botanist Auguste de Saint-Hilaire proved more perceptive about these developments. See, for example, Auguste de Saint-Hilaire, *Viagem*

*pelas províncias do Rio de Janeiro e Minas Gerais*, trans. Vivaldi Moreira (Belo Horizonte: Itatiaia, 1975), 267n400, 274–75.

5. Izabel Missagia de Mattos, "Povos em movimento nos Sertões do Leste (Minas Gerais, 1750–1850)," *Nuevo Mundo Mundos Nuevos* (January 30, 2012), http://journals.openedition.org/nuevomundo/62637. On shipments from Minas Novas, see Wied-Neuwied, *Travels in Brazil*, 275. On conflicts between various groups in the surrounding region, as well as the peace "treaty" with the Botocudo secured by the governor along the Jequitinhonha three years before Wied's arrival, see also B. J. Barickman, "'Tame Indians,' 'Wild Heathens,' and Settlers in Southern Bahia in the Late Eighteenth and Early Nineteenth Centuries," *The Americas* 51, no. 3 (1995): 354–58; Wied-Neuwied, *Travels in Brazil*, 249–50, 275–77; Maximilian A. P. Wied-Neuwied, *Viagem ao Brasil*, trans. Edgar Süssekind de Mendonça and Flávio Poppe de Figueiredo (Belo Horizonte: Itatiaia, 1989), 310.

6. Wied-Neuwied, *Travels in Brazil*, 288–90.

7. Ibid., 181, 289.

8. Ibid., 290–97.

9. Francisco Bethencourt, *Racisms: From the Crusades to the Twentieth Century* (Princeton, NJ: Princeton University Press, 2013), chap. 15; Nicholas Jardine, "*Naturphilosophie* and the Kingdoms of Nature," in *Cultures of Natural History*, ed. N. Jardine, J. A. Secord, and E. C. Spary (Cambridge: Cambridge University Press, 1996).

10. Wied-Neuwied, *Travels in Brazil*, 290–97. For Captain June's Indigenous name, see Wied-Neuwied, *Viagem ao Brasil*, 311.

11. Wied-Neuwied, *Travels in Brazil*, 288, 309; Jurandyr Pires Ferreira, ed., *Enciclopédia dos municípios brasileiros*, 36 vols. (Rio de Janeiro: Institúto Brasileiro de Geografia e Estatística,1957–64), vol. 27, 114.

12. Wied-Neuwied, *Travels in Brazil*, 311–12; Wied-Neuwied, *Viagem ao Brasil*, 286–87.

13. Wied-Neuwied, *Travels in Brazil*, 323–26.

14. John Hemming, *Amazon Frontier: The Defeat of the Brazilian Indians* (Cambridge, MA: Harvard University Press, 1987), 469.

15. Years later, during his travels in North America, Wied would pursue his research under similar circumstances among the peoples of the Great Plains, where he was a "direct witness to forced Indigenous removal, qua genocide, as a result of fierce colonizing efforts." Dearhouse, "Fictionalizing the Indigenous," 16.

16. Bruchac, *Savage Kin*, 176.

17. Manuela Carneiro da Cunha, "Política indigenista no século XIX," in *História dos índios no Brasil* (São Paulo: Companhia das Letras, FAPESP/SMC,

1992), 134. On Blumenbach's skull collection, which became a museum, see Rudolph Wagner, "An Account of the Blumenbachian Museum," in *The Anthropological Treatises of Johann Friedrich Blumenbach* (London: Longman, 1865), 345–55, quoting 351. The original German edition of Wied's travel account featured the illustration of the Botocudo skull as the lead image of its second volume. The image was not included in the English translation. It appears before the index in the Portuguese translation. Later in the century, as anthropology became further established in Brazil, researchers would invoke the alleged small size of Botocudo crania as evidence of their biological inferiority and inaptitude for a modern, civilized existence. Yuko Miki, *Frontiers of Citizenship: A Black and Indigenous History of Postcolonial Brazil* (Cambridge: Cambridge University Press, 2018), 129–32.

18. Wied-Neuwied, *Viagem ao Brasil*, 283–326. For discussion of the skull and related comments about facial features and head shape, see 285–87, 324–25.

19. See, for example, Haruf Salmen Espindola, *Sertão do Rio Doce* (Governador Valadares: Univale, 2005), 139–40; Izabel Missagia de Mattos, "A vida do Borum Kuêk, a repatriação do crânio e o encontro indígena," in *Histórias indígenas: Memória, interculturalidade e cidadania na América Latina*, ed. Izabel Missagia de Mattos et al. (São Paulo: Humanitas, 2020), 64n10.

20. Wied-Neuwied, *Viagem ao Brasil*, 313.

21. Wied did not reveal the conditions under which Guack joined the expedition. His purchase of the Botocudo youth was discovered by an anthropologist who consulted the prince's manuscript diary in the 1970s. See Luís da Câmara Cascudo, *O Príncipe Maximiliano de Wied-Neuwied no Brasil, 1815/1817: Biografia e notas, com versões para o inglês e alemão* (Rio de Janeiro: Livraria Kosmos, 1977), 56–57; Mattos, "Histórias indígenas," esp. 63–66. In the original German, Wied spelled his Botocudo informant's name Quäck; in the English translation, Queck. I have opted for Guack, the spelling in the Portuguese translation, since this is the language of most of the scholarship about him, although even in Portuguese the spelling occasionally varies. Other studies discussing Guack include Christina R. da Costa, "O Príncipe Maximiliano de Wied-Neuwied e sua Viagem ao Brasil (1815–1817)" (master's thesis, Universidade de São Paulo, 2008), esp. chap. 3; Regina Horta Duarte, "Olhares estrangeiros: Viajantes no vale do rio Mucuri," *Revista Brasileira de História* 22, no. 44 (2002); Mattos, "Histórias indígenas," 61–94.

22. Wied-Neuwied, *Viagem ao Brasil*, 314.

23. Wied-Neuwied, *Travels in Brazil*, 138; Wied-Neuwied, *Viagem ao Brasil*, 314–15. For further discussion of alleged Botocudo cannibalism, see Hal Langfur, *The Forbidden Lands: Colonial Identity, Frontier Violence, and the Persistence of*

*Brazil's Eastern Indians, 1750–1830* (Stanford, CA: Stanford University Press, 2006), esp. 243–45.

24. Wied-Neuwied, *Travels in Brazil*, 299, 301, 317, 325.

25. Wied-Neuwied, *Viagem ao Brasil*, 309–23; Costa, "O Príncipe Maximiliano," 86–91.

26. Wied-Neuwied, *Viagem ao Brasil*, 284, 289–91, 293, 318.

27. Ibid., 500–509. Other scientific travelers who, following Wied's example, returned to Europe with Native Brazilians during this period include the Bavarian naturalists Johannes Baptist Spix and Carl Friedrich Philipp Martius, who brought two Indigenous children from Amazonia to Munich, and the Austrian botanist Johann Emanuel Pohl, who brought two Botocudos to Vienna. Maria Leônia Chaves de Resende and Klaus Schönitzer, "Do Novo ao Velho Mundo: Indígenas da Amazônia na Alemanha dos naturalistas Spix e Martius," *Anais de História de Além-Mar* 19 (2018): 204.

28. Dearhouse, "Fictionalizing the Indigenous," esp. 18, 33, 157–65. Also see Vine Deloria Jr., *Red Earth, White Lies: Native Americans and the Myth of Scientific Fact* (Golden, CO: Fulcrum, 1997).

29. Pratt, *Imperial Eyes*, 7, 136.

30. Wied-Neuwied, *Viagem ao Brasil*, 321–26. For a fascinating exploration of the supposed influence of climate, diet, and other environmental factors on skin color in Spanish America, see Rebecca Earle, "The Pleasures of Taxonomy: Casta Paintings, Classification, and Colonialism," *William and Mary Quarterly* 73, no. 3 (2016).

31. On monogenism, Wied cited John B. Sumner, *A Treatise on the Records of the Creation and on the Moral Attributes of the Creator . . .* 2nd ed., 2 vols. (London: J. Hatchard, 1818). Also see Johann F. Blumenbach, "Degeneration of the Species," in *Race and the Enlightenment: A Reader*, ed. Emmanuel C. Eze (Malden, MA: Blackwell, 1997), 79–90; Marvin Harris, *The Rise of Anthropological Theory: A History of Theories of Culture* (Lanham, MD: AltaMira, 2001), 84–85; Naomi Zack, *Philosophy of Science and Race* (New York: Routledge, 2002), 28–31; Aaron Sachs, *The Humboldt Current: Nineteenth-Century Exploration and the Roots of American Environmentalism* (New York: Penguin, 2006), 66–70, 242–43. On cultural relativism, Charles King, *Gods of the Upper Air: How a Circle of Renegade Anthropologists Reinvented Race, Sex, and Gender in the Twentieth Century* (New York: Doubleday, 2019).

32. Michael G. Noll, "Prince Maximilian's *Other* Worlds," *Pennsylvania Geographer* 43, no. 1 (2005): 76.

33. Wied-Neuwied, *Viagem ao Brasil*, 292–93, 315, 320.

34. Duarte, "Olhares estrangeiros," 274–76; Ana Luisa Fayet Sallas, "Narrativas e imagens dos viajantes alemães no Brasil do século XIX: A construção do imaginário sobre os povos indígenas, a história e a nação," *História, Ciências, Saúde-Manguinhos* 17, no. 2 (2010): 419–21.

35. Wied-Neuwied, *Viagem ao Brasil*, 308.

36. For the German and English editions, see Maximilian A. P. von Wied-Neuwied, *Reise nach Brasilien in den Jahren 1815 bis 1817*, 2 vols. (Frankfurt: H. L. Brönner, 1820–21); Wied-Neuwied, *Travels in Brazil*. The imprecise 1940 Portuguese edition, a summary more than a faithful translation, was thoroughly revised and republished in 1958. It has since been repeatedly reprinted. For material not included in the English edition, I have consulted Wied-Neuwied, *Viagem ao Brasil*. On the publication history of Wied's account, see Alicia V. Tjarks, "Brazil: Travel and Description, 1800–1899; A Selected Bibliography," *Revista de Historia de América* 83 (January–June 1977): 242–43; Cascudo, *O Príncipe Maximiliano*; Costa, "O Príncipe Maximiliano," 15–16.

37. Wied-Neuwied, *North American Journals*; Paul Schach, "Maximilian, Prince of Wied (1782–1867): Reconsidered," *Great Plains Quarterly* 14, no. 1 (1994).

38. "[Prince Maximilian]," *Repertory*, 23 June 1818; "[Prince Maximilian]," *Boston Commercial Gazette*, 1 September 1825; "Travels in Brazil," *Commercial Advertiser*, 8 July 1820.

39. Wied-Neuwied, *Travels in Brazil*, 2–4.

40. Carlos Oberacker Jr., "Viajantes, naturalistas e artistas estrangeiros," in *História geral da civilização brasileira*, ed. Sérgio Buarque de Holanda (São Paulo: Difel, 1985), tomo 2, vol. 3: 119.

41. P. L. R. Moraes, "The Brazilian Herbarium of Maximilian, Prince of Wied," *Neodiversity* 4 (2009): 19–20; Regina Horta Duarte, "Facing the Forest: European Travellers Crossing the Mucuri River Valley, Brazil, in the Nineteenth Century," *Environment and History* 10, no. 1 (2004): 33, 41; Duarte, "Olhares estrangeiros," 274–76; Noll, "Prince Maximilian's *Other* Worlds"; Cerue K. Diggs, "Brazil after Humboldt: Triangular Perceptions and the Colonial Gaze in Nineteenth-Century German Travel Narratives" (PhD diss., University of Maryland, 2008), 262. On mutual language instruction, see Wied-Neuwied, *Viagem ao Brasil*, 499. On Guack's remains, see Eduardo T. Girão, "200 anos depois, restos mortais do índio botocudo Kuêk voltam para casa," *Correio Braziliense* (9 May 2011), https://www.correiobraziliense.com.br/app/noticia/ciencia-e-saude/2011/05/09/interna_ciencia_saude,251331/200-anos-depois-restos-mortais-do-indio-botocudo-kuek-voltam-para-casa.shtml.

42. Wied-Neuwied, *Viagem ao Brasil*, 489–96, 517–18. The map follows the index in this Portuguese edition.

43. Ângela Domingues, "O Brasil de Maximiliano de Wied-Neuwied," *Oceanos* 24, no. (1995): 50; Moraes, "Brazilian Herbarium." For a list of Wied's scientific papers, see Costa, "O Príncipe Maximiliano," 15n42.

44. Quoted in Hemming, *Amazon Frontier*, 91. For the French naturalist's voyage along the upper Jequitinhonha River in the company of the army officer Julião Leão, see Saint-Hilaire, *Viagem pelas províncias*, chaps. 25–27.

45. Saint-Hilaire, *Viagem pelas províncias*, 257, 276.

46. Wied-Neuwied, *Viagem ao Brasil*, 313.

47. José Bonifácio de Andrada e Silva, Portaria [decree], Rio, 21 Feb. 1823, BNRJ, DB, C-174, 37, doc. 8; Minister of Finance, "Relação dos objectos que por Portaria da data desta expedida pela Secretaria d'Estado dos Negocios do Imperio á Secretaria de Estado dos Negocios da Fazenda se mandam apromptar para uso dos Indios da Provincia de Minas Geraes," Rio, 21 Feb. 1823, BNRJ, DB, C-174, 37, doc. 9.

48. Provisional Governing Board (*junta*) of Espírito Santo to José Joaquim Carneiro de Campos, Vitória, 13 Oct. 1823, BNRJ, DB, C-174, 37, doc. 10.

49. José Bonifácio de Andrada e Silva, "Apontamentos para a civilização dos índios bravos do Império do Brasil," in *O pensamento vivo de José Bonifácio* (São Paulo: Livraria Martins, 1961), 78–107, esp. 83. Legislation enacted in 1823 and 1824 created Indian directories and ordered directors to employ peaceful means to settle Indians into villages along the Doce River in Minas Gerais and Espírito Santo. See "Decisão 22," 20 Feb. 1823; "Decisão 85," 24 May 1823; "Decreto 31," 28 Jan. 1824, in Manuela Carneiro da Cunha, ed., *Legislação indigenista no século XIX: Uma compilação (1808–1889)* (São Paulo: Universidade de São Paulo, 1992), 111–14, 137. On the perfectibility of Brazil's Native populations and its implications for state policy, see Cunha, "Política indigenista no século XIX," 134, 137; Manuela Carneiro da Cunha, "Pensar os índios: Apontamentos sobre José Bonifácio," in *Antropologia do Brasil: Mito, história, etnicidade* (São Paulo: Brasiliense/EDUSP, 1986), 165–73. Also see Miki, *Frontiers of Citizenship*, 51–52.

50. Maria Leônia Chaves de Resende, "Gentios brasílicos: Índios coloniais em Minas Gerais setecentista" (PhD diss., Universidade de Campinas, 2003), 159–87; Ângelo Alves Carrara, ed., *Uma fronteira da capitania de Minas Gerais: A freguesia de São João Batista do Presídio em 1821* (Mariana: Universidade Federal de Ouro Preto, 1999), 108–9; Judy Bieber, "Mediation through Militarization: Indigenous Soldiers and Transcultural Middlemen of the Rio Doce Divisions, Minas Gerais, Brazil, 1808–1850," *The Americas* 71, no. 2 (2014).

51. A. H. Keane, "On the Botocudos," *Journal of the Anthropological Institute of Great Britain and Ireland* 13 (1884): 205, 207. The maps include, from early in the century, "A Map of the Table Land of Brazil," in John Luccock, *Notes on Rio*

*de Janeiro and the Southern Parts of Brazil; Taken during a Residence of Ten Years in That Country, from 1808 to 1818* (London: Samuel Leigh, 1820), between flyleaf and title page; Carlos Krauss, "Mappa Geral das Colonias S. Leopoldina, S. Izabel, e Rio Novo na Provincia do Espirito Santo," Rio, 1866, GMD, LC; and Carlos Krauss, "Mappa Geral da Provincia do Espirito-Santo relativo as Colonias e Vias de Communicação," Rio, 1866, GMD, LC. As their legends and notations indicate, Krauss's maps were designed to lure European immigrants to settle Brazil's eastern forests. Also see Hemming, *Amazon Frontier*, chap. 18; Izabel Missagia de Mattos, *Civilização e revolta: Os Botocudos e a catequese na Província de Minas* (Bauru: EDUSC, 2004); Maria Hilda Baqueiro Paraíso, *O tempo da dor e do trabalho: A conquista dos territórios indígenas nos sertões do leste* (Salvador: EDUFBA, 2014); Miki, *Frontiers of Citizenship*.

52. Espindola, *Sertão do Rio Doce*, 416, 421.

53. On the repatriation ceremony and the contemporary struggles of the Krenak, see Mattos, "Histórias indígenas"; Girão, "200 anos depois." On the mining disaster, see Clarissa Pains, "Desastre ambiental em Mariana afeta cultura dos índios krenaks," *O Globo* (31 October 2017), https://oglobo.globo.com/brasil/desastre-ambiental-em-mariana-afeta-cultura-dos-indios-krenaks-22012035.

54. André Strauss, et al, "The Cranial Morphology of the Botocudo Indians, Brazil," *American Journal of Physical Anthroplogy* 157 (2015): 214.

### Epilogue

1. Maximilian A. P. Wied-Neuwied, *Viagem ao Brasil*, trans. Edgar Süssekind de Mendonça and Flávio Poppe de Figueiredo (Belo Horizonte: Itatiaia, 1889), 343. The Brazilian naturalist Baltazar da Silva Lisboa confirmed and considered well-founded this hope for inland gold harbored by the inhabitants of southern Bahia. Baltasar da Silva Lisboa, *Memoria topografica e economica da commarca dos Ilheos* (Lisbon: Academia Real das Sciencias de Lisboa, 1823), 231.

2. Auguste de Saint-Hilaire, *Viagem pelas províncias do Rio de Janeiro e Minas Gerais*, trans. Vivaldi Moreira (Belo Horizonte: Itatiaia, 1975), 265n399.

3. John Mawe, *Travels in the Interior of Brazil, Particularly in the Gold and Diamond Districts of That Country* (London: Longman, 1812), 277–79.

4. Maximilian A. P. Wied-Neuwied, *Travels in Brazil in the Years 1815, 1816, 1817* (London: Henry Colburn, 1820), 4.

5. For a map of the earliest expeditions, see Maria Efigênia Lage de Resende, "Itinerários e interditos na territorialização das Geraes," in *História de Minas Gerais: As Minas setecentistas*, ed. Maria Efigênia Lage de Resende and Luiz Carlos Villalta (Belo Horizonte: Autêntica, 2007), vol. 1, 27.

6. Wied-Neuwied, *Travels*, 300; Wied-Neuwied, *Viagem*, 283.

7. Judy Bieber, *Power, Patronage, and Political Violence: State Building on a Brazilian Frontier, 1822–1889* (Lincoln: University of Nebraska Press, 1999), 7–9; Robert M. Levine, *Vale of Tears: Revisiting the Canudos Massacre in Northeastern Brazil, 1893–1897* (Berkeley: University of California Press, 1992), 44–49; David McCreery, *Frontier Goiás, 1822–1889* (Stanford, CA: Stanford University Press, 2006), 1–6; Walter D. Mignolo, *The Idea of Latin America* (Malden, MA: Blackwell, 2005), 58–59, 65.

8. C. R. Boxer, *The Golden Age of Brazil, 1695–1750: Growing Pains of a Colonial Society* (Berkeley: University of California Press, 1969), 60; Darcy P. Svisero, James E. Shigley, and Robert Weldon, "Brazilian Diamonds: A Historical and Recent Perspective," *Gems and Gemology* 53, no. 1 (2017): 8.

9. Luciano Raposo Figueiredo, "A corrupção no Brasil colônia," in *Corrupção: Ensaios e críticas*, ed. Leonardo Avritzer et al. (Belo Horizonte: Universidade Federal de Minas Gerais, 2008), 209–18; Erik Lars Myrup, *Power and Corruption in the Early Modern Portuguese World* (Baton Rouge: Louisiana State University Press, 2015); Ivana D. Parrela, *O teatro das desordens: Garimpo, contrabando e violência no sertão diamantino, 1768–1800* (São Paulo: Annablume, 2009), 86.

10. See, for example, David J. Weber, *Bárbaros: Spaniards and Their Savages in the Age of Enlightenment* (New Haven, CT: Yale University Press, 2005); Paul W. Mapp, *The Elusive West and the Contest for Empire, 1713–1763* (Chapel Hill: University of North Carolina Press, 2011); Daniel H. Usner Jr., *Indians, Settlers, and Slaves in a Frontier Exchange Economy: The Lower Mississippi Valley before 1783* (Chapel Hill: University of North Carolina Press, 1992); Richard White, *The Middle Ground: Indians, Empires, and Republics in the Great Lakes Region, 1650–1815* (Cambridge: Cambridge University Press, 1991).

11. See, for example, Carla M. J. Anastasia, *A geografia do crime: Violência nas Minas setecentistas* (Belo Horizonte: Universidade Federal de Minas Gerais, 2005), 12, 22–23, 99–104, 109; Célia Nonata da Silva, *Territórios de mando: Banditismo em Minas Gerais, século XVIII* (Belo Horizonte: Crisálida, 2007), 36–40, 253–55, 271; Marcia Amantino, *O mundo das feras: Os moradores do Sertão Oeste de Minas Gerais—século XVIII* (São Paulo: Annablume, 2008).

12. Contrast British India, where, as C. A. Bayly argues, "successful intelligence-gathering was a critical feature" of late eighteenth-century imperial domination and longevity beyond the early modern era. C. A. Bayly, *Empire and Information: Intelligence Gathering and Social Communication in India, 1780–1870* (Cambridge: Cambridge University Press, 1999), 365.

13. The historian of independence João Paulo G. Pimenta assesses the matter this way: "We know little or nothing about the political struggles taking place in inland regions, i.e. in those areas where the physical distance from the coast

and the main urban centers certainly implied very specific and particular dynamics in the shaping of political life in all of its sectors, and even less about the question of the implementation, in each part, of a new state apparatus and a new political and social order." João Paulo G. Pimenta, "The Independence of Brazil: A Review of the Recent Historiographic Production," *e-Journal of Portuguese History* 7, no. 1 (2009), http://scielo.pt/scielo.php?script=sci_arttext&pid=S1645-64322009000100006&nrm=iso.

14. For two excellent encapsulations of these developments, which continue to generate countless studies, see Roderick J. Barman, *Brazil*, chaps. 2–4; Jeremy Adelman, *Sovereignty and Revolution in the Iberian Atlantic* (Princeton, NJ: Princeton University Press, 2006), chaps. 6 and 8. For a concise contextualization of these events as part of the broader Latin American independence movements, see Richard Graham, *Independence in Latin America: Contrasts and Comparisons*, 3rd ed. (Austin: University of Texas Press, 2013).

15. Eric Hinderaker and Peter C. Mancall, *At the Edge of Empire: The Backcountry in British North America* (Baltimore: Johns Hopkins University Press, 2003), 5, 175; Patrick Griffin, *American Leviathan: Empire, Nation, and Revolutionary Frontier* (New York: Hill and Wang, 2007), 156–58; Alan Taylor, *The Divided Ground: Indians, Settlers, and the Northern Borderland of the American Revolution* (New York: Vintage, 2006), 97–99; White, *Middle Ground*, 378. Scholarly attention to the backcountry as an important component of the American Revolution is a relatively recent development, crystallizing over the past two decades.

16. Jaime E. Rodríguez O., *The Independence of Spanish America* (Cambridge: Cambridge University Press, 1998), 108, 115, 122 (quoted); John Lynch, *The Spanish American Revolutions, 1808–1826*, 2nd ed. (New York: Norton, 1986), 205–7.

17. Rodríguez O., *Independence*, 185–90; Marixa Lasso, "Race War and Nation in Caribbean Gran Colombia, Cartagena, 1810–1832," *American Historical Review* III, no. 2 (2006): 346; John Lynch, "Bolívar and the Caudillos," *Hispanic American Historical Review* 63, no. 1 (1983): 6–9, 18–21; Lynch, *Spanish American Revolutions*, 213–18; Juan Pablo Dabove, *Bandit Narratives in Latin America: From Villa to Chávez* (Pittsburgh: University of Pittsburgh Press, 2017), 48–51; Jane M. Rausch, *A Tropical Plains Frontier: The Llanos of Colombia, 1531–1831* (Albuquerque: University of New Mexico Press, 1984), chaps. 6–7. On the participation of armed slaves, see Ana Vergara, "Las armas a cambio de la libertad: Los esclavos en la guerra de independencia de Venezuela (1812–1835)," *Relaciones: Estudios de historia y sociedad* 32, no. 127 (2011).

18. For an overview, see Alan Taylor, *American Revolutions: A Continental History, 1750–1804* (New York: W. W. Norton, 2016), chap. 7. Also see Usner, *Indians*, 142–44; Kathleen DuVal, *The Native Ground: Indians and Colonists in the*

*Heart of the Continent* (Philadelphia: University of Pennsylvania Press, 2006), 151–58; Colin G. Calloway, *The American Revolution in Indian Country: Crisis and Diversity in Native American Communities* (Cambridge: Cambridge University Press, 1995).

19. See, for example, Weber, *Bárbaros*, 257–63; Jeffrey A. Erbig Jr. , *Where Caciques and Mapmakers Met: Border Making in Eighteenth-Century South America* (Chapel Hill: University of North Carolina Press, 2020), 158–61; Marcela Echeverri, *Indian and Slave Royalists in the Age of Revolution: Reform, Revolution, and Royalism in the Northern Andes, 1780–1825* (Cambridge: Cambridge University Press, 2016), chap. 5; David J. Weber, *The Spanish Frontier in North America* (New Haven, CT: Yale University Press, 1992), 296–301; Pekka Hämäläinen, *The Comanche Empire* (New Haven, CT: Yale University Press, 2008), 209 (quoted); Jane G. Landers, *Atlantic Creoles in the Age of Revolutions* (Cambridge, MA: Harvard University Press, 2010), chap. 5; Cynthia Radding, *Wandering Peoples: Colonialism, Ethnic Spaces, and Ecological Frontiers in Northwestern Mexico, 1700–1850* (Durham, NC: Duke University Press, 1997), 292–93; Brian DeLay, *War of a Thousand Deserts: Indian Raids and the U.S.-Mexican War* (New Haven, CT: Yale University Press, 2008), 15–16.

20. A possible exception was an uprising in 1824 along the lower Amazon River of allied Natives, free and enslaved Blacks, and mestiços, whose political objectives historians have found difficult to discern beyond a generalized anticolonial anger directed against regional elites. Elsewhere, Krahô and Apinaje warriors briefly joined together to fight royalist forces in Goiás. Mark Harris, *Rebellion on the Amazon: The Cabanagem, Race, and Popular Culture in the North of Brazil, 1798–1840* (Cambridge: Cambridge University Press, 2010), 189–95; Mary C. Karasch, *Before Brasília* (Albuquerque: University of New Mexico Press, 2016), 43.

21. Barman, *Brazil*, 88–91.

22. Edward W. Said, *Culture and Imperialism* (New York: Vintage Books, 1993), xiii.

23. Lauren A. Benton, *A Search for Sovereignty: Law and Geography in European Empires, 1400–1900* (New York: Cambridge University Press, 2010), esp. 1–5, 10–15, 279–83.

# BIBLIOGRAPHY

**Archives and Manuscript Collections**
Arquivo da Casa Setecentista de Mariana, Brazil (ACSM)
Arquivo Histórico do Exército, Rio de Janeiro (AHEx)
Arquivo Histórico Militar, Lisbon (AHM)
Arquivo Histórico do Museu Bocage, Lisbon (AHMB)
Arquivo Histórico do Museu de Ciência da Universidade de Lisboa (AHMCUL)
Arquivo Histórico Ultramarino, Lisbon (AHU)
    Cartografia Manuscrita (CM)
Arquivo do Instituto Histórico e Geográfico Brasileiro, Rio de Janeiro (AIHGB)
Arquivo do Museu Regional de São João del Rei, Brazil (AMRSJDR)
Arquivo Nacional, Rio de Janeiro (ANRJ)
Arquivo Nacional do Torre do Tombo, Lisbon (ANTT)
    Decretamentos de Serviço Fiscalizados e Não Decretados (DSFND)
    Inquisição de Lisboa (IL)
    Ministério do Reino (MR)
    Negócios Militares (NM)
    Registo Geral de Mercês (RGM)
    Tribunal do Santo Ofício (TSO)
Arquivo Público do Estado da Bahia (APEB)
    Seção Colonial e Provincial (SCP)
Arquivo Público Mineiro, Belo Horizonte, Brazil (APM)
    Arquivo Casa dos Contos (CC)
    Seção Colonial (SC)
Arquivo do Tribunal de Contas, Lisbon (ATC)
    Erário Régio (ER)

Arquivo da Universidade de Coimbra, Portugal (AUC)
  Processos dos Professores (PP)
Biblioteca da Academia das Ciências, Lisbon (BACL)
Biblioteca da Ajuda, Lisbon (BA)
Biblioteca Nacional, Lisbon (BNL)
  Coleção Pombalina (CP)
Biblioteca Nacional, Rio de Janeiro (BNRJ)
  Seção de Iconografia (SI)
  Seção de Manuscritos (SM)
  Arquivo Casa dos Contos (CC)
  Arquivo Conde de Valadares (CV)
  Documentos Biográficos (DB)
Biblioteca Pública, Évora, Portugal (BPE)
John Carter Brown Library, Brown University, Providence, RI (JCBL)
Library of Congress, Washington, DC (LC)
  Geography and Map Division (GMD)
Newberry Library, Chicago, IL
Oliveira Lima Library, Catholic University of America, Washington, DC (OLL)

## Printed Materials, Theses, and Dissertations

Abreu, João Capistrano de. *Caminhos antigos e povoamento do Brasil.* Belo Horizonte: Itatiaia, 1989.

Adelman, Jeremy. *Sovereignty and Revolution in the Iberian Atlantic.* Princeton, NJ: Princeton University Press, 2006.

Adelman, Jeremy, and Stephen Aron. "From Borderlands to Borders: Empires, Nation-States, and the Peoples in Between in North American History." *American Historical Review* 104, no. 3 (1999): 814–41.

Aguiar, Melânia Silva de. "A literatura do Setecentos em Minas Gerais: O Arcadismo." In *História de Minas Gerais: As Minas setecentistas,* edited by Mari Efigênia Lage de Resende and Luiz Carlos Villalta, 313–33. Belo Horizonte: Autêntica, 2007.

Alden, Dauril. *The Making of an Enterprise: The Society of Jesus in Portugal, Its Empire, and Beyond, 1540–1750.* Stanford, CA: Stanford University Press, 1996.

———. "The Population of Brazil in the Late Eighteenth Century: A Preliminary Survey." *Hispanic American Historical Review* 43, no. 2 (1963): 173–205.

———. *Royal Government in Colonial Brazil with Special Reference to the Administration of the Marquis of Lavradio, Viceroy, 1769–1779.* Berkeley: University of California Press, 1968.

Alencastro, Luiz Felipe de. *The Trade in the Living: The Formation of Brazil in the South Atlantic, Sixteenth to Seventeenth Centuries*. Translated by Gavin Adams and Luiz Felipe de Alencasto. Albany: State University of New York Press, 2018.

Almeida, Cândido Mendes de, ed. *Codigo Philippino ou Ordenações e Leis do Reino de Portugal*. 14th ed. Rio de Janeiro: Instituto Filomático, 1870.

Almeida, Maria Regina Celestino de. "Land and Economic Resources of Indigenous *Aldeias* in Rio de Janeiro: Conflicts and Negotiations, Seventeenth to Nineteenth Centuries." In *Native Brazil: Beyond the Convert and the Cannibal, 1500–1889*, edited by Hal Langfur, 62–85. Albuquerque: University of New Mexico Press, 2014.

———. *Metamorfoses indígenas: Cultura e identidade nos aldeamentos indígenas do Rio de Janeiro*. Rio de Janeiro: Arquivo Nacional, 2002.

———. *Os índios na história do Brasil*. Rio de Janeiro: FGV, 2010.

Almeida, Rita Heloísa de. *O Diretório dos índios: Um projeto de "civilização" no Brasil do século XVIII*. Brasília: Universidade de Brasília, 1997.

Amantino, Marcia. *O mundo das feras: Os moradores do Sertão Oeste de Minas Gerais—Século XVIII*. São Paulo: Annablume, 2008.

Amantino, Márcia, and Marieta Pinheiro de Carvalho. "Pombal, a riqueza dos Jesuítas e a expulsão." In *A "Época Pombalina" no mundo luso-brasileiro*, edited by Francisco Falcon and Claudia Rodrigues, 59–90. Rio de Janeiro: Editora FGV, 2015.

Anastasia, Carla M. J. *A geografia do crime: Violência nas Minas setecentistas*. Belo Horizonte: Universidade Federal de Minas Gerais, 2005.

———. "Salteadores, bandoleiros e desbravadores nas Matas Gerais da Mantiqueira (1783–1786)." In *Revisão do paraíso: Os brasileiros e o estado em 500 anos de história*, edited by Mary Del Priore, 115–38. Rio de Janeiro: Campus, 2000.

Andrade, Francisco Eduardo de. *A invenção das Minas Gerais: Empresas, descobrimentos e entradas nos sertões do ouro da América portuguesa*. Belo Horizonte: Autêntica, 2008.

Anon. *Novo diccionario da lingua portugueza: Composto sobre os que até o presente se tem dado ao prelo, e accrescentado de varios vocabulos extrahidos dos classicos antigos, e dos modernos de melhor nota, que se achaõ universalmente recebidos*. Lisbon: Rollandiana, 1806.

Apocalypse, Mary. "O tesouro de Isidoro, o garimpeiro." In *Estórias e lendas de Minas Gerais, Espírito Santo e Rio de Janeiro*, edited by Mary Apocalypse, 79–83. São Paulo: Iracema, 1997.

Aranha, Ana. "Escravos do ouro." *Repórter Brasil*, 2018, https://reporterbrasil.org.br/2018/08/resgate-trabalho-escravo-garimpo-ouro-para/ (accessed February 9, 2020).

Araújo, José de Souza Azevedo Pizarro e. *Memórias históricas do Rio de Janeiro e das provincias annexas a jurisdicção do vice-rei do Estado do Brasil.* 9 vols. Rio de Janeiro: Imp. Regia, 1820–22.

Arens, William. *The Man-Eating Myth: Anthropology and Anthropophagy.* New York: Oxford University Press, 1979.

Aron, Stephen. "Convergence, California, and the Newest Western History." *California History* 86, no. 4 (2009): 4–13, 79–81.

Arruda, José Jobson de A. *O Brasil no comércio colonial.* São Paulo: Ática, 1980.

Assis, Maria Emília Aparecida de. "Inácio Correia Pamplona: O 'Hércules' do sertão mineiro setecentista." Master's thesis, Universidade Federal de São de del Rei, 2014.

———. "Inácio Correia Pamplona: Um 'herói' para o sertão mineiro setecentista." *Temporalidades: Revista de História* 6, no. 1 (2014): 67–83.

———. "Uma trajetória de conquista e civilização: Inácio Correia Pamplona e o sertão oeste das Minas Gerais setecentista." *Revista Outras Fronteiras* 2, no. 1 (2015): 133–56.

Balhana, Altiva Pilatti. "A População." In *O Império Luso-Brasileiro, 1750–1822*, edited by Maria Beatriz Nizza da Silva, 19–62. Lisbon: Editorial Estampa, 1986.

Barbosa, Rui. "A Conferência de Alagoinhas (1919)." In *Obras completas de Rui Barbosa*, edited by Américo Jacobina Lacombe, 35–50. Rio de Janeiro: Fundação Casa de Rui Barbosa, 1988.

Barbosa, Waldemar de Almeida. *A decadência das minas e a fuga da mineração.* Belo Horizonte: Universidade Federal de Minas Gerais, 1971.

———. *Dicionário histórico-geográfico de Minas Gerais.* Belo Horizonte: Itatiaia, 1995.

———. *Negros e quilombos em Minas Gerais.* Belo Horizonte: n.p., 1972.

Barickman, B. J. *A Bahian Counterpoint: Sugar, Tobacco, Cassava, and Slavery in the Recôncavo, 1780–1860.* Stanford, CA: Stanford University Press, 1998.

———. "'Tame Indians,' 'Wild Heathens,' and Settlers in Southern Bahia in the Late Eighteenth and Early Nineteenth Centuries." *The Americas* 51, no. 3 (1995): 325–68.

Barker, Francis, Peter Hulme, and Margaret Iversen, eds. *Cannibalism and the Colonial World.* New York: Cambridge University Press, 1998.

Barman, Roderick J. *Brazil: The Forging of a Nation, 1798–1852.* Stanford, CA: Stanford University Press, 1988.

Baubeta, Patricia A. O. de. "Revisiting Camões' Sonnets: Anthologies, Translations, and Canonicity." *Bulletin of Spanish Studies: Hispanic Studies and Researches on Spain, Portugal, and Latin America* 95, no. 2–3 (2018): 169–91.

Bayly, C. A. *Empire and Information: Intelligence Gathering and Social Communication in India, 1780–1870.* Cambridge: Cambridge University Press, 1999.

———. "The First Age of Global Imperialism, c. 1760–1830." *Journal of Imperial and Commonwealth History* 26, no. 2 (1998): 28–47.

Beer, Gillian. "Travel Narratives and Truth Claims." In *Cultures of Natural History*, edited by N. Jardine, J. A. Secord, and E. C. Spary, 322–37. Cambridge: Cambridge University Press, 1996.

Belluzzo, Ana Maria de Moraes, Beatriz Camargo, Mário Pimenta Camargo, and Joaquim José de Miranda. *Do contato ao confronto: A conquista de Guarapuava no século XVIII.* São Paulo: BNB Paribas, 2003.

Benton, Lauren A. *A Search for Sovereignty: Law and Geography in European Empires, 1400–1900.* New York: Cambridge University Press, 2010.

Bergad, Laird W. "After the Mining Boom: Demographic and Economic Aspects of Slavery in Mariana, Minas Gerais, 1750–1808." *Latin American Research Review* 31, no. 1 (1996): 67–97.

———. *Slavery and the Demographic and Economic History of Minas Gerais, Brazil, 1720–1888.* Cambridge: Cambridge University Press, 1999.

Berger, Paulo. *Bibliografia do Rio de Janeiro de viajantes e autores estrangeiros, 1531–1900.* 2nd ed. Rio de Janeiro: SEEC-RJ, 1980.

Bergman, Torbern. *Manual do mineralogico, ou esboço do reino mineral, disposto segundo a analyse chimica.* Lisbon: João Procopio Correa da Silva, 1799.

Bethencourt, Francisco. *Racisms: From the Crusades to the Twentieth Century.* Princeton, NJ: Princeton University Press, 2013.

Bicalho, Maria Fernanda. "As câmaras ultramarinas e o governo do Império." In *O Antigo Regime nos trópicos: A dinâmica imperial portuguesa, séculos XVI–XVIII*, edited by João Luís Ribeiro Fragoso, Maria Fernanda Bicalho, and Maria de Fátima Gouvêa, 189–221. Rio de Janeiro: Civilização Brasileira, 2001.

Bicalho, Maria Fernanda, and Vera Lúcia Amaral Ferlini. *Modos de governar: Idéias e práticas políticas no Império português, séculos XVI–XIX.* São Paulo: Alameda, 2005.

Bieber, Judy. "Mediation through Militarization: Indigenous Soldiers and Transcultural Middlemen of the Rio Doce Divisions, Minas Gerais, Brazil, 1808–1850." *The Americas* 71, no. 2 (2014): 227–54.

———. *Power, Patronage, and Political Violence: State Building on a Brazilian Frontier, 1822–1889.* Lincoln: University of Nebraska Press, 1999.

———. "Uatú Júpú: A History of the Indigenous Rio Doce." *Brasiliana: Journal for Brazilian Studies* 5, no. 2 (2017): 128–53.

Bigelow, Allison M. *Mining Language: Racial Thinking, Indigenous Knowledge, and Colonial Metallurgy in the Early Modern Iberian World*. Chapel Hill: University of North Carolina Press, 2020.

Blair, Ann, and Devin Fitzgerald. "A Revolution in Information?" In *The Oxford Handbook of Early Modern European History, 1350–1750*, edited by Hamish M. Scott, 244–65. Vol. 1, *People and Places*. Oxford: Oxford University Press, 2015.

Bleichmar, Daniela. *Visible Empire: Botanical Expeditions and Visual Culture in the Hispanic Enlightenment*. Chicago: University of Chicago Press, 2012.

Blumenbach, Johann F. "Degeneration of the Species." In *Race and the Enlightenment: A Reader*, edited by Emmanuel C. Eze, 79–90. Malden, MA: Blackwell, 1997.

Bluteau, Rafael. *Vocabulario portuguez e latino*. Lisbon: Pascoal da Sylva, 1720.

Bonavides, Paulo, and Roberto Amaral, eds. *Textos políticos da história do Brasil*. 3rd ed. Vol. 1. Brasília: Senado Federal, 2002.

Borges, Ana. "Mitos e verdades: Mão de Luva e Tiradentes." Jornal A Voz da Serra, www.youtube.com/watch?v=Rn5ye8X-B7A (accessed August 21, 2019).

Bourdieu, Pierre. "Rethinking the State: Genesis and Structure of the Bureaucratic Field." In *State/Culture: State-Formation after the Cultural Turn*, edited by George Steinmetz, 53–75. Ithaca, NY: Cornell University Press, 1999.

Boxer, C. R. *The Golden Age of Brazil, 1695–1750: Growing Pains of a Colonial Society*. Berkeley: University of California Press, 1969.

Brazil, Maria do Carmo. *Fronteira negra: Dominação, violência e resistência escrava em Mato Grosso, 1718–1888*. Passo Fundo: Universidade de Passo Fundo, 2002.

"Brazil, Baptisms, 1688–1935." https://familysearch.org/pal:/MM9.1.1/XNYF-QTT, Teodozia (Teodora) Pamplona, September 3, 1752.

Bruchac, Margaret M. *Savage Kin: Indigenous Informants and American Anthropologists*. Tucson: University of Arizona Press, 2018.

Burmeister, Hermann. *Viagem ao Brasil através das províncias do Rio de Janeiro e Minas Gerais*. Translated by Manoel Salvaterra and Hubert Schoenfeldt. São Paulo: Livraria Martins, 1952.

Burns, E. Bradford. "The Intellectuals as Agents of Change and the Independence of Brazil, 1724–1822." In *From Colony to Nation: Essays on the Independence of Brazil*, edited by A. J. R. Russell-Wood, 211–46. Baltimore: Johns Hopkins University Press, 1975.

Bushnell, Amy Turner. "Gates, Patterns, and Peripheries: The Field of Frontier Latin America." In *Negotiated Empires: Centers and Peripheries in the Americas, 1500–1820*, edited by Christine Daniels and Michael V. Kennedy, 15–28. New York: Routledge, 2002.

Cadena, Marisol de la. "Are 'Mestizos' Hybrids? The Conceptual Politics of Andean Identities." *Journal of Latin American Studies* 37, no. 2 (2005): 259–84.
Calloway, Colin G. *The American Revolution in Indian Country: Crisis and Diversity in Native American Communities*. Cambridge: Cambridge University Press, 1995.
Caminha, Pêro Vaz de. "Letter to King Manuel I of Portugal [1500]." In *The Brazil Reader*, edited by James N. Green, Victoria Langland, and Lilia Moritz Schwarcz, 12–17. 2nd ed. Durham, NC: Duke University Press.
Camões, Luís Vaz de. *The Lusiads*. Translated by Landeg White. New York: Oxford University Press, 2001.
Cañeque, Alejandro. *The King's Living Image: The Culture and Politics of Viceregal Power in Colonial Mexico*. New York: Routledge, 2004.
Carneiro, Edison. *O quilombo dos Palmares*. 3rd ed. Rio de Janeiro: Civilização Brasileira, 1966.
Carneiro, Patrício A. S. "Do sertão ao território das minas e das gerais: Entradas e bandeiras, política territorial e formação espacial no período colonial." PhD diss., Universidade Federal de Minas Gerais, 2013.
Carrara, Ângelo Alves. *Minas e currais: Produção rural e mercado interno em Minas Gerais, 1674–1807*. Juiz de Fora: Universidade Federal de Juiz de Fora, 2007.
———, ed. *Uma fronteira da capitania de Minas Gerais: A freguesia de São João Batista do Presídio em 1821*. Mariana: Universidade Federal de Ouro Preto, 1999.
Carvalho, Sebastião A. B. de. *O tesouro de Cantagalo*. Niterói: Gráfica do Colégio Salesiano, 1951.
Carvalho Júnior, Almir Diniz de. "Índios cristãos: A conversão dos gentios na Amazônia Portuguesa (1653–1769)." PhD diss., Universidade de Campinas, 2005.
Cascudo, Luís da Câmara. *O Príncipe Maximiliano de Wied-Neuwied no Brasil, 1815/1817: Biografia e notas, com versões para o inglês e alemão*. Rio de Janeiro: Livraria Kosmos, 1977.
Castro, Celso Falabella de Figueiredo. *Os sertões de leste: Achegas para a história da Zona da Mata*. Belo Horizonte: Imprensa Oficial, 1987.
Castro, Eduardo Viveiros de. *The Inconstancy of the Indian Soul: The Encounter of Catholics and Cannibals in 16th-Century Brazil*. Translated by Gregory Duff Morton. Chicago: Prickly Paradigm Press, 2011.
Castro, Luiz Paiva de. *O galo é um homem que canta: Mão de Luva, Euclides da Cunha, e Antonio Conselheiro*. Rio de Janeiro: Salamandra, 1980.
Cavalcante, Moema. *Por mares muito antes navegados: A tradição de Camões na poesia colonial brasileira*. Canoas: Universidade Luterana do Brasil, 2001.

Chaves Júnior, José Inaldo. "Reforma dos territórios e das jurisdições nas capitanias do Norte do Estado do Brasil: As atuações do capitão-general Luís Diogo Lobo da Silva e do 'juiz de fora' Miguel Carlos de Pina Castelo Branco na aplicação do Diretório dos índios (1757–1764)." *Locus: Revista de História* 24, no. 1 (2018): 93–120.

Clifford, James. *Routes: Travel and Translation in the Late Twentieth Century*. Cambridge, MA: Harvard University Press, 1997.

Coelho, José João Teixeira. *Instrução para o governo da Capitania de Minas Gerais*. Edited by Caio César Boschi. Belo Horizonte: Secretaria de Estado de Cultura, 1994.

Conklin, Beth A. *Consuming Grief: Compassionate Cannibalism in an Amazonian Society*. Austin: University of Texas Press, 2001.

Corrêa, Carlos H. *Os governantes de Santa Catarina, 1739–1982: Notas biográficas*. Florianópolis: Universidade Federal de Santa Catarina, 1983.

Corrêa, Luís Rafael Araújo. "Feitiço caboclo: Um índio mandingueiro condenado pela Inquisição." PhD diss., Universidade Federal Fluminense, 2003.

Cortesão, Jaime. *Rapóso Tavares e a formacão territorial do Brasil*. Rio de Janeiro: Ministério da Educação e Cultura, 1958.

Costa, Ana Paula Pereira. "Organização militar, poder de mando e mobilização de escravos armados nas conquistas: A atuação dos Corpos de Ordenanças em Minas colonial." *Revista de História Regional* 11, no. 2 (2006): 109–62.

Costa, Antônio Gilberto, Friedrich Ewald Renger, Júnia Ferreira Furtado, and Márcia Maria Duarte dos Santos, eds. *Cartografia das Minas Gerais: Da Capitania à Província*. Belo Horizonte: Universidade Federal de Minas Gerais, 2002.

Costa, Christina R. da. "O Príncipe Maximiliano de Wied-Neuwied e sua Viagem ao Brasil (1815–1817)." Master's thesis, Universidade de São Paulo, 2008.

Costa, Cláudio Manoel. "Vila Rica." In *Obras poeticas de Claudio Manoel da Costa (Glauceste Saturnio)*, edited by João Ribeiro, vol. 2, 148–262. Rio de Janeiro: H. Garnier, 1903.

Costa, Emilia Viotti da. "José Bonifácio de Andrada e Silva: A Brazilian Founding Father." In *The Brazilian Empire: Myths and Histories*, 24–52. Chicago: University of Chicago Press, 1985.

Costa, Iraci del Nero da. *Minas Gerais: Estruturas populacionais típicas*. São Paulo: EDEC, 1982.

Coutinho, José Joaquim da Cunha de Azeredo. *Ensaio economico sobre o comercio de Portugal e suas colonias*. Lisbon: Academia Real das Ciências, 1794.

Couto, José Vieira. "Carta da Nova Lorena Diamantina (1801)." In *Cartografia da conquista do território das Minas*, edited by Antônio Gilberto Costa, 216. Belo Horizonte: Universidade Federal de Minas Gerais, 2004.

———. *Memória sobre a Capitania das Minas Gerais; seu território, clima e produções metálicas*. Belo Horizonte: Fundação João Pinheiro, 1994.

———. *Memoria sobre as minas da capitania de Minas Geraes; suas descrições, ensaios e domicílios próprios, à maneira de itinerário* ... Rio de Janeiro: Laemmert, 1842.

Cunha, Manuela Carneiro da, ed. *Legislação indigenista no século XIX: Uma compilação (1808–1889)*. São Paulo: Universidade de São Paulo, 1992.

———. "Pensar os índios: Apontamentos sobre José Bonifácio." In *Antropologia do Brasil: Mito, história, etnicidade*, 165–73. São Paulo: Brasiliense/EDUSP, 1986.

———. "Política indigenista no século XIX." In *História dos índios no Brasil*, 133–54. São Paulo: Companhia das Letras, FAPESP/SMC, 1992.

Curto, Diogo Ramada. "Naturalismo, indigenismo, reformas e relatos de viagem." In *Cultura imperial e projetos coloniais: Séculos XV a XVIII*, 443–76. Campinas: Unicamp, 2009.

Dabove, Juan Pablo. *Bandit Narratives in Latin America: From Villa to Chávez*. Pittsburgh: University of Pittsburgh Press, 2017.

"Daily Notice of the Marches and Most Noteworthy Happenings in the Expedition Made by Field Officer Regent Inácio Correia Pamplona." In *Colonial Latin America: A Documentary History*, edited by Kenneth Mills, William B. Taylor, and Sandra Lauderdale Graham, 337–52. Wilmington, DE: Scholarly Resources, 2002.

Daniels, Christine, and Michael V. Kennedy, eds. *Negotiated Empires: Centers and Peripheries in the Americas, 1500–1820*. New York: Routledge, 2002.

Dantas, Mariana L. R. *Black Townsmen: Slavery and Freedom in Eighteenth-Century Baltimore, Maryland, and Sabará, Minas Gerais*. New York: Palgrave Macmillan, 2008.

———. "Black Women and Mothers: Social Mobility and Inheritance Strategies in Minas Gerais during the Second Half of the Eighteenth Century." *Almanack* 12 (January–April 2016): 88–104.

———. "'For the Benefit of the Common Good': Regiments of Caçadores do Mato in Minas Gerais, Brazil." *Journal of Colonialism and Colonial History* 5, no. 2 (2004).

Darnton, Robert. "An Early Information Society: News and the Media in Eighteenth-Century Paris." *American Historical Review* 105, no. 1 (2000): 1–35.

Dean, Warren. *With Broadax and Firebrand: The Destruction of the Brazilian Atlantic Forest*. Berkeley: University of California Press, 1995.

Dearhouse, Renae W. "Fictionalizing the Indigenous in German Travel Literature (1772–1834): The Expeditions of Chamisso, Forster, Humboldt, and Maximilian." PhD diss., Stanford University, 2007.

Debret, Jean Baptiste. *Voyage pittoresque et historique au Brésil; ou, Séjour d'un artiste français au Brésil, depuis 1816 jusqu'en 1831 inclusivement.* Vol. 1. Paris: Firmin Didot frères, 1834.

DeLay, Brian. *War of a Thousand Deserts: Indian Raids and the U.S.-Mexican War.* New Haven, CT: Yale University Press, 2008.

Delbourgo, James, and Nicholas Dew, eds. *Science and Empire in the Atlantic World.* New York: Routledge, 2008.

Deloria, Vine, Jr. *Red Earth, White Lies: Native Americans and the Myth of Scientific Fact.* Golden, CO: Fulcrum, 1997.

Dias, A[ntônio] Gonçalves. *Diccionario da lingua tupy: Chamada lingua geral dos indigenas do Brazil.* Leipzig: F. A. Brockhaus, 1858.

Dias, Acácio Ferreira. *O Mão de Luva (fundador de Cantagalo).* Niterói: Imprensa Oficial, 1953.

Dias, Maria Odila da Silva. "Aspectos da Ilustração no Brasil." *Revista do Instituto Histórico e Geográfico Brasileiro* 278 (January–March 1968): 105–70.

Dias, Maria Odila Leite da Silva. "A interiorização da metrópole." In *A interiorização da metrópole e outros estudos,* 7–37. São Paulo: Alameda, 2005.

Diggs, Cerue K. "Brazil after Humboldt: Triangular Perceptions and the Colonial Gaze in Nineteenth-Century German Travel Narratives." PhD diss., University of Maryland, 2008.

Disney, A. R. *A History of Portugal and the Portuguese Empire: From Beginnings to 1807.* 2 vols. Cambridge: Cambridge University Press, 2009.

"Documentário 'O Mão de Luva' é exibido em praça pública, em Cantagalo." 100 anos sem Euclides: projeto cultural, www.projetoeuclides.iltc.br/index.php?page=conteudo&conteudo=impre_noticias&id=212 (accessed March 3, 2012).

Domingues, Ângela. *Viagens de exploração geográfica na Amazónia em finais do século XVIII: Política, ciência e aventura.* Lisbon: Instituto de Historia de Além-Mar, FCSH-UNL, 1991.

———. *Monarcas, ministros e cientistas: Mecanismos de poder, governação e informação no Brasil colonial.* Lisbon: CHAM/FCSH/UNL and Universidade dos Açores, 2012.

———. "Museus, coleccionismo e viagens científicas em Portugal de finais de Setecentos." *Asclepio* 71, no. 2 (2019): 1–19.

———. "Notícias do Brasil colonial: A imprensa científica e política ao serviço das elites (Portugal, Brasil e Inglaterra)." In *Monarcas, ministros e cientistas: Mecanismos de poder, governação e informação no Brasil colonial,* edited by Ângela Domingues, 150–78. Lisbon: CHAM/FCSH/UNL and Universidade dos Açores, 2012.

———. "O Brasil de Maximiliano de Wied-Neuwied." *Oceanos* 24, no. (1995): 39–54.

———. "O Brasil nos relatos de viajantes ingleses do século XVIII: Produção de discursos sobre o Novo Mundo." *Revista Brasileira de História* 28, no. 55 (2008): 133–52.

———. "Para um melhor conhecimento dos domínios coloniais: A constituição de redes de informação no Império português em finais do Setecentos." Supplement, *História, Ciências, Saúde—Manguinhos* 8 (2001): 823–38.

———. *Quando os índios eram vassalos: Colonização e relações de poder no Norte do Brasil na segunda metade do século XVIII*. Lisbon: Comissão Nacional para as Comemorações dos Descobrimentos Portugueses, 2000.

Dooley, Brendan, ed. *The Dissemination of News and the Emergence of Contemporaneity in Early Modern Europe*. Farnham: Routledge, 2010.

Duarte, Regina Horta. "Facing the Forest: European Travellers Crossing the Mucuri River Valley, Brazil, in the Nineteenth Century." *Environment and History* 10, no. 1 (2004): 31–58.

———. "Olhares estrangeiros: Viajantes no vale do rio Mucuri." *Revista Brasileira de História* 22, no. 44 (2002): 267–88.

Dubcovsky, Alejandra. *Informed Power: Communications in the Early American South*. Cambridge, MA: Harvard University Press, 2016.

DuVal, Kathleen. *The Native Ground: Indians and Colonists in the Heart of the Continent*. Philadelphia: University of Pennsylvania Press, 2006.

Earle, Rebecca. "The Pleasures of Taxonomy: Casta Paintings, Classification, and Colonialism." *William and Mary Quarterly* 73, no. 3 (2016): 427–66.

Echeverri, Marcela. *Indian and Slave Royalists in the Age of Revolution: Reform, Revolution, and Royalism in the Northern Andes, 1780–1825*. Cambridge: Cambridge University Press, 2016.

Eigen, Sara, and Mark Larrimore, eds. *The German Invention of Race*. Albany: State University of New York Press, 2006.

Emigh, Rebecca Jean. "What Influences Official Information? Exploring Aggregate Microhistories of the Catasto of 1427." In *Small Worlds: Method, Meaning, and Narrative in Microhistory*, edited by James F. Brooks, Christopher R. N. DeCorse, and John Walton, 199–223. Santa Fe: School for Advanced Research Press, 2008.

Erbig, Jeffrey A., Jr. *Where Caciques and Mapmakers Met: Border Making in Eighteenth-Century South America*. Chapel Hill: University of North Carolina Press, 2020.

Eschwege, Wilhelm Ludwig von. *Brasil, Novo Mundo*. Translated by Domício de Figueiredo Murta. Belo Horizonte: Fundação João Pinheiro, 1996.

———. *Pluto brasiliensis*. Translated by Domício de Figueiredo Murta. 2 vols. Belo Horizonte: Itatiaia, 1979.

Espindola, Haruf Salmen. *Sertão do Rio Doce*. Governador Valadares: Univale, 2005.

Faria, Luciano E., and Carlos A. L. Filgueiras. "A busca por chumbo e prata em Minas Gerais como alternativa às esgotadas minas de ouro e diamantes no século XIX." *Química Nova* 42 (2019): 105–16.

Faria, Sheila de Castro. *A colônia em movimento: Fortuna e família no cotidiano colonial*. Rio de Janeiro: Nova Fronteira, 1998.

———. "Ouro, porcos, escravos e café: As origens das fortunas oitocentistas em São Pedro de Cantagalo, Rio de Janeiro (últimas décadas do século XVIII e primeiras do XIX)." *Anais do Museu Paulista: História e Cultura Material* 26 (2018): 1–42.

Febvre, Lucien. "*Frontière*: The Word and the Concept." In *A New Kind of History: From the Writings of Lucien Febvre*, edited by Peter Burke, 208–17. New York: Harper and Row, 1973.

Ferguson, R. Brian, and Neil L. Whitehead. "The Violent Edge of Empire." In *War in the Tribal Zone: Expanding States and Indigenous Warfare*, edited by R. Brian Ferguson and Neil L. Whitehead, 1–30. Santa Fe: School of American Research Press, 1992.

Ferreira, Francisco Ignacio. *Repertorio juridico do mineiro: Consolidação alphabetica e chronologica de todas as disposições sobre minas, comprehendendo a legislação antiga e moderna de Portugal e do Brasil*. Rio de Janeiro: Typ. Nacional, 1884.

Ferreira, Jurandyr Pires, ed. *Enciclopédia dos municípios brasileiros*. 36 vols. Rio de Janeiro: Instituto Brasileiro de Geografia e Estatística, 1957–64.

Ferreira, Mário Olímpio Clemente. *O Tratado de Madrid e o Brasil meridional: Os trabalhos demarcadores das partidas do sul e a sua produção cartográfica (1749–1761)*. Lisbon: Comissão Nacional para as Comemorações dos Descobrimentos Portugueses, 2001.

Figueiredo, Luciano R. de A. "A corrupção no Brasil colônia." In *Corrupção: Ensaios e críticas*, edited by Leonardo Avritzer, Newton Bignotto, Juarez Guimarães, and Heloisa M. M. Starling, 209–18. Belo Horizonte: Universidade Federal de Minas Gerais, 2008.

———. *Barrocas famílias: Vida familiar em Minas Gerais no século XVIII*. São Paulo: Hucitec, 1997.

———. *O avesso da memória: Cotidiano e trabalho da mulher em Minas Gerais no século XVIII*. Rio de Janeiro: José Olympio, 1993.

Figueirôa, Silvia F. de M., Clarete Paranhos da Silva, and Ermelinda Moutinho Pataca. "Aspectos mineralógicos das 'Viagens Filosóficas' pelo território brasileiro na transição do século XVIII para o século XIX." *História, Ciências, Saúde-Manguinhos* 11, no. 3 (2004): 713–29.

Fiúza, Rubens. *O diamante do Abaeté e outros contos*. Belo Horizonte: Imprensa Oficial, 1988.

Flechor, Maria Helena Ochi. *Abreviaturas: Manuscritos dos séculos XVI ao XIX*. 2nd ed. São Paulo: UNESP, Edições Arquivo do Estado, 1991.

Florentino, Manolo Garcia. *Em Costas Negras: Uma história do tráfico de escravos entre a África e o Rio de Janeiro (séculos XVIII e XIX)*. São Paulo: Companhia das Letras, 1997.

Fonseca, Cláudia Damasceno. *Arraiais e vilas d'el rei: Espaco e poder nas Minas setecentistas*. Belo Horizonte: Universidade Federal de Minas Gerais, 2011.

Fonseca, Fernando Taveira da. "Uma primeira educação do olhar: Universidade e estudantes de Coimbra na transição reformista." In *A universidade pombalina: Ciência, território e coleções científicas*, edited by Ana Cristina Araújo and Fernando Taveira da Fonseca, 13–50. Coimbra: Universidade de Coimbra, 2017.

Forsyth, Donald W. "Three Cheers for Hans Staden: The Case for Brazilian Cannibalism." *Ethnohistory* 32, no. 1 (1985): 17–36.

Fragoso, João Luís Ribeiro. *Homens de grossa aventura: Acumulação e hierarquia na praça mercantil do Rio de Janeiro (1790–1830)*. Rio de Janeiro: Arquivo Nacional, 1992.

Fragoso, João Luís Ribeiro Bicalho Maria Fernanda Gouvêa Maria de Fátima. *O Antigo Regime nos trópicos: A dinâmica imperial portuguesa, séculos XVI–XVIII*. Rio de Janeiro: Civilização Brasileira, 2001.

França, Jean M. C. "A construção de um público." *Hipólito José da Costa e o Correio Braziliense* 30, vol. 1 (2002): 553–604.

Franco, Francisco de Assis Carvalho. *Dicionário de bandeirantes e sertanistas do Brasil: Século XVI, XVII, XVIII*. Belo Horizonte: Itatiaia, 1989.

Freire, José Ribamar Bessa, and Márcia Fernanda Malheiros. *Aldeamentos indígenas do Rio de Janeiro*. Rio de Janeiro: Programa de Estudos dos Povos Indígenas, Universidade do Estado do Rio de Janeiro, 1997.

Freireyss, G. W. "Viagem ao interior do Brazil nos annos de 1814–1815." *Revista do Instituto Histórico e Geográfico de São Paulo* 11 (1907): 158–252.

———. "Viagens a varias tribus de selvagens na capitania de Minas Geraes ..." *Revista do Instituto Histórico e Geográfico de São Paulo* 6 (1900–1901): 236–52.

Furtado, Júnia Ferreira. *Chica da Silva: A Brazilian Slave of the Eighteenth Century*. Cambridge: Cambridge University Press, 2009.

———. *Diálogos oceânicos: Minas Gerais e as novas abordagens para uma história do Império Ultramarino Português*. Belo Horizonte: Universidade Federal de Minas Gerais, 2001.

---. "Enlightenment Science and Iconoclasm: The Brazilian Naturalist José Vieira Couto." *Osiris* 25, no. 1 (2010): 189–212.
---. *Homens de negócio: A interiorização da metrópole e do comércio nas Minas setecentistas*. São Paulo: Hucitec, 1999.
---. "Novas tendências da historiografia sobre Minas Gerais no período colonial." *História da Historiografia* 2 (March 2009): 116–62.
---. *O Livro da Capa Verde: O regimento diamantino de 1771 e a vida no Distrito Diamantino no período da real extração*. São Paulo: Annablume, 1996.
---. *Oráculos da geografia iluminista: Dom Luís da Cunha e Jean-Baptiste Bourguignon D'Anville na construção da cartografia do Brasil*. Belo Horizonte: Universidade Federal de Minas Gerais, 2012.
---. "Pérolas Negras: Mulheres Livres de Cor no Distrito Diamantino." In *Diálogos oceânicos: Minas Gerais e as novas abordagens para uma história do Império Ultramarino Português*, edited by Júnia Ferreira Furtado, 81–121. Belo Horizonte: Universidade Federal de Minas Gerais, 2001.
---. "Tropical Empiricism: Making Medical Knowledge in Colonial Brazil." In *Science and Empire in the Atlantic World*, edited by James Delbourgo and Nicholas Dew, 127–51. New York: Routledge, 2008.
---. "Um cartógrafo rebelde? José Joaquim da Rocha e a cartografia de Minas Gerais." *Anais do Museu Paulista* 17, no. 2 (2009): 155–87.
Garcia, João Carlos, ed. *A mais dilatada vista do mundo: Inventário da colecção cartográfica da Casa da Ínsua*. [Lisbon]: Comissão Nacional para as Comemorações dos Descobrimentos Portugueses, 2002.
Garcia, Romyr C. "O Mão de Luva e os sertões de Serra acima: Garimpos clandestinos e conflitos sociais no Brasil Colônia." *Revista Unifesco—Humanas e Sociais* 4, no. 4 (2018): 246–68.
Garcia, Wolney. "Nas águas do Indaiá uma história de ambição e ódio." Centroeste Urgente, www.centroesteurgente.com.br/centro-oeste-mineiro/nas-aguas-do-indaia-uma-historia-de-amibicoes-e-muito-odio/ (accessed February 5, 2020).
Giraldin, Odair. *Cayapó e Panará: Luta e sobrevivência de um povo Jê no Brasil Central*. Campinas: Unicamp, 1997.
Girão, Eduardo T. "200 anos depois, restos mortais do índio botocudo Kuêk voltam para casa." *Correio Braziliense* (May 9, 2011), www.correiobraziliense.com.br/app/noticia/ciencia-e-saude/2011/05/09/interna_ciencia_saude,251331/200-anos-depois-restos-mortais-do-indio-botocudo-kuek-voltam-para-casa.shtml.
Gomes, Flávio dos Santos. *A hidra e os pântanos: Mocambos, quilombos e comunidades de fugitivos no Brasil (séculos XVII–XIX)*. São Paulo: Polis, UNESP, 2005.

———. *Histórias de quilombolas: Mocambos e comunidades de senzalas no Rio de Janeiro, século XIX*. Rev. ed. São Paulo: Companhia das Letras, 2006.

———. *Palmares: Escravidão e liberdade no Atlântico Sul*. São Paulo: Contexto, 2005.

———. "Seguindo o mapa das minas: Plantas e quilombos mineiros setecentistas." *Estudos Afro-Asiáticos* 29 (March 1996): 113–42.

Gomes, Mauro Leão. "Ouro, posseiros e fazendas de café: A ocupação e a degradação ambiental da região das Minas do Canta Gallo na província do Rio de Janeiro." PhD diss., Universidade Federal Rural do Rio de Janeiro, 2004.

Gould, Stephen Jay. "Linnaeus's Luck?" *Natural History* 109, no. 7 (2000): 18–29.

Gouvêa, Maria de Fátima Silva. "Poder político e administração na formação do complexo atlântico português." In *O Antigo Regime nos trópicos: A dinâmica imperial portuguesa, séculos XVI–XVIII*, edited by João Fragoso, Maria Fernanda Bicalho, and Maria de Fátima Gouvêa, 285–315. Rio de Janeiro: Civilização Brasileira, 2001.

Graham, Richard. *Feeding the City: From Street Market to Liberal Reform in Salvador, Brazil, 1780–1860*. Austin: University of Texas Press, 2010.

———. *Independence in Latin America: Contrasts and Comparisons*. 3rd ed. Austin: University of Texas Press, 2013.

Grandjean, Katherine. *American Passage: The Communications Frontier in Early New England*. Cambridge, MA: Harvard University Press, 2015.

Graulau, Jeannette. "Peasant Mining Production as a Development Strategy: The Case of Women in Gold Mining in the Brazilian Amazon." *Revista Europea de Estudios Latinoamericanos y Del Caribe* 71 (2001): 71–106.

Griffin, Patrick. *American Leviathan: Empire, Nation, and Revolutionary Frontier*. New York: Hill and Wang, 2007.

Guimarães, Carlos Magno. "Escravidão e quilombos nas Minas Gerais do século XVIII." In *História de Minas Gerais: As Minas setecentistas*, edited by Mari Efigênia Lage de Resende and Luiz Carlos Villalta, 439–54. Belo Horizonte: Autêntica, 2007.

———. "Mineração, quilombos, e Palmares: Minas Gerais no século XVIII." In *Liberdade por um fio: História dos quilombos no Brasil*, edited by João José Reis and Flávio dos Santos Gomes, 139–63. São Paulo: Companhia das Letras, 1996.

———. "Quilombos: Classes, estado e cotidiano (Minas Gerais—século XVIII)." PhD diss., Universidade de São Paulo, 1999.

———. *Uma negação da ordem escravista: Quilombos em Minas Gerais no século XVIII*. São Paulo: Icone, 1988.

Hadas, Moses. *A History of Latin Literature*. New York: Columbia University Press, 1952.

Hämäläinen, Pekka. *The Comanche Empire.* New Haven, CT: Yale University Press, 2008.

Hämäläinen, Pekka, and Samuel Truett. "On Borderlands." *Journal of American History* 98, no. 2 (2011): 338–61.

Hamm, E. P. "Knowledge from Underground: Leibniz Mines the Enlightenment." *Earth Sciences History* 16, no. 2 (1997): 77–99.

Harris, Mark. *Rebellion on the Amazon: The Cabanagem, Race, and Popular Culture in the North of Brazil, 1798–1840.* Cambridge: Cambridge University Press, 2010.

Harris, Marvin. *The Rise of Anthropological Theory: A History of Theories of Culture.* Lanham, MD: AltaMira, 2001.

Hemming, John. *Amazon Frontier: The Defeat of the Brazilian Indians.* Cambridge, MA: Harvard University Press, 1987.

Herzog, Tamar. *Frontiers of Possession: Spain and Portugal in Europe and the Americas.* Cambridge, MA: Harvard University Press, 2015.

Higgins, Kathleen J. *"Licentious Liberty" in a Brazilian Gold-Mining Region: Slavery, Gender, and Social Control in Eighteenth-Century Sabará, Minas Gerais.* University Park: Pennsylvania State University Press, 1999.

Hill, John. *Fossils Arranged According to Their Obvious Characters; with Their History and Description; Under the Articles of Form, Hardness, Weight, Surface, Colour, and Qualities; the Place of Their Production, Their Uses, and Distinctive English, and Classical Latin Names.* London: R. Baldwin, 1771.

Hinderaker, Eric, and Peter C. Mancall. *At the Edge of Empire: The Backcountry in British North America.* Baltimore: Johns Hopkins University Press, 2003.

Hixson, Walter L. *American Settler Colonialism: A History.* New York: Palgrave Macmillan, 2013.

Hobsbawm, Eric J. *Bandits.* New York: New Press, 2000.

Holanda, Sérgio Buarque de. *Caminhos e fronteiras.* Rio de Janeiro: J. Olympio, 1957.

———. *Capítulos de literatura colonial.* São Paulo: Brasiliense, 1991.

Homer. *The Iliad.* Translated by Robert Fagles. New York: Viking, 1990.

*Idade de Ouro do Brasil,* 1811.

Instituto Histórico e Geográfico de Bom Jardim. "Lenda: Furnas do Mão de Luva." http://ihgbj.blogspot.com/2009/07/lenda-furnas-do-mao-de-luva.html (accessed February 13, 2016).

Jardine, N., J. A. Secord, and E. C. Spary. *Cultures of Natural History.* Cambridge: Cambridge University Press, 1996.

Jardine, Nicholas. "*Naturphilosophie* and the Kingdoms of Nature." In *Cultures of Natural History,* edited by N. Jardine, J. A. Secord, and E. C. Spary, 230–45. Cambridge: Cambridge University Press, 1996.

José, Oiliam. *Indígenas de Minas Gerais: Aspectos sociais, políticos e etnológicos.* Belo Horizonte: Imp. Oficial, 1965.

Karasch, Mary C. *Before Brasília.* Albuquerque: University of New Mexico Press, 2016.

———. "Damiana da Cunha: Catechist and Sertanista." In *Struggle and Survival in Colonial America,* edited by David G. Sweet and Gary B. Nash, 102–20. Berkeley: University of California Press, 1981.

———. "Interethnic Conflict and Resistance on the Brazilian Frontier of Goiás, 1750–1890." In *Contested Ground: Comparative Frontiers on the Northern and Southern Edges of the Spanish Empire,* edited by Donna J. Guy and Thomas E. Sheridan, 115–34. Tucson: University of Arizona Press, 1998.

———. "Rethinking the Conquest of Goiás, 1775–1819." *The Americas* 61, no. 3 (2005): 463–92.

Keane, A. H. "On the Botocudos." *Journal of the Anthropological Institute of Great Britain and Ireland* 13 (1884): 199–213.

King, Charles. *Gods of the Upper Air: How a Circle of Renegade Anthropologists Reinvented Race, Sex, and Gender in the Twentieth Century.* New York: Doubleday, 2019.

Klein, Herbert S., and Francisco Vidal Luna. *Slavery in Brazil.* Cambridge: Cambridge University Press, 2010.

Knight, David M. "Travels and Science in Brazil." Supplement, *História, Ciências, Saúde-Manguinhos* 8 (2001): 809–22.

Kok, Glória Porto. *O sertão itinerante: Expedições da Capitania de São Paulo no século XVIII.* São Paulo: Hucitec, 2004.

Kraay, Hendrik. *Race, State, and Armed Forces in Independence-Era Brazil, Bahia, 1790s–1840s.* Stanford, CA: Stanford University Press, 2001.

———. "Reconsidering Recruitment in Imperial Brazil." *The Americas* 55, no. 1 (1998): 1–33.

Kury, Lorelai. "Viajantes-naturalistas no Brasil oitocentista: Experiência, relato e imagem." Supplement, *História, Ciências, Saúde-Manguinhos* 8 (2001): 863–80.

Lamas, Fernando G. "Conflitos agrários em Minas Gerais: O processo de conquista da terra na área central da Zona da Mata (1767–1820)." PhD diss., Universidade Federal Fluminense, 2013.

Lamego, Alberto. *A Terra Goitacá á luz de documentos inéditos.* 6 vols. Rio de Janeiro: Garnier, 1913–41.

Landers, Jane G. *Atlantic Creoles in the Age of Revolutions.* Cambridge, MA: Harvard University Press, 2010.

Langfur, Hal. "Cannibalism and the Body Politic: Independent Indians in the Era of Brazilian Independence." *Ethnohistory* 65, no. 4 (2018): 549–73.

———. "Elite Ethnography and Indian Eradication: Confronting the Cannibal in Early Nineteenth-Century Brazil." In *Contesting Knowledge: Museums and Indigenous Perspectives*, edited by Susan Sleeper-Smith, 15–44. Lincoln: University of Nebraska Press, 2009.

———. *The Forbidden Lands: Colonial Identity, Frontier Violence, and the Persistence of Brazil's Eastern Indians, 1750–1830*. Stanford, CA: Stanford University Press, 2006.

———. "Frontier/*Fronteira*: A Transnational Reframing of Brazil's Inland Colonization." *History Compass* 12, no. 11 (2014): 843–52.

———. "Índios, territorialização, e justiça improvisada nas florestas do sudeste do Brasil." In *Os indígenas e as Justiças nas Américas*, edited by Maria Leônia Chaves de Resende, Ângela Domingues, and Pedro Cardim, 157–88. Lisbon: Centro de História da Universidade de Lisboa, 2019.

———. "Introduction: Recovering Brazil's Indigenous Pasts." In *Native Brazil: Beyond the Cannibal and the Convert, 1500–1889*, edited by Hal Langfur, 1–28. Albuquerque: University of New Mexico Press, 2014.

———. "Native Informants and the Limits of Portuguese Dominion in Late-Colonial Brazil." In *The Oxford Handbook of Borderlands of the Iberian World*, edited by Cynthia Radding and Danna Levin Rojo, 209–34. Oxford: Oxford University Press, 2019.

———. "The Return of the Bandeira: Economic Calamity, Historical Memory, and Armed Expeditions to the Sertão in Minas Gerais, Brazil, 1750–1808." *The Americas* 61, no. 3 (2005): 429–61.

———. "Uncertain Refuge: Frontier Formation and the Origins of the Botocudo War in Late-Colonial Brazil." *Hispanic American Historical Review* 82, no. 2 (2002): 215–56.

Langfur, Hal, and Charles F. Walker. "Protest and Resistance against Colonial Rule in Iberian America." In *The Iberian World, 1450–1820*, edited by Fernando Bouza, Pedro Cardim, and Antonio Feros, 617–34. London: Routledge, 2020.

Lara, Mário. *Nos confins do Sertão da Farinha Podre: Povoamento, conquistas e confrontos no Oeste de Minas*. n.p., 2009.

Lasso, Marixa. "Race War and Nation in Caribbean Gran Colombia, Cartagena, 1810–1832." *American Historical Review* 111, no. 2 (2006): 336–61.

Lauderdale Graham, Sandra. "Taming the Wilderness, Minas Gerais, Brazil (1769)." In *Colonial Latin America: A Documentary History*, edited by Kenneth Mills, William B. Taylor, and Sandra Lauderdale Graham, 335–37. Wilmington, DE: Scholarly Resources, 2002.

Lenharo, Alcir. *As tropas da moderação: O abastecimento da Corte na formação política do Brasil, 1808–1842*. São Paulo: Símbolo, 1979.

Lestringant, Frank. *Cannibals: The Discovery and Representation of the Cannibal from Columbus to Jules Verne.* Translated by Rosemary Morris. Berkeley: University of California Press, 1997.

Levine, Robert M. *Vale of Tears: Revisiting the Canudos Massacre in Northeastern Brazil, 1893–1897.* Berkeley: University of California Press, 1992.

Libby, Douglas C. "Reconsidering Textile Production in Late Colonial Brazil: New Evidence from Minas Gerais." *Latin American Research Review* 32, no. 1 (1997): 88–108.

———. *Transformação e trabalho em uma economia escravista: Minas Gerais no século XIX.* São Paulo: Brasiliense, 1988.

Liebersohn, Harry. *Aristocratic Encounters: European Travelers and North American Indians.* Cambridge: Cambridge University Press, 2001.

Linnaeus, Carl. *A General System of Nature: Through the Three Grand Kingdoms of Animals, Vegetables, and Minerals.* Translated by William Turton. Vol. 7. London: Lackington, Allen, 1806.

Lisboa, Baltasar da Silva. *Memoria topografica e economica da commarca dos Ilheos.* Lisbon: Academia Real das Sciencias de Lisboa, 1823.

Lisboa, Karen Macknow. *A nova Atlântica de Spix e Martius: Natureza e civilização no viagem pelo Brasil (1817–1820).* São Paulo: Hucitec, 1997.

Loveman, Mara. "Blinded Like a State: The Revolt against Civil Registration in Nineteenth-Century Brazil." *Comparative Studies in Society and History* 49, no. 1 (2007): 5–39.

———. "The Modern State and the Primitive Accumulation of Symbolic Power." *American Journal of Sociology* 110, no. 6 (2005): 1651–83.

Lowie, Robert H. "The Southern Cayapó." In *Handbook of South American Indians*, edited by Julian H. Steward, 519–20. New York: Cooper Square, 1963.

Luccock, John. *Notes on Rio de Janeiro and the Southern Parts of Brazil; Taken during a Residence of Ten Years in That Country, from 1808 to 1818.* London: Samuel Leigh, 1820.

Luna, Francisco Vidal. *Minas Gerais: Escravos e senhores: Análise da estrutura populacional e econômica de alguns centros mineratórios (1718–1804).* São Paulo: Instituto de Pesquisas Econômicas, 1981.

Luna, Francisco Vidal, and Iraci del Nero da Costa. *Minas colonial: Economia e sociedade.* São Paulo: Livraria Pioneira, 1982.

Lynch, John. "Bolívar and the Caudillos." *Hispanic American Historical Review* 63, no. 1 (1983): 3–35.

———. *The Spanish American Revolutions, 1808–1826.* 2nd ed. New York: Norton, 1986.

Machado Filho, Aires da Mata. *Arraial do Tijuco, cidade Diamantina*. Belo Horizonte: Itatiaia, 1980.

———. *O negro e o garimpo em Minas Gerais*. Belo Horizonte: Itatiaia, 1985.

Machado, José de Alcântara. *Vida e morte do bandeirante*. 1930. Reprint; Belo Horizonte: Itatiaia, 1980.

Magalhães, Basílio de. *Expansão geographica do Brasil colonial*. 2nd ed. São Paulo: Companhia Editora Nacional, 1935.

Malheiros, Márcia. "'Homens de Fronteira': Índios e Capuchinhos na ocupação dos Sertões do Leste do Paraíba ou Goytacazes (séculos XVIII e XIX)." PhD diss., Universidade Federal Fluminense, 2008.

Mallon, Florencia E. "The Promise and Dilemma of Subaltern Studies: Perspectives from Latin American History." *American Historical Review* 99, no. 5 (1994): 1491–515.

Manutchehr-Danai, Mohsen. *Dictionary of Gems and Gemology*. Berlin: Springer, 2000.

Mapp, Paul W. *The Elusive West and the Contest for Empire, 1713–1763*. Chapel Hill: University of North Carolina Press, 2011.

Martins, José de Souza. *Fronteira: A degradação do Outro nos confins do humano*. São Paulo: Contexto, 2009.

Martins, Tarcisio José. *Quilombo do Campo Grande: A história de Minas que se devolve ao povo*. Rev. ed. Contagem: Santaclara, 2008.

Martins Filho, Amilcar, and Roberto B. Martins. "Slavery in a Nonexport Economy: Nineteenth-Century Minas Gerais Revisited." *Hispanic American Historical Review* 63, no. 3 (1983): 537–68.

Matos, Raimundo José da Cunha. *Corografia histórica da província de Minas Gerais (1837)*. 2 vols. Belo Horizonte: Itatiaia, 1981.

Mattos, Hebe Maria. *Das cores do silêncio: Os significados da liberdade no Sudeste escravista—Brasil século XIX*. 2nd ed. Rio de Janeiro: Nova Fronteira, 1998.

Mattos, Izabel Missagia de. *Civilização e revolta: Os Botocudos e a catequese na Província de Minas*. Bauru: EDUSC, 2004.

———. "Considerações sobre política e parentesco entre os Botocudos (Borún) do século XIX: Uma interpretação da articulação de uma rede social e simbólica." *Revista de Antropologia da Universidade Federal de São Carlos* 5, no. 1 (2013): 82–96.

———. "Povos em movimento nos Sertões do Leste (Minas Gerais, 1750–1850)." *Nuevo Mundo Mundos Nuevos* (January 30, 2012), http://journals.openedition.org/nuevomundo/62637.

———. "A vida do Borum Kuêk, a repatriação do crânio e o encontro indígena." In *Histórias indígenas: Memória, interculturalidade e cidadania na América Latina*, edited by Izabel Missagia de Mattos, Chantal Cramaussel, Vânia M. L. Moreira, and Ana Paula da Silva, 61–94. São Paulo: Humanitas, 2020.

Mawe, John. *Travels in the Interior of Brazil, Particularly in the Gold and Diamond Districts of That Country*. London: Longman, 1812.

Maxwell, Kenneth R. *Conflicts and Conspiracies: Brazil and Portugal, 1750–1808*. Cambridge: Cambridge University Press, 1973.

———. *Pombal: Paradox of the Enlightenment*. Cambridge: Cambridge University Press, 1995.

McCreery, David. *Frontier Goiás, 1822–1889*. Stanford, CA: Stanford University Press, 2006.

McQuown, Norman A. "The Indigenous Languages of Latin America." *American Anthropologist*, n.s., 57, no. 3, part 1 (1955): 501–70.

Medick, Hans. "Turning Global? Microhistory in Extension." *Historische Anthropologie* 24, no. 2 (2016): 241–52.

Meinig, D. W. *The Shaping of America: A Geographical Perspective on 500 Years of History*. Vol. 1. New Haven, CT: Yale University Press, 1986.

Mendonça, Marcos Carneiro de. *A Amazônia na era pombalina: Correspondência inédita do governador e capitão-general do estado do Grão Pará e Maranhão, Francisco Xavier de Mendonça Furtado, 1751–1759*. 3 vols. Rio de Janeiro: Instituto Histórico e Geográfico Brasileiro, 1963.

Mercadante, Paulo. *Os sertões do leste: Estudo de uma região; A mata mineira*. Rio de Janeiro: Zahar, 1973.

Merrell, James H. "Indian History during the English Colonial Era." In *A Companion to Colonial America*, edited by Daniel Vickers, 118–37. Malden, MA: Blackwell, 2003.

Metcalf, Alida C. *Go-Betweens and the Colonization of Brazil, 1500–1600*. Austin: University of Texas Press, 2006.

Métraux, Alfred. "The Purí-Coroado Linguistic Family." In *Handbook of South American Indians*, edited by Julian H. Steward, 523–30. New York: Cooper Square, 1963.

Meznar, Joan E. "The Ranks of the Poor: Military Service and Social Differentiation in Northeast Brazil, 1830–1875." *Hispanic American Historical Review* 72, no. 3 (1992): 335–51.

Mignolo, Walter D. *The Idea of Latin America*. Malden, MA: Blackwell, 2005.

Miki, Yuko. *Frontiers of Citizenship: A Black and Indigenous History of Postcolonial Brazil*. Cambridge: Cambridge University Press, 2018.

Millett, Nathaniel. "Borderlands in the Atlantic World." *Atlantic Studies* 10, no. 2 (2013): 268–95.

Mitchell, Timothy. "Society, Economy, and the State Effect." In *State/Culture: State-Formation after the Cultural Turn*, edited by George Steinmetz, 76–97. Ithaca, NY: Cornell University Press, 1999.

Monteiro, John M. *Negros da terra: Índios e bandeirantes nas origens de São Paulo.* São Paulo: Companhia das Letras, 1994.

———. "Rethinking Amerindian Resistance and Persistence in Colonial Portuguese America." In *New Approaches to Resistance in Brazil and Mexico*, edited by John Gledhill and Patience A. Schell, 25–43. Durham, NC: Duke University Press, 2012.

———. "Tupis, tapuias e historiadores: Estudos de história indígena e do indigenismo." Livre Docência thesis, IFCH-Unicamp, 2001.

Monteiro, Rodrigo Bentes, Bruno Feitler, Daniela Calainho, and Jorge Flores, eds. *Raízes do privilégio: Mobilidade social no mundo ibérico do Antigo Regime.* Rio de Janeiro: Civilização Brasileira, 2011.

Moog, Clodomir Vianna. *Bandeirantes and pioneers.* Translated by L. L. Barrett. New York: G. Braziller, 1964.

Moraes, P. L. R. "The Brazilian Herbarium of Maximilian, Prince of Wied." *Neodiversity* 4 (2009): 16–51.

Morais, J. A. David de. "A sífilis nas 'Centúrias de curas medicinais,' de Amato Lusitano." *Cadernos de Cultura: Medicina na Beira Interior, da Pré-história ao Século XXI* 32 (2018): 29–56.

Moreira Neto, Carlos de Araújo. *Índios da Amazônia: De maioria a minoria (1750–1850).* Petrópolis: Vozes, 1988.

Morse, Richard M., ed. *The Bandeirantes: The Historical Role of the Brazilian Pathfinders.* New York: Knopf, 1965.

Motta, Márcia. *Direito à terra no Brasil: A gestação do conflito, 1795–1824.* São Paulo: Alameda, 2009.

Moura, Clóvis. *Dicionário da escravidão negra no Brasil.* São Paulo: Universidade de São Paulo, 2004.

Muaze, Mariana, and Ricardo Salles. *O Vale do Paraíba e o Império do Brasil nos quadros da segunda escravidão.* Rio de Janeiro: 7Letras, 2015.

Myrup, Erik Lars. *Power and Corruption in the Early Modern Portuguese World.* Baton Rouge: Louisiana State University Press, 2015.

Nazzari, Muriel. "Vanishing Indians: The Social Construction of Race in Colonial São Paulo." *The Americas* 57, no. 4 (2001): 497–524.

Nimuendajú, Curt. "Social Organization and Beliefs of the Botocudo of Eastern Brazil." *Southwestern Journal of Anthropology* 2 (1946): 93–115.

Noll, Michael G. "Prince Maximilian's *Other* Worlds." *Pennsylvania Geographer* 43, no. 1 (2005): 65–83.

"Notícia diária e individual das marchas[,] e acontecimentos ma(i)s condigno(s) da jornada que fez o Senhor Mestre de Campo, Regente[,] e Guarda(-)mor Inácio Corre(i)a Pamplona, desde que saiu de sua casa[,] e fazenda do Capote às conquistas do Sertão, até se tornar a recolher à mesma sua dita fazenda do Capote, etc. etc. etc., [1769]." *Anais da Biblioteca Nacional do Rio de Janeiro* 108 (1988): 47–113.

Novaes, Eder Liz. "Joaquim Felício dos Santos: Republicanismo e cultura historiográfica (1860–1871)." Master's thesis, Universidade Federal de Ouro Preto, 2014.

Novaes, Paulo. *Mão de Luva: Romance*. Rio de Janeiro: Nau Editora, 1996.

Novais, Fernando A. *Portugal e Brasil na crise do antigo systema colonial (1777–1808)*. 2nd ed. São Paulo: Hucitec, 1981.

Oberacker, Carlos, Jr. "Viajantes, naturalistas e artistas estrangeiros." In *História geral da civilização brasileira*, edited by Sérgio Buarque de Holanda, 119–31. São Paulo: Difel, 1985.

Oikos Laboratório. "Taquara e Bambu." Universidade Federal de Paraná, http://www.oikos.ufpr.br/produtos/taquaras%20e%20bambus.pdf (accessed October 24, 2015).

Oliveira, José Augusto de, ed. *Conquista de Lisboa aos Mouros (1147): Narrada pelo Cruzado Osberno*. 2nd ed. Lisbon: S. Industriais da C. m. L., 1936.

Oliveira, Luís Valente de, and Rubens Ricupero, eds. *A abertura dos portos*. São Paulo: Senac, 2007.

Oliveira, Rodrigo Leonardo de Sousa. "'Mão de Luva' e 'Montanha': Bandoleiros e salteadores nos caminhos de Minas Gerais no século XVIII (Matas Gerais da Mantiqueira: 1755–1786)." Master's thesis, Universidade Federal de Juiz de Fora, 2008.

Ottoni, Jozé Eloi. "Memória sobre o estado actual da Capitania de Minas Gerais." *Anais da Biblioteca Nacional do Rio de Janeiro* 30 (1908): 303–18.

Outram, Dorinda. *The Enlightenment*. 4th ed. Cambridge: Cambridge University Press, 2019.

Pains, Clarissa. "Desastre ambiental em Mariana afeta cultura dos índios krenaks." *O Globo* (October 31, 2017), https://oglobo.globo.com/brasil/desastre-ambiental-em-mariana-afeta-cultura-dos-indios-krenaks-22012035.

Paiva, Adriano Toledo. *Os indígenas e os processos de conquista dos sertões de Minas Gerais (1767–1813)*. Belo Horizonte: Argumentum, 2010.

Paiva, Eduardo França. "Bateias, carumbés, tabuleiros: Mineração africana e mestiçagem no Mundo Novo." In *O trabalho mestiço: Maneiras de pensar e formas de viver, séculos XVI a XIX*, edited by Eduardo França Paiva and Carla Maria Junho Anastasia, 187–207. São Paulo: Annablume, 2002.

Paquette, Gabriel. *Imperial Portugal in the Age of Atlantic Revolutions: The Luso-Brazilian World, c. 1770–1850*. Cambridge: Cambridge University Press, 2013.

Paraíso, Maria Hilda Baqueiro. "Os Botocudos e sua trajetória histórica." In *História dos índios no Brasil*, edited by Manuela Carneiro da Cunha, 413–30. São Paulo: Companhia das Letras, FAPESP/SMC, 1992.

———. *O tempo da dor e do trabalho: A conquista dos territórios indígenas nos sertões do leste*. Salvador: EDUFBA, 2014.

Parrela, Ivana D. *O teatro das desordens: Garimpo, contrabando e violência no sertão diamantino, 1768–1800*. São Paulo: Annablume, 2009.

Peres, Damião. *Estudos de História Luso-Brasileira*. Lisbon: n.p., 1956.

Perrone-Moisés, Beatriz. "Índios livres e índios escravos: Os princípios da legislação indigenista do período colonial (séculos XVI a XVIII)." In *História dos índios no Brasil*, edited by Manuela Carneiro da Cunha, 115–32. São Paulo: Companhia das Letras, FAPESP/SMC, 1992.

———. "Inventário da legislação indigenista, 1500–1800." In *História dos índios no Brasil*, edited by Manuela Carneiro da Cunha, 529–66. São Paulo: Companhia das Letras, FAPESP/SMC, 1992.

Pijning, Ernst. "The Meaning of Illegality: Contraband Trade in Eighteenth-Century Rio de Janeiro." *Revista do Instituto Histórico e Geográfico Brasileiro* 164, no. 419 (2003): 91–105.

———. "O ambiente científico da época e a viagem ao Brasil do príncipe alemão Maximiliano de Wied-Neuwied." *Oceanos* 24, no. (1995): 26–34.

Pimenta, João Paulo G. "The Independence of Brazil: A Review of the Recent Historiographic Production." *e-Journal of Portuguese History*, no. 1 (2009), http://scielo.pt/scielo.php?script=sci_arttext&pid=S1645-64322009000100006&nrm=iso.

Pinto, Francisco Eduardo. "Potentado e conflitos nas sesmarias da Comarca do Rio das Mortes." PhD diss., Universidade Federal Fluminense, 2010.

Pinto, Renato Venâncio. "Os últimos carijós: Escravidão indígena em Minas Gerais: 1711–1725." *Revista Brasileira de História* 17, no. 34 (1997): 165–81.

Pires, Antonio Olyntho dos Santos. "Viagem aos terrenos diamantíferos do Abaeté." *Annaes da Escola de Minas de Ouro Preto* 4 (1885): 93–166.

Pombo, Nívia. "D. Rodrigo de Sousa Coutinho e a formulação do princípio de unidade política." In *Em terras lusas: Conflitos e fronteiras no Império Português*, edited by Márcia Motta, José Vicente Serrão, and Marina M. Machado, 81–103. Vinhedo: Horizonte, 2013.

Pompa, Cristina. *Religião como tradução: Missionários, Tupi e Tapuia no Brasil colonial*. Bauru: EDUSC, 2003.

Porto, José da Costa. *Estudo sobre o sistema sesmarial*. Recife: Universidade Federal de Pernambuco, 1965.

Portugal, Luís de Almeida. *Cartas do Rio de Janeiro, 1769–1776*. Rio de Janeiro: Instituto Estadual do Livro, 1978.

Portuondo, María M. *Secret Science: Spanish Cosmography and the New World*. Chicago: University of Chicago Press, 2009.

Prado, Fabrício. "The Fringes of Empires: Recent Scholarship on Colonial Frontiers and Borderlands in Latin America." *History Compass* 10, no. 4 (2012): 318–33.

Pratt, Mary Louise. *Imperial Eyes: Travel Writing and Transculturation*. London: Routledge, 1992.

"[Prince Maximilian]." *Boston Commercial Gazette*, September 1, 1825.

———. *Repertory*, June 23, 1818.

Pulteney, Richard. *A General View of the Writings of Linnaeus*. London: T. Payne and B. White, 1781.

Puntoni, Pedro. *A Guerra dos Bárbaros: Povos indígenas e a colonização do sertão nordeste do Brasil, 1650–1720*. São Paulo: Hucitec/Edusp, 2002.

Putnam, Lara. "To Study the Fragments/Whole: Microhistory and the Atlantic World." *Journal of Social History* 39, no. 3 (2006): 615–30.

Radding, Cynthia. *Wandering Peoples: Colonialism, Ethnic Spaces, and Ecological Frontiers in Northwestern Mexico, 1700–1850*. Durham, NC: Duke University Press, 1997.

Radding, Cynthia, and Danna Levin Rojo. "Borderlands: A Working Definition." In *The Oxford Handbook of Borderlands of the Iberian World*, edited by Cynthia Radding and Danna Levin Rojo, 1–27. New York: Oxford University Press, 2019.

———, eds. *The Oxford Handbook of Borderlands of the Iberian World*. Oxford: Oxford University Press, 2019.

Raminelli, Ronald. "Do conhecimento físico e moral dos povos: Iconografia e taxionomia na Viagem Filosófica de Alexandre Rodrigues Ferreira." Supplement, *História, Ciências, Saúde-Manguinhos* 8 (2001): 969–92.

———. *Viagens ultramarinas: Monarcas, vassalos e governo à distância*. São Paulo: Alameda, 2008.

Ramos, Alcida Rita. *Indigenism: Ethnic Politics in Brazil*. Madison: Univeristy of Wisconsin Press, 1998.

Ramos, Donald. "O quilombo e o sistema escravista em Minas Gerais do século XVIII." In *Liberdade por um fio: História dos quilombos no Brasil*, edited by

João José Reis and Flávio dos Santos Gomes, 164–92. São Paulo: Companhia das Letras, 1996.

———. "Single and Married Women in Vila Rica, Brazil, 1754–1838." *Journal of Family History* 16, no. 3 (1991): 261–82.

———. "Social Revolution Frustrated: The Conspiracy of the Tailors in Bahia, 1798." *Luso-Brazilian Review* 13, no. 1 (1976): 74–90.

Rausch, Jane M. *A Tropical Plains Frontier: The Llanos of Colombia, 1531–1831*. Albuquerque: University of New Mexico Press, 1984.

Reis, João José, and Flávio dos Santos Gomes, eds. *Liberdade por um fio: História dos quilombos no Brasil*. São Paulo: Companhia das Letras, 1996.

Resende, Maria Efigênia Lage de. "Itinerários e interditos na territorialização das Geraes." In *História de Minas Gerais: As Minas setecentistas*, edited by Maria Efigênia Lage de Resende and Luiz Carlos Villalta, 25–53. Belo Horizonte: Autêntica, 2007.

Resende, Maria Leônia Chaves de. "'Devassas gentílicas': Inquisição dos índios na Minas Gerais colonial." In *Caminhos gerais: Estudos históricos sobre Minas (séc. XVIII–XIX)*, edited by Maria Leônia Chaves de Resende and Silvia Maria Jardim Brügger, 9–48. São João del Rei: Universidade Federal de São João del Rei, 2005.

———. "Gentios brasílicos: Índios coloniais em Minas Gerais setecentista." PhD diss., Universidade de Campinas, 2003.

Resende, Maria Leônia Chaves de, and Hal Langfur. "Minas expansionista, Minas mestiça: A resistência dos índios em Minas Gerais do século do ouro." *Anais de História de Além-Mar* 9 (2008): 79–103.

Resende, Maria Leônia Chaves de, and Klaus Schönitzer. "Do Novo ao Velho Mundo: Indígenas da Amazônia na Alemanha dos naturalistas Spix e Martius." *Anais de História de Além-Mar* 19 (2018): 189–220.

Reys, Manoel Martinz do Couto. *Manuscritos de Manoel Martinz do Couto Reys, 1785*. Rio de Janeiro: Arquivo Público do Estado do Rio de Janeiro, 1997.

Ribeiro, Márcia Moisés. "Ciência e império: O intercâmbio da técnica e o saber científico entre a Índia e a América portuguesa." In *A "Época Pombalina" no mundo luso-brasileiro*, edited by Francisco Falcon and Claudia Rodrigues, 499–522. Rio de Janeiro: FGV, 2015.

Ribeiro, Mônica da Silva. "'Razão de Estado' e Pombalismo: Os modos de governar na administração de Gomes Freire de Andrada." In *A "Época Pombalina" no mundo luso-brasileiro*, edited by Francisco Falcon and Claudia Rodrigues, 91–124. Rio de Janeiro: FGV, 2015.

Ribeiro, Ricardo Ferreira. *Florestas anãs do sertão: O cerrado na história de Minas Gerais*. Belo Horizonte: Autêntica, 2005.

Ricardo, Cassiano. *Marcha para Oeste: A influência da bandeira na formação social e política do Brasil.* Rio de Janeiro: José Olympio, 1940.

Richter, Daniel K. *Facing East from Indian Country: A Native History of Early America.* Cambridge, MA: Harvard University Press, 2001.

Ricupero, Rodrigo. *A formação da elite colonial: Brasil c. 1530–c. 1630.* São Paulo: Alameda, 2008.

Rocha, José Joaquim da. *Geografia histórica da Capitania de Minas Gerais.* Belo Horizonte: Fundação João Pinheiro, 1995.

Roche, Daniel. "Natural History in the Academies." In *Cultures of Natural History*, edited by N. Jardine, J. A. Secord, and E. C. Spary, 127–44. Cambridge: Cambridge University Press, 1996.

Rodrigues, Aldair Carlos. "Homens de negócio: Vocabulário social, distinção e atividades mercantis nas Minas setecentistas." *História* 28, no. 1 (2009): 191–214.

Rodríguez O., Jaime E. *The Independence of Spanish America.* Cambridge: Cambridge University Press, 1998.

Roller, Heather F. *Amazonian Routes: Indigenous Mobility and Colonial Communities in Northern Brazil.* Stanford, CA: Stanford University Press, 2014.

———. "Autonomous Indian Nations and Peacemaking in Late Eighteenth-Century Brazil." In *The Oxford Handbook of Borderlands of the Iberian World*, edited by Cynthia Radding and Danna Levin Rojo, 641–66. Oxford: Oxford University Press, 2019.

———. *Contact Strategies: Histories of Native Autonomy in Brazil.* Stanford, CA: Stanford University Press, 2021.

———. "River Guides, Geographical Informants, and Colonial Field Agents in the Portuguese Amazon." *Colonial Latin American Review* 21, no. 1 (2012): 101–26.

Romeiro, Adriana. *Paulistas e emboabas no coração das Minas: Idéias, práticas e imaginário político no século XVIII.* Belo Horizonte: Universidade Federal de Minas Gerais, 2008.

Romeiro, Adriana, and Angela Vianna Botelho. *Dicionário histórico das Minas Gerais: Período colonial.* Belo Horizonte: Autêntica, 2003.

Rudwick, Martin. "Minerals, Strata, and Fossils." In *Cultures of Natural History*, edited by N. Jardine, J. A. Secord, and E. C. Spary, 266–86. Cambridge: Cambridge University Press, 1996.

Rugendas, Johann Moritz. *Voyage pittoresque dans le Brésil.* Paris: Engelmann, 1835.

Rupke, Nicolaas, and Gerhard Lauer, eds. *Johann Friedrich Blumenbach: Race and Natural History, 1750–1850.* New York: Taylor and Francis, 2019.

Russell-Wood, A. J. R. *The Black Man in Slavery and Freedom in Colonial Brazil.* London: Macmillan, 1982.

Sachs, Aaron. *The Humboldt Current: Nineteenth-Century Exploration and the Roots of American Environmentalism.* New York: Penguin, 2006.

Safier, Neil. *Measuring the New World: Enlightenment Science and South America.* Chicago: University of Chicago Press, 2008.

Sahlins, Peter. *Boundaries: The Making of France and Spain in the Pyrenees.* Berkeley: University of California Press, 1989.

Said, Edward W. *Culture and Imperialism.* New York: Vintage Books, 1993.

———. *Orientalism.* New York: Vintage Books, 1979.

Saint-Hilaire, Auguste de. *Viagem à Província de Goiás.* Belo Horizonte: Itatiaia, 1975.

———. *Viagem ao Espírito Santo e Rio Doce.* Translated by Milton Amado. Belo Horizonte: Itatiaia, 1974.

———. *Viagem pelas províncias do Rio de Janeiro e Minas Gerais.* Translated by Vivaldi Moreira. Belo Horizonte: Itatiaia, 1975.

Sallas, Ana Luisa Fayet. "Narrativas e imagens dos viajantes alemães no Brasil do século XIX: A construção do imaginário sobre os povos indígenas, a história e a nação." *História, Ciências, Saúde-Manguinhos* 17, no. 2 (2010): 415–35.

Salles, Francisco Antônio de. "Questões de limites entre os estados de Minas e Goyaz." *Revista do Arquivo Público Mineiro* 9, no. 2 (1904): 795–826.

Santos, Antonio Cesar de Almeida. "Poder e territorialização na América portuguesa (segunda metade do século XVIII)." *Revista de Historia Moderna: Anales de la Universidad de Alicante*, no. 36 (2018): 323–48.

Santos, Boaventura de Sousa. "Between Prospero and Caliban: Colonialism, Postcolonialism, and Inter-Identity." *Luso-Brazilian Review* 39, no. 2 (2002): 9–43.

Santos, Catarina Madeira. "Administrative Knowledge in a Colonial Context: Angola in the Eighteenth Century." *British Journal for the History of Science* 43, no. 4 (2010): 539–56.

Santos, Joaquim Felício dos. *Memórias do Distrito Diamantino da Comarca do Serro Frio (Província de Minas Gerais).* 4th ed. 1868. Reprint; Belo Horizonte: Itatiaia, 1976.

Santos, Márcio. *Bandeirantes paulistas no sertão do São Francisco: Povoamento e expansão pecuária de 1688 a 1734.* São Paulo: Universidade de São Paulo, 2009.

Santos, Márcio R. A. dos. *Rios e fronteiras: Conquista e ocupação do sertão baiano.* São Paulo: Universidade de São Paulo 2017.

Schach, Paul. "Maximilian, Prince of Wied (1782–1867): Reconsidered." *Great Plains Quarterly* 14, no. 1 (1994): 5–20.

Schaffer, Simon, Lissa Roberts, Kapil Raj, and James Delbourgo, eds. *The Brokered World: Go-Betweens and Global Intelligence, 1770–1820*. Sagamore Beach: Science History Publications, 2009.

Schiebinger, Londa. "Gender and Natural History." In *Cultures of Natural History*, edited by N. Jardine, J. A. Secord, and E. C. Spary, 163–77. Cambridge: Cambridge University Press, 1996.

Schultz, Kirsten. *Tropical Versailles: Empire, Monarchy, and the Portuguese Royal Court in Rio de Janeiro, 1808–1821*. New York: Routledge, 2001.

Schwartz, Stuart B. "Brazilian Ethnogenesis: Mestiços, Mamelucos, and Pardos." In *Le Nouveau Monde, Mondes Nouveaux: L'experience americaine*, edited by Serge Gruzinski and Nathan Wachtel, 7–27. Paris: EHESS/CNRS, 1996.

———. *Slaves, Peasants, and Rebels: Reconsidering Brazilian Slavery*. Urbana: University of Illinois Press, 1992.

Schwartz, Stuart B., and Hal Langfur. "Tapanhuns, Negros da Terra, and Curibocas: Common Cause and Confrontation between Blacks and Indians in Colonial Brazil." In *Black and Red: African-Indigenous Relations in Colonial Latin America*, edited by Matthew Restall, 81–114. Albuquerque: University of New Mexico Press, 2005.

Schwartz, Stuart B., and Frank Salomon. "New Peoples and New Kinds of People: Adaptation, Readjustment, and Ethnogenesis in South American Indigenous Societies (Colonial Era)." In *The Cambridge History of the Native Peoples of the Americas*, edited by Frank Salomon and Stuart B. Schwartz, 443–501. Cambridge: Cambridge University Press, 1999.

Scott, James C. *Seeing Like a State: How Certain Schemes to Improve the Human Condition Have Failed*. New Haven, CT: Yale University Press, 1999.

Scott, Rebecca J. "Small-Scale Dynamics of Large-Scale Processes." *American Historical Review* 105, no. 2 (2000): 472–79.

Sellers-García, Sylvia. *Distance and Documents at the Spanish Empire's Periphery*. Stanford, CA: Stanford University Press, 2013.

Silva, Antonio de Moraes. *Diccionario da lingua portugueza*. 2 vols. Lisbon: Lacerdina, 1813.

Silva, Antônio de Morais, and Rafael Bluteau. *Diccionario da lingua portugueza composto pelo padre D. Rafael Bluteau, reformado, e accrescentado por Antonio de Moraes Silva natural do Rio de Janeiro*. 2 vols. Lisbon: Simão Thaddeo Ferreira, 1789.

Silva, Antonio Delgado da, ed. *Collecção da legislação portugueza desde a ultima compilação das ordenações*. 6 vols. Vol. 4. Lisbon: Maigrense, 1825.

Silva, Célia Nonata da. *Territórios de mando: Banditismo em Minas Gerais, século XVIII*. Belo Horizonte: Crisálida, 2007.

Silva, Clarete Paranhos da. *O desvendar do grande livro da natureza: Um estudo da obra do mineralogista José Vieira Couto, 1798–1805.* São Paulo: Annablume, 2002.

Silva, Francisco Freire da, and Marlene Rauber. "Memórias, práticas e degradações garimpeiras em Alta Floresta, MT [Mato Grosso]." *Revista Eletrônica das Faculdades de Alta Floresta,* no. 2 (2018), http://refaf.com.br/index.php/refaf/article/view/279 (accessed February 9, 2020).

Silva, José Bonifácio de Andrada e. "An Account of the Diamonds of Brazil." In *Obras científicas, políticas e sociais,* edited by Edgard de Cerqueira Falcão, 56–60. [São Paulo]: [Revista dos Tribunais], 1963.

———. "Apontamentos para a civilização dos índios bravos do Império do Brasil." In *O pensamento vivo de José Bonifácio,* 78–107. São Paulo: Livraria Martins, 1961.

Silva, Maria Beatriz Nizza da. *Sistema de casamento no Brasil colonial.* São Paulo: T. A. Queiroz, Universidade de São Paulo, 1984.

Silveira, Marco Antonio. *O universo do indistinto: Estado e sociedade nas Minas setecentistas (1735–1808).* São Paulo: Hucitec, 1997.

Simon, William J. *Scientific Expeditions in the Portuguese Overseas Territories (1783–1808) and the Role of Lisbon in the Intellectual-Scientific Community of the Late Eighteenth Century.* Lisbon: Instituto de Investigação Científica Tropical, 1983.

Slack, Paul. "Government and Information in Seventeenth-Century England." *Past and Present,* no. 184 (August 2004): 33–68.

Slenes, Robert W. "Os multiplos de porcos e diamantes: A economia escravista de Minas Gerais no seculo XIX." *Cadernos IFCH UNICAMP* 17 (June 1985): 39–80.

Smethurst, Paul. *Travel Writing and the Natural World, 1768–1840.* London: Palgrave Macmillan, 2012.

Soll, Jacob. *The Information Master: Jean-Baptiste Colbert's Secret State Intelligence System.* Ann Arbor: University of Michigan Press, 2009.

Sommer, Barbara A. "Colony of the Sertão: Amazonian Expeditions and the Indian Slave Trade." *The Americas* 61, no. 3 (2005): 401–28.

———. "Negotiated Settlements: Native Amazonians and Portuguese Policy in Pará, Brazil, 1758–1798." PhD diss., University of New Mexico, 2000.

Souza, Evergton Sales. "Igreja e Estado no período pombalino." In *A "Época Pombalina" no mundo luso-brasileiro,* edited by Francisco Falcon and Claudia Rodrigues, 277–306. Rio de Janeiro: FGV, 2015.

Souza, José Antônio Soares. "As Minas do Sertão de Macacu." *Revista do Instituto Histórico e Geográfico Brasileiro* 326 (1980): 21–91.

Souza, Laura de Mello e. *Cláudio Manuel da Costa: O letrado dividido.* São Paulo: Companhia das Letras, 2011.

———. *Desclassificados do ouro: A pobreza mineira no século XVIII*. 3rd ed. Rio de Janeiro: Graal, 1990.

———. *The Devil and the Land of the Holy Cross: Witchcraft, Slavery, and Popular Religion in Colonial Brazil*. Austin: University of Texas Press, 2003.

———. *Norma e conflito: Aspectos da história de Minas no século XVIII*. Belo Horizonte: Universidade Federal de Minas Gerais, 1999.

———. *O sol e a sombra: Política e administração na América portuguesa do século XVIII*. São Paulo: Companhia das Letras, 2006.

———. "Violência e práticas culturais no cotidiano de uma expedição contra quilombolas, Minas Gerais, 1769." In *Liberdade por um fio: História dos quilombos no Brasil*, edited by João José Reis and Flávio dos Santos Gomes, 193–212. São Paulo: Companhia das Letras, 1996.

Spivak, Gayatri Chakravorty. *A Critique of Postcolonial Reason: Toward a History of the Vanishing Present*. Cambridge, MA: Harvard University Press, 1999.

Spix, Johann Baptiste von, and Karl F. P. von Martius. *Reise in Brasilien auf befehl Sr. Majestät Maximilian Joseph I., königs von Baiern, in den jahren 1817 bis 1820 gemacht und beschrieben*. 3 vols. Munich: M. Lindauer, 1823.

———. *Travels in Brazil, in the Years 1817–1820: Undertaken by Command of His Majesty the King of Bavaria*. Translated by H. E. Lloyd. London: Longman, Hurst, Rees, Orme, Brown, and Green, 1824.

Spix, Johann Baptiste von, and Carl Friedrich Phillipp von Martius. *Viagem pelo Brasil, 1817–1820*. Translated by Lúcia Furquim Lahmeyer. 3 vols. Belo Horizonte: Itatiaia, 1981.

Stein, Stanley J. *Vassouras: A Brazilian Coffee County: The Roles of Planter and Slave in a Plantation Society*. 1958. Reprint; Cambridge, MA: Harvard University Press, 1985.

Strang, Cameron B. *Frontiers of Science: Imperialism and Natural Knowledge in the Gulf South Borderlands, 1500–1850*. Chapel Hill: University of North Carolina Press, 2018.

Strauss, André, et al. "The Cranial Morphology of the Botocudo Indians, Brazil." *American Journal of Physical Anthropology* 157 (2015): 202–16.

Stumpf, Roberta Giannubilo. *Filhos das Minas, americanos e portugueses: Identidades coletivas na capitania das Minas Gerais (1763–1792)*. São Paulo: Hucitec, 2010.

Sumner, John B. *A Treatise on the Records of the Creation and on the Moral Attributes of the Creator ...* 2nd ed. 2 vols. London: J. Hatchard, 1818.

Svisero, Darcy P., James E. Shigley, and Robert Weldon. "Brazilian Diamonds: A Historical and Recent Perspective." *Gems and Gemology* 53, no. 1 (2017): 2–33.

Sweet, James H. *Domingos Álvares, African Healing, and the Intellectual History of the Atlantic World*. Chapel Hill: University of North Carolina Press, 2011.

Taunay, Afonso de E. *História geral das bandeiras paulistas.* 11 vols. São Paulo: Ideal, 1924–50.
Tavares, Rui. "Lembrar, esquecer, censurar: A Real Mesa Censória sob Pombal (Portugal, 1768–1777)." *Estudos Avançados* 13, no. 37 (1999): 125–54.
Taylor, Alan. *American Revolutions: A Continental History, 1750–1804.* New York: W. W. Norton, 2016.
———. *The Divided Ground: Indians, Settlers, and the Northern Borderland of the American Revolution.* New York: Vintage Books, 2006.
Tjarks, Alicia V. "Brazil: Travel and Description, 1800–1899. A Selected Bibliography." *Revista de Historia de América* 83 (January–June 1977): 209–47.
"Travels in Brazil." *Commercial Advertiser,* July 8, 1820.
Tschudi, Johann Jakob von. *Viagem às Províncias do Rio de Janeiro e São Paulo.* Translated by Eduardo de Lima Castro. São Paulo: Livraria Martins, 1953.
Twinam, Ann. *Public Lives, Private Secrets: Gender, Honor, Sexuality, and Illegitimacy in Colonial Spanish America.* Stanford, CA: Stanford University Press, 1999.
Usner, Daniel H., Jr. *Indians, Settlers, and Slaves in a Frontier Exchange Economy: The Lower Mississippi Valley before 1783.* Chapel Hill: University of North Carolina Press, 1992.
Vainfas, Ronaldo. *Traição: Um jesuíta a serviço do Brasil holandês processado pela Inquisição.* São Paulo: Companhia das Letras, 2008.
Valadares, Virgínia M. T. *Elites mineiras setecentistas: Conjugação de dois mundos.* Lisbon: Edições Colibri, 2004.
Valadares, Virgínia Maria Trindade. *A sombra do poder: Martinho de Melo e Castro e a administração da Capitania de Minas Gerais (1770–1795).* São Paulo: Hucitec, 2006.
Vandelli, Domingos. *Memórias de história natural.* Porto: Porto Editora, 2003.
Varela, Alex Gonçalves, Maria Margaret Lopes, and Maria Rachel Fróes da Fonseca. "Naturalista e homem público: A trajetória do ilustrado José Bonifácio de Andrada e Silva em sua fase portuguesa (1780–1819)." *Anais do Museu Paulista* 13, no. 1 (2005): 207–34.
Vasconcelos, Diogo [Luís de Almeida Pereira] de. *História média de Minas Gerais.* 4th ed. Belo Horizonte: Itatiaia, 1974.
Vasconcelos, Diogo Pereira Ribeiro de. *Breve descrição geográfica, física e política da Capitania de Minas Gerais.* Belo Horizonte: Fundação João Pinheiro, 1994.
Veracini, Lorenzo. *Settler Colonialism: A Theoretical Overview.* New York: Palgrave Macmillan, 2010.
Vergara, Ana. "Las armas a cambio de la libertad: Los esclavos en la guerra de independencia de Venezuela (1812–1835)." *Relaciones: Estudios de historia y sociedad* 32, no. 127 (2011): 47–85.

Vilardaga, José Carlos. "São Paulo na órbita do império dos felipes: Conexões castelhanas de uma vila da América portuguesa durante a União Ibérica (1580–1640)." PhD diss., Universidade de São Paulo, 2010.

Vives, Vera de. *Descobertos e extravios: História de Maria I e Mão de Luva*. Rio de Janeiro: Editora Record, 1997.

Wagner, Rudolph. "An Account of the Blumenbachian Museum." In *The Anthropological Treatises of Johann Friedrich Blumenbach*, 345–55. London: Longman, 1865.

Wallerius, Johann Gotschalk. *Mineralogie ou description générale des substances du regne mineral*. Paris: Durand, 1753.

Weber, David J. *Bárbaros: Spaniards and Their Savages in the Age of Enlightenment*. New Haven, CT: Yale University Press, 2005.

———. *The Spanish Frontier in North America*. New Haven, CT: Yale University Press, 1992.

Wegner, Robert. *A conquista do oeste: A fronteira na obra de Sérgio Buarque de Holanda*. Belo Horizonte: Universidade Federal de Minas Gerais, 2000.

White, Richard. *The Middle Ground: Indians, Empires, and Republics in the Great Lakes Region, 1650–1815*. Cambridge: Cambridge University Press, 1991.

———. *The Roots of Dependency: Subsistence, Environment, and Social Change among the Choctaws, Pawnees, and Navajos*. Lincoln: University of Nebraska Press, 1983.

Wied-Neuwied, Maximilian A. P. von. *The North American Journals of Prince Maximilian of Wied*. Translated by William J. Orr, Paul Schach, and Deiter Karch. 3 vols. Norman: University of Oklahoma Press, 2008–12.

———. *Reise nach Brasilien in den Jahren 1815 bis 1817*. 2 vols. Frankfurt: H. L. Brönner, 1820–21.

———. *Travels in Brazil in the Years 1815, 1816, 1817*. London: Henry Colburn, 1820.

———. *Viagem ao Brasil*. Translated by Edgar Süssekind de Mendonça and Flávio Poppe de Figueiredo. Belo Horizonte: Itatiaia, 1889.

Wikipedia contributors. "Cantagalo (Rio de Janeiro)." Wikipedia, the Free Encyclopedia, http://pt.wikipedia.org/wiki/Cantagalo_%28Rio_de_Janeiro%29 (accessed March 3, 2012).

Wilson, Kathleen. "Rethinking the Colonial State: Family, Gender, and Governmentality in Eighteenth-Century British Frontiers." *American Historical Review* 116, no. 5 (2011): 1294–1322.

Zack, Naomi. *Philosophy of Science and Race*. New York: Routledge, 2002.

# INDEX

In this index figures are indicated by an italic *f* following the page number

Abaeté River: Couto and, 196, 198–99; garimpeiros and, 196, 212; Isidoro and, 172, 177–78, 196; mining and, 175, 177, 196, 199, 210–11; sertões and, 174

agriculture and farming: Cantagalo and, 148–49; Coimbra and, 130, 141; colonization and, 4, 11, 21, 23, 36, 69, 82, 102, 106, 215; enslaved persons and, 21, 55–56, 148; escaped slaves and, 27, 56; Indigenous peoples and, 14, 81, 83, 93, 128, 138, 141, 149, 235, 239, 248; land grants and, 54, 107; mining and, 21, 36, 56; Pamplona and, 33, 69; Paraíba River and, 149; regulation of, 130; scientific exploration and, 160; sertões and, 23, 296

Albuquerque, Luís de, 313n3

Ambrósio Quilombo, 59, 61, 63

Anastasia, Carla, 344n19, 346n35

Andrade, António Gomes Freire de (Count of Bobadela), 32, 51, 59, 315n8

Andrade, Francisco Eduardo de, 242

anthropology, 223–25, 261–72, 283, 378n17

anthropophagy. *See* cannibalism

anticonquistadors, 227, 261, 271

Araçuaí River, 237

Arcadian tradition of poetry, 47–48

Ataíde e Melo, Pedro Maria Xavier (Viscount of Condeixa), 211, 231, 234

Atlantic Forest: ban on settlement in, 102, 129; colonization and, 102, 129, 237, 276; Indigenous peoples and, 19, 73; international interest in, 223; Jequitinhonha River and, 237; mining and, 73, 87; naturalists and, 223; royal interest in, 222; scholarship on, 87, 223

Atlantic world, 3–4, 25, 71, 77, 160–61, 174, 181, 186, 216, 220, 233, 297–99

backcountry guides and informants: Coimbra and, 131, 135, 140; colonization challenged through, 8–9, 13, 110–11, 150, 215, 298–99;

backcountry guides and informants (*continued*)
    Couto and, 154–55, 158, 164, 169, 181, 197–98, 209, 212; criminality and, 214; escaped slaves and, 219; free people of color and, 219, 238; garimpeiros and, 2, 154, 164, 175, 206; Guack and, 251, 263–64, 265*f*, 267–69, 275, 281, 378n21; Indigenous peoples and, 17, 78–79, 100, 111, 123, 131, 141, 216, 219, 255, 261–64, 267–68, 282; Isidoro and, 173–74, 193, 202–3, 214; naturalists and, 221, 261; Pamplona and, 43, 45, 60, 69; reliability of, 6–8, 73; scientific exploration and, 158, 261–64, 282, 291; smuggling and, 114, 116; sovereignty and, 6–7, 9; territorialization and, 24, 111, 291–92; Wied-Neuwied and, 224–25, 250–51, 261–64, 267–68, 274. *See also* information gathering
Bahia: colonial capital in, 39; colonization and, 215, 234; Indigenous peoples and, 219, 229–30, 254; royal interest in, 222, 230; sertões and, 15; smuggling and, 23, 258; Tailor's Conspiracy and, 161; Wied-Neuwied and, 225–26, 251, 253, 258, 260, 283
Bambuí, 47, 70, 316n12
Bambuí River, 210, 323n1
bandeirantes: colonization and, 19, 36, 69; Couto and, 182–85; enslaved persons and, 19, 44, 69; heroic tradition of, 36–37, 70, 182–84, 287; Indigenous peoples and, 19, 44, 69, 80, 85; information gathering and, 35, 80; Minas Gerais and, 35, 184; mining and, 36, 85, 182, 184, 237; official support for, 36; Pamplona and, 35–36, 70; poetry on, 36–37; quilombos and, 59; scholarship on, 35; scientific exploration and, 227; sertões and, 36, 182, 184
Banks, Joseph, 221
Barbacena, Viscount of (Luís Antônio Furtado de Mendonça), 151, 176
Barbosa, Rui, 2
Barbosa, Waldemar de Almeida, 323n1
Bayly, C. A., 7–8, 383n12
Belmonte, 252, 254
Beltrão, Francisco: appointment of, 173; assessment of expeditions by, 203–10; banderaintes and, 209; garimpeiros and, 165, 190–91, 206–7, 209–10; misinformation suspected by, 204–6, 209–10
Bento (Isidoro's son), 190, 197–202, 206, 209
Bergman, Torben Olaf, 198
Black Legend, 227–28
Blumenbach, Johann Friedrich, 223, 262, 268–69
Board of Royal Finance, 203, 365n54
Bobadela, Count of (António Gomes Freire de Andrade), 32, 51, 59, 315n8
Boccaccio, Giovanni, 48
Bodmer, Karl, 272
Bolívar, Simón, 295
Botocudo Indians: agriculture and, 258; assimilation of, 239, 243–45, 258, 261, 270–71, 275; cannibalism and, 83, 220, 231, 236–38, 263–64, 280; colonization and, 41, 229–30, 235; depictions of, 241*f*, 259*f*; diplomacy of, 220, 290; enslavement of, 231–32, 252; ethnographic description of, 225–26, 228, 261–63, 268–71; expedition contact with, 226, 255–60; independence and, 280–81; information gathering

and, 216–17, 240, 282; intertribal conflict and, 83, 253–54, 290; Jequitinhonha River and, 216, 226, 245, 266, 276; name of, 230; population size of, 312n33; resistance of, 230, 245; scientific exploration and, 250–51, 261–62, 268–69, 281–82; territorialization and, 216; violence against, 140, 216, 276–77; war declaration against, 216, 220, 228, 231–33, 244–47, 251–52, 263, 280; women and, 245, 270
Branco e Abranches, José Luís de Meneses Castelo (Count of Valadares), 42, 64
Brandão, Alexandre Pereira, 69
Bruchac, Margaret, 262
Burmeister, Hermann, 149–50
Butler, John, 294

Cachoeiras de Macacu, 86, 90–91, 133, 137
Câmara, Manuel Ferreira da, 167–68, 211
Caminha, Pêro Vaz de, 84
Caminho Novo, 23, 82, 102, 106–9, 134
Camões, Luís Vaz de, 48–49
Campo Grande, 58*f*, 59, 210
Campos dos Goitacases, 91, 109
cannibalism: Botocudo people and, 83, 220, 231, 236–38, 263–64, 280; colonization and, 220, 232, 236–38, 280; escaped slaves and, 238; Indigenous peoples and, 230–31, 235, 280; information gathering and, 220–21; naturalists and, 236, 264; prevalence of, 236–38, 244, 373n33; scholarship on, 236, 373n33; war declaration justified by, 216, 220, 230–32, 235–36, 247–48, 263, 280; Wied-Neuwied and, 263–64

Cantagalo: agriculture and, 148–49; colonization and, 144; depictions of, 136*f*; as Eldorado of coffee, 149; enslaved persons and, 142–44, 148–49; expeditions and, 135–36, 138, 229; illegal mining and, 147–49; Indigenous peoples and, 141, 149; loss of interest in, 150; military occupation of, 142, 144; origin myth of, 117
cartography. *See* mapmaking
Carvalho e Melo, Sebastião José de. *See* Pombal, Marquis of
Caveleiros, Count of (Rodrigo José de Meneses), 106–9
church: missionaries and, 19, 32, 41, 47, 68, 78–80, 84, 95, 110, 150, 273, 291; priests and, 68, 84, 97, 104–6, 108–9, 114, 127, 131, 139, 248, 285; state-sponsored mission villages and, 102, 104–5, 247
Coimbra, Manoel Soares: agriculture and, 130, 141; backcountry guides and, 131, 135, 140; criminality and, 145; disillusionment of, 144–49, 289; enslaved persons and, 141–43; expedition of, 129–49, 289, 349n5; garimpeiros and, 133–34; illegal mining and, 133–35; Indigenous peoples and, 131–32, 135–41, 144–46; information gathering and, 131–34, 140–41; military command of, 129–32; scholarship on, 129; self-defense of character by, 143–47; smuggling and, 141, 144–47; sources for expedition of, 349n5
colonial militias, 113*f*
colonization: agriculture and, 4, 11, 21, 23, 36, 69, 82, 102, 106, 215; Atlantic Forest and, 102, 129, 237, 276; Bahia and, 215, 234; bandeirantes

colonization (*continued*)
and, 19, 36, 69; bans on settlement and, 82, 89–90, 102, 105–7, 110–11, 115, 120, 128–30; cannibalism and, 220, 232, 236–38, 280; Cantagalo and, 144; challenges to, 8–9, 13, 111, 150, 215, 298–99; Couto and, 182–85; disease and, 82; enslaved persons and, 33, 85, 143; escaped slaves and, 63, 288; free people of color and, 239; frontiers and, 11–14, 22; garimpeiros and, 23, 86–87, 116; Goiás and, 41; Indigenous peoples and, 6, 40–43, 78–79, 82–84, 102, 104–6, 111, 128, 138, 219–20; Jequitinhonha River and, 219, 228, 234, 237, 281; land grants and, 54, 64–68, 107, 248; lifting of bans on, 130, 149, 233–34; mapmaking and, 89, 108, 175; mining and, 51, 116, 129–30; Pamplona and, 29–30, 39–42, 54, 72, 289; Paraíba River and, 90, 94, 115; Rio de Janeiro and, 24, 89–90, 106, 215; São Francisco River and, 27, 30; scientific exploration and, 158, 219–20; sertões and, 6, 9, 13, 21–24, 30–31, 36, 77–78, 82–83, 215, 219, 239, 298–99; sovereignty and, 40, 120, 129–30; travel writing and, 227–28; Vila Rica and, 24; Wied-Neuwied and, 261, 269, 274; women and, 5, 33

Condeixa, Viscount of (Pedro Maria Xavier Ataíde e Melo), 211, 231, 234

contraband. *See* smuggling and contraband

Cook, James, 221

Coroado Indians: cannibalism and, 263; colonization and, 81–82, 102, 104; conversion of, 105; ethnographic description of, 225; incursions against, 106; information gathering and, 102–3, 289; intertribal conflict and, 83, 149; mining and, 132; name of, 83; observation of, 225; protection from colonial authorities of, 84; resistance of, 150; state-sponsored mission villages and, 104–5

Coropó Indians: colonization and, 81–82, 102, 104; conversion of, 105; incursions against, 106; information gathering and, 102–3, 289; intertribal conflict and, 83; mining and, 132; name of, 85; observation of, 225; protection from colonial authorities of, 84; resistance of, 150; state-sponsored mission villages and, 104–5

Costa, Cláudio Manuel da, 36–37, 41, 48

Coutinho, Francisco Inocêncio de Sousa, 44

Coutinho, Rodrigo de Sousa (Court of Linhares), 161, 232

Couto, José Vieira: Abaeté River and, 196, 198–99; backcountry guides and, 154–55, 158, 164, 169, 181, 197–98, 209, 212; background of, 2, 158–59, 161–62; bandeirantes and, 182–85; colonization and, 182–85; deviation during expedition of, 194–95; Enlightenment and, 184, 213; enslaved persons and, 195; expedition of, 154–55, 162–70, 174, 176, 180, 182–206, 212–13, 289–90; frontiers and, 1–2, 11; garimpeiros and, 2, 17, 154, 158, 164–65, 169, 180, 190–95, 197–98, 201–3, 209–10, 290; Goiás and, 194; heroic tradition and, 182–85, 213; independence and, 277; Indigenous peoples and, 234,

277; information gathering and, 2, 17, 164, 174, 200–202; literary techniques and, 185–87, 194–96, 198, 209; mapmaking and, 208, 210; mining and, 154–55, 162–66, 182–83, 185–87, 190–93, 195–200, 203–4; misinformation on expedition of, 188–89, 200–202; results of expedition of, 203–13, 290; São Francisco River and, 162–63, 190, 210; scholarship on, 186, 188–89, 213, 359n20; scientific exploration and, 17, 154, 158, 182, 185, 187–88, 197–204, 210, 212–13, 290; sertões and, 2, 17, 182, 185, 234; smuggling and, 162, 165, 185; Tejuco and, 162, 166, 190, 211; territorialization and, 182, 185; travel writing and, 162–63, 182–88, 190, 194, 196–97, 200, 209; Vila Rica and, 1, 162, 190

criminality and illegality: backcountry guides and, 214; Coimbra and, 145; exoneration through large finds and, 180; free people of color and, 55; garimpeiros and, 23, 51–52, 95, 110, 201, 211; illegal mining and, 52, 74, 85, 88, 90–91, 94, 98–101, 103, 111, 115, 123, 175–76; literary techniques and, 211; military operations against, 17, 74, 103, 115, 130; Minas Gerais and, 21, 67, 115, 288; sertões and, 5, 55, 117, 130, 211; sovereignty and, 120, 130, 288, 298; *vadios* and, 55. *See also* smuggling and contraband

Cunha, Count of (Antônio Álvares da Cunha), 87

Dean, Warren, 223
Dearborn, Renae, 267
Diamond District, 158–59, 165, 177, 180, 206, 210, 212

Dias, Maria Odila Leite da Silva, 331n45
disease, 82, 144, 245, 252
Doce River, 18–19, 89–90, 226, 228, 233–34, 242, 247–48, 258, 281
Domingues, Ângela, 275–76, 309n23

Eldorado myth, 149, 240, 283–84
Enlightenment: commercial reform of, 184; Couto and, 184, 213; information gathering and, 7; naturalists and, 227; noble savage trope of, 227; scholarship on, 21; scientific exploration and, 182

enslaved persons: agriculture and, 21, 55–56, 148; bandeirantes and, 19, 44, 69; Cantagalo and, 142–44, 148–49; Coimbra and, 141–43; colonization and, 33, 85, 143; Couto and, 195; emancipation of, 180; Goiás and, 44; Indigenous peoples and, 22, 35, 40, 231–32, 248, 251, 276; information gathering and, 123; land grants and, 147; legal restrictions on, 56–57; Minas Gerais and, 20–23, 27, 55; mining and, 22, 56–57, 85, 122–23, 125–26, 178–80, 192*f*, 208*f*; Pamplona and, 46, 52, 63; royal dependence on, 143; smuggling and, 122; Vila Rica and, 37*f*

escaped slaves: agriculture and, 27, 56; backcountry guides and, 219; cannibalism and, 238; colonization and, 63, 288; communities of, 29, 56–63, 58*f*, 62*f*, 69–70, 198, 288; expeditions and, 5, 16; frontiers and, 58–59; Goiás and, 58–59; hunting of, 57–59, 63, 106; information gathering and, 238; land grants and, 59–60, 69; legal restrictions on, 56–57; mapmaking and, 61;

escaped slaves (*continued*)
Minas Gerais and, 56, 58–59; Pamplona and, 29, 34, 46, 56, 60–64, 69, 289; property and, 59; punishments for, 56–57; São Francisco River and, 59; scholarship on, 56, 58; sertões and, 28, 58; territorialization and, 58
Eschwege, Wilhelm Ludwig von, 367n74
Espinhaço Mountains, 1, 3, 15, 203, 219, 286
exploration, scientific. *See* scientific exploration

Faria, Sebastião Craveiro de, 122
Farinho, Francisco Pires, 105–6
Farinho, Manoel Pires, 106
farming. *See* agriculture and farming
Ferdinand VII, King, 296
Ferreira, Alexandre Rodrigues, 310n24
Ferreira, Miguel Antunes, 91–94
Figueiró, Count of. *See* Vasconcelos e Sousa, Luís de
First Seminole War (1816-19), 295–96
Forbidden Lands policy: establishment of, 82; failure of, 120, 128; Indigenous peoples and, 128; limits of, 102; mining and, 106, 115; smuggling and, 110–11
free people of color: backcountry guides and, 219, 238; colonization and, 239; criminality and, 55; information gathering and, 238–39; legal restrictions on, 55; Minas Gerais and, 20, 55, 161, 219; Pamplona and, 55; poetry on, 55; racial classification of, 95; scientific exploration and, 290. *See also* garimpeiros
Freyreiss, Georg Wilhelm, 224–26, 263–64, 276

frontiers: colonization and, 11–14, 22; Couto and, 1–2, 11; creative reappropriation of, 13–14; definition of, 11–14, 307n16, 308n20; escaped slaves and, 58–59; external and internal frontiers, 12–13; freedom and, 58–59; Indigenous peoples and, 13–14; information gathering and, 13, 17; scholarship on, 11–13, 22; sertões distinguished from, 11–13. *See also* sertões
Furtado, Francisco Xavier de Mendonça, 41, 89
Furtado, Júnia Ferreira, 213, 312n29, 359n20

*garimpeiros* (prospectors): Abaeté River and, 196, 212; backcountry guides and, 2, 154, 164, 175, 206; Coimbra and, 133–34; colonization and, 23, 86–87, 116; Couto and, 2, 17, 154, 158, 164–65, 169, 180, 190–95, 197–98, 201–3, 209–10, 290; criminality and, 23, 51–52, 95, 110, 201, 211; definition of, 154, 165, 338n31; depictions of, 171f; Goiás and, 205; Indigenous peoples and, 84, 88, 95, 103–4, 127–28, 137; information gathering and, 103, 164, 201–2, 204, 206–7, 211–12; Isidoro and, 165–74, 176–78, 197, 204, 206–7; military action against, 168, 175–76, 205–6; mining and, 175, 180, 211–12; Pamplona and, 46, 62, 69; racial composition of, 190–94; scholarship on, 190–91; scientific exploration and, 181; sertões and, 51, 95; smuggling and, 165, 205, 209; spelling of, 164–65; Tejuco and, 175, 191–93; territorialization and, 164; women and, 190–93

gender, 191, 270; masculinity and, 28, 36, 48–49, 52, 185, 266. *See also* women
Gloved Hand. *See* Henriques, Manuel
Goiás: colonization and, 41; Couto and, 194; enslaved persons and, 44; escaped slaves and, 58–59; garimpeiros and, 205; Indigenous peoples and, 44; land grants and, 59; mapmaking and, 210; mining and, 19, 54; Pamplona and, 41, 47, 54, 70; sertões and, 15–16; smuggling and, 23, 175
Goitacá Indians, 83
Gomes, José: condemnation of, 132–33; illegal mining and, 95, 97–98, 132–33; imprisonment of, 96, 98; information gathering and, 95–96, 100; Inquisition and, 96, 98–99, 111, 132–33; questioning of, 340n39; racial classification of, 96–97, 133
Guack (Botocudo guide), 251, 263–64, 265f, 267–69, 275, 281, 378n21
guides. *See* backcountry guides and informants
Guimarães, Manual Ribeiro, 313n3

Hemming, John, 309n23
Henriques, Manuel (Mão de Luva): arrest of, 107–8, 112, 114, 118–20, 124, 135; condemnation of, 107–8; exile of, 117; illegal mining and, 74, 95–96, 98, 100, 103–4, 107–9, 111–12, 148; Indigenous peoples and, 103–4, 126, 128; information gathering and, 100–102, 120; Inquisition and, 74; marriage of, 118; military raid against, 103, 114, 118–19, 123–26, 136; notoriety of, 91, 103, 116–19; pursuit of, 111–20; scholarship on, 112, 118–19, 123–24; seizure of, 120–28
heroic tradition, 36–37, 70, 182–85, 213
Herzog, Tamar, 12, 307n16, 309n23, 319n20
Hinderaker, Erik, 293
Holanda, Sérgio Buarque de, 303n3, 308n20
Homer, 5, 54
Humboldt, Alexander von, 221, 223, 268–69, 284

Inconfidência Mineira (Minas Conspiracy, 1789), 32, 71, 108, 151, 161
Indaiá River, 195, 207, 211, 359n23
independence of Portuguese America, 3, 9, 251, 277–81, 292–97
Indian Directorate (1758), 40–41, 271
Indigenous peoples: agriculture and, 14, 81, 83, 93, 128, 138, 141, 149, 235, 239, 248; assimilation of, 41–43, 96, 105, 140, 149–50, 247–48, 278; Atlantic Forest and, 19, 73; backcountry guides and, 17, 78–79, 100, 111, 123, 131, 141, 216, 219, 255, 261–64, 267–68, 282; Bahia and, 219, 229–30, 254; bandeirantes and, 19, 44, 69, 80, 85; cannibalism and, 230–31, 234–35, 280; Cantagalo and, 141, 149; Coimbra and, 131–32, 135–41, 144–46; colonial classification of, 78–81, 95–97; colonial Indians, 80–81; colonization and, 6, 40–43, 78–79, 82–84, 102, 104–6, 111, 128, 138, 219–20; complexity of, 78–80; conversion of, 79, 84, 88, 92, 96, 102, 104–5, 123, 128, 137–38, 248; Couto and, 234, 277; depictions of, 81f, 136f, 241f, 259f; disease impact on, 82, 334n10; enslaved persons and, 22,

Indigenous peoples (*continued*) 35, 40, 231–32, 248, 251, 276; frontiers and, 13–14; garimpeiros and, 84, 88, 95, 103, 127–28, 137; Goiás and, 44; identity and, 83, 95; independence and, 277–80, 293–96; information gathering and, 78, 80, 84–85, 88, 94, 102–3, 111, 131–33, 135, 140–41, 150; Inquisition and, 127; intertribal conflict among, 83, 149, 253–54, 290; Jequitinhonha River and, 216, 226, 244–45, 247, 249, 266, 276, 278, 281; Jesuits and, 41; land grants and, 248; literary techniques and, 61, 267, 280; mapmaking and, 11, 89, 103; Minas Gerais and, 22, 41–42, 84, 85, 232–33, 279–80; mining and, 80, 84–85, 88, 90–95, 127; Pamplona and, 29, 34–35, 40–44, 53; Paraíba River and, 83, 85, 90, 137–38, 229, 264; poetry on, 48; policies toward, 40, 78, 80, 94, 105–6, 126–28, 131, 140, 243–44, 249, 277–81, 319n21, 381n49; resettlement of, 137–38; Rio de Janeiro and, 78–79, 81, 110, 140, 219, 230; São Francisco River and, 44; scholarship on, 14, 79–80, 150, 229, 261–62, 267–68, 286; scientific exploration and, 290; sertões and, 22–23, 37–38, 73, 78, 149–50, 198, 233–34, 247, 295–97; smuggling and, 17, 82–85, 90, 94–95, 102–4, 109, 111, 141, 144–45, 237; sovereignty and, 79, 128, 280; state-sponsored mission villages and, 102, 104–5, 247; tame Indians, 80, 94–95, 247; territorialization and, 40, 42, 83, 111, 127, 150, 216, 228–29, 231–33, 279–80; travel writing and, 226–27; war declaration against, 18–19, 40, 41, 94–96, 228–36, 243–49, 280–81; Wied-Neuwied and, 217, 225–28, 247–78, 285–86, 290; wild Indians, 29, 38, 80–81, 89, 103, 198, 226, 253, 261, 278; women and, 91–92, 245, 270. *See also specific tribes*

information brokers and intermediaries, 6–8, 14, 91, 94, 155, 164, 181, 214, 250, 266–67, 291

information gathering: bandeirantes and, 35, 80; cannibalism and, 220–21; challenges of, 6–9, 17–18, 87–88; Coimbra and, 131–34, 140–41; colonization challenged through, 8–9, 13, 110–11, 150, 215, 298–99; Couto and, 2, 17, 164, 174, 200–202; Enlightenment and, 7; enslaved persons and, 123; escaped slaves and, 238; exaggeration in, 7, 33, 43, 70, 85, 94, 174, 197, 205; free people of color and, 238–39; frontiers and, 13, 17; garimpeiros and, 103–4, 164, 201–2, 204, 206–7, 211–12; Guack and, 251, 263–64, 265f, 267–69, 275, 281, 378n21; Indigenous peoples and, 78, 80, 84–85, 88, 94, 102–3, 111, 131–33, 135, 140–41, 150; Isidoro and, 169, 173–74, 196, 201–6, 209; mapmaking and, 7, 24; Minas Gerais and, 110–11; mining and, 85–88, 91, 100–101, 181–82; misinformation and, 7, 18, 44, 72, 100, 181, 291, 298; naturalists and, 216, 220–21, 251, 309n23; Pamplona and, 30, 60, 69, 289; Rio de Janeiro and, 100; royal authorities and, 86–87, 91, 94, 100–103, 109–10; scholarship on, 8, 309n23; scientific exploration and, 17–18, 153–55, 181, 213–14, 289–90, 298; sertões and, 6–7, 9, 23–24, 30, 36, 74, 89, 158, 168, 219, 239, 286;

smuggling and, 78, 101–3, 109–11, 141; sovereignty and, 9; Tejuco and, 211; territorialization and, 15, 24, 42, 290; travel writing and, 227; Wied-Neuwied and, 250–51, 264–68, 283, 378n21; women and, 91–92. *See also* backcountry guides and informants

the Inquisition: Indigenous peoples and, 127; investigations by, 96, 98–99, 111, 132–33, 340n40; mining and, 17; racial classifications and, 96, 133

internal frontier. *See* frontiers; sertões

Isidoro de Amorim Pereira: Abaeté River and, 172, 177–78, 196; backcountry guides and, 173–74, 193, 202–3, 214; background of, 166; as black prospector king, 154, 166; capture, torture, and death claims about, 167–72; Couto's description of, 193; credibility of, 201–6, 209; criminal charges against, 176–77, 204–6, 209; diamond find of, 154, 172, 177, 180, 189, 201, 207, 212; enslavement claims about, 166, 169; escape claims about, 166–67, 169; expedition participation of, 165–66, 171–74, 190, 193–94, 196–97, 201–3, 359n21; family of, 166–67; free status of, 169; garimpeiros and, 165–74, 176–78, 197, 204, 206–7; historical accounts of, 167–70, 177, 202; information gathering and, 169, 173–74, 196, 201–6, 209; mining and, 154, 166–67, 169–73, 176–77, 180, 189, 201, 203–4, 207, 212; mythic status of, 158, 166–70, 214; pardon of, 176–77; São Francisco River and, 193; scholarship on, 166–70, 359n20; scientific exploration and, 181; sertões and, 170; smuggling and, 170; Tejuco and, 166, 168; Vila Rica and, 177, 203

Jequitinhonha River: Atlantic Forest and, 237; colonization and, 219, 228, 234, 237, 281; Indigenous peoples and, 216, 226, 244–45, 247, 249, 266, 276, 278, 281; tense peace along, 216, 226, 244, 276, 278; Wied-Neuwied and, 216, 226, 251–52, 260, 263, 269, 271, 283

Jesuit missionaries, 32, 41, 47, 84, 95, 110, 150, 273

João, Prince Regent (later João VI): cannibalism and, 230–32; expedition appointments of, 1, 148, 174, 224; flight to Portuguese America of, 220–22, 229, 231; independence struggle and, 297; Indigenous peoples and, 230–32; mercantile system abolished by, 222; pardons issued by, 177; ports opened by, 222; return to Lisbon of, 293; rise to kingship of, 222; scientific exploration and, 222–23; war declaration against Botocudo by, 230

Joaquim (Christian Indian captain), 86, 123–24, 127–28, 136, 146

José I, King: death of, 70, 90; expedition appointments of, 38–39; Indigenous peoples and, 40–41; information gathering and, 87; mining and, 87; reassessment following, 70

Kayapó Indians: assimilation of, 140; colonization and, 27, 41–42, 289; enslavement of, 44; expeditions and, 27, 41–44, 289; resistance of, 44; scholarship on, 44; truth and fiction about, 43–44; violence against, 140

La Condamine, Charles Marie de, 310n24
land grants (*sesmarias*): agriculture and, 54, 107; circumvention of limits on, 65–67; colonization and, 54, 64–68, 107, 248; enslaved persons and, 147; escaped slaves and, 59–60, 69; founding rituals and, 68–69; Goiás and, 59; Indigenous peoples and, 248; limits on, 65–67; Minas Gerais and, 64, 67, 107; mining and, 51, 106, 107, 130, 147; Pamplona and, 16, 28, 32–33, 42, 44, 53–54, 60, 64–70, 72, 330n39; process of granting, 327–28n24, 330n38; property and, 64; Rio de Janeiro and, 66; São Francisco River and, 54; scholarship on, 327–28n24; sertões and, 65–68; smuggling and, 106–7; sovereignty and, 64. *See also* property
Lavradio, Marquis of, 90, 338n29
Leão, Julião: Golden Lagoon search and, 284; Indigenous peoples and, 246–47, 249, 253, 259, 261, 272; war declaration criticized by, 249, 274, 278, 280
Léry, Jean de, 273
Linhares, Count of (Rodrigo de Sousa Coutinho), 161, 232
Linnaeus, Carl, 198
Lisboa, Baltazar da Silva, 382n1
literacy and literati, 8, 23–24, 48, 161, 184, 273, 278
literary techniques and narratives: anticonquistadors and, 227, 261, 271; Arcadian tradition, 47; Couto and, 185–87, 194–96, 198, 209; criminality and, 211; exploration and conquest, 28, 50, 87, 154; Indigenous peoples and, 61, 267, 280; itinerary technique, 185; literary devices, 31; mining and, 50; Pamplona and, 28, 31, 33, 38, 46, 53, 63, 313n3; property and, 31; scientific exploration and, 158, 209, 285, 298; travel literature, 227, 267; Wied-Neuwied and, 216, 264, 269–70, 272, 276, 285. *See also* poetry; travel writing
Lorena, Bernardo José de (Count of Sarzedas): exaggeration of expedition results and, 189, 203–4; expeditions organized by, 162, 170, 172–74, 189, 206; Indigenous peoples and, 233–34, 247; mining and, 176, 189; sertões and, 233–34
Lumiares, Count of. *See* Meneses, Luís da Cunha
Lynch, John, 309n23

Macaé, 99
Machado Filho, Airies da Mata, 358n16
Madrid, Treaty of (1750), 9, 35, 310n24
Mancall, Peter, 293
Mantiqueira Mountains, 82, 106
Mão de Luva. *See* Henriques, Manuel
mapmaking: colonization and, 89, 108, 175; Couto and, 208, 210; escaped slaves and, 61; Goiás and, 210; Indigenous peoples and, 11, 89, 103; information gathering and, 7, 24; Minas Gerais and, 89, 112; mining and, 88, 210; Pamplona and, 33, 42, 47, 61–62, 313n3; property and, 130; São Francisco River and, 210; scientific exploration and, 288; sertões and, 89, 103, 175; smuggling and, 88; territorialization and, 130, 288; Wied-Neuwied and, 275
Marcgrave, Georg, 273
Maria, Manoel de Jesus (Padre), 104–6, 108–9, 114, 127

Maria I, Queen, 1, 67, 117, 177, 220
Mariana, 65
Martins, Tarcisio José, 315n7, 325n9, 326n11
Martius, Carl Friedrich Philipp, 379n27
masculinity, 28, 36, 48–49, 52, 185, 266
Mawe, John: assessment of expeditions by, 211; cannibalism and, 177; Cantagalo visit by, 148–49; colonization and, 288; enslaved persons and, 178; expeditions and, 287–88; garimpeiros and, 165; mining and, 177–80, 211, 284, 367n74; scientific exploration and, 284; travel writing and, 170
Maxwell, Kenneth, 162
Mello e Souza, Laura de, 5, 97, 303n3
Melo e Castro, Martinho de, 90, 106–7, 110–11, 129, 150–51
memorials, 160–61, 186–89, 197, 210–11, 233–34. *See also* literary techniques and narratives
Mendonça, Luís Antônio Furtado de (Viscount of Barbacena), 151, 176
Meneses, Luís da Cunha (Count of Lumiares): criticism of, 125–26, 130; enslaved persons and, 143; expeditions and raids ordered by, 108, 123, 130, 175; information gathering and, 175; mining and, 112, 114–15, 117, 175
Meneses, Rodrigo José de (Count of Caveleiros), 106–9
microhistories, 15–16, 298, 309n21
military actions: cannibalism, war declaration justified by, 216, 220, 230–32, 235–36, 247–48, 263, 280; Cantagalo, occupation of, 142, 144; First Seminole War (1816–19), 295–96; against garimpeiros, 168, 175–76, 205–6; Mão de Luva, raid on, 103, 114, 118–19, 123–26, 136; war declaration against Indigenous peoples, 18–19, 40, 41, 94–96, 228–36, 243–49, 280–81
military command of Manoel Soares Coimbra, 129–32
militias, colonial, 113*f*
Minas Conspiracy (1789). *See* Inconfidência Mineira
Minas Gerais: administrative structure of, 39; bandeirantes and, 35, 184; criminality and, 21, 67, 115; decline of mining in, 27, 197; demographics of, 20, 55; enslaved persons and, 20–23, 27, 55; escaped slaves and, 56, 58–59; establishment of, 82; free people of color and, 20, 55, 161, 219; growth of, 20; imperial control over, 20–23; independence and, 279–80, 296–97; Indigenous peoples and, 22, 41–42, 84, 85, 232–33, 279–80; information gathering and, 110–11; initial colonization of, 20–21; land grants and, 64, 67, 107; mapmaking and, 89, 112; mining and, 16–23, 27, 35, 50, 112, 116, 160, 183–84, 197, 286; poetry in, 48; scholarship on, 20–22, 35, 311n28; scientific exploration and, 153–54, 158, 160; smuggling and, 21, 109–11, 129; territorialization and, 110, 129
Minas Novas, 89, 237–38, 254
mining: Abaeté River and, 175, 177, 196, 199, 210–11; agriculture and, 21, 36, 56; Atlantic Forest and, 73, 87; bandeirantes and, 36, 85, 182, 184, 237; boom in, 21, 50, 56–57, 82, 85, 115, 191, 197, 229, 283; Cantagalo and, 147–49; claim jumping in, 50–51, 323n51; Coimbra and, 133–35; colonization and, 51, 116,

mining (*continued*)
129–30; Couto and, 154–55, 162–66, 182–83, 185–87, 190–93, 195–200, 203–4; decline in, 20, 42, 85, 106, 153, 160, 162, 173, 183–84, 197, 232, 287; depictions of, 121*f*, 171*f*; Diamond District and, 158–59, 165, 177, 180, 206, 210, 212; enslaved persons and, 22, 37*f*, 56–57, 85, 122–23, 125–26, 178–80, 192*f*, 208*f*; garimpeiros and, 175, 180, 211–12; Goiás and, 19, 54; illegal operations in, 52, 74, 85, 88, 90–91, 94, 98–101, 103, 111, 115, 123, 175–76; Indigenous peoples and, 80, 84–85, 88, 90–95, 127; information gathering and, 85–88, 91, 100–101, 181–82; Inquisition and, 17; Isidoro and, 154, 166–67, 169–73, 176–77, 180, 189, 201, 203–4, 207, 212; land grants and, 51, 106, 107, 130, 147; literary techniques and, 50; mapmaking and, 88, 210; Minas Gerais and, 16–23, 27, 35, 50, 112, 116, 160, 183–84, 197, 286; mining code, 51–52, 91, 112, 147, 323n51; Pamplona and, 28, 45–46, 50–52; Paraíba River and, 85, 109; Rio de Janeiro and, 35, 109, 222; royal action limiting, 74, 90–91, 115–16, 129–30, 175–76, 323n51; scientific exploration and, 154, 159–60; sertões and, 164, 184, 201, 286–87; sovereignty and, 50, 74; Tejuco and, 196; territorialization and, 19, 111, 116; tools and instruments for, 163*f*; women and, 121*f*, 191–93, 192*f*. *See also* smuggling

mining code, 51–52, 91, 112, 147, 323n51

misinformation, 7, 18, 44, 72, 100, 181, 291, 298

missionaries, 19, 32, 41, 47, 68, 78–80, 84, 95, 110, 150, 273, 291

Moniz, Miguel, 133

Moura, José Pereira Freire: cannibalism and, 237–38, 244; expeditions authorized by, 242–43, 253; Golden Lagoon search of, 283–84; Indigenous peoples and, 237–40, 243–45, 247, 249, 261, 272, 285; information gathering and, 240, 242; mining and, 243; scholarship on, 242; war declaration criticized by, 249, 274, 278, 280

Mucuri River, 226

Napoleon Bonaparte, 18, 179, 210, 215, 222–23, 294

narratives. *See* literary techniques

Nascimento, Belmiro, 193

naturalists: Atlantic Forest and, 223; backcountry guides and, 221, 261; ban lifted on foreign naturalists, 216, 220–23, 273; cannibalism and, 236, 264; depictions of, 256*f*; Enlightenment and, 227; information gathering and, 216, 220–21, 251, 309n23; scientific exploration and, 153, 157–58, 188, 213; stereotypes disseminated by, 221

Noronha, Antônio de, 106

Noronha e Brito, Marcos, 228

Order of Christ, 65, 71, 189

Orosó Indians, 85, 93, 132

Ottoni, José Eloi, 184

Pamplona, Inácio Correia: agriculture and, 33, 69; authority of, 38–40, 42, 64, 318n18; backcountry guides and, 43, 45, 60, 69; background of, 28, 31–32; bandeirantes and, 35–36, 70; colonization and,

29–30, 39–42, 54, 72, 289; commissioning of, 16, 30, 32–33, 36, 38–39, 42; correspondences of, 31, 42; diary of, 30, 33–34, 38, 46–50, 53, 313nn2–3; enslaved persons and, 46, 52, 63; escaped slaves and, 29, 34, 46, 56, 60–64, 69, 289; first expedition of, 32–33, 41; free people of color and, 55; garimpeiros and, 46, 62, 69; Goiás and, 41, 47, 54, 70; Inconfidência Mineira and, 71; Indigenous peoples and, 29, 34–35, 40–44, 53; information gathering and, 30, 60, 69, 289; land grants and, 16, 28, 32–33, 42, 44, 53–54, 60, 64–70, 72, 330n39; leadership style of, 28, 35–36, 46; literary techniques and, 28, 31, 33, 38, 46, 53, 63, 313n3; mapmaking and, 33, 42, 47, 61–62, 313n3; mining and, 28, 45–46, 50–52; Order of Christ membership and, 65, 71; poetry about, 47–50, 54–55; property and, 16, 28, 31, 39, 64, 67–68, 72, 328n24; relation to authorities of, 30–35, 38–40, 70–72; São Francisco River and, 30, 34, 67; scholarship on, 32, 36, 71; self-promotion of, 29–30, 34, 38, 43, 70, 289; sertões and, 30, 32, 39, 53–54, 70, 72; 1769 expedition of, 28, 30, 33–34, 36, 42–46, 52, 60, 69, 317n17; significance of expeditions of, 29–30, 38; sources for expedition of, 313n2; sovereignty and, 34, 72; territorialization and, 29–31, 53, 58, 70, 289; Vila Rica and, 70; wife of, 31
Paracatu, 175, 323n1, 360n30
Paracatu River, 210
Paraíba River: agriculture and, 149; colonization and, 90, 94, 115; Indigenous peoples and, 83, 85, 90, 137–38, 229, 264; mining and, 85, 109; mission village along, 149, 225; smuggling and, 103, 125
Pataxó Indians, 229, 253, 263
Pedro I, Emperor, 277, 293, 297
Pereira, Isidoro de Amorim. *See* Isidoro
Picada de Goiás, 23, 54, 323n1
Pimenta, João Paulo G., 383–84n13
Pinto, Francisco Eduaro, 313n3, 316n11
Piso, Willem, 273
Piuí, 47, 54, 70
poetry, 36–37, 47–50, 54–55
Pohl, Johann Emanuel, 379n27
Pombal, Marquis of (Sebastião José de Carvalho e Melo): colonization and, 10, 27, 32, 89; educational reforms of, 159; Indigenous peoples and, 271; leadership approach of, 27; mining and, 27, 287; modernization and, 161; poetry and, 47; rise to power of, 27; satirization of, 70; secularizing agenda of, 68, 291
Porto Seguro, 237
Portugal, Maurício José, 86, 88, 92, 336n19
Prado, Bartolomeu Bueno do, 59–60
Prates, Manoel Rodrigues, 239–40
Pratt, Mary Louise, 227, 268
property: escaped slaves and, 59; land grants and, 64; limits on accumulation of, 16, 28, 39, 64–65, 67–68, 72; literary techniques and, 31; mapmaking and, 130; Pamplona and, 16, 28, 31, 39, 64, 67–68, 72, 328n24; sertões and, 72; sovereignty and, 64; territorialization and, 72, 130 *See also* land grants
prospectors. *See garimpeiros*
Puri Indians: assimilation of, 278–79; cannibalism and, 236, 263–64;

Puri Indians (*continued*)
colonization and, 41, 149; ethnographic description of, 225, 263–64; expeditions and, 93; information gathering and, 264; intertribal conflict and, 83, 105, 149, 273; land grants and, 248; mining and, 93; name of, 83; Paraíba River and, 229, 264; resistance of, 229; violence against, 105–6, 140

*quilombos* (escaped slave communities), 29, 56–63, 69–70, 198, 288

racial classifications, 78–81, 95–97, 133, 190–94, 250, 269, 290
Raminelli, Ronald, 309n23
Reconquista, 84
Ribeiro, Ricardo Ferreira, 359n20
Rio de Janeiro: colonial capital in, 87; colonization and, 24, 89–90, 106, 215; high appeals court in, 39; Indigenous peoples and, 78–79, 81, 110, 140, 219, 230; information gathering and, 100; land grants and, 66; mining and, 35, 109, 222; royal family's flight to, 210, 215, 222, 230–32, 285, 293; sertões and, 15, 73, 77, 111, 140; smuggling and, 23, 115, 332n1; Wied-Neuwied and, 223, 225
Rio Grande, 59, 92–93, 133, 368n1
Rio Pomba, 104, 106, 114
Rodríguez, Jaime E., 294
Royal Academy of Sciences, 160

Sabará, 165, 173, 205
Sahlins, Peter, 331n47
Said, Edward, 298
Saint-Hilaire, Auguste de, 276–77, 284
San Ildefonso, Treaty of (1777), 9, 35, 310n24

Santos, Joaquim Felício dos, 167–70
São Fidélis, 138, 225
São Francisco River: bridge erected across, 34; colonization and, 27, 30; Couto and, 162–63, 190, 210; escaped slaves and, 59; Indigenous peoples and, 44; Isidoro and, 193; land grants and, 54; mapmaking and, 210; Pamplona and, 30, 34, 67; smuggling and, 23
São João del Rei, 30, 39, 65, 313n2
São Martinho, Pedro Afonso Galvão de, 108–10, 114–15, 119–20, 123–25
Sarzedas, Count of. *See* Lorena, Bernardo José de
Schrader, Heinrich Adolf, 223
scientific exploration: agriculture and, 160; backcountry guides and, 158, 261–64, 282, 291; bandeirantes and, 227; colonization and, 158, 219–20; Couto and, 17, 154, 158, 182, 185, 187–88, 197–204, 210, 212–13, 290; development of, 153–54, 157–59, 181; educational reform and, 159; free people of color and, 290; garimpeiros and, 181; independence and, 286; Indigenous peoples and, 290; information gathering and, 17–18, 153–55, 181, 213–14, 289–90, 298; Isidoro and, 181; literary techniques and, 158, 209, 285, 298; mapmaking and, 288; Minas Gerais and, 153–54, 158, 160; mining and, 154, 159–60; naturalists and, 153, 157–58, 188, 213; preference over previous exploration, 157–58, 181; royal support for, 157–61, 181, 213–14; scholarship on, 274; sertões and, 18, 158, 181; sovereignty and, 181; territorialization and, 158, 181–82, 217, 222; travel writing and, 182,

227; Wied-Neuwied and, 217, 223–25, 250, 272–76
scientific racism, 250, 269, 290
Sellow, Friedrich, 224–25
sertões: Abaeté River and, 174; agriculture and, 23, 296; Bahia and, 15; bandeirantes and, 36, 182, 184; colonization and, 6, 9, 13, 21–24, 30–31, 36, 77–78, 82–83, 215, 219, 239, 298–99; contexts and sources for, 20–25; Couto and, 2, 17, 182, 185, 234; criminality and, 5, 55, 117, 130, 211; definition of, 2, 11–12; depictions of, 45f, 92f, 142f, 183f, 227f; escaped slaves and, 28, 58; forays into, 3, 6, 15–20, 36–38, 298–99; frontiers distinguished from, 11–13; garimpeiros and, 51, 95; Goiás and, 15–16; independence and, 286, 292, 296; Indigenous peoples and, 22–23, 37–38, 73, 78, 149–50, 198, 233–34, 247, 295–97; information gathering and, 6–7, 9, 23–24, 30, 36, 74, 89, 158, 168, 219, 239, 286; Isidoro and, 170; land grants and, 65–68; mapmaking and, 89, 103, 175; methodological approach to, 15–16; mining and, 164, 184, 201, 286–87; modern status of, 299; mythos of, 1–2, 37–38, 168–69; overview of, 9–14; Pamplona and, 30, 32, 39, 53–54, 70, 72; property and, 72; Rio de Janeiro and, 15, 73, 77, 111, 140, 215; scholarship on, 11–12, 30, 168, 288, 292; scientific exploration and, 18, 158, 181; smuggling and, 4, 51, 82, 104; sovereignty and, 15, 128, 181, 215, 283, 298; as state of becoming, 30; Tejuco and, 173; territorialization and, 4, 6, 9, 13–14, 19, 72, 130, 288, 297, 299; transnationalization of, 272–82. *See also* frontiers
*sesmarias*. *See* land grants
settlers. *See* colonization
Silva, Chica da, 169
Silva, Clarete Paranhos da, 213
Silva, Eugênia Luisa da, 31, 41–42
Silva, Joaquim da, 132–34
Silva, José Bonifácio Andrada e, 184, 277–78, 280
Silva, Luís Diogo Lobo da, 32, 89, 104
Silva, Maria da, 118
Silva Xavier, Joaquim José (Tiradentes), 108, 151
slavery. *See* enslaved persons; escaped slaves
smuggling and contraband: backcountry guides and, 114, 116; Bahia and, 23, 258; Coimbra and, 141, 144–47; Couto and, 162, 165, 185; enslaved persons and, 122; garimpeiros and, 165, 205, 209; Goiás and, 23, 175; Indigenous peoples and, 17, 82–85, 90, 94–95, 102–4, 109, 111, 141, 144–45, 237; information gathering and, 78, 101–3, 109–11, 141; Isidoro and, 170; land grants and, 106–7; mapmaking and, 88; Minas Gerais and, 21, 109–11, 129; Paraíba River and, 103, 125; Rio de Janeiro and, 23, 115, 332n1; royal action against, 23, 68, 103–7, 110–12, 115–16, 126, 129, 145, 151, 185, 237; São Francisco River and, 23; sertões and, 4, 51, 82, 104; Tejuco and, 114, 175; territorialization and, 102, 111; Vila Rica and, 120, 134. *See also* mining
Sousa, Tomé de, 40
sovereignty: backcountry guides and, 6–7, 9; colonization and, 40, 120, 129–30; criminality and, 120, 130,

sovereignty (*continued*)
288, 298; Indigenous peoples and, 79, 128, 280; information gathering and, 9; land grants and, 64; mining and, 50, 74; Pamplona and, 34, 72; property and, 64; scientific exploration and, 181; sertões and, 15, 128, 181, 215, 283, 298; territorialization and, 4, 19–20, 72, 99, 110, 129–30, 189, 291, 298

Spanish America, 27, 32, 221, 292–96, 309n23, 364n29

Spix, Johan Baptist, 379n27

Staden, Hans, 273

Sullivan, John, 294

Tailor's Conspiracy (1798), 161

Teixeira, Manuel, 124

Tejuco: Couto and, 162, 166, 190, 211; fame of, 196; garimpeiros and, 175, 191–93; information gathering and, 211; Isidoro and, 166, 168; mining and, 196; sertões and, 173; smuggling and, 114, 175

territorialization: backcountry guides and, 24, 111, 291–92; Couto and, 182, 185; dominion and, 5, 9, 18, 31, 40, 53, 111, 219, 235, 292–93, 298; escaped slaves and, 58; garimpeiros and, 164; Indigenous peoples and, 40, 42, 83, 111, 127, 150, 216, 228–29, 231–33, 279–80; information gathering and, 15, 24, 42, 290; limitations of, 90, 217; mapmaking and, 130, 288; Minas Gerais and, 110, 129; mining and, 19, 111, 116; Pamplona and, 29–31, 53, 58, 70, 289; property and, 72, 130; religious authorization for, 68, 290; scholarship on, 19, 35, 309n23; scientific exploration and, 158, 181–82, 217, 222; sertões and, 4, 6, 9, 13–14, 19, 72, 130, 288, 297, 299; smuggling and, 102, 111; sovereignty and, 4, 19–20, 72, 99, 110, 129–30, 189, 291, 298; Wied-Neuwied and, 253, 261–62

Tiradentes (Joaquim José Silva Xavier), 108, 151

Tocoiós, 237–40, 244–45, 253

travel writing: colonization and, 227–28; Couto and, 162–63, 182–88, 190, 194, 196–97, 200, 209; Indigenous peoples and, 226–27; information gathering and, 227; Mawe and, 170; scholarship on, 226–27; scientific exploration and, 182, 227; Wied-Neuwied and, 226–28, 261–62, 267, 275. *See also* literary techniques

Treaty of Madrid (1750), 9, 35, 310n24

Treaty of San Ildefonso (1777), 9, 35, 310n24

Treaty of Tordesillas (1494), 69

Tupi Indians, 84–85

United States, independence in, 293–95

Valadares, Count of (José Luís de Meneses Castelo Branco e Abranches), 42, 64

Vandelli, Domingos, 159, 355n3

Vasconcelos, Diogo Pereira Ribeiro de, 35, 119, 234

Vasconcelos e Sousa, Luís de (Count of Figueiró): colonization and, 147–48; Indigenous peoples and, 138; information gathering and, 90–91; mining and, 107, 120, 125–26, 147–48; smuggling and, 147

Viçosa, 252

Vila do Príncipe, 179, 238

Vila Rica: administrative structure of, 39; colonization and, 24; Couto and, 1, 162, 190; enslaved persons and, 37*f*; Isidoro and, 177, 203; Pamplona and, 70; poetry about, 36–37; smuggling and, 120, 134
"Vila Rica" (da Costa), 36–37

Wallerius, Johan Gottschalk, 188, 198
war declaration against Indigenous peoples, 18–19, 40, 41, 94–96, 228–36, 243–49, 280–81
Weber, David, 309n23
Wied-Neuwied, Maximilian Alexander Phillip von: backcountry guides and, 224–25, 250–51, 261–62, 267, 274; background of, 223–24; Bahia and, 225–26, 251, 253, 258, 260, 283; cannibalism and, 263–64; colonization and, 261, 269, 274; depictions of, 265*f*; ethnographic writing of, 261–72; expedition of, 216, 224–26, 251–61; Indigenous peoples and, 217, 225–28, 247–78, 285–86, 290; information gathering and, 250–51, 264–68, 283, 378n21; Jequitinhonha River and, 216, 226, 251–52, 260, 263, 269, 271, 283; literary techniques and, 216, 264, 269–70, 272, 276, 285; mapmaking and, 275; motivation for travels of, 285–86; myths of riches and, 283–84; Rio de Janeiro and, 223, 225; scholarship on, 226–27, 267–68, 271–72, 274–76; scientific exploration and, 217, 223–25, 250, 272–76; skull acquired by, 250, 255, 260–62, 281, 378n17; territorialization and, 253, 261–62; travel writing and, 226–28, 261–62, 267, 275; war declaration criticized by, 274, 280
Wilson, Kathleen, 331n47
women: colonization and, 5, 33; garimpeiros and, 190–93; Indigenous peoples and, 91–92, 245, 270; information gathering and, 91–92; mining and, 121*f*, 191–93, 192*f*

Xopotó, 100

The authorized representative in the EU for product safety and compliance is:
Mare Nostrum Group
B.V Doelen 72
4831 GR Breda
The Netherlands

www.ingramcontent.com/pod-product-compliance
Lightning Source LLC
Chambersburg PA
CBHW030601230426
43661CB00053B/1789